The
Judicial
Process

The Judicial Process:

An Introductory Analysis of the Courts of
The United States, England, and France

Third Edition
Revised and Enlarged

Henry J. Abraham

University of Virginia

New York
Oxford University Press
London 1975 Toronto

To Philip

Fourth printing, 1978

Copyright © 1962, 1968, 1975 by Oxford University Press, Inc.
Library of Congress Catalogue Card Number: 74-28873
Printed in the United States of America

Preface
to the
Third Edition

The continued success of *The Judicial Process*, which was initially published in 1962 and revised in 1968, motivated this enlarged third edition, completely revised and updated through November 1974 (including the "Watergate" controversy, the presidential resignation, and the pardon). The book's scope and approach are those of the original edition; yet throughout the pages of the third, a host of changes will be found, roughly one-third of the contents again being new. One procedural innovation since the second edition is the addition of two appendix tables which contain useful, handy, statistical and chronological data on all the Justices of the Supreme Court of the United States to date. A second is the categorization by individuals of Bibliography II (which in the preceding revision was done by topics for Bibliographies I and IV). The four bibliographies have once more been expanded; they now comprise some 3500 listings—the most extensive compilation of its kind extant as an appendix to any book in the field.

I again happily and gratefully acknowledge a profound debt to numerous colleagues who not only encouraged me to undertake this third edition but provided invaluable assistance readily and unselfishly. I am especially beholden to my friend Alan H. Bray, M.A. (Oxon.), of Middle Temple Inn, London, Barrister-at-Law, whose reading and counsel on the expanded sections on England and Wales were crucial (and whose companionship is ever a delight); to David Powell, my colleague at Virginia, who kept an expert eye on the portion dealing with the Soviet Union; and to Dr. Margherita Rendel of the University of London Institute of Education, who proved to be of invaluable aid with the revised materials on France. Of course, Jim Amon and Caroline Taylor of the Oxford University Press did their usual superb editorial work. And I should like to add a special expression of appreciation to E. E. "Dusty" Melton III, my loyal student and research assistant, who was indefatigable and proved to be superb on every count.

H. J. A.

Keswick, Va.
November 1974

Preface
to the
First Edition

When my *Courts and Judges: An Introduction to the Judicial Process* appeared in 1959, I began its Preface by pointing to the general absence of even the most rudimentary knowledge of the judicial process on the part of the vast majority of students of Political Science entering elementary or even advanced courses, and observed that equally striking was the unavailability of accessible materials providing basic data in the field. The measure of success my small book has enjoyed encouraged the writing of the present volume, which is far more ambitious in scope than its predecessor.

This new book is a selective comparative introduction to the judicial process, and seeks to analyze and evaluate the main institutions and considerations affecting the administration of justice under law. The rather extensive coverage of certain significant features and elements of comparative judicial processes was prompted not only by several helpful suggestions by users of the earlier book, but by the continued neglect of these processes in basic textbooks.

An important segment of this work is thus devoted to the judicial process in England and Wales, and France, and—to a necessarily considerably lesser extent in this context—the Soviet Union. Other states are included whenever appropriate, especially in connection with the doctrine and practice of judicial review. Nonetheless, over half of the material deals with the judicial process in the United States.

The detailed Table of Contents obviates capsule explanations of the substance of each chapter in this volume. I have compiled numerous graphs, figures, and charts, all designed to facilitate comprehension. There are two indexes, one general, one for cases. And there are four extensive bibliographies dealing with (1) works in general on American Constitutional Law; (2) biographies and autobiographies of and by Justices of the United States Supreme Court; (3) Comparative Constitutional Law; and (4) Civil Liberties.

Although I have endeavored to be objective in analysis and presentation throughout, in some circumstances it is neither possible nor desirable to shun value judgments; I have thus stated frankly my own opinions where it seemed appropriate to do so.

Once again I express my profound appreciation to the many colleagues who stimulated and urged me on in the writing of this book and whose generous suggestions were so helpful. I am especially grateful to Professors William M. Beaney, David Fellman, Wallace Mendelson, Jewell Cass Phillips, and R. J. Tresolini. Above all, I owe a particular debt of gratitude to Mr. James Wellwood, M.A., of Gray's Inn, Barrister-at-Law, Lecturer in Law at King's College, University of London, for his unselfish counsel and essential criticism on the sections on England and Wales. As they have been throughout my pleasant association with the Oxford University Press, Mr. Byron S. Hollinshead, Jr., and Miss Leona Capeless have been delightful and invaluable co-workers. Mrs. Helen White performed the thankless but so essential task of typing the entire manuscript cheerfully and efficiently. Whatever errors remain are mine. My wife, Mildred, gave me the kind of constant encouragement and confidence that only a devoted partner can provide.

And the book is happily dedicated to one who also helped in his own way.

H. J. A.

Wynnewood, Pa.
February 1962

viii

Contents

Contents

Contents

The
Judicial
Process

I
Introduction:
The Law
and the Courts

Respect for the law is one of the select group of principles which we have come to regard as essential to the effective and equitable operation of popular government. As a democratic principle it is recognized as binding on both the governed and those who govern.

In fostering this principle the role of the judiciary is crucial, for, in the words of Mr. Justice Arthur T. Vanderbilt:

> . . . it is in the courts and not in the legislature that our citizens primarily feel the keen, cutting edge of the law. If they have respect for the work of the courts, their respect for law will survive the shortcomings of every other branch of government; but if they lose their respect for the work of the courts, their respect for law and order will vanish with it to the great detriment of society.[1]

This is true, whether the judicial branch be technically separated from the other two branches of government, as in the United States; partly fused with them, as in France; or largely fused, as in England. The law will be respected as long as it is interpreted and applied within the structures of justice as accepted by the majority of society—in the long run, if not always in the short. Law is, after all, the expressed will of those who rule society.

But the law, in its procedural as well as its substantive aspects, is essentially made and administered by men whose views and interpretations are buffeted by the winds of change through the years, so that it has become a

[1] *The Challenge of Law Reform* (Princeton: Princeton University Press, 1955), pp. 4–5.

"truism that the quality of justice depends more on the quality of the men who administer the law than on the content of the law they administer."[2] Judicial activity, observed Roscoe Pound in one of his lectures, is really the creative element in law. Accordingly, if man's great interest on earth is justice, as Daniel Webster put it, then perhaps a more immediate interest is the securing of the most highly qualified individuals to administer justice impartially with a minimum of chicanery and obfuscation. It follows logically that judges must be assured of an optimum degree of independence and relative freedom from prejudicial pressures from forces both inside and outside of government. Moreover, they must be able to function in a hierarchical structure that is effectively conducive to the performance of the basic task at hand—the impartial administration of justice under law.

They pursue this task through the medium of a court, an institution. As Carl Brent Swisher noted concisely, along with such other characteristics as it may incidentally possess, a court

> . . . determines the facts involved in particular controversies brought before it, relates the facts to the relevant law, settles the controversies in terms of the law, and more or less incidentally makes new law through the process of decision. Over the centuries of Anglo-American history our judiciary has been developed and geared to this process so that it has an integrity or integratedness particuliar to its own. In particular it has a mode of informing the minds of the responsible officers—in this instance the judges—which is unique and which must be kept in sharp focus in any attempt to estimate the capacity of a judiciary to perform competitively in the gray areas which lie between it and institutions which are primarily legislative or executive.[3]

THE NATURE OF LAW

For centuries mankind has discussed the nature of law. In one way or another, it touches every citizen of every nation. The contact may be pleasant or unpleasant, tangible or intangible, direct or indirect, but it is nonetheless a constant force in the lives of people everywhere on the globe. It is essential that we have some understanding of its nature and of the human beings who interpret and administer it.

[2] Evan Haynes, *The Selection and Tenure of Judges* (Newark, N.J.: National Conference of Judicial Councils, 1944), p. 5.

[3] Presidential Address, delivered before the American Political Science Association, New York City, September 8, 1960. (Reprinted in 54 *American Political Science Review* 879–80, December 1960.)

4

"What is Law?" has been asked by priests and poets, philosophers and kings, by masses no less than by prophets. A host of answers might be given, yet the answer to the question remains one of the most persistent and elusive problems in the whole range of thought. For one may well view the entire gamut of human life, both in thought and in action, as being comprised within the concept Law[4] (although a legal system is in fact but part of a larger social order).

It may seem strange that the true essence of such a ubiquitous phenomenon as law should be beyond the grasp of general human understanding. Since law deals with human conduct, in order to grasp its nature it would appear necessary merely to distinguish it from the other factors relating to that conduct: religion, science, morals, ethics, custom. Yet herein lies the difficulty, so ably stated by James Coolidge Carter more than half a century ago:

> Law, Custom, Conduct, Life—different names for almost the same thing—true names for different aspects of the same thing—are so inseparably blended together that one cannot even be thought of without the other. No improvement can be effected in one without improving the other, and no retrogression can take place in one without a corresponding decline in the other.[5]

There is little doubt that law has much in common with all these other aspects of human conduct, yet it is true that it also possesses at least one characteristic unique to it and lacking in all others: its sanction is applied exclusively by organized political government.

Three Historical Categories. Some kind of law has always existed[6]—however inadequate, or even entirely absent, both legal organization and enforcement machinery may have been. First came *primitive* law, based chiefly on primitive custom and lacking even rudimentary machinery and organization. Still prevailing among some of the aboriginal Indian, Oceanic, and Asiatic tribes, it has always been the law of those "preliterate" peoples who,

---

[4] William A. Robson, *Civilization and the Growth of Law* (New York: The Macmillan Co., 1935), p. 3.

[5] *Law: Its Origin, Growth and Function* (New York and London: The Knickerbocker Press, 1907), p. 320.

[6] The earliest known system of written law was the Code of Hammurabi, so named in honor of its founder, a king of Babylonia. It was promulgated about 2050 B.C.—there is considerable disagreement among scholars on the precise decade or even century (estimates vary from 2067 to 1662 B.C.)—and was the embodiment of the existing rules and customs of the land. It presented the idea that justice was man's inherent right, derived from supernatural forces rather than being given by royally bestowed favor.

although un- or under-developed, have nevertheless recognized social rules, and have discovered means of coping with social conflict.

Archaic law, featuring some manner of courts and officialdom—institutions that are basic to every legal system—and introducing certain codes of procedure and substance, arrived on the scene during the early days of Rome and among primitive Germanic and African tribes. However, Moses' *Pentateuch,* given in the fifteenth century B.C., may well lay an earlier claim. Certainly the *Great Sanhedrin,* the seventy-one-man supreme council of the Jewish nation in Greco-Roman days, prior to the destruction of the Temple in Jerusalem by Roman forces in A.D. 70, was a judicial body, headed by a chief justice, which enacted decrees of religious observance *and* interpreted the law of the Hebrews.

Mature law heralded the professionalization of the law. It fathered the law we know today. As Roman law it existed from the third century B.C. to the fall of Rome. As English law it appeared in the twelfth century.

POSITIVE AND NATURAL LAW

The three kinds of law cited above are prongs of *positive law,* the type of law with which we will be concerned throughout this book. It is held to derive from man for the purpose of ruling man; it is a command based upon the relationship between ruler and ruled; its primary nature is that it is *man-made.* It springs from no source higher than the human will. This is what John Chipman Gray alluded to when he defined a man's legal rights as

> . . . power which he has to make a person or persons do or refrain from doing a certain act or . . . acts, as far as the power arises from society.[7]

In other words, according to the tenets of positive law—as defined by John Austin, the English utilitarian jurist (1790–1859) who, inspired by the French social theorist Auguste Comte, became the founder of the analytical school of jurisprudence—law consists of definite rules of human conduct with appropriate sanctions for their enforcement, both of these being prescribed by duly constituted human authority.

Natural Law. But in the eyes of many there is another category of law, *natural law,* known also as "higher law" or "the law of nature." It is law which would be binding upon human societies in the absence of, or as a supplement to, positive law. Witness, for example, its impact upon the American Declaration of Independence and the Constitution;[8] its citation

---

[7] *The Nature and Sources of Law* (New York: Columbia University Press, 1916), p. 19.
[8] Its classic exposition in that connection is Edward S. Corwin's superb *The Higher Law Background of American Constitutional Law* (Ithaca: Cornell University Press, 1929), known to every student of constitutional law and the judicial process.

by conscientious objectors to military conscription; and its invocation by the civil rights movements of the 1950's and 1960's—for instance, by the Reverend Dr. Martin Luther King's exhortations to disobey "unjust" laws. The theory of natural law originated with the Stoics, by whom it was regarded as embodying those rules of justice discernible by right reason. This view was sometimes taken by Roman jurists; the statesman and theorist Cicero (106–43 B.C.), in defining law, was explicit in stating his concept of its essence:

> Law is the highest reason, implanted in Nature, which commands what ought to be done and forbids the opposite . . . the origin of justice is to be found in law, for law is its natural force; it is the mind and reason of the intelligent man, the standards by which justice and injustice are measured.

> I shall seek the root of justice in nature. . . .[9]

Justinian (483–565) adopted Ulpian's (170–228) definition of natural law as that law which "nature has taught all living beings," thus forecasting the modern bionomic view. The Scholastics generally regarded natural law as that part of the divine law which is not directly revealed but is discernible to reason; and the Rationalists of the eighteenth century derived from their analysis of human societies certain *natural rights* as to life, liberty, and the pursuit of happiness—which they regarded as of prior validity to institutional law.[10] Thus it is the thread of rationality that holds the system together and gives a definite order to it:

> . . . the universe obeys God; seas and lands obey the universe, and human life is subject to the decree of supreme law.[11]

It would seem that natural law thus stands on two assumptions: first, the rationality and intelligence of man; second, the existence of a higher *rational* order of things. Since man is presumed to be intelligent, he can hence readily "find" the law—that is, understand the higher rational order.

Without endeavoring to prove or disprove this theory and estimate of man, his history at least places the issue in doubt. At best, it appears that man is as equally capable of capricious action based upon passion as he is of

[9] Cicero, "The Laws," in Francis William Coker, *Readings in Political Philosophy*, rev. ed. (New York: The Macmillan Co., 1955), pp. 145–46.
[10] Webster's *New International Dictionary of the English Language*, 3rd ed. Unabridged (Springfield, Mass.: G. & C. Merriam Co., 1966).
[11] Cicero, op. cit. p. 151.

rational action based upon intelligence. If man's intelligence is placed in doubt, so is his ability to understand a higher rational order. Indeed, it is difficult for man to believe in a higher order or a universal law of justice be-cause of what he sees in real life—as pointed out by Carneades so many years ago. Holmes, who rejected natural law with vehemence and sarcasm—for which he was scathingly attacked in word and in print by prominent Jesuit law professors—regarded it as "mystic overlaw" and the "product of wishful thinking."[12]

Nonetheless, today natural law is identifiable with the abiding sense of justice that pervades the community of man—regardless of its changing sub-stance—a sense of justice based upon a body of rules and customs which the general development of mankind shows to be essential to human society. But it is the positive law that finally governs us as law-abiding members of organized society. And, as we shall presently see, although natural law, like equity, has had marked influence on English common law, "it is not the same as common law and has never absorbed it."[13]

COMMON LAW AND STATUTORY LAW

For our purposes, then, law—broadly speaking—represents the rules of con-duct that pertain to a given political order of society, rules that are backed by the organized force of the community. As it has evolved through the cen-turies, law has been made either by the political representatives of the peo-ple—sometimes rather inaccurately styled "bar-made" law—or it has been "bench-made" by judges and justices. The former type is generally known as *statutory law*, the latter as *common law*. Both will bear close examination, but, at the risk of some oversimplification, the crucial distinction between the two is that between codified written law and unwritten law based on custom and tradition. (The terms "bar-made" and "bench-made" are never used in England; there they are called "statutory" and "judge-made.")

COMMON LAW

Utilized by most English-speaking states, *common law* is variously known also as *English, Anglo-Saxon,* or *Anglo-American law.* Despite its concep-tualization by Lord Coke as "the perfection of reason," it is indeed a vast

[12] See Francis Biddle, *Justice Holmes, Natural Law, and the Supreme Court* (New York: The Macmillan Co., 1961), especially Ch. II, "The Attack on Justice Holmes."
[13] Ibid. p. 31.

and complex instrument of justice. Although at first glance it may well seem chaotic and abstruse, on closer examination it is readily possible to discern a logic which binds the many diverse components that comprise it into a comprehensive and comprehensible entity.[14]

Common law is judge-made, bench-made, law rather than a fixed body of definite rules such as the modern civil law codes. In Roscoe Pound's words, it is a "mode of judicial and juristic thinking, a mode of treating legal problems."[15] He might well have added "a mood." Often based on precedents, it embodies continuity in that it binds the present with the past. Since it thus necessarily grew, and still grows, by virtue of judicial decisions, it is best to explain and analyze it historically.

Historical Background. With the decline and fall of Rome came the growth of Christianity and Christian philosophy. The concept of the state as the highest form of society began to be questioned with the rise of the Christian Church. With the Norman invasion of the British Isles in 1066, "precise and orderly methods into the government and law of England" were introduced.[16] Thus began under the Norman and Angevin monarchs of the eleventh and twelfth centuries the gradual growth of a central administration and the development of the courts of law. The term "common law" was used for the law developed in the King's Courts and was generally employed in order to distinguish between it and that of the ecclesiastical courts. In effect, the concept "common law" was adopted from the *canon law* of the Christian Church, which was the common law of Christendom. The common law of the King's Courts was made by the royal justices from the mass of customary law of the realm and became the common law of England.

There were three great courts of common law: *King's Bench, Exchequer,* and *Common Pleas.* As the routine of these royal courts became firmly established, it was possible to forecast their decisions in terms of similar cases decided by them in the past. However, according to Theodore F. T. Plucknett,[17] the practice of basing decisions upon precedent did not come about because it was the best rule to follow in decision-making, but because it enabled all existing courts to function with a minimum of trouble.

[14] For an excellent description see F. H. Lawson, *The Rational Strength of English Law* (Stevens, 1951).

[15] Roscoe Pound, *The Spirit of the Common Law* (Boston: Little, Brown and Co., 1921), p. 1.

[16] Theodore F. T. Plucknett, *A Concise History of the Common Law,* 5th ed. (Boston: Little, Brown and Co., 1956), p. 11.

[17] Ibid. p. 342.

In many respects the common law reflects the feudal structure whence it was derived. Over a period of centuries the law defining the relationship between the Anglo-Norman monarchs and their tenants-in-chief became the law that was applicable to all Englishmen. At first this dealt solely with private law, but it was gradually extended to cover public law as well. The core of the feudal law was the concept of fealty, which long prevailed after the passing of feudalism. Ruler as well as subject was bound—there were well-defined rights and obligations to be adhered to by all parties. Private rights of freemen were not subject to arbitrary change, and the primary task of the monarch was to preserve and protect the law.

But the groups whose rights the monarch had to acknowledge were limited to the nobility, the landed gentry, and some segments of the rising bourgeoisie. Hence it is hardly astonishing that the common law—which was essentially a law of property, in particular landed property—was "regarded by the politically influential class . . . as its shield."[18] Ordinary freemen had access to the King's Courts only in exceptional circumstances. However, during the twelfth and thirteenth centuries the practice of issuing *royal writs* was introduced, although these covered merely a few classes of civil cases. But early in the reign of Henry II (1154–89)—he was often termed the Father of the Common Law, although some would credit Henry I (1100–1135) with that title—an ordinance proclaiming that no man could be denied his freehold without a royal writ rendered centralization in a royal court inevitable. This was followed by several writs which continued the trend and culminated in the *Assize of Novel Disseisin of 1166*; it ordained that anyone who was denied his freehold could seek immediate remedy in the King's Court. (The Assize also provided for a jury of one's neighbors in questions of fact.) Thus, by 1166 the King was firmly established as the protector of the freehold.

By 1178 the work of the King's Court had become more than King and Council could handle, and five full-time judges were appointed, some of whom would travel about the countryside, settling disputes in each locality according to prevailing custom. They attended to the bulk of the cases, although the monarch and his Council still disposed of "novel and difficult" matters. This arrangement ultimately led to the schema of legal proceedings based on writs, which were promulgated in ever increasing numbers and came to be sold to the litigants at a fixed price. Until the middle of the thir-

---

[18] Sir Charles Ogilvie, *The King's Government and the Common Law: 1471–1641* (Oxford: Basil Blackwell, 1958), p. 6.

teenth century the King issued new writs to deal with a host of new problems. However, the barons became increasingly jealous of his power to make law, and in 1258 the King was forbidden to issue writs without the specific consent of his Council. As new writs could not be issued, the thirty or forty writs then extant were often interpreted and stretched to deal with problems they were not designed to cope with.[19]

With the founding of the Inns of Court as legal "guilds" in the latter half of the thirteenth century (see Chapter II), unofficial reports of cases commenced to be published in annual *Year Books*. These books were records of court proceedings dealing mainly with procedural points for the benefit of practitioners rather than full reports of "casebook law" in the modern sense. Nevertheless, they quite naturally came to serve as a gradually mounting source of precedents and were frequently referred to by those practitioners in the courts. *Stare decisis et non quieta movere*—stand by past decisions and do not disturb things at rest—began to have genuine meaning as a matter of judicial policy. According to Charles Ogilvie, the first inkling of the future English system of case law may be found in the *Dialogus de Scaccario*, written by Richard Fitz-Nigel between 1177 and 1179:

> There are cases where the courses of events, and the reasons for decisions are obscure; and in these it is enough to cite precedents.[20]

Thus were laid the bases on which the common law rests. As society became more complex, so did the law. At first it was made by the royal courts, but from the thirteenth century on it was always accepted as the supreme and fundamental law of the land. (The Divine Right of Kings was a sixteenth-century idea, not a medieval one.) Bracton (Henry of Bratton), a judge of the King's Bench under Henry II (1216–72)—and without equal as a judicial writer until Blackstone came along five centuries later—in his *De Legibus* stated that the King was "under God and the Law . . . for the Law made the King." He was seconded in 1442 by Sir John Fortescue (1394–1476), Chief Justice of the King's Bench, in his remarkable treatise *De Laudibus Legum Angliae*, and by Sir Edmund Plowden (1518–85), probably the foremost common law sage and interpreter of his time. And the great Sir Edward (later Lord) Coke—Attorney General, Member of Parliament, and Chief Justice of the Court of Common Pleas—when called before his King, James I, echoed his three famed predecessors in declaring that the monarch should also be bound by law. When the King told him

19 Ibid. p. 13.
20 Ibid. p. 17.

that he could not be subject "to any man," Coke replied that, agreed, the King "is not subject to any man, but to God and the law." It was Lord Coke who, more than any other man of his time (1552–1634), compiled and analyzed precedents of common law and who was largely responsible for the increasingly accepted practice of reporting cases fully. From these he drew a set of maxims and rules, later to be amplified and explained precisely by Sir William Blackstone. The latter's monumental four-volume work, *Commentaries on the Law of England* (1765–69) was long the bible of legal training in both England and America. Its basic principles remain as useful pillars of English and American law.

Any notion that judges are to serve the popular majority was and is utterly wrong. For while the common law recognized the authority of King and Parliament, it required all men to bow to the law and act within its limits. England's judges have ever abided by their judicial oath to "administer the law without fear or favor." Various attempts were made to displace common (case) law in England by civil (statute) law—to no avail. Common law not only proved victorious, but over the years it was exported to many countries—among them Canada, Australia, New Zealand, India, Pakistan, Israel, and the thirteen colonies that would become the United States. Scotland, although itself a member of the United Kingdom, is an interesting exception. Its existing legal system was derived from Roman law, as were the Continental systems; but it has been greatly influenced by the common law.

Characteristics. As has already been pointed out, common law is predominantly *judge-made law*. Under it the judge is the creator, interpreter, and modifier of laws. Even when he merely "interprets" law, he may well be creating it. To that extent, statutory law, the law enacted by legislative bodies, is tentative. Discussing the benefits of judge-made law, Mr. Justice Cardozo pointed out that the judge can use "free scientific research" when analyzing a problem. By "free" he meant that the common law removes the judge to a very real extent from action by positive authority; by "scientific" he meant that there is an objective element in the judge's decision. Thus he may come closer to the just and the true, for law under the common law system develops by "judicial experience in the decision of cases."[21] For example, in 1972 the United States Supreme Court, invoking the ancient common law of nuisance, declared unanimously that federal district courts may order polluters to stop fouling the environment.[22]

[21] Pound, op. cit. p. 216.
[22] *Illinois v. Milwaukee,* 406 U.S. 91.

Another significant characteristic of common law is the doctrine of *precedent,* under which the judges refer to a previous decision or decisions in order to adjudicate the case at issue. The importance of precedent varies with individual judges, for although common law normally recognizes precedent as binding, judges not only may occasionally depart from precedent when it "appears right to do so," but they may distinguish between various precedents in evolving the new law. Moreover, times and conditions change with changing society, and, "every age should be mistress of its own law"—an era should not be hampered by outdated law. "It is revolting," wrote Mr. Justice Holmes in characteristically forthright language, "to have no better reason for a rule of law than that it was so laid down in the time of Henry IV. It is still more revolting if the grounds upon which it was laid down have vanished long since, and the rule simply persists from blind imitation of the past."[23] It is the readiness of the common law judges to discard that which does not serve the public which has contributed to the survival and adoption of common law, wholly or partly, in so many lands. Nevertheless, although Mr. Justice Cardozo applauded this, he cautioned that while a judge may discard the old and adopt the new, he must remember that the past is often a reflection of the present and he must know and understand it, "for the depths are the foundation of the heights."[24]

Because common law as such is uncodified, it is generally decribed as *unwritten law.* However, case precedents really are not unwritten; they are derived from the principles of law embodied in the judgments of cases which are decided and reported. Presumably most courts keep records, although they are not all required to do so—for example, some Justices of the Peace in certain of the constituent states of the United States of America who, unlike their English counterparts, must follow the precedent of decided cases.

In summary, the common law appears to have three distinct characteristics that together have enabled the system to develop and expand. First is its *vitality and capability to sustain change.* It does not impress its own peculiarities upon any other law; it only aids in the systematic development of a richer and presumably more just law. Second is its *practical quality.* It is unwilling to accept anything a priori and follows the notion that ideally all laws ought to be tested in the courts. Thus, rules and regulations are treated as working hypotheses, continually re-tested in what Munroe Smith called

[23] From an 1897 address, reprinted in his *Collected Legal Papers* (Boston: A. Harcourt, 1920), p. 187.
[24] Margaret E. Hall (ed.), *Selected Writings of Benjamin Nathan Cardozo* (New York: Fallon Law Book Company, 1948), p. 78.

"those great laboratories of the law, the courts of justice."[25] Third is its *rendition of law as a moral obligation to be obeyed*. The results of the laboratory tests of the law are accepted as valid and everyone is obliged to obey them. After all, in the famous words of Mr. Justice Oliver Wendell Holmes, Jr.:

> The common law is not a brooding omnipresence in the sky, but the articulate voice of some sovereign or quasi-sovereign that can be identified.[26]

And as the great jurist put it so well and so hauntingly in his *The Common Law:*

> The life of the law has not been logic; it has been experience. The felt necessities of the time, the prevalent moral and political theories, intuitions of public policy, avowed or unconscious, even the prejudices which judges share with their fellow-men, have had a good deal more to do than syllogism in determining the rules by which men should be governed. The law embodies the story of a nation's development through many centuries, and it cannot be dealt with as if it contained only the axioms and corollaries of a book of mathematics. In order to know what it is, we must know what it has been, and what it tends to become. . . . The very considerations which judges most rarely mention, and always with an apology, are the secret root from which the law draws all the juices of life. I mean, of course, considerations of what is expedient for the community concerned.[27]

Some three decades later Holmes emphasized this ever recurring theme in his opinion for the Supreme Court of the United States in *Gompers v. United States:* "The provisions of the Constitution are not mathematical formulas having their essence in their form; they are organic living institutions transplanted from English soil. Their significance is vital not formal; it is to be gathered not simply by taking the words and a dictionary, but by considering their origin and the line of their growth."[28]

EQUITY

A branch of Anglo-American jurisprudence, born hundreds of years ago and closely related to the common law, *equity* is actually a supplement to the common law. Although the *Court of Chancery* did not appear until the fif-

---

[25] Benjamin N. Cardozo, *The Nature of the Judicial Process* (New Haven: Yale University Press, 1921), p. 23.

[26] *Southern Pacific Co. v. Jensen*, 244 U.S. 205 (1916), at 222.

[27] Oliver Wendell Holmes, Jr., *The Common Law* (Boston: Little, Brown and Co., 1881), pp. 1–2.

[28] 233 U.S. 604 (1914), at 610.

teenth century, equity courts arose in England in the fourteenth century—apparently as early as 1340—as a result of a practice that permitted a disappointed litigant at common law to lay his plight before his sovereign. That is, he could petition the King to "do right for the love of God and by way of charity," the King being empowered to mold the law for the sake of "justice," to grant the relief prayed for as an act of grace, when the common law gave no remedy, or no adequate remedy.

Chancellor and Chancery. The monarch, on the other hand, habitually referred these petitions to his Chancellor. This member of his Council, who until the Reformation was always a cleric, became known as the "Keeper of the King's Conscience." He was the Council's most important member and the Keeper of the Great Seal, an office to which considerable powers were attached. It was he who could, for example, issue a writ of *subpoena,* commanding a person to appear before a duly constituted legal authority. From many points of view the Chancellor was second in power only to his monarch. Ultimately, the volume of these petitions brought about the establishment of a separate court, the *Court of Chancery.* This was the early court of equity. It maintained its separate existence until 1875, when it was merged in the Supreme Court of Judicature by the Judicature Acts of 1873–75. Its jurisdiction is mainly exercised by the Chancery Division of the High Court of Justice; but all courts now administer both common law and equity, with equity prevailing in cases of conflict between them, statutes (Acts of Parliament) being supreme, however.

The United States of America never had *separate* courts of equity on the federal level. But several states retain such separate courts. In others, the same jurist doubles as law judge and equity judge, sitting one day as the former and one as the latter! In others still, no separate equity courts exist at all—the same courts that decide matters of common and statutory law also administer equity.

Defining Equity. But what is equity? We noted that it is a "supplement" to the common law, thus apparently the "conscience" of the law. It is a supplement to the common law in the sense that the principles of equity—which are now part of the fabric of the common law—were developed by the Court of Chancery as an addition to the principles of the medieval common law. Equity began where the law ended, and it is in that role that we know it today. Thus, it created and continues to create precedents. It takes the form of a *judicial decree,* not of a judgment of "yes" or "no." Equity leaves the judge reasonably free to order *preventive* measures—and under some circumstances even *remedial* ones—usually in the form of a writ, such as an *injunction,* or restraining order, designed to afford a remedy not otherwise obtainable, and traditionally given upon a showing of peril. The judge in the original Court of Chancery exercised his decision, since remedies in equity were discretionary—and so they are today.

For instance, in equity an injunction may be issued by a judge to prevent members of a local of the United Steel Workers of America from going out on strike without having banked the furnaces of the Jones and Laughlin Steel Corporation, despite the inapplicability of the permissive injunctive provisions of the Norris-LaGuardia Act in this case, and despite the fact that the union had given due notice to strike in accordance with the requirements of the Taft-Hartley Act. True, the steel firm involved could probably recover monetary compensation for resultant damages from its insurance company, or from the U.S.W. if it should be found that a contractual provision had been violated by the action of the workers. However, the company here is not interested in such money; its sole aim is to prevent its furnaces from the certain destruction that would result from a failure to bank them. Hence the demand for an equity decree in the form of an injunction against the union.

Another illustration, although considerably less in the realm of immediate peril, might be Mr. John Miller's lovely old copper beech on the edge of his private property, directly in the path of a future highway to be built by the Commonwealth of Pennsylvania. The state has every right to chop down the tree under its power of *eminent domain,* provided only that it does so for a public purpose, which a state public highway certainly is, and that it grant just compensation, which it usually does quite liberally in these circumstances. But Mr. Miller is not interested in financial compensation. He wants to continue to enjoy the beauty and shade of the magnificent tree, and the sentimental attachments that go with it—he proposed to his wife under it; his children and grandchildren climbed it with relish for years. Thus, he, too, may appeal to the courts for equity. His chances for success are undoubtedly considerably less than were those of the steel firm mentioned above, but judges are human beings, not automatons.

STATUTORY LAW

Despite the fact that the concept of *statutory law*—variously known as *code, written, Neo-Roman* or *Roman,* or *civil law*—comes to us from ancient Rome, its broad application is essentially a modern one. Whereas the common law has dealt traditionally with matters of a private character, with the relations between individuals, statutory law is more frequently concerned

16

with society as a whole. It is law that originates with specifically designated, authoritative lawmaking bodies—presumably legislatures, but it also embraces executive-administrative decrees and ordinances, treaties and protocols, all of which are committed to paper.

Historical Background. Statutory law developed in and from the homogeneous city-state, exemplified by the Codes of Emperor Justinian I (527–65), the *Corpus Juris Civilis,* which was promulgated about A.D. 535. Hence it is frequently referred to as Roman law and, to confuse teachers and students alike, as *civil* law—which has nothing whatever to do with civil jurisdiction (see below). In contrast to diversified England, with its manifold customs that veritably seemed to cry out for some sort of common law, Rome lent itself ideally to the development of a statutory system, one that could be readily written down, codified. Statutory law had—and has, of course—the advantages of preciseness, simplicity, and clear-cut applicability, although it still remains subject to interpretation by administrators as well as judges.

Enacted by legislative and/or executive-administrative bodies of government, codified and spelled out in writing by the legal profession, the Bar itself, clearly and readily available for all to see—statutory law has survived as the generally accepted law for most of the states of continental Europe, Russia, Latin America, and many of the newly emergent African nations. Justinian's Code had been initially introduced into western Europe in 544 when the Eastern Empire reconquered Italy. But it did not assume genuine significance for the West until the systematic study of Roman law was revived at the Italian universities in the twelfth century.[29] One of its most famous codifiers was Napoleon I, whose Civil Code was published in 1804, his Code of Civil Procedure in 1807, and others subsequently. Indeed, the *Code Napoleon* has been far more enduring than most of the colorful Emperor's military triumphs. Its first major change did not take place until the Gaullist reforms of 1959 that gave France's married women increased property rights.

"MIXING" COMMON AND STATUTORY LAW

England and the United States today have legal systems based on the common law that readily and naturally found its way across the Atlantic Ocean from the Mother Country to the Colonies. But although it must be categorized as a common law system, the Anglo-American legal framework in effect now consists of a mixture of common *and* statutory law. A great deal

[29] A. T. von Mehren, *The Civil Law System* (Englewood Cliffs, N.J.: Prentice-Hall, Inc., 1957), p. 6.

of contemporary law is necessarily statutory; it is coded. However, this is a relatively recent development, for although statutes as a basis of Anglo-American law were not unknown, they played no really significant role until the second quarter of the nineteenth century.

The mixture came into its own largely, although certainly not exclusively, as a result of the perpetuating conservatism of the common law, particularly in the realm of the sanctity of private property, based on the overriding concept of economic *laisser faire*. With the advent of a rising spirit of common social consciousness and responsibility, and a gradual movement toward the service or welfare state on both sides of the ocean, legislative bodies everywhere—but considerably more slowly in the United States than in the United Kingdom—commenced to change or even displace the age-old concepts and practices of the common law in favor of what were viewed as primary considerations of necessary public interest.

Nonetheless, common law remained as an important basis of legislative motivations and actions, and often an enacted statute would—as indeed it still does today—simply spell out certain aspects of the grand sweep of common law. Furthermore, no legislative body—and sometimes not even the executive—is consistently, or even largely, capable of pinpointing in writing all the aspects and ramifications of a statute or order, nor would that necessarily be desirable even if it were possible. The result is interpretation, usually first by administrative units, then often by the courts, and—as we shall have ample opportunity to observe in Chapters V to IX—when courts interpret, they cause statutes to grow or contract. This interpretation becomes part of the statutes and orders, thus giving them meaning in the spirit and application of the common law. Truly, England and America resort to a framework of law that is a generally wholesome blend of common, statutory, and equity law.

Of course, there are certain areas of statutory law where little, if any, discretionary elements remain for the judge. The United States Criminal Code, for example, represents a compendium of laws that prescribe what shall constitute a crime and what the penalties shall be. A judge may have a modicum of leeway regarding the former, but the sole substantive discretion left to him in the realm of the latter is one specifically written into the code. Thus, a particular law may conceivably permit him to exercise his considered judgment as to the severity of a sentence which he is called upon to impose for a given criminal infraction, but this discretion will be strictly limited by the minimum and maximum penalties as provided in it. Moreover, it may well be limited by the nature of the verdict of the jury. Indeed, *criminal law* is becoming more and more codified everywhere among the common law lands, and hence is becoming statutory. The same applies to *public law* generally, although the great bulk of *private* law is still common law. A few words of explanation about these two types of law and some additional legal concepts are in order.

SOME ADDITIONAL LEGAL DEFINITIONS AND CONCEPTS

A few terms and concepts related to notions that play a part in these pages must be elaborated upon here, however briefly. A host of others will be treated throughout the book.[30] We begin with a distinction between the two types of law into which *municipal law*—the law that applies within a state—is normally divided, namely *private* and *public* law.

Private law governs the relationship between private citizens or persons; that is, it regulates the relations of individuals with each other. It is concerned with the definition, regulation, and enforcement of rights in cases where both the person[31] in whom the right inheres and the person upon whom the obligation devolves are private individuals. Obvious examples of private law are the law governing contracts between individuals or corporations and that pertaining to marriage and divorce. In the sense that infractions of the legal obligations inherent in these areas are subject to adjudication by courts, the state is involved, of course, but it is neither the subject of the right nor the object of the duty.

Public law, on the other hand, is a branch or department of law which is very much concerned with the state in its political or sovereign capacities— including the important two subheadings of administrative and constitutional law (to be described presently). Public law deals with the definition, regulation, and enforcement of rights in those cases where the state *is* viewed as the subject of the right or the object of the duty, including criminal law and criminal procedure. In other words, it is that portion of law which is concerned with political conditions and situations—with the powers, rights, duties, capacities, and incapacities that are characteristic of and peculiar to both supreme and subordinate political authority.

[30] A standard legal dictionary, e.g. *Black's Law Dictionary*, will readily supply answers to any others that may occur to the inquiring reader. The definitions used in this section are based in part on its 4th ed. (St. Paul: West Publishing Co., 1957), pp. 1394, 1359, 385, and 67.

[31] In 1886 the Supreme Court declared corporations to be legal "persons" under the Constitution. (See p. 348, *infra.*)

19

Public law applies to and effects the entire people of a nation or state that adopts or enacts it—in contrast to private law, which affects and applies to only one or a few individuals—for it regulates both the relations between individuals and the state and the relations between the branches of the government. Thus, the vast majority of legislation enacted by Congress is in the category of public law—and its statutes are codified, preceded by the term "Public Law_____ [Number]." Social welfare, defense appropriations, subversive activities control, farm subsidies—all these areas of legislation represent illustrations of the vast, diversified content of public law.

Administrative law, which has quite naturally achieved ever increasing prominence over the past few decades, consists of those rules and regulations that are promulgated by the sundry administrative agencies of government that have been empowered to deal with the operation of government under the delegated rule-making authority of the legislative body. That branch of public law prescribes in detail the activities of the agencies involved—such as those concerned with the collection of revenue; regulation of competitive practices; coinage; public health, welfare, safety, and morals; sanitation; and regulation of the armed forces.

Constitutional law is the other great branch of public law. It determines the political organization of a state and its powers while also setting certain substantive and procedural limitations on the exercise of governing power. Because of its position and nature it stands legally above all other types of municipal law, public as well as private. In the United States, with its written Constitution, constitutional law consists of the application of fundamental principles of law based on that document, as finally interpreted by its highest judicial organ, the Supreme Court of the United States. A contemporary example is the famous *Steel Seizure Case.*[32] Believing himself invested with the power to act in his capacity as Commander in Chief and endowed with what he and his advisers viewed as "inherent authority," President Truman seized the steel mills on April 8, 1952, in order to forestall a nation-wide strike in the midst of the Korean War. The owners filed for a writ to enjoin him, charging the absence of both constitutional and legislative authority for his actions. After a series of dramatic skirmishes in the lower federal courts, the United States Supreme Court received the case for adjudication—clearly a matter in the realm of constitutional law. On

---

[32] *Youngstown Sheet and Tube Co. v. Sawyer,* 343 U.S. 579 (1952). The dramatic July 1974 decision in *United States v. Nixon,* 417 U.S. 683, is, of course, another pertinent illustration (see pp. 110, 337, 350).

June 2, 1952, the Court rendered its decision, featured by seven different opinions! But six of the nine Justices did agree on *one* crucial point: that by *usurping legislative power* President Truman had violated the Constitution, and that the seizure of the steel mills was hence *ultra vires*—particularly so since Congress had expressly refused to enact a suggested amendment to the Taft-Hartley Act authorizing such governmental seizures in an emergency.[33]

In brief, constitutional law prescribes generally the plan and method under which the public business of the political organ, known as the state, is conducted. And it differs further from the other types of law we have seen in that it is both enacted and changed either in an extraordinary manner by an ordinary legislative body or by an extraordinary body, such as a constitutional convention, constituted especially for that purpose.

In the United States changes in the letter of the fundamental document are based on the special constitutional amendment provisions of its Article V, which combine extraordinary federal with extraordinary state action. In the United Kingdom, where no formal written constitution and no power of judicial review exist, Parliament is supreme and may affect changes in the constitutional law of the land by ordinary legislation. But it is highly unlikely to tamper with the great cornerstones of its unwritten Constitution —that intriguing British concept consisting of the heritage of the common law, great statutes, important documents, decisions of the courts (other than judicial review), and customs and conventions, that combined constitute the very life blood of the realm. In France the written Constitution of the Fifth Republic may be altered only by extraordinary action of Parliament with the co-operation of the President of France, either with or without ratification by a popular referendum, depending upon the procedure invoked by the President in the course of the initiating stages. And in Switzerland, not only do constitutional alterations by the government call for mandatory ratification by popular referenda, but the Swiss citizens may take the initiative directly by drawing up a proposed constitutional amendment and submitting it for direct popular referendum approval.

[33] Quipped *The Economist* (May 10, 1952) as the case was about to reach the Supreme Court: "At the first sound of a new argument over the United States Constitution and its interpretation, the hearts of Americans leap with a fearful joy. The blood stirs powerfully in their veins and a new lustre brightens their eyes. Like King Harry's men before Harfleur, they stand like greyhounds in the slips, straining upon the start. Last week, the old bugle-note rang out, clear and thrilling, calling Americans to a fresh debate on the Constitution." *The Economist* had an even better time with *United States v. Nixon* in 1974!

21

CIVIL AND CRIMINAL LAW

Another basic distinction of considerable importance which confronts the observer of the judicial and legal process is that between *civil law* and *criminal law*. (The former is not to be equated here with the concept of "civil law" when used as a synonym for statutory or Roman law; here the reference to it is in connection with the subject matter governing in a particular case.) Whether a particular offense is of a civil or criminal nature determines not only the severity of the legal sanction that may be invoked, but frequently the type of tribunal before which the case will be heard. As we shall see in subsequent chapters, some courts are empowered to hear cases involving *both* types of law, as in all three major federal constitutional courts of the United States; but in many instances the judicial hierarchy provides for a separate set of criminal and civil courts, as is the case, to a greater or lesser extent, in both England and France—although many of the English judges are used interchangeably.

Civil Law. A case at *civil law* is normally one between private persons and/or private organizations, for civil law governs the relations between individuals and defines their legal rights. A party bringing suit under it seeks legal redress in a *personal* interest, such as for a breach of contract, a divorce action, a defamation of character, the use of a copyrighted story without permission. Yet while suits at civil law far more often than not are suits among private persons, the government, too, may conceivably be involved. For example, under the Sherman Anti-Trust Act of 1890, as amended, the federal government in the United States is empowered to bring either civil or criminal action against an alleged offender. It has much more frequently brought civil than criminal actions under that statute, probably because the former are not so difficult to win and cause less of an uproar in the interested community.

Criminal Law. A case at *criminal law* is invariably brought by and in the name of the legally constituted government, no matter at what level—national, state, or local—it may arise. Chiefly statutory in the United States, criminal law defines crimes against the public order and provides for appropriate punishment. Prosecution brought under it by the proper governmental authority involves an accusation that the defendant has violated a specific provision of a law, an infraction for which a penalty has normally been provided by statute. Criminal cases comprise such felonies or major crimes as homicide, espionage, sabotage, rape, and perjury, to name but a few. The coverage is as extensive as the lawmakers choose to make it. Since the prosecuting authority in a criminal case is necessarily an agent of the sovereign, the latter's name appears in its title. Hence, assuming one Brown's indictment for murder in Pennsylvania, the case would be docketed for trial as either *The Commonwealth of Pennsylvania v. Brown*, or as *People v. Brown*. Moving to the federal level, one of the cases brought under the membership clause of the Smith Act of 1940 was entitled *United States v. Scales*.[34] However, by far the largest volume of criminal law is still enacted at the state level in the United States and thus is enforced by state officials under state law. Unitary countries, such as France and the United Kingdom, are not confronted with that jurisdictional problem.

But in all cases and at all levels it is the jurists who render the decisions. Alexis de Tocqueville put it well: "Hardly any question arises in the United States that is not resolved sooner or later into a judicial question." To the jurists, then, to their fascinating and significant tasks, and the hierarchical framework in which they perform their duties, we now turn.

[34] 367 U.S. 203 (1961).

23

II
Staffing
the
Courts

SELECTION

What principles should govern the selection of the men who dispense justice? To raise this question brings us face to face with moral, as well as political, questions of the greatest importance. However awe-inspiring their functions may be, our judges are still human beings. As such they make the ultimate decisions in the judicial process. In essence, there are just two basic methods of selection: *appointment* and *election*—no matter who does the actual appointing or electing—although, as we shall see, a compromise between the two modes has been devised and is practiced on certain levels of the judiciary in a good many jurisdictions. A collateral question is whether judges should be members of a career service as in France, chosen from a special group of lawyers as in England, or selected through appointments from the legal profession generally as in the United States. Practices of selection differ in large measure in accordance with the traditions and needs of the country concerned. A crucial consideration here is the very position of the judiciary in the framework of government that provides the rationale for the particular mode adopted and adhered to. Under the Roman law tradition of the Continent, the judiciary is a part of the over-all administrative hierarchy and, as such, represents a position and profession other than that of the ordinary lawyer. Under the common law system, on the other hand, the judges are drawn exclusively from the ranks of the legal profession. Nevertheless, the guiding principles for the selection and tenure of the judiciary in the three countries that concern us most here—Britain, France, and the United States—display a commonly held ideal: judges are expected to be impartial and hence must be given assurance of independence, security, and dignity of tenure. When these are present, the fact that different techniques govern selection in these lands is hardly of great significance. Nevertheless, these techniques must be studied and understood. The process of selection is assuredly more complicated than might be inferred from the otherwise trenchant observation of W. Curtis Bok's imaginary Judge Ulen who quipped: "A judge is a member of the bar who once knew a Governor."[1]

THE TWO CHIEF METHODS

With the important exception of a majority of the (roughly) 12,000 judges in state and local courts, the *appointive* method is employed predominantly in the United States. It is used *exclusively* at the *federal* level of the government, regardless of whether the tribunal concerned is a constitutional or legislative court (a distinction that will be described in detail in Chapter IV). Britain and France use appointment exclusively at all levels.

Appointment. In the *United States* all of the approximately 550 active federal judges are appointed by the President, subject to confirmation by simple majority vote of the Senate. Depending upon the Chief Executive involved, the President's responsibility—a heavy one—has often been largely delegated to the Attorney General and, in practice, to the Deputy Attorney General. This was noticeably true during the later years of the Administration of President Eisenhower, when the selection of members of the federal judiciary was left almost exclusively to Attorney General William P. Rogers and Deputy Attorney General Lawrence E. Walsh. On the other hand, President Lyndon B. Johnson gave Chairman John C. Macy of the U.S. Civil Service Commission a crucial role in the judicial selection process. But three other important factors enter here. *One* is the obvious need for consultation with the United States Senator(s) and/or other seats of political power in the home state of the candidate for judicial office—provided these political figures are of the same party as the appointing authority. Thus, care must be taken that the appointee is not "personally obnoxious" to a home-state Senator, on pain of having the latter invoke the age-old, almost invariably honored, custom of "senatorial courtesy"—a certain death-knell to confirmation by the Senate. The custom is based on the assumption that the President will, as a matter of political patronage, practice, and courtesy,

---

[1] *Backbone of the Herring* (New York: Alfred A. Knopf, 1941), p. 3. H. L. Mencken once observed that "a judge is a law student who marks his own exams."

25

engage in such consultation prior to the nominee's designation—provided that the Senator is a member of the President's party. If the President fails to adhere to the custom, the aggrieved Senator's colleagues will support him on his call for the nominee's defeat, as a matter of fraternal courtesy. Let it be said at once that as a practical matter it is not possible for the Chief Executive to select a candidate for the federal bench and see him confirmed without at least the grudging approval of his Senators. And some powerful Senators of the President's political party will insist not only on the right of prior approval of the President's choice, but also on the right to have particular candidates of their own designated. At the very least, this pertains to the federal district bench.

The *second* factor that has played an increasingly significant role in the appointive process of the federal judiciary in the United States, especially since the latter months of the Truman Administration,[2] is the American Bar Association's twelve-member Committee on Federal Judiciary, established in 1946.[3]

That committee, which was widely utilized subsequently during President Eisenhower's terms of office—a practice continued under Presidents Kennedy, Johnson, and, with the exception of Supreme Court nominees after 1971, Nixon—has generally produced good results and is understandably popular with the legal profession, although there is no unanimity on any evaluation. There are those who believe deeply that the selection of the members of the judicial branch of the government must rest, in fact as well as in name, with the executive branch, its head being specifically charged to do so under Article III of the Constitution; and that the apparent delegation of important aspects of that authority to a private body, no matter how qualified and how representative—a crucial point—is at best questionable, and at worst a dereliction of duty. Nor is the bar free from political or personal biases, as the Committee's contrasting handling of the Fortas and Haynsworth cases in 1969 demonstrated. To cite an earlier case in point, had President Wilson heeded the advice of the A.B.A., Mr. Justice Brandeis would never have been nominated. Furthermore, as an intriguing book-length study of the committee's activities over a period of two decades demonstrated rather convincingly,[4] its membership has been dominated by the

---

[2] The groundwork was laid by President Truman's last Deputy Attorney General, Ross B. Malone.

[3] It consists of one member from each of the eleven federal judicial circuits and a chairman.

[4] Joel B. Grossman, *Lawyers and Judges: The Politics of Judicial Selection* (New York: John Wiley & Sons, Inc., 1965).

"legal establishment." Almost all of its members have been successful lawyers, older, experienced men, partners in large, big-city firms, veterans of local bar association politics. Of the relatively few lawyers the committee had asked to give an evaluation of judicial candidates a decade ago, 70 per cent were officers of local bar associations and 80 per cent were senior partners in "respectable" law firms.[5] At least some diversification has set in, however.[6]

Whatever the merit of demurrers, the committee has become a powerful and respected vehicle in the vital initial stages of the nominating process— at least below the Supreme Court level. After an investigation customarily lasting from six to eight weeks,[7] it reports to the Justice Department on the qualifications of the prospective nominee and rates him in one of four ways: Exceptionally Well Qualified (EWQ), Well Qualified (WQ), Qualified (Q), or Not Qualified (NQ).[8] In a number of cases the consideration of nominees for the federal bench was dropped after the A.B.A.'s committee found them less qualified than others; also its reports have enabled the Justice Department to rule out certain names recommended by the home-state Senator(s).

To illustrate, in September 1961 the Senate confirmed 60 lower court federal judges nominated by President Kennedy, 52 of whom had been rated by the A.B.A. Nine had been rated Exceptionally Well Qualified, 27 Well Qualified, 14 Qualified, and 2 Not Qualified. Yet the two rated Not Qualified—James R. Browning, then the clerk of the U.S. Supreme Court, and Luther Bohanan, an Oklahoman—had sufficiently powerful support to gain confirmation. However, a finding of Not Qualified is not necessarily a reflection on a nominee's character or ability. Thus, the A.B.A.'s committee will not approve anyone who has reached the age of sixty-four, and no one above sixty unless he is ratable at least WQ. President Kennedy's selection

---

[5] Grossman, op. cit. pp. 82–92.

[6] Thus, Professors Richard G. Watson, Rondal G. Downing, and Frederick G. Spiegel, in an article concerned with the members of Missouri's Bar, contend that the notion that the bar is inevitably conservative is *disproved* by the Missouri experience: "Bar Politics, Judicial Selection and the Representation of Social Interests," LXI, *American Political Science Review*, 54 (March 1967).

[7] It is based in part upon the candidate's responses to a 28-page-questionnaire, one question of which asks about the ten most significant cases he has handled.

[8] These categories are not applicable to Supreme Court nominees, however, which began to be rated only as of the 1956 Brennan appointment and then only as Q or NQ to the Senate Judiciary Committee. But after the Haynsworth and Carswell debacles, the committee, as of the Blackman nomination, adopted the following Supreme Court rankings: (a) "high standards of integrity, judicial temperament, and professional competence"; (b) "not opposed"; and (c) "not qualified."

27

of Sarah T. Hughes of Texas[9] to be a federal district court judge was disapproved on that ground, but she was confirmed. In the case of a sitting judge the committee will approve *promotion* up to sixty-eight. The committee is loath to recommend lawyers without trial experience—which was true of both Browning and Bohanan—and it generally insists on fifteen years of experience in "the rough and tumble of legal practice."[10]

Considerably more will be said on the point later, but it should be re-emphasized here that no alert and prudent Chief Executive of the United States would nowadays attempt to designate members of the judiciary *purely* on the basis of political considerations. Too much is at stake in matters of policy and public awareness, and the American Bar Association is a powerful factor in the selection process. Yet, granted the various needs and drives for appointments on the basis of over-all merit and excellence, the political pressures must nevertheless be reckoned with and are disregarded only at the appointing authority's peril. Moreover, a federal judgeship is viewed as such a "plum" by all concerned, in that it represents a potent patronage-whip in the hands of the executive vis-à-vis state politicians as well as Congress.

Both the continuing problem and its flavor are suggested nicely and candidly by this passage in Senator Joseph S. Clark's newsletter of August 11, 1961, to his constituents in Pennsylvania:

> I have forwarded to the Attorney General recommendations to fill additional Judgeships recently authorized by Congress in the United States District Courts in Pennsylvania, and one vacancy in the Court of Appeals for the Third Circuit. I regret that, by custom, Senators have the obligation of making these recommendations after appropriate consultation with their State political leaders. I believe the selection of judges should be entirely nonpartisan and should be made by the Attorney General and the President without Senatorial intervention [a proposal backed unsuccessfully by Attorney General Elliot L. Richardson during his brief tenure under President Nixon in 1973]. Nevertheless, I must live with the rules as they exist until they are changed. After consultations with Governor Lawrence, Democratic State Chairman Otis Morse II, Congressman William J. Green, Jr., and others, I am satisfied that the recommendations made for existing vacancies are men of ability and integrity. The Attorney General and the President will make the final decisions on these Judgeships of course, and may disregard our recommendations if they wish.

[9] Judge Hughes swore in Lyndon B. Johnson in the presidential plane "Air Force 1" after President Kennedy's assassination on November 22, 1963.
[10] Committee member Robert Trescher to author, December 9, 1971.

There is a *third* factor: increasingly demonstrable evidence of the role that sitting members of the Court itself, especially the Chief Justice, may play in consulting with and being consulted by the President in the selection process of a new Supreme Court Justice. Chief Justices Taft, Hughes, Stone, Vinson, Warren and Burger have thus all been involved[11]—Taft more openly and actively than any other. His role in Harding's nomination of Butler was a classic example. In fact, Harding's Attorney General, Harry M. Daugherty, told Henry Taft—William's brother—that he "would not approve anybody for appointment who was not approved by [the Chief Justice]."[12] It is entirely possible to make a good case for the practice—within limits.

In Britain—we are here again almost exclusively concerned with England and Wales (for convenience hereafter referred to as England), since Scotland and Northern Ireland, the two other members of the United Kingdom of Great Britain and Northern Ireland, operate separate court systems—judges are designated by the Crown with little or no surrender to politics. Practically speaking, they are the choices of the Lord Chancellor, the senior law member of the government, who is the Queen's chief adviser on the selection. Since the Lord Chancellor is chosen by the Prime Minister, the latter does have an indirect voice in the selection of judges, however truly small and inaudible that voice is, especially on the middle and higher levels. Among these are the Lords of Appeal in Ordinary (the Law Lords), the Lord Chief Justice, the Master of the Rolls, the President of the Family Division of the High Court of Justice, and the Lord Justices of the Court of Appeal. In the cases of the Lord Chief Justice and the Master of the Rolls, the highest ranking judicial offices, the Prime Minister in effect designates the appointees but acts on the advice of the Lord Chancellor. But it is the Queen who actually issues the commission of appointment.

The Lord Chancellor himself, however, is the politically designated head of the judicial hierarchy of the United Kingdom. In addition, he advises on all appointments to judicial office from the rank of Justice of the Peace to

---

11 For a good description of Taft's role in Harding's designation of Pierce Butler, see David Danelski, *A Supreme Court Justice Is Appointed* (New York: Random House, 1964). See also Alpheus T. Mason, *William Howard Taft: Chief Justice* (New York: Simon and Schuster, 1965) and *Harlan Fiske Stone: Pillar of the Law* (New York: Viking Press, 1956). For a full-scale study of *all* appointments to the Supreme Court through 1973, see Henry J. Abraham, *Justices and Presidents: A Political History of Appointments to the United States Supreme Court* (New York: Oxford University Press, Inc., 1974).

12 Quoted by Mason, *Taft*, op. cit. p. 173.

the higher offices of the English Judiciary. As Speaker of the House of Lords he presides from the Woolsack (a bright red padded bench, its name signifying how important the wool trade was to the British economy in earlier centuries); is a member of the Cabinet; and as head of the Judiciary combines in his person the threefold function of executive, legislator, and jurist —a complete refutation of the principle of separation of powers so dear to Montesquieu. His office—which pays £20,000 ($50,000), the highest British government salary—is older than that of Prime Minister. Since the group of lawyers from whose ranks the Lord Chancellor[13] chooses judges is comparatively small and select, he may know some of them, and when members of the Opposition seem to give promise as competent judges, he will certainly not hesitate to cross party lines to make appointments. If he does not personally know, or know of, a candidate, he will probably consult a senior judge or judges and obtain their views—but *not* their prior approval. Incidentally, barristers must leave the bar when they go on the bench.

No letters of recommendation are accepted, and efforts to put political pressure on the Lord Chancellor are scouted strongly. R. M. Jackson, Reader in Public Law and Administration in the University of Cambridge, in his excellent study on the machinery of justice in England,[14] contends that political considerations have hardly entered the process of judicial selection since 1907—although they died a slower death in the case of the office of Lord Chief Justice; and he insists that, as a consequence, there has been no apparent connection between the "political antecedents" of the judges and their decisions in over a century. However, members of the House of Commons may be appointed to county-court judgeships and also to the High Court.[15]

In *France*, and in many other countries on the Continent, the trained judges are appointed to, rise in, and are promoted from a type of career service which is an adjunct of the general civil service. The de Gaulle Constitution of 1958 specifically makes a point of the time-honored concept that an ideal judge is an impartial judge. There is a Ministry of Justice, but the judges of France (numbering 4200 in 1974) do not really feel its au-

---

[13] On two occasions the title was held by men who were later sainted—Thomas à Becket and Sir Thomas More.

[14] Richard M. Jackson, *The Machinery of Justice in England*, 6th ed. (Cambridge: Cambridge University Press, 1972), p. 378.

[15] For example, in 1962 two of the members of the High Court were from the House of Commons, and the then new President of its Probate, Divorce, and Admiralty Division (now called the Family Division) was the former Solicitor-General, a member of the House.

thority, although the Minister is part of the appointing process. Political patronage plays scarcely a role in their selections. They have all been either schooled as judges for a minimum of twenty-eight months at the École Nationale de la Magistrature in Bordeaux (established in 1959) or have had experience as judges, and they enter the judicial service on the basis of passing competitive examinations.

Theoretically, the President of the Republic, who is charged by the Constitution to be "the guarantor of the independence of judicial authority,"[16] selects the judges; actually, they are chosen either by the eleven-member Conseil Superieur de la Magistrature (High Council of the Judiciary) in the case of the Cour d'Appel and the Cour de Cassation, or by the Minister of Justice, who may consult with, or receive advice from, the High Council, in the case of the lower courts. The High Council consists of the President of the Republic (as le président), the Minister of Justice (as vice president), and nine persons with legal background chosen by the President for a once-renewable term of four years, partly on the recommendation of the Cour de Cassation and the Conseil d'État, as follows: one from the latter; three from the former; three from other courts; and two selected for their general legal knowledge and competence. In any event, the selecting authorities have little choice—considerably less than in England and infinitely less, of course, than in the United States.

The assets and liabilities of the appointive versus the elective method are rather obvious. In general the main argument in favor of appointment hinges on the contention that a candidate for a judicial post who is obliged to run on a partisan ballot cannot possibly serve as an impartial judge, and that he is selected, as Al Smith once put it, "by an electorate who are not really in a position to pass upon the legal and other abilities of the individual."[17] On the other hand, the champions of election on a partisan ballot argue that appointment by a political executive contains even worse features of political beholdenness than election. As is so often the case, neither side of the argument is ipso facto correct on all counts; both contain some merit, and it is easy to oversimplify. Someone, however, has to assume responsibility for staffing the courts; it might as well be the executive, who not only possesses the expertise and has access to all pertinent data, but also is fairly well known to the populace at large on almost all levels and, in fact, is usually the sole officer of government with an all-embracing constituency.

[16] Title VIII, Article 64.
[17] As quoted by Arthur T. Vanderbilt, "Brief for a Better Court System," The New York Times Magazine, May 5, 1957, p. 9.

In a free society, the people—at least in theory—are always in a position to hold him accountable. Making him responsible for unfortunate judicial appointments is more meaningful and more palatable to the electorate than is any arrangement that requires the voters not only to submerge judges into the political arena, but also to become intimately familiar with their adjudicatory record. Whatever the ramifications of this balancing of scales, executive appointment of judges—however it may be subject to input and influence by other sources, private as well as public—has proved to be the preferred method of selection in the United States (with notable state-level exceptions), England, and France. Although compromise arrangements of the type illustrated below may well move onto the scene here and there, there is no chance that election will supplant appointment for the selective process of judges in the vast majority of countries in the free world.[18]

Election. Nevertheless, election of members of that branch of the government is not unknown, even at the national or federal level of governments. In Switzerland, a major exception to the *federal* appointment principle, judges are elected by the two federal chambers—the *Nationalrat* and the *Ständerat*—sitting jointly as the *Bundesversammlung* (National Assembly) to assure that German-, French-, and Italian-speaking members are appropriately distributed on the bench. However, re-election is so usual that to all intents and purposes permanent tenure of office is the result. In a drastically different category, the Soviet Union, too, practices the elective method exclusively, but (a) the victorious candidates serve for short terms only and (b) they have been approved by the political hierarchy of the state in advance of their candidacy.

Election of judges is widespread at the state level of most of the states in America—where recently fully 82 per cent of the nation's state and local court judges were still elected,[19] although by diverse methods. Judges may be elected either by the people (as in Florida) or by the legislature (as in South Carolina and Vermont, where the higher judges are so elected). Judges *sometimes* appear on bipartisan tickets (e.g. Pennsylvania), or even

---

[18] In Israel, recommendations for judicial appointments are made to the Government by an Appointments Committee, consisting of the President of the Supreme Court; two judges from the court containing the vacancy who are chosen by its members; two Bar Association-selected lawyers; the Minister of Justice; and two members selected by the *Knesset* (Parliament). Nominees must come from the ranks of experienced judges, advocates, or legal academicians.

[19] *Time Magazine,* March 30, 1970, p. 48. But *real* contests are relatively rare, and active politicking by judges is usually, although by no means always, regarded as demeaning. A major effort to move to appointment of most New York judges, led by Chief Judge Charles D. Breitel, was under way in 1974.

on a nonpartisan one (e.g. Minnesota) on occasion, but loyal service in partisan politics tends to be a prerequisite for nomination—in line with Jacksonian tradition. Also, while the elective term of office is on the average but eight to ten years, it extends to life for certain judgeships in some states (e.g. Supreme Court of Rhode Island) and to rather lengthy periods in others (e.g. twenty-one years, nonrenewable, for the post of Supreme Court Justice in Pennsylvania). In a few states the concept of supporting the sitting judge has been adopted when he is up for re-election,[20] but this theoretically laudatory practice has been ignored almost as much as it has been observed. Moreover, the mitigating factors that are inherent in the deviations from the straight, partisan, short-term ballot election are found in but a few states, and even in these they are usually confined to the upper echelons of the judiciary.

Other practices worthy of note in this general consideration of selection are those of gubernatorial appointment subject to some legislative consent (e.g. the Delaware Senate) and appointments by courts (e.g. some low level judges and magistrates by high level jurists in Hawaii, Illinois, South Dakota, and Virginia). Massachusetts' gubernatorially appointed judges serve for life; those of New Jersey serve for seven years, and then, if reappointed, serve for life.

A COMPROMISE?

An intriguing attempt at a compromise between the elective and appointive methods of choosing state judges in America has been advanced and popularized in somewhat different versions by a number of states at the Supreme Court and/or other appellate levels. This is the case in California, Missouri, Alaska, Kansas, Colorado, Iowa, Oklahoma, Indiana, Nebraska, Utah, Tennessee, and Vermont. It may also be found at certain low-level, often municipal or metropolitan courts, as in Utah, Tuba County (Oklahoma), Denver County (Colorado), Dade County (Florida), and Birmingham, Alabama. It is designed to minimize political influence and provide a degree of security of tenure, while retaining an element of popular control. Repeatedly and even enthusiastically supported by leading spokesmen of the legal profession and by knowledgeable laymen alike, it has been widely

---

[20] Thus New York State Court of Appeals Associate Judge Stanley H. Fuld, who had demonstrated great talent in twenty years of service on that tribunal, was nominated for the post of Chief Justice on the November 8, 1966, ballot by all four political parties: Republican, Democratic, Liberal, and Conservative.

adopted; its chief obstacle is powerful political opposition, which views this compromise as a genuine threat to the patronage aspects of judicial selection—as well it might be. California and Missouri were the pioneers in the compromise movement.

The California Plan. The first well-known original attempt at a solution to the vexatious problem of judicial selection was the *California Plan,* adopted by referendum vote in 1934. A vigorous campaign for ratification had been started two years earlier by the California State Bar Association, encouraged by its national parent body. The State Bar Association was closely allied with the California Chamber of Commerce. The two powerful state groups had become convinced of the inadequacy of the system under which California then operated—judicial appointment by the Governor with subsequent popular approval, which in their eyes constituted little more than public rubber-stamping of the appointment authority's rank political designations.

Under the California Plan, which applies to the judges of the Supreme Court and District Courts of Appeals only, the Governor nominates *one* person to the Commission on Qualifications. This body is composed of the Chief Justice of the State Supreme Court, the Presiding Judge of the District Court of Appeals of the area concerned, and the Attorney General. If the commission approves the Governor's nominee, the latter is deemed appointed for the duration of *one year only.* At the end of that year he stands for popular election for a full twelve-year term of office—his name being the only one on the nonpartisan ballot. The sole question appearing on the ballot in connection with the nominee's candidacy is "Shall_____ _____ be elected to the office for the term prescribed by law?" There are no limits on the number of terms to which a successful candidate may aspire. Should the electorate's response to the question on the ballot be in the negative, his successor will be designated by the Governor in the same manner, ultimately to go before the electorate as well. In any event, the burden of approval is on the people, who must familiarize themselves with his record—or at least they ought to do so.

The first test of the plan returned the sitting judges by a 2 : 1 affirmative vote, a margin of approval that has steadily widened since that time. Appraisals of the California Plan have been generally favorable, though some have criticized as inadequate what in their view is the essentially negative restriction placed on the Governor's power by the commission. To refuse to confirm a gubernatorial appointment takes a certain amount of courage—not inevitably demonstrated by the commission. There have also been doubts voiced concerning the wisdom of placing a measure of control over judicial appointments, however negative, into the hands of the chief law officer of the state, the Attorney General. Nonetheless, the plan has worked well and has been favorably received by the vast majority of those concerned.

The Missouri Plan. Desirous of adopting a modified version of the California Plan, and learning a tactical lesson from its defeat in popular referenda in 1938 in both Ohio and Michigan, the supporters of the *Missouri Plan* waged a vigorous and enlightened campaign, headed by both professional and lay groups. The movement for its adoption was spearheaded by the Missouri Institute for the Administration of Justice, an educational corporation composed of one-third lawyers and two-thirds laymen, who successfully enlisted the active support of civic, labor, farm, and business organizations. They explained to the electorate the true purpose of the plan: to secure an intelligent and impartial selection of personnel for the bench, to eliminate as much as possible the haphazard results of the elective system, and to relieve the judges of the pressures of political campaigning. And the supporters of the plan pointed out shrewdly that neither the California nor the Missouri Plan was designed to supplant the elective method entirely —that this was clearly a compromise between appointment and election. Characterized by the American Bar Association as the "most acceptable substitute available for direct election of judges," the plan became law in the form of an amendment to Missouri's Constitution in 1940.

The Missouri Plan is mandatory for the judges of the Missouri Supreme Court, the state's other appellate courts, the circuit and probate courts in St. Louis and in Jackson County, and the St. Louis Court of Corrections. It is optional, subject to popular referenda, in the thirty-eight other circuits of the state. Thus, judges of a number of courts, especially those of the lower levels, may well remain outside the compromise plan, as do the judges in California. Under the Missouri version, nonpartisan nominating boards known as the Missouri Appellate Commissions, operating on different court levels, select *three* candidates for every vacant judgeship. For the Supreme Court and the appellate courts, the commission consists of the Chief Justice of the State Supreme Court, the chairman; three lawyers, elected by the state bar, one from each of the three courts of appeals; and three citizens *not* members of the bar, appointed by the Governor, again on the basis of one from each of the three appellate districts. The commissions for the circuit and other lower court judges comprise the presiding judge of the court of appeals district in which the circuit happens to be situated; two members of the bar elected by its own members residing in the circuit involved; and two similarly resident nonbar citizens appointed by the Governor. The members of all these nonsalaried commissions are designated for staggered six-year terms of office, with changes taking effect in alternate years. Since the Governor has a four-year term and can succeed himself but once, it is unlikely that he would appoint all of the lay members. To ensure an additional degree of impartiality, commissioners are permitted to hold neither public office nor an official position in a political party.

The Governor of Missouri is obliged to choose *one* of the three individuals selected by the Appellate Commission and appoint him for *one year*, as under the California Plan. After this probationary period, the appointee must offer himself to the electorate for a full twelve-year term (in the appellate courts) or six-year term (in the trial courts), running unopposed on a separate, nonpartisan judicial ballot at the time of the general election. The question on the ballot, very similar to that of California, is "Shall Judge . . . of the . . . Court be retained in office? Yes (   ) No (   ) (Scratch one)."

Generally deemed to be the most adult and most commendable system of judicial selection extant in the various states, the Missouri Plan embraces a number of commendable features. It combines the democratic notion of accountability to the electorate with an intelligent method of selecting qualified candidates for judicial office. The necessity of facing the electorate on his record provides the judge with an incentive of judiciousness; and the fact that he runs on his own record rather than against that of an opponent allied with a specific political party goes far toward taking the courts out of the more crass aspects of politics. On the other hand, a case could be made for the contention that the awareness of establishing a "good record" for the electorate's eyes and ears may lead to timid and/or "popular" judgments. The results of the Missouri Plan in action, however, do not generally support that theory.

An examination of the election returns for a number of years demonstrates the over-all acceptance of the plan by Missouri's electorate. In 1942 the state went Republican, but two judges of the Supreme Court, both Democrats, were retained by a favorable vote of 2 : 1; six circuit court judges in St. Louis were similarly returned for new full terms in that same election. In 1944 Missouri went Democratic, yet two judges of the Supreme Court, one a Republican and one a Democrat, received the same proportion of the popular vote. In 1946 St. Louis went Republican, but retained its ten circuit judges, all Democrats, seven of those rolling up 4 : 1 majorities. In 1948 the state went Democratic, yet of the two judges retained by Kansas City by an identical vote of 5 : 1, one was a Democrat and one a Republican. In St. Louis, in the same general election, five Democratic and one Republican circuit judge were returned for full terms of office, the Republican and two Democrats receiving 4 : 1 votes, the other three Democrats 3 : 1.[21]

From 1940 through 1970, 179 judicial elections under the plan were held in Missouri: *only one* of these saw a judge *rejected* by the vote of the people—and he received 46.4 per cent affirmative votes.[22] The political parties have respected the plan and, by and large, have made no effort to influence elections under it. The plan has been strongly defended also by the judges, who find themselves in a position to attend to their court dockets free from worries and pressures about forthcoming political campaigns. It is thus not at all astonishing that approximately one-fifth of the states have adopted variations of the Missouri Plan,[23] including a number of states which had defeated the California Plan years earlier.

The two leading plans described represent what is probably a happy compromise between the appointive and elective systems of selection, and they have deservedly engendered considerable support among professionals and laymen. Yet most students of the political scene are inclined to agree that in a representative democracy the appointive system is the more desirable one for the judiciary, provided it is backed up by long—preferably life—tenure and it possesses a genuine degree of independence.[24] Even when one constructs a pattern based on party allegiance, it becomes evident that *appointed* judges are *much* more willing to "vote" against "their" party on the bench than are elected judges.[25] The appointing authority is not beyond accountability—and there is no meaningful substitute for effectively lodged governmental responsibility in a free society.[26] As has been well said else-

---

[21] See Laurence M. Hyde, "Choosing Judges in Missouri," 38 *National Municipal Review* 491 (November 1949).

[22] He was Marion Walter, a circuit judge, prominently identified with the discredited Pendergast machine. See Richard A. Watson—a leading expert on the Missouri plan—"Choosing the Judges," 53 *Judicative* 289 (February 1970).

[23] Alaska, California, Colorado, Iowa, Kansas, Missouri, Nebraska, Oklahoma, Tennessee, Utah.

[24] There are notable exceptions: Stuart Nagel, for example, argued in an interesting article, "Political Party Affiliation and Judges' Decisions," LV *American Political Science Review* 850 (December 1961), that "if judges should have value positions that are representative of the public at large, then it seems arguable that judges (at least on the higher court levels) should be elected, since presumably a judge elected at large will tend to have more representative values than a judge chosen in another manner."

[25] Ibid. pp. 848–49.

[26] Herbert Kaufman, *Politics and Policies in State and Local Governments* (Englewood Cliffs, N.J.: Prentice-Hall, Inc., 1963), p. 60.

where, "on balance our judicial system still represents primarily a compromise between representativeness and neutral competence."[27]

TENURE OF OFFICE

Essential to the independence of the judiciary is the security of tenure, particularly in the case of appointed judges—our main concern here. Without a lengthy term of office, preferably life, adequate remuneration, and stringent constitutional and/or statutory safeguards against removal, the concept of judicial independence becomes a mockery. The record of the three major Western democracies in this regard has been laudatory generally; their practices at the level of the national judicial hierarchies are relatively similar.

THE UNITED STATES

At the *federal* level in the United States of America, all judges of the *constitutional* courts—those appointed under the provisions of Article III of the Constitution (the judicial article)—hold their position during "good behavior," which in effect means for life or until they choose to retire. The other federal judges—those of the *legislative* courts, created under the provisions of Article I of the Constitution (the legislative article)—occupy their positions for whatever period Congress may have prescribed at the time of its establishment of the court or in subsequent legislation. In some instances this has meant "good behavior" tenure for them too, or, frequently, terms of office ranging between four and fifteen years. The constitutional judges have the additional safeguard, stated in Article III, that their ". . . compensation . . . shall not be diminished during their continuance in office." Hence, while their salaries may be increased during their incumbency, they may not be lowered—short of a constitutional amendment of the section concerned. And were a judge of a constitutional court to be removed from office other than in the manner expressly permitted by the Constitution, his salary would indeed be rather drastically "diminished."

Although far from commensurate with the responsibilities and prestige of their office, and infinitely lower than comparable positions in private enterprise, judicial salaries are adequate. In 1974 the annual range on the fed-

[27] An intriguing proposal is advanced by Harold W. Chase in his *Federal Judges: The Appointing Process* (Minneapolis: University of Minnesota Press, 1972), pp. 205ff., in which he calls for the appointment of *all lower federal* courts by the nine justices of the United States Supreme Court alone.

eral level—as will be discussed in more detail in Chapter IV and V—was from $40,000 for judges of the United States Customs Court to $62,500 for the Chief Justice of the United States Supreme Court, his associates receiving $2500 less. But it is hardly for financial gain that a person would aspire to high judicial office. (Compared with those of federal judges, the salaries of state judges are surprisingly good, ranging from an *average* of $26,500 for appellate courts down to $22,500 for all courts in 1974—with New York paying as much as $52,622, plus $6000 in expenses, for its Chief Judge.)

Partly to enable aging jurists to step down from the bench in dignity, and concurrently to render their replacement with younger personnel more palatable, Congress enacted a vastly improved retirement statute in 1937. Under its provisions, federal judges may retire—a more accurate description is "enter inactive status," subject to temporary calls to duty at the discretion of the Chief Justice of the United States—on full pay at the age of seventy after having served ten years on the federal bench, or at sixty-five after having served fifteen years.[28] These requirements are waived in the presence of physical disability, in which case retirement pay is computed in accordance with length of service. Widows and dependents receive an annual purse equivalent to 37.5 per cent of the judge's average salary—if the jurists elected to participate in a contributory "judicial survivors annuity plan."

Despite the liberal provisions of the act, the average federal judge—in particular, the average Justice of the Supreme Court (if such there is)—is reluctant to leave active service. More vacancies occur as a result of death in harness, particularly at the higher levels, than in any other way. Of the ninety-five Supreme Court vacancies between 1789 and 1974, death in of-

---

[28] More than half of the Justices have served fifteen years or more on the highest bench. (Indeed, the members of the U.S. Supreme Court have enjoyed significantly greater longevity than men in the general population. See *Statistical Bulletin*, October 1971, p. 3.) An official example of an assignment order directed to a "retired" member of the Court is the following, issued by Mr. Chief Justice Warren to retired Associate Justice Stanley Reed. "Assignment Order: An order of the Chief Justice designating and assigning Mr. Justice Reed (retired) to perform judicial duties in the United States Court of Claims beginning November 1, 1965, and ending June 30, 1966, and for such further time as may be required to complete unfinished business, pursuant to 28 U.S.C. Section 294 (A), is ordered entered on the minutes of this court, pursuant to 28 U.S.C. Section 295." (Quoted as it was published in *The New York Times*, October 19, 1965.) A somewhat different order saw Mr. Chief Justice Warren assign Mr. Justice Tom C. Clark (retired) to service in the U.S. District Court for Northern California in June 1970. Late in 1965 *retired* Justice Charles E. Whittaker submitted his *resignation* in order to accept a legal position with the General Motors Corporation.

fice was responsible for forty-eight—although, since the passage of the 1937 statute, of twenty-two vacancies, retirement was responsible for twelve, resignation or disability for ten. In the entire twentieth century to date only six Justices have stepped down from the high bench for reasons other than ill health or advanced age: Hughes (to run for President in 1916); Clarke (in 1922, to work for world peace); Byrnes (in 1943, to become F.D.R.'s "Assistant President for Domestic Affairs"); Goldberg (in 1965, to succeed Adlai E. Stevenson at the U.N.); Tom Clark (in 1967, because his son, Ramsey, had become U.S. Attorney General); and Fortas (in 1969, as a result of disclosures of off-Court involvements with financier Louis Wolfson). It is human to cling to power and influence, and it is particularly human to enjoy a role of such significance and nation-wide esteem.[29]

Removal. The removal of federal judges who wish to remain on the bench can only be effected by the process of impeachment and conviction—although it is evidently legal for the Judicial Council of a United States Circuit to discipline one of its federal judges by stripping him of his duties and authority while permitting him to retain both his title and his salary.[30] In accordance with constitutional requirements, impeachment for "Treason, Bribery, or other high Crimes and Misdemeanors"[31] may be voted by a simple majority of the members of the House of Representatives, there being a quorum on the floor. Trial is then held in the Senate, which may convict by a vote of two-thirds of the members of the Senate present and voting, there being a quorum.

Considerable controversy exists as to the exact meaning intended by the framers of Article II, Section 4, when they spoke of "other high Crimes and Misdemeanors." Some—Gerald Ford, for one—have contended that an impeachable offense is whatever a majority of the House views as such (although he came to insist that he had reference only to the appointed members of the judicial branch, not to the elected President). Others, among them the followers of James Madison and Alexander Hamilton, insist, with

[29] Thus, Mr. Chief Justice Taft: "As long as things continue as they are, and I am able to answer in my place, I must stay on the Court in order to prevent the Bolsheviki from gaining control. . . ." (Quoted in C. Herman Pritchett, *The Roosevelt Court* (New York: The Macmillan Co., 1948), p. 18.) Justices Grier, Field, and McKenna, all three in various stages of senility after lengthy service, had to be coaxed off the bench by their colleagues—who were driven to resort to some ingenious devices.

[30] This was done by the Tenth Circuit's Judicial Council in the case of Oklahoma Federal District Court Judge Stephen S. Chandler, in January 1966. He appealed, unsuccessfully, to the Supreme Court for review. (*Chandler v. Judicial Council of the Tenth Circuit*, 382 U.S. 1003 (1966).)

[31] Article II, Section 4.

those Founding Fathers, that the concept of "misdemeanor" is broad enough to encompass "any offense against society" committed by a public official, be it criminal or not. Still others, President Nixon's defense team, for example, claimed that there can be no impeachment in the absence of a criminal act, and that that act, moreover, would have to be an *indictable* offense—while, in the same breath, they insisted that no President can be indicted while in office. A close reading of the Constitution and the works of its framers, and a careful study of the publications of such leading constitutional experts as Harvard Law Professor Raoul Berger, The Committee on Federal Legislation of the Bar Association of the City of New York, and other legal bodies, lead to the considered conclusion that neither a criminal act nor an indictment is a necessary requirement for a vote of impeachment by the House—which should not, however, drive us to embracing the Ford statement as a guide to a proper course of action. The Committee on the Judiciary of the House of Representatives, which voted three articles of impeachment against President Nixon in July 1974, clearly did not.

To date the House of Representatives has initiated a total of thirteen impeachment proceedings, of which ten were directed against federal judges (nine others resigned before formal charges were lodged against them*); one, in 1798, against United States Senator William Blount of Tennessee (charges against him were dismissed by the Senate by a 14 : 11 vote early in 1799 for want of jurisdiction, that body having already voted to expel him, 25 : 1, six months earlier on grounds of conspiracy to seize Spanish Florida and Louisiana with British and Indian help); one, in 1868, against President Andrew Johnson (who was acquitted by the margin of one courageous vote, 35 : 19, the House having charged him 126 : 47); and one, in 1876, against Secretary of War William Belknap (who was subsequently acquitted, 37 : 25). President Nixon *resigned* on August 9, 1974, *before* the House of Representatives took a formal vote on the three counts of impeachment placed against him by its Committee on the Judiciary by votes of 27 : 11 (for obstruction of justice), 28 : 10 (for unconstitutional abuse of power), and 21 : 17 (for failure to comply with a subpoena for tapes as evidence). However, following Nixon's public admission that he had withheld pertinent evidence, and his subsequent resignation, the Committee sent to the House a now *unanimous* report, charging that he had engaged in "deliberate, repeated, and continued deception of the American people" about the

---

* The last one was 7th U.S. Court of Appeals Judge Otto Kerner, former Governor of Illinois, who resigned on July 24, 1974, having been the first federal judge ever to be convicted of a felony (bribery).

Watergate case. The House took no stand on its Committee's conclusions, but officially voted to accept its report, 412 : 3.

Of the ten impeachment proceedings involving federal judges, nine went to trial, with five resulting in acquittals and four in actual removals; the tenth was not pursued by the House—United States District Court Judge Mark H. Delahay, who had been impeached by voice vote, resigned in 1873 before the articles of impeachment could be prepared. The five that ended in acquittal, briefly sketched below, are headed, both chronologically and in importance, by the only impeachment trial to date that has involved a Justice of the Supreme Court, that of Associate Justice Samuel Chase.

(1) *Samuel Chase.* A staunch and partisan convert to the Federalist cause, and one of President Washington's last appointments to the Supreme Court, Mr. Justice Chase was impeached by the House in March 1804 by a vote of 72 : 32. He had made himself obnoxious to the Jeffersonians and others by a long series of injudicious and partisan attacks against them, both on and off the bench; by his "tyrannical trials [of opponents] under the Alien and Sedition Law [of 1798]"; and by his obvious favoritism toward Federalists. His judicial posture was certainly not a happy one, but he had not committed any impeachable offense per se. Even so, the Senate tried him, and with great ceremony. Vice President Aaron Burr presided, and Mr. Chief Justice Marshall was an important defense witness. Chase was justly acquitted in March 1805, the Senate failing to attain the required two-thirds majority for a conviction on any of the eight charges. The result was a signal victory not only for the narrow interpretation of the impeachment process, but also for an independent judiciary. Chase remained on the highest bench until his death in 1811.[32]

(2) *James H. Peck*, a judge of the United States District Court for the District of Missouri, impeached 123 : 49 in April 1830 for "misconduct in office by misuse of contempt power," acquitted in January 1831 by a vote of 22 : 21.

(3) *Charles Swayne*, a judge of the United States District Court for the Northern District of Florida, impeached by voice vote in December 1904 on twelve charges of "padding expense accounts; using railroad property in receivership for his personal benefit; and misusing contempt power," acquitted in February 1905 on all counts by varying votes.

(4) *George W. English*, a judge of the United States District Court for

[32] For an authoritative commentary and interpretation see Richard Tillich, "The Chase Impeachment," 4 *American Journal of Legal History* 49 (1960).

the Eastern District of Illinois, impeached by a vote of 306 : 2 in November 1926 for five counts of "partiality, tyranny, and oppression"; but proceedings in the Senate were dismissed, 70 : 9, when the accused resigned his office that December.

(5) *Harold Louderback*, a judge of the United States District Court for the Northern District of California, impeached in February 1933 by a vote of 183 : 142 on five charges of "appointing incompetent receivers and allowing them excessive fees," acquitted in May 1933 on all counts by diverse votes.

Of the four impeachment trials that resulted in conviction, the first was probably unconstitutional as well as unjust, the second was questionable, and the third and fourth were justified.

(1) *John Pickering*, a judge of the United States District Court for the District of New Hampshire, who was known to be medically insane at the time, was impeached by the House in December 1803 on four counts of "irregular judicial proceedings, loose morals, and drunkenness" by a vote of 45 : 8. In March 1804 the Senate removed him from office by identical 19 : 7 votes on each of the articles. John Adams characterized the Pickering removal as "an infamous and certainly an illegal conviction." Nevertheless, the unfortunate Pickering had been hopelessly insane and an alcoholic for three years.

(2) *West H. Humphreys*, a judge of the United States District Court for the Middle, Eastern, and Western Districts of Tennessee, impeached by voice vote in May 1862 on seven counts of "support of secession and holding Confederate office." In a one-day trial, on June 26, the Senate convicted Humphreys on all charges but one, removing him from office by a 38 : 0 vote and disqualifying him from holding any further office by a 36 : 0 vote.

(3) *Robert W. Archbald*, an associate judge of the United States Commerce Court—which was abolished in 1915—was impeached in July 1912 by a 223 : 1 vote on thirteen serious charges of misconduct in office. The Senate removed him in January 1913 by voice vote, after he had been convicted on five of the articles of impeachment. He was then disqualified from holding any further office by a 39 : 35 vote.

(4) *Halsted L. Ritter* was the last jurist to date to be both impeached and convicted. A judge of the United States District Court for the Southern District of Florida, Ritter was impeached by the House, 181 : 146, in March 1936 on seven counts of "bringing his court into scandal and disrepute," including the receipt of corrupt payments, practicing law while on the bench, and falsifying income tax returns. That April the Senate acquitted him on

43

six of the counts, but found him guilty on the seventh, 56 : 28. A motion to disqualify him from holding any further office lost 76 : 0, however.

The undoubtedly fortunate failure of most impeachment attempts is not an indication of any lack of verbal efforts by legislators who, partly sincerely and partly for constituent consumption, are eager to "get" federal judges—in particular, the Justices of the Supreme Court—usually for decisions that the Congressmen have found repugnant for a variety of reasons. To cite but one modern example: In June 1953 a special subcommittee of five members was created by the House of Representatives to consider the impeachment of Supreme Court Justice William O. Douglas. The resolution for impeachment, which was brought to the House by Congressman W. M. Wheeler (D.-Ga.), charged the jurist with "high crimes and misdemeanors in office," Douglas having granted a brief stay of the scheduled execution of convicted spies Julius and Ethel Rosenberg—a stay which had been set aside by the full Court almost at once. Nothing came of Mr. Wheeler's efforts.[33] (In fact, the attempt would be all but forgotten today were it not for a statement made by Gerald Ford on the floor of the House: "an impeachable offense is whatever a majority of the House of Representatives considers it to be at a given moment in history." Mr. Ford came to regret that assertion two decades later.) Such efforts are not confined to the people's representatives. In February 1957 a group of some two dozen men and women filed with the Clerk of the House of Representatives a petition demanding that the House impeach the entire membership of the Supreme Court. It consisted of foot-long pages headed "Impeach Warren," a battle cry that was taken up with a vengeance by the John Birch Society, which widely advertised "The Warren Impeachment Packet" (obtainable for "One Dollar, Postpaid"). And the Georgia State Assembly, in a colorful brochure decorated with the state flag, distributed "A Resolution Requesting Impeachment of Six Members of the United States Supreme Court"—Justices Warren, Black, Reed, Frankfurter, Douglas, and Clark (Burton, Harlan, and Brennan escaping their wrath, somehow). The main charge: "Unconstitutional . . . pro-Communist racial integration policies."[34]

---

[33] In July 1966 Rep. George W. Andrews (D.-Ala.) introduced another unsuccessful impeachment resolution against Douglas, this one on the ground of his "character," in view of the then sixty-seven-year-old Justice's fourth marriage. (His new wife was twenty-three.) Andrews was joined by Reps. Paul Findley (R.-Ill.) and Thomas G. Abernathy (D.-Miss.). And in 1970 Douglas's congressional enemies—led by Gerald Ford, who by then had become Republican Floor Leader—tried again to impeach him, and again failed!

[34] H.R. No. 174, "A Resolution," adopted on February 22, 1957, pp. 3–12.

The majority of the *states* follow the federal pattern regarding removal of their appointed judges who have lengthy or life tenure, impeachment and conviction being the normal process available. Among the few states that have found it necessary to resort to it are Tennessee, in the case of Criminal Court Judge Raulston Schoolfield, for "corrupt and injudicious conduct," in 1958, and Oklahoma, in the case of its Supreme Court Justice Napoleon Bonaparte Johnson in 1965. But a good many other modes of removal exist in various states. In Massachusetts and New Hampshire judges may be removed by address of the Governor to both houses of the legislature; in California, Utah, Washington, and Wisconsin they may be removed by a joint resolution of the legislature; in Texas, Louisiana,[35] Alabama, and Michigan removal power is vested, on various terms, in the state supreme courts; in Oklahoma (since 1966), Illinois, and New York special courts are provided to hear removal charges. In New York the court is known as the *Court on the Judiciary*. It was created by constitutional amendment in 1948; until then the state legislature held the removal power. The court heard its first case in 1959, at which time it considered the removal of two judges, Kings County jurists Nathan R. Sobel and Samuel S. Liebowitz. It voted not to remove either of them, although it did "censure" them both for their public demeanor. In 1963, however the court ousted New York Supreme Court Justice Louis L. Friedman and New York Claims Court Judge Melvin H. Osterman, in two separate actions. Two other jurists—Michael M. D'Auria and Mitchell D. Schweitzer—resigned in 1971 and 1972, respectively, rather than face action by the Court on the Judiciary. And in December 1973 the court removed Supreme Court Justice Joseph P. Pfingst, who had been under suspension for having been convicted of concealing a monetary conflict of interest.[36] In several western states, sitting judges may be recalled from office by popular vote—an in-

[35] In November 1970 the Louisiana Supreme Court, acting on the recommendation of the State Judicial Commission, by a 6 : 1 vote removed from office Judge Edward A. Haggerty, Jr., who had been arrested in a vice squad raid on a "stag party" in a local motel a year earlier. (*In re Judge Edward A. Haggerty, Jr.*, La. 241 So. 2d 469.)

[36] Friedman was removed by a 4 : 2 vote for having engaged in "unethical judicial conduct" and having violated the "concept, spirit, and letter" of the canons of judicial ethics. He unsuccessfully appealed for U.S. Supreme Court review (*Friedman v. Court on the Judiciary*, 375 U.S. 10 (1963), *certiorari* denied). Osterman was removed by unanimous vote for his refusal to sign a waiver of immunity and answer questions before a New York grand jury investigating the 1963 New York State Liquor license scandals. His appeal to the U.S. Supreme Court also met with a denial of review (*Osterman v. Court on the Judiciary*, 376 U.S. 914 (1964), *certiorari* denied). Pfingst had unsuccessfully petitioned for Supreme Court review of his conviction. (*Pfingst v. Court on the Judiciary*, 412 U.S. 941, *certiorari* denied.)

triguing and controversial manifestation of "direct democracy," of which the referendum and the initiative are both illustrations.

BRITAIN

The British have come a long way since the days of James I (1603–25) and Charles I (1625–49), when the English judges held their office *durante bene placito nostro* ("according to our good pleasure"). Most, but not all, English judges today, very much like their cousins in the United States, enjoy what to all intents and purposes is tenure for life. But since The Courts Act of 1971, "the Lord Chancellor may remove a circuit judge from office on the ground of incapacity or misbehaviour."[37] Recorders—lower judges— are removable for "failure to comply with any requirements" of their appointment.[38] The custom of appointing judges for indefinite terms of office during their "good behaviour" dates back to the Act of Settlement of 1701, which provided that judge's "commissions" be made *quam diu se bene gesserint* ("as long as they will have performed well"). One significant recent change must be noted, however. As a result of the mandate of the Judicial Pensions Act of 1959 and the Courts Act of 1970 a seventy-two-year retirement limit for judges of the superior and circuit courts has been adopted for all appointments at that level, with a possible three-year extension. Recorders retire at seventy-two, but Higher Court judges may stay until seventy-five. Retirement pensions are paid on a graduated scale that rises from one-quarter of basic salary after five years of service to a maximum of half of the annual salary after fifteen years.

For practical purposes, the English judges, notably those of the superior courts, are irremovable, the Judicature Act of 1925 providing that all judges except the Lord Chancellor hold office "during good behaviour subject to a power of removal by His [now Her] Majesty on an address presented to His [now Her] Majesty by both Houses of Parliament."[39] However, the judges of the county courts are deemed to be removable at the insistence of the Lord Chancellor for "inability" and "misbehaviour" under various statutes, e.g. the County Courts Act of 1959. The justices of the peace are also removable for similar reasons of "misconduct" or "proved incapacity." In fact, the English judges are not protected in any way from a change by statute; Parliament retains its fundamental power to alter their tenure and emoluments of office. Suffice it to say that it is highly unlikely to do so in

[37] Sec. 17(4).
[38] Sec. 21(6).
[39] Sec. 12(1) of 15 & 16 G.O., Ch. 49.

a detrimental sense! In any event, a dismissal of a judge for political reasons is impossible today for all practical purposes. Indeed, since the Act of Settlement of 1701, *only one* English judge has been removed on any grounds (although official complaints have been lodged against seventeen). That single removal took place in 1830, when Sir Jonah Barrington, a superior judge—a judge in admiralty—was deprived of his office by petition of both houses of Parliament as a result of an inquiry into the Irish courts of justice carried out during that year.

The salaries of the judges, which range between £6550 (for circuit judges) and £20,000 (for the Lord Chancellor, which includes the salary payable to him as Speaker of the House of Lords), are set by Act of Parliament,[40] but are, in effect, set by the Lord Chancellor with the consent of the Minister of the Civil Service. The executive branch may not move to reduce these while the recipients hold office, and the legislature is similarly enjoined since judicial salaries do not even come up for parliamentary review. A further indication of effective judicial independence is the parliamentary custom that no questions at all may be asked about the conduct of courts in particular cases. Moreover, according to two court rulings now firmly regarded as *res judicata* in England,[41] a judge may not be held for civil or criminal proceeding because of anything he may have said or done in his judicial capacity, even if it is alleged to have been malicious or in bad faith. Given these cherished safeguards of judicial strength and independence, the English bench has reciprocated in full measure with a record of efficiency and impartiality not likely to be readily matched anywhere in the free world today. Sir Ivor Jennings was quite correct when he contended in 1954 that "no allegation" of partiality or corruption or political influence is ever made against judges of the United Kingdom.[42]

FRANCE

The career judges of the Fifth French Republic who, as we have seen, comprise a branch of the national civil service, also have life tenure. There is no doubt that they are at least as secure today as are their English and American counterparts. But it took a considerable while to attain that cherished goal. During the *ancien régime* judicial office went customarily to the favorites of the monarch, and especially to those who could afford to pay for

---

[40] See Sec. 1(2) of the Ministerial and Other Salaries Act of 1972.
[41] *Anderson v. Gorrie*, 91 L.J.K.B. 897 (1922), and *Heddon v. Evans*, 35 T.L.R. 642 (1919).
[42] *The Queen's Government* (London: Penguin Books, 1954), p. 147.

47

it. *La révolution* replaced that interesting system of patronage *cum* purchase with popular election of judges—which was not much of an improvement, if any. Napoleon Bonaparte grandly eliminated that method and announced the principle of "irremovability," which, in practice, meant rather complete dependency upon *him*. A period of minor changes and ameliorations was effected by the institutions and individuals that succeeded the colorful Corsican until the days of the Third Republic, barely a century ago, when the status of the French judges improved—without, however, reaching a truly separate status.

Irremovability as an avowed policy for the career judiciary was resuscitated by a proclamation of the Provisional Government a few days after V-E Day in 1945. It was made a part of the basic document of the de Gaulle Republic by the specific verbiage of the Constitution of 1958, which asserts that these judges are "irremovable." Actually, that is technically incorrect, for they *are* removable—but solely for "misconduct in office," and then only upon the recommendation of the High Council of the Judiciary, which acts as a disciplinary court for judges. When it sits as such, the President of the *Cour de Cassation* is its presiding officer.

The judges of France are not so well paid as those across the Channel,[43] but there is no evidence that they are in any sense more susceptible to corruption or injudiciousness than their English counterparts. Strengthened even more by the specific proviso of the de Gaulle Constitution making the President of the Republic the "guarantor of the independence of the judicial authority," and by the genuine protective power of the High Council of the Judiciary, they enjoy an extensive degree of both professional freedom and authority.

QUALIFICATIONS AND MOTIVATIONS: THE UNITED STATES

Although attitudes and practices regarding tenure of office do not differ significantly among the American, British, and French judiciaries, substantial —indeed, crucial—distinctions become immediately apparent in any consideration of the qualifications—background, experience, and training—of the judges in these three countries. They represent distinctions that flow

[43] The average salaries of the French judges in 1974 ranged from approximately NF 29, 850 ($5970) for the lowest echelon to NF 96,069 ($19,216) for the highest, not counting certain allowances that might add up to 20 per cent. (Data provided by M. André Arnaud, Service de Presse et d'Information, Ambassade de France, June 10, 1974.)

rather logically from different traditions and theories regarding the role of government in society, and they are attuned to what, for better or for worse, are deemed to be the needs and experiences of each land. With these thoughts in mind we turn to a consideration of the problem of judicial qualifications in the United States.

BASIC PREREQUISITES?

In contrast to the specialized requirements that obtain in Britain and France, there is but one standardized prerequisite for qualification as a United States *federal* judge today—the LL.B. or J.D. degree of the aspirant. However, the possession of that degree is neither a constitutional nor a statutory requirement for appointment: yet custom would automatically exclude from consideration anyone who did not have it. Moreover, the legal profession, which, as already noted, has a very real voice in today's appointive process, would remonstrate so determinedly that the political powers of the government involved would assuredly acquiesce. Still, at the *state* and local level not even the LL.B. is necessary in many instances![44]

Theoretically, any graduate of an accredited bona fide school of law with his eye on a federal judgeship may thus look forward to an appointment to the coveted niche—provided that he is politically "available" *and* acceptable to the executive, legislative, and private forces that, in the order enumerated, constitute the powers-that-be which underlie the paths of selection, nomination, and appointment in the judicial process. In the final analysis, of course, it is the President and his immediate advisers concerned—here usually the Attorney General and his Deputy—who take the crucial step of submitting the nominee to the Senate. Thus, all of America's chief executives, except William Henry Harrison, Zachary Taylor, and Andrew Johnson, have succeeded in seeing at least one nominee attain membership on the highest court of the land—which will be our chief concern in these particular pages. Of the three exceptions, the first two were removed too quickly by death, and Johnson was the victim of congressional machinations which successfully prevented him from filling several Supreme Court vacancies. Table I illustrates the number of Justices each President appointed and who *actually served*, including those not ultimately confirmed by the Senate. An example of the latter is John Rutledge, who was designated Chief Justice by President Washington in 1795. The Senate, by a vote of 10 : 14, refused to confirm the President's recess appointment of the man whom it had approved as Associate Justice in 1789, but who had resigned that post less than two

44 See Ch. IV, infra, pp. 138–40 and fns. 4–6.

years later without ever sitting—although he had served on circuit duty—in order to accept the post of Chief Justice of the Supreme Court of South Carolina (and hence is listed as only one Washington appointment). Counting Mr. Justice Rutledge thus just once, and Justices E. D. White, Hughes, and Stone twice—since those three all actually served both as Associate Justice *and* as Chief Justice and were appointed by a different President in each instance—the 100 individual Justices who had served on the Court as of the beginning of the 1973–74 term provided thirty-four Presidents with 103 successful appointments.

JUDICIAL EXPERIENCE AND ITS ABSENCE

In view of the minimal basic requirement of the LL.B. or J.D., it is hardly astonishing that many a newly appointed United States jurist lacks practical judicial experience.[45] Among the appellate courts, this has been especially true of United States Supreme Court designees; those of the court level immediately below, the United States (Circuit) Court of Appeals, have often had some lower court experience on the United States District Court—the federal trial court. Among the 100 individual Justices who served on the Supreme Court between 1789 and the end of 1974, only twenty-two had ten or more years of previous judicial experience on any lower level, federal or state, at the time of their appointment, and forty-two had no judicial experience whatsoever. Yet, as Table II demonstrates, the list of the totally inexperienced contains many of the greatest and most illustrious names in America's judicial history. Among them are six of the fifteen Chief Justices (eight if one does not count Hughes's and Stone's years as Associate Justices)—Marshall, Taney, S. P. Chase, Waite, Fuller, and Warren—and Associate Justices Story, Miller, Bradley, Brandeis, and Frankfurter, to name a few.

In a learned essay calling for selection of Supreme Court justices "wholly on the basis of functional fitness," Mr. Justice Frankfurter argued keenly that neither judicial experience nor political affiliation nor geographic considerations ought to play a significant role in the appointment of these highest jurists, whose job he viewed as necessarily requiring the qualities of *philosopher* ("but not too philosophical," commented his student Paul A.

---

[45] By way of contrast, in addition to other requirements, nominees to the intermediate appellate judiciary in Pakistan, for example, must have a minimum of ten years of judicial experience; and they need fifteen years for appointment to the Pakistan Supreme Court (including five years at the intermediate appellate level).

Freund), *historian, and prophet*.[46] Even though ill-equipped to do so (the task requires "poetic sensibilities" and the "gift of imagination"), he must "pierce the curtain of the future . . . give shape and visage to mysteries still in the womb of time." He must "have antennae registering feeling and judgment beyond logical, let alone quantitative proof."[47] Thus, Frankfurter asserted:

> One is entitled to say without qualification that the *correlation between prior judicial experience and fitness for the Supreme Court is zero*. The significance of the greatest among the Justices who had such experience, Holmes and Cardozo, derived not from that judicial experience but from the fact that they were Holmes and Cardozo. They were thinkers, and more particularly, legal philosophers.[48]

And on this point Mr. Justice Frankfurter was fond of quoting the distinguished Judge Learned Hand, who for so many years rendered outstanding service on the United States Court of Appeals for the Second Circuit (New York, Connecticut, and Vermont), but who never attained his richly merited promotion to the Supreme Court:

> I venture to believe that it is as important to a judge called upon to pass on a question of constitutional law, to have a bowing acquaintance with Acton and Maitland, with Thucydides, Gibbon and Carlyle, with Homer, Dante, Shakespeare and Milton, with Machiavelli, Montaigne, and Rabelais, with Plato, Bacon, Hume, and Kant as with books which have been specifically written on the subject. For in such matters everything turns upon the spirit in which he approaches the questions before him. The words he must construe are empty vessels into which he can pour nearly everything he will. Men do not gather figs of thistles, nor supply institutions from judges whose outlook is limited by parish or class. They must be aware that there are before them more than verbal problems; more than final solutions cast in generalizations of universal applicability. They must be aware of the changing social tensions in every society which make it an organism; which demand new schemata of adaptation; which will disrupt it, if rigidly confined.[49]

Attitudes Toward Experience. Yet the experience factor for Supreme Court Justices, although more or less dormant during some Administra-

[46] To which, in a conversation with the author in May 1964, Mr. Justice Brennan added "inordinate patience."

[47] *Of Law and Men* (New York: Harcourt, Brace & Co., 1956), p. 39.

[48] Felix Frankfurter, "The Supreme Court in the Mirror of Justices," 105 *University of Pennsylvania Law Review* 781 (1957). (Italics supplied.)

[49] As quoted in *The New York Times Magazine*, November 28, 1954, p. 14.

TABLE I

NUMBER OF PRESIDENTIAL APPOINTMENTS OF UNITED
STATES SUPREME COURT JUSTICES WHO ACTUALLY
SERVED ON THE COURT (arranged chronologically)

President	Dates in Office	Number of Appointments
Washington	1789-1797	10
J. Adams	1797-1801	3
Jefferson	1801-1809	3
Madison	1809-1817	2
Monroe	1817-1825	1
J. Q. Adams	1825-1829	1
Jackson	1829-1837	6 (5)[a]
Van Buren	1837-1841	2 (3)[a]
W. H. Harrison	1841	0
Tyler	1841-1845	1
Polk	1845-1849	2
Taylor	1849-1850	0
Fillmore	1850-1853	1
Pierce	1853-1857	1
Buchanan	1857-1861	1
Lincoln	1861-1865	5
A. Johnson	1865-1869	0
Grant	1869-1877	4
Hayes	1877-1881	2
Garfield	1881	1
Arthur	1881-1885	2
Cleveland	1885-1889; 1893-1897	4[b]
B. Harrison	1889-1893	4
McKinley	1897-1901	1
T. Roosevelt	1901-1909	3
Taft	1909-1913	6
Wilson	1913-1921	3
Harding	1921-1923	4
Coolidge	1923-1929	1
Hoover	1929-1933	3
F. D. Roosevelt	1933-1945	9
Truman	1945-1953	4
Eisenhower	1953-1961	5
Kennedy	1961-1963	2
L. B. Johnson	1963-1969	2
Nixon	1969-1974	4
Ford	1974-	1
		104

[a] Jackson had nominated Catron, but the latter was not confirmed until Van Buren had taken over.
[b] Two in each of his two terms, which were split by Harrison's single term.

TABLE II

PRIOR JUDICIAL EXPERIENCE OF U.S. SUPREME COURT JUSTICES AND THEIR SUBSEQUENT SERVICE

| Justice | Year Nominated | Number of Years of Prior Judicial Experience | | | Years of Service on Supreme Court[a] |
		Federal	State	Total	
Jay*	1789	0	2	2	6
J. Rutledge*[b]	1789 and 1795*	0	6	6	2
Cushing	1789	0	29	29	21
Wilson	1789	0	0	0	9
Blair	1789	0	11	11	7
Iredell	1790	0	½	½	9
T. Johnson	1791	0	1½	1½	2
Paterson	1793	0	0	0	13
S. Chase	1796	0	8	8	15
Ellsworth*	1796	0	5	5	4
Washington	1798	0	0	0	31
Moore	1799	0	1	1	5
Marshall*	1801	0	0	0	34½
W. Johnson	1804	0	6	6	30
Livingston	1806	0	0	0	17
Todd	1807	0	6	6	19
Story	1811	0	0	0	34
Duval	1811	0	6	6	24
Thompson	1823	0	16	16	20
Trimble	1826	9	2	11	2
McLean	1829	0	6	6	32
Baldwin	1830	0	0	0	14
Wayne	1835	0	5	5	32
Taney*	1836	0	0	0	28
Barbour	1836	6	2	8	5
Catron	1837	0	10	10	28
McKinley	1837	0	0	0	15
Daniel	1841	4	0	0	19
Nelson	1845	0	22	22	27
Woodbury	1845	0	6	6	6
Grier	1846	0	13	13	24
Curtis	1851	0	0	0	6
Campbell	1853	0	0	0	8
Clifford	1858	0	0	0	23
Swayne	1862	0	0	0	19
Miller	1862	0	0	0	28

* Indicates Chief Justice and date of his appointment and/or promotion.

a Counted as of date of receipt of commission, following Senate confirmation.

b Rutledge's nomination as Chief Justice was rejected by the Senate, but he did serve in the post as a recess appointee for four months.

TABLE II (*Continued*)

| Justice | Year Nominated | Number of Years of Prior Judicial Experience | | | Years of Service on Supreme Court[a] |
		Federal	State	Total	
Davis	1862	0	14	14	15
Field	1863	0	6	6	34½
S. P. Chase*	1864	0	0	0	8
Strong	1870	0	11	11	10
Bradley	1870	0	0	0	22
Hunt	1872	0	8	8	10
Waite*	1874	0	0	0	14
Harlan, Sr.	1877	0	1	1	34
Woods	1880	12	0	12	7
Matthews	1881	0	4	4	8
Gray	1881	0	18	18	21
Blatchford	1882	15	0	15	11
L. Q. C. Lamar	1888	0	0	0	5
Fuller*	1888	0	0	0	22
Brewer	1889	6	22	28	21
Brown	1890	16	0	16	16
Shiras	1892	0	0	0	11
H. E. Jackson	1893	7	0	7	2
White*	1894 and 1910*	0	1½	1½	27
Peckham	1895	0	9	9	14
McKenna	1898	5	0	5	27
Holmes	1902	0	20	20	30
Day	1903	4	3	7	19
Moody	1906	0	0	0	4
Lurton	1909	16	10	26	5
Hughes*c	1910 and 1930*	0	0	0	17
Van Devanter	1910	7	1	8	27
J. R. Lamar	1910	0	2	2	6
Pitney	1912	0	11	11	10
McReynolds	1914	0	0	0	27
Brandeis	1916	0	0	0	23
Clarke	1916	2	0	2	6
Taft*	1921	8	5	13	9
Sutherland	1922	0	0	0	16
Butler	1922	0	0	0	17
Sanford	1923	14	0	14	7
Stone*c	1923 and 1941*	0	0	0	23

c Had had no judicial experience when appointed as *Associate* Justice.

TABLE II (*Continued*)

| Justice | Year Nominated | Number of Years of Prior Judicial Experience | | | Years of Service on Supreme Court[a] |
		Federal	State	Total	
Roberts	1930	0	0	0	15
Cardozo	1932	0	18	18	6
Black	1937	0	1½	1½	34
Reed	1937	0	0	0	19
Frankfurter	1939	0	0	0	23
Douglas	1939	0	0	0	36½
Murphy	1940	0	7	7	9
Byrnes	1941	0	0	0	1
R. H. Jackson	1941	0	0	0	13
W. Rutledge	1943	4	0	4	6
Burton	1945	0	0	0	13
Vinson*	1946	5	0	5	7
Clark	1949	0	0	0	18
Minton	1949	8	0	8	7
Warren*	1953	0	0	0	16
Harlan	1955	1	0	1	16
Brennan	1956	0	7	7	
Whittaker	1957	3	0	3	5
Stewart	1958	4	0	4	
White	1962	0	0	0	
Goldberg	1962	0	0	0	3
Fortas	1965	0	0	0	4
Marshall	1967	3½	0	3½	
Burger*	1969	13	0	13	
Blackmun	1970	11	0	11	
Powell	1971	0	0	0	
Rehnquist	1971	0	0	0	

tions, such as those of President Franklin D. Roosevelt, is sometimes revitalized by others, as it was by that of President Eisenhower. Roosevelt paid little, if any heed to it, whereas Eisenhower, after his initial appointment of Mr. Chief Justice Warren, insisted that his nominees have at least *some* judicial experience, no matter how slight. Of the nine men who sat on the Court as a result of President Roosevelt's appointments (or promotion to Chief Justice in the case of Stone), neither Mr. Chief Justice Stone nor Associate Justices Reed, Frankfurter, Douglas, Byrnes, and Jackson had any judicial experience whatsoever, while Mr. Justice Rutledge served on the Court of Appeals for the District of Columbia for four years, and Justice Black served one and a half years and Justice Murphy seven years on state tribunals. President Truman followed his predecessor's habit of ignoring judicial background: of his four appointees, Associate Justices Burton and Clark had none at all, Mr. Chief Justice Vinson had five years, and Associate Justice Minton had eight years of prior service on the lower federal bench. President Eisenhower's four appointees subsequent to that of the Chief Justice—Associate Justices Harlan, Brennan, Whittaker, and Stewart —all had seen some prior service, although the total number of years for the four comprised but fifteen. Neither Associate Justices White and Goldberg, appointed by President Kennedy, nor Fortas, appointed by President Lyndon B. Johnson, had had any judicial experience, whereas Johnson's other appointee, Thurgood Marshall, had spent three and a half years on the federal bench below the Supreme Court. President Nixon's first two appointees, Mr. Chief Justice Burger and Associate Justice Blackmun, had served thirteen and eleven years, respectively, on lower federal benches, but Associate Justices Powell and Rehnquist had had no prior judicial experience at all when nominated.

Congress, too, is hardly of one mind on the matter of the necessity or even the desirability of judicial experience as a prerequisite for appointment to the highest court in the land. Bills are continually introduced that would require future nominees to the Supreme Court to have upwards of five years of experience on lower court benches. In the 89th Congress, and again in the 91st, for example, thirteen bills of this type were sponsored by members on both sides of the aisle in both houses of Congress. But all of these measures failed of enactment. Moreover, many legislators agree with what is clearly a majority of the closest observers of the Supreme Court, as well as with the thesis of Mr. Justice Frankfurter, that judicial experience, because of the special nature of that Court's work, is not essential. The Supreme Court is not a trial court in the sense that the federal district courts below are, nor is it called upon to deal with a particular judicial constituency as are these courts of first instance and, to a considerably lesser extent, the federal courts of appeals that lie immediately above the district courts in the judicial hierarchy. Further, there is very little transition or connection between the experience in the lower federal constitutional courts and that of the highest—the procedural and jurisdictional frameworks are quite different. The type of private litigation at common law, so prevalent below, is practically extinct at the bar of today's Supreme Court; the highest Court is almost exclusively occupied with questions of public law, led by cases at constitutional law or with constitutional overtones, review of administrative actions, and other related questions. Experience on the courts below may well be theoretically desirable—although there are some observers who would not even grant that much—but it should not become a *requirement* for qualification for the Supreme Court. Again returning to Mr. Justice Frankfurter and Judge Learned Hand, the business of the Supreme Court today is "with the application of rather fundamental aspirations," what Judge Hand called *moods*, that are embodied in constitutional provisions such as the due process of law clauses of the Fifth and Fourteenth Amendments—clauses and concepts that were quite evidently deliberately designed "not to be precise and positive directions for rules of action." In the words of Mr. Justice Frankfurter:

> The judicial process in applying them involves a *judgment on the process of government.* The Court sits in judgment, that is, on the views of the direct representatives of the people in meeting the needs of society, on the views of Presidents and Governors, and by their construction of the will of legislatures *the Court breathes life, feeble or strong, into the inert pages of the Constitution and the statute books.*[50]

Small wonder that this function calls for a combination of philosopher, historian, and prophet![51]

A *Case Study.* A brief survey of the judicial experience of the members of the 1974–75 Supreme Court may aid in demonstrating that even if that specific qualification is largely, or even wholly, absent in many instances, experience in other relevant areas of public service is often abundantly present. Of the members of the 1974–75 Court, which began its term on October 7, 1974, only five had past judicial experience, and in all but two or at most three of these cases it was rather negligible: as already noted, Mr. Chief Justice Burger had served thirteen years on the U.S. Court of Appeals for the District of Columbia, and Mr. Justice Blackmun eleven on the U.S. Court of Appeals for the Eighth Circuit. Mr. Justice Brennan had seen seven years of service on New Jersey state courts. But Mr. Justice Stewart had had a mere four on the U.S. Court of Appeals for the Sixth Circuit, and Mr. Justice Marshall three and a half on the Second Circuit Court of Ap-

---

[50] Frankfurter, "The Supreme Court in the Mirror of Justices," op. cit. at 793. (Italics supplied.)

[51] In an article entitled "Characteristics of Supreme Court Greatness," Stuart S. Nagel, a close observer of the Court, sees the following as "the important characteristics": ". . . a brilliant intellect, an ability to write well, a deep knowledge of law and society, a willingness to work hard, a strong personality, an ability to get along with one's colleagues, and a high level of succeess in one's prior convictions." (56 *Journal of the American Bar Association* 959, October 1970.)

peals. Justices Douglas, White, Powell, and Rehnquist came to the Court without any prior judicial service.

Yet *all* of the members of the 1974–75 Court had a record of considerable experience in *public life*, and that frequently of an administrative nature, in addition to or in place of whatever judicial experience they might have had. Thus, in 1969, upon his designation as Chief Justice at the age of sixty-one, Warren Earl Burger had practiced law for twenty-three years; had been politically active in his native Minnesota; and for three years had been Assistant Attorney General, leading the criminal division of the U.S. Department of Justice. William O. Douglas had practiced law, had taught it for almost a decade, and had been both a member and the chairman of the U.S. Securities and Exchange Commission for three years when President Roosevelt appointed him in 1939 at a youthful forty-one (only four Justices were appointed at a younger age). William J. Brennan, Jr., had practiced law for fifteen years, was a decorated army officer during World War II, and had served the State of New Jersey when Governor Driscoll appointed him, at the age of forty-three, to the state bench in 1949. Potter Stewart had practiced law for more than a decade and had served on the City Council of Cincinnati for five years when he first entered the federal judiciary in 1954, at the age of thirty-nine. Byron R. White—that rare phenomenon of both Rhodes Scholar and professional athlete (known as "Whizzer White")— had practiced law for fourteen years and was U.S. Deputy Attorney General when his wartime friend President Kennedy sent him to the highest bench in 1962. White was then forty-five. President Johnson's second appointment, Thurgood Marshall—the first Negro to reach the highest Court—had practiced law for three decades, much of it constitutional law at the bar of the Court he was destined to join; had been a nationally known leader in the civil rights movement; had served on the Second Circuit Court of Appeals from 1962 to 1965; and was the U.S. Solicitor General when the President thus honored him in 1967. Harry A. Blackmun, President Nixon's second appointee, had practiced law in a Minneapolis firm for twenty-five years when he was named to the U.S. Court of Appeals for the Eighth Circuit by President Eisenhower in 1959, aged fifty-one. Lewis F. Powell, the third Nixon appointment (made late in 1971), sixty-four years old, had a long and distinguished career as a legal practitioner and civic leader in Virginia, including the chairmanship of the Richmond public school board in the late 1950's, and had been President of the American Bar Association. Nixon's fourth, William H. Rehnquist, a youngish forty-seven when he was sent to the Court concurrently with Powell, had clerked for Mr. Justice Robert H.

Jackson, had practiced law and been active in Arizona politics for a good many years, and was serving as U.S. Assistant Attorney General in charge of the Office of Legal Counsel at the time of his appointment to the Court.

If—for the sake of argument—one were to grant the wisdom of judicial experience as a pertinent requirement for Supreme Court nominees, a background rich in nonjudicial experience, such as those just described, does not compensate in and of itself for the lack of actual experience on a lower bench. However, it does indicate that the men—there have been no women on a federal court level *higher than* the Court of Appeals (the first at that level was Judge Florence Allen of the Sixth Circuit[52])—who come to the Supreme Court of the United States, and for that matter to the

---

TABLE III

OCCUPATIONS[a] OF SUPREME COURT
DESIGNEES AT TIME OF APPOINTMENT[b]

Federal Officeholder in Executive Branch	22
Judge of Inferior Federal Court	22
Judge of State Court	21
Private Practice of Law	18
U.S. Senator	8
U.S. Representative	4
State Governor	3
Professor of Law	3
Associate Justice of U.S. Supreme Court[c]	2
Justice of the Permanent Court of International Justice	1

a Many of the appointees had held a variety of federal or state offices, or even both, prior to their selection.

b In general, the appointments from state office are clustered at the beginning of the Court's existence; those from federal office are more recent.

c Justices White and Stone, who were *promoted* to the Chief Justiceship in 1910 and 1930, respectively.

---

52 Of the 702 active *and* senior federal judgeships extant as of the spring of 1974, only seven (five active and two senior) were held by women. (The first female federal judge was the Coolidge-appointed Genevieve R. Cline to the United States Customs Court in New York in 1928.) Judge Allen was appointed to the Sixth Circuit by President Roosevelt in 1934 from her position as the first woman on the Ohio State Supreme Court. She became Chief Judge of the Circuit in 1958—another "woman's first"—and retired from the bench at the age of seventy-five in 1959. She died in 1966. Her earliest trail-blazing feat as a woman was her service on the Cleveland (Ohio) Court of Common Pleas from 1920 to 1922, whence she was elected to the seven-member Ohio Supreme Court. She had served for two six-year terms when F.D.R.'s call to the federal bench came.

lower federal courts, have had lengthy *legal* experience. Moreover, *all* of the 100 men who have actually *sat* on the highest bench, except Mr. Justice George Shiras (1892–1903), had engaged in at least *some* public service at various levels of government, often elective, or had participated in political activity. Nevertheless, unlike the jurists of France, for example—who are schooled and trained as jurists—a great many of the judges of the major courts in the United States have no *judicial* background—as distinguished from a *legal* one. England relies on still another system, to be discussed presently. Table III indicates the occupations of the Justices (using the full figure of 103 here) as of the time of their appointment to the Supreme Court.

THE JUSTICES IN COMPOSITE

Whatever individual exceptions may be applicable, and keeping in mind the subjective attitude many an observer brings to bear on the qualifications and performance of the Justices of the Supreme Court of the United States, the caliber of that select group has been all but universally high. Indeed, no other unit of American government can readily match its general record of demonstrable competence and achievement. An over-all analysis of the background and characteristics of the 100 Justices to date (1974–75 term) would produce the following composite:

> Native-born (there have been but six exceptions); male (there have been no women to date—late 1974); Caucasian (the first Negro was appointed in 1967); generally Protestant (there have been six Catholic and five Jewish Justices); fifty to fifty-five years of age at the time of appointment; Anglo-Saxon ethnic stock (all except fifteen); upper middle to high social status; reared in an urban environment; member of a civic-minded, politically active, economically comfortable family; B.A. and LL.B. or J.D. degrees; held some type of public office; generally well-educated.[53]

MOTIVES THAT UNDERLIE APPOINTMENTS[54]

The only person who knows with certainty why a man is appointed to the Supreme Court is the President of the United States himself. However, his-

---

[53] For two studies corroborating this "composite," see John R. Schmidhauser, "The Justices of the Supreme Court: A Collective Portrait," 3 *Midwest Journal of Political Science* 1 (1959), and his *The Supreme Court: Its Politics, Personalities and Procedures* (New York: Holt, Rinehart and Winston, Inc., 1960), Ch. 3 *passim.*

[54] Much of the material in this section and in that on the role of the Senate is derived from Henry J. Abraham, *Justices and Presidents: A Political History of Appointments to the United States Supreme Court* (New York: Oxford University Press, 1974), Chs. I–III.

torians and students of the judicial process can come close to the truth by interpreting the facts at their disposal; thus a study of the records of the thirty-four Presidents who have sent men to the Supreme Court—an evaluation of their reasons for making the choices they did—points to several criteria that have been predominant in influencing presidential decisions. The following four have probably been the most important: (1) objective merit, (2) personal friendship, (3) balancing representation on the Court, and (4) political and ideological compatibility.

When a President considers the objective merit of a candidate, he attempts to determine whether he possesses the ability and background requisite for a mastery of the vital and complicated issues that reach the Supreme Court. To achieve that end, he might look to the candidate's basic intellectual acumen; reputation for legal scholarship; competence in a particular area of the law; experience as a judge, lawyer, legislator, or executive; integrity and morals; judicial temperament; work habits. Even age may be relevant. If the nominee is too young he may be lacking in judgment, wisdom, and experience; if too old, retirement, illness, or death may intervene.

Personal friendship is difficult to measure, but assuredly it has influenced a considerable number of nominations. In Taft's choice of Horace H. Lurton; in Wilson's of Louis D. Brandeis; in Truman's of Harold H. Burton; and in Kennedy's of Byron R. White, to cite some obvious illustrations, personal friendship figured prominently. Other examples are Truman's appointments of Mr. Chief Justice Fred M. Vinson and Associate Justices Tom C. Clark and Sherman Minton. It was probably the crucial consideration in the case of Minton, although the Indianan was a good Democrat and had seen eight years of service, however colorless, on the federal appellate bench. The most obvious and most discussed case in recent years was Lyndon Johnson's choice of Abe Fortas. Long Fortas's intimate personal friend, L.B.J. time and again urged him to accept a vacancy. Perhaps prophetically, Fortas was demonstrably reluctant. But he ultimately bowed to the President's entreaties and, with considerable lack of enthusiasm, accepted appointment to the seat vacated by Mr. Justice Goldberg when he resigned to become United States Ambassador to the United Nations in 1965.

Balancing religious and geographical representation has also influenced Presidents in their choice of Supreme Court nominees. Of the four factors, religious representation is the least defensible and the most emotion-charged. Yet no matter how undesirable it may be in theoretical terms, it is not only here to stay but, considering present-day group consciousness, it will very likely be joined by representation by sex.

The widespread notion that all sections of the land should be represented on the bench—to date the Justices have come from thirty-one of the fifty states—cannot be dismissed readily. (See Table IV.) It has considerable appeal as a matter of political equity. It was a primary consideration among almost all of the nineteenth-century Presidents; thus, Lincoln's successful search for "an outstanding trans-Mississippi lawyer" (Samuel F. Miller) and a Californian (Steven J. Field, a Democrat); and Cleveland's insistence on geographic appropriateness, best exemplified by his choice of a Chief Justice (Melvin Fuller). Among recent Presidents strongly influenced by the "geography factor" Richard Nixon stands out. Yet after the Haynsworth and Carswell rejections, he abandoned his much-publicized quest for a "Southern strict-constructionist" by choosing Judge Harry A. Blackmun, long time Minnesotan, and Blackmun's close friend, Mr. Chief Justice Burger, who was not only a Northerner but a resident of a state already "represented" twice on the Court.

On the other hand, a determined President will not permit geography to stand in the path of a desired appointment. Woodrow Wilson proved this with his insistence on the confirmation of Brandeis, notwithstanding the

---

TABLE IV

THE 31 STATES FROM WHICH THE
103 SUPREME COURT APPOINTMENTS WERE MADE[a]

New York	15	Iowa	2
Ohio	9	Louisiana	2
Massachusetts	8	Michigan	2
Virginia	7	Minnesota	2
Pennsylvania	6	North Carolina	2
Tennessee	6	Arizona	1
Kentucky	5	Colorado	1
Maryland	4	Indiana	1
New Jersey	4	Kansas	1
Alabama	3	Maine	1
California	3	Mississippi	1
Connecticut	3	Missouri	1
Georgia	3	New Hampshire	1
Illinois	3	Texas	1
South Carolina	3	Utah	1
		Wyoming	1

[a] The state where the appointee then resided, not necessarily the state of his birth.

---

presence on the bench of Holmes, a fellow citizen of Massachusetts; so did Hoover when he finally appointed Cardozo in the face of the Court presence of fellow New Yorkers Stone and Hughes.

The religious factor is based upon the notion that there should be a "Roman Catholic seat" and a "Jewish seat" on the Supreme Court. A development of dubious communal wisdom, the concept of religious-group representation has become one of the facts of American political and judicial life (see Table V)—although it has been less of an emotional problem in the courts than it has in the makeup of election slates in minority-conscious cities, for example.

Six men have occupied the "Catholic seat" to date: Mr. Chief Justice Roger B. Tancy (Jackson, 1835); and Associate Justices Edward D. White (Cleveland, 1894—he was promoted to Chief Justice by Taft, 1910); Joseph McKenna (McKinley, 1898); Pierce Butler (Harding, 1922); Frank Murphy (Roosevelt, 1940); and William J. Brennan (Eisenhower, 1956). With the exception of the seven years between Mr. Justice Frank Murphy's death in 1949 (when President Truman deliberately ignored the unwritten rule of the "reserved" seat and nominated Protestant Tom C. Clark to the vacancy created by Murphy's death) and Mr. Justice William J. Brennan, Jr.'s nomination in 1956, a Roman Catholic has been on the Supreme Court continually since the White appointment.

The "Jewish seat" was established in 1916 with the appointment of Louis D. Brandeis. That tradition too was broken when, in 1969, President Nixon successively nominated three Protestants (Haynsworth, Carswell, and Blackmun) to succeed Fortas. In 1971 Nixon had two opportunities to "atone" for this, but he again nominated two more Protestants, Lewis F. Powell, Jr. and William H. Rehnquist. Questioned on the continued "oversight" at one of his infrequent news conferences, Nixon gave the logical response: that merit, rather than religion, should and must govern—a laudable aim, provided it is in fact invoked. The five occupants of "the Jewish seat" to date have been Louis D. Brandeis (Wilson, 1916), Benjamin N. Cardozo (Hoover, 1932), Felix Frankfurter (Franklin D. Roosevelt, 1938), Arthur J. Goldberg (Kennedy, 1963), and Abe Fortas (Johnson, 1965).

In June 1967 Lyndon Johnson designated Thurgood Marshall, the first Negro ever to be nominated to the Supreme Court. The President, leaving no doubt that the nominee's race was probably the major factor in his decision, told the country: "I believe it is the right thing to do, the right time to do it, the right man and the right place."[55] It is fair to conjecture that

[55] *The New York Times*, June 14, 1967, p. 1.

there now exists a "black seat" on the bench that is at least as secure as the Catholic and the Jewish seats. It is also highly likely that a "woman's seat" will be established, too—probably within the current decade. The presidential campaign of 1972 featured public assurances by both candidates that a woman would be appointed: George McGovern promised that "the next vacancy" would go to a woman, and Nixon, already on record with his abortive Mildred Lillie nomination, spoke repeatedly of his desire to nominate "a qualified woman."

Political and ideological compatibility often go hand in hand in influencing presidential choices for the Supreme Court. Among the points a President is almost certain to consider are the following: (1) whether his choice will render him more popular among influential interest groups; (2) whether the nominee has been a loyal member of the President's party; (3) whether the nominee favors presidential programs and policies; (4) whether the nominee is acceptable, or at least not "personally obnoxious," to his home-state Senators; (5) whether the nominee's judicial record, if any, meets the incumbent president's criteria of constitutional construction; (6) whether the President is indebted to the nominee for past political services; and (7) whether he feels "good" or "comfortable" about his choice.

It is an unwritten law of the judicial nominating process that the President will not normally select an individual from the ranks of the political opposition. To lessen charges of "court-packing," however, this rule is purposely relaxed now and then, but only within "political reason"—which seems to have meant roughly to the tune of 10 per cent of all appointments to district and appellate tribunals and 15 per cent to the Supreme Court. In at least thirteen instances of the latter, including two promotions to the

---

TABLE V

ACKNOWLEDGED RELIGION OF THE 101 INDIVIDUAL
JUSTICES OF THE SUPREME COURT (at time of appointment)

Episcopalian	26	Jewish	5
Unspecified Protestant	25	Methodist	4
Presbyterian	17	Congregationalist	3
Roman Catholic	6	Disciples of Christ	2
Unitarian	6	Lutheran	1
Baptist	5	Quaker	1

---

post of Chief Justice, the appointee came from a political party other than that of the President. Thus Whig President John Tyler appointed a Democrat, Samuel Nelson, and Republican Presidents Abraham Lincoln, Benjamin Harrison, William H. Taft, Warren G. Harding, Herbert Hoover, Dwight D. Eisenhower, and Richard M. Nixon appointed nine Democrats. Taft alone appointed three! The nine Justices and their nominators were Stephen J. Field (Lincoln); Howell E. Jackson (Benjamin Harrison); Horace H. Lurton, Edward D. White (to Chief Justice) and Joseph R. Lamar (Taft); Pierce Butler (Harding); William J. Brennan (Eisenhower); and Lewis F. Powell, Jr. (Nixon). And Democratic Presidents Woodrow Wilson, Franklin D. Roosevelt, and Harry S Truman appointed three Republicans: Louis D. Brandeis (Wilson); Harlan F. Stone to Chief Justice (F.D.R.); and Harold D. Burton (Truman). Some would add, as a fourteenth case, F.D.R.'s selection of Felix Frankfurter, who labeled himself an Independent. What accounted for these thirteen or fourteen appointments from the ranks of "the other" party?

Crossing Party Lines. The naming of *Nelson* by President Tyler came after Tyler had been defeated by Democrat James K. Polk in the election of 1844. Eager to have history show at least one of his own nominees attain the Supreme Court, the "lame duck" Tyler—after three of his four first Whig choices had to be withdrawn because of obviously decisive opposition, and the fourth one, John Spencer of New York, was rejected by the Senate 26 : 21—then designated Nelson, who had not been an active political figure.

In 1863 *Field,* who was to serve longer than anyone but Douglas to date on the Court (34¾ years), was chosen by Lincoln largely for three reasons: First, Field came from California, a part of the country not then represented on the Court—in fact, Congress created a tenth seat for that purpose—and even though he had been a Buchanan Democrat as late as 1861, Lincoln felt his nominee would help to "fuse" the Northern cause by preserving the loyalty of California and strengthening its political ties. Second, Field's many influential friends, including California's Governor Leland Stanford, put considerable pressure on the President. Third, Field's brother, David Dudley Field, a bitter and vocal opponent of slavery, had played a considerable role both in the organization of the Republican party and in Lincoln's nomination as its standard-bearer in 1860.

Harrison's choice of *Jackson* was motivated by reasons similar to those that governed the Tyler-Nelson case. Cleveland had already defeated Harrison when the vacancy on the Court occurred, the Democratic Senate was in no mood to confirm the Republican lame duck President's partisan choice, and, happily, Harrison and Jackson, who had served in the Senate together, were close friends—as were their wives.

The Taft appointments of *Lurton* and *Lamar* and his promotion of *White*, all three Southern Democrats appointed by a good Republican, are attributable to a combination of personal friendship or esteem, ideological kinship, and politico-sectional expediency. Taft and Lurton had served together for eight years on the U.S. Circuit Court of Appeals for the Sixth Circuit, where they had become fast friends. Taft, who had been its Chief Judge, was very much impressed with the legal and judicial ability of the Tennessee Democrat who had succeeded him as Chief Judge when the future President went to the Philippine Islands. Conservative kinsmen, they were usually at one in their opinions from the bench and in their general philosophy of government. Taft called the nomination of his friend Lurton "the chief pleasure of my administration."[56] Although Joseph R. Lamar of Georgia was not as close to Taft personally as Lurton was, he readily met Taft's standards of conservatism and his general ideological bent. For example, the two men saw eye to eye on the tariff—a matter of the utmost importance to the President. And Taft perceived in the appointment of the Confederate Army veteran an additional opportunity for strengthening his position among Southern political leaders who, if they would not vote for him at election time, would at least help him with his legislative program. He promoted White—then in his seventeenth year on the Court—in part because he considered him the ablest administrator among the Justices on the bench; in part because his fellow Justices apparently had petitioned the President to designate him rather than Hughes,[57] who had seemed to have the proverbial inside track ("White, Not Hughes, for Chief Justice," was the front-page headline in *The New York Times*[58] when the announcement was made); and in large part because in Taft's eyes he had voted "right" on the bench—among his votes there was one to uphold a military tariff in the Philippine Islands at the time Taft was Governor there.[59]

Wilson's hotly contested nomination of *Brandeis*, a registered Massachusetts Republican, was confirmed by the Senate by a vote margin of 47 to 22,

[56] Silas Bent, *Justice Oliver Wendell Holmes* (New York: Garden City Publishing Co., 1932), p. 248.
[57] George Shiras III, *Justice George Shiras* (Pittsburgh: University of Pittsburgh Press, 1953), p. 130.
[58] December 12, 1910.
[59] Cf. William Howard Taft, *Our Chief Magistrate and His Power* (New York: Columbia University Press, 1916), pp. 99–102.

after a delay of more than four months. Of the 47 affirmative votes, 44 were cast from the 45 Democratic Senators present and voting; the three Republican votes in favor came from Senators Robert M. La Follette (Wisc.), George W. Norris (Neb.), and Miles Poindexter (Wash.). Twenty-one of the 22 negative votes came from the Republican Senators present and voting.[60] The lone Democratic negative vote was cast by Senator Francis G. Newlands of Nevada. Twenty-seven Senators, including the influential Borah, did not vote at all.[61] Brandeis, the famed "People's Lawyer," as Wilson was fond of calling him, was a personal friend of the President and a close ideological ally—a political and social liberal who shared Wilson's philosophy of life and government and who had worked hard for him in the 1912 campaign. It was primarily these two factors and his great regard for Brandeis's character and ability that prompted Wilson to ignore the sectional factor (Massachusetts was then already "represented" by Holmes); possible repercussions because of the nominee's religion (he was the first person of Jewish persuasion to reach the Supreme Court); and the danger during the 1916 election year of designating a controversial personage such as Brandeis in the face of the violent opposition of the most influential segment of the bar and the business community, particularly in his New England home base. Ironically, despite his convictions regarding the "curse of bigness," Mr. Justice Brandeis never wrote an opinion in favor of the Government in an antitrust case!

Harding's choice of *Butler*—vigorously promoted by Mr. Chief Justice Taft—had three motives. First, the President liked his record of almost four decades of service in the law and in public life; second, and probably most important, Harding found Butler's ideological ultra-conservatism to be entirely sympathetic (he became one of the two leading avowed reactionaries on the bench); and third, the President deemed it politically advantageous to appoint a man who combined what would seem to be the desirable factor of being a "safe" Democrat—most Democrats refused to regard Butler as one of their number in roughly the same fashion as the Republicans did Brandeis—with that of being a member of a then "unrepresented" minority

---

[60] Among these were illustrious and powerful men such as: Henry A. du Pont, Henry Cabot Lodge, George Sutherland (a future colleague of the nominee!), Warren G. Harding, and Albert B. Fall. The remaining twenty-seven Senators did not vote; but twelve—all Republicans—were paired *against*, and twelve—ten Democrats and two Republicans (Moses E. Clapp of Minnesota and Asle J. Grenna of North Dakota)—*for*; three Senators were absent and were not recorded at all.

[61] For a fascinating account of the Brandeis nomination and confirmation battle, see A. L. Todd's *Justice on Trial: The Case of Louis D. Brandeis* (New York: McGraw-Hill Book Co., 1964).

religion (Roman Catholic) and a native Minnesotan, only the second nominee born west of the Mississippi to reach the bench. Initially rejected by
the Senate, Butler was renominated by Harding on the following day and
ultimately won confirmation easily—though he was veritably scorched by
large segments of the public press.

The *Cardozo* appointment was almost literally forced upon President
Hoover by the country, despite the fact—conceivably detrimental or even
fatal in the case of other nominees, depending upon circumstances—that
the nominee came from New York, already "represented" on the bench at
that time by Mr. Chief Justice Hughes and Mr. Justice Stone, and that he
was Jewish, a religion already "represented" by Mr. Justice Brandeis. Hoover
raised these points during a command-visit by Republican Senator Borah of
Idaho, chairman of the Committee on Foreign Relations, who had been
very vocal in urging the Cardozo appointment—along with many others, including Mr. Justice Stone. (Stone, who was to play a major role in persuading the President to designate the man whom he had introduced to him
initially, even offered to resign his own seat on the Court if that was what it
would take to see his fellow New Yorker nominated.) Hoover handed Senator Borah a list of the names of several prominent individuals he was considering for the vacancy on the Court left by Mr. Justice Holmes's resignation. The last name on the list was that of the Chief Judge of the New York
State Court of Appeals, Benjamin N. Cardozo. "Your list is all right," commented Senator Borah, "but you handed it to me upside down!"[62] When
the President then strongly urged that his visitor consider the geographical
situation involved, and mentioned "possible religious and sectarian repercussions," Senator Borah told him in no uncertain terms that "Cardozo belonged as much to Idaho as to New York" and that geography should no
more bar him than the presence of two Virginians on the high bench—John
Blair and Bushrod Washington—should have prevented President John
Adams from naming John Marshall Chief Justice.[63] Furthermore, Borah
told Hoover, ". . . anyone who raises the question of race [*sic*] is unfit to
advise you concerning so important a matter."[64] When the President bowed
to what was all but unanimous professional as well as popular clamor for the
Cardozo appointment, he became the recipient of much praise, typical of
which was Senator Clarence Dill of Washington's remark that ". . . when

---

[62] Claudius O. Johnson, *Borah of Idaho* (New York: Longman's, Green and Co., 1936).
p. 452.
[63] *The New York Times,* January 30, 1932.
[64] Johnson, loc. cit. p. 453.

President Hoover appointed Judge Cardozo . . . he performed the finest act of his career as President."[65]

President Franklin D. Roosevelt promoted *Stone*—who had been one of his professors at Columbia University Law School—largely as a manifestation of unity in the face of the incipient war crisis. When Mr. Chief Justice Hughes announced his intention to retire, speculation as to his successor revolved around Stone and the then Attorney General Robert H. Jackson. Roosevelt's heart was on the side of Jackson—who desperately craved the Chief Justiceship—but he deemed it wiser and more politically astute and appropriate at this turbulent juncture of history to name Stone. In fact, he discussed the matter with Jackson, who agreed heavyheartedly and later, having become an Associate Justice of the Court, wrote that the need for judicial leadership and the "desirability for a symbol of stability as well as of progress" were evidently the reasons for Stone's elevation "in the interest of the [fostering of the] judiciary as an institution."[66] Moreover, the retiring Chief Justice himself had strongly urged Stone's elevation on the basis of his record, and had suggested that Roosevelt consult Mr. Justice Frankfurter in the matter. Frankfurter told the President:

> . . . when war does come, the country should feel you are a national, the Nation's President, and not a partisan President . . . [to bolster this assessment] you [should] name a Republican, who has the profession's confidence, as Chief Justice.[67]

President Truman's nomination of *Burton*—the first of his four—is far too readily dismissed merely as a reward to "an old Senate crony."[68] The Republican Senator from Ohio and mayor of Cleveland had served well and closely with the then Senator Truman on the latter's Special Committee To Investigate the National Defense Program (the "Truman Committee"). Unquestionably, Truman's personal affection for Burton was a factor in the appointment. But there were assuredly others: the advice given to the President that he designate a Republican to replace the retiring Mr. Justice Roberts, a Republican; Mr. Chief Justice Stone's advance approval of the nominee because of his valuable legislative experience; Truman's belief in Burton's judicial temperament; the absence of anyone from Ohio on the

---

[65] *The New York Times*, March 2, 1932.
[66] Alpheus T. Mason, *Harlan Fiske Stone: Pillar of the Law* (New York: The Viking Press, 1956), p. 573.
[67] Ibid. p. 567.
[68] For example, see Glendon A. Schubert, *Constitutional Politics* (New York: Holt, Rinehart and Winston, Inc., 1960), p. 38.

bench; the assumption that the nominee's Senate seat would be filled by a Democrat, as indeed it subsequently was, by the incumbent Governor Lausche (though he was a rather unpredictable Democrat); plus the faithful support Burton had given to the Democratic party on foreign policy, and even on some domestic policy, throughout his tenure in the Senate.

President Eisenhower chose New Jersey Democrat *Brennan* for a variety of reasons. The President's initial choice had been that state's able Chief Justice, Arthur T. Vanderbilt, who had achieved an outstanding national reputation as head of the then recently reorganized New Jersey court system. Because of his advanced age and failing health (he died in 1957), Vanderbilt declined the appointment, but he highly recommended the nomination of his colleague and protégé, Associate Justice Brennan of the State Supreme Court. This recommendation was strengthened by the support of Secretary of Labor James Mitchell, a New Jersey Republican; the two Republican Senators from New Jersey, Clifford P. Case and Alexander H. Smith; and Democratic Governor Robert B. Meyner. Moreover, it was the very eve of the 1956 election, and the choice of a Roman Catholic from the metropolitan East would hardly hurt the President in the impending campaign. With only Republican Senator Joseph R. McCarthy of Wisconsin voting "no," the Brennan nomination was confirmed by the Senate in March 1957.

The most recent selection of a Supreme Court nominee from the opposition party is President Nixon's late 1971 choice of nominal Democrat Lewis F. Powell, Jr. Yet that distinguished Virginia ideological conservative seemed ideally fitted for the President's expressed qualifying criteria of "a philosophy for the Constitution similar to my own"—which he was fond of styling, not overly helpfully, as "strict construction." Powell did not meet the Nixon guidelines of "right age" (at sixty-four he was some ten years older than the preferred age) nor of "broad experience as an appeals judge" (he had no judicial experience whatsoever). But Powell came from a milieu sympathetic to the President both politically and personally: he was a recognized, visible leader of the Virginia Bar; he had seen important local and state civic service; he was a recent past President of the American Bar Association; and his writings in the "law-and-order" sector could not have been more pleasing to Mr. Nixon. Hence his professed formal party allegiance on the Democratic side was of small moment. Mr. Justice Powell's subsequent service on the Court proved the President's judgment of his third appointee's jurisprudential philosophy to be generally sound—but not without at least some "disappointments," e.g. the Justice's authorship of a unanimous

TABLE VI

AVOWED POLITICAL AFFILIATION OF THE
104 SUPREME COURT JUSTICES (at time of selection)

Federalists	13	Republicans	40
Whig	1	Independent	1
Democrats	49		

opinion by the high bench (Mr. Justice Rehnquist not participating) clearly and unequivocally denying the existence of any "inherent" independent presidential power to wiretap in instances of suspected subversive *domestic* elements.[69]

There will always be some crossing of party lines, particularly at the lower court levels, in order to maintain at least the appearance of nonpartisanship

[69] *United States v. United States District Court for the Eastern District of Michigan,* 407 U.S. 297 (1972).

TABLE VII

PERCENTAGES OF FEDERAL JUDICIAL APPOINTMENTS
ADHERING TO THE SAME POLITICAL PARTY AS
THE PRESIDENT, 1888–1974

President	Party	Percentage
Cleveland	Democratic	97.3
B. Harrison	Republican	87.9
McKinley	Republican	95.7
T. Roosevelt	Republican	95.8
Taft	Republican	82.2
Wilson	Democratic	98.6
Harding	Republican	97.7
Coolidge	Republican	94.1
Hoover	Republican	85.7
F. D. Roosevelt	Democratic	96.4
Truman	Democratic	90.1
Eisenhower	Republican	94.1
Kennedy	Democratic	90.9
L. B. Johnson	Democratic	93.2
Nixon	Republican	93.7
Ford	Republican	

in the judicial process and to placate the opposition, but the practice may be safely viewed as the exception rather than the rule (as Table VI and the following statistics indicate). Many a President has been told by his political advisers to stay on his side of the fence, where surely there are just as many qualified and deserving lawyers as on the other side. "Think Republican," Republican National Chairman Rogers C. B. Morton frankly urged President Nixon when the latter was presented with his initial opportunity to fill two seats on the Supreme Court in the Spring of 1969.[70] As Table VII amply demonstrates, Morton's sentiments are not confined to *his* political party! If the percentage of "other party" Supreme Court appointees has been higher than that of the lower federal courts, it is because the President recognizes that what matters more than anything else is the ideological compatability of the candidate—what Teddy Roosevelt referred to as the nominee's "real" politics.

"PACKING THE COURT" AND THE NOMINEES' "REAL" POLITICS

Whatever the merits of the other criteria attending presidential motivations in appointments may be, what must be of overriding concern to any nominator is his perception of the candidate's "real" politics. The Chief Executive's crucial predictive judgment concerns itself with the nominee's likely future voting pattern on the bench, based on his past stance and commitment on matters of public policy, insofar as they are reliably discernible.[71] All Presidents have tried to thus "pack" the bench to a greater or lesser extent.

[70] *The New York Times,* May 17, 1969, p. 1.
[71] An illuminating illustration is President Kennedy's selection of his long-time friend and ideological kinsman, Deputy Attorney General Byron J. White, to fill the first vacancy on the Court during his brief Administration. As *Washington Star* reporter James E. Clayton reported the decision: "Thinking back on the process months later, the Attorney General [Robert F. Kennedy] tilted back in his chair and said: 'You wanted someone who generally agreed with you on what role government should play in American life, what role the individual in society should have. You didn't think about how he would vote in a reapportionment case or a criminal case. You wanted someone who, in the long run, you could believe would be doing what you thought was best. You wanted someone who agreed generally with your views of the country.' Both he and the President believed that White and Arthur J. Goldberg met that test. They could not be as sure of the others on the list [Paul A. Freund of Harvard University and Judge William H. Hastie of the U.S. Court of Appeals for the Third Circuit]." Quoted in Clayton's *The Making of Justice: The Supreme Court in Action* (New York: E. P. Dutton & Co., 1964), p. 52.

In the public eye Court-packing has been most closely associated with Franklin D. Roosevelt. Having had not a single opportunity to fill a Court vacancy in his first term (1933–37), and seeing his domestic programs consistently battered by the Court, the frustrated President attempted to get his way all at once. His "Court-packing bill," however, died a deserved death in the Senate.

It is not surprising that Court-packing and the name of President Roosevelt have become synonymous. Yet even such popular heroes as Jefferson, Jackson, and Lincoln followed similar courses of action in the face of what they considered "judicial intransigence and defiance." Their approach was not so radical as Roosevelt's, but they very likely would have been sympathetic to his efforts. George Washington, though broadly regarded as far removed from "politics," had insisted that his nominees to the Court meet a veritable smorgasbord of qualifications. In fact, every President who has made nominations to the Supreme Court has been guilty of Court-packing in some measure. It is entirely understandable that a President will choose men who will share his own philosophy of government and politics, at least to the extent of giving him a sympathetic hearing. Theodore Roosevelt, for example, in discussing the potential candidacy of Horace H. Lurton with Henry Cabot Lodge, put the issue well:

> The nominal politics of the man has nothing to do with his actions on the bench. His real politics are all important. . . . He is right on the Negro question; he is right on the power of the federal government; he is right on the Insular business; he is right about corporations, and he is right about labor. On every question that would come before the bench, he has so far shown himself to be in much closer touch with the policies in which you and I believe.[72]

Lodge concurred in substance, but he replied that he could see no reason "why Republicans cannot be found who hold those opinions as well as Democrats."[73] Consequently, he strongly urged the candidacy of a Republican, whom T.R. then duly nominated—William H. Moody, Attorney General of Massachusetts.

Thus, concern with a nominee's real politics is a fundamental issue, and examples abound. It prompted Republican Taft to give half of his six appointments to Democrats who were kindred souls; Republican Nixon to ap-

[72] Henry Cabot Lodge, *Selections from the Correspondence of Theodore Roosevelt and Henry Cabot Lodge, 1884–1918* (New York: Charles Scribner's Sons, 1925), Vol. II, pp. 228, 230, 231.
[73] *Ibid.* p. 229.

point Democrat Powell; Democrat Roosevelt to promote Republican Stone; and Democrat Truman to appoint Republican Burton. Yet there is no guarantee that what a President perceives as real politics will not fade into a mirage. Hence Charles Warren, eminent chronicler of the Court, observed that

> nothing is more striking in the history of the Court than the manner in which the hopes of those who expected a judge to follow the political views of the President appointing him are disappointed.[74]

Few have felt the truth of that statement more keenly than Teddy Roosevelt did when Oliver Wendell Holmes, Jr., whose early "anti-administration" opinions in antitrust cases (notably in *Northern Securities v. United States*)[75] were entirely unexpected. A bare 5 : 4 majority in that case did uphold the Government's order, under the Sherman Anti-Trust Act, dissolving the Northern Securities Company, brainchild of E. A. Harriman and J. J. Hill, the wealthy and powerful owners of competing railroads who had organized the company in order to secure a terminal line into Chicago. Roosevelt had won that important litigation, but he was furious about his recent appointee's "anti-anti-trust" vote in the case. He stormed: "I could carve out of a banana a Judge with more backbone than that!"[76] Holmes reportedly merely smiled when told the President's remark and noted his intention to "call the shots as I see them in terms of the legal and constitutional setting." Later, during T.R.'s second term of office (1905–9) Holmes expressed his sentiments to a labor leader at a White House dinner: "What you want is favor, not justice. But when I am on my job, I don't give a damn what you or Mr. Roosevelt want."[77]

James Madison, having refused to heed his political mentor, Thomas Jefferson, was similarly chagrined with his appointment of Mr. Justice Joseph Story. Jefferson had warned him that Story was an inveterate Tory who would become a rabid supporter of Mr. Chief Justice Marshall, and he was right: Story not only instantly joined Marshall's approach to constitutional adjudication and interpretation, but he even out-Marshalled Marshall in his nationalism. Perhaps even more chagrin was felt by Woodrow Wilson when his appointee James C. McReynolds proved himself at once to be the antithesis of almost everything his nominator stood for and believed in.

[74] *The Supreme Court in United States History*, rev. ed. (Boston: Little, Brown, and Co., 1926), Vol. II, p. 22.
[75] 193 U.S. 197 (1904).
[76] As quoted by James E. Clayton, op. cit. fn. 71, p. 47.
[77] As quoted by Arthur Krock, *The New York Times*, October 19, 1971, p. 431.

More recently, Harry Truman observed that ". . . packing the Supreme Court simply can't be done . . . I've tried and it won't work. . . . Whenever you put a man on the Supreme Court he ceases to be your friend. I'm sure of that."[78] Future Presidents may well be advised to heed the admonition of Zechariah Chafee, Harvard's famed expert on the judicial process, who contended that in order to forecast the behavior of a future jurist it is wiser to consider the books in his library than the list of clients in his office.

There is indeed a considerable element of unpredictability in the judicial appointing process. To the often-heard "Does a person become any different when he puts on a gown?" Mr. Justice Frankfurter's sharp retort was always, "If he is any good, he does!" In the words of Alexander M. Bickel, "You shoot an arrow into a far-distant future when you appoint a Justice and not the man himself can tell you what he will think about some of the problems that he will face."[79] And late in 1969, reflecting upon his sixteen years as Chief Justice of the United States, Earl Warren pointed out that he, for one, did not "see how a man could be on the Court and not change his views substantially over a period of years . . . for change you must if you are to do your duty on the Supreme Court."[80] It is a duty that, in many ways, represents the most hallowed in the governmental process of the United States.

ON THE ROLE OF THE UNITED STATES SENATE

That the Senate takes its confirmation role seriously is documented by its refusal to confirm 26 of the 136 Supreme Court nominees forwarded to it in the less than two centuries of our history. True, even when counting the Senate's refusal to vote on the Fortas promotion, only four have been voted down during the present century, but, as the experiences of the Nixon Administration demonstrate, the possibility is ever present. Yet a return to the nineteenth-century record of one rejection for every three nominees would appear to be highly unlikely nowadays.

Just why were the twenty-six rejected? Among the more prominent reasons have been: (1) opposition to the nominating President, not necessarily to the nominee; (2) the nominee's involvement with a visible or contentious issue of public policy (i.e., "politics"); (3) opposition to the record of

---

[78] Lecture at Columbia University, New York City, April 28, 1959.
[79] As quoted in *Time Magazine*, May 23, 1969, p. 24.
[80] Comment to Anthony Lewis, "A Talk with Warren on Crime, the Court, the Country," *The New York Times Magazine*, October 19, 1969, pp. 128–29.

the incumbent Court, which the nominee was presumed, rightly or wrongly, to have supported; (4) senatorial courtesy (closely linked to the consultative nominating process); (5) a perceived "political unreliability" of the nominee; and (6) an evident lack of qualification or the limited ability of the nominee. Usually several of these reasons figure in the rejection of a nominee, not one alone; the purpose of the previous list is merely to suggest some applicable prototypes.

Thus, a number of candidates were rejected because of Senate opposition to the nominating Chief Executive. For example, John Quincy Adams's nomination of John J. Crittenden in 1828 was "postponed" by the Senate in a strictly partisan vote of 17 : 23 two months after the nomination. The "loyalist" Democrats in the Senate thereby foiled Adams's last-minute Whig appointment and preserved the vacancy so that it could be filled instead by the President-elect, strong-party Democrat Andrew Jackson. In 1844 Whig President John Tyler sent six nominations to the upper house—which disapproved five and confirmed but one, the outstandingly qualified Chief Justice Samuel Nelson of New York's highest court. Of the former, John C. Spencer, an erstwhile Whig who had accepted high cabinet posts under Tyler and whom the "loyalist" Whig followers of Henry Clay regarded as a traitor, was rejected by a formal roll call vote of 21 : 26; and action regarding Edward King—who was nominated twice—Ruben H. Walworth, and John M. Read was postponed by the Senate chiefly because of the mistaken expectation of the Clay Whigs that their leader would defeat James Polk in the presidential election of 1844. In 1852 action on George E. Badger, one of Whig President Millard E. Fillmore's nominees—despite the fact that Badger was then a United States Senator (Whig) from North Carolina—was postponed indefinitely and no action at all was taken on his two others, Edward A. Bradford and William E. Micou. The purpose of the anti-Fillmore maneuvers was to preserve court vacancies for incoming Democratic President Franklin Pierce, yet Pierce succeeded in filling only one of them, he too falling victim to similar Senate tactics. Democrat James Buchanan's nomination of Jeremiah S. Black in December 1860, one month before his term ended, fell 25 : 26, chiefly because Republican Senators wanted to hold the seat for Abraham Lincoln to fill. In 1866 Union President Andrew Johnson nominated his gifted Attorney General, Henry Stanberry, but the Senate's hostility to Lincoln's successor was such as to frustrate every attempt he made to fill a Supreme Court vacancy. Congress even went so far as to *abolish* the vacancy (thus "icing" Johnson's nominating impotence). A century later, in 1968, the Senate refused to approve Lyndon

B. Johnson's attempt simultaneously to promote Abe Fortas to Chief Justice, and to replace him with Judge Homer Thornberry of the United States Court of Appeals for the Fifth Circuit. Johnson failed largely because most members of the Senate "had had it" with the lame-duck President's nominations. Victory-scenting Republicans also wanted such plums as Supreme Court appointments for themselves; they had not had an opportunity to fill a vacancy on the bench since President Eisenhower's appointment of Mr. Justice Potter Stewart ten years earlier.

A good many illustrations are on record in which nominees failed to receive senatorial confirmation because of their involvement with public issues. Thus in 1795 the Senate rejected John Rutledge as Chief Justice by a vote of 10 : 14 even though he had been serving as such for four months on a recess appointment, Congress not being in session. On John Jay's resignation from the Chief Justiceship Rutledge had asked Washington for the appointment, but he now found his fellow Federalists voting against him because of his vigorous opposition to the Jay Treaty of 1794. The Federalist Senators refused to confirm a public figure who actively opposed the Treaty they had championed so ardently—even though he was able to meet Washington's stiff criteria for service on the highest bench. Their cause was aided by an all-but-unanimous denunciation by the Northern Federalist press. In 1811, James Madison's nomination of Alexander Wolcott fell 9 : 24 because the Federalist Senators, eagerly backed by the press, opposed Wolcott's vigorous enforcement of the embargo and nonintercourse acts when he was United States Collector of Customs in Connecticut. There was however, also some genuine question as to Wolcott's legal qualifications.

The rejection of James K. Polk's nomination in 1845 of fellow Democrat George W. Woodward of Pennsylvania, although in part due to the opposition of Pennsylvania's Independent Senator Simon Cameron on the basis of "senatorial courtesy," was largely a result of what was termed Woodward's "gross nativist American sentiments." Chiefly because of these alleged sentiments, which were particularly offensive to Irish Americans, five Democratic Senators joined Cameron and a phalanx of Whigs to defeat the nomination by a vote of 20 : 29. The President, however, saw the action as a power play calculated to weaken his Administration at the very outset. On December 15, 1869, Republican President Ulysses S. Grant nominated his eminently qualified and popular Attorney General Ebenezer R. Hoar. The debate over his nomination dragged on for seven weeks, until February 3, 1873, when Hoar was finally rejected by a vote of 24 : 33. Hoar had antagonized most of the Senators by his consistent refusal to back senatorial nominations for judgeships; by his publicly uncompromising insistence on "non-political" appointments throughout the government; and by his early championship of civil service reform. Moreover, he had made enemies of fellow Republicans by his outspoken opposition to the proposed impeachment of President Andrew Johnson. Few professional politicians appreciated Judge Hoar's high standards of excellence and assertive political independence, and the Court was deprived of an unusually promising candidate.

Another issue-oriented rejection was that of John J. Parker, United States Fourth Circuit Court of Appeals Judge (Hoover, 1930). A prominent and distinguished Republican leader in North Carolina for many years, and an outstanding jurist, Judge Parker fell victim to the sustained opposition of the American Federation of Labor and the National Association for the Advancement of Colored People. Still, the Senate would not have had the votes to defeat the nomination—Parker lost by a two-vote margin, 39 : 41— had they not been aided by the anti-Hoover Progressive Republicans, including such prominent and influential Senators as Hiram Johnson of California, Robert M. La Follette, Jr., of Wisconsin, George W. Norris of Nebraska, and such powerful mavericks as William Borah of Idaho. The A.F.L.'s chief grudge against the nominee stemmed from the impression that he was "unfriendly" to labor and that it was he who had handed down an opinion affirming a lower court decision upholding "yellow dog" contracts.[81] However, a close reading of Judge Parker's opinion in the case indicates neither approval nor disapproval of "yellow dog" contracts; rather, it reflects the jurist's belief that he was bound by a United States Supreme Court precedent.[82] Yet the impression of anti-labor bias lingered, fostered by A.F.L. President William Green and other influential labor spokesmen— who, on the other hand, did concede that Judge Parker's integrity, high standards, and professional qualifications were not in question. The NAACP contended that the nominee was opposed generally to Negro participation in politics and especially to Negro suffrage. Thus, Walter White of the NAACP leadership pointed out that Judge Parker, while stumping North Carolina as a gubernatorial candidate in 1920, had made an unfortunate remark: "The participation of the Negro in politics is a source of evil and danger to both races and is not desired by the wise men in either race or by the Republican Party of North Carolina."[83] Parker had uttered the state-

[81] *United Mine Workers v. Red Jacket Consolidated Coal and Coke Co.*, 18 F. 839 (1927).

[82] *Hitchman Coal and Coke Co. v. Mitchell*, 245 U.S. 229 (1917).

[83] *Hearings Before the Subcommittee of the Committee on the Judiciary, U.S. Senate, on the Confirmation of John J. Parker to Be an Associate Justice of the Supreme Court of the United States*, 71st Cong., 2d sess., 1930, p. 74.

ment in response to repeated taunts and charges by his Democratic opponents that he intended to enfranchise Negroes and to alter the North Carolina Constitution to accommodate "them." Ironically, it was Judge Parker —he continued to sit on the Fourth Circuit bench after his rejection—who would write some of the earliest and most significant pro-Negro opinions on desegregation. Among them was *Rice v. Elmore* (1947), in which he sustained United States District Court Judge J. W. Waring's outlawing of South Carolina's machinations to bar Negroes from primary elections.[84]

The next outright rejections were Judges Clement F. Haynsworth, Jr. and G. Harrold Carswell, both Nixon nominees, almost forty years later. Although their involvement with civil rights did play a considerable role in their rejection, especially in that of Carswell, the overriding and ultimately decisive margin of defeat lay elsewhere: in Haynsworth's case it was the question of judicial ethics; in Carswell's case it was lack of professional qualification. To his basic specifications Mr. Nixon had added his desire to choose a Southern jurist of conservative judicial bent. Of course the Court already had at least one Southern strict constructionist, indeed, a constitutional literalist of the first magnitude, in the person of the distinguished Mr. Justice Hugo Lafayette Black of Alabama, but that was not exactly what the President had in mind. Haynsworth was a native of South Carolina and a Harvard Law School alumnus, a relatively able jurist meriting a "B-minus" grade in the minds of most Court watchers, fit all of the President's specifications—and, perhaps even more significantly, those of such influential Southern Senators as Strom Thurmond (R.-S.C.), James O. Eastland (D.-Miss.), and John L. McClellan (D.-Ark.). He was also supported by the Attorney General, John Mitchell.

Most of the Senate seemed disposed to confirm Judge Haynsworth for the Fortas vacancy (see below). But to the President's anger, frustration, and embarrassment, the hearings of the Senate Committee on the Judiciary provided clear evidence of the nominee's patent insensitivity to financial and conflict-of-interest improprieties. Apparently, as with Fortas, no actual legal infractions had taken place—but how could the Senate confirm Haynsworth when it had played such an activist role in causing Fortas's resignation? It could not—and among those who vocally opposed the South Carolinian and voted against his confirmation were such anti-Fortas, strict-constructionist leaders as Senators Robert Griffin (R.-Mich.) and Jack Miller (R.-Iowa). Down went the Haynsworth nomination by a vote of 55 : 45 on November 21, 1969—largely for the reasons indicated, although

[84] 165 F. 2d 387. (It sustained 72 F. Supp. 516, also decided in 1947.)

he had also drawn considerable labor and minority-group fire for allegedly anti-civil libertarian and anti-civil rights stands. The livid President Nixon, however, chose to lay the blame for his nominee's defeat upon "anti-Southern, anti-conservative, and anti-constructionist" prejudice, and he vowed to select another "worthy and distinguished protagonist" of Southern, conservative, and strict constructionist persuasion.[85]

To the dismay of those Senators who had counseled confirmation of Judge Haynsworth lest a successor-nominee be even less worthy of the high post, the President, again on the recommendation of Attorney General Mitchell, quickly countered by nominating Judge G. Harrold Carswell of Florida, a little-known and little-distinguished ex-United States District Judge with only six months of experience on the United States Court of Appeals for the Fifth Circuit. "He is almost too good to be true," Mr. Mitchell was reported to have said.[86] The appointment was an act of vengeance —one intended to teach the Senate a lesson and to downgrade the Court. The Senate, intimidated by the President and the Attorney General, was disposed to confirm him. But suspicious reporters and researchers soon cast serious doubt on that "almost too good to be true" classification of the nominee. Immediately damaging was the discovery of a statement Carswell had made to a meeting of the American Legion on August 2, 1948, while he was running for a seat in the legislature of his native Georgia. "I yield to no man as a fellow candidate or as a fellow citizen in the firm, vigorous belief in the principles of White Supremacy, and I shall always be so governed."[87] To be sure, the nominee, pointing to his youth and inexperience (he was twenty-eight at the time), now disavowed that statement and any racism as well. But an examination of his record on the bench did more than cast further doubt on his objectivity in racial matters. While serving as United States Attorney in Florida, Carswell had been involved in the transfer of a public, municipally owned Tallahassee golf course—built with $35,000 of federal funds—to the status of a private club. It was a move obviously designed to circumvent a contemporary Supreme Court decision proscribing segregation in municipal recreation facilities.

Still, the Administration appeared to have the votes for Senate confirmation, given the vivid memories of the Haynsworth battle, the intensive wooing of doubtful Senators by the White House and the Justice Department,

[85] *The New York Times,* November 22, 1969, p. 20.

[86] Richard Harris, *Decision* (New York: E. P. Dutton & Co., Inc., 1971), p. 11.

[87] As quoted by Harris, op. cit. pp. 15–16; in *The New York Times,* January 23, 1970, p. 16; and by Senator Birch Bayh (D.-Ind.) in *Congressional Record,* Vol. 116, p. 6, p. 7498, 91st Cong., 2nd sess.

and the natural predisposition to give the President his choice, all things being equal. But things were far from equal, for as the Carswell opponents continued their attack it became apparent that—quite apart from the controversy surrounding his civil rights record—the candidate was patently inferior, simply on the basis of fundamental juridical and legal qualifications. If Judge Haynsworth had merited a "B-minus" grade, Judge Carswell scarcely merited a "D" on the scale of relevant ability. Senator Roman Hruska (R.-Neb.), the President's floor manager of the nomination, made a fumbling, pathetic attempt to convert the candidate's mediocrity into an asset: "Even if he is mediocre there are a lot of mediocre judges and people and lawyers. They are entitled to a little representation, aren't they, and a little chance? We can't have all Brandeises, Cardozos, and Frankfurters, and stuff like that there."[88] Hruska's remarkable assertion was seconded by Carswell-supporter Senator Russell Long (D.-La.), who intoned:

> Does it not seem . . . that we have had enough of those upside down, corkscrew thinkers? Would it not appear that it might be well to take a B student or a C student who was able to think straight, compared to one of those A students who are capable of the kind of thinking that winds up getting us a 100-percent increase in crime in this country?[89]

This line of argument failed to convince the doubtful Senators. Instead, they became increasingly aware of the lack of ability of the nominee, who, among other debilitating features, held the dubious record of having been reversed by appellate courts more than any of the other federal jurists then sitting except eight! Yale Law School Dean Louis H. Pollak styled the Carswell nomination as one of "more slender credentials than any Supreme Court nominee put forth in this century";[90] perhaps even more tellingly, the distinguished William Van Alstyne, Professor of Law at Duke University, opposed the nomination. Van Alstyne, an ardent and vocal backer of the Haynsworth nomination, now testified: "There is, in candor, nothing in the quality of the nominee's work to warrant any expectation whatever, that he could serve with distinction on the Supreme Court of the United States."[91] When the final vote on confirmation came on April 9, 1970— three months after the nomination—the President's choice went down by a vote of 51 : 45. Among the "noes" were such significant Republican votes as those of Margaret Chase Smith of Maine, Winston L. Prouty of Ver-

[88] As quoted by Harris, op. cit. p. 110.
[89] *Congressional Record*, op. cit. p. 7487.
[90] Harris, loc. cit.
[91] As quoted by Harris, op. cit, p. 56.

mont, Marlow W. Cook of Kentucky, and Richard S. Schweiker of Pennsylvania.

It was indeed a bitter defeat for the President. Not only had he seen two nominees rejected within less than five months, but his carefully devised "Southern strategy" had suffered a serious blow. His reaction was swift and vitriolic. Conveniently ignoring the basic issues for his candidates' defeats, he blamed them instead on sectional prejudice, abject politics, and philosophical negations, and told the country:

> . . . I have reluctantly concluded that—with the Senate as presently constituted—I cannot successfully nominate to the Supreme Court any federal appellate judge from the South who believes as I do in the strict construction of the Constitution. . . . Judges Carswell and Haynsworth have endured with admirable dignity vicious assaults on their intelligence, their honesty, and their character. . . . When all the hypocrisy is stripped away, the real issue was their philosophy of strict construction of the Constitution—a philosophy that I share. . . .[92]

Quite to the contrary, several distinguished federal jurists in the South were eminently qualified to serve, jurists who indeed shared the President's philosophy of government and politics, and whom the Senate assuredly would have confirmed. It could not, in good conscience, given the Fortas precedent, the public concern, and the nature and role of the Supreme Court, have confirmed Haynsworth or Carswell, especially not Carswell. The latter, ironically, was soon to be defeated by his constituents in the Florida senatorial primary, during which he was photographed with a lettered sign around his neck reading "Heah Come 'de Judge." It is an intriguing thought that had Haynsworth been nominated *after* Carswell, he might well have been confirmed.

President Nixon followed up his blast against the rejections with the petulant suggestion in a well-publicized letter to Senator William B. Saxbe (R.-Ohio) that the Senate had denied him the right to see his choices appointed. That right, he insisted, had been accorded all previous Presidents— a patently false statement, in the face of the twenty-six rejections of nominees to the Court on record. Moreover, the President's collateral suggestion to Saxbe and the nation, that senatorial advice and consent to nominations (which is *expressly* provided for in Article II, Section II, Clause 2 of the Constitution) is merely a pro forma requirement, is utterly incorrect with

[92] From the President's nation-wide television address of April 9, 1970, quoted in *The New York Times*, April 10, 1970, p. 1, and in *Time Magazine*, April 20, 1970, p. 9.

regard to nominations to the judiciary in general and the Supreme Court in particular. Mr. Nixon, fully familiar with the contrary judgment of practically all students of constitutional law and history, as well as with Hamilton's equally contrary assertions in *The Federalist Papers* (#76 and 77), must have been aware of how wrong he was. His anger and frustration were understandable, but his historical misstatement was a distinct disservice to country, Constitution, and Court.

The Senate's refusal to accept closure in 1968 in order that the Senators might vote on the promotion of Mr. Justice Fortas—no such vote was ever taken—has been variously attributed to his "record" on the high bench on such contentious issues as obscenity and criminal justice. In fact, although those issues were dramatically vocalized by such powerful and committed opponents to the nomination as Senators Strom Thurmond (R.-S.C.) and John L. McClellan (D.-Ark.), they were not an important reason for the nomination's failure. It was fought with such ardor largely because of deep-seated opposition to the jurisprudential philosophy of the "Warren Court," whose approach to constitutional interpretation had resulted in the inevitable disaffection of numerous groups and individuals, both public and private. The Court's stance and record of "judicial activism" on such emotion-charged issues as desegregation, reapportionment and redistricting, criminal justice, separation of church and state, civil disobedience, and freedom of expression were bound to offend as well as to please.

Coming, as it did conveniently, at the close of the Johnson Administration, the Fortas nomination readily served as target and symbol of the pent-up frustrations against the Warren Court—but against the Court as a unit rather than against the individual Justices. One of the famous episodes surrounding the attacks against Fortas occurred early in the hearings on the nomination by the Senate Judiciary Committee, when Senator Thurmond shouted at Fortas: "Mallory! Mallory! I want that name to ring in your ears!" Thurmond's reference was to Andrew Mallory, a nineteen-year-old black from South Carolina who was arrested in 1954 on a charge of choking and raping a thirty-eight-year-old Washington woman while she was doing her laundry. After a seven-hour interrogation by the police *prior* to his arraignment, Mallory had confessed. The trial was delayed for a year because doubts had been raised that he understood the proceedings against him, but ultimately Mallory was sentenced to the electric chair. He appealed to the Supreme Court on the grounds of coerced confession. In 1957, in what became the celebrated case of *Mallory v. United States*,[93] the

[93] 354 U.S. 449.

Court unanimously reversed Mallory's conviction on the ground that the failure of the police officer to bring him before a magistrate "forthwith" constituted an "unnecessary delay," in violation of (congressionally sanctioned) federal rules of criminal law procedure, thereby giving "opportunity for the extraction of a confession." Released, Mallory resumed a life of drifting and crime which culminated in his 1960 arrest in Philadelphia and his subsequent apprehension for burglary, assault, and rape. He was convicted on the assault count, served eleven years in jail, and barely six months after his release in 1971 attacked and robbed a couple in a Philadelphia park. When discovered by two policemen, he aimed a gun at one and was killed by the other. It was the so-called "Mallory Rule," as pronounced by the Supreme Court in 1957, that Senator Thurmond referred to in his outburst at Justice Fortas. Yet Fortas had never been connected with the case and had not even been appointed to the Court until 1965, eight years after the Mallory decision! (The "Mallory Rule" itself was modified by Congress in the Omnibus Crime Control Act of 1968.) Other charges were leveled at the nominee, some of them concerning decisions in obscenity cases rendered long before Fortas ever sat.

Senatorial courtesy, the fourth in our list of reasons for Senate refusal of Supreme Court nominations, has already been discussed. A fifth is broadly styled as "political unreliability," as perceived by the Senate. Perhaps the most obvious example of the application of this reason is another among the several unsuccessful Grant nominations—that of former Attorney General Caleb Cushing, who was the President's choice to assume the Chief Justiceship in 1874, following the death of Salmon P. Chase. Cushing's age —seventy-four—was noted prominently during debate, but the real reason for his rejection was the Senate's not-entirely-erroneous belief that Grant's close personal friend was a political chameleon. Indeed, Cushing had been in turn a Regular Whig, a Tyler Whig, a Democrat, a Johnson Constitutional Conservative, and, at last, a Republican. He had proved himself a first-rate legal practitioner and scholar; nevertheless, with opposition from almost all political factions growing daily, Grant withdrew Cushing from consideration.

A final reason for Senate refusal of a nominee is simply real or apparent lack of qualification to sit on the Supreme Court. Of course the concepts of "quality" and "ability" are subject to diverse analysis; yet a number of ascertainable standards and guidelines clearly exist. A nominee's age, experience, and record in and out of public life are all available guidelines. Ulysses S. Grant, in choosing his Attorney General George H. Williams to fill the vacancy caused by the death of Chief Justice Chase, thus evoked an entirely justifiable storm of adverse reactions. Williams had seen service in the Senate and had been Territorial Governor of Oregon, but his record as Attorney General was undistinguished and his talents as a lawyer were clearly mediocre (it was alleged that he had unnecessarily lost several important cases in private as well as public litigation). Both the bar and the press were severely critical of his achievements and his promise. Stunned and hurt by that reaction, and despairing of a lengthy confirmation battle, Williams asked President Grant to withdraw his nomination in early January 1874.

It is fair to conclude that Presidents have avoided nominating patently unqualified individuals to the high tribunal, although a number of rather weak nominations have slipped past the Senate, such as James C. McReynolds (Wilson), Pierce Butler (Harding), Sherman Minton (Truman), and Charles E. Whittaker (Eisenhower).[94] The one nominee on whose lack of qualification almost all fair-minded observers now agree is G. Harrold Carswell. With the calm hindsight of history President Nixon's choice still merits the characterization of a spite nomination. It is fortunate that the Senate simply would not accept Carswell.

Would any of the twenty-six who failed in being confirmed have been approved if they had been members of the Senate at the time of their nomination? The evidence is persuasive that they would have: the Senate almost invariably treats as a *cas d'honneur* the presidential designation of a sitting member—and, normally, although not as predictably, of a past colleague in good standing. Among the many illustrations are Senators James F. Byrnes (D.-S.C.) and Harold H. Burton (R.-Ohio). Byrnes, highly respected and very much a member of the Senate's "inner club," was confirmed unanimously without even being scrutinized by the Committee on the Judiciary when President Roosevelt nominated him in 1941.[95] Burton's nomination, although that of a Republican by a Democratic President (Truman), was unanimously confirmed in 1945 on the same day it reached the Senate, which was then controlled by a Democratic majority.

That the special treatment accorded senatorial colleagues is normally reserved to those actually serving is demonstrated by the case of ex-Senator

[94] For a ranking of all Justices through Thurgood Marshall (1967), based on a poll conducted by sixty-five experts in 1970, see Appendix "A" in Henry J. Abraham, *Justices and Presidents: A Political History of Appointments to the United States Supreme Court* (New York: Oxford University Press, Inc., 1974).

[95] After barely fifteen months, Byrnes resigned to become F.D.R.'s "Assistant President for Domestic Affairs."

85

Sherman Minton of Indiana. Minton, who had been defeated for re-election in 1940, largely because of his ardent espousal of the New Deal, was serving as a judge on the United States Court of Appeals for the Seventh Circuit when President Truman selected him for the Court in 1949. In part because of his support of the "Court-packing bill," the Senate judiciary committee voted 5 : 4 to ask him to testify before it. Minton refused, pointing to his position as a jurist and questioning the propriety of testifying lest conflicts arise concerning pending litigation. The committee relented and reported his nomination favorably, 9 : 2. But the Senate, led by prominent Republicans, took a formal vote on recommittal of Minton's nomination. It lost 45 : 21; thereafter he obtained quick confirmation, 48 : 16.

A notable exception to the unwritten rule of the all but automatic approval of senatorial colleagues was Franklin D. Roosevelt's controversial nomination of Senator Hugo LaFayette Black (D.-Ala.) in August 1937. Black's nomination was referred to the judiciary committee for full hearings, an action not taken since 1888. The initial reasons for that action, over the strong objections by the Chairman of the Committee, Senator Henry Ashurst (D.-Ariz.), were Black's strong support of the President's 1937 "Court-packing bill," his ardent New Deal partisanship, and his ruthless public investigations of the utility lobby. The attempt to increase the size of the Court was anathema to a majority of the Senate and the bar. And the controversy was compounded and exacerbated by rumors that Black had once been—and some alleged he still was—a member of the Ku Klux Klan in his native Alabama. Even so, the Committee ultimately approved the nomination by a vote of 13 : 4 (two Democrats and two Republicans voting against him), and the Senate confirmed him 66 : 15, nine Republicans and six Democrats voting "nay." Meanwhile, reporter Ray Sprigle of the *Pittsburgh Post-Gazette* came up with evidence that Black had indeed belonged to the KKK. Black, however, faced the charges squarely, and in a candid, dramatic broadcast to the American people admitted a two-year KKK membership in the mid-1920's, but pointed to his established liberal record and vowed to be a fair and impartial jurist. During his tenure on the Court, which lasted more than a third of a century, he kept his word.

The last test of the Senate's refusal to refer nominations of Senators to the Judiciary Committee came with Burton in 1945; no Senator has since been nominated. It was precisely the recognition of that rule which prompted leading supporters of President Nixon to urge him to nominate a Senator after Judge Haynsworth's rejection in 1969. Evidently the President briefly toyed with the idea of nominating John Stennis (D.-Miss.) or

Sam Ervin (D.-N.C.), both Southern Senators generally supportive of his "strict construction" views, but in his determination to "teach the Senate a lesson" he chose Carswell. Yet it will be recalled that one of "The Six" he had under consideration for the Black and Harlan vacancies in 1971 was Senator Robert C. Byrd (D.-W. Va.), a man infinitely less qualified to serve on the Court than his colleagues Stennis and Ervin. Whether or not Nixon seriously contemplated the Byrd nomination, there is but scant doubt that his colleagues would have given their approval. Yet those same colleagues would have been far less likely to approve someone of equally marginal qualifications from outside the halls of the Senate.

In general, opposition to the confirmation of a Supreme Court Justice seems to reflect the existence of deep-seated concern in the nation. In the early years of the Court's history, relatively little concern was shown about the potentially "unfortunate effects" of Justices of uncertain, or certain, convictions. It became more frequent and noticeable as the influence of the Court became more apparent. At the present time, when there are so many issues in which large numbers of people are deeply concerned, almost every appointee is made to run the gauntlet; he may even feel slighted if his appointment is unopposed, since this could be interpreted as a sign that he is not regarded as a man who carries very much weight. The nomination and confirmation procedure has become one more battleground on which large issues are fought out before the public eye.

QUALIFICATIONS AND EXPERIENCE: THE SPECIAL CASES OF ENGLAND AND FRANCE

In endeavoring to explain and analyze the staffing of the courts of England and France, and in comparing their respective judiciaries, it is necessary to remain cognizant of the two different types of law that govern the systems concerned—the common or Anglo-Saxon or Anglo-Norman law in England, and the civil or Roman law in France. There are fundamental differences between the laws of the two countries—and far greater ones become apparent, of course, in contrasting one or both with the prevalent norms and practices in the United States. But it is above all the very position of the judiciary that provides the key to these differences. Under the Roman law tradition of the Continent, the judiciary is a part of the administrative-executive hierarchy (as will be explained in considerable detail in Chapter VI) and it constitutes a *profession* distinctly separate from that of the practicing lawyer. Where the common law tradition holds, however, the legal profession is practically an autonomous body, the judges being drawn from its ranks—notwithstanding the different mode and mood of selection that governs in England and Wales as compared with that of the United States, where the common law tradition also holds.

Nevertheless, we have already observed that a common ideal, that of impartiality of the appointees, is held by all three lands for both selection and tenure of their judiciaries, and that each is therefore willing, as it must be, to protect their independence and provide a large measure of immunity in order to achieve it. But the techniques of training and selecting judges and ensuring their impartiality differ widely.

ENGLAND

Unlike the United States, England divides its legal profession into two major groups: the *solicitors* and the *barristers*—and it is impossible to be both *concurrently*. The former deal mainly with the general public; they conduct about 95 per cent of the ordinary legal business of the country, leaving the remaining highly important work of advocacy in the courts to the barristers, who see the layman only when so instructed by a solicitor. The best analogy of the difference between the two groups is found in medicine: the difference between the general practitioner and the consultant. Barristers are consultants for the solicitors—the latter do all the ordinary work of the law and call in the barristers when they need their services, either for advice or for conducting a case in court.

The Solicitors. The "office lawyers" of the judicial structure, the solicitors are obviously its workhorses. It is they who deal directly with the clients, who do the routine legal office work, and who prepare the spadework for cases to be argued at the bar of the higher courts by the barristers. But they also enjoy the right of audience in the magistrates and county courts, and, at the discretion or "direction" of the Lord Chancellor, under section 12 of the Courts Act of 1971, at certain limited proceedings, in the Crown Court; in fact, they do a great deal of advocacy in these several courts. They handle practically all of the drawing-up of legal documents, such as transfer of property. In short, the approximately 17,000 practicing solicitors do the bulk of England's ordinary legal work. Having determined to become a solicitor on the conclusion of his educational career, and having undergone additional legal training, the aspirant then takes a number of special professional examinations. Passing these, he becomes a "Solicitor of the Supreme Court" and commences his career. He will also probably join the Law Society, a voluntary association of solicitors with certain statutory powers. Every *prac-*

ticing solicitor must become a member of this society. Incidentally, university training is not an absolute requirement—over half of the solicitors are not university products.

The Barristers. It is the approximately 2700 practicing barristers who comprise England's *best-known* legal talent. Their chief function is to render legal advice to clients (in the great majority of cases, on instructions given to them by solicitors), either generally or in preparation for trial, and, of course, to conduct cases. Thus, they argue all cases in the higher courts—cases which, by custom and tradition, are almost always given to them directly by the solicitors who have processed them in a preliminary manner, rather than by the clients themselves. The barristers are professionally specialized and usually—although not inevitably—highly experienced members of the legal profession. It is from their ranks that the Lord Chancellor normally selects the judges on behalf of the Crown. Indeed, with the exception of justices of the peace, the English and Welsh judges were always appointed from the ranks of practicing barristers until the passage of the Courts Act of 1971, when solicitors became eligible for the posts of Recorder or Circuit Judge.[96]

The barristers are divided into two groups, or ranks: "Junior Barristers" and "Queen's Counsel." The latter are referred to colloquially as "Silks" from the fact that they are entitled to wear a silk gown instead of the "stuff" gown wore by the Junior Barristers. The two gowns are different in style also: those worn by the "Juniors" are like academic gowns with flowing sleeves, those of the "Silks" have simpler lines. One becomes a "Silk" upon the recommendation of the Lord Chancellor, on reaching top status in the profession, seldom until the completion of ten years' successful practice—although it should be noted that some very distinguished lawyers never "take Silk." The "Silks" constitute the elite among the barristers, and they receive higher fees than the junior barristers. Their main tasks include appearances in court, where they must be accompanied by a "Junior." It is from the ranks of Queen's Counsel that judges are mainly chosen. Yet sometimes a man may become a judge without being a "Q.C."—e.g. Lord Chief Justice Parker was made a judge as a "Junior." He had been Junior Counsel to the Treasury, the Government advocate for Crown business in the High Court. Normally those who have "taken Silk" for at least seven

---

[96] A Recorder must now be a barrister or solicitor of at least ten years' standing; a Circuit Judge a barrister of at least ten years' standing or a Recorder who has held that judicial office for at least five years. A County Judge, however, must have been a barrister for at least seven years, a Lord Chief Justice of Appeal for at least fifteen.

years, and, in the cases of the higher courts, for at least ten years, may expect to be considered for a judgeship in the event of a vacancy. But the number of superior court judges is low, and when one of the promotions does come it is viewed with a certain awe and respect by the legal profession and the public at large. Judges of the High Court are *invited* to become such by the Lord Chancellor—i.e. they do not solicit the post—whereas those of the County Court are appointed from the ranks of those who have *applied* to the Lord Chancellor for consideration of appointment.

All barristers are members of one of the four historic *Inns of Court* in London: Lincoln's Inn, Gray's Inn, Inner Temple, and Middle Temple.[97] In effect, they constitute both a "law school" and a corporate professional organization. Separate colleges, each with its own hall, chapel, and library, they arose as a result of the lawyers' custom of living together during terms. Self-governing, historic organizations—officially dating back roughly to the time of Edward I (1272–1307)—the Inns of Court have differing histories, but they were generally modeled upon the old trade guilds, to which they owe their origin. An Inn of Court was not so much a School of Law as a School for Englishmen (as Sir John Fortescue so well described it in his epic *De Laudibus Legum Angliae*.) The outlook developed in a university (Oxford and Cambridge) was purely scholastic; that in an Inn of Court was eminently national. In an Inn of Court the students lived together as one community. Fortescue describes the Inns of his time (fifteenth century) as not merely places for the students of the law, but as universities or schools of all commendable qualities. There, students as well as members of the bar would study, live, work, eat, and pray. But now they are no longer residences in the full sense of the term—although quite a few barristers still do live there, sometimes with their families.

In the past, under the tutelage of barristers, England's future lawyers were thus trained in the Inns rather than in a university law school, where

---

[97] The Inner and Middle Temples derive their names from the round temple which was built by the Knights Templar in 1160, and stood, until they were almost entirely destroyed—as were the other two inns—in the London Blitz, between the Strand and the Thames. They were rebuilt and rededicated in the early 1960's. What is now known as the Inner Temple covers what used to be the consecrated portion of the grounds surrounding the Temple Church. The Middle Temple covers what used to be the unconsecrated part. Gray's Inn derives its name from Reginald de Grey, Justician of Chester, who lived there in the thirteenth century. (Sir Francis Bacon, one of Gray's Inn's most famous members, planned and planted its lovely gardens, where he loved to walk and talk with such statesmen as Sir Walter Raleigh.) Lincoln's Inn owes its name to the Earl of Lincoln, who was a member of the King's Council, also in the thirteenth century.

Roman or civil law and canon law, as opposed to the common law, were taught. Today, these students may attend the lectures of the Council of Legal Education, a joint committee for education from the four Inns of Court. They are tested by examiners of the council, and on passing the examination, and having kept their "dining terms" for three years, they apply to the "Benchers," the governing body of the Inn, for admission as a barrister. This "dining term" rule is a relic of the days when students of the common law lived in the Inns of Court and had to frequent the hall of their Inn for dinner, for the exercises in "mooting," and for other forms of learning before becoming barristers. To this day they must dine in the hall on three nights in each dining term.

Once admitted to the bar, the young barrister remains under the general jurisdiction of his Inn of Court throughout his career—in fact, for life— and it is his Inn which constitutes both his professional protector and his disciplinarian. A full measure of *esprit de corps* flows naturally from life and membership in the Inn. Disciplinary problems are further under the supervision of the General Council of the Bar, a special body elected by the members of the Bar to act for it in a wide range of matters. Authority to expel a barrister for misconduct is given to the "Benchers" of the Inn of which he is a member. Disciplinary and other matters affecting the Bar generally also now come under the jurisdiction of the Senate of the Four Inns of Court, which has representative members of the four Inns and of the Bar Council.

The legal education provided by the Law Society for solicitors, who have numerous offices at the Inns but do not study there, differs from that given to the barristers. It is based on intensive courses, practical training, and a year's compulsory attendance at a recognized law school. The future barrister, on the other hand, must pass the bar examinations which involve a background in general legal principles, despite the fact that he may not have had specific training in these, that he often does not attend the elaborate series of lectures provided by the Council of Legal Education, and that he is not required to have practical training. However, recently a pledge has been exacted from candidates to spend six months as pupils in chambers.

The reason the future solicitor is given a thorough practical training in a solicitor's office by being apprenticed to the latter for three years, if a university product, and five years, if not, is because solicitors are entitled to practice from the moment they are admitted and can do legal work of practically any kind *at once* for the general public. But a barrister is never employed directly by a member of the public; he is employed, or instructed, by a solicitor—and in practice is a highly trained lawyer before he gets work of any importance from a solicitor.

Even given the possibility of a judicial appointment, his attractive social status, and the "psychic income" he may receive from his membership in the profession, the future of the barrister's branch of that profession is nevertheless undergoing some examination. One of the several significant considerations is his relatively low income, which has undoubtedly been a factor in the gradually declining number of practising barristers. As of the end of 1971, the number practicing was 2714 (including 167 women) of whom 733 practiced wholly or mainly in the provinces.

Yet whatever the problems of the parent profession may be—and they have been exaggerated at times—the English judges are very likely the most highly esteemed, the most independent, and, relatively speaking, the most generously paid in the West. There is little doubt that these three factors account in considerable degree for the universally higher quality of British justice, properly so often cited and envied by much of the rest of the world.

FRANCE

The Republic of France, together with several other states on the continent of Europe, goes considerably further than Britain in distinguishing between judges, public prosecutors, and officials of the powerful Ministry of Justice on the one hand, and privately practicing lawyers on the other. Although there is a clear-cut distinction between the British solicitor and the barrister, both are nonetheless members of the legal profession and may commence their advanced legal training together. In France, however, the bench is a separate career; it is not viewed as a reward for legal excellence or renown as it is in both Britain and the United States.

A future French student of the law must decide at the very outset of his schooling whether he wishes to become either a private lawyer or else a judge or prosecutor or go to the Justice Ministry. If the former, he attends law school and chooses among three specialties open to him: *avocat*, roughly akin to the British barrister; *avoué*, the approximate equivalent of the British solicitor—although the two aforementioned specialties were, in effect, fused in September 1972[98]—or *notaire*—a lawyer especially trained in drafting and registering of legal papers, related in name only to the American notary public, who need not be a lawyer. These three groups comprise the French *legal*, not *judicial*, profession. The French law student desirous

[98] Pierre Drai, "Les 'Gens' de Justice," *Les Cahiers Français*, 156–57, Septembre–Decembre 1972 (*La Documentation Française*, Paris, 1972).

92

of becoming a judge of the lower or appellate courts or a public prosecutor or member of the Ministry of Justice follows a totally separate path of training, for—as has been explained earlier—the judiciary of France is, in effect, a branch of the government, a part of the civil service.

Training for a Judgeship. Until the judicial reforms of 1958–59 took place, after finishing law school prospective members of the judiciary would initially gather some experience, a sort of apprenticeship, in a law office. From there they usually moved on to a minor office in a local court, while awaiting appointment. In the meantime, when they deemed themselves sufficiently qualified, they would take an examination and, if successful, could then look forward to the anticipated placement in the judicial system. It was common practice to be first assigned public prosecutor and then gradually effect promotion to a judgeship.

However, since 1959, as a result of a governmental decree designed to broaden and further professionalize their background, experience, and training, all potential applicants for judgeships as well as legal posts in the executive branch are also required to attend the *École Nationale de la Magistrature* (National School for Jurists) for twenty-eight months: the first eleven of these are spent at the school's site in Bordeaux in seminars, lectures, extrajudicial training (e.g., forensic medicine and criminology); in the next seventeen the applicants gain practical experience in Paris and in the provinces. After a battle of examinations, and now having selected their careers, the candidates conclude their training with a special two-month pre-appointment training period. The hopeful who wish to become students there are selected on the basis of competitive examinations, both in legal subjects and in the general liberal arts. The students, who are paid by the government for attending the *École Nationale*, must be law school graduates and under twenty-seven years of age. The successful graduate is then assigned to one of the courts of first instance, the *tribunaux d'instance*, in accordance with his class standing—assuming he wishes to become a judge. But he is also eligible for the *parquet*[99] (the office of the public prosecutor) or for service in the Ministry of Justice. The National School for Jurists was purposely designed to do for the judiciary what the National School of Administration (*École Nationale d'Administration*) has done so well for the upper echelons of the general civil service—to create a competent, reputable, and esteemed group of public servants.[100]

[99] Explained in Ch. III, *infra*, especially pp. 101–2.
[100] Early in 1967 the American Bar Association endorsed President Johnson's plan to establish a Federal Judicial Center—with the Chief Justice of the United States as

In the United States and, to a more modified extent, in Britain, the selection of a lawyer as a judge customarily represents the culmination of a long and quite frequently distinguished career in the law—subject to certain obvious political contingencies in the United States. But in France the judge is chosen from the *judicial profession*, for which he prepared by special schooling and examination—a profession just as medicine, teaching, and the law are. Although he is not particularly well paid, he enjoys considerable prestige and a high social rating. We shall now see him and his confrères in action on the bench.

Chairman of its Board—in the Administrative Office of the U.S. Courts (See Ch. IV, *infra*) to train federal court employees, including federal judges, and to foster programs of continuing education for them. A bill to enact the proposal into law was passed by Congress in December 1967. Other tasks of the Center include keeping abreast of computer technology, conducting and stimulating research on methods to speed the handling of cases, and reducing case backlogs.

III
Courts,
Courtrooms,
and Juries

TYPES OF COURTS: TRIAL AND APPELLATE

Each of the countries discussed in this book has a system of courts designed to serve its own needs and choice. Some have similar features, but no two are truly alike. Speaking broadly, however, each of these systems—and in fact practically every known judicial system in the world—has endeavored to separate the jurisdiction of *trial* (first instance) and *appellate* (review) courts. Some courts do fulfill both functions, but in that event—if justice is to have any meaning at all—they will at the very least have separate dockets for each area. This applies, for example, to the English Crown Court and the French *Cour d'Assise*. In a rather limited sense, the Supreme Court of the United States is also constitutionally empowered to exercise jurisdiction in the trial as well as in the appellate area—termed *original* and *appellate* by Article III of the Constitution, where these designations are found. However, that high tribunal's original jurisdiction docket is usually empty; seldom, if ever, has it exceeded more than a fraction of 1 per cent of the volume of cases handled by the Court. The overwhelming number of cases and controversies that reach the highest tribunal in the American judicial hierarchy do so under its appellate jurisdiction. In fact, as will be explained in more detail in Chapter V, the Supreme Court may, save in the instance of litigation involving two or more of the fifty states, share its original jurisdiction with courts below—i.e. its original jurisdiction is thus *concurrent* with them—which, in effect, means that seldom, if ever, will the Supreme Court decide such a case in its role of a trial court.

TRIAL COURTS

Trial courts perform the function their title clearly implies: they *try* cases in the first instance, as tribunals of original jurisdiction. Cases commence there because they are statutorily required to do so. More often than not they are also completed there upon the pronouncement of the verdict of guilt or acquittal—which may or may not, depending upon organizational requirements and choice, have come about as a result of a trial by jury. Rather obvious illustrations of trial courts of varied jurisdiction are a United States District Court; a Court of Common Pleas in the Commonwealth of Pennsylvania; a French *Tribunal de Grande Instance*; and the Queen's Bench Division of the High Court of Justice of England and Wales.

Again depending somewhat upon the law of the land and governmental subdivision concerned, both law and fact are taken into account at the bar of a trial court, and both parties to the litigation, plaintiff as well as defendant, are presumably accorded a full opportunity to present their respective sides of the case or controversy. In common law countries, such as most of the English-speaking lands, a single judge customarily—but by no means always—presides over a trial alone; in statutory law systems, such as those found in most continental European states, normally three or more judges sit *en banc*. When a jury sits in a case, the judge *charges* (instructs) it at the conclusion of the presentation of pertinent evidence in the law and in the procedures attendant upon the case. The jury then returns a verdict upon completion of its deliberations, which may last from a few hours to several days.

APPELLATE COURTS

The *raison d'être* of a court of appeals is to provide a forum for review of decisions rendered in trial court. Such appeals are presumably limited to questions of law at issue in the litigation below, but in some circumstances they may also deal with questions of fact, either collaterally or on their own merits. In any event, it is often extremely difficult to separate categorically matters of law and fact, and the final word on such a distinction, if it is crucial to the question of the grant of the petition for review, will necessarily lodge in the appellate tribunal itself. In large measure, this decision depends upon the tribunal's statutory authority and the extent and nature of the discretionary review powers given to it. Some appellate courts *must* accept all cases properly presented to them for review—such as the United States (Circuit) Court of Appeals, which has no effective discretionary power to decline to accept appellate petitions. Others—for example, the United States Supreme Court—possess all but complete statutory *discretionary* authority as to whether or not to accept a case brought before them for review from below, although in theory there are *some* cases of mandatory review (as will be shown in Chapter V). Still other appellate tribunals, the British House of Lords for one, have discretionary power to accept or reject cases, but are guided to a considerable degree by certification from the court below (here the Court of Appeal). Courts of appeals are usually multiple-member bodies; as a rule, three or more judges sit *en banc* to hear the appeal without a jury.

A well-known appellate court, in addition to those already named above, is England and Wales's important Court of Appeal (for civil and criminal cases). That court is empowered to *retry* a case, a departure from the normal role of appellate tribunals—but solely on the ground of fresh evidence having become available, and subject to the court's judgment that a retrial is indeed appropriate in the interests of justice.[1] It thus retries cases but rarely. The *Cour de Cassation*, at the apex of the regular French judicial system, is another example of a court of appeals. In some appellate courts, such as the criminal division of the English Court of Appeals, appeals may be instituted only by the defendant. In the United States, although the federal government may usually appeal an adverse decision of a trial court on a point of law—unless it involves "double jeopardy"—it is barred from appealing on a point of fact; this means that, in effect, the government cannot appeal an adverse verdict in a criminal proceeding on the basis of the factual evidence presented in court on pain of violating the double jeopardy safeguards of the Fifth Amendment to the United States Constitution. Until the Supreme Court so ruled in 1969, that Bill of Rights provision did not automatically apply to the states.[2]

COURTROOM PROCEDURE: GENERAL

There are essentially two methods by which society, through its judicial and legal organs, may approach a member of its body politic accused of an of-

---

[1] See Administration of Justice Act of 1964 (Sec. 5).

[2] *Benton v. Maryland*, 395 U.S. 784. The 1960's had witnessed an increasing number of "applications," "absorptions," or "incorporations" of provisions of the Bill of Rights, by virtue of a series of landmark rulings of the Supreme Court. For a full discussion of this intriguing constitutional problem, see the author's *Freedom and the Court: Civil Rights and Liberties in the United States*, 2d ed. (New York: Oxford University Press, 1972), Ch. III, "The Applicability of the Bill of Rights to the States."

fense—either by presuming his innocence until it has effectively succeeded in proving him guilty under due process of law, or by presuming his guilt unless he successfully disproves that assumption under similar processes.

"INNOCENT-UNTIL-PROVED-GUILTY": THE ACCUSATORIAL PROCEDURE

It is a cornerstone of Anglo-Saxon justice that an accused is presumed innocent until proved guilty beyond a reasonable doubt. Few, if any, concepts are more deeply rooted in our traditions. Admittedly, there have been violations of that principle from time to time, especially during periods of war and other emergencies when an occasional departure from it has been justified on the grounds of constitutionally sanctionable expediency, however distasteful. Thus, writing painfully for a divided (6 : 3) bench that ". . . hardships are part of war, and war is an aggregation of hardships. . . ." Mr. Justice Black, one of the outstanding civil libertarians ever to sit on the Supreme Court of the United States, upheld the compulsory evacuation of 112,000 persons of Japanese ancestry from their homes on the West Coast—among them some 70,000 native-born American citizens, none of whom had been *specifically accused* of disloyalty.[3] On the whole, however, the record of the common law countries, such as Britain and the United States, has been good in this regard. The layman may quite naturally be quick to adjudge a person guilty in his own mind, and he is sometimes joined by the press, particularly in America; but the Anglo-Saxon legal profession on both sides of the Atlantic Ocean, and throughout the English-speaking world, has done its best to adhere to the time-honored principle that a person is presumed innocent until he has been proved guilty beyond a reasonable doubt by due process of law. As Mr. Justice Brennan wrote for the Supreme Court in a decision highly unpopular with Congress and the public at large, in which the Court by a vote of 7 : 1 reversed the conviction of one Clinton Jencks, a suspected Communist perjurer who had not been permitted to attempt to impeach testimony given to the Federal Bureau of Investigation, on the basis of which he had been convicted in the trial court: ". . . the interest of the United States in a criminal prosecution . . . is not that it shall win a case, but that justice shall be done."[4] And, in the words of Mr. Justice Frankfurter's majority opinion in a coerced confession case in 1961, ". . . ours is an accusatorial and not an inquisitorial system—a system in

---

[3] *Korematsu v. United States,* 323 U.S. 214 (1944).

[4] *Jencks v. United States,* 353 U.S. 657 (1957), at 668. With some paraphrasing, he in effect was quoting Mr. Justice Sutherland's opinion in *Berger v. United States,* 295 U.S. 78 (1935), at 88.

which the State must establish guilt by evidence independently and freely secured and may not by coercion prove its charge against an accused out of his own mouth."[5] Of course, this jurisprudential posture applies equally to any civil proceeding, whether or not the government is a party to it. In the summary words of one of Mr. Justice Jackson's opinions concerning one attorney's right to compel another to disclose certain papers involved in the litigation concerned, "A *common law* trial is and always should be an adversary proceeding."[6]

Thus, the presumption of the innocence of the accused, until proved otherwise, is transformed into courtroom procedure in the Anglo-Saxon countries. Essential to it are the ancient, basic safeguards inherent in that philosophy of the law, safeguards which, to a greater or lesser degree, are fundamental to the notions of liberty and justice that pervade the political system of the liberal democratic West. Among these are the privilege against self-incrimination; the right to cross-examine witnesses; the writ of *habeas corpus*—perhaps the most basic right of all—and many others in the same general category.

The Judge's Role. An important feature of the accusatorial type of procedure is that the judge does *not*—except as noted below, and in rare instances in order to call forth certain types of evidence, usually of a technical nature—insert himself into the substantive questioning during the trial. Quite naturally, he does—indeed he must—hand down rulings on various motions, points of order, and other problems that may arise during the course of the trial. He is—or certainly he is expected to be—in complete charge of courtroom procedure, and as such possesses a considerable residue of what in legal parlance is termed *judicial discretion*. In this connection, that intriguing compound noun demands an application

> . . . enlightened by intelligence and learning, controlled by sound principles of law, of firm courage combined with the calmness of a cool mind, free from partiality, not swayed by sympathy nor warped by prejudice nor moved by any kind of influence save alone the overwhelming passion to do that which is just. . . .[7]

In that discretion, the judge will question a witness only to avert grave injustice, not to advance the case for either side. He is not in any sense an ac-

[5] *Rogers v. Richmond*, 365 U.S. 534, at 540–41.
[6] *Hickman v. Taylor*, 329 U.S. 495, at 516 (1946). (Italics supplied.)
[7] *Davis v. Boston Elevated Railway*, 235 Mass. 482, at 496–97. Quoted by Felix Frankfurter, *The Case of Sacco and Vanzetti* (Boston: Little, Brown and Co., 1927), pp. 90–91.

tive elicitor of truth regarding the testimony presented. In essence, he is an independent arbiter between the state and the individual or between the litigating parties. This is a concept basic to the common law adversary proceeding mentioned by Mr. Justice Jackson, a system that "sets the parties fighting." According to Professor Max Radin, one of the giant interpreters of jurisprudential theory and practice, that system has been in vogue since its adoption in Rome in the fourth or fifth century B.C., when—for better or for worse, and quite conceivably the latter—the judge's task changed from determining the truth to the umpiring of a competition.[8] There is little doubt that many, probably most, of today's lawyers would have great difficulty of conceiving of a trial as anything else. It is thus often viewed, not at all inaccurately, as a grim game.

"GUILTY-UNTIL-PROVED-INNOCENT": THE INQUISITORIAL PROCEDURE

In France, to use the most obvious example, a different philosophy regarding the legal process obtains. Not independent arbiters, the French judges are part of the machinery of the state, and courtroom procedure in criminal trials is characterized by the *inquisitorial* method, known as the *enquête*. Here the presumption may almost be regarded as implicitly one of guilt, although it may be doubted that any civilized land actually proceeds on such an assumption. Indeed, Max Radin refers to the notion of presumption of guilt as a "curiously persistent calumny," and views the presumption of innocence as "inherent in the French Declaration of the Rights of Man and the Citizen."[9] Still, so much painstakingly accumulated preliminary investigation by a professional judge—the *juge d'instruction* (examining magistrate)—has already preceded the courtroom trial that the judge or judges presiding at the trial may all but presume the defendant to be guilty of the offense charged. Nonetheless, the presiding judges actively, often vehemently and acidly, participate in the courtroom questioning of witnesses as well as of the accused—who, incidentally, cannot invoke the Anglo-Saxon privilege of refusing to take the stand on grounds of possible self-incrimination. Yet had the investigating judge been unable to find any evidence of apparent guilt, the accused would very likely never have been brought to trial. In a sense, this preliminary "investigation" (the *enquête*) is an advanced, combined form of grand jury investigation and indictment—

[8] Max Radin, "The Permanent Problems of the Law," 15 *Cornell Law Quarterly* 10–11 (1929).
[9] *The Law and You* (New York: Mentor M34, 1948), p. 99. Prof. Radin took specific exception to my above characterization in an interview shortly before his death on June 22, 1950.

still so prevalent in the American courts—but with the significant distinction that whereas the *enquête* in France is conducted by professional magistrates, the American grand jury is composed entirely of laymen.

The "Juge d'Instruction" and the "Enquête." The office of the *juge d'instruction*—which is not a uniquely French institution—combines the powers of a prosecutor and a magistrate, but the *juge d'instruction* is not a member of the prosecution *per se*. His function is to determine the truth on behalf of the state, with the aid of the police. Yet he may commence an investigation only upon notification by a member of the *parquet*, i.e., the public prosecutor (*procureur*),[10] who must have been advised of the crime by the police. The powers of the *juge d'instruction* are awesome indeed. He may call witnesses and badger them. He may ask suspects to re-enact the alleged crime. He may open mail and tap telephone wires. He may even keep people in jail indefinitely—the revered Anglo-Saxon institution of the writ of *habeas corpus* is unknown in France.[11] He may commission experts to investigate and report on special aspects. But perhaps the most potent weapon in his considerable arsenal is the famous *confrontation de témoins* (confrontation of witnesses), which is unlike anything in Anglo-American legal procedure. When two or more witnesses tell contradictory stories, the *juge d'instruction* calls them into his office together for a *confrontation*. There, under his watchful and experienced eyes and ears, and in the presence of a court official who writes down every uttered syllable, each witness is quoted repeatedly, with the other(s) invited to point out "errors" or "discrepancies" in his testimony. The questioning of witnesses by the *juge d'instruction* may proceed after the *confrontation*—presumably it also took place before—with a witness's lawyer being present in all instances. As a result of the *confrontation*, perjured testimony in criminal cases has been almost eradicated.

When all the evidence, including that of the police, has been procured in a case, and both the defense and prosecution lawyers—the latter headed by the *procureur*—have had access to the complete *dossier*, the *juge d'instruction*, who will usually consult the *procureur*, can now send the case to trial on his own authority. Since he is highly unlikely to do so unless he has become convinced of the presence of guilt, the resultant trial itself turns largely into a public verification of the accumulated record, *including* any previous criminal record. In the event of a statutorily designated *serious*

[10] The role of *parquet* is roughly similar to that of the United States Attorney General and his associates when they act as public prosecutors.

[11] Some disagreement exists on this point, with some observers contending that he can do so only for twenty days.

crime, the entire record of the investigation must be reviewed before it is admitted to trial by a *chambre d'accusation,* a judicial body at the appellate court level.

Although the broad powers accorded to the *juge d'instruction* are sometimes criticized even by French legal scholars as being akin to a "star chamber" proceeding, that charge is grossly exaggerated. The *juge d'instruction* operates in a system which simply refuses to concede to the contending parties control over the presentation of evidence—either its submission or its impeachment by cross-examination. During the trial such control becomes the duty of the presiding judge. In the absence of cross-examination, the data procured by the *enquête* are necessary to ensure the accuracy of testimony. However "tough" it may have been, the *enquête* is characterized by a patient, painstaking discovery procedure, one that has presumably solved mysteries and eliminated discrepancies in testimony. All the evidence is recorded in the *dossier,* enabling the *juge d'instruction* and the *procureur* to build the case against the accused. But it does more: it permits the presiding judge to conduct the trial free from the "games" inherent in the adversary process, especially as it is so frequently practiced in American courtrooms.

In its final impact, the French system of the *enquête* would appear to be at least as effective as the Anglo-American accusational method, in which all the evidence is brought out for the first time, almost in the manner of a contest, by testimony and cross-examination in open court before trial judge and jury. A grand jury indictment, after all, requires only a *prima facie* case. One may well contend that a criminal trial in a French court is an investigation rather than a battle between two opposing platoons of learned counsel—a "sporting theory" battle that above all in America, according to one legal authority, denotes "a bitter adversary duel" rather than a disinterested investigation—in which the duelers indulge in trickery and fight with "make believe" evidence that often bears scant relation to the facts at issue.[12]

"VOX DEI" OR "VOX POPULI" IN ACTION: THE JURIES

There is no doubt that the institution of the jury is at once one of the most fascinating and one of the most controversial aspects of the judicial process —and that justice in the West owes a great debt to the jury system. Yet it is hardly astonishing that many a curse has been uttered against a jury and what it stands for, even while the other party to the litigation at hand has

---

[12] See James Marshall, *Law and Psychology in Conflict* (Garden City, N.Y.: Doubleday & Co., Inc., 1969), p. 7.

voiced a prayer of gratitude in its behalf! Sundry types of juries exist; but essentially a jury is a group of ordinary citizens of predetermined number whom a duly constituted public official has called together for the purpose of answering a question. Used in Athens as long ago as five or six centuries before the birth of Christ, they went to Rome some ten centuries later, and then to France in the ninth century. The modern Western world traces their origin to the England of almost 800 years ago, where, in the early stages, they were regarded simply as a body of men to aid the monarch in dispensing justice by attesting to certain facts—that is, the jurors did not determine guilt or innocence, but instead were *witnesses*. Whatever their age, they have been praised and attacked ever since. Although many countries, not necessarily excluding dictatorships, still resort to juries—apart from English-speaking lands they exist today largely in Austria, Belgium, Denmark, Greece, Norway, some Latin-American countries, and some Swiss cantons—the institution has clearly suffered a decline. This is more true of the *grand jury* than it is of the *trial* (*petit*) *jury*, but both types have experienced decreased usage, especially in England and Wales, where the grand jury was abolished by the Administration of Justice (Miscellaneous Provisions) Act of 1933, and where the use of the trial jury in civil cases was seriously curtailed by the same law. Today, that jury is used in less than 5 per cent of all cases in the British Isles (to be exact, juries serve in less than 1 per cent of *civil* cases, but they *are* used in all "*grave*" *criminal* ones where there is a plea of "not guilty"). In France, of course, the grand jury is not at all employed, because of the role of the *juge d'instruction*. Juries are still widely used in the United States, particularly on the federal level.[13] In many of the fifty states, however, juries, notably grand juries, have fallen into at least partial disuse. Indeed, more and more trials everywhere are decided by judges sitting without a jury, sometimes as a result of statutory or constitutional provisions, sometimes by the agreed-upon choice of the parties to the suit. Today it seems almost unbelievable that the courts of Athens in the fifth century B.C. were composed of a jury only—there was no judge at all! Moreover, the more significant the nature of the case, the greater the number of the jurors. Thus Socrates was tried by a panel of 501 in the fourth century B.C., and Alcibiades's trial on charges of treason in the fifth featured 1501 jurors. These able Attics were drawn from all over the Athenian communities by a complicated but apparently popular lot system.[14]

---

[13] Still, even here the vast majority of cases are disposed of without juries.
[14] See Charles P. Curtis, *It's Your Law* (Cambridge: Harvard University Press, 1954), p. 102.

The foundation of the English jury system is traceable to the French empire under the Carolingian kings. As part of their successful attempt to unite their empire, a procedure called the *inquisition*, or *inquest*, was devised. Carried out by representatives of the monarch, its purpose was to call together various bodies of neighbors in order to ask questions and explain the sovereign's "immemorial" rights. The Norman conquerors subsequently carried the concept of the inquest to England, where they used it first in the compilation of the 1086 *Domesday Book*. This tome, which listed the ownership of all English land, was compiled from data obtained from royal administrators who gathered neighbors together in various parts of the country and used them as their source of information. This served to establish the right of the state to obtain data from its citizenry, and thus furthered the concept of the jury system.

The first true juries were used to discover facts under the various writs of the *Possessory Assizes*, e.g. litigant neighbors decided who was dispossessed and who owned a certain piece of land under the writ of *Novel Disseisin* ("newly dispossessed"). Thus, trial by jury was closely linked with the protection of possessions; indeed, Norman dukes and English kings sometimes specifically granted, both to private persons and to churches, the privilege of having their rights ascertained by this method. However, these juries merely filled a particular need at a particular moment in English history; they were permitted to die out and are hence not the bona fide predecessor of the modern English jury. The latter institution—initially used for civil cases only—was founded under King Henry II in the sixth decade of the twelfth century. Today, it would look strange in its original form, for then it represented what in effect was a combination grand jury and trial jury that enabled the accusing body (the modern grand jury) also to pass judgment on the guilt of the accused (the modern trial jury). Ultimately these two functions were separated, heralding the now axiomatic difference between them.[15]

THE GRAND JURY

The chief distinction between a grand jury and a petit (trial) jury is that the former does not pass on a defendant's innocence or guilt. The grand jury merely determines whether, in its considered judgment, sufficient evi-

<hr>

[15] See Frederick G. Kempin, Jr., *Development of the Common Law* (Philadelphia: Lecture Note Fund, University of Pennsylvania, 1959), I-3-2 and I-3-7. For an excellent source on the origin and history of the jury, see F. W. Maitland, *The Constitutional History of England* (Cambridge: Cambridge University Press, 1961).

dence exists or has been brought to its attention to justify a trial on criminal charges. (Grand juries do not ordinarily sit in civil charges.) A trial jury, on the other hand, determines whether to convict or acquit. Hence a grand jury does not return a verdict; it listens to a bill of evidence presented to it by the legal representative of the prosecuting authority, who must draw up the formal written accusation, and who almost invariably dominates its deliberations—given the absence of a judge or other "neutral" in the grand jury room. The grand jury then decides whether or not the evidence warrants an *indictment*, also known as a *true bill*—which it returns in approximately 95 out of 100 instances. In effect, an indictment thus charges one or more persons with having committed a felony or misdemeanor. The party called before the grand jury does not actually have an opportunity to give his full story; if he is indicted his day will come in the courtroom in the event of a trial. Nor may he bring counsel into the jury room, though he may retire to an antechamber to consult with counsel. He is entitled to know the names of, yet not confront—let alone cross-examine—witnesses that have appeared before the grand jury, but little else—except, of course, the evidence presented at the preliminary hearing before the committing magistrate. There is no *right* to appear before the grand jury; one is invited or ordered to come before it—and there is no right to advance notice of the nature and scope of the crime being investigated. When the grand jury does not find sufficient evidence, it issues what is known as an *ignoramus*, or a *no bill*, in which case the would-be defendant is not brought to trial.

By most accounts, the institution of the grand jury antedates the Magna Charta of 1215, but its origin is a source of considerable disagreement. Some have claimed to find its traces among the Athenians, but Athenian history, while mentioning the trial jury repeatedly, is quite silent on any body of citizens whose duty it was to accuse. The first grand jury, then called a *presenting jury*, was created as an accusatory body—composed of twelve knights or twelve "good and lawful men" in each community—by the Assize of Clarendon in 1166 under King Henry II. It provided

> . . . that inquiry be made in each county and in each hundred, by twelve lawful men of the hundred and four lawful men of every township—who are sworn to say truly whether in their hundred or township there is a man accused of being or notorious as a robber, or a murderer or a thief, or anybody who is a harborer of robbers, or murderers, or thieves, since the king began to reign. And this let the justices and sheriffs inquire, each before himself.[16]

[16] Ibid. p. 7.

Interestingly enough, this provision was not intended to protect the liberties of freemen, but rather to protect the monarch's interests. By 1352, in the reign of Edward III, the principle that a man's indictors were not to serve both as grand and trial jurors was firmly established. The modern concept of the grand jury dates from 1368, when Edward III impaneled twenty-four men to act as county inquisitorial boards. It was not until three centuries later, however, that a grand jury became truly independent: in two successive cases—*Colledge's Case* and *Earl of Shaftesbury's Case*[17]—for the first time refused to return an indictment, on the grounds of *ignoramus*, that it "knew nothing." According to at least one historian, the immediate reason for the *ignoramus* in one of the cases was that the sheriff and many of the grand jurors were friends of the Earl of Shaftesbury![18]

Information. In England and Wales, where the grand jury was abolished as a result of the aforementioned statute of 1933 after a century of increasing disuse, and in many parts of the United States, the fast and easy method of *information* has been adopted in its place. This is a simple and efficacious device whereby the public prosecutor merely submits his charges in the form of an affidavit of evidence, supported by sworn statements, to a court of original jurisdiction. Usually a preliminary hearing has been held before a committing magistrate here, too, and after these brief procedures the accused is ready to stand trial. In France, the *enquête* by a professional judge performs the functions of the grand jury. Only in the United States is the common law heritage of that body still relatively popular.

The documented history of the process of information is not nearly so complete as that of the grand jury and the trial jury. However, Blackstone noted in his *Commentaries* that "there can be no doubt that this mode of prosecutions by information filed on record by the King's Attorney General, or by his coroner or master of the crown office in the Court of the King's bench . . . is as ancient as the common law itself."[19] Although its usage lagged until the twentieth century, the process did figure prominently in the famous case of Peter Zenger, commonly recalled as a milestone in the battle against press censorship. In 1735 an attempt was made to indict that courageous editor of the *New-York Weekly Journal* for libel against the conduct of the royal government, as personified by Governor William Cosby. When the grand jury—symbolizing its independence in North America—

[17] 8 How St. Tr. 550 (1681) and 8 How St. Tr. 759 (1681).
[18] George J. Edwards, Jr., *The Grand Jury* (Philadelphia: George T. Bisel Co., 1906), p. 29.
[19] IV *Commentaries on the Laws of England* 309. (Ch. 23, "Of the several Modes of Prosecution.")

ignored the bill of charges against him, Zenger was then held on the basis of an information filed by the attorney general of the province. After a celebrated trial in which he was ably defended by famed Philadelphia attorney Andrew Hamilton, Zenger was acquitted. It was the English settlers who had brought the grand jury with them from their native land, together with all of the other civil rights they had enjoyed there. America's revolutionaries thought of it later as a means to prevent political prosecutions, but it was never tested for that purpose after the founding of the new nation.

Grand Jury Guarantees Today. The opening sentence of the Fifth Amendment to the Constitution of the United States in effect guarantees grand jury action on the *federal* level. Exempting members of the armed forces, it specifies that no person may be held for a "capital, or otherwise infamous crime," unless on a presentment or indictment of a grand jury. But the grand jury provision of the Fifth Amendment is not applicable to the *states*, the Supreme Court of the United States having held repeatedly and consistently that its absence in these constituent parts of the nation does not in and of itself violate those "fundamental principles of liberty and justice which lie at the base of all our civil and political institutions."[20] Indeed, less than one-half of the fifty states—twenty as of late 1975—still retain the grand jury system, and some of these utilize it solely to investigate crime and corruption among public officials in a limited number of cases, such as homicide and treason. The balance of the states have replaced it with the device of information, which may be also employed by the federal government in noncapital cases[21] at the district court level—as it was in the 1972–74 Watergate scandals in the instance of one-time counsel to President Nixon, John W. Dean III—and, generally, in civil cases, a famous early example of which is the 1886 case of *Boyd v. United States.*[22]

The standard federal or grand jury today consists of a panel of between twelve and twenty-three members, who are chosen at random from the local register of voters. The appropriate judge selects the foreman and his deputy. Unlike the trial jury, it need not be unanimous even at the federal level, but a minimum of twelve jurors—more, often sixteen, in some jurisdictions

20 *Palko v. Connecticut*, 302 U.S. 319 (1937). See also *Hurtado v. California*, 110 U.S. 516 (1883). The Supreme Court again refused to consider its "incorporation" in 1968. (*Gyuro v. Connecticut*, 393 U.S. 937.)

21 The future availability of capital punishment on *any* level of government in the United States was placed into serious constitutional doubt by a 5 : 4 decision of the Supreme Court in 1972, which ruled that capital punishment, as then constituted, violated the prohibition against "cruel and unusual punishment" of the Eighth and Fourteenth Amendments. (*Furman v. Georgia*, 408 U.S. 238.)

22 116 U.S. 616.

—must agree on an indictment or an *ignoramus,* and sixteen constitute a quorum. A grand jury is usually impaneled for a period of three to eighteen months at a time—unless discharged earlier by the judge to whom it reports —and it is called together (and paid $20.00 to $25.00 a day at the federal level in 1974) during that time whenever need for its services arises, usually a few days each week. Since no one is being "tried," its proceedings are secret—all witnesses are heard *in camera*—and may not be released to the public. The latter *caveat,* which is protective of both the accused and the grand jurors, is an essential aspect of the grand jury, and a traditional one. As already explained, not only are no defense attorneys allowed to be present, but not even a judge is permitted in the grand jury room. All witnesses thus testify alone. The grand jury normally deliberates with remarkable speed: The prosecutor appears before it; briefly outlines his case; and asks for an indictment. He almost always gets his wish.

Presentments. Grand juries may do considerably more than determine the sufficiency or lack of evidence submitted to them; they may also, and often do, conduct certain types of public investigations, enabling them to hand up a finding known as a *presentment.* Such an action represents a formal accusation against one or more individuals, made on the grand jury's own motion, calling attention to alleged illegal or improper activities—but *not* including an indictment. The first presentment on record came in England in 1683, charging certain Whigs, including the Earl of Macclesfield, with disloyal and seditious conduct. The accused brought an action for libel, but the court held for the grand jury, thus establishing the propriety of its report.[23]

Presentments have a habit of stirring up the public as well as the bar, quite frequently giving rise to general anguish. Thus, when a New York grand jury during the "quiz-show" scandals in 1959 on its own initiative handed up a presentment highly critical of the television and radio industry, General Sessions Court Judge Mitchell D. Schweitzer impounded and permanently sealed it. He declared that no grand jury had a right to return a report dealing with the activities or morals of a *private* individual or corporation. A bill designed to embody Judge Schweitzer's position in a law subsequently failed to pass the New York State legislature.[24] However, the matter was reopened tangentially two years thereafter, when the New York State Court of Appeals ruled 4 : 3 in the *Wood* case that a grand jury has

---

[23] 10 How St. Tr. 1330 (1684).

[24] A similar bill, but one which outlawed *all* presentments, had passed in 1946 but was vetoed by Governor Dewey.

the following choices: return an indictment, dismiss the charge, or remain silent.[25] Since this case involved *public* officials only, the ban seemed to have been extended to all elements of the citizenry. The action in the suit was brought by one James F. Wood, the foreman of a Schenectady county grand jury, to compel Judge Charles M. Hughes of the New York Supreme Court to make public a report the jury had filed on its own motion regarding the county highway department.

The narrowly decided *Wood* case, which overruled a prerogative in existence since 1688, serves to put the role of the grand jury and its problems into proper focus. The majority decision, written by Judge Stanley H. Fuld —and applauded by most of the lawyers' associations of the State of New York—declared that the jury involved made an inquiry which, by its own admission, failed to find that there was "willful and corrupt conduct" by a public official. The phrase quoted came from the statute under which the jury had been impaneled and charged, yet the jurors had simply decided to chart a course of action on their own, one that was both unauthorized and publicly deprecatory of reputations. The dissenters, on the other hand, urged that such action by the grand jury was simply a reaffirmation of a basic American principle under common law and of considerations of ethics in government—namely, that an authorized body of citizens may, indeed must, take appropriate action to counter the suppression or burial of evidence of "tyranny and corruption in public office." In April 1961 Judge Schweitzer augmented his earlier action by expressly warning four grand juries he impaneled that "under no circumstances" were they to submit a presentment to his court. And the New Jersey State Supreme Court ruled that presentments must not be used to rebuke individuals in the absence of conclusive proof of wrongdoing. On the other hand, Philadelphia Common Pleas Court Judge Joseph E. Gold permitted a 1962 special grand jury charged to investigate municipal corruption in Philadelphia to hand up a stinging presentment in 1963, publicly naming individuals as well as organizations.[26] When, in 1964, the New York legislature finally agreed on a bill to deal with grand jury presentments, it turned out to be a compromise: under it a grand jury is empowered to criticize a public official or employee,

---

[25] *Wood v. Hughes*, 212 N.Y. S. 2d 33 (1961).

[26] For details of the presentment, see *The Philadelphia Inquirer*, March 9, 1963, p. 1. The most celebrated "runaway" grand jury is the one that, in 1935, requested Governor Herbert Lehman of New York to supersede the District Attorney, who, the jury said, was trying to hamstring its investigation into organized vice and racketeering. The Governor responded by naming Thomas E. Dewey as special prosecutor, and indictments and convictions followed.

but *only* if its main purpose is to recommend remedial administrative or legislative action. And U.S. District Judge John J. Sirica agonized for two weeks in early 1974 ere he disposed of his "Watergate" Grand Jury's sealed presentment regarding President Nixon's involvement in the case by forwarding it, sealed, to the U.S. House of Representatives' Committee on the Judiciary for its consideration in weighing the bringing of impeachment charges against the President. No wonder he agonized! It was later revealed that the Grand Jury in that presentment had cited Nixon, 19 : 0, as an "unindicted co-conspirator." It had refrained from indicting him only because Special Prosecutor Leon Jaworski had expressed the opinion that a President was not indictable—an issue the Supreme Court pointedly refused to come to grips with in its momentous 8 : 0 "tapes" decision against the President late in July 1974 (*United States v. Nixon* and *Nixon v. United States.*)

Whatever one's judgment of the merits of the above developments may be, there is little doubt that while grand juries have traditionally been vested with broad powers to investigate crimes, such powers are not, and cannot be, either unlimited or unbridled. Grand juries are not powers unto themselves, but are essentially lay bodies whose actions are subject to judicial scrutiny and remedial relief. In that role grand juries have existed for such interesting and significant investigatory and stand-by purposes as juvenile delinquency, waterfront crime, narcotics traffic, subversive activities, quizshow manipulation, corruption, "kick-backs," tax evasion (e.g., the Agnew case in 1973), and the "Watergate" scandals of 1972–74, to name but a few of the myriad assignments given to a panel of these jurors. Necessarily, they become fairly well steeped in their particular area of jurisdiction. And they have often done a good job. The grand jury may well be cumbersome, amateurish, time-consuming, annoying, emotional, and a fifth wheel in the legal process, but on balance—as was well demonstrated by the persistent 1973–74 "Watergate" grand jury—it does appear to serve as a potentially powerful arm of direct democracy—if one is willing to accept the philosophy of the instituiton in the first place and if one has faith in the competence and intelligence of one's fellow citizens.

THE TRIAL OR PETIT JURY

Normally, when the average person or the public press refers to a jury, he has the trial or petit jury in mind. In some areas, e.g. in parts of Pennsylvania, it is known as the *traverse* jury, a term deriving from medieval days when Norman French was beginning to displace Latin as the official language of the Court of England. As has been indicated, the trial jury has suffered a decline in many parts of the world, but it is still a popular institution. In England and Wales it is employed mainly, but limitedly, in criminal cases, only very sparingly in civil cases; the same is true of France, possibly more so. In Switzerland only ten of the twenty-five cantons permit its use in criminal cases, none in civil cases. Its last important, and evidently secure, stronghold in the Western world is in the United States, where the concept of a trial by a jury of one's peers still thrives.

In England and Wales, where trial by jury, first for civil and later for criminal cases, effectively commenced during the reign of King Henry II (1154–89), the accused is still entitled—as indicated earlier—to such a trial for all serious crimes and for a very limited number of substantial civil infractions. With certain important qualifications, this jury may be demanded in all English and Welsh courts save in the highest and the lowest, but the privilege may be waived if the defendant so wishes. A jury is always impaneled in criminal cases if the accused pleads not guilty to an indictable offense. However, since 1933 the courts in England and Wales have been given considerable discretion as to whether or not to call a jury in a case; it is hence not astonishing that this discretion has been used widely to prevent a jury impaneling. If a trial jury is employed in a case, it is compiled as far as possible from local people, and consists of ten to twelve persons whose verdict of guilt or acquittal was, for 700 years, required to be unanimous. But the requirement of unanimity became a thing of the past when Parliament enacted legislation in 1967 and 1971 permitting English juries to convict by a 10 : 2, 10 : 1, or 9 : 1 majority.[27] There are a number of reasons for the decline of the trial jury in England and Wales, among which the more important are first, the belief that a judge sitting alone can perform the jury's functions at least as well, and usually better; second, the desire for a speedy trial; and third, the fact that the litigants rather than Her Majesty's government pay the jurors' fees.

The French Republic resorts to jury trials solely at the level of the assizes, the courts of original jurisdiction for serious crimes. Trial by jury has no deep roots in France. Indeed, although it once did exist as part of customary procedure in some parts of the country, in the fifteenth century, it disappeared during the reign of Charles VII, not to be reimported from England until the Revolution. Today, it consists of nine local *citoyens* (who sit with one or more judges); there is no unanimity requirements, and frequently the verdict is rendered by a simple majority vote. The French have no great

[27] In Scotland, where juries may consist of fifteen persons in some cases, a simple majority of 8 : 7 suffices to convict.

111

fondness for the jury system, and their adherence to the inquisitorial mode in the judicial process leaves little or no genuine purpose for the existence of a trial jury per se. In any event, they generally view the jury as an instrument designed to becloud and confuse the issues in a case.

But the United States, where a total of approximately two million jurors serve in some 200,000 cases each year, has remained broadly faithful to the concept of a trial by jury. Indeed, 80 per cent of the world's criminal jury trials take place here. This is necessarily true at the level of the *federal* courts because of the express requirements of the Sixth and Seventh Amendments to the Constitution. The Sixth ascertains a trial by jury in *all* federal criminal cases; the Seventh does the same for all civil cases where the value of the controversy exceeds the sum of $20—which today to all intents and purposes means in practically every instance. Although all fifty states had also provided for at least *some* type of trial by jury, the specific guarantees of the federal Bill of Rights did not automatically apply to them until the Supreme Court, in 1968, ruled that this procedural right was "implicit in the concept of ordered liberty."[28] The highest tribunal had long insisted that a defendant in a state proceeding be given a *fair trial*, on pain of a violation of the Fourteenth Amendment's due process of law and equal protection of the laws clauses. Among the several state practices affecting juries that had *inter alia* been held thus to constitute an *unfair* trial, are *systematic* exclusion of Negroes from juries[29] and the labeling of black jurors with brown, and white jurors with white, selection tickets.[30]

However, since each of the states may prescribe its own brand of jury system, a variety of practices exists—and many of these would be unconstitutional if practiced by the federal authorities. Thus, some states grant no jury trials in civil cases at all, others do in just a handful. The frequency of jury trials may thus vary widely—from only 3 per 100,000 accused in Connecticut to 144 per 100,000 in Georgia just a few years ago.[31] At the federal level, it

---

[28] *Duncan v. Louisiana,* 391 U.S. 145. But, ruled the Court in 1970, it does not reach crimes classified by *states* as "misdemeanors," *if* the penalty therefor does *not* exceed six months' incarceration. (*Baldwin v. Connecticut,* 399 U.S. 66.)

[29] *Norris v. Alabama,* 294 U.S. 587 (1935); *Hill v. Texas,* 316 U.S. 400 (1942); *Patton v. Mississippi,* 332 U.S. 463 (1947); *Whitus v. Georgia,* 385 U.S. 545 (1967).

[30] *Avery v. Georgia,* 345 U.S. 559 (1953). On the other hand, if non-whites in an assembled jury pool are excluded from jury duty on the basis of the use of intelligence tests administered equitably to all members in the pool, such exclusion is not *ipso facto* a *prima facie* denial of due process. (See *Donaldson v. California,* 404 U.S. 968, 1971, certiorari denied.) Nor is the systematic exclusion of young people such a denial. (*Ross v. United States,* 410 U.S. 990, 1973.)

[31] *Time Magazine,* August 12, 1966, p. 26.

112

is generally possible to *waive* a trial by jury, *provided* that common consent of the parties to the suit and of the judge assigned to the case is obtained,[32] but many states will not permit such a waiver, especially in certain criminal cases.[33] Other significant procedural differences between federal and state practices pertain to the *size* of juries and the requirement of *unanimity*. As a result of a series of significant Supreme Court decisions in the late 1960's and early 1970's, the following constitutional posture has emerged: *Federal* juries must still render *unanimous verdicts* in both *civil* and *criminal* cases, but the English common law tradition of having twelve jurors is no longer constitutionally required in *civil* cases;[34] all but eleven of the federal courts either permitted[35] six-member juries or even required them[36] as of 1974–75. *State* juries were long ago deemed not to be controlled by the federal unanimity jury rule,[37] and the states had adopted a host of diverse numerical requirements in both civil and criminal cases which passed judicial muster repeatedly. They were exempted from the rule again by two 1972 Court decisions which specifically sanctioned a 10 : 2 Oregon criminal jury verdict[38] and a 9 : 3 Louisiana one,[39] with Mr. Justice White's opinion for the 5 : 4 majority holding that, in non-capital cases such as these, non-unanimous rulings could equally well serve "the interests of the defendant in having the judgment of his peers interposed between himself and the officers of the state who prosecute and judge him. . . ."[40] (But the Court hedged as to the precise cut-off point where even lower numerical non-unanimity would con-

---

[32] In 1965, in *Singer v. United States*, 380 U.S. 24, the Supreme Court ruled unanimously that a defendant in a federal trial does *not* have a constitutional right to insist on trial by a judge rather than by a jury if the government insists on a jury.

[33] According to the seminal study by Harry Kalven, Jr., and Hans Zeisel, *The American Jury* (Boston: Little, Brown and Co., 1966), regional custom apparently determines whether a defendant will waive jury trial, with the percentage of jury waivers varying from a high of 79 per cent in Wisconsin to 3 per cent in the District of Columbia and to 0 per cent in Montana! Also significant is the category of crime: Jury waiver occurs in 70 per cent of drug violation cases (where the judge is presumed to be less emotionally involved than lay jurors), whereas the jury is waived in only 13 per cent of homicide cases. (Pp. 20–26)

[34] *Colgrove v. Battin*, 413 U.S. 149 (1973).

[35] *Report* of the Administrative Office of the United States Court for 1974.

[36] E.g., the United States District Court for the Southern District of New York, which mandated the six-man civil jury for all of its twenty-seven judges as of August 1, 1973. (See *The New York Times*, July 22, 1973, p. 16.)

[37] *Minneapolis & St. Louis Railroad Co. v. Bombolis*, 214 U.S. 211 (1916). The Court had set a standard for twelve-member *federal* juries in 1898 in *Thompson v. Utah*, 170 U.S. 343, when Utah was still a federal territory.

[38] *Apodaca v. Oregon*, 406 U.S. 404 (1972).

[39] *Johnson v. Louisiana*, 406 U.S. 356 (1972).

[40] *Apodaca v. Oregon*, loc. cit. at 411.

stitute a denial of due process of law.) Juries of less than twelve on the state level had been Court-approved for some time—even as small a panel as Florida's six-member criminal trial jury,[41] one of which convicted, and another subsequently acquitted, Clarence Earl Gideon in his celebrated constitutional battle regarding the incorporation of the right to counsel in all criminal cases.[42] Today, approximately 80 per cent of the states authorize jury verdicts by 75 per cent of the jurors in civil cases, with 20 per cent of the states extending this form of split verdict also to non-capital criminal cases. Half of the states authorize various types of trials with juries of less than twelve members, often six.[43] The governing question concerning these state practices at the bar of the United States Supreme Court is not a matter of comparison or method, but the essential one of whether or not the defendant received a fair trial under conditions of due process of law.

SELECTION AND IMPANELING OF JURIES

Since the enactment by Congress of the Jury Selection and Service Act of 1968—largely the work of Senator Joseph D. Tydings (D.-Md.)—federal grand and petit juries in the United States must be drawn by lot from the voting-registration lists of area or district citizens by the jury clerk, who uses these names to form a jury panel, or *venire*. The statute, long requested by public and private observers, became all but a foregone conclusion when a federal court of appeals ruled that a particular defendant's rights had been violated precisely because his jury had not been selected from "a cross section" of the community,[44] but under the so-called "key man" system.

The "key man" system, widely used until 1968 on the federal as well as the state level, still obtains in many of the latter jurisdictions. Under it, the

41 *Williams v. Florida*, 399 U.S. 78 (1970). Mr. Justice White here again expressed his conviction that size has no bearing on the essential feature of a jury, which he viewed as the "interposition between the accused and his accuser of the common sense judgment of a group of laymen, and in the community participation and shared responsibility that results from that group's determination of guilt or innocence." (At 100.)

42 *Gideon v. Wainwright*, 372 U.S. 335 (1963).

43 Why twelve was initially selected for a jury's composition remains a mystery. However, that number has been mathematically significant ever since the days of the Sumerians, 5000 B.C., and also has religious significance: twelve signs of the Zodiac; twelve tribes of Israel; twelve Christian apostles.

44 *Scott v. Walker*, 358 F.2d 561 (1966). Because he viewed the prospective jury list in Erie County, N.Y. (Buffalo), to be less than a true "cross-section," State Supreme Court Justice Edward Brovenzano discharged the entire juror list of 110,000 for the county in July 1974! (*The New York Times*, July 4, 1974, p. 1.)

jury clerk asks "upstanding" citizens of the community to submit names of individuals whom *they* believe to be potentially qualified jurors—with the panel ultimately selected from these lists by the clerk. A time-and-practice-honored system, it nonetheless lent, and lends, itself to the possibility of considerable mischief, and it is entirely conceivable that, sooner or later, the states too will either abandon it voluntarily or do so as a result of court action.

In England and Wales juries are selected by the sheriff from a list of householders compiled by local authorities; in France they are chosen from departmental lists of citizens of thirty years of age and over who possess all civic and political rights. In Switzerland juries sitting with the Criminal Chamber of the Federal Tribunal to try certain criminal cases are *elected* by the people for six-year terms on the basis of one juror for each 3000 inhabitants. Happily, in more and more jurisdictions, notably in the United States, automation has entered, with electronic data-processing systems increasingly taking over the task of clerks who pick names from mahogany drums or glass jars to choose the jurors to be called for service, thus reducing to an average of twenty minutes a process that formerly took two days! Theoretically, every adult of voting age is eligible for jury duty and may expect a call, unless he has served for more than a year in prison on a criminal charge and has not been pardoned for that offense.[45] This limiting proviso is statutorily applicable only to the federal government, but most of the fifty states now have the same, or at least a similar, requirement. While everyone else of voting age may thus expect to get a jury call at one time or another, it is not only relatively easy to avoid jury duty—which, incidentally, is one of the chief criticisms leveled against the jury system—but entire segments of the body politics are exempt either by permissible judicial rule, by law, or by custom. Among the occupational groups exempt almost automatically in the vast majority of jurisdictions, especially in the United States, are professionals such as lawyers (a jury composed of arguing and battling lawyers would indeed be an interesting experience!); physicians (too busy to serve); members of the armed forces (often absent from the community); officers of all three branches of government (possible conflict of interest), policemen and firemen (indispensable professionally); clergymen (a jury must deliberate, not pray); teachers (essential occupation);

---

[45] The official qualifications for *federal* jurors—which are similar to those in the several states—are: (1) U.S. citizenship; (2) attainment of at least eighteen years of age; (3) one year's residence in the district; (4) no prior conviction punishable for more than one year unless pardoned or amnestied; (5) ability to read, write, and understand English; and (6) no mental or physical disabilities that would hamper efficient jury service.

and others in similar capacities. Other busy employed people can normally avoid jury service by submitting affidavits of indispensability from employers. Still others, such as nursing mothers and those with a large family of young children, will normally have to do little more than to write a letter to the court concerned in order to be excused by the judge.[46] But a failure to do at least that much may conceivably result in a citation for contempt of court, which occurred in the case of one thirty-seven-year-old Waterloo, Iowa, mother who repeatedly and knowingly flouted requests for an explanation by the court and finally found herself sentenced to be incarcerated for six months, in Rockwell City Women's Reformatory, for criminal contempt.[47]

If none of the reasons cited is acceptable to the court as a bona fide excuse, an irresponsible citizen can, of course, still evade his civic duty by confessing to one of the many otherwise validly disqualifying factors in jury impaneling. Among these are confession of prejudice for or against one of the litigants (although in England there is no right to *examine* a jury for prejudice); acquaintance with either party to the suit, however slight; allegation of sympathy with, or opposition to, certain pertinent philosophies of life involved in the case, no matter how tangentially; and so forth. In fine, only those who are really willing and able to serve will normally do so in the long run. On the other hand, in 1968 the Supreme Court ruled 6 : 3 that persons expressing general conscientious scruples against the death penalty could no longer automatically get off, or be kept off, juries in capital cases; and that, consequently, no death sentence could stand if it had been propounded by a jury that had been *purged* of all persons who said that they opposed the death penalty or had conscientious scruples against it.[48]

Challenges. Jurors may naturally be removed from a panel for any of the above reasons or a myriad of others by the procedure of appropriate *challenges* (first given credence by Roman tribunals during the Empire's heyday, when one was allowed to object to a jury trying any particular case), which are granted to both the defense and the prosecution as a matter of

---

[46] Under new rules adopted following the enactment of the 1968 statute, the U.S. District Court for the Southern District of New York (Manhattan) now excuses the following *on written request:* Lawyers; persons over 70; actively engaged ministers and members of religious orders; women with children under ten; practicing physicians, dentists, and registered nurses; persons who have served on juries thirty days in the preceding two years; sole proprietors of businesses who have no help; teachers, supervisors or administrators of schools; and anyone living more than fifty miles from the Foley Square Court House.

[47] *The Philadelphia Inquirer*, May 18, 1952, p. 13.

[48] *Witherspoon v. Illinois*, 391 U.S. 510.

116

regular courtroom procedure in England and in France as well as in the United States. However, English juries are not subject to examination by counsel for "prejudice," nor is there a right to have an all black or white or an all male or all female jury.

Most frequently employed in the United States, challenges are essentially of two types, *peremptory* and *for cause*. They play a major role in the adversary process. A peremptory challenge entitles either one of the parties to the suit to request the removal of a would-be juror by *fiat*—no reason need be given; the mere request, whatever the motivation, will be honored. As the Supreme Court held in 1965, in a 6 : 3 decision written by Mr. Justice White, ". . . the essential nature of the peremptory challenge is that it is one exercised without a reason stated, without inquiry, and without being subject to the court's control."[49] It is a critical, often crucial element in the lawyer's strategy. What *is* subject to court control, however, is the *number* of these challenges granted—although that is often determined by statute. It is customary to permit the defense more peremptory challenges, than the prosecution, but this is not inevitably the case. In federal trial courts, three such challenges per juror are normally permitted each side, depending on the nature of the offense. On occasion a flat ten have been authorized. But in the 1974 Mitchell-Stans trial for perjury, conspiracy, and obstruction of justice, which resulted in the defendants' acquittal, U.S. District Court Judge Lee P. Gagliardi, citing "acute pre-trial publicity, assigned twenty peremptory challenges to the defense yet only eight to the prosecution. In Pennsylvania, the usual rule for murder cases is twenty for the defense and twenty for the prosecution. In the sensational trial of Richard Speck, who was ultimately convicted of the murder of eight student nurses in Chicago in 1966, Illinois Judge Herbert C. Paschen, endeavoring to be scrupulously fair and guarding against reversals on appeal, permitted the unprecedented total of 320 peremptory challenges! Each side was permitted twenty for *each* of the eight murder charges—and a grand total of 2500 jurors was questioned![50] On the other hand, in the famed "Pentagon Papers" (espionage, theft, and conspiracy) federal trial of Dr. Daniel Ellsberg and Anthony J. Russo in 1973, the defense was allowed a total of fourteen such challenges, the prosecution only six. When a panelist is challenged for *cause*, however, the challenger must be in a position to advance a bona fide reason for his demand for the disqualification, and it will have to be one sufficiently related to the substantive or procedural aspects of the litigation involved in

[49] *Swain v. Alabama*, 380 U.S. 202, at 220.
[50] See the accounts in *Time Magazine*, March 24 and April 7, 1967.

order to be acceptable in the eyes of the court. But there are no limits to the *number* of challenges for cause.

These challenges, whose procedures are regulated by the court concerned, not infrequently delay the impaneling of the trial jury for days, occasionally even for weeks. For instance, it took four months to select the twelve-member jury in the 1971 Connecticut murder trial of Bobby G. Seale—with a total of 1550 jurors being called to the venire, 1035 of whom were questioned.[51] And the arduous and delicate task of selecting a jury to sit in the trial of the eleven top-echelon members of the Communist Party-U.S.A. in Judge Harold Medina's U.S. District Court for the Southern District of New York in 1949 consumed a total of six weeks. Because of the nature of the charges of the case, which ultimately resulted in the conviction of all eleven (although with varying sentences),[52] both defense and prosecution were painstaking in their questioning of the prospective jurors, many of whom managed to extricate themselves from serving by simply acknowledging that they could not possibly have an open mind regarding the guilt of the accused. It is not astonishing, therefore, that jury selection has not only become an art but a game, albeit a grim one, in which defense and prosecution often go to extreme lengths to jockey for a jury panel favorable to their side. Thus in 1972 defense attorneys employed psychologists and handwriting analysts to help select the Angela Davis jury—which acquitted her. A team of social scientists went to Harrisburg, Pa., three months prior to the trial of Father Philip Berrigan—who was accused of plotting to raid draft boards, blow up heating tunnels in Washington, D.C., and kidnap Dr. Henry A. Kissinger—to help the defense in its efforts to get a "sympathetic" jury impaneled from the final venire of forty-six prospective jurors. Their suggested "ideal" was "A female Democrat with no religious preference and a white collar or skilled blue collar job."[53] The jury that tried Dr. Carl Coppolino for murder in New Jersey in 1966 was one selected from a panel of 275 which had been the object of the closest professional scrutiny and weeks-long attention by experienced Asbury Park lawyer Joe Mattice, who had been hired by the crack defense attorney, F. Lee Bailey, "to pick

[51] *The New York Times*, March 12, 1971, p. 43.

[52] *United States v. Dennis*, 72 F. Supp. 417 (1949).

[53] After some sixty hours of deliberations, the jury—nine women and three men—reported itself "hopelessly deadlocked" on all of the charges and found Father Berrigan and Sister Elizabeth McAllister guilty simply of "letter smuggling." (*The Philadelphia Sunday Bulletin*, May 6, 1973, p. 10xf.) For an account of the operation of the team of social scientists at work here (and in two other famed cases), see *Time Magazine*, January 28, 1974, p. 60.

the jury" that would acquit. It did.[54] The jury that acquitted Messrs. Mitchell and Stans was constructed with the professional aid of one Marty Herbst, the president of a self-styled "communications think tank," following a profile that called for blue-collar workers, primarily Roman Catholics, who earned an average of $8000 to $10,000 annually and who read the *Daily News*. The profile had no place for Jews (none were impaneled), for people with college degrees (none were impaneled, although one alternate, who ultimately served, did have one), for people Herbst called "limousine liberals" (there were none). As Herbst told Martin Arnold of *The New York Times* (May 5, 1974, p. 1), "We wanted people who were home established, to the right, more concerned with inflation than Watergate"—jurors who would associate the dour John Mitchell with John Wayne, as Herbst put it. It is no wonder that after the acquittal the prosecutor bitterly remarked that he had lost the case at the impaneling stage. He might have explained, too, that, while the defense had employed its own impaneling tactics, the composition of the jury was also in no small measure determined by Judge Gagliardi, who eliminated an unusually large number of potential jurors at the *voir dire* "for possible prejudice" because they were "politically interested" and "better educated"! That kind of action taken by a trial judge, although a controversial practice, is neither uncommon nor illegal.

In a completely different vein, it has proved so difficult at times to impanel a jury that clerks of courts literally have had to stoop to grabbing people off the streets in search of a trial panel, under the traditional common law right of going to the streets "to impress citizens into duty"—which is what happened on two occasions to strolling unemployeds near City Hall in Philadelphia in 1965 and 1966, and to a U.N. Delegate taking a walk in Paterson, New Jersey, in 1958. A judge in Kentucky, in an unsuccessful attempt to impanel jurors for a case involving the murder of two deputy sheriffs in 1962, sent out state troopers, and New Jersey sheriffs collared seventeen Morristown residents for service within forty minutes on an October day in 1967.[55]

Blue Ribbon Juries. Among the charges voiced frequently against juries, both grand and petit, are that they merely give vent to the established community prejudices; that they are utterly unqualified to render judgment; and that, worse still, they are composed quite consistently of people who not

[54] See the colorful account by Joe McGinnis in *The Philadelphia Inquirer*, December 19, 1966, p. 29.

[55] *The New York Times*, April 15, 1962; ibid. October 26, 1967. (This was for the trial of the black poet and playwright LeRoi Jones and two others on a weapons charge following the bloody Newark, N.J., riots in 1967.)

only are uninformed in civic affairs, but are actually not interested. In Illinois, at least for a while, the names of those persons who consistently failed to vote were placed at the top of prospective jury lists. This interesting practice was apparently based on the assumption that nonvoters make excellent jurymen! In large part to meet the general criticism of unsatisfactory juries, some states in America have statutorily adopted either a special jury test, or, more commonly, the *blue ribbon jury*. This device, as used at various times and in sundry jurisdictions of a quarter of the states,[56] sees judges of certain courts giving potential veniremen a series of test questions involving legal terminology that the jurors would almost certainly encounter. If an otherwise eligible juror misses more than one or two of these chiefly multiple-choice and matching questions, disqualification is almost certain.

Blue ribbon juries (then called *struck juries*) made their first appearance in England in 1730. They were employed solely at the level of the King's Bench and only for "trials of great consequence," or when the subject matter of the case was beyond "discussion of the ordinary freeholder." Court officials would choose forty-eight men who were "competent, intelligent, and less prejudiced than the ordinary juror." Somewhat later, the privilege to impanel such a blue ribbon or "special" jury was extended to all courts, who could authorize it for either of the above two reasons or, generally, when an ordinary jury "could not be impaneled." However, they were finally statutorily abolished in England in 1971.

It is hardly astonishing that the institution of the blue ribbon jury would ultimately face a test at the bar of the highest court of the United States. It came in 1947, not surprisingly involving the New York County special jury —which, in existence since the turn of the century, consisted of a "special jury" panel of some 3000 eligibles out of a total pool of 60,000 veniremen— and it was closely followed by a similar test barely one year later.[57] By the narrowest of margins, 5 : 4, the Supreme Court of the United States upheld the statute and the practice against the dual challenge that it violated both the due process of law and the equal protection of the laws clauses of the Fourteenth Amendment to the Constitution. The majority of the Court contended that the professionals and white collar workers, so dominant on the jury, could well come from widely varying salary groups, and that neither clause cited requires that a jury must represent all components of society. As Mr. Justice Jackson wrote for the majority in the first case: "So-

[56] E.g., Ala., Del., Ind., Mich., N.Y., N.J., Tenn., Vt., Va., W.Va.
[57] *Fay v. New York*, 332 U.S. 261 (1947) and *Moore v. New York*, 333 U.S. 565 (1948).

ciety also has a right to a fair trial. The defendant's right is a neutral jury. He has no constitutional right to friends on a jury."[58] Furthermore, the majority felt that a state might reasonably use blue ribbon juries as a means of rendering the administration of justice more efficient. But four Justices— Murphy, Black, Douglas, and Rutledge—dissented vigorously. Their opinion was written by Justice Murphy, who had been President Franklin D. Roosevelt's Attorney General. He insisted that an accused person was entitled to be tried by a jury fairly drawn from a true cross section of the population, and that a blue ribbon jury simply could not be representative.

> One is constitutionally entitled to be judged by a fair sampling of all one's neighbors, . . . not merely those with superior intelligence or learning . . . The vice lies in the very concept of "blue ribbon" panels—the systematic exclusion of all but the "best" or most learned or most intelligent of the general jurors. Such panels are completely at war with the democratic theory of our jury system, a theory formulated out of the experience of generations.[59]

The majority decision in that case has never been overruled and thus stands as *res judicata*. Yet its abolition on the *federal* level by the terms of the 1968 statute may well herald its demise in the states as well—although, without a judicial decision to the contrary, its constitutionality prevails. A blue ribbon jury may be both unfair and undemocratic, but these qualifications do not render it *ipso facto* unconstitutional. Furthermore, it may be well to reiterate that the notion that juries should be composed of men and women from all walks of life is a relatively recent one. At its English origins, the jury was composed of favorites of the Crown, men of position, or men who were indebted to the Crown. In the early history of the jury in the United States, it comprised a handful of propertied men. Several decades passed before being male and owning property, to name but the two more obvious qualifications, were no longer prerequisites to participation in jury duty.

THE TRIAL JURY AT WORK

A trial jury (which always contains one or more alternates to guard against a case of sudden indisposition of a juror) sits *en banc* throughout the course of the trial. It does so no matter how long the trial may take, and the jurors are compensated, generally inadequately, on a daily fee basis.[60] Each of its

[58] *Fay v. New York*, loc cit. at 288.
[59] *Moore v. New York*, loc cit. at 570.
[60] It is difficult to pinpoint an "average" daily juror's fee, but in 1973 it ranged between $10.00 and 20.00 daily—the former figure being the state, the latter the federal average.

members is presumed to listen impartially and with an open mind to both sides of the case; is not to discuss the trial with anyone, no matter how near or dear; and, at least in theory, is not permitted to read, view, or hear any media of communication that might have a conceivable bearing on the ongoing trial. In fact, most judges ban *any media whatsoever* during the trial. The latter requirement may well be an illusory one: there is every reason to believe that, regardless of a juror's conscientiousness and dedication, few public-spirited individuals would in fact literally deny themselves the news of the day. However, if either side in the litigation succeeds in presenting incontrovertible proof of such an aberration, it may move for a mistrial or even a directed verdict of acquittal. The jurors are not permitted to take notes; they are to "register the evidence as it is given, on the tablets of [their] memory and not otherwise."[61] When the presiding judge has delivered his charge (see below) to the jury at the end of the trial, the jury retires for its deliberation until it reaches a verdict—which, according to the findings of a host of knowledgeable students of the jury system, they have decided *prior* to their deliberations![62]

If the deliberative proceedings stretch into the night, the jury is locked up ("sequestered") in a near-by hotel and subsequently continues its work on the following day or days. According to the results of research on jury deliberations conducted by one expert, 50 per cent of the average jury's deliberation time is spent exchanging "personal experiences," 25 per cent on "procedural matters," 15 per cent on reviewing facts, and exactly 8 per cent on discussing the judge's instructions.[63] If, after a reasonable period of time and repeatedly unsuccessful balloting, a trial jury is unable to arrive at a verdict of guilt or acquittal, the judge will declare it to be a *hung jury*, dismiss it, and remit the case to the docket for a trial *de novo* before an entirely different judge and jury. *But* the average judge will battle hard to avoid a deadlock. Thus, U.S. District Judge Edward Weinfeld of New York declined to accept the request of a long-deadlocked jury in 1962; sent it back to a midtown hotel with orders to return to his court at 9 a.m. It did, redeliberated, and later that day returned a verdict of "guilty."

"*Hung*" *Juries.* A famous example of a hung jury was that of the first

---

[61] Indiana Supreme Court, as quoted by L. L. Bromberger, "Jurors Should Be Allowed to Take Notes," 32 *Journal of the American Judicature Society* 57–8 (1948).

[62] Donald M. Gillmor, *Free Jury and Free Trial* (Washington, D.C.: Public Affairs Press, 1966), pp. 201–10.

[63] *Ibid.* quoting Rita M. James, "Status and Competence of Jurors," 64 *American Journal of Sociology* 563 (1959).

Alger Hiss case,[64] in which the jury deadlocked 8 : 4 for conviction after countless ballots, and Federal District Judge Samuel Kauffman declared it hung. Not long thereafter, Hiss was convicted of perjury in a new trial and with a new jury before Federal Judge Henry W. Goddard.[65] A sensationalized illustration of not just one but two hung juries in succession was the highly publicized Finch-Tregoff murder-conspiracy case in California. The first trial ended in a hung jury in March 1960, after thirteen weeks of courtroom action, with the jury hopelessly deadlocked upon after thirty-seven hours of deliberation. At that time it stood 10 : 2 for convicting Dr. R. Bernard Finch, but 8 : 4 for his mistress Carole Tregoff's acquittal. The retrial was completed in November 1960, and again ended in a hung jury, this time having lasted seventeen weeks, with the jury taking fifty-nine ballots during seventy full hours of active deliberation. Mr. Edwin Fry, foreman and the only male on the jury, reported that the twelve jurors had unanimously found Dr. Finch guilty of the murder of his wife, but were divided 9 : 3 on the degree of murder to be charged—three jurors stubbornly insisting on a second-degree finding. On Miss Tregoff the jury had split 9 : 3 on the degree as well as the guilt—and that same count held against both regarding the conspiracy charge! Another seemingly interminable trial finally resulted, ending the fiasco in March 1961 with a clear-cut verdict against the two defendants: both were found guilty of conspiracy, Dr. Finch being convicted of first-degree murder and conspiracy to commit murder, Miss Tregoff of second degree murder and conspiracy to commit murder. Both were given life sentences. She was on parole in 1969, he in 1971, after having served eight and ten years, respectively. A recent example of two hung juries in succession following an initial, reversed conviction—with the government then despairing of a fourth trial—was that of Black Panther co-founder Huey Newton, who had been charged with the killing of Oakland, California, policeman John Frey in a 1967 gun battle. Newton had been found guilty of manslaughter in his initial trial in 1968, but a new trial had been ordered by the California Supreme Court because of judicial error in the charge to the first jury. In the two subsequent trials the jury deadlocked, i.e. was "hung," 6 : 6 and 11 : 1 for conviction—but one determined juror can, of course, hang any jury that requires unanimity.[66] (Reference is some-

---

[64] *United States v. Hiss.* Jury hung in August 1949.

[65] *United States v. Hiss,* 88 F. Supp. 559 (1950). See also *United States v. Hiss,* 107 F. Supp. 128 (1952).

[66] See the accounts in *The Philadelphia Inquirer,* August 9, 1971, p. 1, and *The Philadelphia Evening Bulletin,* December 16, 1971, p. 68g.

times made to a *hanging jury*, which is a *grand jury* that has earned a reputation for almost certain indictments.)

INSTRUCTING THE JURY: THE JUDGE'S CHARGE

One of the highlights of a trial in the pertinent federal and state courts of
the United States, and a crucial point in its evolvement, is the presiding
judge's *charge* to the trial jury upon completion of testimony, arguments,
and motions by all concerned. It comes after the summations by the prosecution and the defense, the latter customarily speaking last. Much thought
goes—or should go—into this charge, which is intended as an exposition of
the law and is delivered orally in most, although not all, cases.[67] The judge
must take great care to ascertain that its contents are clear, to the point,
comprehensive, and illuminating, and that they pose readily discernible alternatives to the jury panelists, who may well ask for further instructions on
details. But the jury may not take copies of the charge to the jury deliberation room, nor may they tape-record it. It is a highly complicated business
for them. Thus, in the words of an appellate tribunal:

> The trial judge should not as a rule limit himself to stating good set terms
> of law culled from the codes and the reports. Jurors need not legal defini-
> tions merely. They require proper instructions as to the method of applying
> such definitions after reaching their conclusions on the facts.[68]

Moreover, the judge must see to it that his charge is scrupulously fair to
both sides in the dispute. But it is of overriding importance to the accused.
It should be "the safeguard of fairness and impartiality and the guarantee
of judicial indifference to individuals."[69] Many a charge has, ultimately,
been instrumental in causing a mistrial; many another has been found to
be defective on points of law by appellate courts. In brief, the judge's charge
to the jurors, which is almost always necessarily complicated, sums up the
case, pinpoints the chief issues involved, and concludes with the admonition
that the jury must bring in a verdict of "guilty" or "not guilty"—addressing
itself to each of the charges and/or counts at issue and, if a choice is permissible under law in homicide cases, determining the degree of punish-

---

[67] An interesting study of jury-charging attitudes by 50 randomly-selected federal district court judges in 1970, conducted by Jerry K. Frye of Texas Christian University,
pointed, a.o. to: the extreme importance judges assign to *oral* instructions; to its
"meaningfulness" to the jurors; an average length of 1½ hours; a strong disinclina-
tion to permit any written material to accompany the jury to the deliberation room;
and considerable confidence in the average juror's listening and comprehension ability.
(See letter to author, plus chart, dated February 5, 1970.)
[68] *People v. Odell*, 230 N.Y. 481 (1921), at 487–88.
[69] Ibid. at 488.

ment. Any verdict of "guilty" must have taken into account the absence of *reasonable doubt,* often a very difficult problem. There are no in-between stages of a verdict, although in some cases, in some of the fifty American states, juries are empowered to mitigate their judgment of guilt in homicide cases by a recommendation of mercy, which is normally binding upon the judge. It was just such a binding recommendation by the third jury in the Finch-Tregoff murder case that saved Finch from the electric chair.

Under certain limited circumstances, a judge may express a value judgment on the evidence in charging his jury, but this is valid only in isolated instances, and, indeed, has been judicially interdicted in others—e.g., in Pennsylvania.[70] Superior Judge Leroy Dawson in the second Finch-Tregoff case startled courtroom observers by telling the deadlocked jury that the evidence showed "a willful and deliberate taking of human life." When one of the defense attorneys repeatedly attempted to stop the judge from reading his comments, he found himself twice cited for contempt. Judge Dawson cited a 1934 amendment to the California Constitution as his authority and a San Diego case in 1958 as his precedent.[71] Since his own case resulted in a hung jury, Dawson's action was not challenged further. On the other hand, judges everywhere are free to comment upon a jury's verdict once that has been announced, although many jurists believe that practice, too, to be at least unwise if not unethical; but it is not illegal unless expressly interdicted by constitutional, statutory, or judicial mandate.

Setting a Verdict Aside. In *civil* cases, but generally not in *criminal* cases save for a few states that permit it, a judge may *reverse* the jury's verdict. This frequently occurs in so-called *negligence* cases, in which jury lawlessness, in the form of excessive verdict, is not uncommon. A federal case of this nature, one which was widely featured in the public press in 1959 because of an open clash between Justices Whittaker and Douglas, was *Inman v. Baltimore and Ohio Railroad.*[72] A District of Columbia jury had held the railroad negligent in stationing Inman where he could be knocked down by a drunken driver, and it awarded him $25,000. However, the judge who presided over the trial in the United States District Court set the verdict aside as being "irrational."[73] When the United States Court of Appeals upheld

---

[70] Philip R. Goldsmith, "Judges' Comments to Jurors Curbed," *The Philadelphia Inquirer,* April 22, 1972, p. 8.

[71] *The Sunday Bulletin* (Philadelphia), November 6, 1960, p. 1.

[72] 361 U.S. 138.

[73] An example of a state court reversal of a verdict is the action by Philadelphia Court of Common Pleas, Judge Theodore L. Reimel in setting aside a $25,000 verdict by a jury for a local attorney's claim for fees due as being "excessive and perverse." (*The Evening Bulletin,* January 16, 1962, p. 13.)

the district judge, Inman appealed to the United States Supreme Court, which, in a 5 : 4 opinion, affirmed the judgment below. What provoked the headlined outburst by Mr. Justice Douglas, and his insistence that the Supreme Court has a duty to enforce the guarantee of a jury trial and to prevent the lower courts from setting too strict a standard, was Mr. Justice Whittaker's concurring opinion. In it Whittaker had scoffed at the idea that the railroad had been negligent and suggested that the only way that it could have prevented the accident was to have the employee encased in an army tank. This, in the full glare of an "Opinion Monday" (to be described in detail in Chapter V), Mr. Justice Douglas denounced, in person and from the bench, as "smart-alecky." Barely one year later, however, with Justices Black and Douglas dissenting vehemently, the Supreme Court itself, for the first time in twenty-four years, reversed a jury's verdict awarding damages to an injured railroad worker.[74] Judge Charles E. Wyzanski, Jr., of the federal trial court below had upheld the jury's verdict, but denounced it in no uncertain terms, asserting the case was devoid of "any evidence of negligence." He had refrained from setting it aside solely because he felt bound by what until then had been Supreme Court doctrine in these cases.[75] Of course, courts may also reverse and remand an award as being "too low," although this occurs far less frequently. Thus, the U.S. Court of Appeals for the Second Circuit held a $32,000 jury-awarded payment to a widow for the death of her husband killed in an automobile accident "as grossly inadequate," basing the decision on what Judge Irving R. Kaufman noted as the unfair influence of the trial judge's charge to the jury.[76]

The judges may also set aside a jury verdict if it is clearly based upon an obviously mistaken notion of the law involved in a case. Yet all these practices in American courts are a far cry from Continental systems, where the trial judge is permitted, if not expected, to comment upon the weight of the evidence and the credibility of witnesses throughout the course of the trial, and to allow the jury to know his opinion on the merits of the case.[77] On the other hand, the average judge in the United States, too, has the power in all cases to order a verdict of *directed acquittal* before a case goes to the jury—a motion made often by defense counsel almost as a routine matter, but granted rarely. If granted, however, it is not subject to reversal by any

---

[74] *New York, New Haven, and Hartford v. Hennagan,* 364 U.S. 441 (1960).
[75] Ibid. As reported in 272 F. 2d 153, at 155–56 (1959).
[76] *Caskey v. The Village of Wayland,* 362 F. 2d 1789 (1967).
[77] In sixteenth-century England—and until 1670—the so-called "writ of atteint" (the remote ancestor of today's "directed verdict") enabled a judge to refuse to accept *any* jury verdict he did not approve, no matter *what* the evidence. A new trial was then held, customarily, and with a larger jury.

higher court on the *federal* level. Moreover, the judge may take a case out of the jury's hands if it becomes evident that there are only questions of law involved, no facts being in dispute at all. And among the myriad of reasons why a judge may order a *retrial* is the finding of a clear case of basic confusion among the jurors—one that obviously affected the verdict in such a fashion that there is grave doubt in the mind of the presiding judge that the jury has fulfilled its part in seeing that justice is done. Thus, in a New Jersey automobile accident case the jury had returned from its deliberations, and its foreman upon being asked by the judge, "Have you agreed upon a verdict, Mr. Foreman?", answered, "My name isn't Foreman. My name is Admerman." When the trial judge refused to recognize this interesting reply as a sufficient reason to declare a mistrial, defendant Naomi Haberli appealed to the Appellate Division of the New Jersey State Superior Court, which unanimously ordered a retrial, citing Mr. Admerman's response, as well as the grossly excessive award granted by his fellow jurors, as a *prima facie* example of the type of "basic confusion" necessitating a new trial.[78] But it should be understood that no trial or appellate judge will readily tamper with a jury's verdict, no matter what his private opinion may be.

"General" and "Special" Verdicts. On the basis of the somewhat questionable assumption that the jury fully comprehends the judge's instructions concerning the applicable substantive legal rules, it is usually required to return a *general* or *over-all* verdict in favor of one party or another. Theoretically, as already indicated, this jury verdict is based on the *facts* of the case, the judge himself having determined the rules of *law*—although it is not always possible to separate facts and law, and the U.S. Supreme Court has repeatedly dismissed challenges to statutory provisions that make juries the sole judges of the law as well as the facts in criminal trials.[79] In practice, however, the general verdict permits the jury to do what it pleases: it gives no details, simply reports its decision, and no one either really knows or may safely predict just what facts a jury found from the evidence. Judge Jerome Frank, a life-long and severe critic of the jury system as a fact-finding institution, viewed the judge's charge as little more than an elaborate ceremonial routine, and he argued that of all the possible ways that could be devised to arrive at the falsity or truth of testimony, ". . . none could be conceived that would be more ineffective than trial by jury."[80] He and many other legal authorities have long contended that *special*, or *fact*, verdicts—employed

[78] *The New York Times*, December 15, 1960, p. 27.
[79] See, for example, *Giles v. Maryland*, 372 U.S. 767 (1962).
[80] Jerome Frank, *Courts on Trial* (Princeton: Princeton University Press, 1949), p. 20. (Italics supplied.) This is one of *the* great books on the judicial process.

127

in England for centuries, and reconfirmed with the Courts Act of 1971—in which the jury is asked to answer a *specific* question of fact, are a far preferable method of arriving at a verdict that is just to all concerned. In a special verdict procedure, which is now used in several of the fifty states, and was authorized for federal *civil* suits in 1938 (but is very rarely used), the trial judge charges the jury to report its findings—presumably even if these are simply beliefs—about certain particular issues of fact raised during the course of the trial, facts which a jury should be able to weigh and determine with a modicum of accuracy and reliability. To those facts thus "found" the judge then applies the appropriate legal rule. Whatever the type of jury verdict advocated, the degree of perfection one may expect from the human institutions that comprise the judicial process is necessarily a limited one.

English and Welsh judges employ a charge rather similar to that found in the tribunals of the United States, but they provide somewhat more guidance to the jury during the trial. No charge is used in the courts of France. Instead, the French presiding judge, who actively directs the proceedings in the courtroom by interrogating the accused and witnesses, submits to the jury—in the infrequent instances of its presence in a case—a list of questions which the nine panelists are required to answer with a simple "yes" or "no." Standard examples of these queries would be, "Did the accused prove his alibi?"; "Was the accused present at the scene of the crime when it was committed?"; "Was the act of homicide one of self-defense?"; and, always, "If you find the defendant guilty, were there any extenuating circumstances?" Clearly, by his interrogation the judge tries to give to the jury the most lucid picture possible as a matter of guidance. The jury, its members voting individually and in secret, answers these questions specifically and thereby reaches its verdict—if necessary by a *majority* vote, in contrast to the *unanimity* requirements of the American federal judicial system. However, should the divisions among the jurors prove to be uncomfortably close, such as 7 : 5 or even 6 : 6, the presiding judge may assume the power of determining the verdict with the aid of the two associate judges (there are always three judges at the assise-trial level). But in that event the verdict is almost certain to be one of acquittal.

In West Germany today the entire courtroom examination in criminal trials is conducted by the judges, while the prosecuting attorney and counsel for the defense sit mute and take notes. Counsel is privileged to put a question only when the judges have completed an examination calculated to bring out fully and fairly all that a witness might tell. Jurors are taken from a local list of "outstanding" citizens and impaneled for a term of one year. Judge and jury sit on the bench together and participate jointly and equally in deliberation on a case—a procedure known as a *fused* jury.

JURIES: BLESSING OR EVIL?

It is not easy to be objective about juries—and few observers are. Certainly there is but little doubt that juries throughout the Western world have declined both in significance and esteem during the past century. Often, when they are not held in utter contempt by their professional critics, they are merely tolerated as a necessary, and at times admittedly convenient, evil. In large measure, the juries have brought this opprobrium on themselves—no matter how innocent and perhaps even understandable their response to the demands of the legal process may be. But it is not easy to defend the institution in the face of so many jury-created fiascos.

Thus, we again turn to the aforementioned Finch-Tregoff case, this time the first 1960 trial, to find the jury at its worst. According to an interview (!) granted to United Press International by one of the members of the panel of five men and seven women that had just been declared a hung jury:

> . . . at one point a near fight broke out. At the height of one heated debate, a male juror threatened to throw another [a female] out of a window and turned over the jury table—he used to be a boxer—before she ran to the door. She was hysterical and pounded on the door for the bailiff.[81]

A different woman juror also readily and beamingly gave an interview to U.P.I., reporting that at least three "propositioning" notes had been passed to one of her female colleagues on the panel. An extra bailiff was then brought in to stand guard at another woman's hotel room door after those notes came to light.[82] A further illustration is the young mother from Bedford, Indiana, who confessed that as a member of a jury panel in the 1950's she had voted to convict the accused of rape—despite the fact that she believed him to be innocent. She did so against her own judgment, she readily admitted, because "I knew I had those children at home and we would never get out of there if we tried to argue it out with the others."[83] Similar "interviews" were granted by jurors in the Wallace Butts-Curtis Publishing Co. 1963 libel suit. And to conclude the unfortunately almost inexhaustible

[81] *The New York Times,* March 13, 1960, p. 42.
[82] Ibid. But judges may enjoin interviews (e.g. *U.S. v. Driscoll,* 276 F. Supp. 333, 1967).
[83] As quoted by John F. X. Irving, "The Jury May Be Out Permanently," 6 *National Review* 177 (September 1958).

instances of the kind of antics that have served to bring widespread oppro-brium on the institution: In March 1961, under the guise of registering a *coup* in what it called "public service," the Hearst Corporation-owned sta-tion WBAL-TV in Baltimore induced, evidently without any difficulty, nine of twelve jurors to appear before the studio camera and re-enact their deliberations that resulted in the conviction of one Melvin Davis Rees, Jr., for murder and kidnapping. This intriguing performance, which featured in great detail the thoughts and reasoning that culminated in the verdict, came on the evening *prior to* the scheduled sentencing of the convicted man! As a result, defense counsel succeeded in obtaining at least a temporary post-ponement of sentencing, and he raised a series of legal questions based upon this jury TV debut—which the *Baltimore News Post*, also a Hearst-owned medium, termed "a reportorial breakthrough of the traditional silence of the jury room."[84] Considerations of law, ethics, morals, and taste were evi-dently deemed insignificant.

Evil? It is tempting to underscore the questioning of the efficacy of the institution of the jury—which Balzac once defined as "twelve men to de-cide who has the better lawyer," and Herbert Spencer called "a group of twelve people of average ignorance"—by noting that there is considerable evidence that the average jury reaches its verdict in most instances by a kind of "happy" compromise. Not being able to agree on a financial award in a civil case, for example, each panelist will write down his own figure, then the jury will add the total, divide it by the number of jurors, and thus attain peace of mind! In homicide cases a host of revelations again and again points to jury compromises. Thus, unless they are expressly forbidden to do so by statute or by the judge's charge, jurors will frequently decide a case of murder by "compromising" between first-degree murder and acquittal by settling for a second-degree conviction—even if not justifiable by the facts in the case. For example, the 1967 Naples, Florida, jury that convicted Dr. Carl Coppolino of the poison-murder of his first wife, Carmela, brought in a verdict of murder in the *second* degree—when, obviously, the very use of poison carries with it premeditation, which calls for a *first*-degree murder conviction. Evidently, the jury had "compromised." Sometimes the flip-of-the-coin or lot method is employed in order to get the nasty business over with. Or, as was demonstrated in a Hancock County, Kentucky, case, the jury became so confused as a result of its own deliberations that it formally "retracted" an already rendered verdict![85]

[84] See Jack Gould's article in *The New York Times*, March 25, 1961, p. 49.
[85] *The New York Times*, April 15, 1962, Sec. 4, p. 8E.

Even with the best of intentions, it may well be almost impossible for the wandering mind of the ordinary juror to overcome conclusively the histrionics that so often characterize presentation by counsel. Both prosecution and defense generally conduct what is to all intents and purposes a legal sporting combat, with each side following evidence by counter-evidence, examination by cross-examination, witness by counter-witnesses, each one sworn to tell the truth, the whole truth, and nothing but the truth. Not infrequently, this alleged search for the truth results in statements in open court that are clearly out of order. But even if the judge so holds, as he often does, and asks the jury to disregard the statement at issue, it has been uttered, of course, and it is conjectural at best whether it can be wiped from the jurors' minds. To arrive at the truth behind what one long-time observer of juries styled "the curtain of flimflam and obfuscation"[86] the jury may well have to decide which side, in its judgment, seemed to tell fewer lies, and in that way reach a verdict. Hence, in the words of Judge Frank, based on his many years of active experience in the legal and judicial processes:

> . . . the jury is the worst possible enemy of the "supremacy of the law." For "jury-made law" is, par excellence, capricious and arbitrary, yielding the maximum in the way of lack of uniformity, of unknowability. . . . To my mind a better instrument than the usual jury trial could scarcely be found for achieving uncertainty, capriciousness, lack of uniformity, disregard of the [rules], and unpredictability of decisions.[87]

Accordingly, he and others would prefer the trial judges to hear and decide cases alone, the assumption being that judges are presumably trained in the law, which jurors are not, and that they function in a setting which is open to considerably more scrutiny than juries. Yet the "Chicago Jury Project"[88] pointed to a significant 83 per cent agreement on verdicts between judges and juries!

Blessing? A natural and main source of endorsement of the jury system is the trial lawyer, who has a vested interest in influencing it—even if this is done by persuading the generally bewildered jurors that black is really white. Few, if any, defense lawyers in a criminal case would argue against it. But the venerable institution's defense does not need to rest its case on such pragmatic grounds. Many a legal scholar, far from decrying the factors of

---

[86] David A. Dressler, "Trial by Combat in American Courts," 222 *Harper's Magazine* 32 (April 1960).
[87] Frank, op. cit. pp. 123, 132.
[88] See p. 152 and fn. 93, *infra.*

emotion, prejudice, and sympathy that are undeniably major determinants in jury verdicts, holds that these very factors advance the cause of justice because they represent the "socially adapted intuitive law" of the various communities to which we belong. Thus, Thomas Lambert of the American Trial Lawyers Association noted in 1968 that "the glory of the jury is its beautiful lawlessness. . . . [It represents] the yeasty independence of the average man over officialdom."[89] Charles P. Curtis and Harold J. Berman have contended repeatedly that the jury reflects "the intuitive part of us," which they view as a necessary counterbalance to the equally essential "intellectual part of us" in the judge.[90] This is particularly appropriate if one keeps in mind that, in the final analysis, the first and foremost function of a jury is to choose between conflicting testimony, testimony so frequently beclouded by histrionics and legalistics as to render an "intuitive" judgment all but inevitable—at least up to a point. Something can certainly be said for the time-honored principle of being judged by a group of one's peers. Moreover, much of the adverse criticism would appear to depend on which side of the case one's interests lie, and whether the jury sits in a civil or criminal case.

One of the most articulate and influential champions of the jury system was the distinguished John Henry Wigmore, who advanced four main arguments in favor of the principle: First, that it prevents popular distrust of official justice since it gives the average member of the body politic a share in the political process. Second, that it provides for some necessary flexibility in legal rules and regulations in that it enables an adjustment of the "general rule of law to the justice of a particular case," whereas the judge is rightly expected to be consistent and consequential in his rulings for all. Third, that it educates the ordinary citizen in the administration of justice by cultivating the judicial habit in him and by creating in him a respect for law and order, thus making him conscious of his duty to society and his share in the governmental process. Fourth, that it ameliorates the verdict because it is based on the amalgam of a host of temperaments and viewpoints.[91] In essence, this is a plea on behalf of the institution based on the recognition of the role of common sense in the judicial process. It is a plea echoed by Law Professors Harry Kalven, Jr., and Hans Zeisel of the University of Chicago after a monumental study of the jury system, involving the

---

[89] *Time Magazine*, July 26, 1968, p. 80.
[90] See Curtis, op. cit. pp. 101–4.
[91] As discussed and quoted by William Wirt Blume, "The Place of Trial in Criminal Cases," 43 *Michigan Law Review* 64–65 (1944).

questioning of 550 judges who presided over 3576 jury trials across the country. Their conclusion was that the freedom of a jury to inject its own sense of justice is one of the greatest strengths of the system. But it also acknowledged that "jury legislation," or the jury's conscious modification of the law to make it conform to community views of what it ought to be, was a factor in fully 50 per cent of the disagreements between judge and jury of what *the law* in a given case *is*.[92]

Unquestionably, the Wigmore roster of exhortation is subject to serious exception—especially since it is based, at least in part, on a rather optimistic, happy, and sanguine view of human nature and a belief in the willingness as well as the ability of the average citizen to accept and adapt himself to these laudatory notions of participation in the responsibilities of society and state. Some of the illustrations presented in connection with the adverse criticism of the institution would appear to raise some crucial doubts regarding Professor Wigmore's analysis. Be that as it may, despite its shortcomings the jury system has been generally regarded by the public at large as a laudable instrument in the quest for justice. "It is so justly regarded," once applauded Joseph H. Choate,

> as the best and perhaps the only known means of admitting the people to a share in maintaining their wholesome interest in the administration of justice. . . ."[93]

The ultimate questions remain, however: Is it? And does it? It is difficult to still the haunting doubts.

FROM OFFENSE TO TRIAL: A PROCEDURAL NOTE

The practices and customs that characterize the judicial process differ widely in the various jurisdictions discussed herein; this also applies to the procedures followed in the lengthy and often difficult path that leads from the commission of the offense to its ultimate adjudication in or out of the courtroom—for the vast majority of cases are in fact settled by mutual agreement before they reach the trial stage. Indeed, on the whole it is only the so-called trouble cases that actually traverse the tedious process through the entire courtroom sequence. The purpose of this procedural note is to

92 The study, Ford Foundation-financed, and known as the "Chicago Jury Project," was published under the title *The American Jury* (Boston: Little, Brown and Co., 1966). See pp. 111, 114.
93 As quoted by Justice Bernard Botein, *Trial Judge* (New York: Simon and Schuster, 1952), p. 195.

illustrate, in necessarily brief and generalized fashion, the various stages that confront participants in a full-length legal proceeding. The model employed, which will distinguish between civil and criminal cases, is a typical jurisdiction in the United States of America. And it should be noted that the very nature of an American court case requires the presence of the following four conditions: (1) an adversary process, (2) a justifiable issue, (3) ripeness for judicial determination, and (4) an actual disposition.[94]

PROCEDURE IN CIVIL CASES

A civil case is one in which individuals or groups bring adjudicable actions in court against other individuals or groups by whom they contend to have been wronged. *Step 1* is the *commencement of the action* by the *plaintiff*, the party bringing the suit, against the *respondent* or *defendant*. If it is a matter of an *appeal* rather than the bringing of an initial suit, the party who appeals is known as the *appellant*, the other side as the *respondent* or *appellee*. The plaintiff or appellant may also be termed *petitioner*. A word of caution: while it is easy to determine who the two sides to a respective suit are at the initial stage of a new suit, once that proceeding has reached the various appellate stages it is considerably more difficult, and the only safe way to do so is to read the first few paragraphs of the case. In order to bring his suit, a plaintiff will have to do at least three things: (1) select the correct and proper tribunal; (2) have the defendant or his possessions brought before it; and (3) present his charges and ask for appropriate remedies.

In order to achieve the second requirement, the plaintiff must ask the proper authorities to serve a *summons*, which is issued after the petitioner has "sworn it out." Presumably it will be obeyed. Failure to respond to the summons will normally result either in a judgment against the respondent by default or in contempt proceedings. An even more compelling order to appear is a *subpoena*, a writ that, unlike the summons, must always be served on the respondent or witness in person; it directs his appearance on pain of being held in contempt of court (or of whatever other judicial or quasi-judicial authority may be empowered to issue the writ). A subpoena *duces tecum*, a related writ, requires the respondent to *bring something* along, a specific document, for example. If the respondent resides outside of the court's jurisdiction, but owns property therein, the latter may be *attached* in order to commence a suit, but only if the property attached is itself the subject matter of the suit. If it is not, the respondent cannot be brought into

[94] See Ch. IX, *infra*, in this connection.

court by attachment of business property, even if he resides within the jurisdiction.

Closely related to the three tasks the plaintiff performs in order to commence the action is an attempt by the two parties to the suit to narrow the factual and legal issues involved by virtue of an exchange of one formal written statement, or a series of them, stating the claim at issue. Such statements are called *pleadings*. These follow logically as a result of the plaintiff's initiation of his *complaint*. *Step* 2 is designed solely to formulate the issues in the case and consists of the formal pleadings, now presumably involving the legal battery for both sides. This stage of the pleadings features the formal exchange of documents between the two sides, with the respondent required to file an *answer*. Often the lawyers are able to settle matters at this stage, but since we are here concerned with a sketch of the entire procedure, we assume that instead of there being acquiescence or agreement, the future defendant will file a *motion to dismiss* the complaint, sometimes also known as a *demurrer*. If the plaintiff rejects these formal counterclaims, the stage will now have been set for the docketing of the case on the calendar of the court of proper jurisdiction. A *pretrial conference with the judge* may conceivably settle matters at this juncture and avoid an actual trial—it will very likely serve to narrow further some of the problems involved. The next formal stage is the trial itself.

The nature and character of *step* 3, the *trial*, depend largely on whether the issue between the litigants is one of law or one of fact. If the issue is solely one of *law*, the court receives the case via a legal *argument* presented by the attorneys for both sides. Since there are no facts to be determined, jury and witnesses are not called; the judge decides the dispute strictly on the basis of the law, as he sees it. But if the dispute is either "mixed" or strictly of *facts*, the case will be tried before judge and jury, depending somewhat upon its nature and, as has been described earlier in the chapter, depending on whether or not a jury trial is waived by mutual consent where that is possible and desirable. The next four steps, *verdict, judgment, appellate review* (if any), and *enforcement*, if not self-explanatory, have already been delineated above or will be discussed in subsequent chapters.

PROCEDURE IN CRIMINAL CASES

Because of the very nature of the offense, the procedure in a criminal case is *ipso facto* both more formal and more elaborate, and it involves the machinery of the state to a much more important degree. Above all, the state, as was demonstrated in Chapter I, necessarily is a party to the suit—at least in the sense that it is responsible for the prosecution of the offense. It is responsible because criminal proceedings pertain to actions by individuals or groups who are charged with having committed one or more antisocial acts that society, through its governmental processes, has defined as a "crime" in public law. *Step 1* in a criminal case, therefore, is very simply the *apprehension* of the prospective defendant within the territorial limitations of the governmental jurisdiction concerned—i.e. unless he voluntarily surrenders to the authorities, he is literally caught and arrested, either in the act of commission, while fleeing, or as a result of an arrest warrant, which the arresting officer must obtain in advance from properly constituted authority. *Step 2*, closely related to the first, sees the arrested person—who, if he is indigent, is entitled to the appointment of counsel as of the arrest stage— brought before a magistrate (known formerly as a "Commissioner" on the federal level[95]) for the *preliminary* examination, in order to determine whether he shall be released or shall be *held to answer*. If the latter, the accused will be held either in *custody* or released on *bail* to await the decision of the public prosecutor or the grand jury on the question of whether or not an *information* or an *indictment* shall be filed against him. The preliminary examination is a crucial and highly significant stage in criminal procedure— if for no other reason than that well over one-half of those arrested are released here, which customarily closes the books on the matter.

Step 3 repesents the formal *accusation* by grand jury indictment or by the process of "information," depending upon the statutory requirements or practices in the several jurisdictions concerned. This is logically followed by the *arraignment* and pleading—although the accused may already have entered a plea at the preliminary hearing stage—constituting *step 4*. An arraignment consists simply of the official, formal reading of the terms of the indictment or information to the accused by the court of jurisdiction. The arraignment concludes with the question, "How do you plead?"—giving the accused the choice of *"guilty"* or *"not guilty."*[96] Here the two parties often

---

[95] See p. 163, *infra*, for a brief explanation of this office. See also Charles A. Lindquist, "The United States Commissioner: An Evaluation of the Commissioner's Role in the Judicial Process," 39 *Temple Law Quarterly* 138 (Winter 1966).

[96] Under some circumstances the accused may plead *nolo contendere*, or "no contest,"— specifically, "I do not wish to contend"—by which he throws himself upon the mercy of the court. In effect an admission of guilt without so stating formally, the *nolo contendere* penalties are potentially the same as for the plea of guilty; but the judge more often than not displays leniency in such cases—some say if for no other reason than that that plea saves time, effort, and money. Vice President Spiro T. Agnew's plea of *nolo contendere* in federal district court in October 1973, to a charge of income tax evasion, is a famous case illustration. (Concurrently he announced his resignation from the high office—to which he was succeeded by Gerald Ford.)

try to reach a settlement to avoid a formal trial: known as "plea bargaining," it is conducted between the prosecution and the defense, frequently with the assistance of the judge.[97]

Step 5 is the *trial* itself, if there is one at all—if not, the judge's verdict takes its place, as happens in many, but not all, pleadings of guilty. A host of proceedings, with which we need not concern ourselves here, antedates the trial—including various motions for dismissal of the case, change of pleadings, placing of dispositions, request for changes of *venue*, plea bargaining, possible dismissal or change of charges. The trial is conducted by the judge, either with or without a jury as the case and jurisdiction may mandate, and the process terminates with the next four steps: *verdict, judgment and sentencing, appellate review*, if any, and *execution of the sentence imposed*, if any. Of course, no bare procedural sketch such as this can take into account the sundry aspects and ramifications of the manifold practices, procedures, and safeguards that surround this fascinating aspect of the judicial process; this should be regarded merely as the outline of its essential framework.

Despite the relatively drastic distinctions in judicial theory and practice between the common law lands and the statutory law lands of the free West, the justice meted out under both legal systems is similar in its ultimate degree of fairness, if not in its efficiency. Each system is characterized by obvious advantages and disadvantages, and each features methods that are peculiar to the needs or predispositions of the particular governmental jurisdiction concerned. As is so pre-eminently true of most practices in the realm of free government, they, too, are specifically adapted to the needs of the people directly involved. They are steeped in their own culture and tradition, and it is sheer folly for outsiders to endeavor to impose their own systems—even in theory. Sir Stafford Cripps once remarked wisely that methods and institutions of government are not simply commodities of international commerce, thus echoing the statement made by Alexis de Tocqueville in his *Democracy in America* in 1831:

> The more I see of this country [the United States] the more I admit myself penetrated with this truth: that there is nothing absolute in the theoretical value of institutions, and that their efficiency depends almost always on the original circumstances and the social conditions of the people to whom they are applied.

[97] Plea bargaining played a prominent role in the Agnew case and in many "Watergate" ones.

IV
Courts at Home:
I The Lesser Tribunals

A DUAL SYSTEM OF COURTS

As a result of the federal system that prevails in the United States, the national government and fifty state governments all make and enforce law. In effect, this means that there exist, side by side, two major court systems—one could even say fifty-one—which are wholly distinct bodies, in the sense that they are created under different basic authorities—the respective national and state constitutions. The jurisdiction of these two systems may, and in some highly significant instances does, regularly "merge" at the bar of the final interpretative authority of the United States Supreme Court. However, such a "merger" can come about only if a *substantial* federal question has been validly raised in the proper state court below and, all remedies at the state level having been duly exhausted, that question has been successfully brought to what is in all but a handful of cases the *discretionary* attention of the Supreme Court. It is axiomatic that the path to the highest court in the land is long, expensive, arduous, and difficult—thus it is not traveled frequently. Other than in this appellate process, and possibly in the vexatious and procedurally intricate realm of injunctive relief, the national and state courts in the United States are separate entities. Nonetheless, it should be noted that through its constitutional power to establish *"inferior* courts,"[1] Congress possesses the power to draw a rigid line between the *jurisdiction* of these federal and state courts. But it has not seen fit to do so except in certain civil rights areas—notably, some types of

[1] U.S. Constitution, Art, III, Sec. 1, Par. 1. (Italics supplied.)

racial discrimination[2]—and in a number of fields of relatively narrow jurisdiction, such as matters involving admiralty, bankruptcy, copyright, and patent.

THE STATE COURTS

It is in the courts of the fifty states that the great majority of the legal business of the American public begins and ends. The character, jurisdiction, quality, and complexity of these courts vary considerably from state to state in accordance with the myriad considerations of public policy, need, size, and constitutional practice that characterize the heterogeneous component parts of the nation. Every state constitution either establishes a judicial branch for its invariably tripartite government or, either in whole or in part —as is true for the national level under Article III of the Constitution of the United States—authorizes the legislature to provide for a judicial system. Although the terminology and structure among the state courts differ significantly, a discernible structural pattern does exist. The base consists of a system of justices of the peace and trial courts, with the pyramid gradually winding its way upward through a more or less elaborate appellate system, culminating in a supreme court (not invariably termed "Supreme Court," however).

THE JUSTICE OF THE PEACE

With rare exception, the lowest court at the state level—and there are those who would put the noun "court" into quotation marks in this particular connection—is the *Justice of the Peace*, originally a fourteenth-century Anglo-Saxon office. The officeholder is often, and sometimes irreverently, referred to as the "J. P." (standing for "Justice for the Plaintiff," in some eyes). He is also occasionally styled *squire* and, increasingly in many cities, e.g. New York, *magistrate*. By no means necessarily a lawyer, this official is usually elected for a two- to six-year term in counties, townships, and towns; but sometimes he is appointed for a term of similar length by the executive in the cities. The office he fills has an honorable and, indeed, ancient tradition which came to the colonies from England. It was initially designed to aid in the administration of justice in minor matters at the local level. Today the Justice of the Peace, who is usually also a notary public, still performs a modicum of court work, but many of his duties are quasi-legislative,

[2] For example, see certain provisions of the Civil Rights Acts of 1957, 1960, and 1964 and the Voting Rights Act of 1965, as amended in 1970.

quasi-judicial, and quasi-administrative, including, characteristically, performance of civil marriages. Most of these tasks are performed on a fee basis —probably a regrettable practice in view of its close link to meting out justice. He does, however, retain at least the appearance of a court of first instance in minor civil and criminal matters. In the former, his jurisdiction normally extends only to cases involving less than $200; in the latter, it is limited almost exclusively to misdemeanors.

With some notable exceptions, again usually confined to some urban areas—e.g. New York City, where the magistrates have legal background, are appointed for ten-year terms of office, and receive about $35,000 annually, an unusually high figure for that office, which normally commands a far lower remuneration—the Justice of the Peace's lack of training and qualifications is exceeded only by his sure-fire penchant for convictions, which have averaged 96 per cent in civil cases and 80 per cent in criminal cases.[3] A study made in 1956 of the minor judiciary of North Carolina, pointed out that not a single J. P. in that state then had a law degree; that 75 per cent had never gone to college; and that 40 per cent had never even attended high school![4] A similar study for Virginia a decade later showed that, of 411 past and present members of the Association of Justices of the Peace of Virginia, a mere four were lawyers, 71 per cent had never gone to college, only five of the 29 per cent who did were graduated, and 18 per cent were not even high school graduates.[5] In Oregon only nine of seventy J. P.'s had law degrees in 1966.[6] Even in such a cosmopolitan city as Philadelphia, only six of its twenty-eight elected magistrates held a law degree in 1968. All this represents an unfortunate state of affairs, for, given suitable attributes of integrity and proper qualification, the Justice of the Peace might well still provide able and inexpensive adjudication and settlement of minor legal problems in the judicial process. On the other hand, Phila-

---

[3] In 1962 in Pennsylvania, of 63,040 criminal cases handled by the then 4305 J.'s, 51,997, or about 83 per cent, resulted in conviction; another 6375, or 10 per cent, were bound over for court trial; and 4668, or about 7 per cent, were dismissed (XI *Horizons for Modern Governments* 5, May 1963, p. 4). For examples of conviction rates from 95 to 99.2 per cent in Michigan, Mississippi, and Tennessee counties, see Mitchell Dawson, "The Justice of the Peace Racket," in Robert Morlan, *Capitol Courthouse and City Hall*, 3rd ed. (Boston: Houghton Mifflin Co., 1966), pp. 144–45.

[4] Isham Newton, "The Minor Judiciary in North Carolina" (Unpublished Ph.D. Thesis, University of Pennsylvania, 1956).

[5] "Justice of the Peace in Virginia: A Neglected Aspect of the Judiciary," 52 *Virginia Law Review* 151 (January 1966), describing a survey conducted by Weldon Cooper of the Institute of Government of the University of Virginia.

[6] *The Christian Science Monitor*, May 9, 1967, p. 5.

delphia's then Chief Magistrate, Joseph J. Hersch, insisted in a 1961 interview, seconded in 1968 by his successor, John Patrick Walsh, that the job of a magistrate is "more social than legal"; he decried the increasing clamor for a law degree, stating:

> A law degree doesn't make a magistrate more qualified. Living with people is more essential than going to a law library to find out what it's all about. . . . If you take Purdon's law books away from them [the lawyers], they're out of business.[7]

THE MUNICIPAL COURT

Again because of varying needs, different nomenclature attends the *Municipal Court*, the next higher level of court ordinarily found in the several states. Some of the more common designations are *Traffic Court, City Court, Night Court,* and *Police Court.* The Municipal Court, whatever it may be called, is almost always a court of original jurisdiction, and normally also the first court of record[8] in the judicial hierarchy of the state. Its jurisdiction is customarily limited to about $500 to $1000 in civil cases, and to misdemeanors where it does have criminal jurisdiction. The municipal-level courts provide the parties before them with a fast and inexpensive procedure, and they are generally staffed by judges who possess legal training.[9]

THE COUNTY COURT

The next court in line is the workhorse of the average state judiciary, the *County Court.* It is a court of general civil and criminal jurisdiction, covering as a rule, three major types of cases and controversies: ordinary civil beyond the limit of the court of jurisdiction just below; criminal except for routine misdemeanors; plus probate and inheritance. As its name implies, the County Court's geographical jurisdiction is limited to the level of that subdivision of the state. If juries are used by a state judiciary at all—and they usually are, although there is still no *state* obligation always to provide juries under the wording and interpretation of the Bill of Rights in the

---

[7] Interview with author, December 18, 1961.

[8] Although all courts are, presumably, required to keep records today, the expression "court of record" is still used to distinguish between courts presided over by members of the minor judiciary (magistrates or justices of the peace) and other courts of original jurisdiction presided over by judges.

[9] Frequently found at the Municipal Court level, but usually not regarded as a court of record, is the *Court of Small Claims.* Its jurisdiction is usually limited to claims of $200.00 or less; there are low fees, no juries, often no appeals (except for a trial *de novo*), sometimes not even counsel.

141

federal Constitution—they will be found here. Although Philadelphia, for one, has a separate tribunal called the County Court (with jurisdiction over juveniles, domestic relations cases, certain crimes, and some civil matters), a whole coterie of allied or subsidiary courts is either present at this level or takes the place of the County Court. Among these may well be all or some of the following, often self-explanatory, judicial county helpmates: *Common Pleas* (a court to hear and determine civil cases, usually where the amount in controversy is in excess of $5000); *Oyer and Terminer* (a criminal court with jurisdiction over capital crimes and other felonies—e.g. murder, manslaughter, treason, robbery, rape, kidnapping); *Quarter Sessions* (a predominantly criminal court with jurisdiction over a few technical civil cases and over crimes not tried by Oyer and Terminer, which usually meets four times annually, and sometimes consists of the same personnel as Oyer and Terminer); *Orphans*; *Probate* (for wills, estates, and deeds); *Juvenile* (for youthful offenders); *Domestic Relations*; *Surrogate* (similar to Probate in some counties); *Chancery* (specializing in equity matters); and *Equity*.[10]

THE INTERMEDIATE COURT OF APPEALS

Beyond the County Court lies the intermediate court, or courts, of appeals, usually termed *Appellate Division, State Appellate Court, Superior Court,*

---

[10] A highly promising "non-court" system of case-disposition in the judicial process is Philadelphia's (and Pittsburgh's) fascinating system of "compulsory arbitration" of civil cases involving claims of up to $3000 (and voluntarily up to $10,000). Actually found administratively at the level of the County Court in Philadelphia since its statutory adoption by the state in 1958, it consists of teams of three-member lawyer panels who hear and decide a vast number of cases that would otherwise linger on the court dockets. The lawyers are appointed by the Arbitration Commissioners from an alphabetical list of volunteers: No matter how long a hearing takes, the lawyers are each paid a nominal fee of $30.00 per case, the chairman $50.00. The average cost per "trial" to date has been but $82.50! Not only their time and expertise, but also their quarters and any necessary secretarial help, are provided by these volunteer members of the bar. The atmosphere of the proceedings is judicial and judicious, but rules of evidence are given liberal construction. Any appeals taken from a panel's decision is heard by a County Court judge *de novo* with or without a jury. But very few cases are in fact appealed, and the successful processing of an average of 8000 cases annually by these arbitration panels is proof positive of the system's success and common sense. (For details see the *Annual Reports* of the Commissioner of the Compulsory Arbitration Division of the County Court of Philadelphia, 1958ff.) Philadelphia, beset—as are almost all jurisdictions—by clogged dockets, is also moving lesser *criminal* offenses out of the regular court structure. Charges that carry penalties of two years or less imprisonment are handled by *special* judges who settle the cases without a jury. Any defendant dissatisfied with the result may have a formal court trial, but to date less than 4 per cent have so requested. This has resulted in a marked decrease of untried cases.

or *Intermediate Court of Appeals.* The jurisdiction of this tribunal is almost wholly appellate—certain writs being the exception in some states. It receives and adjudges appeals from decisions of the County Court and the Municipal Court, and, in rare cases, from others. More often than not its decisions are final, although it is, of course, possible to go up from here to the final level since it is an *intermediate* appellate court. Only about half of the states resort to such an intermediate stage, but all of the larger ones do. Some of these have an elaborate structure, indeed: Thus, New York has an intricate system of more than 150 appellate courts at this level; and the appellate structure of California enabled Caryl Whittier Chessman to file fourteen appeals in its system (which he augmented with twenty-eight appeals to the federal courts between 1948 and 1960 in an ultimately unsuccessful battle to escape San Quentin's gas chamber). Happily, in recent years several states have taken considerable strides toward the adoption of more integrated hierarchical judicial pyramids—in large measure owing to the fine example set by New Jersey under its Chief Justice, Arthur T. Vanderbilt, in the 1950's—Virginia's 1973 reorganization being a case in point.

THE FINAL COURT OF APPEALS

At the apex of each state system lies its *Final Court of Appeals,* which receives and adjudicates appeals on major questions emanating from the courts below, normally from the intermediate appellate level. It will not lightly accept cases that are merely concerned with questions of fact; its main purpose is to find the law. Usually this highest state court is known as the Supreme Court, but not always. In New York, for instance—where the "Supreme Court" is a trial court at the lower rung of the state judiciary and its lowest court of record—the high tribunal is called the *Court of Appeals;* in Maine it is termed the *Supreme Judicial Court.* It has the last word in the state on all constitutional questions. Its decisions are final and authoritative as to state and, by virtue of the unitary structure involved, local law. Although there are some exceptions,[11] the United States Supreme Court insists that "all remedies below" must have been exhausted before it will consider a request for review from a party that "lost" in the final court of appeals of a state. Nevertheless, if a federal question of a substantial nature is allegedly involved, and if that question has been properly raised below, a chance, however slim, does exist that the highest court in the land will accept the case for review. In rare instances, the Supeme Court of the United States theoretically *must* accept a case appealed from the highest

[11] *Fay v. Noia,* 372 U.S. 391 (1963), governing certain types of *habeas corpus* appeals.

court—but, as will be described in the next chapter, this presumed duty is not without significant loopholes.

THE FEDERAL COURTS

When we look at the other prong of the "dual system of courts" at issue, we are confronted with the federal system, which is in many ways considerably less varied and confusing than the understandably heterogeneous state system(s). Certainly the federal courts are infinitely less numerous and, indeed, the hierarchical and jurisdictional arrangements of the three major constitutional courts—demonstrated in Chart A below—are readily comprehensible and clear-cut. Nevertheless, there is more to the structure and organization of the federal system of courts than is immediately apparent. Above all, there are two major *types* of federal courts from the point of view of their creation and functions: the *constitutional* courts and the *legislative* courts. Briefly, the former are created under Article III, the judiciary article of the Constitution, whereas the latter are created under Article I, its legislative article. Consequently, the safeguards of tenure, salary, and independence which accrue to judges of the constitutional courts by virtue of the expilcit and inherent safeguards of Article III are not necessarily present for the judges of the legislative courts. However, since they are created by Congress, nothing prevents that body from clothing the judges of the legislative courts by statute with the same or similar prerogatives as are constitutionally guaranteed to those of the constitutional courts. In fact, even before Congress changed the status of three erstwhile legislative courts—the United States Court of Claims,[12] the United States Customs Court, and the United States Court of Customs and Patent Appeals[13]—to that of constitutional courts in 1953, 1956, and 1958, respectively, it had already granted them the same "good behavior" tenure provisions enjoyed by the judges of the constitutional courts. A more significant difference between the two types of courts is that the legislative courts are endowed with functions that are nonjudicial, i.e. legislative and administrative, as well as judicial. Moreover, while they are tied into the constitutional appellate structure for certain

---

[12] The constitutionality of the change was challenged, but it was upheld by the Supreme Court in a 5 : 2 decision in 1962. (*Glidden Co. v. Zdanok*, 370 U.S. 530). It held the Court of Claims to be a court properly created under Article III of the federal Constitution, and that therefore its judges may sit on all federal district and appellate courts.

[13] The same verdict as that accorded to the constitutionality of the Court of Claims was applied in a challenge to the United States Court of Customs and Patent Appeals, and for the same reasons. (*Lurk v. United States*, 370 U.S. 530.)

purposes, they are primarily created to aid in the *administration* of specified congressional statutes. Nonetheless, their judgments are as much *res judicata*—authoritative settled law—as are those of the constitutional courts.

THE FEDERAL LEGISLATIVE COURTS

As its basic power for the establishment of *legislative* courts, Congress utilizes Article I, Section 8, Clause 9, which extends to it "the power to create tribunals inferior to the Supreme Court." The lawmakers then expressly or implicitly join that fundamental power via the "necessary and proper" clause, the famous "implied powers" clause (I-8-18) of the Constitution, with that congressional authority in the particular field in which the court is to perform its main function—for example, the taxing power (I-8-1) for the United States Customs Court (now a constitutional court), or the power to "make rules for the government and regulation of the land and naval forces" (I-8-14) for the United States Court of Military Appeals. Other legislative courts have existed in the past, of which the defunct (as of 1915) *United States Commerce Court*, created under congressional power over interstate and foreign commerce (I-8-3), is an example. But today, if we exempt the now officially transformed United States Court of Claims, United States Court of Customs, and United States Court of Customs and Patent Appeals, there are only two bona fide legislative courts: the United States Court of Military Appeals and the several Territorial Courts. Some observers would contend that the *United States Tax Court* ought to be classified as a legislative court. Its sixteen members, who are appointed by the President with the advice and consent of the Senate for fifteen-year terms at $40,000 annually, and who are removable in the same manner as members of the independent regulatory commissions, do have the official designation of judges. Yet in a very real sense the United States Tax Court is an adjunct of the executive branch, a quasi-administrative agency independent of the Internal Revenue Service, rather than a court per se. The Tax Court and its subdivisions have jurisdiction to review governmentally-proposed deficiency assessments of income, gift, self-employment, and prior excess profits taxes that have been challenged by the taxpayer concerned. The United States Commissioner of Internal Revenue is, necessarily, always the defendant party. This court, which may hold hearings anywhere in the United States, is a busy agency.[14]

[14] Its removal from the executive branch was strongly recommended by the Hoover Commission, but no action to that effect has been taken to date despite considerable congressional interest.

The United States Court of Military Appeals. This "G.I.'s Supreme Court" was created in 1950 as part of the revised Uniform Code of Military Justice, which Code had been created earlier largely because of the severe criticism heaped upon the military's concepts and practice of justice before, and especially during and after, World War II. That system of justice, steeped in the court-martial tradition, had been predominantly concerned with notions of military efficiency and chain of command, and had lodged all but dictatorial powers in the persons of the various commanding officers. Other than the unlikely "court of last resort" in the person of the President of the United States, all appeals from its judgments went to higher military commanders. The new code altered this arrangement drastically and dramatically by granting accused military personnel new rights before a court-martial and by creating the civilan *Court of Military Appeals*, which Mr. Chief Justice Warren dubbed the "civilian supreme court of the military." *De minimis* this meant that service personnel now had a genuine appellate tribunal to apply and interpret military law (while retaining their right of eventual appeal to the Secretary of Defense and his subordinates, and, of course, the President). In effect, the door was opened for civilian observance and at least a modicum of civilian control, and as the 1950's ripened into the 1960's it became clear that the service man had gained considerably more: the application of most of the Bill of Rights. Thus, in 1965 military personnel were assured that the Sixth Amendment's right to counsel entitled them not only to a lawyer in a military case, but to a *trained* lawyer. In April 1967 the "G.I.'s Supreme Court" ruled 2 : 1 that the limitations on police interrogation and confessions announced in 1966 by the Supreme Court of the United States in its historic *Miranda v. Arizona* decision[15] must also be applied in military law, because, in the words of the majority opinion written by Judge Homer Ferguson, it announced standards for the enforcement of the Fifth Amendment, which is binding on *all* federal courts—including the C.M.A.[16] And the Military Justice Act of 1968, authored by Senator Sam J. Ervin (D.-N.C.), contains sweeping safeguard provisions, including—for the first time—bail and insulation of military legal officers from local command pressure on court-martial decisions. The law permits defendants to demand trial by a military judge alone, instead of a jury of officers, in general courts-martial cases; and, if the defendant objects, forbids a single officer to act as prosecutor, defense counsel, judge, and jury in summary courts-martial.

[15] 384 U.S. 436.
[16] *United States v. Tempia,* 16 USCMA 629 (1967), at 635.

The United States Court of Military Appeals is staffed by three judges who receive $42,500 annually; they must be appointed from civilian life, but may hold a reserve commission in "any armed force." They are nominated for staggered fifteen-year terms of office by the President, subject to confirmation by the Senate—and are eligible for reappointment. The President, who has the power to designate the Chief Judge, may remove a member of the court only for neglect of duty or because of a mental or physical disability. No more than two of the judges may be from the same political party. Those who had been appointed through 1974 had all had judicial and/or other public service, not necessarily excluding past military duty.[17]

This court, which determines its own rules of procedure, is authorized to review *at its discretion* decisions of courts-martial involving bad-conduct discharges and prison sentences of more than one year, on being petitioned by the accused serviceman, provided that the petition had already been passed upon by a Board of Review appointed by the Judge Advocate General. The court *must* review all courts-martial decisions, as affirmed by a Board of Review, involving general or flag officers—i.e. generals and admirals; all those cases in which the death penalty was decreed below, regardless of the rank of the accused; and all cases certified for its review by the Judge Advocate General after initial review by a Board of Review (a group of officers who are attorneys in civilian life and who, during their term of service, are stationed in the office of each service's Judge Advocate General). However, the court's powers of review extend solely to matters of law, not of fact—although that line, as we shall have occasion to note repeatedly, is sometimes a very fine one.

An illustration of one type of decision the Court of Military Appeals may render is the case of one Russo, a member of the Air Force, whom a duly convened court-martial had found guilty of premeditated murder and sentenced to death. On reviewing the record of the case, the staff judge advocate recommended approval of the sentence by the convening authority, but concurrently recommended that it be commuted to a dishonorable discharge from the Air Force, coupled with life imprisonment. When the Board of Review received the case, it indicated its belief that the suggested commutation was appropriate. However, it held that it was ". . . powerless to effect the change in penalty . . . [because] Congress had not granted that power to Boards of Review." Hence, it affirmed both the findings of

---

17 For example, as of the time of his appointment in 1956 by President Eisenhower, Judge Homer Ferguson had been an attorney-at-law, a judge, a United States Senator, and Ambassador to the Philippine Islands; he had seen no military service.

147

guilt and the originally imposed sentence. Since this judgment involved a death penalty, and had been approved by the Board of Review below, review by the Court of Military Appeals was mandatory. In a decision written again by Judge Ferguson, the court denied various other points of appeal advanced by Russo, but held that both a court-martial convening authority and a Board of Review have the authority to lessen the severity of a death penalty. The court then reversed the judgments below and returned the record of the Russo trial to the Judge Advocate General of the Air Force for action consistent with its decision.[18] More than half of all cases to date heard there have won reversals in the Court of Military Appeals. One that did not was that brought by First Lt. William L. Calley, who thus unsuccessfully appealed from the twenty-year court-martial sentence meted out for his role in the slaying of "at least twenty-two" Vietnamese civilians in the 1968 My Lai massacre. In 1974 that sentence was reduced by the Secretary of the Army and his conviction overturned by a federal district court.[19]

There is no direct appeal from the final judgments of the Court of Military Appeals. However, the United States Supreme Court, as well as the other federal constitutional courts, could quite conceivably exercise jurisdiction to review or "pick up" a case in an *habeas corpus* proceeding—such as claims of illegal detention, illegal procedure, or deprivation of fundamental constitutional rights. In 1953, the Supreme Court did indicate that it had that power in a much-discussed case that featured four separate opinions; but a majority of the Justices went on to point out that under the law federal constitutional court review would probably be limited to determinations of military court jurisdiction and considerations of "fair claims of justice."[20] Justices Black and Douglas dissented vigorously, contending that *all* of the rights under the Fifth and Sixth Amendments of the United States Constitution should be held to apply to military, as well as civilian, trials. Regardless of the merits of the dissent, or of speculation on how the highest tribunal would "go" today, the Fifth Amendment issue has become moot in the face of the Court of Military Appeals' aforementioned 1967 confession and interrogation case,[21] in which Judge Ferguson wrote:

> The time is long since past when this court will lend an attentive ear to the argument that members of the armed forces are, by reason of their status, *ipso facto* deprived of all protections of the Bill of Rights.

[18] *United States v. Russo,* 11 USCMA 252, 29 CMR 168 (1960).
[19] *United States v. Calley,* 22 USCMA 534 (1973).
[20] *Burns v. Wilson,* 346 U.S. 137, at 144, 147.
[21] *United States v. Tempia,* op cit. at 635, fn. 16.

Without necessarily guaranteeing the application of *all* aspects of the Bill of Rights in *all* circumstances to service personnel, the Ferguson opinion, coupled with reforms readily undertaken by the armed forces themselves (led by the Air Force), the broad sweep of the Supreme Court's decisions in matters affecting Amendments Four, Five, Six, Seven, and Eight in the 1960's, and the impact of the Ervin Military Justice Act of 1968, it seems safe to say that the service man's constitutional protection now comes very close to that of the American in mufti. Moreover, the Supreme Court further liberalized the rights of servicemen with a 1969 holding that gave the *civil* courts authority over "off-base, non-service connected" offenses committed *in the United States* in peacetime.[22]

The Territorial Courts. Perhaps the several Territorial Courts are in a slightly different category than the standard legislative courts, but they are established by Congress under its power to "make all needful rules and regulations respecting the territory or other property belonging to the United States. . . ." (IV-3-2). Created for, and located in, such diverse areas as the Canal Zone (1912), Guam (1900), Puerto Rico (1900), and the Virgin Islands (1917), these courts have jurisdiction that is, necessarily, extremely varied.[23] Generally—but specifically excluding Puerto Rico, where they have federal jurisdiction only, Puerto Rico having a set of separate local courts— it includes matters analogous to those in the jurisdiction of state and local courts *as well as* the federal District Courts. The judges of the Territorial Courts are appointed in the usual manner by the President and confirmed by the Senate; but their term of office, which varies from four to eight years, represents an uncommonly brief period for members of the federal judiciary. In creating the various Territorial Courts, Congress has generally followed the wise policy of tailoring them to specific local needs, while retaining the *fundamental*, as distinguished from the *formal*, safeguards of the Constitution of the United States.

EX-LEGISLATIVE "SPECIAL" CONSTITUTIONAL COURTS

Until their conversion by Congress from their status as legislative to that of constitutional courts in the 1950's, the three most important and best known of these federal legislative courts were the Court of Claims, the Court of Customs, and the Court of Customs and Patent Appeals. Although they are now constitutional courts, they nevertheless still occupy a

---

[22] *O'Callahan v. Parker*, 395 U.S. 258.
[23] For statistical purposes *only*, these courts and their judges have been counted throughout this work as "U.S. District Courts."

special niche in the federal court system; they may be regarded as special constitutional courts with special court duties. Despite their new station, they thus still perform, or at least may be viewed as performing, certain quasi-legislative and quasi-administrative functions. However, there is no doubt that public laws by Congress specifically changed their former status, and it must be assumed theoretically that Congress will henceforth not bestow upon these three the kind of nonjudicial powers that have always been considered inappropriate for members of the constitutional courts.

The United States Court of Claims. Created in 1855, after four earlier bills seeking to establish it had failed, the Court of Claims consists of seven judges (paid $42,500 annually) who, aided by fifteen "commissioners" who report on their findings, adjudicate citizens' suits for damages against the Government of the United States. Most, but certainly not all, of these suits represent claims arising out of public contracts. Others involve just compensation for the taking of private property for public use. Some represent suits for injuries caused by negligent or wrongful behavior of a government employee. The court is, in fact, an institutionally arranged denial of the age-old theory that the sovereign cannot be sued. Through the Court of Claims, sometimes referred to as "the keeper of the nation's conscience," the federal government does in fact permit itself to be sued by affected persons—and thus becomes the only proper defendant—but only within rather narrow limits, such as the contractual disputes already mentioned. Because of the volume of these complaints and the time consumed in their adjudication, the existence of the Court of Claims, with its jurisdiction extending to territories and possessions as well as the United States proper, represents a genuine blessing to the general courts, whose dockets might otherwise be clogged considerably more than they already are. Moreover, the Court of Claims as well as the other specialty-area courts are a welcome time-and-trouble-saving device for Congress itself; for there is no question that a good many of the matters now handled and adjudicated by these courts would otherwise have come to the halls of the federal legislature in the form of requests for special or local bills, or of amendments to general statutes.

Essentially, the jurisdiction of the Court of Claims is thus limited to *original* jurisdiction in all contractual, tax, injury, and other *non-tort*[24] claims against the Government of the United States.

It does, however, possess a very limited power of *concurrent appellate re-*

---

[24] A tort is any wrongful act, *other than a breach of contract*, for which an injured party may bring a civil action against the alleged wrongdoer.

view with the United States Circuit Courts of Appeals in certain tort actions against the federal government decided in the United States District Courts. Decisions of the Court of Claims are subject to Supreme Court review in appropriate instances, and some of the latter's more famous cases did in fact "come up" from the Court of Claims, among them *Humphrey's Executor (Rathbun) v. United States*,[25] which arose out of a suit against the United States to recover a sum of money allegedly due the deceased Humphrey. In 1931 Humphrey had been reappointed a member of the Federal Trade Commission for a second seven-year term; in 1933 President Franklin D. Roosevelt removed him. Contending that he had been illegally removed, Humphrey—and, upon his death, his executor, one Rathbun—sued to recover his salary. The Court of Claims, evidently somewhat uncertain of its grounds, certified (see Chart B, p. 202, *infra*) some questions regarding the President's removal power to the Supreme Court. That tribunal subsequently held unanimously that the Chief Executive had no authority to remove summarily members of independent regulatory commissions clothed with quasi-legislative, quasi-judicial, quasi-executive powers, thereby decisively restricting his power of removal. This decision stands today, reaffirmed and reinforced by a 1958 case which involved President Eisenhower's dismissal of War Claims Commissioner Wiener.[26]

The United States Court of Customs and Patent Appeals. In 1910, utilizing the severally delegated powers to regulate commerce with foreign nations and among the states (I-8-3), to levy taxes (I-8-1), and "to promote the progress of science and useful arts" (I-8-8), Congress established the Court of Customs and Patent Appeals. Its five members, appointed in the customary manner, receive $42,500 per annum and now serve "during good behavior." The functions of the court are primarily threefold: to review (1) decisions of the *Customs Court* regarding duties levied on goods imported into the United States and the classification of such goods; (2) those of the *Patent Office* regarding decisions on patents and trademarks; and (3), on a more legally restricted scale, those of the *Tariff Commission* relating to import practices.

For example, in one case on record the Tariff Commission, on reviewing an appeal by an importer, held that the attempted importation and sale of certain synthetic sapphires and rubies described in an established United States patent represented not only "unfair methods of competition," but also "unfair acts in importation," both of which tended substantially to in-

[25] 295 U.S. 602 (1935).
[26] *Wiener v. United States*, 357 U.S. 349.

jure the industry of the patent's owner. The commission consequently recommended proceedings against the importer involved, and the latter appealed to the Court of Customs and Patent Appeals. The court held that the evidence at hand amply supported the findings below that the patent owner's industry was operated efficiently and economically within the United States; that the imported stones fell within the description of the patented articles; that the patent had been properly secured; that the importer's actions had a tendency substantially to injure the aforesaid owner within the meaning of the statute; and that where no holding of invalidity of patent was alleged, it would be regarded as valid.[27]

A rather different instance of the work of the court concerned an action in August 1955 by President Eisenhower, who, pursuant to a recommendation of the Tariff Commission, had set certain new import duty rates on bicycles manufactured abroad. However, in so doing he had neither acted within the time limit prescribed by law nor really followed the Tariff Commission's advice—instead his announced rates represented a *compromise* with it. The importers filed a suit in the Customs Court which held against the United States Government. The latter appealed on the legal issue involved to the Court of Customs and Patent Appeals. The court ruled that, by following the course of action described, the President had violated the basic statute, which provides that Tariff Commission recommendations must either be accepted or rejected outright.[28] All parties concerned acquiesced in that 1960 decision. The Court of Customs and Patent Appeals, unlike the Court of Claims, possesses only *appellate* jurisdiction, and it is confined to matters of law. Appeals from its decisions may go to the Supreme Court.

The United States Customs Court. The largest of the three courts at issue, the Customs Court has nine members—of whom no more than five may be members of the same political party—who receive $40,000 annually, a somewhat lower salary than the other two courts. A successor of the United States Board of General Appraisers, and with roots extending back to pre-Revolutionary days, the modern version of the court was created by Congress in 1926 under its commerce and taxing powers. Sitting in three sections or divisions of three judges each, this special court, which meets in New York headquarters and all other ports of entry in both the continental United States and the territories and insular possessions, has jurisdiction to review the rulings and appraisals on imported goods by collectors of cus-

---

[27] *re Von Clemm,* 229 F. 2d 441 (1955).
[28] *United States v. Schmidt Pritchard & Co.,* 47 CCPA 152, C.A.D. 750.

toms. As we have seen, appeals from its decisions go to the Court of Customs and Patent Appeals, although, in rare instances, it is possible to go directly to the Supreme Court.

An illustration of the work of the Customs Court is a case involving International Packers, Ltd., in 1959. The firm contended that it should be permitted to deduct from the appraised value of goods imported from Argentina a certain percentage of the purchase price it had to pay to the Argentine authorities on their export. The United States Government's customs officials rejected this claim. On bringing action for ajudication in the Customs Court, the plaintiff convinced that body that the 15 per cent levy exacted by the Argentine Government was a "necessary expense from the place of shipment to the place of delivery." Accordingly, the court ruled that the percentage involved was properly allowable as a deduction in computing the United States value of the merchandise under the Tariff Act."[29]

Review of tariff controversies by the Court of Customs is not limited to the statutory provisions of the various congressional enactments. The right to sue before it applies to practically every legal controversy between an importer-taxpayer and the federal government. The fact that the Secretary of the Treasury or some other public official might have handed down an administrative ruling does not preclude an appeal to this interesting watchdog-court.

THE FEDERAL CONSTITUTIONAL COURTS

We now turn to the three chief *constitutional* courts, the United States District Courts, the United States (Circuit) Courts of Appeals, and the United States Supreme Court—but the most important of these, the Supreme Court, will be the sole subject of the next chapter. All three were created under Article III of the United States Constitution. In its key Section 1, that article mentions only "one supreme court," but it goes on to point to "such inferior Courts as the Congress may from time to time ordain and establish." The two lower of these three constitutional courts hence owe their origin to one of the very first acts passed by the First United States Congress, the Judiciary Act of 1789, of which Senator Oliver Ellsworth, who had been a delegate from Connecticut to the Constitutional Convention and who was soon to be the second Chief Justice of the United States, was a leading author. The act established and fairly well spelled out the national system of constitutional courts, which, as has been

[29] *International Packers, Ltd. v. United States*, 171 F. Supp. 854.

demonstrated, received no hierarchical additions until the Court of Claims was designated a constitutional court in 1953, followed by the Customs Court in 1956 and the Court of Customs and Patent Appeals in 1958. These six courts and their judges are clothed with the significant and essential benefits of life (literally, "good behavior") tenure, irreducible salary, prestige, and independence. In the opinion of many an observer of the American scene, including the author of this book, there are no positions of greater desirability and prestige in the entire structure of American government than those occupied by the members of the three leading constitutional courts.

General Jurisdiction. Omitting the jurisdiction (discussed above) of the several "special" federal courts, constitutional as well as legislative, the general jurisdiction of these three chief federal constitutional courts is amazingly well spelled out by Article III, Section 2, of the Constitution. In what is surely one of the most succinctly worded segments of the basic document, the first sentence of the first paragraph of that section makes clear at once that the judicial power of the United States "shall extend to all Cases, in Law and Equity, arising under this Constitution, the Laws of the United States, and Treaties made, or which shall be made under their Authority. . . ." Thus, in addition to announcing the sweeping realm of over-all jurisdiction, that wording comes to grips with one of the crucial aspects of the jurisdictional process, namely that it is limited to "Cases" (and "controversies," by implication). This signifies the necessity of the presence of a bona fide case or controversy involving litigants of opposing points of view who bring to the federal courts a genuine conflict of interest. In the absence of these fundamental elements, the three constitutional courts have no jurisdiction—which pinpoints the important truth that they neither can nor will accept manufactured or trumped-up cases or controversies devoid of the essential elements described, nor can or will they render *advisory* opinions per se.[30] This collective ban is as applicable to official as it is to private personages, and even extends to the influential government official who might feel the urge of convenience to run to the chambers of the Supreme Court with a fervent plea for an opinion on the legality of an issue, be it pending or dormant. Thus, as early as 1792, the Supreme Court declined to advise the government because it deemed the advisory function to be one more properly belonging to the Cabinet—a precedent that has not been violated.[31]

---

[30] For a detailed analysis of the "case or controversy" and other "maxims" of the judicial process, see Ch. IX, *infra*.

[31] *Hayburn's Case*, 2 Dallas 409.

154

After having disposed of that crucial aspect, the constitutional paragraph at issue goes on to outline the particular type of jurisdiction available to these courts. Generally speaking, these fall into two groups or classifications: (1) those that are based on the character or nature of the *subject matter* of the *case*; and (2) those that are based on the character or nature of the *parties* to the suit. Under group (1) the courts may hear and dispose of cases and controversies in law and equity arising under:

(1) the Constitution, a federal law, or a treaty;

(2) admiralty and maritime laws.

Under the necessarily larger and more complex group (2) the courts may hear and dispose of cases and controversies in law and equity if:

(a) the United States is a party to the suit;

(b) one of the fifty states is a party to the suit (*but,* in accordance with the provisions of the Eleventh Amendment, *not* if the suit was commenced or prosecuted *against* a state by either an individual—*any* individual—or by a *foreign* country);

(c) they are between citizens of different states;

(d) they affect ambassadors and other bona fide representatives, duly *appointed,* of an accredited *foreign* country;

(e) they arise between citizens of the *same* state because of a dispute involving land grants claimed under titles of two or more states.

However, despite this very specific and extensive jurisdiction it does not necessarily follow that the federal courts will inevitably exercise it. There is no barrier in the language of the Constitution against congressional assignment of certain aspects of it (theoretically, probably even all of it!) to the fifty states, either on a concurrent or even exclusive basis—for example, the requirement that the value of a controversy in civil suits between citizens of different states must exceed $10,000 in order to qualify for original federal jurisdiction. Moreover, Congress may distribute the seven areas of federal jurisdiction among the various federal courts. It has done so and continues to do so in accordance with felt need, more often than not as a result of suggestions by the members of the judicial branch itself.

Overlapping Federal and State Jurisdiction. Whether or not Congress assigns concurrent or even exclusive jurisdiction in *federal* matters to *state* courts, it is axiomatic, of course, that in some areas the *state* courts have *exclusive* jurisdiction. It may be possible to raise a *federal issue* in a matter arising under state law or the state constitution, but the *original* jurisdiction of state courts over their own affairs is exclusive, as is that of the federal courts in their own sphere. However, there are some areas in which *both*

155

court systems have jurisdiction[32]—as in the case of bank embezzlement involving a federally insured bank, or in that of the theft of an automobile that subsequently crosses state lines—and where, consequently, the guilty party or parties are subject to prosecution and punishment by *both*. The United States Supreme Court has held repeatedly that such dual prosecution and even dual punishment violates neither the Bill-of-Rights ban against double jeopardy nor the "due process of law" clause under the Fourteenth Amendment.[33]

As indicated above, Congress has purposely granted *exclusive* jurisdiction over certain federal matters to the states. More often than not it has done this to reduce the federal work load in otherwise routine areas, such as the vast realm of diversity of citizenship disputes—i.e. suits between citizens of different states.[34] For these cases it enacted the requirement of a minimum

---

[32] The over-all problem of jurisdiction remains a major bone of contention: For as long as a defendant can appeal an unfavorable verdict from state to federal courts, and as long as state courts can "distinguish" federal court orders, finality is often both illusory and elusive. See the perceptive book by Judge Carl McGowan of the U.S. Court of Appeals for the District of Columbia, *The Organization of Judicial Power in the United States* (Evanston: Northwestern University Press, 1969).

[33] See *Bartkus v. Illinois,* 359 U.S. 121 (1959) and *Abbate v. United States,* 359 U.S. 187 (1959).

[34] More than one-quarter of all civil federal cases now fall into that category of litigation!

CHART A
THE JURISDICTION OF THE THREE MAJOR FEDERAL CONSTITUTIONAL COURTS OF THE UNITED STATES

COURTS CREATED UNDER ARTICLE III OF THE FEDERAL CONSTITUTION[a]

1 *Supreme Court of the United States,* 9 judges, has:

Original jurisdiction in actions or controversies:
1. Between the United States and a state.[b]
2. Between two or more states.
3. Involving *foreign* ambassadors, other *foreign* public ministers, and *foreign* consuls or their "domestics or domestic servants, not inconsistent with the law of nations."[b]
4. *Commenced by a state against* citizens of another state or aliens, or *against* a foreign country.[b] (N.B.: If these actions are *commenced by the citizen or alien against a state,* or by a foreign country *against* a state, the suit must *begin in state court,* according to the provisions of Amendment XI.)

Appellate jurisdiction from:
1. All lower federal *constitutional* courts; most, but not all, federal *legislative* courts; and the *territorial* courts.
2. The highest state courts having jurisdiction, when a "substantial federal question" is involved.

11 *United States* (*Circuit*) *Courts of Appeals*, 97 judges, have:

Appellate jurisdiction *only* from:
1. U.S. District Courts.
2. U.S. Territorial Courts, the U.S. Tax Court, and some District of Columbia Courts.
3. The U.S. Independent Regulatory Commissions.
4. Certain federal administrative agencies and departments (for review, but also for *enforcement* of certain of their actions and orders).

94 *United States District Courts*, approximately 400 judges, have:

Original jurisdiction *only*[c] over:
1. All crimes against the United States.
2. All civil actions arising under the Constitution, laws, or treaties of the United States, wherein the matter in controversy exceeds $10,000 (unless the U.S. Supreme Court has jurisdiction as outlined above).
3. Cases involving citizens of different states or citizens and aliens, provided the value of the controversy is in excess of $10,000.[b]
4. Admiralty, maritime, and prize cases.
5. Review and *enforcement* of orders and actions of certain federal administrative agencies and departments.[b]
6. All such other cases as Congress may validly prescribe by law.

[a] For the purposes of this chart, the three "special" courts (U.S. Court of Claims, U.S. Court of Customs, and U.S. Court of Customs and Patent Appeals) are omitted.
[b] *Jurisdiction not exclusive*—i.e. while, according to Article III of the Constitution, cases are to originate here, legal arrangements may be made to have them handled by a different level court. For example, Congress has the power to give the federal District Courts *concurrent original jurisdiction* over cases affecting foreign ambassadors and *some* cases in which a state is a party to the suit. See *United States v. Ravara*, 2 Dallas 297 (1793); *Bors v. Preston*, 111 U.S. 252 (1884); and *Ames v. Kansas*, 111 U.S. 449 (1884). And in late 1964 the Supreme Court declined to review a Ninth Circuit Court decision that United States District Courts have jurisdiction over suits *by the United States against a state.* (*California v. United States*, 379 U.S. 817).
[c] A case can be made for the contention that it also has a measure of *appellate* jurisdiction, involving certain actions tried before especially designated U.S. Commissioners.

value of $10,000 as the admission ticket to the federal court of jurisdiction, here the United States District Court. Going beyond that proviso, however, Congress has seen fit to grant *concurrent* jurisdiction in diversity of citizenship cases to the states even when the value meets or exceeds $10,000—provided the parties to the suit are willing to go there. As a further aid to the

157

over-docketed federal courts, especially the work-horse District Courts, Congress in the late 1950's enacted a long overdue statute dealing with the citizenship status of corporations for purposes of legal actions. As a result, corporations are now viewed as "citizens" not only of the states in which they have been incorporated—which had been the case heretofore—but also as "citizens" of those states in which they have their principal place of business, regardless of their status of incorporation in them.

On the other hand, Congress has seen fit to vest *exclusive* original jurisdiction in the federal courts in a number of areas: suits between two or more of the fifty states (Supreme Court only); cases involving *foreign* ambassadors and other accredited *foreign* representatives; all bankruptcy proceedings; and all prosecutions for violations of *federal* criminal laws. Chart A demonstrates the over-all jurisdiction of the three major federal constitutional courts.

The United States District Courts. By all odds the workhorses of the federal judiciary, the ninety-four District Courts, with their some 400 judges—perpetually an insufficient total—comprise the trial courts of the federal system. Established under the Judiciary Act of 1789, their jurisdiction extends to the initial trial of almost all civil and criminal cases arising in the vast realm of federal jurisdiction. It is here that the United States Government commences, and usually ends, its prosecutions—e.g. the government's victorious antitrust suit against the electrical appliance concerns for illegal price-fixing, which began and terminated in the United States District Court for Eastern Pennsylvania in Philadelphia in February 1961, Judge J. Cullen Ganey rendering the famous decision that saw a number of astonished top executives go to jail.[35] It is here also that most suits arising under the federal statutes begin and end—viz., one Paul Abrikossoff's action to recover certain property that had been disposed of by the Alien Property Custodian under the Trading with the Enemy Act.[36] And it is here that the trial (petit) juries sit in the federal system; they do so in roughly half of all cases commenced at that level. The District Courts have *original* jurisdiction only. However, when necessary, they do have the obligation to *enforce* as well as review actions and orders of certain federal administration agencies and departments; certain actions tried before United States Magistrates,

[35] Case not reported in F. Supp. See Reporter's Transcript in Office of the Clerk, U.S. District Court, Eastern District of Pennsylvania. Also see Clerk Gilbert W. Ludwig's letter to author, dated June 8, 1961.
[36] *Abrikossoff v. Brownell*, 145 F. Supp. 18 (1956).

158

formerly known as Commissioners (see below), may be reviewed by them; and certain other classes of cases may be *removed* to them from the state courts under certain specific statutory authorization. Hence, in the vast majority of instances, the decisions of the District Courts are, in effect, final. And there is a veritable flood of business: they now decide upwards of 325,000 cases annually. In 1974, to cite one busy year, a total of 330,697 proceedings were *commenced* in the District Courts.[37] No wonder delays are common here—as well as elsewhere in the undermanned, overly litigous American judicial system. At the level of the *federal* courts the time interval between the point when a case was "at issue" and the trial itself ranged from 4.1 months to 39.1 months in 1959; from 3.9 to 48.7 months in 1965–66; and from 1.0 months to 52.0 months in 1972–73. In the *state* courts, it varied from 1.0 months to 52.9 months in 1959; from 4.3 to 69.5 months in 1965–66; and from 0.7 months to 58.1 months in 1972–73.[38] A poignant and pertinent illustration: a ten-year-old girl, Nancy Verona, was hit by a car while riding her bike. When her case at last came to trial, she was a young mother, aged nineteen, who brought her baby to the court with her![39]

Each of the fifty states of the Union, the District of Columbia, Puerto Rico, Guam, the Canal Zone, and the Virgin Islands contains at least one federal district with a District Court and a District Court Judge, who receives $40,000 annually. There is no cutting across state lines, but in many instances the large number of cases to be adjudicated compels a subdivision of labor within a particular district. Most districts today have two or more judges—although there were still seven districts in early 1974 with but one each.[40] The Southern District of New York (New York County—Manhattan—Bronx County, and the adjacent suburban counties to the north), with its high proportion of complex commercial litigation, had the 1975

---

[37] To be precise: 103,530 civil; 37,667 criminal; and 189,500 bankruptcy cases—representing an over-all increase of about 30 per cent in seven years (*Annual Reports* of the U.S. District Courts).

[38] See the symposium, "Lagging Justice," 328 *The Annals of the American Academy of Political and Social Science* (March 1960); the series by Howard James in *The Christian Science Monitor*, "Crisis in the Courts," April–July 1967, and James's book, *Crisis in the Courts*, rev. ed. (New York: David McKay Co., Inc., 1971), *passim*; the statistics cited by Victor G. Rosenblum in James W. Fesler (ed.), *The 50 States and their Local Governments* (New York: Alfred A. Knopf, 1967), pp. 434–35; and the *Annual Reports* of the Administrative Office of the United States Courts.

[39] Cited by Louis Banks, "The Crisis in the Courts," 64 *Fortune Magazine* 86 (December 1961), at 88.

[40] Canal Zone, Guam, Louisiana (middle), Maine, New Hampshire, Wisconsin (western), and Wyoming.

maximum—twenty-seven.[41] Almost half of all litigation occurs in the twelve District Courts that are located in the larger metropolitan areas. The Chief Justice of the United States (the Chief Justice of the Supreme Court) has the authority to transfer district judges temporarily from their home circuit to a more congested one, but only with their consent. These judges are then known as "visiting judges." It was as Visiting Judge for the Eastern District of Arkansas that United States District Judge Ronald N. Davies, whose home district was North Dakota, issued the now famous injunction[42] against Governor Orval E. Faubus and other state officials of Arkansas in September 1957, after they had actively interfered with an earlier court order upholding the Little Rock School Board's desegregation plan.[43] Judge Davies had been temporarily transferred to help deal with a mounting backlog of cases. To cite one other procedural example: in order to remedy a staggering backlog of civil jury cases in the United States District Court for the Southern District of New York, Mr. Chief Justice Warren, acting on the urging of Chief Judge Sidney Sugarman of that court in 1968, assigned ten district judges from other parts of the country (one each from Oregon, California, Iowa, Kansas, Utah, Tennessee, New Mexico, and the Eastern District of New York, and two from Connecticut) to help clear the accumulation. The team did just that within two months.

But no matter how many judges may be permanently or temporarily assigned to a federal district, it is customary for a lone District Court judge, sitting with a jury—unless that institution has been validly waived—to preside over a trial in the roughly 400 localities where they now are held in the United States. However, in some instances of particular importance, Congress has statutorily provided for adjudication by *Three-Judge District Courts*. They customarily consist of two district judges and one circuit judge, the Judicial Code providing that at least one judge must be from the circuit—the next higher echelon in the judicial system. As a matter of practice, the Chief Judge of the Circuit Court involved, rarely, if ever, assigns more than that absolute minimum. Suits required to be heard by these Three-Judge District Courts—from which lies direct appeal to the Supreme Court of the United States as a matter of right—are usually those seeking to restrain by an *injunction* the enforcement, operation, or execution of both federal and state statutes and orders of state administrative agencies on

[41] Columbia, Dutchess, Greene, Orange, Putnam, Rockland, Sullivan, Ulster, and Westchester.
[42] *United States v. Faubus*, 156 F. Supp. 220 (1957).
[43] *Aaron v. Cooper*, 143 F. Supp. 855 (1956).

grounds of *unconstitutionality*, or orders issued by the Interstate Commerce Commission. A few other instances are also provided by statute, some of these injunctions to cover certain violations of the federal antitrust laws. Considerable sentiment exists for the discontinuation of the use of these Three-Judge tribunals, for they have unquestionably added to the judicial workload in general and Supreme Court review in particular (2.7 per cent of the Court's docket in 1971–72 and 22 per cent of total cases decided on the merits). Mr. Chief Justice Burger is a leading spokesman for abolition.[44]

The busy judges of the District Courts are provided with a number of assistants to carry on their tasks, all of whom are appointed by the judges themselves (some were mentioned in an earlier chapter). Among them are the United States Magistrates, Law Clerks, Bailiffs, Court Reporters, Stenographers, Clerks, Probation Officers, and, as of 1971, professional administrators to relieve the chief judges of management duties at the appellate level as well as here. These positions are more or less self-explanatory, except for that of the important *United States Magistrate*, who, as has been pointed out, is in charge of some of the preliminary steps involved in the pre-trial process. He may issue arrest warrants; he may hear evidence in order to determine whether to hold an accused person for grand jury action— in which case he may set the bail—he may assume jurisdiction in certain minor federal offenses when the defendant waives his right to a federal judge and jury; he is active in pre-trial and discovery proceedings and considers preliminary petitions; he appoints legal counsel for indigent defendants under the Criminal Justice Act of 1964; he may try petty cases and, in most jurisdictions, mete out sentences of up to six months' imprisonment and/or $500.00 in fines. The Federal Magistrates Act of 1968, under which magistrates are appointed by the District Court judges for eight- and four-year terms of office, requires all magistrates to hold a law degree (unless "none is available" for service with such a degree). In early 1974 there were 68 full time and 400 part-time magistrates. Salaries are geared to work loads, but gone are the days when magistrates—then called commissioners—were paid out of court fees.[45]

The two most significant officers at the district level are the *United States Marshal* and the *United States Attorney*. The latter, appointed for each of

---

[44] See the "Freund Report," published by the Federal Judicial Center, January 1973; *The New York Times*, August 15, 1972, p. 1; and U.S. News and World Report, Aug., 21, 1972, p. 41, for illustrative commentary.

[45] For an excellent article on this little-known office, see Charles A. Lindquist, "The United States Commissioner: An Evaluation of the Commissioner's Role in the Judicial Process," 39 *Temple Law Quarterly* 138 (Winter 1966).

the districts by the President with the advice and consent of the Senate, functions under the authority of the Attorney General (rather than that of his District Judge), who also appoints a number of Assistant United States Attorneys, often in conjunction with the patronage wishes of influential members of his political party. The U.S. Marshal,[46] appointed in the same manner as the U.S. Attorney, makes arrests; guards and transports prisoners; determines where a prisoner is to serve his sentence; disburses federal judicial funds; serves court orders, writs, and processes;[47] guards and transports all federal court documents, from jury notices to Supreme Court orders; ascertains the security of witnesses; generally maintains the decorum of the courtroom of the District Court of the United States; and, when called upon, aids in riot control. In 1973 there were 94 such marshals and 749 deputy and chief deputy marshals.[48]

The United States (Circuit) Courts of Appeals. Standing immediately above the United States District Courts in the federal constitutional court hierarchy are the eleven United States (Circuit) Courts of Appeals, which are essentially what their name implies: *appellate* courts only. They do, however, have a statutory obligation to *enforce*, when necessary, as well as review, actions of a host of federal executive agencies that are clothed with quasi-judicial functions. Among these, to cite but a few, are certain rulings of the National Labor Relations Board; wage orders of the Administration of Wage and Hour Division of the Department of Labor; and orders under antitrust or unfair practice laws of the Interstate Commerce Commission, the Federal Communications Commission, the Civil Aeronautics Board, and the Board of Governors of the Federal Reserve System. But even if we are to classify aspects of the review and enforcement of the activities of these quasi-judicial units of the federal government as original jurisdiction —and they are that only by stretching the concept considerably—the vast majority of the work of the United States Courts of Appeals is clearly appellate. In effect, it is at once the first and last stop for appeals from below in all instances save those that go on up to the United States Supreme

---

[46] The origin of the office traces back to medieval England, where the Old French word *mareshal* (groom) came to mean a sort of royal sheriff in charge of procuring witnesses for the monarch.

[47] This is a task that frequently takes considerable ingenuity. For example, to serve a desegregation injunction on the evasive and defiant Alabama Governor George Wallace in 1963, one deputy marshal stowed away in the men's room aboard the Governor's plane!

[48] See *Annual Report* of the United States District Courts. Appointees must have attained a qualifying grade on the Treasury Enforcement Examination and have at least five years of investigative experience.

Court and those few that are permitted to bypass it from below en route to the Supreme Court. Other than the appeals from the highest state courts of record, which go directly to the Supreme Court without touching the other federal courts, the Circuit Courts of Appeals may be validly bypassed only if: (1) such a decision is made by the Three-Judge District Courts, as explained above; (2) there is a direct appeal statutorily authorized to the Supreme Court from a limited number of ordinary District Court cases, such as a case where a federal statute has been held unconstitutional by a District Court and the United States is a party to the suit; and (3) it is shown that a case is of "such imperative public importance as to justify the deviation from normal appellate process and require immediate settlement [in the Supreme Court]."

But in all other instances, both civil and criminal, the Circuit Court of Appeals is the natural appellate tribunal for the approximately 6,500 cases— an increase of 125 per cent in a mere seven years!—that now come up to it annually from the United States District Courts in the fifty states, the District of Columbia, and the territories, and from the many independent regulatory commissions, agencies, and cabinet departments that are endowed with quasi-judicial powers and functions. In effect, it *finally* decides approximately 85 per cent of all federal cases. For example, the Court of Appeals for the District of Columbia, sometimes referred to as the Eleventh Circuit, held, on reviewing the denial of one Shachtman's passport application by the Department of State, that the latter had violated the due process of law clause of the Fifth Amendment in the circumstances at issue.[49] The Department of State subsequently complied with the court's mandate. Illustrations of cases arising from a decision of a District Court rather than that of an administrative agency or department are the (unsuccessful) appeal to the United States Court of Appeals for the Second Circuit by Alger Hiss for reversal of his conviction on perjury charges in connection with the theft of United States Government documents and the (equally unsuccessful) appeal by President Nixon to the Court of Appeals for the District of Columbia from Judge John J. Sirica's order to turn nine of the "Watergate Tapes" over to him for scrutiny.[50]

Although officially stripped of the term "circuit" in 1948, the courts on this important level in the federal judicial process are still generally referred to as "Circuit Courts." There are ten such numbered circuits in the United

[49] *Shachtman v. Dulles,* 225 F. 2d 938 (1955).
[50] *United States v. Hiss,* 185 F. 2d 822 (1950) and *Nixon v. Sirica,* 487 F. 2d 700 (1973), respectively.

States plus the unnumbered eleventh one, known as the *Court of Appeals for the District of Columbia:*[51]

First Circuit:	Maine, Massachusetts, New Hampshire, Rhode Island, Puerto Rico.
Second Circuit:	Connecticut, New York, Vermont.
Third Circuit:	Delaware, New Jersey, Pennsylvania, Virgin Islands.
Fourth Circuit:	Maryland, North Carolina, South Carolina, Virginia, West Virginia.
Fifth Circuit:	Alabama, Florida, Georgia, Louisiana, Mississippi, Texas, Canal Zone.
Sixth Circuit:	Kentucky, Michigan, Ohio, Tennessee.
Seventh Circuit:	Illinois, Indiana, Wisconsin.
Eighth Circuit:	Arkansas, Iowa, Minnesota, Missouri, Nebraska, North Dakota, South Dakota.
Ninth Circuit:	Arizona, California, Idaho, Montana, Nevada, Oregon, Washington, Hawaii, Alaska, Guam.
Tenth Circuit:	Colorado, Kansas, New Mexico, Utah, Oklahoma, Wyoming.

Each of these circuits is theoretically headed by one of the nine Justices of the United States Supreme Court. They are by tradition said to be "riding circuit"—the junior Justices usually, but not necessarily, being assigned the two "extra" circuits. Indeed, this is what the Justices used to do, literally, at the beginning of America's nationhood, but the practice fell into disuse approximately three-quarters of a century later. Today, lack of time prevents them from more than nominal participation, although they continue to be faithfully and formally "assigned" at the beginning of each term. And, of course, they do retain the power to act on certain pleas that arise from court actions, particularly dispositive orders, in "their" circuits. A typical illustration is Mr. Justice White's refusal to set aside an Oklahoma District Court decision that had nullified the state's May 1964 primary and had ordered a new primary for that September on a "one-man, one-vote" basis. White, as the Justice in administrative charge of the Tenth Circuit, of which Okla-

[51] In 1933 the United States Supreme Court ruled that both the United States District Court for the District of Columbia *and* the United States Court of Appeals for the District of Columbia are at the same time "constitutional" *and* "legislative" courts. (*O'Donoghue v. United States*, 289 U.S. 516.) In 1930 it had held that "it is recognized that the courts of the District of Columbia are not created under the judiciary article of the Constitution but are legislative courts. . . ." (*Federal Radio Commission v. General Electric Company*, 281 U.S. 464, at 468.) But, of course, *O'Donoghue* governs today.

homa is a part, simply wrote "stay denied"—and "that," in Mr. Justice Holmes's language, "was that!"

The eleven Circuit Courts of Appeals comprise a total of ninety-seven judges—salaried at $42,500 annually—who, except for the judges of the District of Columbia, must be residents of the assigned circuit during the time they serve and even thereafter—because, though they may have retired, they are still subject to assignments by the Chief Justice of the United States. Each of the Circuit Courts has a Chief Judge, who, upon reaching the voluntary retirement age of seventy, retains his powers as a full-fledged member of his court—assuming he neither chooses to retire nor has accumulated sufficient time to do so on full salary—but ceases to be head of the court involved. This arrangement also applies in the District Courts, but not in the Supreme Court. From three to nine judges may sit *en banc* to hear cases, although there are usually only three in view of the work load; a quorum is two. Proceedings before the Courts of Appeals are conducted on the basis of the record made below—i.e. before the United States District Courts or one of the administrative agencies. The most important cases are selected for oral argument, while the lesser are decided solely on the basis of submitted documents (except in the Second Circuit, which hears oral argument in *all* cases). But new evidence may not be presented at the bar of this appellate tribunal, just as it may not be introduced in the appellate cases reaching the highest ranking court in the Amercian judicial hierarchy, the Supreme Court of the United States.

ADMINISTERING THE FEDERAL JUDICIARY

Before turning to the Supreme Court in the next chapter, something should be said about the administration of the federal judicial system. Considerable thought may well have been given for many years to the establishment of a centralized administrative structure for these courts, but it was actually not until shortly prior to the second quarter of this century that the judicial and legislative branches, particularly the former, recognized the urgency of the problem to the extent of doing something about it—other than to declaim and exhort on what had become an increasingly deplorable state of administrative anarchy. Fortunately, Congress yielded to mounting pressure by bar, bench, and interested laymen, and the establishment of the Judicial Conference of the United States and the Administrative Office of the United States Courts in 1922 and 1939, respectively, effected considerable improvement.

The Judicial Conference of the United States. The 1922 statute requires "the Chief Justice . . . to submit to Congress an annual report of the proceedings of the Judicial Conference and its recommendation for legislation." This is done faithfully and to considerable advantage by the "Chief," who is head of that body. In addition to him, it consists of the chief judge of each of the eleven federal judicial circuits, a district court judge from each of these circuits—chosen for a term of three years by the judges of the Circuit at its annual Judicial Conference—the Chief Judge of the United States Court of Claims, and the Chief Judge of the Court of Customs and Patent Appeals. The Judicial Conference meets at least once a year for the legislatively established purpose of making a "comprehensive survey of the conditions of business in the courts of the United States and [of preparing] plans for assignment of judges to or from circuits or districts where necessary." It is also required to submit suggestions to the various courts "in the interest of uniformity and expedition of business." This vital body of prestigious and influential experts has made an excellent job of keeping abreast of the needs of an efficient judiciary and has done its utmost—in conjunction with the Administrative Office of the United States Courts, for which it establishes policy—to realize these needs. In that capacity, to cite an example of its administrative and personnel role, it sent out the following admonition to all federal judges: "No justice or judge of the United States shall serve in the capacity of officer or director or employe of any corporation organized for profit."[52] In 1968 it called on all federal trial courts to adopt rules limiting what lawyers may say publicly about criminal cases.[53]

Although not all of the Judicial Conference's policy recommendations have either been adopted, or adopted speedily, by Congress—this applies especially to those involving the creation of new judgeships—the legislative branch has displayed considerable regard for the wisdom of the Judicial Conference and its committees. Thus, in 1958 Congress passed a Conference-recommended law authorizing the Judicial Conference to set up committees of judges, lawyers, and law professors to study the rules of procedure in the federal courts. On receiving the committees' recommendations, the Judicial Conference passes judgment on them and then sends them on to the Supreme Court for its action. Adopted changes become effective in ninety days unless they are specifically disapproved by Congress during that time. Congress also acquiesced in the Conference's request for federally ap-

[52] As quoted in its *Annual Report* for 1973.
[53] *The Philadelphia Evening Bulletin*, September 20, 1968, p. 12f.

propriated funds for the defense of the indigents in federal courts, a move which resulted in the Criminal Justice Act of 1964.[54]

The Administrative Office of the United States Courts. This judicial housekeeping agency (and veritable gold mine of statistics) is the executive arm of the Judicial Conference. It is headed by the director, who is appointed by the Chief Justice of the Supreme Court.[55] The director possesses no administrative jurisdiction vis-à-vis the Supreme Court, but he and his subordinates are crucially involved in the administrative business of the subordinate federal courts. (Indeed, an increasing number of the fifty states have begun to establish similar bodies—e.g. California, Iowa, New York, and Pennsylvania.) Among these tasks are the compilation of the suggested budgets; determination of personnel needs; examination of the dockets; auditing of accounts; procurement and allocation of supplies; preparation of all vital statistics in connection with the business of the courts (its *Annual Report* has become essential for all those interested in the judicial process); and all such other duties as may be assigned to the director and his staff by either the Supreme Court or the Judicial Conference—both of which are headed by the Chief Justice of the United States. The Administrative Office of the United States Court has become an essential arm of the judicial system; it has been widely and justly acclaimed; it has, in effect, become indispensable to the orderly and successful operation of the courts. Judge John J. Parker, who characterized it at the time of its creation in 1939 as "probably the greatest piece of legislation affecting the judiciary since the Judiciary Act of 1789,"[56] was quite correct in his analysis. Nonetheless, constant efforts to bring about further improvement in the operation and function of the courts, high as well as low, are essential. The establishment, in 1967, of the Federal Judicial Center as the research and training agency of the federal judicial system, with the Chief Justice of the United States as Chairman of the Board, is a highly commendable step in the right direction.[57] So is the creation of State/Federal Judicial Councils in almost all of the states (to alleviate friction between the two jurisdictions and to resolve overlapping between the two court systems), this largely due to the

---

54 See the article on the subject and related issues by Anthony Lewis, *The New York Times*, October 14, 1964.

55 The director also serves on the board in charge of the new Federal Judicial Center (mentioned in Ch. II, *supra*).

56 As quoted by James Willard Hurst, *The Growth of American Law: The Law Makers* (Boston: Little, Brown and Co., 1950), p. 114, 454.

57 For a brief sketch of the Center's functions, see fn. 100, p. 93, Ch. II, *supra*. In 1973, the F.J.C. provided training for 1600 federal judicial employees, including 129 judges (See *The New York Times*, Jan. 7, 1974, p. 16C.)

efforts of Mr. Chief Justice Burger; the Chief Justice's call for a National Institute of Justice (to devise proposals to ameliorate varied aspects of the judicial process); and the 1972 creation of the National Center for State Courts (to assist those courts in research and development to meet new burdens of adjudication).[58] There remains much room, of course, for additional improvement.

[58] See the interview with Mr. Chief Justice Warren E. Burger, "New Ways to Speed up Justice," *U.S. News and World Report*, August 21, 1972, pp. 38–46, and "Burger Renews Plea for Agency," *The New York Times*, December 7, 1972, p. 31.

V
Courts at Home:
II   The Supreme Court

AT THE ZENITH: THE UNITED STATES
SUPREME COURT

The most dazzling jewel in the judicial crown of the United States is the revered and often controversial United States Supreme Court. It is the sole court mentioned specifically in Article III or in any other part of the Constitution, all other federal courts having been created by statute. The Supreme Court, the national symbol of justice, stands at the very pinnacle of the judiciary: there is no higher court, and all others bow before it—or, at least, are expected to do so. It is, in Alpheus Thomas Mason's words—so prophetic for 1974—"the American counterpart of the British Crown, but unlike a queen on the throne, the Court has real power. It can bring Congress, President, state governors and legislators to heel."[1] At times having had as few as five, and at other times as many as ten, Justices in the first eighty years of its venerable history, the Court has stood at nine ever since the first term of President Grant in 1869. Prior thereto, as dictated by various policy considerations, its membership, which is congressionally fixed, comprised five in 1789, six in 1790, seven in 1807, nine in 1837, ten in 1863, and eight in 1866.

The Supreme Court consists of the Chief Justice and eight Associate Justices, the former being rewarded since 1969 with an annual salary of $62,500, the latter with $60,000 each.[2] But the nonsalary compensations, frequently

[1] "Judicial Activism: Old and New," 55 *Virginia Law Review* 411 (1969).

[2] An illustration of petty congressional pique vis-à-vis the Supreme Court, motivated chiefly by its momentous and trail-blazing civil rights and civil liberties decesions of the 1950's and 1960's, was the refusal of Congress in 1964 and again in 1965 to give the Chief Justice and his associates on the Court the same $7500 pay increase granted all lower federal court judges. Instead, the members of the highest tribunal had to settle for a $4500 raise.

called "psychic income" by college professors, are undoubtedly considerable. (The retirement prerogatives were discussed in Chapter II.)

ORIGINAL JURISDICTION

The United States Supreme Court has both *original* and *appellate* jurisdiction, but it exercises the former only in rare instances. Moreover, the Eleventh Amendment to the Constitution, ratified in 1798, has seriously abridged that phase of its work by removing from its, and the lower federal courts', jurisdiction all those cases in which one of its own citizens or one of another state or of a foreign country, or even a sovereign foreign country itself, wishes to sue one of the states of the United States. In effect, the Eleventh Amendment enacted the necessity of obtaining *a state's permission to sue it* in all litigation involving the above-mentioned categories.

The Eleventh Amendment was adopted as a direct result of a Supreme Court decision in 1793 in the case of *Chisholm v. Georgia*.[3] There the Court, in a broad decision, but in accordance with the terminology of Article III of the Constitution, held 4 : 1 that one Chisholm, a citizen of one state (South Carolina), could sue another state (Georgia) in the federal courts—an outrageous and shocking pronouncement in the eyes of citizens with confirmed states-rights views. It was especially galling since the matter involved debts owed to a then deceased British creditor, one Robert Farquhar, a merchant who had resided in Charleston, S.C., for whom Chisholm acted as an executor. (But it ought to be noted that the debts were for supplies sold in 1777 to Georgia in full accordance with the wishes and at the direction of Georgia's Executive Council.) The Supreme Court's judgment triggered instantaneous and profound opposition. For example, the lower house of the legislature of the State of Georgia passed a bill to punish by hanging "without benefit of clergy" any person endeavoring to aid in the enforcement of the decision! Merely two days had passed after the announcement in *Chisholm v. Georgia* when the future Eleventh Amendment was introduced into both houses of Congress.

Thereafter, the *original* jurisdiction docket of the Supreme Court became a very minor factor in its work. Not counting *memorandum orders* (to be explained later), at the outset of its 1974–75 term the Court had *rendered decisions* under the original jurisdiction clause of the Constitution —Article III, Section 2, Paragraph 2, as amended—in only 141 cases since its

---

[3] 2 Dallas 419. Actually, *Chisholm* involved the review of a case which had reached the Court from the Circuit Court below, entitled *Farquhar v. Georgia* (*Farquhar's Executor v. Georgia*). (Case File, Records of U.S. Circuit Court, District of Georgia, Case A, Box 1.)

first term in 1789.[4] The cases that now still commence under it do so as a *matter of right* under its provisions. Theoretically, these comprise the following four categories of cases or controversies: (1) those between the United States and one of the fifty states; (2) those between two or more states; (3) those involving *foreign* ambassadors, other *foreign* public ministers, and *foreign* consuls, or their "domestics or domestic servants not inconsistent with the law of nations"; and (4) those *commenced by a state* against citizens of another state or aliens, or *against* a foreign country. (But note that if these actions are *commenced by the citizen[5] or alien or even the foreign country[6]* against a state, that litigation *must begin in state court*, in accordance with the provisions of the Eleventh Amendment.)

However, the Supreme Court does not exercise *exclusive* original jurisdiction even in the four categories cited, with the sole exception of cases or controversies involving two or more of the several states. There it, and it alone, exercises original jurisdiction. But Congress, with the hearty approval of the Court, has extended *concurrent original* jurisdiction to the federal District Courts in litigation affecting category (3) and in *some*, but not all, cases in categories (1) and (4) in which a state is party to the suit at issue. Hence, most of the cases the Supreme Court has heard on its original jurisdiction docket have indeed involved two or more states. For example, the nine successive actions the State of Virginia filed against West Virginia in the lengthy and trying history of their debt controversy were all heard at the bar of the Supreme Court.[7] More recent controversies have involved Michigan and Ohio in a possession dispute over a 200-square-mile tract in the Maumee Bay area of mineral-rich Lake Erie,[8] California and Arizona in their persistent water squabbles,[9] a river boundary dispute between Louisiana and Texas,[10] Delaware's unsuccessful attempt to have the Court declare unconstitutional the electoral college vote count in presidential elections,[11] and the evidently eternal Virginia–Maryland "war of the oyster beds."[12] All of

---

[4] For a detailed analysis, including a list of 123 of these cases, see "The Original Jurisdiction of the United States Supreme Court," 11 *Stanford Law Review* 665–719 (July 1959).

[5] See *Hans v. Louisiana*, 134 U.S. 1 (1890).

[6] See *Monaco v. Mississippi*, 292 U.S. 313 (1934).

[7] E.g. *Virginia v. West Virginia*, 246 U.S. 565 (1918).

[8] *Michigan v. Ohio*, 386 U.S. 1029 (1967).

[9] *Arizona v. California*, 370 U.S. 906 (1961); ibid. 373 U.S. 546 (1963); ibid. rehearing denied, 375 U.S. 892 (1963).

[10] *Texas v. Louisiana* (410 U.S. 702 (1973).

[11] *Delaware et al. v. New York et al.*, 385 U.S. 895 (1966).

[12] E.g. *Virginia v. Maryland*, 355 U.S. 946 (1958).

these cases must, and do, commence in the Supreme Court. Yet if a determination of *facts* is required, the Court here often utilizes the device of referring these disputes to a special *master*—frequently an ex-jurist—for a hearing and report to it, as it did in the Virginia–Maryland oyster dispute, the Western water litigation cases, and in a 1966 suit by Ohio against Kentucky in a dispute over their boundary.[13]

APPELLATE JURISDICTION

The primary task of the Court is *appellate*. In that capacity it serves as the final arbiter in the construction of the Constitution of the United States, and it thus provides a uniform interpretation of the law—although its very power to do so also enables it to change its mind from case to case. However, at least to a considerable degree, it attempts to adhere to precedent, the aforementioned doctrine known as *stare decisis*, i.e. let the decision stand—giving to precedents the authority of established law. (We shall examine this philosophy of law and the extent of its success in Chapter VIII.)

Appellate cases come to the Supreme Court from the subordinate federal courts and the state courts of last resort (which are usually, but not always, the state supreme courts). Actually, there are five different sources of the appellate cases that reach the Court: (1) the state court of last resort having jurisdiction in a particular action, provided that a federal question has been raised validly, and further provided that all remedies have been duly exhausted below; (2) the United States Circuit Courts of Appeals; (3) the United States District Courts; (4) the United States Court of Claims and the United States Court of Customs and Patent Appeals in *judicial* rather than *administrative* matters; and (5) one of the legislative or territorial courts, if permissible under the laws that establish it.[14]

WRITS OF REVIEW

Cases or controversies normally reach the Supreme Court for purposes of review under its appellate jurisdiction in one of three principal ways—with each member of the Court considering every application for review: (1) on

---

[13] The three masters involved in these three decisions were, respectively, retired U.S. Supreme Court Associate Justice Stanley F. Reed, retired U.S. District Judge Simon H. Rifkind, and retired U.S. Court of Appeals Judge Percy Foreman. Masters' reports are normally accepted by the Court, but not always—e.g., in 1974 the Court rejected a master's proposal in connection with a longstanding dispute between New York and Vermont over water pollution in Lake Champlain. (*Vermont v. New York*, 415 U.S. 270.)

[14] Ch. 81, Title 28, U.S. Code.

a writ of appeal, as a matter of right (usually simply called *appeal*); (2) on a writ of *certiorari*, as a matter of Court discretion (usually simply called *certiorari* or *cert.*); and (3) by certification. The old writ of *error*, a common law process roughly akin to today's writ of appeal, was statutorily discontinued in the federal courts in 1928. It brought the entire record of a proceeding in a lower court before the Supreme Court for its consideration of "errors of law," allegedly committed below. We may also quickly dispose of *certification*. Rarely employed, it presents the Court with even less cases than those on its original jurisdiction docket. It covers "any question of law in any civil or criminal case in which instructions are desired" by the lower court, usually a Court of Appeals or the Court of Claims.

Appeal. In the instance of a writ of *appeal*, the aggrieved party—known as the *appellant*, the answering party is the *appellee* or *respondent*—has an absolute, *statutorily granted right* to carry a case to the United States Supreme Court, which in theory must review it. However, since 1928 the high tribunal has had the very considerable discretionary power to reject such an appeal on the ground that the federal question, otherwise validly raised, is "insubstantial." Moreover, the federal question must have been validly raised early in the state court, and even then the Supreme Court may not take the case if the state court's judgment can be sustained on an independent ground of state law. This highly significant multiple discretionary element in the area of the Court's so-called compulsory appellate jurisdiction caused it to dismiss 91.3 per cent of the appeals and petitions presented to it in the 1972–73 term. Of these, at least half were rejected "for want of a substantial federal question,"[15] the balance on other jurisdictional grounds. An average of 50 to 60 per cent of the writs of appeal are dismissed or the judgment below affirmed without printing the record or oral argument— and Mr. Justice Douglas contended in an important statistical article that, as a rule, the Court actually grants no more than 15 per cent.[16]

Hence, the appeal is used but sparingly, to date in only about 9 per cent of all cases or controversies *presented* to the Court—but Douglas claimed that this 9 per cent constitutes 90 per cent of all "meritorious" cases.[17] Yet whatever the practice, there are a total of five instances in which an aggrieved party may resort to it: (1) if a state court of last resort has declared

---

[15] One earlier example was the Court's refusal to interfere with a Connecticut law that allows a person injured by a drunk to sue the person who sold the drink! (*Albanese v. United States*, 350 U.S. 845, 1955, *certiorari* denied.)

[16] William O. Douglas, "The Supreme Court and its Case Load," 45 *Cornell Law Quarterly* 401 (Spring 1960), at 410.

[17] Ibid. at 409.

a federal law or treaty, or parts thereof, unconstitutional;[18] or, (2) if a state court *upholds a state law* or a provision of a state constitution *against a substantial challenge that it conflicts* with a provision of a federal law or treaty, or the United States Constitution;[19] (3) if any federal court declares a federal law or treaty, or parts thereof, unconstitutional, provided the United States is a party to the suit;[20] (4) if a federal Court of Appeals *strikes down a state law as being contrary* to a federal law, treaty, or the Constitution;[21] and (5) in certain statutorily specified cases from the federal District Courts and all other "courts of the United States" (e.g. if a case, required to be heard by any three-judge federal District Court, has resulted in an order granting or denying an injunction).[22] By far the largest number of cases on appeal come to the Supreme Court either from a state court of last resort —usually its highest court—or from one of the special three-judge courts at the federal District Court level (which must include at least one federal Circuit Court of Appeals judge). Many of the segregation-integration cases have reached the Supreme Court via the latter route.[23]

Certiorari. In all other cases involving a "federal question of substance" the disappointed litigant in a suit has *no right* to appeal to the Supreme Court the adverse decision he sustained; *however*, he does have the *privilege* of petitioning the highest bench in the land to grant him a writ of *certiorari*. Generally, each such petition,[24] a copy of which goes to every Justice with a record of the proceedings below, comprises the two sides' arguments both for and against its grant—the party bringing the action known as the *plaintiff* or *petitioner*, the other as the *respondent*. Ninety per cent of the cases decided by the Supreme Court reach it by that method, and most of these come to it from the Circuit Court of Appeal. (Neither in *certiorari* nor in *appeal* proceedings is a formal printed record necessary until such time as the writ of *certiorari* is granted or the appeal noted.) However, forty copies of the petition must be filed within thirty to ninety days after final judgment in the lower courts, and they must be accompanied by a $100 fee.

---

[18] E.g. *Reynolds v. Katzenbach*, 248 F. Supp. 593 (1965), consolidated with *South Carolina v. Katzenbach*, 383 U.S. 301 (1966).

[19] E.g. *Torcaso v. Watkins*, 367 U.S. 488 (1961).

[20] E.g. *Missouri v. Holland*, 252 U.S. 416 (1920).

[21] E.g. *Reynolds v. Sims*, 377 U.S. 533 (1964).

[22] E.g. *Wickard v. Filburn*, 317 U.S. 111 (1942).

[23] E.g. *Brown v. Board of Education of Topeka*, 347 U.S. 483 (1954).

[24] The petition must set forth the basis for the Court's jurisdiction; frame the questions presented for review; state the facts material to a consideration of those questions; and, in the words of Mr. Chief Justice Vinson, "explain why it is vital that the questions involved be decided finally by the Supreme Court."

The grant of *certiorari*—a Latin term meaning "made more certain," or "better informed"—signifies the willingness of the Supreme Court to review a case, based upon a written petition initiated by the plaintiff together with a reply from the other side, which often urges a denial of *certiorari*. A grant of the petition directs the lower court to send up the record in the case for review so that the decision "may be made more certain." Needless to say, the Court is quite chary of granting its writs of *certiorari*, and unless it detects an issue of substantial significance or controversy in the case, or happens to be especially interested in it, chances are that the application for the writ will be rejected with a terse *"certiorari* denied"—as is evident from the published listing of a large number of petitions thus disposed of. The Court's own Rule 19 states that *certiorari* will be granted only "when there are special and important reasons therefor." Among these, according to the language of Rule 19 of the Court's Revised Rules of 1967, are the following: (1) where two federal Circuit Courts of Appeals or two three-judge federal District Courts have rendered conflicting decisions (e.g. in one case, two diametrically opposed judgments involving the constitutionality of the so-called Blue Laws were handed down by two three-judge federal District Courts, sitting in Boston and Philadelphia, striking down and upholding such Massachusetts and Pennsylvania laws, respectively,[25] and, in another case, equally opposing judgments, this time on the constitutionality of the Public Accommodations Title of the Civil Rights Act of 1964, were rendered by two three-judge courts in the *same* circuit—the Fifth —in Atlanta and Birmingham, respectively, upholding and striking down that title of the Act[26]); (2) where a state court or a federal appellate court has passed on an important question of federal law on which the Supreme Court has never passed;[27] (3) where these lower courts have rendered a decision that conflicts with applicable precedent established by the Supreme Court;[28] or (4) where a federal court has so far departed from the accepted canons of judicial proceedings as to call for exercise of the Supreme Court's power of supervision.[29] In any case, as Mr. Justice Frankfurter viewed the Court's power to control its docket, ". . . [it] carries with it the responsibil-

[25] *Crown Kosher Super Market v. Gallagher*, 176 F. Supp. 466 (1959), and *Two Guys from Harrison-Allentown v. McGinley*, 179 F. Supp. 944 (1959).
[26] *Heart of Atlanta Motel v. United States*, 231 F. Supp. 393 (1964), and *McClung v. Katzenbach*, 233 F. Supp. 815 (1964).
[27] *Furman v. Georgia*, 408 U.S. 238 (1972).
[28] E.g. *Biddle v. Perovich*, 274 U.S. 480 (1927), and *United States v. O'Brien* plus *O'Brien v. United States*, 391 U.S. 367(1969).
[29] E.g. *United States v. District Court (United States v. Haley)*, 371 U.S. 18 (1962).

ity of granting review only in cases that demand adjudication on the basis of importance to the operation of our federal system; importance of the outcome merely to the parties is not enough."[30] In an address to a group of Illinois lawyers he illustrated what the Chief Justice, who plays an important role in *certiorari* grants, might say:

> This is a very interesting and important question . . ., but we can't do any better than Judge Julian Mack [late judge of the United States Court of Appeal] did with it below. He really knows more about this field of law than the rest of us. I suggest we deny this petition for *certiorari*.[31]

This posture is symptomatic of what Mr. Justice Frankfurter used to term the need for "alert deference" to lower court opinions in general. It echoes Mr. Chief Justice Vinson's contention that the Supreme Court "is not, and never has been, primarily concerned with the corrections of errors in lower court decisions. . . . [Its] function is, therefore, to resolve conflict of opinions on federal questions of wide import under the Constitution, laws and treaties of the United States, and to exercise supervisory power over the lower courts."[32]

Still, a case of substance is not necessarily a "big" or "major" case. For example, the Supreme Court once reached down to the Police Court of Louisville, Kentucky, to set aside, as a violation of the due process of law clause of the Fourteenth Amendment to the Constitution, two $10 fines for loitering and disorderly conduct.[33] This case symbolizes the willingness of the highest court in the land to look at the smallest matters if it is necessary to do so to ensure justice. Here, in a criminal conviction, one Sam Thompson, a man who had been convicted of disorderly public conduct for "shuffling" in a cafe, took his claim of lack of evidence successfully to the Supreme Court on *certiorari* because, under Kentucky law, the fines involved were too small to be reviewed by any state appellate court.[34] Speaking for the unanimous Court, Mr. Justice Black noted: "Our examination of the record presented in the petition for *certiorari* convinced us that *although the fines here are small, the due process questions presented are*

---

[30] Quoting from *Wilkerson v. McCarthy*, 336 N.J., 53 (1949).

[31] As quoted by Anthony Lewis, "How the Supreme Court Reaches Decisions," *The New York Times Magazine*, December 1, 1957, pp. 51–54.

[32] Address to the Annual Meeting of the American Bar Association, St. Louis, Mo., September 7, 1949. See also Mr. Justice Harlan's similar sentiments in *Cohen v. California*, 403 U.S. 15 (1971).

[33] *Thompson v. City of Louisville et. al.* 362 U.S. 199 (1960).

[34] Actually, it was the family for whom he worked who urged Thompson to appeal his case, for they felt that the police had been harassing him; they hired Louis Lusky, a distinguished lawyer with an abiding interest in civil liberties, to take the case.

substantial and we therefore granted *certiorari* to review the police court's judgment."[35] And, in the oral argument before the Court, the case was given *twice* the customary time allotted!

Since the Court has complete discretionary power over grants of *certiorari*—a power bestowed upon it by the necessary and desirable "Judges Bill" of 1925,[36] which was largely the creation of Mr. Chief Justice Taft and Mr. Justice Van Devanter—it denies between 85 and 90 per cent of all *certiorari* applications, and does not usually explain its reason for the denial.[37] Prior to the 1925 statute, the Court's appellate jurisdiction was obligatory to the extent of some 80 per cent of its business. Gone are the days when the Court, its docket jammed with mandatory appeals, was expected to devote an all-too-large portion of its valuable time and energy merely to correct errors of lower courts which primarily affected the rights of parties to a particular case or controversary. Today, it must concentrate on those cases whose resolution will have immediate importance far beyond the particular facts and parties involved. On the other hand, the Court has never forgotten the oft-quoted admonition of Mr. Chief Justice Marshall in *Cohens v. Virginia,* back in 1821:

> It is most true that this Court will not take jurisdiction if it should not: but it is equally true that it must take jurisdiction if it should. The judiciary cannot, as the legislature may, avoid a measure because it approaches the confines of the Constitution. We cannot pass it by because it is doubtful. With whatever doubts, with whatever difficulties, a case may be attended, we must decide it if it be brought before us. We have no more right to decline the exercise of jurisdiction which is given than to usurp that which is not given. The one or the other would be treason to the Constitution.[38]

Indeed, a glance at the subject matter represented on the Court's 1974–75 docket points to a veritable smorgasbord, ranging the alphabetical gamut from "abortion" to "zoning discrimination." However, there exists a distinct tendency on the Court's part to favor reviews sought by the federal government as a petitioning party. This is true both in terms of fully-discussed cases and in the decisions of the Chief Justice (and the Clerk of Court) to "special list" cases for possible review in the first place.

In order to grant *certiorari*, at least *four* of the Justices must vote to do

---

[35] Ibid. at 203. (Italics supplied.)
[36] 43 Stat. 936.
[37] An examination of a twenty-five-year period (1948–73) indicates that it does so in barely 1 percent of all such denials.
[38] 6 Wheaton 264, at 404.

so. At this stage each Justice, without any consultation with the others, reaches his own conclusion as to whether the application should be granted or denied. A working rule devised by the Court itself, this Rule of Four also applies to noting probable jurisdiction on writs of appeal—an interesting development in view of the important distinction which, theoretically, governs the two writs. Of course, the Court can also change its mind on a grant for review; there is nothing to prevent it, on thinking the matter over, from ultimately dismissing a writ as having been "improvidently granted."[39] According to a statute of 1863, however, *six* Justices constitute a quorum to hand down a decision.[40] This means that a plurality of four Justices can *decide* a case. In the event of a tie vote, the decision of the lower court stands as the final word in the controversy at issue.[41] But a single Justice may—unless, or until, overruled by action of his brothers on the bench—grant a stay of execution or a writ of *habeas corpus*. A pertinent illustration of this significant prerogative is the grant of a request for a stay of execution, although denying a request for a writ of *habeas corpus*, by Mr. Justice Douglas, in the sensational case of the convicted atom spies, Ethel and Julius Rosenberg, in June 1953. While vacating the stay of execution just twenty-four hours after it had been granted, Mr. Chief Justice Vinson took note inferentially of the intemperate reaction in the public press, and especially in Congress (where bills of impeachment were at once introduced in the House of Representatives), by writing that "Mr. Justice Douglas had power to issue the stay. No one has disputed this, and we think the proposition is indisputable."[42]

Considerable disagreement exists, not only among the many observers of

[39] E.g. *Cichos v. Indiana*, 385 U.S. 76 (1966), a state double jeopardy case which it had originally accepted for review, and the "smut" case of *Carlos v. New York*, 396 U.S. 119 (1969). Ditto *Nixon v. United States*, 418 U.S. 000 (1974).

[40] Early in 1970, when Mr. Justice Harlan abruptly removed himself from an important case involving oil shale mining rights, the niceties of judicial ethics dictated the cancellation of a Supreme Court hearing in mid-argument—for Harlan's departure left but five Justices on the bench. (*The New York Times*, January 22, 1970, p. 22.)

[41] E.g. Maryland's highest court's 1971 finding that the Swedish film *I Am Curious (Yellow)* was obscene. (*Grove Press, Inc. v. Maryland State Board of Censors*, 401 U.S. 480.)

[42] *Rosenberg v. United States*, 346 U.S. 273 (1953), at 285. Each Supreme Court Justice is responsible for considering appeals for stays in *any* matters which come up in his circuit. However, if someone seeking a stay is turned down by the Justice presiding over his circuit, the petitioner can further appeal to *any or all* of the *other* members of the Court for relief. When Douglas was savagely attacked for granting the Rosenbergs' stay, Senator William Langer (R.-N.D.) offered him solace: "Douglas, they have thrown several buckets of shit over you. But by God, none of it stuck. And I am proud." (*Go East, Young Man. The Early Years: The Autobiography of William O. Douglas* (New York: Random House, 1974), p. 469.)

the Court, but among the Justices themselves, as to the true meaning of a denial of an application for a writ of *certiorari*. Mr. Justice Jackson viewed "sincere worthiness" as a tacit agreement by a quorum of the Justices that the decision below is good enough to stand. "The fatal sentence," he wrote, "that in real life writes finis to many causes cannot in legal theory be a complete blank."[43] Mr. Justice Frankfurter, however—in what is probably a majoritarian view of the issue—always insisted that no significance attaches to the denial of *certiorari*, that it "in no wise" implies Court approval of the decision below. All it means, he would point out, is that, for reasons seldom, if ever, disclosed, six or more Justices evidently do not think that a case ought to be adjudicated on its merits. On one occasion he spelled out his reasoning:

> . . . [it] seemed . . . to at least six members [of the Court] . . . that the issue was either not ripe enough or too moribund for adjudication; that the question had better wait for the perspective of time or that time would bury the question or, for one reason or another, it was desirable to wait and see; or that the constitutional issue was entangled with nonconstitutional issues that raised doubt whether the constitutional issue could be effectively isolated; or for various other reasons not related to the merits.[44]

No matter which of these two contrasting views may be "correct," the effect in the eyes of the disappointed petitioner is necessarily the same: at least for the present, he has lost.[45]

WORK LOAD

All cases to be disposed of are placed on one of the Court's three dockets: the *Original,* the *Appellate,* and the *Miscellaneous.* In the 1973–74 term the Court had more cases (5079) on these dockets and *disposed* of more (3876) with finality than ever before. But of those many cases the Court disposed, it decided only 468 *on the merits,* with *full written opinions* handed down in just 147 cases—an average number—the remainder being disposed of either *per curiam* or by *memorandum orders—*e.g. "affirmed," "reversed," or "dismissed" ("vacated"). Yet it must be recognized that the

---

43 Concurring opinion in *Brown v. Allen,* 344 U.S. 443 (1953), at 543.
44 Dissenting opinion in *Darr v. Burford,* 339 U.S. 200 (1950), at 227. See, similarly, Mr. Justice Brennan's statement in "State Court Decisions and the Supreme Court," 31 *Pennsylvania Bar Association Quarterly* 399-400 (1960).
45 Not infrequently, one or more disappointed Justices will write an *opinion,* or a note, on the Court's refusal to grant *certiorari* in a certain case—e.g. Mr. Justice Douglas's lengthy one from the Court's refusal to hear a test of the constitutionality of New York's criminal syndicalism state in 1968. (*Epton v. New York,* 390 U.S. 29.)

CHART B
UNITED STATES SUPREME COURT REVIEW

CASES NORMALLY REACH THE U.S. SUPREME COURT FOR PUR-
POSES OF *REVIEW* (as distinct from original jurisdiction) IN ONE OF
TWO PRINCIPAL WAYS:
  (1) on APPEAL, i.e. as a matter of right;
  (2) on a writ of *CERTIORARI*, as a matter of Court discretion.
(A third way, by CERTIFICATION, will be omitted for present purposes.
It is rarely used—presenting the Court with even less cases than those on its
original docket. It covers "any question of law in any civil or criminal case as to
which instructions are desired" by the lower court, usually a Court of Appeals
or the Court of Claims.[a] The old writ of ERROR, a common law process
strongly akin to (1) above, was statutorily discontinued in the federal courts in
1928. It brought the entire record of a case proceeding in a lower court before
the Supreme Court for its consideration for alleged "errors of law" committed
below.)

N.B. Title 28 of the United States Code, formulated as a result of congressional
legislation, governs the types of review available to an appellant. (See Secs.
1257 and 1254.)

I. *Cases reaching the U.S. Supreme Court on APPEAL* (i.e. the Court reviews
   because it *must*).
   A. *From the State Court of Last Resort* having statutory jurisdiction in any
      particular case (usually, but not always, the *Highest State Court*, which
      normally, but not always, is the State Supreme Court).
      1. When a state court has declared a federal law or a federal treaty, or
         provisions thereof, unconstitutional.
      2. When a state court has *upheld* a state law or a provision of the state
         constitution *against* the challenge that it *conflicts* with the federal Con-
         stitution, a federal law, a federal treaty, or any provision thereof.

   B. *From the U.S. (Circuit) Courts of Appeals:*
      1. When a state law or a provision of a state constitution has been *invali-
         dated* because of a conflict with a federal law, a federal treaty, or a
         provision of the federal Constitution.
      2. When a federal law has been held *unconstitutional, provided* the
         United States, or one of its agencies, officers, or employees is a party to
         to the suit.

---

[a] One of the very infrequent illustrations of its use is that by the Fifth United States
Circuit Court of Appeals in 1963, which certified the question of whether its criminal
contempt citation of Governor Ross R. Barnett and Lieutenant Governor Paul B.
Johnson, Jr., of Mississippi necessitated a trial by jury. The intermediate appellate tribunal was evenly divided (4 : 4) when it turned to the Supreme Court in this ticklish
case, which had arisen out of the admission of Negro James H. Meredith to the University of Mississippi at Oxford. (*United States v. Barnett*, 375 U.S. 805.) The highest
tribunal ruled 5 : 4 against Barnett and Johnson (ibid., 376 U.S. 681) in 1964. But
one year later the Circuit Court cleared the two because of "changed circumstances
and conditions." (Ibid. 346 F. 2d 99.)

C. *From the U.S. District Courts:*
1. When a federal statute has been held *unconstitutional, provided* the United States, or one of its agencies, officers, or employees is a party to the suit.
2. When the United States is a party to a *civil* suit under the federal interstate-commerce, communication, or anti-trust laws.
3. When a *special three-judge District Court*[b] (which must include at least one circuit judge) has granted or denied an interlocutory or permanent injunction in any proceeding required to be heard by such a court. (These three-judge courts usually sit in suits brought to *restrain enforcement, operation, or execution of federal or state statutes or orders of state administrative agencies* on the grounds of unconstitutionality; *or* because of an order of the Interstate Commerce Commission.)

D. *From "Any Court of the United States"* (comprising the *constitutional, legislative,* and *territorial* courts)—and specifically including, a.o., the *Court of Claims,* the *Court of Customs and Patent Appeals,* etc.:
1. When a federal statute has been held *unconstitutional* in any *civil* action, suit, or proceeding, *provided* the United States, or one of its agencies, officers, or employees is a party to it.

II. *Cases reaching the U.S. Supreme Court on a writ of* CERTIORARI (i.e. because a minimum of four Supreme Court Justices has agreed to a review.) Writs of *certiorari* are granted or denied at the *discretion* of the Court—subject always to the latent power of Congress to define and limit the *appellate* power of the Court.
A. *From the State Court of the Last Resort having statutory jurisdiction* in any particular case (usually, but not always, the Highest State Court, which normally, but not always, is the State Supreme Court).
1. In all cases, *other than* those for which the remedy is APPEAL (see I, A, 1 & 2 above), in which a *"substantial federal question"* has been properly raised. (The Court itself determines just what constitutes such a question.)

B. *From U.S. (Circuit) Courts of Appeals* (and, in all pertinent cases, from the *U.S. Court of Claims,* and the *Court of Customs and Patent Appeals*):
1. When a decision involves the *application or interpretation* of a federal law, a federal treaty, the federal Constitution, or provisions thereof.
2. Where the U.S. Court of Appeals has *upheld* a state law or a provision of a state constitution *against* the challenge that it conflicts with a federal law, a federal treaty, the federal Constitution, or provisions thereof.

[b] In an important public interview, Mr. Chief Justice Burger strongly urged the abolition of these tribunals, which accounted for 22 per cent of all Supreme Court cases in recent years—a class of cases that by statutorily granted right thus come *directly* to it and "must" be accepted for review. (*U.S. News & World Report,* August 21, 1972), p. 41.) See a similar call for their abolition by the Federal Judicial Center's Freund Committee Report, January 1973, *et seq.*

181

Court does *act* on each and every case of which it disposes, whatever the nature of that disposition. The large number of cases docketed and disposed of, representing a major increase in the work load over previous years, came almost entirely in the so-called *miscellaneous* cases, which are largely handwritten or typewritten papers filed by indigent persons, often prison inmates, and, unlike the formal petitions for *certiorari* on the appellate docket, need not follow a particular form or even contain material normally considered essential in petitions. This category of cases rose sharply, to a record of 1969. Indigents obtain authority to file from the federal *in forma pauperis* statute,[46] which gives to a citizen of the United States the right to enter proceedings in any federal court, provided he executes such an oath. Of course, this does not guarantee a Supreme Court review—although of the cases the Court heard in its 1973–74 term more than half came to it *in forma pauperis!* Of course, it did summarily vacate or reverse a fair number of other lower court decisions challenged by indigent persons. The purpose of this interesting statute clearly was to protect indigent persons—a large proportion of whom, according to a bitter remark by Mr. Justice Jackson, represent "our convict population." And Mr. Justice Douglas, certainly a sympathetic friend of the underdog, commented, in an address before the Cornell University Law School in April 1960, that the claims made in these pauper cases "are often fantastic, surpassing credulity . . . [and] are for the most part frivolous." Nevertheless, many vital criminal cases have reached the Court via this path—indeed, they have increased almost twentyfold since 1930, and today represent about one-half of all case filing's. Among them was the momentous *Gideon v. Wainwright*[47] in 1963, which resulted in the overruling of the *Betts v. Brady*[48] precedent which had stood for two decades. Clarence Earl Gideon had petitioned the Supreme Court for a writ of *habeas corpus* in a hand-penciled letter from his Florida prison cell.[49] Of the total number of 5079 cases filed during the 1973–74 term, 1203 were not disposed of, and thus went over to the 1974–75 docket. That residue represented the largest number of cases carried forward to a new term since the Clerk of the Supreme Court began to keep these statistics in 1930.

Although there is some disagreement among the Justices themselves on

[46] 28 USC 1915 (a). See also Supreme Court Rule 53.5.
[47] 372 U.S. 335.
[48] 316 U.S. 455 (1942).
[49] See the superb book on the *Gideon* case by Anthony Lewis, *Gideon's Trumpet* (New York: Random House, 1964), which, in addition to its basic story, is highly instructive in the judicial process.

the point, notably on the part of Douglas, who insisted time and again that the Court is "underworked—not overworked,"[50] most observers of the work of the Court believe firmly that it is overburdened with cases. In large measure, this is due to the flood of petitions that reach it; but to some degree it may also be due to the fact that the Court has persisted in taking cases which are at best trivial, sometimes dealing simply with matters of fact, without presenting any truly imperative constitutional questions. This, of course, is a matter of judgment. Yet it would seem that at least in tax cases or in railroad and maritime injury-negligence cases, particularly the latter, which usually involve a question of fact as to who was at fault in the accident, the Court has at times unnecessarily overextended itself in granting petitions for review. That a good many of the Justices feel quite strongly about the matter is indicated by a veritable stream of comments by Mr. Justice Frankfurter, who, in case after case in this field, would pen a comment to the extent that "the case . . . is so trivial that the Court should dismiss its grant of review as improvident." And in one dispute, answering in the affirmative the question whether a jury should hear the case of a wrench falling on a seaman's "left great toe," Mr. Justice Harlan, speaking for a minority of four Justices, delivered a three-page dissent that began:

> At the opening of a term which finds the court's docket crowded with more important and difficult litigation than in many years, it is not without irony that we should be witnessing among the first matters to be heard a routine negligence . . . case involving only issues of facts. I continue to believe that such cases, distressing and important as they are for unsuccessful plaintiffs, do not belong in this Court.[51]

Mr. Justice Frankfurter went even further here, contending the Court should not even have agreed to consider such an issue in the first place; and he once again voiced his long-standing lament against consideration of minor negligence cases. Among several suggestions advanced in 1972–73 by the blue-ribbon Study Group on the Case Load of the Supreme Court, usually referred to as the Freund Committee (after Prof. Paul A. Freund of Harvard University Law School), was one to abandon the appellate jurisdiction of the Court and leave a writ of *certiorari* as the only means of ob-

[50] E.g., again in an interview on December 7, 1972 (*The Daily Progress*, Charlottesville, Va., p. 2). His colleague Brennan formally seconded Douglas in an interesting article in 59 *American Bar Association Journal* 835 (August 1973), "Justice Brennan Calls National Court of Appeals Proposal 'Fundamentally Unnecessary and Ill Advised.'"
[51] *Michalic v. Cleveland Tankers, Inc.*, 364 U.S. 325 (1960), at 332–33.

taining review by the Supreme Court. In other words, direct appeals to the highest judicial body, whether from a one-judge court under the antitrust Expediting Act or from a three-judge court convened to consider the constitutionality of a state or federal statute, would be abolished other than via *certiorari*. Congress had the proposal before it again in 1974.

An intriguing, and possibly highly significant, decision by the Court during its 1960–61 term gave Mr. Justice Frankfurter additional reasons for expounding on the theme of unwise, non-jurisdictional, unnecessary case work. Over his lone fifty-eight-page dissenting opinion, the eight-man majority held that policemen and other local officials who violated a citizen's constitutional rights under the Civil Rights Act of 1871 could be sued for damage in *federal* courts *even if these officials acted without state authority*. Frankfurter in his dissent not only charged the majority with violating federal-state relationships—relying heavily on the legislative history of the act as he saw it to prove his point—but he also decried what he viewed as rank court interference. Envisaging a veritable flood of petitions, he insisted that the broad construction adopted here by the Supreme Court made the federal Constitution

> a law to regulate the quotidian business of every traffic policeman, every registrar of elections, every city inspector or investigator, every clerk in every municipal license bureau in this country.[52]

Whatever the number of cases docketed, it ought to be fairly obvious that the lawyer who grandiosely and proudly informs both his client and the public press that "we'll fight this case all the way to the Supreme Court," really means that *if* the funds are present he will *attempt* to do so—unless a pauper's oath is involved the standard case will consume a solid outlay of upward of $10,000—and *if* the Court will grant review he will *endeavor* to convince it of the righteousness of his client's case. An average case takes from two to five years to reach the highest bench. The preparation and printing of the record and the writing of briefs alone normally consume five months. Seldom does the Court actually *hear oral arguments* on more than 125 to 150 of the cases it disposes of annually; the balance is dismissed on procedural or some other jurisdictional ground. Of those actually heard, formal *written opinions* by the Court are usually handed down in 75 to 85 per cent of the cases, the others being decided *per curiam*—an anonymous opinion expressing the summary judgment of the Court as a whole and not the opinion of a single Justice with whom the others concur. In other

[52] *Monroe v. Pape*, 365 U.S. 167 (1961).

words, a *per curiam* is an *unsigned,* normally very brief, opinion for the Court, applying *res judicata* (settled law), its authorship unknown to the outside world—although, in Professor Schubert's opinion, "it seems probable that most . . . are written by the Chief Justice or for him by one of his . . . law clerks."[53] For example, it was employed in the initial disposition of the controversial 1972 *Capital Punishment Cases.*[54] Usually *per curiam* opinions are written for a unanimous Court, but there are exceptions. For instance, in 1966 Mr. Justice Clark wrote a formal dissenting opinion to the Court's *per curiam* in *Riggan v. Virginia*[55] in which he was specifically joined by his colleagues Black, Harlan, and Stewart. There, the now readily identifiable majority of five (Warren, Douglas, Brennan, White, and Fortas) reversed *without briefs or arguments* a lower court decision upholding the validity of a search warrant isued by a Virginia tribunal. Considerable criticism about the increasing resort to *per curiam* decisions has ensued. However, it may very well be that this simply represents an attempt by the Court to resolve the conflict between rendering fully reasoned opinions and affording the finality of Supreme Court ajudication to as large a number of litigants as possible. Or it may simply represent a stopgap expedient—such as the Court's *per curiam* decision in a group of obscenity cases in 1967,[56] an area that has deficd a firm, universally applicable rule of law—notwithstanding continuing attempts to determine one.[57]

Reconsideration. A petitioner whose request for review has bccn *denied* by the Court for one or more of the reasons discussed above is not, of course, barred from trying again. Accordingly, some sanguine souls are rather persistent in these efforts—although they rarely, if ever, succeed unless their new petition serves to convince four Justices of the merits of the renewed appeal. Among well-known illustrations of such unsuccessful attempts are the cases of Morton Sobell, convicted of complicity in the atomic espionage casc of Ethcl and Julius Rosenberg, and the doomed Caryl Chcssman. Sobell filed eight formal petitions for review of his con-

---

[53] Glendon Schubert, *Judicial Policy-making: The Political Role of the Courts* (Glenview, Ill.: Scott, Foresman and Co., 1965), p. 73. The statement concerning the role of the law clerks is subject to considerable doubt, however. (See, in this book, pp. 237–40, *infra.*)

[54] *Furman v. Georgia,* 408 U.S. 238.

[55] 384 U.S. 152.

[56] *Redrup v. New York, Austin v. Kentucky, and Gent v. Arkansas,* 386 U.S. 767 (decided together).

[57] See, for example, the Court's dubious try in a series of 5 : 4 decisions handed down in 1973. (*Miller v. California* 413 U.S. 15 and *Paris Adult Theatre v. Slaton,* 413 U.S. 49.)

viction between 1953 and 1958; all were denied by the Court without comment.[58] Chessman filed fully sixteen petitions for review with the Court between his conviction in 1948 for seventeen crimes (including kidnapping, attempted rape, sex perversion, robbery, and car theft) and his execution in 1960, prompting even Mr. Justice Douglas to comment: "The conclusion is inevitable that Chessman is playing a game with the courts, stalling for time. . . . This is not a case of a helpless man who was given no opportunity to participate in the settlement of the record."[59] Chessman's battle ended in failure only after he had filed a total of forty-two appeals with various federal and state courts! The struggle covered twelve years, caused extensive debates on the merits of capital punishment, and made Chessman's name a household word throughout the world.[60] A rare occurrence in this realm of the judicial process is a Court-*solicited* or -encouraged reconsideration, such as that specifically requested by the 1961–62 bench when, in granting review to prison inmate Gideon,[61] it requested argument on the specific *quaere*[62] whether it should now reconsider its 1942 ruling in *Betts v. Brady*.[63]

Rehearing. On the other hand, it is also possible for a *defeated* litigant to petition the Supreme Court for a *rehearing* within twenty-five days after the announcement of an unfavorable decision, in the dim hope that the Court, in the person of one or more of the Justices, may undergo a change of mind on rehearing the case. This is especially true when the original decision was a very close one and featured a sharply divided Court. But under the Court's

---

[58] He came close with his ninth attempt, in 1968, when he gained the votes of three of the necessary four Justices (Douglas, Harlan, and Brennan). He was released after his tenth appeal one year later.

[59] *Chessman v. Teets*, 354 U.S. 156 (1957), at 170.

[60] Chessman's record years on death row were exceeded in 1966 by the thirteen years spent by both Edgar Labat and Clifton Alton Poret, two blacks who had been convicted of raping a young white woman in 1950. However, not only were they released from death row, but they were ordered freed from jail by the Fifth United States Circuit Court of Appeals because they had been convicted by juries from which blacks were *systematically* excluded. Their death row record was exceeded in turn by Edgar H. Smith, freed in 1971 after having served more than fourteen years for the murder of a fifteen-year-old girl.

[61] *Gideon v. Cochran*, 370 U.S. 908 (1962).

[62] "Should this Court's holding in *Betts v. Brady*, 316 U.S., be overruled?" In *Betts* the Court had held 6 : 3 that indigent state criminal defendants are automatically entitled to state-furnished counsel *only in capital criminal cases*—unless certain "special circumstances" attended the case (and, in the Court's judgment, they did not in *Betts*).

[63] 316 U.S. 455 (1942). When the *Gideon* decision came down in 1963, *Betts v. Brady* stood unanimously overruled—in a triumphant opinion for the Court by Mr. Justice Black, one of the three dissenters in *Betts* (*Gideon v. Wainwright*, 372 U.S. 335).

186

rules, such a rehearing may not be granted unless a member of the *majority* in the original decision votes for one—and the Court in effect granted only six rehearings between 1940 and 1965, to cite an otherwise especially active quarter-century. Nevertheless, every litigant has the right to seek a rehearing.

A notable illustration of one of the infrequent successes gained by a petitioner on rehearing—one of but three such victories in the twenty-five year period indicated—was the group of "military justice" cases, involving Mesdames Clarice Covert and Dorothy Smith-Krueger, both civilians, who killed their unfaithful Master Sergeant and Colonel spouses with ax and knife, respectively, while with them at overseas bases. The cases were argued together at the bar of the Supreme Court initially in 1956, the constitutional issue being the validity of the section of the United States Uniform Military Code of Justice that authorized the military trial of civilians accompanying the armed forces abroad.[64] The Court upheld the disputed section in a 5 : 3 decision, delivered by Mr. Justice Clark, while the three dissenters—Warren, Black, and Douglas—protested they were being rushed at term's end; and Mr. Justice Frankfurter refused to participate other than to file a "reservation," because of "lack of adequate time to consider" the issues involved and "their complexity." Clearly, this was the type of decision in which counsel for defendants might well see a distinct hope for a rehearing. A motion for one was duly filed; it was accepted by a 5 : 3 vote, the three original dissenters and Mr. Justice Frankfurter being joined in approving the petition for rehearing by Mr. Justice Harlan, a member of the original majority.[65] Matters certainly seemed to look up for the widows!

The case was duly reargued early in 1957, and during the waning days of that term the Court handed down its decision, reversing itself by declaring the section in question unconstitutional by a 6 : 2 vote.[66] Only Justices Clark and Burton remained of the former majority; Justices Minton and Reed having retired from the Court; Mr. Justice Harlan having changed his mind; and a new member, Mr. Justice Brennan, joining the majority. The ninth member, Mr. Justice Whittaker, just appointed to replace Mr. Justice Reed, did not participate in the decision. It should be reemphasized, however, that a grant of a petition for rehearing is the exception to the rule. An indication of a possible chance for one, but certainly no assurance, is, of course, an officially announced change of mind from the bench—such as

[64] *Kinsella v. Krueger*, 351 U.S. 470 and *Reid v. Covert*, 351 U.S. 487 (June 11, 1956).
[65] *Reid v. Covert* and *Kinsella v. Krueger*, 352 U.S. 901 (November 5, 1956). On petition for rehearing.
[66] *Reid v. Covert* and *Kinsella v. Krueger*, 354 U.S. 1 (June 10, 1957). On rehearing.

Mr. Justice Douglas's announcement, in the *New York Prayer Case*,[67] that he *now* believed the *New Jersey Bus Case* of 1947, in which he had provided the crucial fifth vote,[68] to have been wrongly decided! Yet the latter has never been overruled.

Reargument. A related, but distinct, practice is an order for *reargument*, in which the Court—for reasons best known to itself—orders a case back on the docket for reargument rather than hand down a decision. At the end of what became known as the "libertarian 1956–57 term," it did this in ten cases that had already been briefed and argued before it. The famed *Segregation Cases*[69] represent a pertinent earlier example. Initially argued in December 1952, they were ordered reargued in December 1953 and were decided in May 1954. A more recent illustration is the aforementioned controversial water-dispute case between Arizona and California, which the Supreme Court ordered reargued in 1962—as an original jurisdiction case—despite the fact that the Court had spent a week hearing arguments in that complex litigation during the preceding January. A crucial reason for this order was Chief Justice Warren's voluntary disqualification—he had been Governor of California—coupled with Mr. Justice Frankfurter's illness and Mr. Justice Whittaker's retirement, Whittaker's successor—Mr. Justice White—not having heard the initial arguments. A decision was ultimately handed down, in June of 1963, with the Chief Justice not participating, but with both Mr. Justice Goldberg—who had replaced the then retired Mr. Justice Frankfurter—and Mr. Justice White taking part and siding with the 7 : 1 Black majority opinion.[70] A later petition for a rehearing by the "loser," California, was denied.[71]

THE UNITED STATES SUPREME COURT AT WORK

The concluding sections above illustrated a marginal function of the Court. But how does this most impressive and most dignified of all governmental bodies in the United States *generally* conduct its work? Since 1873 it has customarily sat for thirty-six weeks annually, from the first or second Mon-

---

[67] *Engel v. Vitale*, 370 U.S. 421 (1962), at 443.
[68] *Everson v. Board of Education of Ewing Township*, 330 U.S. 1.
[69] *Brown v. Board of Education of Topeka*, 347 U.S. 483 (1954), and *Bolling v. Sharpe*, 347 U.S. 497 (1954).
[70] *Arizona v. California*, 373 U.S. 546.
[71] 375 U.S. 892 (1963). *United States v. Brewster*, 404 U.S. 1055 (1972), which dealt with the range and extent of senatorial immunity, represents an even more recent and pertinent illustration of a reargument order.

day in October until the end of June. Now and then, as in the 1971 *Pentagon Papers Case* and in the dramatic Nixon Tapes ruling of 1974,[72] the Court may briefly extend its term because of the felt necessity to render a decision prior to adjournment. And on rare occasions, such as in the case involving the Little Rock, Arkansas, school desegregation crisis in August-September 1957[73] and the case of the seven German saboteurs in 1942,[74] a Special Session may be convened, although there have been only four such sessions in this century. Yet it must be stated at once that the business of judging, at least at the level of the federal government, is a year-round occupation, regardless of formal sessions.

All of the Court's sessions are now held in its own magnificent Greek-style, Corinthian-order, white marble structure, at 1 First Street, N.E., near Capitol Hill in Washington, D.C. The Court's present home,[75] constructed in 1935, was patterned after the Temple of Diana at Ephesus. The noble words "Equal Justice Under Law" are carved above the majestic entrance, over the great bronze doors. Its resplendent 82- by 91-foot courtroom has a 44-foot dome, supported by twenty-four Ionic columns of light Siena Old Convent marble from Liguna, Italy, and Ivory Vein marble walls from Alicante, Spain. The carvings on the walls depict both real and symbolic judicial figures (on one wall those of the pre-Christian era, on the other those of the Christian). Here convenes the Supreme Court of the United States, its nine Justices clad in black judicial vestments—which Judge Jerome Frank always wanted to banish.[76] They are seated behind the raised half-hexagon bench of marble and Honduran mahogany in high-backed swivel chairs of varying size which stand against a background of full purplish red draperies.

[72] *The New York Times Co. v. United States* and *United States v. The Washington Post Co.*, 403 U.S. 713, and *United States v. Nixon*, 417 U.S. 683, respectively.

[73] *Cooper v. Aaron*, 358 U.S. 1.

[74] *Ex parte Quirin*, 317 U.S. 1.

[75] The first term of the Supreme Court was the February Term, 1790. It began on February 2 of that year and was held in the Royal Exchange Building in New York City, which was then the seat of the federal government. In February 1791 it, along with the Capital, moved to the (now restored) Supreme Court Building on Fifth and Chestnut streets in Philadelphia; it met there and in City Hall until 1810, when it moved to Washington, to the office of the Clerk of the Senate (on the main floor of the East Wing of the then still unfinished Capitol Building). It remained there until its own chamber in that edifice was readied in 1808—although it had to meet briefly in private homes when the British had used Supreme Court documents to set fire to the Capitol. In 1860 it moved to what is now known as the "Old Senate Chamber," where it stayed until 1935, when the Cass Gilbert-designed present structure was ready for occupancy.

[76] See his amusing "The Cult of the Robe" in his classic *Courts on Trial: Myth and Reality in American Justice* (Princeton: Princeton University Press, 1949), Ch. XVIII.

FIGURE I
THE 1974–75 COURT
1. Mr. Chief Justice Burger

2. Mr. Justice Douglas	3. Mr. Justice Brennan
4. Mr. Justice Stewart	5. Mr. Justice White
6. Mr. Justice Marshall	7. Mr. Justice Blackmun
8. Mr. Justice Powell	9. Mr. Justice Rehnquist

10. The Clerk's Desk   11. The Marshal's Desk

12. Counsel's Desk

At the appointed hour, the drapes part and from behind them appears the Chief Justice, followed by the eight Associate Justices, *seriatim* in order of seniority. They, as well as all those assembled in the courtroom, remain standing until the Marshal has completed his time-honored introduction: "Oyez, Oyez, Oyez! All persons having business before the Honorable, the Supreme Court of the United States, are admonished to draw near and give their attention, for the Court is now sitting. God save the United States and this Honorable Court" (a remark that has been the butt of a number of tasteless jokes).[77] The Justices' seats are arranged according to length of continuous service on the bench; the Chief Justice sits in the center, flanked by the Senior Associate Justice on his immediate right, the second-ranking on his immediate left, then alternating in that manner in declining order of seniority.

ORAL ARGUMENT

In this impressive setting, guarded by its special thirty-three-man police detail on round-the-clock security, and attended by four high-school-age pages[78] (since 1963 mercifully no longer in knickers, long black stockings, and double-breasted jackets), the Court listens to oral arguments—in the cases it has agreed to hear—for the first four days in two weeks out of each month. Its Justices spend the other two weeks behind closed doors in consideration of cases and writing of opinions. Forty copies of the printed briefs of the oral arguments—one set going to each Justice[79]—have to be filed with

---

[77] At the Court's first session of each new term in October, the Chief Justice will announce, as Warren E. Burger did on that occasion in 1974: "I have the honor to announce that the October, 1974, term of the Supreme Court of the United States has convened." (October 7, 1974.)

[78] For the first time in its 182-year history the Court, in September 1972, appointed a *girl* page—fourteen-year-old Deborah Gelin of Rockville, Md.

[79] All printed documents filed in the Court must be 6⅛″ by 9¼″ in size, with type no smaller than 11-point, "adequately leaded," and the paper must be "opaque and unglazed."

the Clerk of the Court well in advance—to be exact, within forty-five days after the case is placed on the docket by the party bringing suit—and the answering brief has to be filed thirty days thence. The briefs, which are filed in accordance with prescribed format and are preferably no longer than twenty-five pages, generally state the facts, issues, questions to be presented, decisions of lower courts, and all relevant legal arguments, together with the statutes and citations of cases to which they apply. (As already explained, those bona fide paupers whose cases are treated on the special miscellaneous docket may file handwritten or typewritten briefs). Oral argument, now heard on designated days from 10:00 a.m. to noon and from 1:00 p.m. until 3:00 p.m.,[80] is at once the most significant and the most fascinating aspect of the *public* portion of the Court's work. (Of the 300 seats available, 112 are allotted to the press, the Justices' families, and members of the bar, the remaining 188 being available to the general public strictly on a "first come, first served" basis. Usually there are two public queues for those seats—one a three-minute-stay line, the other a "stay as long as you wish" one.) There is at least a chance that skillful oral arguments, in supplementing the printed brief by oral emphasis,[81] may sway members on the spot, although this is far less likely in the great than in the small cases. Still, first impressions count—and Mr. Justice Douglas, for one, has insisted that ". . . oral arguments win or lose the case."[82] The pressure on the arguing lawyers, who must speak from the floor level, is enormous, naturally. They are frequently questioned sharply by the Justices, who often have a bench memorandum prepared before the argument, and their questions may conceivably forecast the ultimate decision of the Court, although in few, if any, instances is it possible to give an accurate prognosis. Some Justices (e.g. Douglas) customarily ask very few questions; others (Frankfurter was a prime example) have a habit of asking a great many. John P. Frank reported that in one particular case he witnessed—perhaps a somewhat extreme illustration—the Justices interrupted counsel 84 times during 120 minutes of oral argument, with 93 questions and interpolations chargeable to Mr. Justice Frankfurter alone![83] Woe unto counsel who is ill-prepared or uncertain of himself—and the Justices frown on reading from

---

[80] From 1873 until 1961 the Court met from noon until 4:30, and from 1898 until 1970 it allowed but half an hour for lunch. Then Mr. Chief Justice Burger adopted the more humane break of one hour which is now in force.
[81] See John M. Harlan, "What Role Does Oral Argument Play in the Conduct of an Appeal?" 41 *Cornell Law Quarterly* 6 (1955).
[82] *The Philadelphia Inquirer*, April 9, 1963.
[83] *The Marble Palace* (New York: Alfred A. Knopf, 1958), pp. 104–5.

the prepared text. In fact, Rule 44 of the Court states that it looks "with disfavor" on such a practice. But the Justices may also well prove to be helpful to counsel. Thus, during one oral argument heard in the 1960–61 term, Mr. Justice Frankfurter sharply questioned an obviously flustered lawyer several times, only to see Mr. Justice Douglas intervene each time with a helpful answer! "I thought *you* were arguing this case," shot Frankfurter to the grateful counsel, who responded, "I am, but I can use all the help I can get."[84] It should be clear that the Court, as Frankfurter once put it, does not see itself as "a dozing audience for the reading of soliloquies, but as a questioning body, utilizing oral argument as a means for exposing the difficulties of a case with a view to meeting them."[85]

Unlike the old days, especially during Mr. Chief Justice John Marshall's reign, when argument seemed often interminable, and when a Daniel Webster would sometimes address the Court with mounting eloquence for days, present-day lawyers are severely limited in the time granted to them for argument. Normally, the limit is one hour for each side, sometimes merely a half-hour. One of the rare suspensions of the time limit rule took place in the case of *United Steel Workers of America v. United States*,[86] involving the legality of the injunctive provisions of the Taft-Hartley Act. In the average term only about 250 hours of argument are allotted to the attorneys for their oral presentations.[87] They use a lectern to which two lights are attached; five minutes before time is up a white light flashes; when the second light, appropriately a red one, flashes, the lawyer must stop instantly—unless he is granted permission by the Chief Justice to continue. According to one of Mr. Chief Justice Hughes's law clerks, the "Chief" was so strict on the score of time that he once stopped a leader of the New York Bar in the middle of the word "if"; and, on another occasion, upon being asked by the same attorney how much time remained, Hughes replied icily, "Fourteen seconds, Mr. Counsel."[88]

To argue cases at the bar of the Supreme Court a lawyer must be admitted to practice before it. This is now a relatively routine matter, one

---

[84] As reported by Anthony Lewis in "The Justices' Supreme Job," *The New York Times Magazine*, June 11, 1961, p. 31. (Italics supplied.)

[85] From "Memorial for Stanley M. Silverberg," in Philip Elman (ed.), *Of Law and Men* (New York: Harcourt, Brace & Co., 1956), pp. 320–21. (Which does not mean that there has never been any dozing on the bench!)

[86] 361 U.S. 49 (1959). Six hours were provided in that case. Another was *Arizona v. California*, sixteen hours (!), in January 1962. A third was *Brown v. Board #* 2 in 1955, for which fourteen hours were allotted.

[87] In the 1968–69 term, for example, 220 hours.

[88] Edwin McElwain, "The Business of the Supreme Court as Conducted by Chief Justice Hughes," 63 *Harvard Law Review* 6 (1949).

which requires two sponsors, three years of good standing before the highest court of a state, and payment of a $25 fee. Gone are the days, in vogue until 1970, when the Chief Justice would formally welcome and chat with each lawyer newly admitted to practice before the Court. The $25 "admission fee" is used by the Supreme Court to cover travel and printing expenses of Court-assigned lawyers who represent indigent parties that come before it. Admission may, however, be revoked—as occurred, for example, in the case of attorney Wilmer D. Rekeweg of Paulding, Ohio, in June 1967. Because of certain professional aberrations resulting in his disbarment from the practice of law in all courts of Ohio by order of the Supreme Court of Ohio, the Supreme Court of the United States, after a "show cause" procedure, suspended and then disbarred him in a special Order which read: ". . . it is ordered that the said Wilmer D. Rekeweg be, and he is hereby disbarred, and that his name be stricken from the roll of attorneys admitted to practice before the bar of this court."[89] A similar fate befell G. Gordon Liddy, one of the convicted "Watergate" burglars, who was disbarred late in 1973.

The Solicitor General. The *Solicitor General* is the third-ranking official in the U.S. Department of Justice, following the Attorney General and the Deputy Attorney General. Because of its special relationship to the Supreme Court, the post of Solicitor General has always enjoyed a high reputation in legal circles; has been eagerly sought by members of the legal profession; and has not infrequently been filled by legal scholars—viz., President Kennedy's 1961 appointment of Professor Archibald Cox of Harvard University Law School; President Johnson's of Cox's Dean, Erwin N. Griswold, in 1967 (succeeding Thurgood Marshall); and President Nixon's of Yale Law School Professor Robert M. Bork in 1973.

The Solicitor General is in charge of all of the government's litigation in the Supreme Court, which comprises in excess of 50 per cent of the Court's total work load. He and his staff argue all of the government's cases before it. His office supervises all government briefs filed in the Court, and he must personally approve, or disapprove, any case before the government takes it to the Court. Moreover, the Solicitor General—whose post pays $48,500 (1974)—has supervisory authority over other government appeals. Only if he gives his approval may the government appeal from an adverse decision in a trial court.[90] Sometimes, much to the chagrin of certain mem-

---

[89] "Actions in United States Supreme Court," June 5, 1967 (as reported in *The New York Times,* June 6, 1967). (Order 1346 Misc.)

[90] It must of course be remembered that both the federal and state governments are checked by the formidable Fifth (and Fourteenth) Amendment safeguards against double jeopardy.

bers of both the executive and legislative branches, the Solicitor General's office exercises its commendable tradition of alertness toward any unfairness in government cases. When he detects such unfairness, the Solicitor General will usually file a "Confession of Error" in the Supreme Court, in which he asks that it set aside a victory won by the government in the lower court. Although this practice is of the very essence of justice—which, after all, should be the aim of all litigation—it may be doubted that a large number of private counsel would be similarly willing to forgo a victory. All too frequently litigation is viewed as a courtroom battle between two opposing teams of high-powered trial lawyers bent upon "victory" rather than upon the triumph of justice.

BEHIND CLOSED DOORS

Each Friday during the Court's term is *Conference Day*.[91] On that day— there are about thirty each term of Court—the Justices, summoned by a buzzer five minutes before the hour, meet in a strictly closed session, usually from 10:00 a.m. until 5:30 or 6:00 p.m. with less than one hour for lunch, in the beautiful, oak-paneled conference chamber, under the chairmanship of the Chief Justice, whose offices are adjacent to it.[92] The role of the "Chief" is that of *primus inter pares*, although some have tended to be more *primus* than *pares*, and vice versa (as we shall presently see). Here the Justices discuss the cases they have heard, as well as all pending motions and applications for *certiorari*—although upwards of three-quarters of the latter are dismissed without even having merited conference discussion. Among petitions Mr. Justice Brennan thus considered frivolous in 1973 were the following propounded questions: "Are Negroes in fact Indians and therefore entitled to Indians' exemption from federal income taxes?" "Are the federal income tax laws unconstitutional insofar as they do not provide a deduction for the depletion of the human body?" "Is the Sixteenth Amendment unconstitutional as a violation of the Fourteenth Amendment?" and "Does a ban on drivers' turning right on a red light constitute an unreasonable burden on interstate commerce?" These are just some of the examples given in an August 1973 article in the *ABA Journal*. Each Justice is expected to be ready to indicate his tentative stand, which he normally will have noted on his copy of the agenda, having been previously advised which cases would be up for discussion—generally those just heard

[91] Until changed by Mr. Chief Justice Warren, Saturday was "Conference Day."
[92] Late in 1969, the new Chief Justice, Warren Burger, announced that henceforth the conference chamber would serve as the Chief Justice's official receiving room for Ambassadors and other visiting dignitaries, as his own office was too small.

by the Court on the four "argument days" during that week or those recently heard in the course of conferences meeting during the two recess weeks in which no oral arguments are presented. The conference "list" may run from 25 to 150 items; 75 is about normal. The importance of this traditional conference, or for that matter any conference of appellate judges at which law cases and controversies are reviewed, was well stated by Mr. Justice Jesse W. Carter of the California Supreme Court:

> . . . [The conference] is not a prayer meeting where everyone is expected to nod "amen"; it is more like a battleground where opposing philosophies meet in hand-to-hand combat.[93]

The Justices are seated around a large rectangular conference table, each chair bearing a nameplate. In accordance with a tradition established by Mr. Chief Justice Fuller in 1888, all will have shaken hands with one another on entering the room. The Chief Justice sits at the south end and the Senior Associate Justice at the north end. Three of the other Justices sit on one side, four on the other, but not necessarily in the usual order of seniority.[94] Looking down on this scene is the sole portrait in the room— that of Mr. Chief Justice John Marshall. The incumbent Chief Justice, whose personality and administrative talent loom large in these meetings, customarily gives his own view first in the case up for discussion, and he is followed by the other Justices in order of seniority. Each Justice must be prepared to recite and do so persuasively—if he feels strongly about an issue involved. Upon completion of this phase of their deliberations, the nine members of the Court take a tentative vote on the case, the Justice with the lowest seniority voting first this time, presumably so that he will not be influenced by the votes of his more experienced brothers—a somewhat debatable rationale. Each Justice has a hinged, lockable docket book, in which all votes are duly recorded.

The Role of the Chief Justice. Although he is theoretically merely *primus inter pares*—and he does have but one vote among nine—the "Chief" has a potential influence that may well outweigh that of any ordinary presiding officer. Mr. Justice Hughes suggested some reasons for this:

> Popular interest naturally centers in the Chief Justice as the titular head of the Court. He is its executive officer; he presides at its sessions and its conferences, and announces its orders. By virtue of the distinctive func-

[93] As quoted in *The New York Times*, March 16, 1959, p. 31.
[94] In a letter to the author, dated September 28, 1970, Mr. Justice Brennan described the Court's seating arrangement at that time as follows: "On the Chief's right sit Justice Marshall, myself and Justice Douglas in that order. On his left sit Justice Stewart, Justice White, Justice Blackmun, and Justice Harlan in that order."

tion of the Court he is the most important judicial officer in the world; he is the Chief Justice of the United States.[95]

Several of his functions lend themselves ideally to the exercise of that influence: One is the chairmanship of the Court's own conference, including his highly important role in the sifting of writs of *certiorari*, the other his assignment of opinions (to be more fully described later in this section). When the "Chief" opens discussion of a case by giving his own views first, he has an excellent opportunity to state the case as he sees it, to indicate the questions to be decided, and to give his opinions on the issue or issues involved. This "speak first" rule is a far from inconsiderable power, for there is a good chance that his initial analysis of a problem will have at least some influence on that of others in the room. It is, of course, by no means inevitable that the man who selects the issues to be discussed will dominate or determine the ultimate results—to which the lasting and profound differences in reading the meaning of the Constitution among Justices on a host of issues bear witness. Still, there is a chance, and often a good chance, that he may do so. An interesting example, gleaned from the Harold H. Burton papers, is Mr. Chief Justice Warren's role in speaking first in the Court's Conferences on the *1954 and 1955 Segregation Cases.*[96]

And there are other tasks, implied or actual, that confront a Chief Justice and play a role in history's regard of him as an effective or ineffective leader. Among them is his ability to keep peace among the several Justices, who are often deeply divided along intellectual as well as personal lines. Justices Jackson and Black, for example, became increasingly hostile during the waning days of Mr. Chief Justice Stone's tenure, resulting, or so it is believed, in President Truman's compromise "peacemaker appointment" of Fred Vinson as Stone's successor on the latter's death in 1946. Vinson, a person of far less judicial and intellectual stature than Stone, had a reputation as a conciliator and, apparently, succeeded at least in keeping the feud between the two Justices *en famille.* Mr. Justice McReynolds, a confirmed anti-Semite, refused even to speak to his newly appointed colleague, Mr. Justice Brandeis, from 1916 to 1919. Mr. Chief Justice White was unable to alter the situation, but the amiable and popular Mr. Chief Justice Taft apparently succeeded in mitigating it somewhat. Still, McReynolds caused Taft constant difficulties, too. For instance, he refused to sit for the Court's

---

[95] As quoted in *The New York Times,* June 24, 1969, p. 25.

[96] *Brown v. Board of Education of Topeka,* 347 U.S. 483 (1954); *ibid.* 349 U.S. 294 (1955); and *Bolling v. Sharpe,* 347 U.S. 497 (1954). See the account by S. Sidney Ulmer in *Courts as . . . Small Groups* (New York: General Learning Press, 1971), pp. 23–26; Warren obituary, *The New York Times,* July 11, 1974, p. 35A.

annual photograph in 1924 because he would have found himself seated next to Brandeis in seniority—and no photo was taken! And two years earlier he had refused to accompany the Court to a Philadelphia ceremony, writing to Taft: "As you know, I am not always to be found when there is a Hebrew abroad. Therefore, my 'inability to attend' must not surprise you."[97] Other McReynolds quirks were almost constant carping at practically every opinion authored by Stone, whom he disliked for philosophical reasons, and his overt hostility toward Mr. Justice John H. Clarke. McReynolds, who, as Wilson's Attorney General, had played a role in Clarke's appointment to the bench, felt "betrayed" because Clarke failed to vote on the Court as McReynolds thought he should and would. While he was by no means able to stop entirely the public barbs exchanged on the bench on occasion between, for example, Justices Frankfurter and Whittaker on the one hand, and Justices Black and Douglas on the other, Mr. Chief Justice Warren apparently smoothed over many a ruffled feeling, despite his personal involvement in an outburst or two, as some of the illustrations to follow will indicate. Yet it is vital to be aware of a basic fact of life on the Court: *no* Chief Justice can command the beliefs of his associates—and the Court has never really lacked for both strong personalities and strong convictions.

Another significant facet of the "Chief's" work is to keep an eye on the clock during the conference, with a view of getting its tasks accomplished. Although there has been disagreement on the extent of the Court's burden, there is little doubt that the pressure of case work is enormous. Unless a firm hand rules the conference, time will flee, especially as the Justices are, quite naturally, given to extensive speaking—Mr. Justice Oliver Wendell Holmes, Jr., interestingly enough, being a notable exception. No Chief Justice since Marshall controlled his flock so firmly as did Hughes, whom most students and observers of the Court, as well as those who served with him on the high tribunal, have generally regarded as the most effective—even if on occasion somewhat arbitrary—organizer, leader, and disciplinarian along these lines since Marshall's taut judicial regime.[98]

For example, Hughes would accord an average of three and one-half min-

---

[97] As quoted by Alpheus T. Mason in his *William Howard Taft: Chief Justice* (New York: Simon and Schuster, 1965), pp. 216–17.

[98] Which does not mean that even Hughes was able to control the idiosyncracies of the cantankerous Mr. Justice McReynolds, who, upon being informed by a messenger from the Chief Justice that it was time to convene for a Court session, sent the messenger packing with the reply that he did "not work for" the Chief Justice. As reported by James F. Simon, *In His Own Image: The Supreme Court in Richard Nixon's America* (New York: David McKay Co., Inc., 1973), p. 55.

utes of conference time, and no more, to a petition for *certiorari*—having himself gone through and thoroughly analyzed all of them *before* the conference and being fully prepared to make recommendations on each to his colleagues. And he would often force the end of a discussion that he viewed as unprofitable or dilatory by intoning: "Brethren, the only way to settle this is vote. So let us do just that—now." Mr. Justice Stone, whose philosophy of his role as "Chief" was drastically different, declined to put any time on either *certiorari* discussions or on a particular series of cases. Stone simply refused to engage in what he viewed as "high pressure tactics." Thus, where Hughes finished a conference docket in four hours, Stone would require four days for a similar docket. This did not make Stone a less qualified jurist, but it probably made him a far less effective "Chief" than Hughes— or Taft, another effective and popular Chief Justice, whose caliber, however, was certainly considerably below that of Stone as a *jurist*. (Taft was infinitely happier as Chief Justice than as President; he regarded the former office as possessing both more power and more prestige than the latter.) Some observers, although distinctly a minority, believe that the virtues of Hughes as Chief Justice were overstated and those of Stone underrated. One of these, John P. Frank, a law clerk for Mr. Justice Black, complained that Hughes's tactics of "business efficiency" meant that ". . . discussion in conference was perforce a statement of conclusions more than an exchange of mutually stimulating ideas . . ." and he charged the Chief Justice with "intellectual flexibility for the sake of the appearance of unanimity."[99] Be that as it may, Mr. Chief Justice Hughes was immensely popular as a leader of his bench, and he was the only member of the Court to whom Mr. Justice McReynolds would defer. We have Mr. Justice Frankfurter's word that ". . . if he made others feel his moral superiority, they merely felt a fact . . . all who served with him recognized [his] extraordinary qualities. . . . To see him preside was like [seeing] Toscanini leading an orchestra."[100] Mr. Justice Black attested to his own "more than impersonal and detached admiration [for Hughes's] extraordinary intellectual gifts."[101] And Mr. Justice Roberts wrote that "Men whose views were as sharply opposed as those of Van Devanter and Brandeis, or those of Sutherland and Cardozo, were at one in their admiration and affectionate regard for their presiding officer."[102] There is little, if any, doubt that Charles

[99] John P. Frank, "Harlan Fiske Stone: An Estimate," 9 *Stanford Law Review* 629n (1957).
[100] *Of Law and Men,* op. cit. pp. 133, 148.
[101] Black to Hughes, June 3, 1941. Hughes Papers.
[102] New York County Lawyers' Association, December 12, 1948.

Evans Hughes was the epitome of a great Chief Justice. And history may well place Earl Warren into a similar bracket—perhaps even higher, next to John Marshall. For to both Warren and Marshall the Court was more than "a mystically passive weigher of 'the law,' but also a participant, along with other agencies of the government, in the practical process of realizing the objectives set out in the Constitution's preamble."[103]

ASSIGNING AND WRITING OPINIONS

As Eugene V. Rostow wrote when he was Dean of the Yale School of Law, "Judges must write down their reasons for a decision because they are partners with us, the citizenry, in an agreed procedure for reaching responsible decisions.[104] The practice of writing the Opinion of the Court[105] goes back to the days of Mr. Chief Justice John Marshall. Prior to his adoption of this time-saving procedure, the Justices usually, but not always, delivered their opinions *seriatim*[106]—a practice still prevalent with the Law Lords of the British House of Lords, and one that Jefferson, as President, wanted to institutionalize in the face of Marshall's powerful objections. For Marshall believed that the Court's power and prestige would be enhanced if it were to speak with a single voice. Today, full opinions are written for the Court (some of these *per curiam*, as we have seen) in all cases heard by it on the merits, other than those decided by memorandum order. However, if there is a tie vote, no opinion is written, and the Court does not announce on which side of the tie the Justices stood. In the event of a tie vote, the decision of the highest court below, from whence the case came to the Supreme Court, is sustained; e.g. the Court's 4 : 4 vote in the case of *Bailey v. Richardson*[107] affirmed the 2 : 1 upholding of the loyalty dismissal of Dorothy

103 Alpheus Thomas Mason, "Judicial Activism: Old and New," 55 *Virginia Law Review* 424 (1969). Fred Graham placed Warren just below Marshall and above Taney in an interesting evaluative article, "180 Years of Chief Justices: Some Nonentities, Some Giants," *The New York Times*, June 24, 1969, p. 25.

104 *The Sovereign Prerogative: The Supreme Court and the Quest for Law* (New Haven: Yale University Press, 1962), p. 89.

105 John P. Frank, a careful observer and student of the Court, once divided the writing styles of the Justices into four categories: "legal lumpy," "legal massive," "rock-bottom contemporary," and "legal lucid." *The Marble Palace* (New York: Alfred A. Knopf, 1958), pp. 295ff.

106 A well-known illustration is the group of *seriatim* opinions by Associate Justices Chase, Paterson, and Iredell in the 1796 case of *Hylton v. United States*, 3 Dallas 171.

107 341 U.S. 918 (1951). For a recent illustration, see the Court's 4 : 4 split (Mr. Justice Lewis F. Powell, a prominent Richmond educational leader, abstaining) in the 1973 Richmond school consolidation case. (*School Board of Richmond v. Bradley*, 411 U.S. 913.)

Bailey by the federal government in the Court of Appeals for the District of Columbia. In this instance the even division of the Court came about as a result of Mr. Justice Tom Clark's failure to participate in the case; since he had been the United States Attorney General at the time of Miss Bailey's travail and dismissal, he deemed it unethical to be involved in the disposition of her appeal.

Abstentions. The members of today's Supreme Court, unlike most members of Congress, are extremely cautious about even the faintest taint of conflict of interest, be it of a social, economic, personal, or political nature. (Even though, as a fledgling member of the Court in 1972, Mr. Justice Rehnquist, notwithstanding the highly critical reaction of large segments of the legal and academic communities, refused to disqualify himself in at least three 5 : 4 decisions that had been within his jurisdiction as an official in the Justice Department prior to his appointment to the Supreme Court— but he did *not* participate in *United States v. Nixon.*) Among the Justices, "When in doubt, do not sit" is a firmly established custom, partially reinforced by two federal statutes and a canon of the American Bar Association.[108] This was not always so, particularly not in the early days of the Court —witness Marshall's refusal to disqualify himself in *Marbury v. Madison,*[109] in which he was personally and directly involved.

The work load of preparing opinions of the Court is usually very well distributed. If the Court is unanimous, or if the Chief Justice is in the majority, he may—and often does—write the opinion of the Court himself. In the latter instance, provided he speaks for at least four other Justices, it would be known as the *majority opinion.*

But, of course, nothing prevents him from asking another member of the Court, either when it is unanimous, or when he is on the side of the majority, to write the opinion. The only exception to this practice is the longstanding tradition of permitting every newcomer to the Court to select the first opinion he will write. Gone long ago are the days of Mr. Chief Justice Marshall who, especially during his early years on the bench, would himself write practically every opinion—no doubt at least partly because his fellow Justices were rather lethargic (some would say browbeaten). In fact, during

---

[108] For their exact verbiage, see Title 28, Sec. 454, U.S.C.A., Title 28, Sec. 455, U.S.C.A., and the Fourth Canon of the American Bar Association's Canons of Judicial Ethics. The frequent abstentions of the then still recently appointed Mr. Justice Thurgood Marshall in his first term on the Court (1967–68)—largely because he had been Solicitor General of the United States as well as a prominent civil rights attorney—caused considerable consternation. By the end of the first five months of the term he had abstained in 31 of the 44 formally decided cases!

[109] 1 Cranch 137 (1803).

his first four full years (1801–5) he personally authored all save two of the opinions of the Court![110] Mr. Chief Justice Warren, on the other hand, assigned 80 per cent of all the Court's opinions during his sixteen-year tenure.[111]

When the Chief Justice is on the minority side of a decision, however, the Senior Associate Justice on the side of the majority either writes the opinion of the Court himself or assigns it to one of the other members among the majority. All assignments are made by sending a formal note to the prospective author. The 1972–73 term serves as an illustration of an equitable distribution of the work load of preparing *opinions of the Court:* Mr. Chief Justice Burger led with nineteen opinions; Mr. Justice Powell wrote seventeen; so did Justice White; Justices Douglas, Stewart and Rehnquist, sixteen; Blackmun, fourteen; Brennan, thirteen; and Marshall, twelve. (Twenty-four opinions were *per curiam.*) Of the sixty-seven *concurring opinions* filed, Mr. Justice Blackmun led his brothers with eleven; Mr. Justice Stewart was next, with ten. Mr. Justice Douglas headed the Court in the 178 *dissenting opinions* filed, with fifty-three(!), followed by Justice Brennan, twenty-nine, Marshall and Rehnquist, twenty-one, Stewart, sixteen, White, fourteen, the Chief Justice, nine, Powell, eight, and Blackmun, seven. In all cases disposed of, whether by full opinion or memorandum order, the Justices cast six hundred and sixty-one dissenting *votes,* led by Mr. Justice Douglas, who wrote one hundred and seventy-three. As a rule, *unanimous opinions* are rendered in a minority of full opinion cases, averaging 25 to 30 per cent through the years; thus the Court was unanimous in 30.1 per cent of its full opinions again in its 1973–74 term. Memorandum orders, which, quite naturally, enjoy a far higher degree of unanimity, were up to 49.4 per cent.[112]

Dissenting Opinions. As these statistics demonstrate, dissenting and concurring opinions as well as simple dissents and concurrences are quite common.[113] Yet only when the former method of registering disagreement with the decision and/or the opinion of the majority is employed does the prac-

---

[110] In all, he wrote 519 of his Court's 1106 opinions, dissenting only nine times in his 34½ years on the high bench; and he wrote 36 of the 62 decisions involving constitutional questions.

[111] Ulmer, *op. cit., Courts* . . . (New York: General Learning Press, 1971), p. 22.

[112] Several good sources for these statistics exist; among others, the *Annual Report of the Director of the Administrative Office of the U.S. Courts,* and the law reviews, especially the November issue of the *Harvard Law Review.*

[113] Apparently there exists a tradition—albeit not an unbroken one—that precludes *any* qualifying opinion in a decision involving a new Justice's *first* opinion for the Court. See Wallace Mendelson's "Neo-Behavioralism—A Rebuttal," 57 *American Political Science Review* 952 (December 1963), fn. 7.

tice become meaningful for the governmental process. A simple *dissent*, without explanation, such as "Mr. Justice Butler dissents" in *Palko v. Connecticut*,[114] ranks as a vote on the other side; but it says little to the expert and layman alike, save that a Justice, for reasons known only to himself, chose to dissent. It is entirely possible, of course, for honest, competent men to arrive at sharply divided opinions in a case; hence, *dissenting opinions*, both short and long, are quite common. In fact, the first *reported* decision of the Supreme Court was rendered by a divided Court, Justices William Cushing and Thomas Johnson dissenting from the Court majority's grant of an injunction to Georgia.[115] As one of the best-known dissenters, Mr. Justice Holmes, said, "General propositions do not decide particular cases." One of the classic statements on the subject was made by the then ex-Associate Justice and future Chief Justice Charles Evans Hughes:

> A dissent in a court of last resort is an appeal to the brooding spirit of the law, to the intelligence of a future day, when a later decision may possibly correct the error into which the dissenting judge believes the court to have been betrayed.[116]

This from the pen of a jurist who rarely wrote dissenting opinions himself, who rarely dissented, and who exerted a greater dominance over the Court than any other Chief Justice save Marshall! Hughes often expressed the view that there is no reason to expect more unanimity on difficult problems of law than in the "higher reaches" of physics, theology, or philosophy. Mr. Justice Carter, the colorful state of California jurist mentioned earlier, was fond of observing: "I welcome dissents, for they test the soundness of my own opinions. . . . The dissenting opinion is . . . a forecast of things to come. The writers of dissents are usually men who look forward—not back, nor to the immediate present, but to the future."[117] Or, as Roscoe Pound once remarked, ". . . dissenting opinions may be the symptom of life in the law of time."[118] To Thomas Reed Powell they were ". . . most valuable equilibrators in the undulating course of the law."[119] And in his very last public statement on the last day of his sixteen-year tenure as Chief Justice of the United States, Earl Warren, responding to President Nixon, said:

[114] 302 U.S. 319 (1937).
[115] *Georgia v. Braisford*, 2 Dallas 402 (1792).
[116] C. Evans Hughes, *The Supreme Court of the United States* (New York: Columbia University Press, 1928), p. 68.
[117] As quoted in *The New York Times*, March 16, 1959, p. 31.
[118] "Preface," in *Justice Musmanno Dissents* (Indianapolis: Bobbs-Merrill, 1956).
[119] "The Logic and Rhetoric of Constitutional Law," 15 *Journal of Philosophy, Psychology, and Scientific Method* 654 (1918).

"We do not always agree [on the bench]. I hope the Court will never agree on all things. I am sure that its virility will have been sapped because it is composed of nine independent men who have no one to be responsible to except their own conscience."[120]

Many among the most memorable opinions of the Court initially on the dissenting side have eventually become majority opinions—especially some by famed spokesmen of erstwhile minority viewpoints, such as Justices William Johnson, Harlan, Sr., Holmes, Brandeis, Stone, and Black. One obvious example is the lone Harlan dissenting opinion in 1896, his eloquent remonstrance against the "separate but equal" doctrine in Plessy v. Ferguson[121] which became the unanimous opinion of the Court in 1954 in Brown v. Board of Education of Topeka.[122] Another is the lone dissenting opinion of Stone in 1940 in the Gobitis case;[123] Stone argued forcefully, but unsuccessfully, against the compulsory flag salute required by the Minersville, Pennsylvania, school district even from those who found it to be religiously objectionable. Scarcely three years later this became the opinion of the Court when a majority of six held a similar West Virginia Board of Education requirement to be an unconstitutional attachment of freedom of religion in the Barnette case.[124] Mr. Justice Cardozo, also a frequent dissenter, viewed the dissenting opinion as an entirely proper place for recording "the best inspiration of the time," for instruction in moral values still battling for general acceptance in the political process.[125] "It's grand to fight," once remarked Mr. Justice Black. "The Supreme Court does disagree. I hope it always will. It does have men who express their differences. I hope it always will have. Because I subscribe to the theory that there is no progress when differences are stifled."[126] It was Black who was given the honor of writing the opinion for the unanimous Court in the 1963 Gideon case, which extended to indigents the right to be furnished counsel in non-capital as well as capital criminal cases—a decision that overruled the Betts case of 1942 in which Black had vigorously dissented (joined by his brothers Douglas and Murphy).[127]

[120] As quoted in The New York Times, June 24, 1969, p. 1.
[121] 163 U.S. 537. Harlan's memorable words: "Our Constitution is color-blind, and neither knows nor tolerates classes among citizens" (at 559).
[122] 347 U.S. 483.
[123] Minersville School District v. Gobitis, 310 U.S. 586.
[124] West Virginia State Board of Education v. Barnette, 319 U.S. 624 (1943).
[125] Benjamin M. Cardozo, Selected Writings (New York: Fallon Publishers, 1947), p. 274. (Edited by Margaret E. Hall.)
[126] Quoted in The New York Times, June 5, 1961, p. 10.
[127] See fns. 47, 48, and 63, supra.

There is little doubt that a dissenting opinion is preeminently the result of a profoundly held conviction; consequently, it may well be regarded as strengthening rather than weakening the authority of a particular case. However, it may also serve to muddy the waters, to force extremist positions, and to confuse the public. For example, there are those students of the *Dred Scott* case—and not necessarily only the apologists for Mr. Chief Justice Taney—who contend that Taney's extremist position for the majority was a reaction to the extremist position taken by the politically ambitious Mr. Justice McLean in his dissenting opinion.[128] (It should be noted here that dissent is *much* less common in the fifty state courts, where the average rate of dissent at the highest appellate level is but one case in ten.)[129]

Concurring Opinions. At times the reasoning of the Justice assigned to write the opinion of the Court may not be palatable to all of the members of the majority side. In that event, one or more *concurring opinions* may be written—an increasingly frequent practice during the past few decades. Broadly speaking, it usually signifies the concurrence of its author in the *decision*, but not in the reasoning of the Court. One illustration would be the two separate concurring opinions of Justices Black and Douglas in the 8 : 0 decision of the Supreme Court in *Rochin v. California*.[130] While agreeing with the Court that the State of California had engaged in grossly brutal, and hence obviously illegal, conduct in its apprehension and conviction of Rochin, a narcotics peddler, the two Justices strongly disagreed with the *ground* on which the Court based its reversal of Rochin's conviction: violation of the due process of law clause of the Fourteenth Amendment of the U.S. Constitution. In the firmly held judgment of Black and Douglas, California had actually violated individual liberty safeguards specifically enumerated in the Bill of Rights—in fact thus contending, as they had done ever since their appointment to the Court in 1937 and 1939, respectively, that the specific provisions are per se applicable to the states (via the Fourteenth Amendment) as well as to the federal government.

[128] In his essay on "politically minded" Justices, Alexander M. Bickel calls McLean the "most notoriously so." See his *Politics and the Warren Court* (New York: Harper & Row, 1965), p. 135. Indeed, McLean was a presidential candidate of sorts five times: in 1832 as an Anti-Mason; in 1836 as an Independent; in 1848 as *both* a Whig and a Free-Soiler; in 1852 he refused the Native American party's nomination; in 1856 came his most serious candidacy, as a Republican. No doctrinaire he! See Francis P. Weisenburger, *The Life of John McLean: A Politician on the United States Supreme Court* (Columbus: Ohio State University Press, 1937).

[129] See the interesting article by Robert J. Sickles, "The Illusion of Judicial Concensus," 59 *American Political Review* 100 (March 1965).

[130] 342 U.S. 165 (1952).

Another example of the use of the concurring opinion is that by Mr. Justice Frankfurter—a frequent "concurrer"—in *Cooper v. Aaron* (*The Little Rock Case*),[131] which was decided in the Special Session in the summer of 1958. There, not only in order to show its continuous unanimity in cases basically following *Brown v. Board of Education*,[132] but also to make clear that those Justices (Harlan, Brennan, and Whittaker) who had not participated in *Brown* were at one with the remaining six members of that historic opinion, the Supreme Court issued its opinion in the form of a joint authorship, with the names of each of its nine unanimous members specifically listed *seriatim* at the head of the "Opinion of the Court." However, Mr. Justice Frankfurter was obviously deeply grieved and disturbed by the clear flouting of the law and the crass defiance of the federal judiciary by the officials of the State of Arkansas, led by Governor Orval E. Faubus, so much so that he was moved to write a separate concurring opinion, which was issued and published some weeks thereafter. In it, he gave what in effect was a profound and moving lecture to the country in general, and the South in particular, on the meaning of "the supreme Law of the Land" and the federal system. Written with scholarship and feeling, this independent statement nevertheless probably diminished somewhat the effect of the joint opinion of the Court. There are many legal scholars who are convinced that, whereas *dissenting* opinions are both eminently justifiable and necessary, *concurring* opinions are neither—that they are frequently nothing more than ego-manifestations and/or "quibbling," which would more profitably be confined to footnotes in the body of the majority opinion. Yet there is no doubt that the concurring opinion is a significant tool in the judicial process.

Techniques of Assignment. The preceding discussion raises the interesting problem of the selection of the opinion writers by the Chief Justice, or by the Senior Associate Justice when the duty of designation devolves upon him. Giving due attention to the need of distributing the work load relatively evenly (and, as explained earlier, permitting a Court newcomer to select his own first opinion to write), the average Chief Justice's assignments —approximately 80 to 85 per cent of the cases—may well be said to follow a fairly common pattern. It is a pattern, based upon the considerable influence that governs the actions of the "Chief" in making his selections, that will take account of all of the following considerations: First, the so-called "great," "big," or "important constitutional" cases—although these are necessarily somewhat subjective concepts—should be authored by the

131 358 U.S. 1 (1958).
132 347 U.S. 483 (1954).

"Chief" himself, e.g. Mr. Chief Justice Warren speaking for the unanimous Court in *Brown v. Board of Education*[133]—of which, as he was quoted after his retirement, he had written "every blessed word."[134] Or Mr. Chief Justice Hughes's majority opinion for the narrowly divided Court (5 : 4) in the immensely significant case of *West Coast Hotel Co. v. Parrish*,[135] upholding the State of Washington minimum wage law for women—sometimes, perhaps flippantly but probably not altogether unjustly, called "the-switch-in-time-that-saved-nine" case. Here the Court departed from its erstwhile stubborn adherence to the narrow construction of the concept of "freedom of contract" under the Fifth and Fourteenth Amendments to the Constitution by overruling the specific precedent of *Adkins v. Children's Hospital*[136] (in which it had struck down [5 : 3] a similar, though federal, law for the District of Columbia). That departure clearly indicated a change of position by the Chief Justice *and* Mr. Justice Roberts. The latter's switch was especially significant because before that he had normally represented the "swing vote" between the so-called pro- and anti-New Deal factions on the Court. His new stance heralded more or less clear sailing, at least on constitutional grounds, for the legislative programs enacted by the then still high-riding New Deal Roosevelt Administration. And in 1974 it was Mr. Chief Justice Burger who wrote the momentous opinion for his unanimous Court in *United States v. Nixon*.

Second, no matter what the importance of a case, the selection of a Justice to write the opinion must take into account the possible importance of the decision as a precedent. Justices may well differ in their views on whether the decision should be lodged on a broad or a narrow construction of the issue and on the ground on which the decision is to be based. For instance, the movie *Lady Chatterley's Lover* had been banned by the New York State Board of Regents on grounds of a statutory provision that forbade showing of films that present "acts of sexual immorality, perversion or lewdness" as being "desirable, acceptable, or proper patterns of behavior," and the Court agreed *unanimously* that the movie did not fall under that ban. But a majority of only five Justices (Warren, Black, Douglas, Brennan, and Stewart) would join in Stewart's opinion for the Court, holding that particular provision of the New York licensing statute to be unconstitutional as a violation of the Fourteenth and First Amendments. There

[133] Ibid.
[134] As quoted by James F. Simon, *In His Own Image: The Supreme Court in Richard Nixon's America* (New York: David McKay Co., 1973), p. 55.
[135] 300 U.S. 379 (1937).
[136] 261 U.S. 525 (1923).

were five *concurring* opinions, of which the principal opinion by Harlan (joined by Frankfurter and Whittaker)—while agreeing that the New York statute could not be validly applied in this case—argued that the Court should have reversed New York on *statutory construction* grounds without reaching the *constitutional issues*. Frankfurter also penned an individual concurrence, and Clark noted that he concurred "in the result." Black and Douglas, although members of the majority of five, joined one another in the two remaining concurring opinions, in which they contended that this statute, like all other prior censorship of movies, should be thrown out as being "unconstitutional on its face" as a prior restraint on freedom of speech and press.[137] Obviously, here the Chief Justice's assignment had to take into account which prospective authorship would be sufficiently acceptable, or least offensive, to five Justices—in this case, evidently Stewart's.

Third, although some observers would disagree, there is considerable evidence that the "Chief" is conscious of an element of "public relations" in designating his opinion writer. This is particularly true in cases that are undoubtedly going to be unpopular to a sizable segment of the population. In other words, he is not unmindful of the importance of making a decision acceptable to the public, or, when necessary, of coating the bitter pill that must be swallowed. A fascinating illustration of this point was brought to light by Professor Alpheus T. Mason in his fine biography, *Harlan Fiske Stone: Pillar of the Law*.[138] In 1944 the Court conference on the Texas "White Primary" case, *Smith v. Allwright*,[139] had clearly evidenced that all of the Justices save Roberts were agreed that this constitutionally challenged Texas statute was unconstitutional as a violation of the Fifteenth Amendment. The South was bound to react with great vehemence. Mr. Chief Justice Stone assigned the opinion to Mr. Justice Frankfurter, an eloquent stylist and a profoundly serious and scholarly jurist, not given to pamphleteering. One day after the conference, having discussed his strong misgivings with some of the Justices, Mr. Justice Jackson—a good friend of the principals involved—wrote a highly unusual, and, indeed, probably quite unprecedented, letter to the Chief Justice, candidly and fervently suggesting that the nature and the importance of the issue in the case were so far-reaching and made of such emotional matter that the Frankfurter selection was bound to "grate on Southern sensibilities." He explained:

---

[137] *Kingsley International Pictures Corporation v. Regents*, 360 U.S. 684 (1959)—which featured a total of six opinions.
[138] (New York: The Viking Press, 1956), pp. 614–15.
[139] 321 U.S. 649 (1944).

> Mr. Justice Frankfurter unites in a rare degree factors which unhappily excite prejudice. In the first place, he is a Jew. In the second place, he is from New England, the seat of the abolition movement. In the third place, he has not been thought of as a person particularly sympathetic with the Democratic party in the past.[140]

Jackson went on to point out that he realized that a consideration of every one of the listed factors was utterly distasteful, and that he mentioned them only with the greatest reluctance and "frank fear of being misunderstood." He had, of course, discussed the matter with Frankfurter and had advised him of his intention to write to the Chief Justice. Evidently persuaded by Jackson's argument, Stone, with Frankfurter's knowledge and agreement, substituted Mr. Justice Stanley Reed, who was: (a) an old-line Kentuckian; (b) a Protestant; (c) a native-born, in contrast to Mr. Justice Frankfurter, who had been born in Vienna; and (d) a Democrat of long standing. This did not render the wounds of the South any less severe, but at least they were administered, in a manner of speaking, by a one-time kinsman.

In the same general vein, the Chief Justice will normally make it a practice to assign so-called "liberal" opinions of the Court to "conservative" Justices and so-called "conservative" opinions to "liberal" Justices—again in the hope of making them more palatable. Thus, Mr. Chief Justice Stone assigned to one of the Court's leading liberals, Mr. Justice Black, the majority opinion in what has been widely labeled as the worst racist decision in this century's history of the tribunal, *Korematsu v. United States*.[141] There the Court upheld 6 : 3 the forcible exclusion of 112,000 persons of Japanese ancestry, including 77,000 native-born American citizens, and their removal from their West Coast homes to inland war relocation centers. Although not one of these evacuees had been specifically accused of disloyalty, the Black opinion upheld the exclusion order as a valid emergency measure necessitated by the facts of life of wartime, as an "exercise of power of the government to take steps necessary to prevent espionage and sabotage in an area threatened by Japanese attack." When the Court, in a 7 : 1 opinion in 1957, severely limited the application of the Smith Act in the prosecution of Communist party leaders and members, Mr. Chief Justice Warren assigned the case to a member usually found on the "conservative" side, Mr. Justice Harlan.[142] And when the Court, in the emotion-

---

[140] Mason, loc. cit. p. 615. Mr. Justice Frankfurter was not exactly pleased about the publicity given this event.
[141] 323 U.S. 214 (1944).
[142] *Yates v. United States*, 354 U.S. 298.

charged field of religion, in 1963 decided 8 : 1 that no state or locality may either require or sanction the recitation of the Lord's Prayer or the reading of verses from the Holy Bible in the public schools, the Chief Justice assigned that delicate case to Mr. Justice Clark, a Presbyterian who was active in the affairs of his church. (He was joined, in separate concurring opinions, by the Court's only Catholic, Mr. Justice Brennan, and its only Jew, Mr. Justice Goldberg).[143] Such strategy, if that it be, is not always employed, but it is resorted to with sufficient regularity to make a distinct pattern, mild and unpredictable though it may be.

Fourth, when the conference has indicated a split decision, no matter how many Justices may be in the latent minority, the Chief Justice will endeavor to assign the opinion to a Justice whose views come closest to the would-be dissenters, without, however, being one of them. The theory here is that the Justice would, in this case—and probably in others—be a "center Justice," whose "middle" approach would be acceptable, more or less, to both majority and minority.[144] For example, in *United States v. Butler*[145] a majority of six declared the Agricultural Adjustment Act of 1933 unconstitutional, as an illegal use by Congress of its powers over taxation and commerce at the expense of the principle of "dual federalism." This was one of thirteen New Deal laws or provisions thereof that the Court would invalidate on constitutional grounds in little more than one year's time during 1935–36. Reasoning that an opinion by one of the four "ultra-conservative" justices—Butler, McReynolds, Van Devanter, and Sutherland—would only serve to increase the fury of both the executive and legislative branches, Mr. Chief Justice Hughes assigned Mr. Justice Roberts to speak for the Court. The latter wrote an opinion that adopted the broad Hamilton-Story interpretation of the "general welfare" clause of the Constitution (I-8-1), but struck down the particular tax at issue as substantially an illegal regulation of local affairs. There is evidence that the Chief Justice went along with the majority only because Roberts wrote the opinion—and there was enough in that opinion to permit the minority of three, and their allies on both ends of Pennsylvania Avenue, to nourish hopes for a better day! It came scarcely a year later.

The critical role of the Chief Justice in assigning opinions is thus axiom-

---

[143] *Abington School District v. Schempp* and *Murray v. Curlett*, 374 U.S. 203.

[144] For an able and extensive discussion of this and related points, see the interesting paper by David J. Danelski, "The Influence of the Chief Justice in the Decisional Process of the Supreme Court," presented at the 1960 American Political Science Association Meeting, New York City, September 9, 1960.

[145] 297 U.S. 1 (1936).

atic. Much depends upon his skill, diplomacy, tact, and sheer powers of persuasion. On retiring, Mr. Chief Justice Warren was frankly proud of the record of "his" Court on that score: "During all the years I was there I never had any of the Justices urge me to give them opinions to write, nor did I ever have anyone object to any opinion that I assigned to him or anyone else."[146] No other "Chief," in the opinion of Mr. Justice Frankfurter, a long-time member of the bench who served under four Chief Justices and knew three others, "equalled Chief Justice Hughes in the skill and wisdom and disinterestedness with which he made his assignments." Pointing out that Hughes's governing consideration was always "what was best for the Court as to the particular situation," he closed his observations with this wise admonition:

> The grounds for the assignment may not always be obvious to the outsider. Indeed, they are not always so to the members of the Court; the reasons normally remain within the breast of the chief justice. But these involve, if the duty is wisely discharged, perhaps the most delicate judgment demanded of the chief justice.[147]

Yet no matter how hard he may try, or how skillful he may be, a Chief Justice cannot compel unanimity. As we have already seen, separate opinions are the rule rather than the exception. It is thus not at all uncommon to find five, six, seven, eight, and occasionally even nine opinions in a single case. The *Dred Scott Case*,[148] the *Licence Case*,[149] the 1971 *Pentagon Papers Case*,[150] and the 1972 *Capital Punishment Cases*[151] each featured nine such opinions! The *Steel Seizure Case*[152] had seven; the *Connecticut Birth Control Case*,[153] *Baker v. Carr*,[154] and the 1973 *Abortion Cases*[155] each six;

146 Comment to Anthony Lewis, "A Talk with Warren on Crime, the Court, the Country," *The New York Times Magazine*, October 19, 1969, p. 130.
147 *Of Law and Men*, op. cit. pp. 137, 142. Frankfurter regarded Marshall, Taney, and Hughes as the greatest Chief Justices.
148 19 Howard 393 (1857): Taney (Opinion of the Court); Wayne, Nelson, Grier, Daniel, Campbell, and Catron (Concurring Opinions); and McLean and Curtis (Dissenting Opinions).
149 7 Howard 283 (1849).
150 *The New York Times v. United States* and *United States v. The Washington Post*, 403 U.S. 713.
151 *Furman v. Georgia*, 408 U.S. 238.
152 *Youngstown Sheet & Tube Co. v. Sawyer*, 343 U.S. 579 (1952).
153 *Griswold v. Connecticut*, 381 U.S. 479 (1965).
154 369 U.S. 186 (1962).
155 *Roe v. Wade*, 410 U.S. 113, and *Doe v. Bolton*, 410 U.S. 179.

Dennis,[156] the *Bible Reading Cases,*[157] and *Ginzburg v. United States*[158] each five opinions. The practice of writing separate opinions may be valuable and intriguing, yet it hardly lends itself to certainty in the judicial process. However, certainty is not inevitably an end in itself; indeed, certainty and unanimity in the law are generally possessed only under a dictatorial system of government—to which, in fact, they are indispensable.

Drafting and Circulating Opinions. Following the assignment of opinions—which does not take place at the Conference itself, but formally, in writing, a few days thereafter—the laborious task of drafting commences. The power of persuasion by the author, presumably actively supported by the Chief Justice, whenever feasible, looms large in this phase of the judicial decision-making process. An opinion, as Mr. Justice Holmes once commented, must not only be informative and persuasive, it must show that the ". . . judge can dance the sword dance; that is he can justify an obvious result without stepping on either blade of opposing fallacies."[159] Again, we know but little of what takes place during these backstage activities, but from those few sources that are available—papers, biographies, former law clerks, various memoirs, and, lately, the research of persistent political scientists[160]—we do acquire an outline of this terminal phase of the preparation of a Supreme Court opinion, collective as an end product but with the distinct imprint of the minds and labor of nine individuals. As opinions are drafted, and on whatever side of the tentative decision they may be, printed "proof" copies are circulated by their authors among the members of the Court. These copies—indeed all of the Court's publications—are composed by a special unit of printers who labor in secrecy (to the extent of locking themselves in during working hours) and utilize the basement of the Court building for their work rather than the Government Printing Office. A private Supreme Court library, with a staff of fourteen and all conceivable facilities, is at the disposal of the Justices and their law clerks at all times.

Depending upon comments by his brothers, an author of an opinion may

---

156 *Dennis v. United States,* 341 U.S. 494 (1951).
157 *Abington School District v. Schempp* and *Murray v. Curlett,* 374 U.S. 203 (1963).
158 383 U.S. 463 (1966).
159 Alpheus T. Mason, reviewing *The Holmes-Einstein Letters* (New York: St. Martin's Press, 1965), in *The New York Times Book Review,* November 22, 1964.
160 See, for example, some of the important work concerning the innards of the Conference by lawyer-political scientists David J. Danelski of Cornell University and Walter F. Murphy of Princeton University. See also the excellent article by J. Woodford Howard, Jr., "On the Fluidity of Judicial Choice," 52 *American Political Science Review* 43 (March 1968) which, relying heavily on the Murphy papers, provides fascinating and important insights.

draw additional drafts in an attempt to gain adherence, or a concurrence rather than a dissent; or he may use any one of the other devices that may soften disagreement where disagreement exists, or make more forceful an opinion where unanimity seems attainable. Mr. Justice Brennan reported that once he circulated ten printed drafts before one was accepted as the Opinion of the Court.[161] This labor of persuasion is undertaken irrespective of how the several Justices may have voted in conference, the theory being that there is always hope for their views to win out in future years. The process of opinion writing is frequently a difficult and laborious task, sometimes running into months, occasionally even years. The opinion for *Brown v. Board of Education* was in various stages of writing from 1952 to 1954, probably largely owing to Mr. Chief Justice Warren's herculean efforts to obtain not only a unanimous Court, but also a single opinion, undoubtedly a delicate and difficult matter on the subject at issue—the declaration of unconstitutionality of compulsory racial segregation in the public schools.[162] Although still very much a case of conjecture, apparently the last holdout on the Court was Mr. Justice Reed. It is certain that this decision was the collective product of inordinately painstaking labor.[163]

We do know of many specific cases of persuasion—"bargaining" would not at all be an inappropriate term here—thanks to the papers left by the Justices. In one instance, Mr. Justice Butler, who had voted in conference to reverse the decision of the lower court, evidently succumbed to the persuasive powers of his colleague Stone. Sending a copy of his "surrender" to Mr. Chief Justice Taft, who ever tried to turn a dissenting opinion into silent acquiescence, he wrote to case-author Stone as follows:

> I voted to reverse. While this sustains your conclusion to affirm, I still think reversal would be better. But I shall in silence acquiesce. Dissents seldom aid in the right development or statement of the law. They often do harm. For myself I say: "lead us not into temptation."[164]

It is quite clear that all of the Justices, at one time or another, are thus will-

161 "Inside View of the High Court," *The New York Times Magazine*, October 6, 1963.
162 For a surprising view that strongly *disapproves* of this obviously so deliberately planned and achieved unanimity, see Charles S. Hyneman, *The Supreme Court on Trial* (New York: Atherton Press, 1963), pp. 211–14.
163 According to Yale Law Professor Fred Rodell, three Justices (evidently Reed and Jackson plus either Burton, Clark, or Minton) came close to dissenting, and the bare minimum of four had voted to grant *certiorari* in the case. See his "It is the Earl Warren Court," *The New York Times Magazine*, March 13, 1966, p. 93.
164 As quoted by Danelski in "The Influence of the Chief Justice in the Decisional Process of the Supreme Court," pp. 19–20. See fn. 144, *supra*.

ingly constrained by group and institutional concerns.[165] About another and later Stone opinion, Mr. Chief Justice Hughes wrote to him: "I choke a little at swallowing your analysis, still I do not think it would serve any useful purpose to expose my views."[166] Although, as Chief Justice, Stone exercised far less persuasive pressure than Hughes, he did work for unanimity whenever possible. At times, this would involve—as it does quite frequently—a switch from a decisional ground initially agreed upon to another. For example, in one of the cases brought during Stone's tenure, *Edwards v. California*,[167] he successfully persuaded Mr. Justice Byrnes to change his conference vote. Now delivering the opinion of the Court, Byrnes's switch resulted in adopting a *ground* for the decision on which five members of the Court could agree—the interstate commerce, rather than the "privileges and immunities" clause of the Constitution. Four Justices concurred in the decision, thus rendering it unanimous, but indicated their preference for the latter ground. An extreme example of the drive for agreement was provided in a difficult double jeopardy case in 1959, when Mr. Justice Brennan wrote the opinion of the Court *and a separate opinion* in which he expressed views he had evidently been unable to persuade his colleagues to accept, stating that ". . . it cannot be suggested that in cases where the author is the mere instrument of the Court he must forego expression of his own convictions."[168] It is essential to recognize that Justices may shift positions between the Conference and their final vote—a "testament," as Prof. Howard put it, "to the limitations of conference and the effectiveness of the argumentation system."[169]

Much of what has been said of the backstage give-and-take is documented by an excellent study by Professor Alexander M. Bickel of Yale University Law School—who was one of Mr. Justice Frankfurter's law clerks—titled *The Unpublished Opinions of Mr. Justice Brandeis*.[170] Based on the private papers of Louis Dembitz Brandeis as they relate to his career as Justice of

---

[165] See Howard's article, *op. cit.*, for ample corroborative evidence on this point.

[166] Danelski, *loc cit.* at p. 21. The case was *Sanford v. Commissioner*, 308 U.S. 39 (1939).

[167] 314 U.S. 160 (1941).

[168] *Abbate v. United States*, 359 U.S. 187 (1959), at 196, fn. 1. Other similar illustrations which are cited by Brennan are the actions of Mr. Justice Jackson in *Wheeling Steel Corporation v. Glander*, 337 U.S. 562 (1949), at 576, and those of Mr. Justice Cardozo in *Helvering v. Davis*, 301 U.S. 619 (1937), at 639–41.

[169] *Loc cit.* p. 47. (Mr. Justice Brennan told me that post-Conference "line-up" switches are far more common than is generally believed.)

[170] (Cambridge, Harvard University Press, 1957.) Subtitled, *The Supreme Court at Work*.

the Supreme Court of the United States from 1916 to 1939, the book is rich in illustrations of the persuasive processes that accompany the drafting of opinions for ultimate delivery. One or two examples will suffice: A photograph of a note from Holmes to Brandeis indicates that Holmes had revised his opinion in *Bullock v. Florida*[171] by adopting the result Brandeis had urged upon him. Having been persuaded by Brandeis's point of view, Holmes did so willingly enough; but his note showed much concern lest his changed opinion cause dissatisfaction among the former majority and perhaps result in a reassignment of the case to someone else. That did not happen, however.[172]

In another instance, it was Brandeis's turn to give in. He had felt quite strongly about the construction of a statute at issue in a 1924 railroad case opinion, which had been assigned to Mr. Justice McReynolds.[173] In discussing the case some years later with the then Professor of Law Felix Frankfurter, Brandeis said that he had told the Chief Justice (Taft) that "he couldn't stand for" McReynolds's opinion, that it contained too much that would "bother us in the future." Mr. Justice Van Devanter, continued Brandeis,

> worked with McReynolds and made changes, and the Chief asked me whether that will remove my sting. The corrections weren't adequate, and finally the Chief took over the opinion and put out what is now the Court's opinion and I suppressed my dissent, because, after all, it's merely a question of statutory construction and the worst things were removed by the Chief.[174]

On the other hand, the persuasion *cum* bargaining may well be blunt and direct, as evidenced by a memorandum sent by the usually gentle Mr. Justice Stone to Mr. Justice Frankfurter: "If you wish to write [the opinion] placing the case on the ground which I think tenable and desirable, I shall cheerfully join you. If not, I will add a few observations for myself."[175]

Toward the End Product. By far the most important fact revealed by this glimpse into the Supreme Court's inner sanctum is that many, if not all, of the Court's opinions, though ostensibly the work of one man, are really the product of many minds, in the sense that the Justice who writes the opinion

[171] 254 U.S. 513 (1921).
[172] Bickel, loc cit. insert between pp. 118–19, last photographic plate.
[173] *Railroad Commission of California v. Southern Pacific Railway Co.*, 264 U.S. 331.
[174] As quoted and described by Bickel, loc cit. pp. 209–10.
[175] Quoted by Mason in *Harlan Fiske Stone*, op. cit. p. 501. (Stone's letter was dated January 20, 1941.)

often has to add to, delete, or modify his original draft in order to be able to retain the support of his colleagues, many of whom are far from agreeing with him or with each other. If this involves changes of mind, even reversals, so be it—such behavior is very human. In fact, one close student of the Court's 1940 decade was tempted to avow that hardly any decision during that period "was free from significant alteration of vote and language before announcement to the public."[176] Moreover, studies based on the Justices' papers make abundantly clear that Justices of *all* ideological persuasions ponder, bargain, and argue in the course of reaching their decisions —even at the risk of compromising their ideologies.[177] Those who see facile niches and categories for the Justices may need to do a bit more applied research. It is essential to recognize that each member of the Court participates in each and every stage of the consideration of a case. Once we grasp this, we can readily understand why a considerable number of the Court's decisions are vague or contain several apparently contradictory statements. Since the views reflected in a given opinion are rarely identical, it may well turn out to be either ambiguous or maintain several varying postures, in order that each man who supports it will be able to reconcile it with his own particular position. A pertinent example is the laborious forging of Mr. Chief Justice Stone's majority opinion in *In Re Yamashita*,[178] in which the Court upheld the conviction by a United States military commission of the Japanese general who was accused of violating the laws of war in failing to prevent his troops from committing atrocities against American and Philippine citizens. The decision is quite unclear on the question of whether the due process clause of the Fifth Amendment is binding on such a military commission. On the whole, the opinion tends to give the impression that the answer to this question is in the negative, but some slight support can be found for the contrary view. According to Professor Mason, Stone's biographer, the latter's original draft contained the assertion that Yamashita's trial would have to adhere to the requirement of this clause. However, to meet at least in part the objections of Justices Black and Reed, who apparently were of the opinion that these commissions were not bound by the provisions of the due process clause, Stone deleted the assertion and made some confusing additions which Black and Reed could more or less reconcile with their own views on this matter.[179] The end product, though it did

---

[176] *Howard*, op. cit. p. 44.
[177] See, for example, *ibid.* pp. 55–56.
[178] 327 U.S. 1 (1946).
[179] Mason, op. cit. pp. 667–69.

not entirely satisfy either its readers or the bench as a whole, at least had the virtue—if that it be—of receiving the support of the majority of the Court.

Secrecy of Deliberations. Even though these various data undoubtedly are intriguing and are important to an understanding of the Supreme Court, the absolute secrecy that attends the backstage work and deliberations of the Supreme Court—the "Purple Curtain," as Professor Fowler Harper once called it—is essential. Until 1910 it was customary for two page boys to be present, but since that time (the Justices suspected a "leak" by one or more of the pages in a decision) no one save the nine Justices is present in the conference; no record of the discussions is kept. When clerks bring messages, the Justice who is junior in seniority—no matter what his chronological age—goes to the door to get them. There simply are no leaks. This is not to say, however, that no leaks have ever occurred. The most serious of these on record came in connection with the *Dred Scott* case.[180] There not only did the pro-slavery Mr. Justice John Catron evidently tell President-elect James Buchanan the "line-up" of the Justices in the pending decision one month prior to its announcement, but segments of the Northern press published the dissenting opinion of Mr. Justice Curtis. The incoming President, troubled and weak, used the Catron information in his inaugural address on March 4, 1857, and told the country that the Court would soon settle the much disputed territorial question. Two days later Mr. Chief Justice Taney delivered the 7 : 2 opinion of the Court—which, as history proved all too soon, did anything but settle the problem. Indeed, it acted as a catalyst in bringing on the Civil War.

However, that instance was a rare and crass exception. Complete secrecy does, and must, exist. The Court can neither open its backstage deliberations to the public nor hold news conferences. To do either would fatally affect its position as well as its effectiveness. For a description of what goes on behind the doors, we depend almost entirely on the kind of papers and biographies of the Justices discussed above, duly analyzed by scholars; and, on occasion, on revelations, usually appearing after the death of the Justice involved, by their former law clerks. Yet even these revelations are more often than not confined to matters of procedure. This is emphatically as it should be. We know enough of the operation and functions of the highest court in

---

[180] *Dred Scott v. Sandford,* 19 Howard 393 (1857). See Stanley I. Kutler, *The Dred Scott Decision: Law or Politics* (Boston: Houghton Mifflin Co., 1967), and Vincent C. Hopkins, S. J., *Dred Scott Case* (New York: Atheneum, 1967), for two thorough analyses of the case.

the land to enable us to appreciate, study, and, we hope, understand them in the context of the Court's significant role in the process of free government. To repeat, the secrecy of the Court's proceedings behind that "Purple Curtain" is a necessary by-product of its work. In a widely read article endeavoring to explain Mr. Justice Roberts's famous so-called "switch-in-time" to the side of the "liberals" on the Court in 1937, Mr. Justice Frankfurter viewed the Court's reticence in these terms:

> Disclosure of Court happenings not made public by the Court itself, in its opinions and orders, presents a ticklish problem. The *secrecy that envelops the Court's work is not due to love of secrecy or want of responsible regard for the claims of a democratic society to know how it is governed.* That the Supreme Court should not be amenable to the forces of publicity to which the Executive and the Congress are subjected is essential to the effective functioning of the Court. But the passage of time may enervate the reasons for this restriction, particularly if disclosure rests not on tittle-tattle or self-serving declarations. . . .[181]

OPINION DAY

The final stage in the Supreme Court's decision-making process occurs on *Opinion Day.* On that important occasion, usually[182] on three Mondays of each month during the term, the entire Court meets in solemn public session and announces, or "hands down," the decisions it has reached. Other than those disposed of *per curiam* or decided by memorandum order, the now made-public cases—all of which are filed with the Clerk of the Court—cover the full reasoning of the Court and set forth all viewpoints expressed by the Justices. Commencing with the junior Justice, and proceeding in order of seniority, the various opinions are either read verbatim or are paraphrased or summarized by their authors as the spirit and the occasion may dictate; sometimes simply the decision is given. Mr. Justice Whittaker read from his text, while Mr. Justice Frankfurter never looked at his, but would

---

[181] "Mr. Justice Roberts" 104 *University of Pennsylvania Law Review* 313 (1955). (Italics supplied.) For further insights "behind the scenes," see Walter F. Murphy, *Elements of Judicial Strategy* (Chicago: University of Chicago Press, 1964), especially Ch. III, "Marshalling the Court."

[182] Until April 11, 1965, when Mr. Chief Justice Warren announced that he and the Court saw no reason why decisions should be announced only on Mondays, that day of the week was in fact "reserved" for that purpose. And in the 1970–71 term of "his" Court, Mr. Chief Justice Burger commenced a pointed—although but marginally successful—effort to *avoid* Mondays, chiefly to vitiate the high overtime payments to printers in the Court's printshop incurred by first-day-of-the-week pressures.

expound from memory. Thus techniques vary widely.[183] The reading of the opinions may run from fifteen minutes to several hours[184]—although the Chief Justice would almost certainly try to discourage the latter. Nevertheless, a visitor to the Supreme Court Chamber on an Opinion Day ought to be prepared for an average session of two hours' continuous duration.[185] This interesting practice of announcing opinions orally is not generally followed in the lower courts, where a case is "announced" simply by filing its disposition with the clerk. Prior to the Chief Justiceship of Charles Evans Hughes, the Court's announcements were even lengthier, for the Justices generally persisted in reading opinions word for word, not infrequently in an unrelieved monotone. Hughes, however, sensing a golden opportunity—in the words of Edwin McElwain, who was one of his law clerks—to make "a public demonstration of the dignity and responsibility of the Court to the bar and to the thousands of visitors who came to the new Supreme Court Building during his regime,"[186] not only encouraged paraphrasing and summarizing of opinions, but also impressed upon his brothers of the bench the need to deliver them forcefully and convincingly. The Chief Justice himself was such an impressive figure—with his magnificent head, white beard, and sonorous voice, that visitors to an Opinion Day, hearing him deliver one of his opinions with dramatic impact, often likened him to a latter-day Moses—a concept not entirely displeasing to Hughes, not so much for himself, but for Court and Law.

Even after the Justices have assembled for the announcement of their opinions, should any one of their number have some last-minute qualms regarding one about to be handed down, all he has to do is to ask the Chief Justice to "let it go over"—such is the concern with each Justice's sensibilities. It cannot be emphasized too strongly that *each and every Justice* passes on all aspects of a case, at *each* of its stages; the Court most emphatically does not function by committee, panel, or section. The now published opin-

---

183 See Donald D. Gregory and Stephen L. Wasby, "How To Get an Idea from Here to There: The Court and Communication Overload," 3 *Public Affairs Bulletin* 5 (November–December 1970), *passim*.

184 One of Mr. Justice Holmes's many virtues was brevity, which one of his most ardent on-the-bench admirers, Mr. Justice Robert H. Jackson, attributed to Holmes's lifelong practice of writing his opinions in longhand while *standing* at a desk of draftsman's height. When fatigue set in, Holmes would write finis to the opinion. See Eugene C. Gerhart, *Robert H. Jackson: Lawyer's Judge* (Albany: Q Corporation, 1961), pp. 109–10.

185 The 1901 *Insular Cases* took six hours to deliver.

186 "The Business of the Supreme Court as Conducted by Chief Justice Hughes," 63 *Harvard Law Review* 20 (1949).

ions presumably confine themselves to the issue involved in the various cases, but the voicing of profoundly held beliefs, and at times even a swipe at a colleague, is quite common. Thus, cleavages among the Justices of an intellectual, policy, and, at times, even personal nature become apparent in the written opinions—no matter how skilled an arbiter the Chief Justice may be. Fortunately, less frequent are *ad hoc* outbursts from the bench on Opinion Day; these are not found in the written record, but they do occur. Perhaps the most famous one is Mr. Justice McReynolds's explosion in 1935, while reading his dissent in the *Gold Clause Cases*,[187] when he veritably screamed from the bench: "This is Nero at his worst. The Constitution is gone!"

Judicial Tempers. To give brief, contemporary illustrations of this aspect of Opinion Day: In November 1960, Mr. Justice Douglas, having just heard Mr. Justice Whittaker read the 6 : 3 opinion for the Court in a tax case, commented acidly from the bench that the issue decided this day was "narrow and technical"; that he would not have filed a dissent had not the "majority's error been so egregious"; and he closed with the observation: "But six make the law, and sometimes very bad law." Earlier that year, Mr. Justice Frankfurter had characterized as a "judicial somersault" an opinion for the Court by Mr. Justice Stewart in a criminal law case.[188] On Opinion Monday, March 30, 1959, Mr. Justice Frankfurter, while reading the majority opinion upholding the successive federal and state trials of one Bartkus for the same criminal act, against the charge of double jeopardy, made a passing reference to "the so-called Bill of Rights." When Mr. Justice Black's turn came to read his dissent in the case, he declared passionately: "This case concerns the Bill of Rights, not the 'so-called Bill of Rights!' "[189] Eight years later, the normally gentle Black, dissenting from a new interpretation of the constitutionality of eavesdropping in the *Katz* case, accused his brothers of being "language-stretching judges" whose aim was to "rewrite" the Constitution, who lacked "scholarship, common sense and candor," who had engaged in "clever word juggling."[190] On an Opinion Monday in April 1971, the usually affable Mr. Justice Brennan began his dissent from the Court's 5 : 4 decision ruling that some foreign-born U.S. citizens

[187] *Norman v. Baltimore & Ohio Railroad Co.* 294 U.S. 240.
[188] *Elkins and Clark v. United States,* 364 U.S. 206 (1960).
[189] As reported by Anthony Lewis, "Justice Black at 75: Still the Dissenter," *The New York Times Magazine,* February 26, 1961, p. 74.
[190] Comment from the bench in *Katz v. United States,* 389 U.S. 347, on December 18, 1967.

could lose their citizenship merely on certain residential grounds by bitterly observing: "Since the Court this term has already downgraded citizens receiving public welfare, and citizens having the misfortune to be illegitimate, I suppose today's decision downgrading citizens born outside the United States should have been expected."[191]

During the waning days of the 1960–61 term, the public and the Court were treated to two serious *ad hoc* outbursts from the bench on two Opinion Days, involving Mr. Chief Justice Warren and, again, Mr. Justice Frankfurter. In the first instance, a sharp dissent by the latter provoked on oral rebuttal by the former, which was even more unusual because the Chief Justice, on the side of the 5 : 4 majority, had written no opinion in the case. But in stating his dissent, Mr. Justice Frankfurter took nearly fifteen minutes to sharpen the written language and heighten his criticism of the majority opinion in the criminal case at issue. Evidently hurt and annoyed by Frankfurter's tone of voice and the contents of his summation, the Chief Justice told the courtroom that "since so much has been said here that was not in any written opinion," he wanted to add a word as to why he joined the majority.[192]

And an even more serious manifestation of judicial temper-flaring occurred several Opinion Days later, again featuring the same two Justices. The Court, once again by a 5 : 4 vote, as is so frequently the case in criminal cases involving Bill-of-Rights interpretations, had reversed the murder conviction of one Willie Lee Stewart. In a ringing dissent, Mr. Justice Frankfurter, going far beyond anything he had written, accused the majority of "plucking out" of the lengthy trial record an isolated episode, and suggested that judges find in the record "what the mind is looking for." He went on to categorize the majority opinion as an "indefensible example of finicky appellate review of criminal cases," and warned against "turning a criminal appeal into a quest for error." When he had finished, Mr. Chief Justice Warren leaned forward, his face deeply flushed, and with evident emotion stated that the dissent just heard was not a proper statement of an opinion, but rather a

> lecture . . . a closing argument by a prosecutor to a jury. It is properly made, perhaps, in the conference room [of the Court], but not in the court room. . . . The purpose of reporting an opinion [here] is to inform the public and is not for the purpose of degrading this Court.

[191] *Rogers v. Bellei*, 401 U.S. 815.
[192] As reported in *The New York Times*, March 21, 1961, p. 18.

Warren then turned to Frankfurter, who was seated to his immediate left, and whispered an invitation to respond. Frankfurter said: "The Chief Justice urges me to comment on what he said, but of course I won't. I have another case."[193] Yet at the end of the session the two adversaries were engaged in friendly and cordial conversation! Even Supreme Court Justices are human. . . .[194]

Ratio Decidendi and Obiter Dictum. It is important to distinguish—although this is sometimes far more easily said than done—between the *ratio decidendi* of an opinion and the frequently present *obiter dictum* or *obiter dicta. Ratio decidendi* refers to the essence, the vitals, the necessary legal or constitutional core of the decision; *obiter dictum* is a more or less extraneous point, presumably unnecessary to the decision, made by the author of an opinion. In other words, the former constitutes the legal rule to be followed and adhered to; the latter is an expression of a brief, viewpoint, or sentiment, which, at least in theory, has no binding effect. It is not surprising, however, that, on occasion, an *obiter dictum* lives long after the *ratio decidendi* has been forgotten! Moreover, as U.S. District Court Judge P. M. Hall of California once put the matter, "I am not unmindful of the fact that in the last analysis the Judges of the Supreme Court are the final arbiters as to what is or is not *dicta* in a previous opinion."[195] Mr. Justice Brennan once observed that *obiter dicta* reflected "the gas on the stomach felt by the Justice at the time he was writing the decicion."[196] But it is the *ratio decidendi* that makes the decided case one of record and renders the

---

[193] As reported in *The (Philadelphia) Evening Bulletin*, April 25, 1961, p. 3, and in *The New York Times*, April 25, 1961, p. 27. (The case is *Stewart v. United States*, 366 U.S. 1.)

[194] Since the exchanges described above took place, there have been other memorable judicial outbursts—among them an unusually sharp attack by Mr. Justice Douglas on his brother Black in *Arizona v. California*, 373 U.S. 546 (1963); an acid exchange between Black and Mr. Justice Harlan in the congressional redistricting case of *Wesberry v. Sanders*, 376 U.S. 1 (1964); Harlan's scathing attack on the entire Court in the key reapportionment cases of 1964, headed by *Reynolds v. Sims*, 377 U.S. 533; Mr. Justice White's sarcastic references to his colleague Goldberg's reasoning in the now famous case of *Escobedo v. Illinois*, 378 U.S. 478 (1964); Mr. Justice Black's blistering attack on what he regarded as the "loosest construction of the Constitution in this court's history" by its two leading alleged and avowed "strict constructionists," Mr. Chief Justice Burger and Mr. Justice Blackmun, in the "gratis divorce proceedings case" of *Bodde v. Connecticut*, 401 U.S. 371 (1971); and the latest to date, Mr. Justice Stewart's angry charge in a 1974 repossession case (*Mitchell v. W. T. Grant Co.*, 416 U.S. 600) that "recent changes in the Court's composition—instead of principles of law—caused a break with precedent less than two years old!" There are, and presumably will always be, others.

[195] *Odikubo v. Bonesteel*, 60 F. Supp. 916 (1945) at 930, fn. 28.

[196] Remark made to me, December 18, 1969.

matter at issue *res judicata*, i.e. a matter upon which a competent court of law has passed judgment.

One of the most famous expounders of the *obiter dictum* was Mr. Chief Justice John Marshall, who delighted in employing that technique as a medium for the constitutional education of the public. His celebrated opinions in *Marbury v. Madison*,[197] *McCulloch v. Maryland*,[198] and *Gibbons v. Ogden*,[199] for example, are full of *dicta* which history has so merged with the *ratio decidendi* in these cases as to make the two concepts almost indistinguishable. Nor has that approach become extinct in our own day, to which illustrations on two levels of the judiciary bear witness: In the case of *Shachtman v. Dulles*,[200] three judges of the U.S. Circuit Court of Appeals for the District of Columbia held unanimously that the grounds for the Secretary of State's denial of a passport to the petitioner constituted an arbitrary, and hence unconstitutional, denial of due process of law under the Fifth Amendment. That was the *ratio decidendi* of the case, but the author of the opinion of the tribunal, Circuit Judge Fahy, in an interesting *obiter dictum*, based the privilege of a passport upon the "natural right" to travel, "to go from place to place as the means of transportation permit." At the level of the Supreme Court, *Watkins v. United States*[201] dealt with the refusal of a former labor organizer, John T. Watkins, to answer certain questions put to him by a subcommittee of the House Committee on Un-American Activities, which was investigating "Communist activities in the Chicago area." In a 6 : 1 decision, speaking through Mr. Chief Justice Warren, the Court set aside Watkins's conviction for contempt of Congress in the District Court below because neither Congress nor the Committee had ever satisfactorily apprised him whether the questions he had refused to answer were "pertinent to the subject under inquiry." This failure on the part of the legislature was thus held to render the conviction void on the ground of vagueness under the due process of law clause of the Fifth Amendment. Here we have the *ratio decidendi* of the *Watkins* case. But, resorting to the device of the *obiter dictum*, Mr. Chief Justice Warren also discussed matters, however related, which had not really been specifically raised by the petitioner Watkins in his allegations. In the face of charges of "overstatement" and "lily-gilding," Warren's long and fervant *dictum* clearly represented a lecture to Congress—and, he hoped, to the public at large—on the

197 1 Cranch 137 (1803).
198 4 Wheaton 316 (1819).
199 9 Wheaton 1 (1824).
200 225 F. 2d 938 (1955).
201 354 U.S. 178 (1957).

rights of individuals and Congress's abuse of its power to investigate. In it was this admonition: "We have no doubt that there is no congressional power to expose for the sake of exposure."[202] Another important example is the Court's footnote *dictum* in *United States v. Barnett*,[203] which indicated that anyone convicted of criminal contempt by a judge could not be given a sentence more severe than might be imposed for a "petty offense."

After the announcement and reading of an opinion the case is presumably finished, insofar as the members of the Court are concerned, and no further public comment thereon will normally emanate from the Justices. On rare occasion, however, the public reception of a decision may move a Justice to further comment. This occurred, for example, as a result of the *New York Prayer Case*,[204] when Mr. Justice Clark seized upon the occasion of a public speech to take note of the decision's critical reception by "explaining" his vote as a member of the majority. Referring to the Court's 8 : 1 judgment that New York's state-composed twenty-two-word nondenominational prayer for use in the state's public schools constituted a violation of the principle of separation of church and state as imbedded in Amendments I and XIV, he stated simply: "No to me means no. That is all the court decided, not that there should be no recognition of a supreme being."

COMPLIANCE

When officially announced as decided, the case becomes binding on all lower federal courts and on all state courts when and where applicable. It is now *the* controlling opinion, *res judicata*—the law of the land—as enunciated and/or interpreted by its highest tribunal. It is then duly recorded and published by the federal government in an invaluable series of volumes known as the *United States Reports,* which, duly compiled and edited by the Supreme Court's Reporter of Decisions, constitute the sole *official* record of the actions of the Court. There are also several unofficial publications available.[205] (The *Reports* and their forerunners are on file back to 1790.) However, although compliance with the Court's decisions may be expected to be a foregone conclusion insofar as the lower *federal* courts are concerned—Chapter VIII will discuss some of the problems of compliance,

---

202 Ibid., at 200.
203 376 U.S. 681 (1964), at 695 fn. 12.
204 *Engel v. Vitale*, 370 U.S. 421 (1962).
205 For example, the *Supreme Court Reporter* and the *Lawyers' Edition of the Opinions of the United States Supreme Court.*

and of enforcement by *nonjudicial* governmental bodies generally—it is not always necessarily simple and automatic.

By Federal Courts. For example, in September 1960, Judge Ashton Williams of the U.S. District Court for South Carolina disqualified himself from a desegregation suit on the ground that *he* considered the Supreme Court's decision and subsequent order in *Brown v. Board of Education*[206] to be unconstitutional. He announced that another judge would have to hear the case, brought by four Charleston Negroes, which involved compulsory segregation of the Charleston municipal golf course. Contending that the Supreme Court's decision barring separate facilities for whites and blacks in such public recreational facilities was based "on constitutional grounds," he nonetheless stepped aside rather than disobey, and declared: "Since as a Federal judge I have to follow that decision I will disqualify myself because I have taken an oath to sustain the Constitution."[207]

Another U.S. District Court jurist, the then eighty-seven-year-old Judge William H. Atwell of Texas, went considerably further in 1956; he simply *refused* to carry out the desegregation ruling of the Court, and resorted to every conceivable judicial roadblock to prevent it. Although his ruling had been reversed by the Fifth U.S. Circuit Court of Appeals,[208] after his initial rejection of the plaintiffs' petition,[209] he again refused to set a date of desegregation of the Dallas school district because such a step would cause "civil wrongs." In order to make quite clear where he stood on the issue, Atwell announced:

> I believe that it will be seen that the [Supreme] Court based its decision on no law but rather on what the Court regarded as more authoritative, more psychological knowledge. . . . It will be recalled that in 1952, Mr. Justice Frankfurter said it [the Supreme Court] was not competent to take judicial notice of "claims of social scientists."[210]

The Court of Appeals, naturally, again reversed the second Atwell decision in short order.[211] But far from acquiescing, Judge Atwell now embarked upon a course of action in the opposite extreme by ordering all Dallas schools integrated in the middle of the academic year![212] This decision was

---

[206] 347 U.S. 483 (1954) and 349 U.S. 294 (1955).
[207] As reported in *The New York Times*, September 8, 1960, p. 27.
[208] *Brown v. Rippy*, 233 F. 2d 796 (1956).
[209] *Bell v. Rippy*, 133 F. Supp. 811 (1955).
[210] *Bell v. Rippy*, 146 F. Supp. 485 (1956), at 486.
[211] *Borders v. Rippy*, 247 F. 2d 268 (1957).
[212] 2 *Race Relations Law Reporter* 985 (1957).

also reversed by the higher court.[213] Three or four years later, Atwell retired permanently—he had been recalled for temporary duty—and another federal District Court judge ultimately ordered a "mild" form of desegregation. This was broadened and amended by the Fifth Circuit Court of Appeals in accordance with the Supreme Court's 1954 and 1955 mandates,[214] with desegregation scheduled to begin on a one-grade-a-year basis in September of 1961[215]—which indeed it did, without incident. It should be pointed out, however, that the nature of the implementation order, as handed down by the Court in the second *Brown* case,[216] was tailor-made for dilatory tactics by federal District Court judges. It vested in them inherent authority to use their discretion in ordering desegregation by suggesting that they take notice of the peculiarities of the local situation. In effect, they were guided solely by the Court's mandate that the judges require a "prompt and reasonable start toward full compliance" and that they take such action as may be necessary to bring about the end of racial segregation in the public schools "with all deliberate speed."[217]

But lest the impression arise that all defiance and deviation from the law as stated by the Court are confined to the segregation-integration controversy, we have another, and quite different example, this one involving an eminent jurist, Chief Judge John J. Parker of the Fourth U.S. Circuit Court of Appeals. In 1940 the Supreme Court had held 8 : 1 in the first of the *Flag Salute Cases*[218] that Pennsylvania could validly require children of Jehovah's Witnesses attending public schools to salute the flag, despite claims of violation of their constitutionally guaranteed freedom of religion. Only Mr. Justice Stone had dissented. But no Supreme Court reversal having taken place two years later, Judge Parker held an *identical* West Virginia statute unconstitutional.[219] He went to some length to point out that this really was not defiance, since three members of the 1940 majority

---

[213] *Rippy v. Borders,* 250 F. 2d 690 (1957).

[214] *Brown v. Board of Education,* 347 U.S. 483 (1954), and ibid. 349 U.S. 294 (1955).

[215] *Boston v. Rippy,* 275 F. 2d 850 (1960).

[216] Loc. cit. 349 U.S. 294 (1955).

[217] Ibid., at 296. The term "all deliberate speed" was suggested by Mr. Justice Frankfurter, who lifted it from Mr. Justice Holmes's opinion in *Virginia v. West Virginia,* 222 U.S. 17 (1911), at 30—a case dealing with a monetary controversy between the two states. After more than fourteen years of "deliberate speed" compliance, the Court unanimously abandoned that doctrine in October 1969, ordering desegregation "at once" by and for all school systems so as henceforth to "operate now and hereafter only unitary schools." (*Alexander v. Holmes County Board of Education of Mississippi,* 396 U.S. 19. Rehearing denied, 396 U.S. 976 (1969).)

[218] *Minersville School District v. Gobitis,* 310 U.S. 586 (1940).

[219] *Barnette v. West Virginia,* 47 F. Supp. 251 (1942), at 253.

had publicly confessed error on the occasion of a different case involving another constitutional claim by Jehovah's Witnesses,[220] and that two others[221] had retired from the bench in the two-year interim, thus leaving the supporters of the compulsory flag salute in a minority of three.[222] His analysis and implied prediction proved to be correct, because the Court did specifically overrule itself, 6 : 3, when that very same West Virginia case[223] reached it—but, of course, Judge Parker could neither safely predict that event, nor did it lessen the fact of his deviation.[224]

As a final example of defiance or deviation on the lower federal court level, we have the astonishing case of the then eighty-six-year-old U.S. District Court Judge T. Whitfield Davidson of Dallas. In 1962, fully four years after he had been ordered to do so by the Supreme Court of the United States, Judge Davidson refused resolutely to impose a $506.11 penalty on a Texas farmer who had wilfully and illegally exceeded his planting allotment of wheat under federal regulations by forty-three acres. The venerable judge simply insisted upon his own conclusions that the statute involved was unconstitutional—despite several Supreme Court holdings to the precise contrary[225]—and he further ruled that the highest court had no jurisdiction in the case at bar! When the federal authorities ultimately appealed Judge Davidson's obstructions to the Supreme Court, the latter made clear—in a curt and unsigned opinion—that it did indeed have jurisdiction and that it wanted its orders carried out forthwith "without delay."[226] They were! Had they not been, the Court could have issued a writ of *mandamus* to him—as it did in 1969 to U.S. District Judge John F. Dooling, Jr., of Brooklyn, who not only had ignored a trial jury's guilty verdict *and* dismissed the grand jury's indictment against four members of the "Mafia," but had ignored a writ by the U.S. Court of Appeals for the Second Circuit.[227]

However, these illustrations of deviations by lower court *federal* judges

---

[220] *Jones v. Opelika*, 316 U.S. 584 (1942), at 623–24. The three were Justices Black, Douglas and Murphy.

[221] Mr. Chief Justice Hughes and Mr. Justice Byrnes.

[222] Justices Roberts, Reed, and Frankfurter. The six constituting the new majority were the new Chief Justice (Stone); the three "confessors-of-error" (Black, Douglas, and Murphy); and the two newcomers to the bench, Justices Jackson and Rutledge.

[223] *West Virginia State Board of Education v. Barnette*, 319 U.S. 624 (1943).

[224] For an enlightening article on compliance generally, see Walter Murphy, "Lower Court Checks on Supreme Court Power," 53 *American Political Science Review* 1017–31 (December 1959).

[225] The leading—and unanimous—decision was *Wickard v. Filburn* 317 U.S. 111 (1942), which upheld the constitutionality of the Agricultural Adjustment Act of 1938.

[226] *United States v. District Court (United States v. Haley)*, 371 U.S. 18.

[227] *Perzico v. United States*, 395 U.S. 911 (1969).

are exceptions to the general rule of compliance with the orders emanating from the highest tribunal. There may be disagreement with such an order, but one must, and may, expect that it be followed. The comments below by U.S. District Court Judge Charles E. Wyzanski, Jr., of Boston are in the best tradition of compliance, no matter how extensive the substantive disagreement. At issue was one of those time-consuming negligence cases, involving a trial jury's grant of $30,000 in damages to an injured New Haven Railroad worker, one Mrs. Henagan. The New Haven, upon receiving the jury's verdict in Judge Wyzanski's court, asked him to set it aside. He replied that he would if he could, but that he was not free to do so because the Supreme Court had consistently held in favor of railroad employees in similar cases, and that the Court's precedent commanded his obedience. But he went on to indicate his feelings in no uncertain terms:

> I cannot read the record as a whole in a way to find any evidence of negligence [by the New Haven]. But I know that my method of reading the record is different from that of a majority of the Supreme Court of the United States as exhibited in past cases, and I hope *I am a lawful judge*, and I recognize the limits of my authority whether appellate judges do or not.[228]

Ironically, as matters developed, the Supreme Court, for the first time in a quarter of a century in a Federal Employers' Liability Act case, a short time thereafter reversed a jury verdict by a 6 : 2 majority because it found insufficient negligence on the part of the railroad—and the case was that of Mrs. Henagan![229]

It should also be noted that the Court, by special order, may bypass proceedings in the lower federal courts—although this is not commonly done, as Congressman Adam Clayton Powell (D.-N.Y.) found out in 1967 when he unsuccessfully sought a Supreme Court order to bypass the U.S. Court of Appeals, where his appeal from an adverse decision from a U.S. District Court on his exclusion from the U.S. House of Representatives then lodged. However, an example of a successful plea is a 1964 antitrust action under the Clayton Act commenced by the federal government against the El Paso Natural Gas Co. There, Mr. Justice Douglas directed that El Paso divest it-

---

[228] *New York, New Haven, & Hartford v. Henagan*, as reported in 272 F. 2d 153 (1959), at 155–56. (Italics supplied.) For a similar stance see the statement of U.S. Court of Appeals for the Fifth Circuit in *Griffin v. Breckenridge*, 410 F. 2d 817 (1969), a case it wanted to overrule but did not, because "[s]ince we may not adopt what the Supreme Court has expressly rejected, we obediently abide the mandate in [*Collins v. Hardyman*, 341 U.S. 651, 1951]."

[229] *New York, New Haven, & Hartford v. Henagan*, 364 U.S. 441 (1960).

227

self of a firm it had acquired "without delay"—and without "further proceedings in the lower courts," an order from which only Mr. Justice Harlan dissented.[230]

By State Courts. When it comes to compliance with Supreme Court decisions by *state* courts, an entirely different element enters. In effect, the Supreme Court has no power to make a *final determination* of any case in which it reviews *state* court judgments. All it can do in these instances is to *decide the federal issue and remand* it to the state court below for final judgment "not inconsistent with this opinion."[231] Because the state courts possess the power to raise new issues after they receive the case back from above, they are provided with an opportunity to evade the substantive effects of the reversal by the Supreme Court in a number of ways.[232] And once a new issue is raised, the ultimate disposition of the case may, of course, go either way. A notorious illustration is the case of Virgil Hawkins, a Florida Negro, who was denied admission to the University of Florida Law School. After lengthy legal stratagems, delays, and assorted maneuvers on all levels of the judiciary over a period of nine years, Hawkins was finally ordered admitted by the U.S. Supreme Court after the Florida Supreme Court continued to stall—yet he was in fact never allowed to go to the University, and he gave up.[233] That this whole matter of spotty and often unpredictable state court compliance is not an illusory conclusion is well demonstrated by, for instance, certain statistics gathered and published by the *Harvard Law Review* some years ago.[234] For example, from 1941 to 1951, the Supreme Court remanded 175 cases to the various state courts for further proceedings "not inconsistent with this judgment." In forty-six of these (almost 27 per cent of the total), further litigation ensued, with twenty-two

---

[230] *United States v. El Paso Natural Gas Co.*, 376 U.S. 251.

[231] E.g., see the grisly history of the case of *Williams v. Georgia*, 349 U.S. 375 (1955) and 350 U.S. 950 (1956).

[232] E.g. the New York State Court of Appeals' "reviving" of that state's eavesdropping law in 1967 (*People v. Kaiser*, 286 N.Y. 52 & 801), notwithstanding the U.S. Supreme Court's mandate of unconstitutionality pronounced six months earlier in *Berger v. New York*, 388 U.S. 41.

[233] Among the seven Hawkins cases were: *Florida ex rel Hawkins v. Board of Control*, 347 U.S. 971 (1954); ibid. 350 U.S. 413 (1956); and ibid. 355 U.S. 839 (1957). See the account of the Hawkins dilemma in Walter F. Murphy and C. Herman Pritchett, *Courts, Judges, and Politics* (New York: Random House, 1961), pp. 606–18.

[234] See the two *Notes*, "Final Disposition of State Court Decisions Reversed and Remanded by the Supreme Court, October Term 1931 to October Term 1940," 55 *Harvard Law Review* 1357 (1942), and "Evasion of Supreme Court Mandates in Cases Remanded to State Courts since 1941," 67 *Harvard Law Review* 1251 (1954).

of the parties who *won* in the Supreme Court now *losing* in the state courts as a result of the final judgment below. In the decade immediately preceding, the Court had reviewed 187 state court cases and remanded them. In 34 of these (somewhat above 18 per cent), new issues were raised below, and in a mere nine of these did the ultimate state court decision favor the party who had "won" in the Supreme Court of the United States.

Whatever the difference in the degree of compliance with the decisions of the highest court in the land,[235] it is fair to conclude that their nationwide impact is often uneven. The many diverse local conditions that characterize the federal system are all but tailor-made for considerable latitude in compliance. This fact of constitutional life clearly accounts for the spotty, often utterly absent compliance in the 1954 and 1955 decisions concerning desegregation, yet, conversely, also for the amazingly speedy acceptance and compliance, however varied, with the reapportionment-redistricting decision of the 1960's, following the historic Supreme Court ruling in *Baker v. Carr*.[236] On the other hand, some public school districts, egged on by local and state authorities, openly defied, and others circumvented by "interpretations" that seemed to ignore, the language of the Supreme Court's ruling in the *Prayer and Bible Reading Cases* of 1962 and 1963.[237] Indeed, nearly 13 per cent of the nation's public schools—and 50 per cent of those in the South—were continuing their defiance as the 1960's turned into the 1970's.[238] And until the Court issued its contentious but specific and plainly understood rules in its historic criminal justice decision in *Miranda v. Arizona*,[239] different state courts—even so sophisticated a court as the Supreme Court of New Jersey—interpreted the decision in *Miranda's* antecedent, *Escobedo v. Illinois*,[240] in a host of diverse, frequently

---

[235] For a study that found no significant degree of difference in the compliance rate of federal and state courts, see Edward N. Beiser, "A Comparative Analysis of State and Federal Judicial Behavior: The Reapportionment Cases," LXII *American Political Science Review* 788 (September 1968).

[236] 369 U.S. 186 (1962). Barely six years later all but a handful of states had either complied voluntarily or done so as a result of U.S. District Court orders. What had once been an average deviation of close to 11 per cent in population representation had sunk to less than 1 per cent—an amazing manifestation of compliance!

[237] See, for example, "The Supreme Court and the Bible Belt: Tennessee Reaction to the 'Schempp' Decision," by Robert H. Birkby, X *Midwest Journal of Political Science* 3 (August 1966). Also see Henry J. Abraham and Robert R. Benedetti, "The State Attorney General: A Friend of the Court?," 117 University of Pennsylvania Law Review 6 (April 1969).

[238] *The New York Times*, March 26, 1969, p. 1.

[239] 384 U.S. 436 (1966).

[240] 378 U.S. 478 (1964).

clearly defiant, ways. If properly supported by responsible public and private sources of power and influence, the Court will of course ultimately generally have its way, more or less—unless it is reversed by legislative action or constitutional amendment, or if it overrules or modifies its own decisions (of which much more will be said in Chapters VII and VIII). But it must be accorded appropriate executive support—as it was in Little Rock, Arkansas, Oxford, Mississippi, and Tuscaloosa, Alabama—for, as will be emphasized and re-emphasized in these pages, the Court's only effective power is the power to persuade: purse and sword are in other hands.

OUTSIDE INFLUENCES ON COURT PERSONNEL

Much has been written and pronounced on various outside sources that allegedly prey upon and lobby the Court and endeavor to influence its decision-making process. A good deal of this commentary has been exaggerated; much has been spurious; some has been made with nothing less than evil intent and ill will; and some has been sheer nonsense. Of course, the Justices are subject to "influence." Any governmental body with the power to make significant discretionary choices—which the Court assuredly possesses—may be expected to be a target of interest groups and interest seekers. But it is an entirely different type of "influence" than that normally associated with lobbying. Let it be stated at once and unequivocally, the sort of lobbying and the button-holing and back-slapping approaches used to influence (1) legislators and (2) executives and administrators, not only would not work with the members of the federal judiciary in general, and the Justices of the Supreme Court in particular, but would meet with withering disdain. As the British would say, "this simply is not done!" Moreover, the so welcome and necessary independence of the federal judiciary, and the almost Olympian position of awe, if not necessarily always majoritarian regard and esteem, the Justices rightfully enjoy in the popular mind would militate against any of the myriad approaches, ingenuous or ingenious, to which the average official or unofficial lobbyist resorts in Washington and the various other seats of federal and state power in the United States of America. If, however, we mean by "influence" a well-reasoned and ably written brief, be it by one of the litigants or a brief *amicus curiae* (see below); a persuasive oral argument on behalf of an issue at bar; a timely, thoughtful, and convincing book, monograph, speech, or law review article on the general or specific issue; a strategically timed use of a bona fide test case—*that* type of influence, as well as the intriguing concept of the "climate of public opinion" (to be discussed in Chapter VII), falls into a different category. In the final analysis, here the Justices remain the complete masters of their own house.

In elaborating somewhat on the several sources of outside influence that may bear upon the Court, we may omit the more obvious and self-explanatory, such as the well-written brief, the persuasive oral argument, and most literature. Some others do deserve separate treatment, including the alleged "gray eminences" behind the Justices, the law clerks.

LEGAL PERIODICALS

Articles that appear in law reviews and other legal periodicals undoubtedly have exerted a formative influence on the law for some time. This is only natural, since the best legal thinking finds expression in these periodicals (only the top law students "work on" law reviews while in law school). The jurists are part of the legal process and are quite naturally generally familiar with the thinking that presents itself in the pages of the reviews; indeed, they must be familiar with it if they wish to keep their finger on the pulse of the profession and, as Mr. Justice Holmes put it so cogently, "the felt necessities of the times." In a pioneering article based on work leading to his doctorate, Chester A. Newland presented the results of a close study of the use made by the Supreme Court of legal periodicals during the period between 1924 and 1956.[241] In most cases the law review and other articles cited by the Justices constituted minor references in the opinions concerned, although a few seemed to be close to the *ratio decidendi*. An avowed and indeed acknowledged illustration of the latter is Mr. Justice Brandeis's significant opinion in the landmark case of *Erie v. Tompkins* of 1938,[242] which overruled the century-old precedent on the judicial application of common law laid down in *Swift v. Tyson*.[243] Brandeis made a point of crediting "the research of a competent scholar"—Charles Warren's article, "New Light on the History of the Federal Judiciary Act of 1789," 37 *Harvard Law Review* 49 (1923).[244] In any event, there were numerous references in each term after 1937, with an average of twenty-five opinions (or

---

[241] "Legal Periodicals and the United States Supreme Court," 3 *Midwest Journal of Political Science* 58–74 (February 1959).
[242] 304 U.S. 64.
[243] 16 Peters 1 (1842). As a result of *Erie*, the Judicial Code now provides that "the laws of the several states . . . shall be regarded as rules of decision in trials at common law in the courts of the United States." Equity, admiralty, and criminal cases are excluded from the clause's operation, however.
[244] 304 U.S. 64, at 72–73.

about one-quarter of the number handed down by the Court in a typical term) citing a total of between forty and seventy periodicals. Not surprisingly, the Justices varied in the frequency of use they made of these references, depending, more or less, on their scholarly bent and interest. Of the Justices appointed after 1937 and before 1957 who cited legal periodicals in at least twenty opinions during that period, Mr. Justice Rutledge, with a per-term average of 7.4 opinions, headed the list; next came Mr. Justice Frankfurter with 5.5; third was Mr. Justice Jackson with 4.1; low man was Mr. Justice Burton with 2.0. For whatever significance it may have, the statistics indicate also that the four most frequently cited journals during the thirty-two year period covered by Professor Newland's study, and the number of times they were referred to, were: *The Harvard Law Review* (399); *Yale Law Journal* (194); *The Columbia Law Review* (176); and *The Michigan Law Review* (165).

There is little doubt that reliance on the legal periodicals by both bar and courts during the past generation or so has increased. Although difficult to determine objectively, this particular genre of the written word exerts a formative influence, and it does, of course, represent an outside influence. Yet it may well be asked how much "outside" this particular type of influence is. Moreover, commentators as well as students of the legal process hardly agree upon its extent. To cite one of the more extreme points of view on the matter, in a speech in the House of Representatives, Congressman Wright Patman (D.-Tex.) viewed any reliance upon legal periodicals as all but evil and sinister, and contended that it was subversive of traditional judicial processes:

> In adopting and relying upon such pseudo-legalistic papers disseminated by the lobbyist-authors thereof the result is that the theories advanced by these pretended authorities were presented and received by the Court in an ex parte fashion.[245]

Replying to Patman in his article, Professor Newland charged the veteran Congressman with "some measure of naïveté," and pointed out that if law reviews and other legal journals were not to limit their interests solely to the past, they were bound to be vehicles for the expression of views on current policy issues.[246] He concluded his observations by putting the problem into its proper focus:

[245] *Congressional Record*, 85th Cong. 1st sess., Vol. 103, Part 12, p. 16160.
[246] Newland, op. cit. pp. 73–74.

Critics may properly object that some views expressed in legal periodicals and adopted by the courts are contrary to policies which they deem desirable. But no greater unanimity of opinion usually exists among law faculties and reviews than exists on the Supreme Court. Legal periodicals appear to be "political" in somewhat the same way that the Courts are.[247]

TEST CASES

Since the American federal judicial system is based on the concept of litigation by virtue of an actual case or controversy brought before the courts by parties directly concerned, who must have standing to sue either as individuals or as personally and directly involved members of a class (see Chapter IX), the solution of an issue in the judicial process depends upon the decision handed down by the tribunal having jurisdiction. Consequently, neither the United States Supreme Court nor any of the lower constitutional courts can decide an issue unless it is before it. Here the employment of "test cases" becomes *a fortiori* crucial, and both the timing and the presentation of the case are of the utmost importance. So long as the plaintiff or petitioner is a bona fide litigant it does not matter whether or not he pays for the almost always considerable expenses involved; nor does it matter to the outcome whether he personally is vitally interested in the decision. Provided that he is directly involved and is willing to go to court, it is of no legal significance that, in effect, he may thus well act as a front or a foil. Some states do have laws against "barratry"—a form of induced litigation—but it is extremely difficult to prove that barratry has been practiced, unless a litigant so acknowledges. This is particularly unlikely in those "class action" cases epitomized by the segregation-integration controversy. The first really important case in that realm came before the Supreme Court through the auspices of a Missouri Negro, Lloyd Gaines, to whom that state had statutorily denied admission to its public law school,[248] but who mysteriously disappeared just a few days prior to his significant 7 : 2 victory in the Court. (Gaines was never heard from again.) Ever since that time, test cases have been brought with increasing frequency by blacks who have been discriminated against—with the active encouragement, backing, and financing of the interest groups such as the National Association for the Advancement of Colored People (NAACP). It is neither surprising nor subject to doubt that that organization, dedicated to the aim inherent in its title, has acted, and will assuredly continue to act, very much like a strategy board of a field

[247] Ibid. p. 74.
[248] *Missouri ex rel Gaines v. Canada*, 305 U.S. 337 (1938).

command, with due regard to the manifold tactical and strategic problems that beset such a command. In that sense, it resorts to the device of the test case to get its day in court, as do a host of other organizations for their own purposes.

Another illustration of the practice is the concerted drive by the Jehovah's Witnesses to obtain a maximum of religious freedom, as the Witnesses conceive of it, through the device of testing in the courts what they consider to be restrictions and attacks upon their members. During the second quarter of this century, individual members of that sect, actively supported by the parent body, brought more than fifty bona fide test cases to the Supreme Court. Of these they won all but five! Nor is this practice confined to so-called minority groups. Almost every segment of the body politic has resorted to the device of the test case to gain—or lose—a point. The question arises, just how much pressure or influence-peddling on the Court is involved here? Those who suspect a burglar under every judicial bed quite naturally view test cases as an all but subversive scheme. Yet test case or regular case, a case is a case, provided it meets the jurisdictional requirements of the Court. And the line between a "plotted" or "instigated" case and a "real" or "natural" one is so thin that it almost defies detection except in the most obvious instances. Moreover, the Court is the master of its own calendar and will not accept frivolous litigation, much less hand down a decision on it. Finally, if an issue of constitutional magnitude is duly and properly brought before the Court—all legal remedies below having been exhausted, and all the requirements of the judicial process having been met —and the Court has agreed to review it, does it *really matter* whether the issue was instigated or just happened in the natural course of events?

THE BRIEF *Amicus Curiae*

Closely related, indeed often essential, to the technique of test cases encouraged and supported by interest groups is the resort to the brief *amicus curiae*. It is a partisan brief filed by an outside individual or group—almost always a formal organization in the latter category—who is not a litigant in the suit but who is vitally interested in a decision favorable to the side it espouses. Long gone is the original concept of the *amicus curiae*—namely, that it "acts for no one, but simply seeks to give information to the Court."[249] The device of the brief *amicus curiae*, i.e. "friend of the court"— which may well be a misnomer in some situations—enables the interested party filing these briefs to enter the case, however tangentially, either by

[249] *Campbell v. Swasey*, 12 Ind. 70 (1859), at 72.

234

way of a written statement, or by participating in oral argument, or both. But there are obstacles as well as limitations to the filing of an *amicus curiae*. If all parties consent to the filing of such a brief, the Supreme Court's rules require its own acquiescence thereto. However, such mutual consent by the litigants is by no means always readily forthcoming. In that event, a party may petition the Court itself for permission to file an *amicus curiae*, a request which may or may not be granted, depending entirely on the judgment of the Justices.[250] Moreover, in cases in which the United States Government is a party to a suit, which is true of approximately one-half of the total number of all cases before the Supreme Court, consent for leave to file briefs *amici curiae* must be given by the Solicitor General before the Court will admit them. In general, that high government official has been quite willing to do so, but on some occasions the Court has granted organizational requests for briefs *amici curiae* over his refusal to consent. The same general approach is true of cases involving *state* government—as was demonstrated by the Supreme Court's acceptance of briefs *amici curiae* in the 1965 case testing Connecticut's birth control statute over that state's objections.[251]

Who files these briefs? Theoretically any interested party may do so; in practice, however, most briefs *amici curiae* have come from active civic organizations and other pressure groups and, not surprisingly, from the federal government itself via the Solicitor General. According to an authoritative study of applicants for leave to file during relatively recent times,[252] most requests have been filed by the following organizations: the American Civil Liberties Union (a tireless and effective battler for civil rights and liberties); the NAACP (persistent and broadly successful spokesman for the Negro); the American Jewish Congress (in roughly the same category as the ACLU, but with emphasis on cases concerning matters involving its own particular interests); and the chief interest group for the vast labor movement, the AFL-CIO. Also very active have been the American Bar Association; sundry consumer groups (often lead by Ralph Nader in the 1970's); various veterans' pressure groups, led by the American Legion; and, quite often of late in matters involving reapportionment-redistricting, sexual discrimination, and segregation-integration (but not only those), the

---

250 Thus, in *Lemon v. Kurtzman*, 397 U.S. 1042 (1969), probable jurisdiction noted, the Court *granted* one motion to file an *amicus curiae* and *denied* another.

251 *Griswold v. Connecticut*, 381 U.S. 479. See the illuminating article in *Time Magazine*, February 26, 1965, pp. 50–51.

252 Clement E. Vose, "Litigation as a Form of Pressure Group Activity," 319 *Annals of the American Academy of Political and Social Science* 20–31 (September 1958).

United States Government.[253] Such requests have often, but by no means always, been granted.

To cite a specific example of the successful use of an *amicus curiae* by the last, the Government filed such a brief in the 1960 case of *Boynton v. Virginia*[254] through the auspices of Solicitor General J. Lee Rankin. Here a bus terminal restaurant in Richmond, Virginia, segregated passengers according to color, regardless of their destination. The plaintiff rested his brief on the equal protection of the laws clause of the Fourteenth Amendment, under which so many cases in the area of racial segregation had been won by Negro petitioners. However, the Solicitor General's brief *amicus curiae* used an entirely different approach, contending that since the restaurant involved was an "integral part" of a bus line's interstate passenger service, the Interstate Commerce Act of 1887—a federal statute—forbade such segregation. More or less ignoring the litigants' arguments and briefs, the Supreme Court fastened upon the contents of Mr. Rankin's *amicus curiae* and decided 7 : 2 in the plaintiff's favor. Mr. Justice Whittaker, however, in a dissenting opinion in which he was joined by Mr. Justice Clark, chided the Court majority for deciding the case on the commerce clause which had been raised *solely* by the Government as *amicus curiae*.

Unless the evidence is as clear-cut as it was in the above instance, it is very difficult to determine how far, if at all, the Court's decision and opinion make use of briefs, *amici curiae*. What some commentators in this field report as the gospel's truth is not infrequently laced with conjecture and sheer guesswork, and some of it with prejudiced motivation. On the other hand, it would be fair to state that the flood of briefs *amici curiae* filed by the NAACP in the area of its own special interest had at least some persuasive influence in the outcome of the many cases handed down by the Court in the fifteen years between the end of World War II and 1960, for example—in which cases the cause espoused by the NAACP gained fifty victories! A specific illustration of one of these is the momentous decision by the Court in *Shelley v. Kraemer*,[255] the most important of the *Restrictive*

---

[253] In one fairly typical stretch of six terms of Court (1962–68), the U.S. government participated as *amicus curiae* in 121 cases (roughly 15 per cent of the total number of cases heard by the Court). Roughly half of these 121 dealt with race and apportionment matters. See Samuel Krislov, *The Role of the Attorney General as* Amicus Curiae (Washington, D.C.: American Enterprise Institute for Public Policy Research, July 1968), pp. 71–103. In the 1970's, discrimination other than on the basis of race replaced apportionment as the Government's second major concern.

[254] 364 U.S. 454.

[255] 334 U.S. 1 (1948).

Covenant Cases.[256] That case held the record for the number of main briefs and briefs *amici curiae* filed and accepted until 1963: nineteen by the NAACP and others favorably disposed to its point of view; five by opposing groups, chiefly real-estate interests; and one by Solicitor General Philip B. Perlman on behalf of the U.S. Department of Justice, siding with the black plaintiff.[257] Speaking for the unanimous six-man Court—Justices Reed, Jackson, and Rutledge having disqualified themselves from participation— Mr. Chief Justice Vinson ruled that although racially restrictive *private* covenants did not in themselves violate the Fourteenth Amendment of the Constitution, *court enforcement* of such contracts would constitute state action and thereby violate the equal protection of the laws clause of that Amendment—a signal victory for the cause of the NAACP.

Other illustrations of the use of briefs *amici curiae* on *both* sides are *Gideon v. Wainwright*, the influential 1963 decision that extended the right of indigents to be assigned counsel for *non*capital as well as capital criminal cases, and *De Funis v. Odegaard*, which, in 1974, raised the delicate question of "reverse discrimination" in university admissions.[258] In the former, twenty-four such briefs were filed on behalf of Clarence Earl Gideon, two on behalf of Warden Wainwright of Florida. In the latter, which was mooted by the Court, eight were filed for law student Marco De Funis, nineteen for University of Washington President Charles Odegaard.

Surely, briefs *amici curiae* may, and sometimes do, influence members of the Court. To acknowledge that entirely plausible, and in many cases quite conceivably salutary, phenomenon is one thing; to lower it to the level of a sinister or subversive cops-and-robbers plot is quite another. In this realm of alleged outside influence, as well as in those discussed earlier, the fact remains that, when all is said and done, the Justices have the final word on whether or how far, if at all, they permit themselves to be influenced within the accepted framework of the judicial process.

THE LAW CLERKS

In a somewhat different category among the "pressures" on the Court are its law clerks. Depending upon the point of view advanced, these able and intelligent young aides to the Justices, all recent law-school graduates in

[256] Ibid. plus *Hurd v. Hodge*, 334 U.S. 24 (1948) and *Barrows v. Jackson*, 346 U.S. 249 (1953).
[257] Clement E. Vose, *Caucasians Only: The Supreme Court, the NAACP, and the Restrictive Covenant Cases* (Berkeley and Los Angeles: University of California Press, 1959), Ch. 8.
[258] 372 U.S. 335 and 416 U.S. 312, respectively.

their mid-twenties, are either in the category of a private secretary aide-de-camp to their Justices or in that of a gray eminence, a sort of judicial Rasputin—indeed, the veritable power behind the throne! Thus, in an angry speech on the Senate floor, U.S. Senator John Stennis (D.-Miss.), a vigorous critic of the Court's attitude on segregation and subversion cases, took pains to call for an investigation of the activities of the clerks; the establishment of statutory minimum qualifications for them; and their confirmation by the Senate just like the Justices themselves—all this because of what the Senator termed "their ever-increasing importance and influence." The law clerks, he said, might be occupying roles in government far more important than those occupied by undersecretaries and assistant secretaries of the executive branch, and that:

> To the extent that they participate in shaping the work of the court, they are deciding vital questions of national effect. Within the Judicial branch, these are equivalent to policy-level decisions in the executive branch.[259]

Yet we have the word of ex-law clerk after ex-law clerk that their influence on the Justices to whom they were assigned was nil in so far as the actual judicial decision-making process was concerned. John P. Frank, once clerk to Mr. Justice Black, wrote that, in his years at the court, "my Justice made approximately one thousand decisions, and I had precisely no influence on any of them."[260] Dean Acheson, one of several of Mr. Justice Brandeis's law clerks who later rose to national prominence, reported that his Justice would sometimes let him work on a draft opinion, largely for the sake of criticism, but:

> When I finished my work on a draft which had been assigned to me or got as far as I could, I gave it to him. [As is evident from the Brandeis files] he tore it to pieces, sometimes using a little, sometimes none [of it].[261]

"Judging is not delegated!" snapped Mr. Justice Brennan once in response to a reporter's taunt.[262] And of all the law clerks who have written or otherwise reported on their experiences behind the "Purple Curtain," only one, William H. Rehnquist—who was appointed to the Supreme Court by President Nixon late in 1971 from his former position of U.S. Assistant Attorney General—suggested the possibility of some "*unconscious* slanting of ma-

---

[259] As reported in *The New York Times*, May 7, 1958, p. 27.
[260] *The Marble Palace* (New York: Alfred A. Knopf, 1958), p. 119.
[261] As quoted by Bickel, op. cit. p. 92.
[262] *Time Magazine*, June 5, 1964, p. 67.

terial by clerks."[263] But even he, who had served as Mr. Justice Jackson's clerk in the 1952–53 term, readily admitted that the notion of the law clerk "exerting an important influence on the cases actually decided by the Court, may be discarded at one . . . I certainly learned of none."[264] During his often heated confirmation hearings, a memorandum came to light in which Rehnquist had argued to Jackson that the "separate but equal" doctrine in education should not be overturned because it "was right and should be reaffirmed."[265] Yet Jackson subsequently joined the unanimous Court in declaring that doctrine unconstitutional in 1954.[266]

These law clerks, almost without exception, have gone on to notable careers.[267] Just who are they, and how are they selected? As indicated above, they are recent law-school graduates of the highest caliber, and all were men until the first two women, Lucille Loman and Margaret Corcoran, were appointed by Justices Douglas and Black, respectively, in 1944 and 1966. Each is chosen by an individual Justice to work for him for a year, sometimes for two. The practice was initiated by Mr. Justice Horace Gray in 1882. He paid his clerks out of his own pocket until 1886, when Congress provided $1600 a year for a "stenographic clerk" for each Justice. That figure had risen to $17,500 by 1974.[268] Today (1975) each Associate Justice selects three, the Chief Justice four. Since 1972 the Chief has also been entitled to an "Administrative Assistant to the Chief Justice," a post created by Congress to help him in his planning, leadership, and administrative responsibilities for the federal judiciary; and Congress also authorized such an official for each of the Associate Justices, instead of the third clerk. But Mr. Chief Justice Burger stirred strong opposition from a majority of his colleagues in 1974 when he proposed that, henceforth, each member of the Court be given one *permanent* law clerk—in addition to temporary (yearly) ones—an arrangement which he and Mr. Justice White experimented with that year. Some Justices do their own clerk-selecting, either by personal in-

---

263 "Who Writes Decisions of the Supreme Court?" *U.S. News and World Report,* December 13, 1957, p. 275.

264 Ibid.

265 *The New York Times,* December 7, 1971, p. 20c.

266 *Brown v. Board of Education of Topeka,* 347 U.S. 483 (1954), and *Bolling v. Sharpe,* 347 U.S. 497 (1954).

267 E.g. Dean Acheson (U.S. Secretary of State), Francis Biddle (U.S. Attorney General), Irving Olds (president of U.S. Steel), David Riesman (famed professor of sociology), Byron White (Associate Justice of the Supreme Court of the United States).

268 Until 1973, when each of the Justices was at last assigned two secretaries, they had to content themselves with just one, plus the use of the stenographic "pool."

terview or by considering written data, almost always the former; others rely chiefly on experts' recommendations—viz., Mr. Justice Frankfurter, whose clerks were chosen for him by Professors Sachs and Freund at the Harvard Law School—as Mr. Justice Brennan's are now. From there Professor of Law Felix Frankfurter sent a number of his own outstanding students, sometimes referred to as "Felix's Happy Hot Dogs," to the Court as clerks (and to government service with the New Deal). In short, the clerks are really the purely personal patronage of the Justices, who are free to base their selections on whatever criteria they desire. John P. Frank avowed that his Justice, Mr. Justice Black, tried "to get Southern boys—and tennis-players where possible."[269] Mr. Justice Stewart preferred Yale Law School graduates, Mr. Chief Justice Warren Californians, Mr. Justice Clark graduates of lesser known law schools. Mr. Justice Harlan usually chose one boy from Harvard and one from a New York City law school, and Mr. Justice Douglas usually turned to a West Coast law school for his choice. The 1965–66 term of the Court saw nineteen law clerks chosen by the nine members of the court, Mr. Chief Justice Warren selecting three, Mr. Justice Douglas one, all others two, plus one assigned jointly to retired Justices Reed and Burton, who were still "on call" for lower federal court spot tasks, as assigned by the Chief Justice. The young men came from ten different law schools; six from Harvard University; three each from Yale University and the University of Pennsylvania; two each from the University of Virginia and Stanford University; and one each from Columbia University, the University of Texas, and the University of North Carolina.

Exactly what work a Justice assigns or delegates to his clerk depends upon the former's inclination—or, as Mr. Justice Jackson once stated, "on the Justice's temperament and experience." Apparently, most, but by no means all, of the Justices—Justices Frankfurter and Brennan,[270] are on record as being notable exceptions to the practice—use their clerks to wade through the manifold petitions for *certiorari* that are filed annually. Typically, a law clerk may read such a petition and the opposing party's response, and then type or pen a brief memorandum to his Justice stating the issues involved and setting forth arguments for and against a grant of the desired writ. Suffice it to note that the Justice concerned will, of course, make up his own mind, yet the *certiorari* work by the clerks may well become crucial in the Court's endeavor to handle the ever-mounting case

[269] *The Marble Palace*, op. cit. pp. 115–16.
[270] See 59 *American Bar Association Journal* 836 (August 1973) for Mr. Justice Brennan's assertions on the issue.

load.[271] Some of the Justices may go somewhat further in employing their clerks, asking for a so-called bench memorandum on a particular case now and then. Such a memorandum may note whether the case is properly before the Court, state what federal issues are presented and how these were decided by the courts below, summarize the positions of the parties pro and con on the grant of the writ, propound certain approaches and points of precedent, and thereby suggest questions to be asked of counsel by the Justices during oral argument. The most intensive task performed by the law clerks is probably that of the necessary drudgery of research once an opinion has been assigned to a particular Justice. Here commences the time-consuming chore of investigating, of sorting and checking precedents, citations, historical data, congressional records—the host of materials so vital to the decision-making process. Beyond that, the chief role of the law clerk is to serve as a foil, friend, critic, sounding board. In the final analysis, however, as one former clerk wrote:

> In the course of my year, we never changed the Justice's mind on the result of any case. Our influence was close to nil. There was the fullest discussion, but he made the decisions. . . . The judge will listen if you say that some statement in his draft opinion is too broad or that a case is cited incorrectly. But if you tell him that such-and-such a constitutional amendment doesn't mean what he believes, you might as well stay in bed.[272]

The clerks are important tools for the Justices in the judicial process, perhaps indispensable ones, yet they are hardly classifiable as powers behind the throne. Essentially, they are law *clerks*—able, intelligent, and undoubtedly often, if not always, of considerable procedural aid to their Justices. But they are not members of the Court in any sense of the term. And, as has been contended repeatedly in connection with the entire matter of influence upon it, the Supreme Court of the United States is, in fine, master of its own house—which does not, however, mean that it is not aware of the existence of other houses both in and out of the governmental compound.

As we conclude this extensive consideration of the Supreme Court of the United States at work, it is both easy and natural to assent to a perceptive statement made by *The New York Times'* Supreme Court reporter Anthony Lewis as he left his seven-year coverage of the Court for a new assign-

---

271 For an interesting analysis which contends that the Court could not function without the clerks' *certiorari* role, see Arthur S. Miller, "High Court Secrets," *The New York Times*, November, 17, 1971, p. 45m.
272 As quoted anonymously in *The New York Times*, October 14, 1957, p. 29.

ment in London in 1965: "The wonderful thing about the Supreme Court is that it does its work. It decides, as it has to decide. There has never been a Rules Committee to save the Justices on tough problems. . . . [T]he Supreme Court . . . is the last stronghold of personal responsibility for decision."[273]

[273] *The New York Times Magazine*, January 17, 1965, pp. 56–58.

VI
Courts
Abroad

Wherever appropriate, reference has been made to the practices and theories of jurists and judicial systems of sundry lands, since the comparative element is one of the essential characteristics of this work. Newly emergent states of the world adapt their needs to the legal and social patterns of older ones. The United States has both profited from and contributed to other systems. Basically English in origin and design, features of its judicial system and process nevertheless both resemble, and differ drastically from, its progenitor as well as that of others. The legal systems of England and Wales, France, and the Soviet Union are most useful in an analysis in this connection. In the following pages a relatively brief view of the courts of these three countries will be presented.

THE COURTS OF ENGLAND AND WALES

It is incorrect to think of the courts of "Great Britain" or of the "United Kingdom" as a unified judicial system. For there exist actually *three different systems* in the United Kingdom of Great Britain and Northern Ireland: one for England and Wales; one for Scotland; and one for Northern Ireland. Only at the ultimate appellate level of the House of Lords is it possible to speak with accuracy of a unified system for the United Kingdom; because that body in its judicial role represents the final court of appeals—in those very few cases that manage to reach it—from the judgments of the highest courts of Scotland and Northern Ireland as well as from those of

England and Wales. The following description is of the judicial system of England and Wales—for convenience hereafter referred to as "England"—unless specified otherwise.[1]

In the United States the *same* tribunals ordinarily have *both* civil and criminal jurisdiction, with some minor exceptions for certain low level state courts, such as the Court of Small Claims in Pennsylvania. But in the England of today justice is meted out in two separated judicial hierarchies, one for civil cases and one for criminal cases—although the judges are often the same. This separation is based upon the Supreme Court of Judicature (Consolidation) Act of 1925, as amended, the progeny of a series of Judicature Acts that commenced in 1873. That statute brought order into what had been a truly bewildering array of distinct tribunals—e.g. some seven or eight leading courts had original jurisdiction in civil cases! However, unlike France, neither England nor the United States has a bona fide system of administrative courts—although some of the English administrative courts, e.g. Railway Rate Tribunals, existed long before World War II, and others have begun to make their appearance since the war; also some of the special and/or legislative tribunals in the United States are at least quasi-administrative.[2]

THE CRIMINAL COURTS' HIERARCHY

It is perhaps somewhat unorthodox to discuss the criminal courts hierarchy before that of the civil courts, but the English structure lends itself peculiarly well to such a procedure—in part because of a considerable amount of interchange of judges between the two hierarchies, despite the rigid structural segregation inherent in the system. Jurisdiction over criminal offenses has been exercised as a separate entity for some 700 years.

The Justice of the Peace and the Stipendiary Magistrate. At the base of the criminal courts hierarchy in England is the unpaid, volunteer lay magistrate, the *Justice of the Peace*, who must live within 15 miles of the judicial area of jurisdiction. His is an office established by law in 1326 or 1327 during the reign of Edward II. Approximately 4000 "J.P.s" are at work today. In the larger cities there is instead the *Stipendiary Magistrate*—London alone, where he is called Metropolitan Magistrate, has roughly thirty-five of

---

[1] These courts are presided over by judges who wear wigs—either shoulder-length ("full-bottomed") or short—and robes of office, with the color of their robes depending upon the law they administer. The common law judges as well as those who administer to the criminal law wear scarlet robes; the others wear black.

[2] See Chapter IV, *supra*, for details.

these officials—who, unlike his cousin, the Justice of the Peace, must be a full-time professional lawyer, usually a barrister, and is paid. With the exception of the Duchy of Lancaster, where they are designated by its own Chancellor, the magistrates at this lowest level of the criminal hierarchy are appointed on behalf of the Crown by the Lord Chancellor after careful screening and recommendation by local advisory committees in each county. This politically designated officer, who was discussed earlier,[3] is not only the highest judicial officer in the British system, he is also a member of the Cabinet, its foremost legal adviser, and a member as well as *ex officio* presiding officer of the House of Lords.

Sitting *en banc* without a jury, the Justice of the Peace or Stipendiary Magistrate, in his role as a tribunal of first instance, is exclusively a court of summary jurisdiction for criminal offenses. But he may also double as a committing judicial officer by holding an accused for action by a higher court in the event of "indictable" offenses. These would normally require grand jury action at the federal level in the United States; but in England, since the statutory abolition of the grand jury in 1933, the process of "information" has replaced it. Except for minor matters, trials at this lowest level of original jurisdiction are conducted by one, two, or three justices of the peace, but by only one stipendiary magistrate—a vital distinction between the two types of similar officials. The chief function of these officials is to try relatively minor criminal offenses, although they have an important jurisdiction in certain domestic relations—matrimonial, bastardy, and rate cases, and some administrative functions, such as licensing—and, as indicated, determine whether there is sufficient evidence to commit the offender for trial before a jury in a higher court.

Many of the offenses handled by the J.P. or the Stipendiary Magistrate concern traffic violations with limited fines. Generally speaking, his jurisdiction is restricted to cases involving a maximum fine of £100 or a six-months jail sentence or both—although there are exceptions, such as customs cases. In many instances the accused is permitted the option of a trial before the Justice of the Peace or the Stipendiary Magistrate or before a higher judge (and jury, when appropriate). Experience has demonstrated that the accused will often choose the former because of considerations of expeditiousness, but he may have a right to trial and wish to exercise it.

Still at the same level of the judiciary, when two or more justices of the peace or one stipendiary magistrate are sitting, a *Court of Petty Sessions* is said to exist. As will be explained subsequently, appeals from this level are

[3] See Chapter II, *supra*.

possible either to the Court of Quarter Sessions or to a three-judge Divisional Court of the Queen's Bench Division of the High Court of Justice, depending upon the nature of the appeal, and provided that the defendant did not plead guilty—although in London he is free to appeal even in the latter event if the sentence is more than one month in prison or a fine of more than £3. Appeals in matrimonial cases go to the Divisional Court of the Probate, Divorce, and Admiralty Division of the High Court of Justice.

The Crown Court. Immediately above the J.P. level is the *Crown Court*, established by the Courts Act of 1971; it replaced the fourteenth-century *Court of Quarter Sessions* and the twelfth-century *Assize Courts*. Clothed with appellate as well as original jurisdiction, it is the first court in which an accused, given the proper circumstances, is entitled to a trial by jury. The Crown Court is statutorily enabled to sit anywhere in England and Wales, and is staffed by High Court judges, the newly created Circuit judges, and Recorders. They sit with justices of the peace in case of appeals and committals of sentence, but no more than nine members of the Court may sit *en banc* in any given case. In some boroughs the Court consists merely of the paid *Recorder*, selected from barristers of at least five years' experience. He sits only occasionally as such, however, and continues in practice as a barrister. Ordinarily, the Court's session is presided over by a professional Circuit judge or, on limited occasions, by a High Court judge "on circuit" from the Queen's Bench Division of the High Court of Justice (a civil court) in London. It was Lord Parker, the Lord Chief Justice, who, in his capacity as a judge of its Queen's Bench Division, presided over the important Philby-Blake spy trial that took place in the spring of 1961 in England's capital. (The Lord Chief Justice, who is England's highest judicial officer, is the head of the Queen's Bench Division.)

Because of the nature of the offenses tried before them—all trials on indictment, including all major felonies such as homicide, robbery, larceny, and rape—the assizes always sit with a jury. Much traditional pageantry and fanfare attend their sessions, the proper judicial manner being very much in evidence. The Crown Court for Metropolitan London is the Central Criminal Court, widely known as the "Old Bailey" because of the name of the building where it meets for its twelve sessions annually, one each month.[4]

---

[4] "Bailley" was the tenth-century English word for "enclosure," and the Old Bailey stands on the site of an enclosure, originally part of Newgate Prison, where public executions took place until 1868.

Appeals from judgments of the Crown Court are possible to the next higher level court, the Court of Appeal, both on points of law and fact. On the former, any convicted defendant may appeal; and he may do so on a point of fact with leave of the Crown Court judge or that of the Court of Appeals itself. The latter permission is mandatory for an appeal against the sentence itself.

The Court of Appeal. Appeals from the two lower levels in the hierarchy, to which only the defendant is entitled—the Government may not appeal from a verdict of acquittal—were formerly taken directly to the *Court of Criminal Appeal*, created in 1907. Recently, however, the separate Court of *Criminal Appeal* was abolished, and its functions taken over by a *criminal division* of the *Court of Appeal*—an arrangement of chiefly administrative importance. Appeals come to the criminal division in the same way they used to go to the Court of Criminal Appeal, assuming the necessary jurisdiction is present and leave to file has been obtained. It is the most important tribunal of appellate jurisdiction in the criminal hierarchy of England. Sitting without a jury, it hears appeals based on the transcripts of the evidence taken at the trial. The Court of Appeal is composed of the legally qualified and salaried judges of the Queen's Bench Division of the High Court of Justice. Usually there are three members—the quorum—but whatever the number, it must be uneven.

Because of the stipulated assumption that any appeal constitutes a "retrial," the Court of Appeal has the power to revise—i.e. alter or vary—the original sentence in three situations: (1) if it is not legally justified; (2) if it was based on improper evidence; and (3) if the length or severity of the sentence points to an error in "some matter of principle" by the trial court. The Court of Appeal may even substitute conviction of another offense for the initial one if it appears that the defendant should have been convicted for it rather than for the one for which he was convicted below. But it has no power to order a trial *de novo* unless there has been a mistrial in the lower court.

The House of Lords. In rare instances, the accused—never the prosecutor—has one last and very much restricted path of appeal, from the Court of Appeal to the *House of Lords* (an institution to be more fully described in connection with the civil hierarchy). Yet such an appeal is possible only when a point of law of "general public importance" is involved, and leave to file for appeal to that august body must be given by the Court of Appeal or the Divisional Court of the Queen's Bench Division of the High Court of Justice—or by the House of Lords itself if refused by the aforementioned tribunals. Such appeals have averaged "somewhat under three a year."[5] Moreover, since the House of Lords habitually confines its rulings on the specific, often narrow, point of law involved—here very much like the Supreme Court of the United States—broad legal pronouncements are unlikely indeed.

Until a statutory change was effected in 1960, permission to appeal to the House of Lords was even more circumscribed than the present procedure. Leave to appeal could be granted only by the Attorney General, the senior law officer of the Crown, and then only if the point of law involved was deemed of "*exceptional* public importance." Thus, in the famous Guenther Padola loss-of-memory murder case of 1959, the Attorney General, Sir Reginald Manningham-Buller, refused to grant such permission. All other channels of appeal had previously been exhausted, and the Old Bailey jury had decided in the trial court that the alleged amnesia was faked. The accused consequently paid the ultimate penalty.

THE CIVIL COURTS' HIERARCHY

Although some of the terminology will be similar and some of the judicial personnel, in fact, the same, the existing hierarchical distinctions between the criminal and civil courts are highly pertinent to a proper understanding of the judicial process in England. Again, we commence at the lowest level of the courts.

The County Court. The court of first instance in civil matters is the *County Court*—so called by virtue of the adoption of the ancient name of the local courts of the county in early Anglo-Norman times, despite the fact that the jurisdiction of these tribunals today does not necessarily coincide with county boundaries. Indeed, it has nothing to do with them. The districts they serve are arranged so that a County Court is within ready reach everywhere; they are subject to geographic alteration by the Lord Chancellor. The more than 500 county courts are grouped into over fifty circuits, with at least one judge for each such circuit, who holds court in each district at least once a month. The judges—called "circuit judges" since the Courts Act of 1971—are appointed by the Crown on the advice of the Lord Chancellor—again with the exception of those in the Duchy of Lancaster, as in the case of the justices of the peace. To qualify, they must be barristers

---

[5] Richard M. Jackson, *The Machinery of Justice in England*, 6th ed. (Cambridge: Cambridge University Press, 1972), p. 152. This is an excellent book, and one of the very few relatively up-to-date ones available on the British judiciary. It presents a superb explanation and analysis of its subject matter.

FIGURE 2
THE CRIMINAL AND CIVIL COURTS OF ENGLAND AND WALES

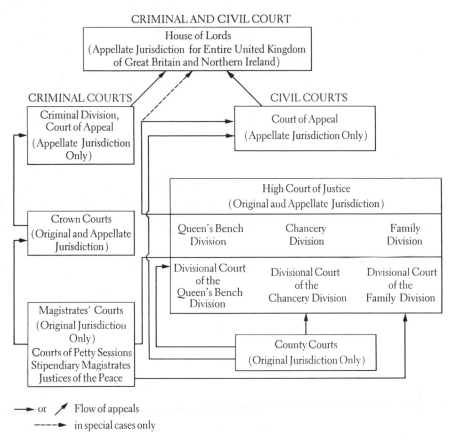

→ or ↗ Flow of appeals

----→ in special cases only

in good standing with at least seven years of experience. They retire at seventy-two or, exceptionally, at seventy-five.

The County Court judges—who are well paid, as is generally true of Britain's jurists—live in their districts and hold court once or twice a month in appropriate towns, referred to as their circuit, depending upon the work load docketed. Each County Court is assigned a *Registrar*, a solicitor appointed by, and subject to removal by, the Lord Chancellor, who is not only in charge of the court's office staff, but who may also act as a lesser judge. By leave of his county court judge, and in the absence of objections by any of the parties, the Registrar deals mainly with matters not involving more than £75; but he may exercise wider jurisdiction with the consent of the litigants.

The jurisdiction of the County Court, although strictly limited statutorily, is extensive, and the number of cases commenced at this level is vast. In 1968, for instance, a total of 1,509,558 proceedings were entered here.[6] Broadly speaking, the large majority of cases fall into the area of actions based on contract and tort claims up to a maximum of £750, with a handful of exceptions—e.g., libel and slander. Yet most of these cases do not exceed £150 in value. Other areas of County Court jurisdiction include equity matters up to £750, real-estate actions up to £400, and a limited range of admiralty and bankruptcy matters. And a highly significant field of its jurisdiction arises under so-called "social" or "collectivist" statutes, a by-product of today's welfare state. Since 1934, an appeal from the County Court must be taken directly to the Court of Appeal, thus by-passing the next higher court level.

The High Court of Justice. Immediately above the County Court in the hierarchy of the civil courts stands the *High Court of Justice*—an ancient institution deriving from the Norman *curia regis*, which was the monarch's personal instrument for the dispensing of justice. It has chiefly original, but also some divisionally restricted, appellate jurisdiction. This famous tribunal, established in 1873, is now staffed by three presiding officers and seventy-five distinguished *puisne* judges[7] who have had a minimum of ten years of experience as barristers—many have had twenty or twenty-five. The three divisions of the "High Court," as it is commonly called, thus comprise: the forty-three-member *Queen's Bench Division*, plus its presiding officer, the Lord Chief Justice, who ranks immediately after the Lord Chancellor in the judicial hierarchy; the eleven-member *Chancery Division*, plus its non-sitting presiding officer, the Lord Chancellor; and the President and eighteen judges of the *Family Division* (formerly known as the *Probate, Divorce, and Admiralty Division*).

---

[6] *Ibid*. p. 33.

[7] The first woman to be appointed to the High Court of Justice was County Court Judge Elizabeth Lane, Q. C., who reached her country's No. 3 tribunal in August 1965. A minor crisis arose over what to call the first woman judge. Would it be "Mr. Justice" or "Your Lordship"? Not at all, decreed the Lord Chancellor, Lord Gardiner. Upon her confirmation by Queen Elizabeth, it was announced that "henceforth and hereafter" Dame Elizabeth Lane would be addressed as "The Honorable Mrs. Justice Lane" and, inside the court room, as "My Lady" and "Your Ladyship." (*The Christian Science Monitor*, September 19, 1965.) Another woman was appointed in 1974.

Of the three, the Queen's Division is by far the largest and busiest, partly because its judges must—as was explained above—participate also in the work of the criminal courts as a matter of exercising original jurisdiction, and partly because, with three or five of its judges sitting as the *Divisional Court* of the Queen's Bench Division, it hears certain appeals in criminal cases from the courts of summary jurisdiction, i.e. the Justice of the Peace and Stipendiary Magistrate Court and the Crown Court. Coupled with its jurisdiction over the general field of the common law, its work range thus extends to: (1) ordinary civil actions; (2) its appellate and supervisory jurisdiction *en banc* in its mantle of Divisional Court of the Queen's Bench Division; (3) appellate functions exercised by a single judge; and (4) its limited original criminal jurisdiction.

As the presiding officer of the Queen's Bench Division, the Lord Chief Justice enjoys a considerable degree of authority and prestige. In his capacity he is the directing figure of the criminal courts of England. Members of the British legal circles are fond of stating that the Lord Chief Justice is in somewhat the same position as the Pope in that what he says on any given occasion may influence not only the other judges but also the lawyers, the magistrates, and even the police.[8] He is indeed a towering figure on the scene of government, and he is regarded with much awe, confidence, and respect.

The Chancery Division has exclusive jurisdiction in some cases, and concurrent jurisdiction with the Queen's Bench Division in others. In the extensive former category are equity matters of bankruptcy, companies, execution of trusts, wardships, patent cases, foreclosures of mortgages, etc. Appeals from county courts in bankruptcy matters lie to a *Divisional Court of the Chancery Division.*

The Family Division has jurisdiction in the areas implied by its name: giving valid title to the estate of deceased persons; matrimonial decrees as to divorce, nullity, restitution of conjugal rights, judicial separation, presumption of death, and dissolution of marriage; and declaration of legitimacy. Its *Divisional Court* hears appeals from the Magistrates' Courts level in matrimonial cases. The Family Division (remember Admiralty) also has jurisdiction over various matters affecting ships under maritime law. In popular lingo, the Family Division is often referred to as the "Wrecks" Division, because it is said to deal with "wills, wives, and wrecks." Lord Goddard, who was Lord Chief Justice for twelve years, amended this ancient

[8] See *The New York Times,* March 23, 1961.

jest—he said that it deals with "wrecks of wills . . . marriages . . . and ships."[9]

In addition to its specialized jurisdiction just explained, the High Court of Justice has over-all jurisdiction in all cases that are eligible for hearings in the County Court as well as those that lie outside that tribunal's jurisdiction. But, if it is asked to take cases under its original jurisdiction when these can be handled by the County Court, e.g. routine controversies with a value of less than £500 to £750, even the successful plaintiff must pay court costs. Together with the Court of Appeal, the High Court of Justice forms the *Supreme Court of Judicature* which sits continually in London. It is a body that is actually neither supreme nor a court, but serves as a type of cover-all for these two entirely separate branches of the civil courts system.

The Court of Appeal. Appeals from any of the Divisions of the High Court of Justice go to the *Court of Appeal*,[10] which consists of the Lord Chancellor; former Lord Chancellors; the Lords of Appeal in Ordinary; the Lord Chief Justice; the Master of the Rolls (England's third highest judicial officer); and the President of the Family Division of the High Court as members *ex officio;* plus eight Lord Justices of Appeal, the regular sitting members, who must have had fifteen years of experience as barristers or been High Court judges. But of the *ex officio* members, only the Master of the Rolls actually sits with the regular sitting judges—normally three in number—of the Court of Appeal. Its appellate jurisdiction extends to points of law arising out of civil cases from the County Court or the High Court of Justice.

Appeals on points of law coming from the County Court reach the Court of Appeal as a matter of right if the amount of the claim involved exceeds £20, or when the remedy is an injunction. In other appeals the judge below must give permission. In the cases coming from the High Court, appeal is automatic on points of law but not on points of fact. If the Court of Appeal grants an appeal, retrial of the case will normally take place below; however, it may also reconsider the evidence itself, but without taking new testimony from witnesses.

The House of Lords. From the Court of Appeal, if the matter of law involved is deemed to be of sufficient importance, there remains the final path

---

[9] Lord Goddard, "Organization and Jurisdiction of the Courts of England," 44 *Journal of the American Judicature Society* 62 (August 1960). (See his entire article for a fine description, pp. 60–65.)

[10] The Administration of Justice Act of 1969 provides for appeals in some cases directly from the High Court to the House of Lords, thus "leapfrogging" the Court of Appeal.

of appeal to the *House of Lords* (an expensive—£1000 for printing costs alone is an average expenditure—and uncommon one) provided that the appeal has been certified by the Court of Appeal[11] or granted by the House of Lords itself, a historic right dating back to the practices of the Norman institution of the *magnum concilium*, the Great Council. The Lords do not, of course, sit in a mass body for that purpose—there are over 1000 members (though only about 200 actually attend!). Instead, the legal section of the House of Lords comprises a small, highly skilled, distinguished group of judicial experts, the nine *Law Lords*, known as the *Lords of Appeal in Ordinary*, plus the Lord Chancellor, the presiding officer of the House of Lords. These ten officials—who thus constitute the final court of appeal—are augmented by any other peer who has held, or now holds, high judicial office under the Crown.

This small group of appellate[12] experts was created originally by the Appellate Jurisdiction Act of 1876 to supplement the judicial strength of the House of Lords. It remains the sole kingdom-wide judicial body, and as such always has some members from Scotland and, on occasion, one from Northern Ireland. These few dignitaries, who have backgrounds of at least fifteen years as barristers in England or Northern Ireland or as practicing advocates in Scotland, or of two years in high judicial office, who are all professional, paid judges with life peerages, and who ordinarily take no part whatever in the political business of the Lords, thus constitute the Supreme Court of the United Kingdom of Great Britain and Northern Ireland. But unlike the Supreme Court of the United States and the other United States federal and state courts, neither the House of Lords nor any other English or Welsh court, no matter how high, possesses the power of judicial review (which will be fully described in the following chapter).

The Judicial Committee of the Privy Council. One other major appellate tribunal, sitting somewhat astride the regular court system just described, exists in the British Isles. It is the important *Judicial Committee of the Privy Council*, which constitues the final court of appeal for cases from the

---

[11] A famous illustration of a refusal by the Court of Appeal so to certify an appeal was the case of Dr. Robert A. Soblen in 1962. The sixty-one-year-old psychiatrist had fled the United States while under a life sentence for wartime espionage for the Soviet Union, and asked Britain to grant him asylum. The British Home Office refused, and Soblen commenced a lengthy, ultimately unsuccessful series of legal maneuvers to escape deportation. He later committed suicide rather than be sent back to the States.

[12] The House of Lords has *original* jurisdiction in civil cases of claims to peerages and decisions as to disputed elections. (In criminal matters it has both original and appellate jurisdiction, but it is very rarely exercised.)

ecclesiastical courts of the Church of England, colonies, protectorates, trust territories, the Isle of Man, and the Channel Islands. It is also available as the ultimate appellate body for all those members of the Commonwealth that might wish to avail themselves of its services. But in recent years, with the rare exception of isolated cases from Ceylon, New Zealand, Australia, Ghana, Jamaica, and Malaya, Commonwealth members have normally preferred to adjudicate their problems in their own judicial structure. This is conclusively the case with India and Pakistan, for example. However, the Judicial Committee of the Privy Council did constitute the final court of appeal from Canada on constitutional matters until 1949, when the right to appeal to it was abolished there by statute.

Only privy councilors are eligible for membership on the Judicial Committee. In practice, most of the work has been done by the Law Lords of the House of Lords, but other high judicial officers from the United Kingdom, as well as from the Commonwealth and other jurisdictions the Judicial Committee serves, have participated in its functions.

THE COURTS OF FRANCE

If imitation may be regarded as indication of approval, the popularity and acceptance of the French judicial system among the older as well as the newer states of the world represent such approval in the highest degree. The French administration of justice, far more than the Anglo-American, has become a model abroad. To a large extent this is attributable to its base—those legendary civil, criminal, penal, commercial, and procedural codes, drafted under the often personal direction of Napoleon Bonaparte at the end of the eighteenth and especially at the beginning of the nieneteenth century, culminating in the famous, and still very much alive, *Code Napoleon*. With full justice the French codes have been called "well-balanced pieces of jurisprudential art, utterly systematic and conveniently accessible."[13] Here French logic was truly at its best.

Yet the judicial structure which applies the codes—which, of course, have been periodically amended—is far from a simple and readily comprehensible one. A maze of tribunals stud the countryside—just as in Napoleon's time, despite a number of revisions in the hierarchy of one of the two major court systems under the de Gaulle Republic in 1959, 1963, 1965, and 1967,

---

13 Robert G. Neumann, *European and Comparative Government*, 4th ed. (New York: McGraw-Hill Book Co., 1968), p. 330.

and under his successor, Georges Pompidou, in 1972. The French authorities have gone so far as to take due public cognizance of the problem in an official governmental release, which noted that "judicial organization in France is exceptionally complex," but they went on to point out that "it is the product of successive contributions from centuries of our history, and in it, tradition continues to play a very important role."[14] This acknowledgment may not be of much comfort to the student of the system, but it does serve as an explanation. The government bulletin might have added that one of the reasons for the complexity and profusion of the French courts is the generally admirable notion that justice should be provided quickly, efficicently, inexpensively, and conveniently—very much like any other government service!

TWO MAJOR DIVISIONS

The courts of France are characterized by two quite separate and distant hierarchies: first, the *ordinary* or *regular* courts; second, the *administrative courts*. (A substructure of commercial and certain other special courts need not concern us at this juncture; they may be viewed as falling generally under the ordinary courts—although appeal from some of them lies to the Conseil d'Etat.) In case of doubt as to proper jurisdiction, the eight-member *Tribunal des Conflits* (Tribunal of Conflicts), created especially for that umpire-role, and headed by the Minister of Justice—who votes only in case of a tie—determines, unappealably, to which of the two major court systems a case goes.

Again, the chief reason for this division of responsibility between the two judicial hierarchies is an historic one. Fearful that the ordinary courts might interfere with the administrative or executive branch of the government, the legislative bodies of France, dating all the way back to the days of the Revolution, wrote into laws and constitutions specific provisions that expressly forbade judicial bodies to intervene. For example, the Law of December 22, 1789, provided: ". . . Judicial power should not trouble local administrative agencies in the exercise of their functions." And that of August 16–24, 1790, spelled the matter out more clearly:

> The judicial functions are and will remain forever separate from the administrative functions. The judges will not be allowed, under penalty of forfeiture, to disturb in any manner whatsoever, the activities of the ad-

[14] As quoted in Taylor Cole (ed.), *European Political Systems*, 3d ed. (New York: Alfred A. Knopf, 1959), p. 234.

255

ministrative corps, nor to summon before them the administrators, concerning their functions.[15]

This was all very well in theory, but it soon became clear that someone or something would be needed to check certain administrative excesses of power beyond the mediating and advisory services rendered by the *Conseil d'Etat* on matters in dispute between the citizen and the government. Hence the eventual adoption of the system of administrative courts—comprising the *Conseil* plus developing subordinate administrative tribunals—designed to check administrative abuses and at the same time retain the cherished principle of separation of powers insofar as the judicial and executive-administrative functions are concerned. The separated hierarchies have flourished, and they survive essentially unchanged in design and principle, although not in certain organizational structure and nomenclature.

THE ORDINARY OR REGULAR COURTS' HIERARCHY

On March 1, 1959, the de Gaulle government effected the first group of several contemporary judicial reforms, chiefly designed to give the courts a corps of more specialized judges and to distribute these more equitably geographically in a rearranged system of ordinary courts, geared more closely to modern demands and realistic population distribution. The effect of these changes, as augmented in 1963, 1965, and 1967, and most recently and extensively in 1972, is reflected in the following description.

The Court of Instance (TRIBUNAL D'INSTANCE). The first de Gaulle Reorganization Bill abolished the time-honored, but outdated, lowest of the ordinary courts, the local *Juge de Paix*—again our friend, the Justice of the Peace—and replaced that popular institution with a new local court of first instance in all minor civil cases, the *Tribunal d'Instance*. Theretofore *juges de paix*—with law diplomas, unlike most of their English and American counterparts—had brought justice, more or less, to the 3040 cantons of France by way of a completely informal, inexpensive, and often inconsequential procedure in the usual type of petty, chiefly civil, infractions, which obliged them to "ride circuit." Since 1959, however, the new *tribunaux d'instance*, numbering 455, have existed in the capitals of the various *arrondissements*—the administrative geographical levels above the canton. Each of the new courts may have several judges—who are required to live

---

[15] Stephan Riesengeld, "The French System of Administrative Justice: A Model for American Law," 18 *Boston University Law Review* 48 (1938). See also Margherita Rendel's excellent work, *The Administrative Function of the French Conseil d'Etat* (London: Weidenfeld and Nicolson, 1970).

in the area of jurisdiction of the tribunal—but decisions are rendered by a single judge. The *tribunaux d'instance* and their judges have been given considerably more effective adjudicatory power than that possessed by the old *juges de paix*. Indeed, they are fully intended to become the most important basic unit in the revised judicial system, as the 1972 reforms again demonstrated.

The Court of Major Instance (TRIBUNAL DE GRANDE INSTANCE). The old civil *Court of First Instance* (*Tribunal de Première Instance*), of which one was located in every *arrondissement*, gave way to the newly created *Tribunal de Grande Instance*. The erstwhile criminal section of this level, the *Correctional Court* (*Tribunal Correctionnel*), has been retained, but was moved to the criminal side of the judicial structure (see Figure 3). In place of the original 359 courts, the new 172 *tribunaux de grande instance* have unlimited civil jurisdiction throughout the *département*—the highest administrative subdivision in France—not merely in a single *arrondissement*.[16] According to the number of inhabitants and the "degree of economic activity,"[17] the larger *départements* are entitled to two or more of the tribunals. Each case is tried by several judges sitting *en banc*, usually three, but always comprising an uneven number, with the decision reached by majority vote. Appeals from the *tribuneaux de grande instance* lie to the Courts of Appeals.

The reforms established *Police Courts* (*Tribuneaux de Police*) as the basic tribunal for minor offenses on the *criminal* side of the organizational ledger. Numbering 455 like the *tribuneaux d'instance*, its judge (or judges) may well be the same individual as that at the basic civil level. The Police Court's jurisdiction is limited to offenses not exceeding penalties of sixty days in prison and/or small fines.

At the next higher level of the criminal hierarchy of the ordinary courts are the aforementioned Correctional or Criminal Courts (*Tribuneaux Correctionnels*). Like their counterparts on the civil side, the *tribuneaux de grande instance*, there are 172 units, comprising three or more judges. Their jurisdiction extends to more serious offenses, covering penalties of up to five years' imprisonment and fines upward of F.F. 200.

The Assize Court (COUR D'ASSISE). The original tribunal for most criminal cases above the *tribuneaux correctionnels* and for most appeals is the *Assize*

[16] A major structural and organizational rearrangement of regional and local government began to take place in France in 1973–74 which, if carried through, could well herald a wholesale restructuring of the administrative subdivisions and thus prompt major changes in judicial organization as well.

[17] *Ambassade de France*, French Affairs Bulletin No. 84 (May, 1959), p. 32.

Court (*Cour d'Assise*). Its *original* jurisdiction thus extends to all major criminal cases, such as homicide. It does not sit with a jury when acting as an appellate tribunal; rather, a lot-chosen jury of nine "*de simples citoyens*" (plain citizens), plus three judges sit in cases of original jurisdiction. (A verdict of guilty requires a majority of eight votes.) There are ninety-five assizes, one in each *département*, each being usually staffed with three judges from the twenty-seven units of the courts of appeal above. However, depending upon the work load and the availability of personnel, two of the three judges may be drafted from a local lower tribunal, but the presiding judge is invariably a member of the *Cour d'Appel*.

The Court of Appeal (cour d'appel). The 1959 and subsequent reforms did not make any substantial changes in the structure of the *Court of Appeal* (*Cour d'Appel*), the appellate tribunal for civil cases from below, and none at all in the number of the twenty-seven judicial districts (*Chambres*) —each of which includes several *départements*—in which one of these tribunals operates. However, the jurisdiction of the *Cour d'Appel* was naturally extended not only to take appeals on all matters of fact from both the civil and criminal courts below, but also to include the special courts alluded to earlier, and other newly created ones, particularly in the field of social and economic legislation. Thus, in addition to criminal appeals from the *assises*, and civil ones from the *tribuneaux de grande instance*, appeals to a *Cour d'Appel* may come from such as any one of the following (in addition to the considerable number of appeals that come up from the *tribunaux de grande instance* in the regular hierarchy below): The *Labor Conciliation Board* (*Conseil de Prud'hommes*), composed of an equal number of employers and employees who, chosen by their own groups for six years (one-half retiring every three years), hear disputes arising out of industrial contracts and arbitrate these; the *Commercial Court* (*Tribunal de Commerce*), consisting of businessmen elected by their local peers for two-year terms to act in certain statutorily designated commercial cases; the *Juvenile Court* (*Tribunal pour Enfants*) one judge sitting for three years, chosen from a *tribunal de grande instance*; the *Farm Lease Court*, found at the seat of each *tribunal d'instance*; and the *Social Security Commission*, which consists of one judge from the *tribunal d'instance* plus two representatives of "interested parties." All of these special courts have several court units throughout the country. Each of the twenty-seven courts of appeal, with from three to five judges sitting—seven in the Parisian tribunal—hears a case before it entirely *de novo*; their decisions on points of *fact* are final. On points of *law* further appeal lies to the Cour de Cassation.

In 1963, Parliament created a complicated and controversial special tribunal to combat "subversive activity," the *Permanent Court of State Security* (*Cour de Sûreté de l'État*), largely as a direct result of terrorist activity by both civil and military elements involved in the government's attempts to settle the difficult problem of Algeria. The tribunal consists of civilian judges and senior military officers; there is no jury. The sole appeal from its decisions is to the *Cour de Cassation*.

The Supreme Court of Appeal (*Cour de Cassation*). At the pinnacle of the regular courts of France stands its Supreme Court of Appeal (*Cour de Cassation*). Although it was largely unaffected by the Judicial Reorganization Acts of 1959, 1963, and 1965, the 1967 reforms did reach it. Appropriately sitting in Paris—as ever, the heart and pulse of *la patrie*—it consists of 83 judges, or, more precisely, 77 counselors (*conseillers*), the Chief Justice (*Premier Président*), and 5 presidents of sections. Its jurisdiction, which is interpretatively final in both civil and criminal cases on points of *law*, extends throughout the French Republic. The high tribunal enjoys great prestige and respect.

The *Cour de Cassation* is divided into five sections (*chambres*) of fifteen judges, each headed by a *président*—a favorite French title—with the entire tribunal presided over by the First President, or Chief Justice. Seven judges constitute a quorum to hear a case. Two sections deal with civil matters (personal and family status and property); one of these, known as the Screening Section, receives and evaluates all petitions and requests for review, conducts a preliminary inquiry into their merits, dockets those it deems worthy of review by the court, and rejects all others. The other three *chambres* handle commercial, social, and criminal matters, respectively. Like the House of Lords, but unlike the Supreme Court of the United States, the *Cour de Cassation* has no original jurisdiction; all cases that come to it through the hierarchy of the ordinary courts do so by way of appeal from the assizes (a majority of the cases) and the courts of appeal below.

Casser, the French for "to break," or "to smash," indicates the actual role of this respected and dignified tribunal. That role is distinctly limited, for the *Cour de Cassation* rules only on the legal appropriateness of the decision rendered—i.e. it merely passes judgment on *the point of law involved in the decision*, emphatically not on the substance of the case. It neither "decides" nor "retries" a case. It simply possesses the power to quash—*casser*—the legal point of a case, and *then to remand it below for retrial* by a court of the same rank as the one from which it came, but not to the

259

FIGURE 3
THE REGULAR (ORDINARY) COURTS OF THE FIFTH FRENCH REPUBLIC (1974)

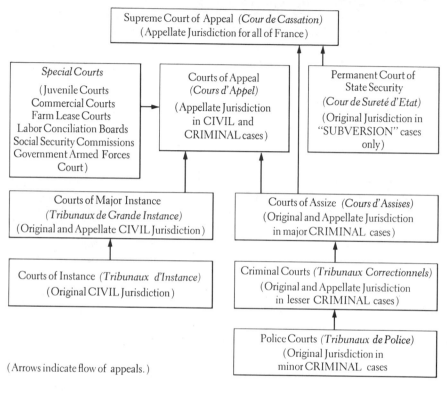

Supreme Court of Appeal *(Cour de Cassation)*
(Appellate Jurisdiction for all of France)

Special Courts
(Juvenile Courts
Commercial Courts
Farm Lease Courts
Labor Conciliation Boards
Social Security Commissions
Government Armed Forces
Court)

Courts of Appeal
(Cours d'Appel)
(Appellate Jurisdiction
in CIVIL and
CRIMINAL cases)

Permanent Court of
State Security
(Cour de Sureté d'Etat)
(Original Jurisdiction in
"SUBVERSION" cases
only)

Courts of Major Instance
(Tribunaux de Grande Instance)
(Original and Appellate CIVIL Jurisdiction)

Courts of Assize *(Cours d'Assises)*
(Original and Appellate Jurisdiction
in major CRIMINAL cases)

Courts of Instance *(Tribunaux d'Instance)*
(Original CIVIL Jurisdiction)

Criminal Courts *(Tribunaux Correctionnels)*
(Original and Appellate Jurisdiction
in lesser CRIMINAL cases)

(Arrows indicate flow of appeals.)

Police Courts *(Tribunaux de Police)*
(Original Jurisdiction in
minor CRIMINAL cases

same court. In the event of a second appeal in a case that it had sent back down initially, the Court will give an authoritative interpretation which *must* be followed by the lower tribunal. In sum, the *Cour de Cassation*'s legal holdings are binding on all lower courts.

In no sense does the *Cour de Cassation*, "an offspring of the revolutionary legislators' profound distrust of the judges,"[18] have the power of judicial review—although in 1974 President Giscard d'Estaing's government promised to consider its adoption in a future reform of the judiciary. Indeed, as the Court itself ruled, in a case involving the newspaper *Le National*, a law which had been "deliberately promulgated according to constitutional

[18] Mauro Cappelletti, *Judicial Review in the Contemporary World* (Indianapolis: The Bobbs-Merrill Co., Inc., 1971), p. 13.

forms" is beyond attacks on grounds of unconstitutionality under the French system of separation of powers.[19] The absence of judicial review is a deficiency of power which the French courts have shared with their friends across the Channel. However, a system of what might be called quasi-judicial review, lodged in an extra-judicial body lying outside the judicial hierarchy, the *Constitutional Council* (*Conseil Constitutionnel*)—to be described in the following chapter—was adopted by the Constitution of the Fifth Republic as a successor to its rather anemic relative of the Fourth Republic, the *Constitutional Committee* (*Comité Constitutionnel*). But, as will be readily perceived, the French system of quasi-judicial review is a far cry from the bona fide power and authority vested in the United States judiciary—although it is now (late 1974) undergoing some strengthening.

ADMINISTRATIVE TRIBUNALS GENERALLY

We now turn to what is unquestionably the more interesting, because more novel, second judicial hierarchy in France, the popular and entirely separate *administrative courts*, which are more or less foreign to the Anglo-Saxon world. Despite some post-World War II modifications, the United Kingdom and the United States still hold, by and large, to the ancient Anglo-Saxon principle that "the King can do no wrong"—which, in effect, signifies that the sovereign, the state, cannot be sued without its expressed consent. This concept of governmental immunity—dating from the reign of Henry II (1154–89)—has its legal roots in the prerogatives of the King of England, who was the "Fountainhead of Justice and Equity" under the law of the feudal state. During the sixteenth century, the personal immunity of the monarch was enlarged to include that of the state—hence the King (State) can do no wrong. Accordingly, in the Anglo-Saxon world of our day the acts of government officials are viewed as the acts of ordinary citizens and are judged by exactly the same rules of law and before the same courts. After all, it is one of the underlying principles of the philosophy of democratic government that any citizen is presumably capable of participating in it (a notion dear to the heart of President Andrew Jackson—and popularized well by him—who used it to justify, and some erroneously contend, to invent, the "spoils system"). Thus, as one of Britain's great students of government, A. V. Dicey, put it often, every government official, from the Prime Minister on down to the lowliest clerk, is "under the same responsibility for every act done without legal justification as any other citizen."[20]

[19] See VII *Political Studies* 51–53 and 60–61 (February 1959).
[20] For example, see his *Introduction to the Study of the Law of the Constitution*, 10th ed. (New York: The Macmillan Co., 1961).

This has meant that a British or American citizen who believes himself to have been aggrieved or injured by a government official in either of the two lands and wants to take action would *have to sue that official*—who, in turn, would have to justify his actions at the bar of the regular courts. Thus, if Citizen John Smith believes that he has been wronged or maltreated by Sheriff James Doe in the latter's capacity as an officer of the law, he may bring suit. But such a suit must be brought against Sheriff James Doe, in a regular court of jurisdiction, *not* against Doe's state of Virginia, whose laws he was presumably enforcing (or not against the United States, if the arresting officer had been a federal official), and the suit will normally read *Smith v. Doe*. Moreover, to collect damages, which would presumably come out of Doe's pocket, Citizen Smith must demonstrate successfully that Sheriff Doe has exceeded his discretionary authority under the law—an extremely difficult task in most instances.

Whatever the underlying philosophical justifications for personal liability of governmental officials, its practical implications are often unsatisfactory, to say the least, and may well be fraught with danger both to the individuals involved and the system which they serve and under which they live. Among these implications and the lessons of experience are: the possibility that an official may perform his duties timidly or haphazardly, or that he may not perform them in accordance with his most considered judgment but according to expediency; the difficulty, already alluded to, of collecting from an individual government servant; the question why, in performing a duty for his government, he should be personally responsible in the first place. Moreover, there are the inevitable delays in getting a case docketed in the courts; the slowly grinding judicial process, especially in as large and litigation-happy a country as the United States; and the inconvenience and expense of bringing a case to court. All these represent factors that may well, and often do, outweigh any monetary recompense that might eventually accrue to the plaintiff.

In recognition of these very real problems, England and the United States have gradually begun to provide tribunals in which the state may be sued directly. No abandonment of the old philosophy of a single, unified judiciary has taken place, nor is it likely to take place in the near future. However, both countries have shown considerable interest in the institution of the Scandinavian *ombudsman*,[21] a sort of "people's watchdog" over ad-

[21] See the compendium on the *ombudsman*, edited by D. C. Rowat, *The Ombudsman: Citizen's Defender*, 2d ed. (London: Allen & Unwin, 1968), containing chapters on Britain and the United States; the chapter on the United States is my "The Need for Ombudsmen in the United States." See also my "Denmark's *Folketingets Ombudsmand*: A People's Watchdog," 20 *Public Administration Review* 152 (Summer 1960),

ministrative abuses, who commands a good deal of influence and esteem, though little direct power, and who disposes of some thousand cases annually with dispatch and expertise. Indeed, with the enactment of the Parliamentary Commissioner Act of 1967, Britain adopted a limited, rather restricted and watered down version of it.

Moreover, both Britain and the United States have taken some tangible steps in the direction of rendering matters a bit more palatable to government employees and citizens alike. Thus, Britain adopted the Crown Proceedings Act of 1947, which, under certain circumstances, makes the government responsible for the actions of its servants. Purposely provided with many loopholes and exceptions, the act nevertheless now enables ordinary citizens to sue the government in the same manner and before the same tribunals "as if the Crown were a fellow-citizen." Hence, the injured or aggrieved party sues the state as a matter of right.[22] Furthermore, the act makes government departments responsible for common law as well as statutory duties. However, it should be noted that the act confines itself, more or less, to the *non-law-enforcing* agencies of government, thus leaving unchanged the path of claims that might arise under the law-enforcing units, such as police, military services, foreign affairs. Nevertheless, this unquestionably valuable statute does represent a wholesome and welcome change.[23]

What the above statute did for Britain, the Tort Claims Act of 1946 had done, broadly speaking, for the United States one year earlier, insofar as the federal government is concerned. Under it, a citizen who feels he has been injured or aggrieved by an employee of the federal government, or the government itself, may bring suit in any civil action, other than a breach of contract—which is not a tort—against the United States for negligence or wrongful acts, no maximum monetary ceiling existing on the claim. It is also possible to make claims of less than $1000 directly to the head of any federal agency alleged to be responsible for a loss caused by "negligent or wrongful act of omission of an employee," but the agency is *not required* to sanction such claims. Appeals under the provisions of the Tort Claims Act may be taken to the Court of Claims and, under certain conditions, to the regular constitutional court hierarchy.

---

and the compendium, edited by Roy V. Peel, "The Ombudsman or Citizen's Defender: A Modern Institution," 377 *The Annals* (May 1968), pp. iii–240.

[22] Thus, if a citizen is run over by a Post Office van, he can sue the Post Office instead of proceeding against the Attorney General by Petition of Right.

[23] For a brief evaluation of the Act, see Harry Street, *Government Liability: A Comparative Study* (Cambridge: Cambridge University Press, 1953).

The Court of Claims, established in 1855, as was demonstrated in some detail in Chapter IV, is itself a vehicle for citizens to sue the federal government for damages, and as such represents a modification of the "sovereign-can-do-no-wrong" principle. But its limited jurisdiction is confined to contractual, tax, and other non-tort claims against the Government of the United States. The Tort Claims Act contains, as does its British counterpart, many deliberate exceptions and ambiguities. For example, it excludes

> . . . any claim based upon an act or omission of an employee of the Government exercising due care, in the exercise of a statute or regulation, whether or not such statute or regulation be valid, or based upon the exercise or performance or the failure to exercise or perform a discretionary function or duty on the part of a federal agency or an employee of the Government, whether or not the discretion involved be abused. . . .[24]

but, hopefully, it personifies a salutary trend in adjudication.[25] In effect, the act, together with the Court of Claims and the United States Tax Court (see pp. 150–51, *supra*), represents one of three forms of "consent in advance," under which a citizen may now bring suit against the federal government.

THE FRENCH ADMINISTRATIVE COURTS

The hierarchy of courts that administers the *droit administratif* in France is very much part and parcel of the governmental system, however separated it is from the ordinary courts. To the French—and to many careful observers in the Anglo-Saxon world as well—theirs is the only logical system of supervising the administrative branch of the government, not only because of its rapid, convenient, and efficient adjudicatory process, but also because of

[24] It should not be forgotten, of course, that in both countries exist numerous *quasi-judicial* agencies and/or tribunals that, among other duties, *adjudicate administratively* claims upon the government. These are, for example, the "independent" regulatory commissions and agencies in the United States, and the ministerially appointed "special administrative tribunals" in the United Kingdom—established to deal with cases arising out of the application of social policy, e.g. the Licensing Authority for Public Service Vehicles. An important development in connection with these British tribunals was the creation of the Council on Tribunals, established under the Tribunals and Inquiries Act of 1958, following the Franks Committee Report; it is charged with general supervision over all British administrative tribunals. For a perceptive explanation and analysis, see H. W. N. Wade, "The Council on Tribunals," *Public Law* 351 (1960).

[25] For an article that is still informative on the status of the doctrine of tort liability in the several states of the United States, see Robert A. Leflar and Benjamin E. Kantrowitz, 29 *New York University Law Journal* 1363 (1954), especially the "Five Major Groupings," pp. 1407–8.

the expertise inherent in the judicial personnel that staff its administrative courts. This is even more remarkable because the French administrative courts are actually more closely linked to the executive than to the judicial branch. Evolving gradually since revolutionary days, the predominantly "judge-made" *droit administratif* has a long and honorable history, beginning with the creation of the first *Council of State* (*Conseil d'État*) under Napoleon Bonaparte in the year VIII (1799).

The structure of the French administrative court system is infinitely less complicated than the regular court system. It consists of but two levels: first, the *Regional Councils* or *Administrative Tribunals* (*Tribunaux Administratifs*), since they are arranged no longer in *départements*, as of yore, but in twenty-three national regions plus Paris; second, the famous multipurpose, and powerful, *Council of State* (*Conseil d'État*) at the apex. (There is also a number of special collateral administrative tribunals, sometimes known as "inferior councils"—such as the *Council of Public Instruction* (*Conseil d'Instruction Publique*) and the *Draft Review Board* (*Conseil Militaire de Revision*), which may be omitted for present purposes.)

The Regional Councils (TRIBUNAUX ADMINISTRATIFS). It is to the *Tribunal Administratif* of his region that a French citizen with a complaint against the administrative branch of *La République* turns initially. In almost all instances involving the *droit administratif*, the *Tribunal Administratif* acts as the administrative court of first instance. It has power either to annul an illegal decision or action, or to cause payment of damages. It is staffed by able, experienced civil servants of whom three-quarters have been recruited either directly from the *École Nationale d'Administration* (see below), or from the administrative branch itself—provided they have law degrees—or they are merit appointees who have passed competitive examinations; a few have come from political or semi-political posts.[26] The caliber of the four to six members of each *tribunal administratif*—one *président*, of course, and three to five *conseillers*—is almost always outstanding even at this first instance level.

The administrative court system of France is both simple and inexpensive: all a plaintiff at the bar of his *Tribunal Administratif* has to do is to execute and file the official complaint form which costs practically nothing. Normally, the tribunal will conduct the investigation of the complaint by way of written statements to both sides of the complaint. Sometimes an

---

[26] Margherita Rendel, "The Political Impact of the French *Conseil d'État*." Paper presented at the meeting of the International Political Science Association, Montreal, Canada, Aug. 21, 1973, p. 3.

oral hearing is held, at which the litigants may either present arguments personally or through legal counsel. When the tribunal is ready to render a decision it will do so publicly; usually that settles the matter. Far more often than not, the complaining *citoyen* wins his suit, and can then look forward to speedy compensation from the public treasury for any damages. So prevalent have been these citizen victories that considerable criticism has ensued among both legal scholars and practitioners, who believe that the administrative court system has caused the French Government to be "too tough on itself," that there exists what might be viewed as a distinct bias *against* it.

The Council of State (LE CONSEIL D'ÉTAT). With its appellate jurisdiction from the *tribunaux administratifs*—approximately 20 to 25 per cent of the lower tribunals' decisions are appealed[27]—as well as original jurisdiction in certain stipulated "important" and/or "delicate" cases, the *Conseil d'État* justly enjoys enormous prestige. Actually, it is far more than a merely administrative tribunal; only one of its five sections—a most renowned one, the *Litigation Section* (*Section du Contentieux*)—deals with the *droit administratif*. The other four are concerned with drafting of legislation for the cabinet; giving advisory opinions on legislative and executive matters; supervising rules of public administration; and performing other significant functions in the governmental process. In the words of one of the foremost students of the *Conseil d'État*, it is its policy "to ensure a reasonable and proper administrative method, and to try to advise consistency and completeness, so that administrative agencies are not driven to sketching or twisting the law in order to carry out their policies."[28] Plainly, it will insist on what it regards as proper procedures.

Roughly one-half of the Council's membership of 261, headed titularly by the Minister of Justice but effectively by its vice president, works in the administrative court section, and its personnel is uniquely trained and qualified. The members of that Litigation Section are recruited in two ways, as are those of the other branches of the council: The "second class auditors" —those who enter the council at the bottom of the ladder—are drawn from graduates of the three-year course at the justly celebrated *École Nationale d'Administration*, which provides expert personnel destined for the highest levels of the corps of civil servants in France. Admission to the *École* is by

---

[27] *Les Cahiers Français*, No. 156–157, Septembre–Décembre 1972, "La Justice," Notice 1 (Paris: La Documentation Française, 1972).
[28] Margherita Rendel, *The Administrative Function of the French* Conseil d'État, *op. cit.*, p. 248.

stiff competitive examination, most of the applicants having had some train-ing in the law or in political science. The school graduates only about 150 students annually—a figure that represents at most 5 per cent of the initial applicants—and those who do obtain their diplomas are indeed highly trained and qualified. The personnel of the higher echelons of the council come from either the upper levels of the ministries, the ranks of the prefects or the legal profession, or are promoted from lower echelons. France is justly proud of her distinguished corps of *conseillers* in the Council of State; it is truly an elite civil service body and richly merits its great prestige and acclaim.

Nine subsections, numbered chronologically, constitute the section of the council which handles the *droit administratif*. Each of these subsections consists of a *président* and a number of *conseillers*. Although roughly half of the subsections operate independently in readying cases for decision, they may hear cases either singly or in pairs. Important cases are considered by the full "judicial section," consisting of the presiding officers of the eleven subsections plus two members of the subsection(s) where the report of the case was prepared. The highest organ of the *Conseil d'État* is its General Assembly, for which are reserved cases of "extreme importance." It is com-posed of the seventeen highest officers of the council, in this instance in-cluding four *conseillers* from its administrative sections. Decisions by all of these organs are of equal weight, and they are final and binding.

Review Procedure. As already illustrated briefly, the procedure for ob-taining review in the French administrative court hierarchy is as simple as it is inexpensive. In large measure, it is inexpensive because the French state assumes responsibility for investigating both the facts and the law involved in a plaintiff's petition. Moreover, since under the French inquisitorial pro-cedure the judiciary plays an active role throughout the judicial process, the role of the petitioner is reduced to a summary statement as to the alleged facts and the relief prayed. He may request either of two types of review ac-tions: (1) proceedings for the annulment of an *ultra vires*—beyond powers —administrative act (*recours pour excès de pouvoir*); or (2) proceedings to order some type of affirmative administrative action, such as payment of monetary damages (*recours de pleine jurisdiction*). Most petitions for re-view fall into the first category. Having received the petition, the adminis-trative tribunal takes over; petitioner need not even retain legal counsel in the first type of case unless he chooses to do so. In any event, he need not worry, his interests will be amply guarded by the mills of the *droit adminis-tratif*. Moreover, the Council of State, *on its own cognizance*, has added a

267

third ground for review going beyond the concept inherent in *ultra vires*— i.e. an official action beyond the scope of legal authority—namely, the famous French administrative law concept of *détournement de pouvoir*, best translated as rank *abuse* of power. In its eyes, *abuse* of power is a concept different from that of an illegal *application* of power, which is governed by the first review category under *ultra vires*. Its deliberations are secret.

Once the Council of State has granted the availability of review, it must define the extent or scope of its reviewing power on the merits. This is especially true in the first category cases, under which the legality of an administrative action may be challenged on three grounds, all of which fall under the *ultra vires* concept: (1) lack of jurisdiction; (2) failure to observe procedures defined by law; (3) error of law. To these three the special category of abuse of power is then added.

Even President de Gaulle had to bow to a Council ruling in 1962 under the *détournement de pouvoir* category: He had set up a special military tribunal to try terrorists who aided European extremists in Algeria. But when the lawyer for one of the leaders of the terrorist secret army charged de Gaulle with "an illegal administrative act" in setting up the tribunal, and took the matter to the Council of State, the latter agreed and ruled it illegal indeed! (One year later Parliament created the Court of State Security described earlier.) On the other hand, later that year the Council found itself impotent in the face of its defiance by de Gaulle in connection with his call for a national referendum on direct election of the *Président* (see p. 298, *infra*). It did, however, win a qualified victory over him in May 1968 when, following its declaration of unconstitutionality of de Gaulle's proposed national referendum on his leadership during a series of sustained student uprisings, the *Président*—sensing a hostile political climate—yielded. (Yet he won an unprecedented victory in the national *elections* he then called instead of the abortive referendum.) The *Conseil d'État's* role of constitutional watchdog, manifested in these illustrations, prompted one expert, Professor Mauro Cappelletti, to assert that it has come near to assuming the power to invalidate statutes *per se*—since it seems now ready to review "all *executive* acts, decrees, and ordinances, even those legislative in nature . . . in adversary, party-initiated proceedings for conformity with applicable statutes, the provisions of the Constitution, and the general principles of law."[29] But it still lacks actual power to declare a law unconstitutional.

Evaluation. It is hardly surprising that the Council of State is literally swamped with petitions for action and review! The same applies to the

---

[29] *Judicial Review in the Contemporary World*, *op. cit.* p. 18. Margherita Rendel (see fns. 27, 28, and 30 of this chapter) concurs readily.

lower rung of the administrative court system. The French people look up to it as a reliable and virile guardian of individual rights against administrative encroachment. Moreover, they have great faith in the ability of these high-class civil servants to dispose of the thousands upon thousands of cases that reach them every year—as well they might. Small wonder that Anglo-Saxon states have given considerable thought to the adoption of a similar system. The Task Force of the Second Hoover Commission in the United States, for one, urgently suggested some form of administrative court system for our federal government.

Not only does the French system provide for fuller review of administrative action than the average Anglo-Saxon one, but the cost of litigation is smaller; accessibility to the courts is greater; review is more easily available; scope of review is larger; state liability for damages is less circumscribed; and settlement is far more prompt and efficient. The French state, whatever the wisdom of its philosophy of government here may be, simply considers itself totally liable for service-connected faults of public officers and state agencies. That liability has even been extended to cover most cases in which the damage is caused by personal fault of public officials, for the administrative courts have held that such faults are often inseparably connected with the administrative service of which the official is an agent. In such cases, the state indemnifies the damages to the injured citizen, and the officer at fault becomes personally liable to the state.

Yet not only does the French state accept liability for fault under the *droit administratif*, but as outlined earlier, also for risk. In other words, if proper administrative action results in an unequal burden on, or a social injustice to, a citizen, the state bears the cost of equalizing the burden—without the need to introduce a private bill in the legislature. In effect, the *droit administratif* is developing in the direction of absolute liability to ensure equitable sharing among all citizens of the burden of government action. This may well be far from an unmixed blessing, but the French administrative court system, with the *Conseil d'État* standing at its apex, has operated so successfully and has proved to be such a bulwark against arbitrary actions by the centralized state that it richly merits the careful attention that has been extended to it increasingly by students and practitioners of government alike. And the political implications of its jurisdictional growth in constitutional matters—perhaps "its most important development in the last quarter of [the] century"[30]—will undoubtedly enhance that attention.

[30] Margherita Rendel, "The Political Impact of the French *Conseil d'État*," *op. cit.* p. 12.

A NOTE ON THE JUDICIARY OF THE SOVIET UNION

Because of the oligarchical nature of the effective instrumentalities of government in the Union of Soviet Socialist Republics, law and judiciary—the entire judicial process—are in a category of their own. Despite the series of mild reforms that were adopted in the mid and late 1930's and the far more significant ones of the post-Stalin era, especially those of 1957–59 and 1961–63, law in Russia of today is still employed principally as a tool of the state; it is utilized for purposes of conformity; it is an organ of state power *par excellence*. The rights of the citizens under such a system are often illusory. Moreover, certain rights specifically enumerated under the Constitution of the USSR, are qualified by such tellingly realistic phrases as ". . . unless otherwise provided by law . . . ," such as Article III of the Constitution of the 1936, as amended, dealing with the right to public trial.[31] However, the post-1953 Soviet law reforms have rendered this and a host of other substantive and procedural concepts more meaningful—if in a limited manner.[32]

Although theoretically all law is inherently coercive and conformist, the fundamentally arbitrary characteristic of Soviet law is a logical by-product of the traditional concept of Marxism, where law is viewed as an instrument of domination, as a coercive tool of the state in its transition from socialism to communism, where the *duties* of a citizen prevail over his *rights*. This characteristically coercive interpretation has been embraced quite naturally by the Soviet jurists, who follow Lenin's dictum that law is "nothing if there is no apparatus adapted to coerce people into observing its provisions."[33] Hence the absence of meaningful guarantees to freedom under Soviet rule. It should be noted, however, that the legal system and machinery of justice in the Soviet Union—which in its outward structure and functioning was derived largely from the French system—grinds in an entirely different manner when it deals with an ordinary transgression, that is, one not involving the state as a politico-economic institution per se. In the former case, adjudication will be effected by the tribunals involved in roughly the same manner known throughout the world; but in the latter, law becomes the po-

[31] *Constitution (Fundamental Law) of the Union of Soviet Socialist Republics* (Moscow: Foreign Languages Publishing House, 1962), p. 91.

[32] For an informative analysis see Harold J. Berman, "Legality vs. Terror: The Post-Stalin Law Reforms," in Gwendolyn M. Carter and Alan F. Westin (eds.), *Politics in Europe: 5 Cases in European Government* (New York: Harcourt, Brace & World, Inc., 1965), pp. 179–205.

[33] Quoted by George C. Guins, *Soviet Law and Soviet Society* (The Hague: Martinus Nijhoff, 1954), p. 45.

litical organ of state power, the instrument of the class that constitutes the regime of the land, a mere adjunct of state power in pursuit of conformity within Soviet society.

THE ABSENCE OF AN INDEPENDENT JUDICIARY

There is not—indeed there cannot be—a truly independent judiciary under Soviet Rule. Although the Constitution provides that "Judges are independent and subject only to the law,"[34] any meaningful power to check and balance the other branches of the government—assuming there are purposeful distinctions at all—is necessarily illusory. On the contrary, both the legislature and the judiciary are instruments—Stalin called them "transmission belts"—of the party. There have been criticisms in the Soviet press of direct party interference in certain cases, but this happens rarely. The judges are, after all, politically reliable—almost all are party members—and thus need neither instructions nor "cues."

The judiciary does not, of course, possess the power of effective judicial review. If that power exists anywhere at all in the USSR—really an academic question—it resides in the Presidium of the Supreme Soviet, which is specifically charged under the Constitution with the "interpretation of the laws."[35]

Moreover, throughout the judicial hierarchy, both the professional and the lay judges, known as *assessors*, are *elected* for short terms of office—not exceeding five years—by legislative bodies (*soviets*) or residents of the districts in which they serve, *and* they are all subject to recall at any time. Either faithful party members or politically acceptable "non-party Bolsheviks," these judges—aged twenty-five and over—represent the political power of the state, and the eyes of the dominant elements of Soviet society are constantly fixed upon them.

THE COURT HIERARCHY

One of the most salient features of the judicial hierarchy of the USSR is its high degree of centralization, despite the federal structure of the government and despite the myriad courts in the various and manifold geographic subdivisions below. The sole "federal" court is the Supreme Court of the USSR, which enjoys corrective power over the lower courts. But more im-

[34] Constitution of December 5, 1936, Art. 112.
[35] *Ibid.* Art. 14, d. The "Supreme Soviet" is the highest legislative body in the USSR, which meets infrequently. Its "Presidium" is its small "executive committee," which functions continuously; it issues decrees which have the force of law, but it has no administrative responsibilities; its tasks are essentially executive and ceremonial.

portant is the overriding supervisory power of the "boss" of the entire judicial system, the Procurator-General, the "supreme overseer of Soviet legality," who will be described more fully below.

The Comrades' Court. At the lowest level of the Soviet judiciary is the *Comrades' Court*, a rather unique institution that actually falls outside the regular hierarchy. More appropriately, these units, which may be found at local levels everywhere in the land, have been called "social" or "honour courts."[36] Staffed by local citizens for the adjudication of disputes between individuals, comrades' courts are organized as *ad hoc* bodies in villages, farm co-operatives, apartment houses, factories, or any other place of work or dwelling where they might be needed to deal with the sundry petty offenses that invariably take place among people everywhere, whatever their political philosophy may be. The "judges" of the Comrades' Court in a particular unit or locality are normally elected for each case that arises by the membership of the residential or occupational unit concerned, or they may comprise all those present at a meeting of that unit. Their jurisdiction was materially extended with the 1963 court reforms, so they can now deal with petty hooliganism, petty thefts in the case of first-time offenders, petty speculation, plus a host of other minor infractions. They may also levy reprimands and small fines; order an offender to apologize; administer "public censure"; propose that an offender be evicted from his dwelling; propose that he be transferred to a job paying less; or require the payment of damages to the victim of up to 50 rubles ($70.00 in 1974). Probably the most important cases tried by these courts—which since 1963 may also operate in factories and other places of work to make non-obligatory recommendations to management for "corrective action"—are those involving breaches of "labor discipline" and "standards of behavior in communal apartments." In the words of a leading authority on Soviet courts, the basic aim is "reform" of the "anti-social offender" and "the entire procedure is conceived as a lesson in communist morality."[37]

But since these comrades' courts are really not recognized as courts per se, their decisions are subject to annulment by the level immediately above, the People's Court. This is true for all judgments *except* a new classification, devised in 1959, and confirmed and expanded in 1963, concerning decisions of special comrades' courts in connection with "speculators, hooligans, unemployed elements, etc." and generally "unsocialist behavior." Those found

[36] Robert G. Neumann, op. cit. pp. 627–28.
[37] Harold J. Berman, *Justice in the U.S.S.R.*, rev. ed., enl. (New York: Vintage Books, 1966), pp. 289–91.

272

FIGURE 4
THE JUDICIARY AND PROCURACY OF THE USSR

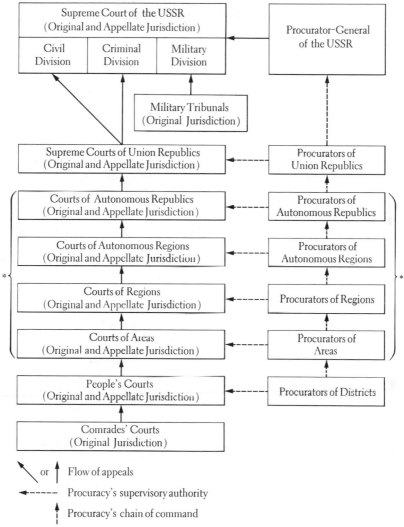

* These provincial or territorial subdivisions and levels are not necessarily present everywhere in the USSR, nor do they necessarily carry identical nomenclature in the various
jurisdictions marked. This fact pertains to the procuracy as well as the courts.

273

guilty of one of these offenses at a meeting of "friends and neighbors" constituted as the Comrades' Court of jurisdiction, may be punished by banishment from their place of residence.[38] The People's Court above may not review that type of decision, although the local *soviets* (legislatures) do have that power.

The People's Court. If we omit the level of the quasi-tribunal just discussed, the base of the Soviet judiciary is actually occupied by the *People's Court*. Organized on a district basis throughout the Soviet Union, the people's courts are strictly courts of original jurisdiction in both criminal and civil cases—except for their tangential supervisory power over the comrades' courts. As the workhorse courts of the entire system, the people's courts handle the bulk of the minor criminal and civil cases in the USSR. The Council of Ministers of the pertinent Union or Autonomous Republic concerned determines the number of these courts to be established in each district (*raion*). They are locally staffed by one judge, as chairman, and two assessors; the former is elected by the inhabitants of the district for five years and the latter for two. The judge is not statutorily required to be a professional, although he usually is; the assessors, being "lay judges," have no formal judicial or legal background.

Assessors, who come from all walks of life and who usually serve only for a brief period—perhaps up to two weeks annually—are emphatically not to be regarded as jurors in the typical Western sense. No juries as the West knows them exist in the Soviet Union—although there have been periodic suggestions, ignored by the authorities, that they be introduced. When the assessors hear and decide a case, they act as judges and have a full voice and vote on the various aspects of the facts and law of a case as well as in the decision itself. Although the views of the professional judge on the People's Court normally prevail, the assessors do play a role, however minor, and are part and parcel of the judicial process there.[39]

The Courts of the Region, Autonomous Region, and Autonomous Republic. Now matters become somewhat more complicated. At the next level, or really at the next three levels, lie the intermediate courts, arranged according to territorial divisions that bridge the hierarchical gap between the level of the People's Court and that of the *Supreme Court of the Union*

---

[38] Neumann, loc. cit. p. 628.

[39] In the United States, Vermont's Constitution provides for an intriguing system of laymen or "side judges" in the county courts of that state. They are elected in each county to serve with a judge. It should also be noted that the institution of "assessors" is present, whatever its particular nomenclature, in several countries of Continental Europe and in European-based legal systems elsewhere.

Republic. Not *all* multiple rungs of these intermediate courts will inevitably be present in *all* union republics, certainly not in the smaller ones—although sometimes there will even be a fourth (the Area)—but they are sufficiently standardized to represent a definite pattern. Their jurisdiction is both original and appellate. In the exercise of the appellate function, they review decisions coming to them from the sundry people's courts of their respective territories, and when an appeal has been decided by a minimum of three regular judges sitting *en banc* it is final.

The courts of the regions, autonomous regions, and autonomous republics have original jurisdiction in the more serious criminal and civil cases. Among the former, according to the revised criminal code, are "anti-state activities, crimes against administrative order when they involve particular danger to the state, the pillaging of socialist property, and other important economic crimes." In the realm of civil jurisdiction lies cases involving the state and social institutions, public enterprises, and organizations. The work of these courts is usually performed by panels of five professional judges and assessors, holding the titles of chairman, deputy chairman, members, and people's assessors, all of whom are elected for five-year terms by the *soviets* of the areas or regions concerned.

The Supreme Court of the Union Republic. In each Union Republic— the largest constituent part of the federal structure of the Soviet Union— lies a *Supreme Court of the Union Republic*, constituting the highest judicial body of that division. Its members, headed by five professional judges —but also comprising the ubiquitous assessors—are elected for five-year terms by the Supreme Soviet of the Union Republic. These high courts have both original and appellate jurisdiction. In the latter sphere of their work, they are empowered to set aside the decisions of any inferior court in the Republic; and appellate decision rendered here becomes final and binding. Related to that jurisdiction is their power to supervise all inferior courts by receiving and acting on "protests" against verdicts rendered below, coming to them from the Procurator-General or the Chairman of the Supreme Court of the USSR or by the corresponding officials of the lower echelons—one of the more intriguing practices in the Soviet Union, which, in effect, institutionalizes double jeopardy at the discretion of the state! The Supreme Court of the Union Republic has original jurisdiction in the more serious criminal and civil cases, including those involving infractions committed in office by the higher officials of government in the Republic. Its decisions are final.

The Supreme Court of the USSR. At the pinnacle of the judicial hier-

275

archy in the Soviet Union stands the *Supreme Court of the USSR*, classified by Article 104 of the Constitution of 1936 as its "highest judicial organ." Elected by the Supreme Soviet of the USSR for five-year terms of office, its membership consists of a chairman, two vice chairmen, nine professional judges, and twenty people's assessors. Moreover, attached to it as members *ex officio* are the fifteen chairmen of the supreme courts of the union republics, but these do not necessarily sit on a steady basis. The regular members of the Supreme Court are divided into three specialized *collegia* (panels), one each for civil, criminal, and military matters, but the entire Court is charged to meet at least once every three months in plenary session (the *plenum*). The chairman may preside over any case before the Court and he has the power to relieve or discharge any inferior court in the Soviet Union of a case in order to "protest" it in plenary session—sessions that are invariably attended by the Procurator-General.

Despite the implications of the Supreme Court's division of labor and jurisdiction, it is basically a court of review and appeals, a supervisory court. As such it also has the authority to recommend, even to draft for the Supreme Soviet, legislation dealing with the judicial system. Yet, as already explained, the Supreme Court emphatically lacks the power of judicial review; nor does it possess the authority to interpret laws, a function theoretically reserved, as is the former, to the Presidium of the Supreme Soviet of the USSR. But it may give advice to the Presidium in cases of interpretation. Nevertheless, the civil and criminal *collegia* do serve as tribunals of original jurisdiction in cases of exceptional nation-wide significance. When it exercises original jurisdiction, a *collegium* consists of one professional judge as chairman and two assessors; in its appellate or review jurisdiction all its members are regular judges. The remaining *collegium*, the military, has jurisdiction in a small number of particularly significant cases of treason, espionage, and other high crimes against the state. It may also review appeals from, and protests against, the judgments of lower military tribunals. Except in the sense that there is always the possibility of an appeal to the Presidium of the Supreme Soviet, decisions of the Supreme Court of the USSR are final and binding. But far more significant on the scales of power and authority in the judicial system of the Soviet Union than any court is the Procurator-General and his own extensive hierarchy of procurators throughout the land.

THE PROCURATOR-GENERAL

The best indication of the subordination, centralization, and lack of independence of the judicial hierarchy in the Soviet Union is the existence of the *Procurator-General*, sometimes known as Public Prosecutor or Public Procurator. No official associated with the legal or judicial process of comparable authority exists anywhere else today—certainly not in the free world. An institution conceived by Tsar Peter the Great in 1722 and revived by Lenin after a five-year lapse in 1922, the Procurator-General combines his position atop the entire judiciary with that of watchdog of the application and interpretation of criminal law on all levels of government, either directly or indirectly, as well as all civil law. Chosen by the Supreme Soviet of the USSR for a term of seven years, the Procurator-General, in turn, has considerable input in the appointment by the Secretariat of the various procurators for five-year terms on the lower levels throughout the USSR (see chart below). His is truly a centralized and centralizing posture, and although he is technically responsible for his actions to the Supreme Soviet, in effect he is responsible solely to the Communist party's top echelon, the Politbureau and the Secretariat. His subordinate procurators, too, are independent of all local organs of government; as guardians of local conformity they are responsible solely to their chief, the Procurator-General in Moscow —and, of course, to top party authorities (sometimes even to subordinate ones).

Powers and Functions. Always held by a high-ranking, trusted member of the Communist party, the position of Procurator-General is eagerly sought and influential. Andrei Vyshinsky, who occupied the office during the famous purge trial years in the late 1930's, whence he steadily advanced, ultimately to become Foreign Minister and the Soviet Union's Representative to the United Nations, described the Procurator-General as the "watchman of socialist legality, the leader of the policy of the Communist party and of Soviet authority, the champion of socialism."[40] Even if this appraisal be somewhat embellished, it comes close to the verities of a system of law in which the Procurator-General personifies an omnipotent force. In Nikita Khrushchev's words, he "must stand guard over the laws of the Soviet Union."[41]

In addition to his basic authority, outlined in Article 113 of the Constitution—namely to ensure the strict observance of the law by all ministries and institutions as well as by all officials and citizens of the Soviet Union at large and, under a 1955 statute, to exercise the function of "general superviser" over the legality of acts of all state organs"—the Procurator-General

---

[40] *The Law of the Soviet State* (New York: The Macmillan Co., 1948), p. 537.
[41] Quoted in Glenn G. Morgan, *Soviet Administrative Legality: The Role of the Attorney General's Office* (Stanford: Stanford University Press, 1962), citing *Izvestia* of January 25, 1958. Professor Morgan's fine book is exclusively devoted to the Soviet procuracy.

possesses the following prerogatives: He may conduct a *juge d'instruction* type of pre-trial preliminary investigation (as may also the KGB—the secret police—and the regular police); he may act in the nature of a Scandinavian *ombudsman* (see pp. 262 ff., *supra*), which the Soviet Union claims to have invented; he has the right to appear in any civil case on behalf of either party at any point during a trial; he may re-open a completed or closed trial by means of the now familiar "protest"—although the period of time during which this can be done seems to have been shortened from five years to two by the reforms of 1957; and he may review the judgment of any court, regardless of whether the case was adjudicated in a lower court or the *plenum* of the Supreme Court of the USSR. Moreover, he sits with the latter and thus has a strategic perch from which to operate. In brief, he and his subordinates combine the basic authority of bringing people to justice before the judiciary with that of supervising the execution of the laws by all institutions of government, public officials, and private citizens. This represents a unique and awe-inspiring compendium of power, but one that is not inconsistent with the dissent-stifling, dissent-punishing system under which he functions.

VII
Judicial Review:
I   The Supreme Power

DEFINING JUDICIAL REVIEW

Certainly the most controversial and at the same time the most fascinating role of the courts of the United States in general, and of the Supreme Court in particular, is the exercise of the power of *judicial review*. It is commonly viewed with almost equal amounts of reverence and suspicion. Edward S. Corwin regarded it as "American democracy's way of hedging its bet."[1] Although about sixty countries had adopted some form of judicial review by late 1974, in its full majesty and range it is a power that the *ordinary* courts —i.e. those that are part of the formal judicial hierarchy—of only a handful of lands possess effectively. Chief among these are Australia, Brazil, Burma, Canada, India, Pakistan, and Japan, of whom all except Japan have federal systems of government.[2] Experience has demonstrated that those countries that have exhibited stable or moderately stable traditions of judicial review are generally characterized by: (1) regime stability; (2) a competitive political party system; (3) significant horizontal power distribution; (4) a strong

[1] Review of Benjamin F. Wright's article, "Growth of American Constitutional Law," 56 *Harvard Law Review* 487 (1942).
[2] For an informative summary discussion, see K. C. Wheare, *Federal Government*, 4th ed. (New York: Oxford University Press, 1964), Ch. IV, "The Constitution, the Courts, and the Law." Judicial review in *Switzerland* is confined to cantonal legislation. *India's* Supreme Court has been flexing its muscles increasingly. Thus, in February 1970 it struck down 10 : 1 Prime Minister Indira Ghandi's Bank Nationalization Act, ruling that the July 1969 takeover of the fourteen biggest banks was "hostile discrimination" since other Indian banks and foreign banks were excluded. (*The New York Times*, February 11, 1970, p. 1.)

tradition of judicial independence; and (5) a high degree of political freedom.[3]

Briefly stated, judicial review is the power of any court to *hold unconstitutional and hence unenforceable any law, any official action based upon a law, or any other action by a public official that it deems*—upon careful, normally painstaking, reflection and in line with the canons of the taught tradition of the law as well as judicial self-restraint—*to be in conflict with the Basic Law, in the United States its Constitution.* In other words, by invoking the power of judicial review, a court applies the *superior* of two laws, which at the level of the federal judiciary of the United States signifies the Constitution instead of the legislative statute or some action by a public official allegedly or actually based upon it.

In the United States, which will serve as the chief subject in this treatment of judicial review, this highly significant instrument of power—"the principled process of enunciating and applying certain enduring values of our society"[4]—is possessed theoretically by *every* court, no matter how high or low on the judicial ladder. Although admittedly it happens rarely, it is not at all impossible for a judge in a low-level court of one of the fifty states to declare a federal law unconstitutional; such a decision would quite naturally at once be appealed to higher judicial echelons for review. Conscious of the nature and purpose of federalism and the need to permit legislative bodies to act in accordance with their judgment, no matter how unwise that may well be at times, courts are understandably loath to invoke the judicial veto. Yet their power to do so, and especially that of the Supreme Court of the United States, serves as an omnipresent and potentially omnipotent check upon the legislative branches of government. While that highest tribunal, in a total of 110 or 111 cases (depending upon the count), has to date (Fall 1975) declared but 116 provisions of *federal* laws unconstitutional out of a total of over 75,000 public and private laws passed, some 900 *state* laws and provisions of *state* constitutions have run wholly or partly afoul of that judicial checkmate since 1789—some 800 of these coming after 1870. An example of the latter action is the Court's unanimous ruling in *Torcaso v. Watkins*[5]: there it struck down a provision of the Maryland Con-

---

[3] See the perceptive paper by Donald P. Kommers, "Cross-National Comparisons of Constitutional Courts: Toward a Theory of Judicial Review," presented at the Annual Meeting of the American Political Science Association, Los Angeles, Calif., September 11, 1970.

[4] Alexander M. Bickel, *The Least Dangerous Branch* (Indianapolis. The Bobbs-Merrill Co., 1962), p. 58.

[5] 367 U.S. 488 (1961).

stitution on the ground that to compel officeholders to declare belief in God constituted a "religious test for public office" that invaded the individual's right to religious freedom. In many ways, the Court's power over state actions is of more significance to the federal system than the much more publicized and more well-known power over federal actions.

Tables VIII and IX illustrate in some detail the power of judicial review over *legislative enactments* as exercised by the Supreme Court at the *federal level only*. But it is interesting to note that more statutes of the State of Louisiana have been declared unconstitutional than those of any other state—Louisiana being the only one of the 50 to employ *civil law* as its judicial system. Regarding the sparse number of federal statutes held unconstitutional by the post-"anti New Deal" Supreme Court in recent times, the thirty-six provisions of congressional enactments that as of this writing (Fall 1974) have fallen since 1937—actually since 1943—all but two did so because they infringed certain personal rights and liberties safeguarded under the Constitution. Those thirty-six instances were:

(1) *Tot v. United States* (1943).[6] A statutory presumption that a known criminal in possession of firearms or ammunition must have carried them in violation of the Federal Firearms Act of 1938, Section 2(f), was invalidated 8 : 0 as a violation of the due process of law clause of the Fifth Amendment.

(2) *United States v. Lovett* (1946).[7] Section 304 of the Urgent Defense Appropriation Act of 1943, which barred the salaries of certain specifically named federal employees, was struck down 8 : 0 as violative of the constitutional prohibition against a Bill of Attainder.

(3) *United States v. Cardiff* (1952).[8] Section 704 of the Food, Drug, and Cosmetic Act, which deals with factory inspection, fell 8 : 1 as unconstitutionally vague under the due process clause of the Fifth Amendment.

(4) *Bolling v. Sharpe* (1954).[9] The federal companion case to the *Public School Segregation Cases*,[10] involving an 1862 federal statute that, insofar as pertinent here, provided for separate schools for white and black children, was unanimously held unconstitutional as a violation of the due process of law clause of the Fifth Amendment.

(5) *United States ex rel Toth v. Quarles* (1955).[11] The Court 6 : 3 held unconstitutional Article 3A of the Uniform Code of Military Justice when

[6] 319 U.S. 463.
[7] 328 U.S. 303.
[8] 344 U.S. 174.
[9] 347 U.S. 497.
[10] *Brown v. Board of Education of Topeka, Kansas, et al.*, 347 U.S. 483 (1954).
[11] 350 U.S. 11.

applied to a *former* member of the United States Air Force as violative of the guarantees of the civilian judicial process inherent in Article III of the Constitution.

(6)–(8) *Reid v. Covert* and *Kinsella v. Krueger* (1957), later coupled with *Kinsella v. Singleton* and *Grisham v. Hagan* and *McElroy v. United States* (1960).[12] These cases concerned a series of related decisions in which the Court—over a three-year period—dealt with several aspects of Article 2(11) of the Uniform Code of Military Justice, and, by votes ranging from a high of 7 : 2 to a low of 5 : 4, found some of these unconstitutional as applied to various civilians accompanying the armed forces. The pertinent sections of the Code in these multiple cases fell as violative of the individuals' rights under Article III and Amendments V and VI of the Constitution, including the right to a trial by jury, indictment by grand jury, and public trial in a civilian court before an impartial jury of one's peers.

(9) *Trop v. Dulles* (1958).[13] Here the narrowly divided Court struck down section 401(G) of the Nationality Act of 1940, holding that Congress had exceeded its military and expatriation powers in making desertion in time of war punishable by expatriation. The Court ruled 5 : 4 that to expatriate for such a reason constituted "cruel and unusual punishment," forbidden by Amendment VIII.

(10) and (11) *Kennedy v. Mendoza-Martinez* and *Rusk v. Cort* (1963).[14] Although these two cases were decided together (and under the same citation), the Court's 5 : 4 decision in effect held two sections of different congressional statutes unconstitutional as violative of procedural safeguards found in Amendments V and VI. Thus affected were Section 349 (a) (10) of the Immigration and Nationality Act of 1952 and Section 401 (j) of the Nationality Act of 1940, which had provided for automatic expatriation of United States citizens who, in order to evade military service, either fled the country or refused to return upon draft-board notification.

(12) *Schneider v. Rusk* (1964).[15] In another citizenship decision the Supreme Court here invalidated 5 : 3 Section 352 (a) (1) of the 1940 Nationality Act, chiefly on due process of law grounds under the Fifth Amendment. Section 352 had deprived *naturalized* American citizens of their citizenship if they returned to the territory of their birth and then resided there for more than three years.

[12] 354 U.S. 1; 361 U.S. 234; 361 U.S. 278 and 361 U.S. 281, respectively.
[13] 356 U.S. 86.
[14] 372 U.S. 144.
[15] 377 U.S. 163.

(13) *Aptheker v. Secretary of State* (1964).[16] Here a 6 : 3 majority of the Court declared unconstitutional on its face Section 6 of Title I of the Subversive Activities Control Act of 1950, which proscribed the application for or the use of a United States passport by any member of an organization required to register under the Act's provisions. The Court held that Section 6 ". . . too broadly and indiscriminately restricts the right of travel and thereby abridges the liberty guaranteed by the Fifth Amendment."

(14) *Lamont v. Postmaster-General* and *Fixa v. Heilberg* (1965).[17] In its *first* decision voiding an Act of *Congress* on the ground that it violated the freedom of speech guarantee of the First Amendment, the Court unanimously declared unconstitutional a section of the Postal Services and Federal Employees Salary Act of 1962, which provided that all mail matter originating abroad, except first class mail, that the Secretary of the Treasury held to be "communist political propaganda" was to be detained and that the addressee was to be notified that it could be delivered to him only if he sent a card stating that desire.

(15) *United States v. Brown* (1965).[18] The Court, in one of its rare applications of the Bill of Attainder rule, held 5 : 4 that Section 504 of the Labor-Management Reporting and Disclosures (Landrum-Griffin) Act of 1959, making it a crime for a member of the Communist party to serve as an officer or employee of a labor union, was in fact such an unconstitutional piece of legislation.

(16) *United States v. Romano* (1965).[19] Unanimously, the Court reversed a conviction under a federal statute providing that the presence of a defendant at the site of an illegal still was sufficient to authorize a conviction for possession and control of that still, unless the defendant satisfactorily explained his presence to the jury. It held such a statutory presumption of guilt to be an unconstitutional violation of substantive due process of law under the Fifth Amendment.

(17) *Afroyim v. Rusk* (1967).[20] Here, in an enormously significant decision, the Court ruled 5 : 4 that Congress lacks the constitutional authority to pass *any* laws that strip American citizens of their nationality *without their express consent*. Specifically, it declared unconstitutional that section of the already tattered Nationality Act of 1940 which deprived United

---

[16] 378 U.S. 500.
[17] 381 U.S. 301.
[18] 381 U.S. 437.
[19] 382 U.S. 136.
[20] 387 U.S. 253.

States citizens of their nationality if they voted in a foreign election—and thereby overruled a 1958 decision that had held 5 : 4 to the contrary.[21]

(18) *United States v. Robel* (1967).[22] On that term's last Opinion Day, the Court 6 : 2 struck down as an unconstitutional infringement of the freedom of association guarantees of the First Amendment a section of the much-battered Subversive Activities Control Act of 1950 that made it a crime for Communist party members to work in defense plants.

(19) and (20) *Marchetti v. United States* and *Grosso v. United States* and *Haynes v. United States* (1968).[23] Here, in three separate 7 : 1 decisions delivered simultaneously, the Court declared unconstitutional as a violation of the Fifth Amendment's privilege against compulsory self-incrimination pertinent sections of the Gambling Tax Act of 1951 in the first two cases named and the Firearms Act of 1934 in the third.

(21) *United States v. Jackson* (1968).[24] A section of the "Lindberg Anti-Kidnapping Law" (1201A of Title 18 of the Criminal Code), dealing with pleas and sentencing, fell as violative of the self-incrimination and jury guarantees of Amendments V and VI, respectively.

(22) *Washington v. Legrant* (1969).[25] The Court declared unconstitutional as a violation of due process of law a District of Columbia statutory provision that denied welfare assistance to those residents of the District who had not resided there for at least one year prior to their application for assistance.

(23) and (24) *Leary v. United States* (1969).[26] Unanimously, the Court here struck down two federal laws dealing with marijuana controls as violative of the Fifth Amendment's guarantees against compulsory self-incrimination. One required payment of a .tax for transportation of marijuana; the other established that anyone with marijuana in his possession upon entrance into the United States could be presumed to have imported it knowingly.

(25) *Schacht v. United States* (1970).[27] Down unanimously, on grounds of crass violation of First Amendment freedom of expression grounds, went a quaint federal law that made it a crime for an actor to wear United States

21 *Perez v. Brownell*, 356 U.S. 44.
22 389 U.S. 258.
23 390 U.S. 39, 390 U.S. 62, and 390 U.S. 85, respectively. (Involved two separate laws, the two cases first cited coming under the first.)
24 390 U.S. 569.
25 394 U.S. 618.
26 395 U.S. 6.
27 398 U.S. 258.

military apparel in a theatrical production if the portrayal reflected "discredit" on the armed forces—it was perfectly acceptable to wear it if it was a "favorable" portrayal!

(26) *Oregon v. Mitchell* (1970).[28] While the Court *upheld* 5 : 4 a newly enacted federal law that provided for the lowering of the voting age to eighteen in *national* elections, it ruled unconstitutional—Mr. Justice Black switching to the other side—a collateral provision of the law that would also have lowered the voting age similarly for *state and local* elections as violative of Article I, Sec. 2 of the U.S. Constitution governing state electoral authority.

(27) and (28) *Blount v. Rizzi* and *United States v. The Book Bin* (1971).[29] Two so-called "mail block" laws were unanimously held to constitute unconstitutional invasions of First Amendment guarantees of freedom of expression, since they authorized the Post Office Department to cut off postal service to mail order houses that deal in pornography, without providing prompt judicial review of the issues of "pornography."

(29) *Tilton v. Richardson* (1971).[30] A provision of the Federal Higher Educational Assistance Act of 1963 here fell unanimously afoul of First Amendment strictures against the violation of the principle of separation of Church and State, by permitting church-affiliated schools to use buildings erected with federal construction funds for religious purposes after a twenty-year hiatus.

(30) *Chief of Capital Police v. Jeannette Rankin Brigade* (1972),[31] saw another unanimous declaration of unconstitutionality of a federal statute, one enacted in 1882, on First Amendment invasion grounds. The law, adjudged an impermissibly vague restriction of free speech and assembly, had banned "all unauthorized demonstrations" on the grounds of the U.S. Capitol.

(31) *Richardson v. Davis* and *Richardson v. Griffin* (1972).[32] Here the Court struck down 6 : 3, as an unconstitutional infringement of due process of law guarantees under the Fifth Amendment, Section 203 (a) of the Social Security Act of 1935, as amended, which provided that "illegitimate children get benefit payments only to the extent payments to widows and other children of wage earners do not exhaust 'maximum family' benefits."

---

[28] 400 U.S. 112.
[29] 400 U.S. 410.
[30] 403 U.S. 672.
[31] 409 U.S. 972.
[32] 409 U.S. 1069.

TABLE VIII

U.S. SUPREME COURT DECLARATIONS OF
UNCONSTITUTIONALITY OF FEDERAL LAWS, I.

(Arranged chronologically in accordance with tenure of Chief Justices.)[a]

Time Span	Chief Justice	Number of Declarations of Unconstitutionality	Commentary
1789–1801	Jay	0	
	J. Rutledge	0	Weak, placid Court.
	Ellsworth	0	
1801–1835	Marshall	1	1803: *Marbury v. Madison.*
1836–1864	Taney	1	1857: *Dred Scott v. Sandford.*
1864–1873	Chase	9	1870: *Legal Tender Cases.*
1874–1888	Waite	8	1883: *Civil Rights Cases.*
1888–1910	Fuller	14 (15)	1895: *Income Tax Cases.*
1910–1921	White	13	1918: *Child Labor Case.*
1921–1930	Taft	13	1923: *Minimum Wage Case.*
1930–1936	Hughes	14	Of these, 13 came in 1934–36!
1936–1941	Hughes	0	The New Deal Court emerges.
1941–1946	Stone	2	New Libertarian emphasis.
1946–1953	Vinson	1	Abstemious Court.
1953–1969	Warren	21	High watermark of Libertarian- ism.
1969–Present[a]	Burger	12	Chiefly First and Fifth Amend- ment concerns.
		109 (110)	

[a] As of October 1974.

(32) and (33) *United States Department of Agriculture v. Murry* and *United States Department of Agriculture v. Moreno* (1973).[33] By votes of 5 : 4 and 7 : 2, respectively, the Court here sanctioned challenges to the constitutionality of Sections 5(b) and 3(e) of the Food Stamp Act of 1964 as violations of due process of law under the Fifth Amendment. In the former instance, the program denied eligibility to certain household residents on "over-age" grounds, in the latter to "unrelated" persons; the Court's majorities regarded both provisions at war with the legislation's stated purpose.

[33] 413 U.S. 508 and 413 U.S. 528, respectively. (Involved two separate decisions governing two distinct sections of the statute.)

(34) and (35) *Frontiero v. Richardson* (1973).[34] With only Mr. Justice Rehnquist in dissent, the Court struck down as violative of the due process of law clause of the Fifth Amendment sections of 37 and 10 U.S.C. that provided for greater statutory dependency benefits to servicemen than to servicewomen.

(36) *Jiminez v. Weinberger* (1974).[*] Again with only Mr. Justice Rehnquist dissenting, the Court declared unconstitutional on due process grounds a provision of the Social Security Act of 1935, as amended—42 U.S.C. 416 (h) (3) (B)—which denied benefits to illegitimate children of a disabled mother just because they were born after the disability began.

State legislation, too, has thus—with generally minor exceptions[35]—been held unconstitutional largely because of infringement of civil rights and liberties, although a number of instances involved cases of state interference with national interests, especially in the realm of interstate commerce.

After the famous decision in *Marbury v. Madison*[36] in 1803 in which Mr. Chief Justice Marshall enunciated the doctrine of judicial review—although it was not really the first instance of its application[37]—no other federal legislation was declared unconstitutional by his Court during the remaining thirty-two years of his long tenure (thirty-four years).[38] Nevertheless, the Marshall Court wielded immense power and, guided by the dominant figure of the great Chief Justice, probably did more than either of the other two branches of the national government to make the young United States a strong, vigorous, powerful nation, and its Constitution a living, effective, elastic Basic Law. Not until Mr. Chief Justice Taney's crucial decision in *Dred Scott v. Sandford*[39] in 1857 was another federal statute struck down by the Court; and the greatest crisis evoked by that power of the Supreme Court did not arrive until, dominated by the doctrinaire conservatives among the so-called Nine Old Men, the Court declared unconstitutional no less than thirteen New Deal laws in 1934–36.

---

[34] 411 U.S. 677. (The provisions of the two separate statutes were disposed of in the same case.)
[*] 417 U.S. 628.
[35] E.g. *Wood v. Lovett*, 313 U.S. 362 (1941), and *Morey v. Doud*, 354 U.S. 451 (1957).
[36] 1 Cranch 137.
[37] See this chapter, pp. 305–9, and fns. 79–87.
[38] The Circuit Court of Appeals for the District of Columbia did strike down by a vote of 2 : 1 a congressional statute in *U.S. v. Benjamin More* only six months after *Marbury v. Madison*.
[39] 19 Howard 393.

TABLE IX

U.S. SUPREME COURT DECLARATIONS OF
UNCONSTITUTIONALITY OF FEDERAL LAWS, II[a]

Under Chief Justice	Recorded Declaration Number	Citation of Case and Year Decided	Vote
Marshall	1	1 Cranch 137 (1803) *Marbury v. Madison,*	6 : 0
Taney	2	*Dred Scott v. Sandford,* 19 Howard 393 (1857)	7 : 2
Chase	3	*Gordon v. United States,* 2 Wallace 561 (1865)	8 : 2
Chase	4	*Ex parte Garland,* 4 Wallace 33 (1867)	5 : 4
Chase	5	*Reichert v. Felps,* 6 Wallace 160 (1868)	8 : 0
Chase	6	*The Alicia,* 7 Wallace 571 (1869)	8 : 0
Chase	7	*Hepburn v. Griswold,* 8 Wallace 603 (1870)	4 : 3
Chase	8	*United States v. DeWitt,* 9 Wallace 41 (1870)	9 : 0
Chase	9	*The Justices v. Murray,* 9 Wallace 274 (1870)	9 : 0
Chase	10	*The Collector v. Day,* 11 Wallace 113 (1871)	8 : 1
Chase	11	*United States v. Klein,* 13 Wallace 128 (1872)	7 : 2
Waite	12	*United States v. Reese,* 92 U.S. 214 (1876)	7 : 2
Waite	13	*United States v. Fox,* 95 U.S. 670 (1878)	9 : 0
Waite	14	*Trade Mark Cases,* 100 U.S. 82 (1879)	9 : 0
Waite	15	*United States v. Harris,* 106 U.S. 629 (1883)	8 : 1
Waite	16	*Civil Rights Cases,* 109 U.S. 3 (1883)	8 : 1
Waite	17	*Boyd v. United States,* 116 U.S. 616 (1886)	7 : 2

[a] As of October 1974.

TABLE IX (*Continued*)

Under Chief Justice	Recorded Declaration Number	Citation of Case and Year Decided	Vote
Waite	18	*Baldwin v. Franks,* 120 U.S. 678 (1887)	7 : 1
None[b]	19	*Callan v. Wilson,* 127 U.S. 540 (1888)	8 : 0
Fuller	20	*Monongahela Nav. Co. v. U.S.,* 148 U.S. 312 (1893)	8 : 0
Fuller	21	*Pollock v. Farmers' L. & T. Co.,* 157 U.S. 429 (1895)	6 : 2
Fuller	21A	*Pollock v. Farmers' L. & T. Co.,* 158 U.S. 601 (1895)	5 : 4
Fuller	22	*Wong Wing v. United States,* 163 U.S. 228 (1896)	8 : 0
Fuller	23	*Kirby v. United States,* 174 U.S. 47 (1899)	6 : 2
Fuller	24	*Jones v. Meehan,* 175 U.S. 1 (1899)	9 : 0
Fuller	25	*Fairbank v. United States,* 181 U.S. 283 (1901)	5 : 4
Fuller	26	*James v. Bowman,* 190 U.S. 127 (1903)	6 : 2
Fuller	27	*Matter of Heff,* 197 U.S. 488 (1905)	8 : 1
Fuller	28	*Rassmussen v. United States,* 197 U.S. 516 (1905)	9 : 0
Fuller	29	*Hodges v. United States,* 203 U.S. 1 (1906)	7 : 2
Fuller	30	*Employers' Liability Cases,* 207 U.S. 463 (1908)	5 : 4
Fuller	31	*Adair v. United States,* 208 U.S. 161 (1908)	6 : 2
Fuller	32	*Keller v. United States,* 213 U.S. 138 (1909)	6 : 3
Fuller	33	*United States v. Evans,* 213 U.S. 297 (1909)	9 : 0
White	34	*Muskrat v. United States,* 219 U.S. 346 (1911)	9 : 0
White	35	*Coyle v. Oklahoma,* 221 U.S. 559 (1911)	7 : 2

[b] Mr. Chief Justice Waite died before the case was heard and was not replaced by Mr. Chief Justice Fuller until after it had been decided.

TABLE IX (*Continued*)

Under Chief Justice	Recorded Declaration Number	Citation of Case and Year Decided	Vote
White	36	*Choate v. Trapp,* 224 U.S. 665 (1912)	9 : 0
White	37	*Butts v. Mer. & Miners' Co.,* 230 U.S. 126 (1913)	9 : 0
White	38	*United States v. Hvoslef,* 237 U.S. 1 (1915)	8 : 0
White	39	*Thames & Mersey Mar. Ins. Co. v. United States,* 237 U.S. 19 (1915)	8 : 0
White	40	*Hammer v. Dagenhart,* 247 U.S. 251 (1918)	5 : 4
White	41	*Knickerbocker Ice Co. v. Stewart,* 253 U.S. 149 (1920)	5 : 4
White	42	*Eisner v. Macomber,* 252 U.S. 189 (1920)	5 : 4
White	43	*Evans v. Gore,* 253 U.S. 245 (1920)	7 : 2
White	44	*United States v. Cohen Grocery Co.,* 255 U.S. 81 (1921)	6 : 2
White	45	*Weeds, Inc. v. United States,* 255 U.S. 109 (1921)	6 : 2
White	46	*Newberry v. United States,* 256 U.S. 232 (1921)	5 : 4
Taft	47	*United States v. Moreland,* 258 U.S. 433 (1922)	5 : 3
Taft	48	*Child Labor Tax Case,* 259 U.S. 20 (1922)	8 : 1
Taft	49	*Hill v. Wallace,* 259 U.S. 44 (1922)	9 : 0
Taft	50	*Keller v. Potomac Electric Co.,* 261 U.S. 428 (1923)	9 : 0
Taft	51	*Adkins v. Children's Hospital,* 261 U.S. 525 (1923)	5 : 3
Taft	52	*Spalding & Bros. v. Edwards,* 262 U.S. 66 (1923)	9 : 0
Taft	53	*Washington v. Dawson,* 264 U.S. 219 (1924)	7 : 2
Taft	54	*Miles v. Graham,* 268 U.S. 501 (1925)	8 : 1
Taft	55	*Trusler v. Crooks,* 269 U.S. 475 (1926)	9 : 0
Taft	56	*Myers v. United States,* 272 U.S. 52 (1926)	6 : 3

TABLE IX (*Continued*)

Under Chief Justice	Recorded Declaration Number	Citation of Case and Year Decided	Vote
Taft	57	*Nichols v. Coolidge,* 274 U.S. 531 (1927)	9 : 0
Taft	58	*Untermyer v. Anderson,* 276 U.S. 440 (1928)	6 : 3
Taft	59	*National Life Insurance Co. v. United States,* 277 U.S. 508 (1928)	6 : 3
Hughes	60	*Heiner v. Donnan,* 285 U.S. 312 (1932)	6 : 2
Hughes	61	*Booth v. United States,* 291 U.S. 339 (1934)	9 : 0
Hughes	62	*Lynch v. United States,* 292 U.S. 571 (1934)	9 : 0
Hughes	63	*Panama Refining Co. v. Ryan et al.,* 293 U.S. 388 (1935)	8 : 1
Hughes	64	*Perry v. United States,* 294 U.S. 330 (1935)	5 : 4
Hughes	65	*Railroad Retirement Bd. v. Alton R. R.,* 295 U.S. 330 (1935)	5 : 4
Hughes	66	*Schechter Poultry Corp. v. United States,* 295 U.S. 495 (1935)	9 : 0
Hughes	67	*Louisville Joint Stock Land Bank v. Radford,* 295 U.S. 555 (1935)	9 : 0
Hughes	68	*United States v. Constantine,* 296 U.S. 287 (1935)	6 : 3
Hughes	69	*Hopkins Federal Savings and Loan Association v. Cleary,* 296 U.S. 315 (1935)	9 : 0
Hughes	70	*United States v. Butler,* 297 U.S. 1 (1936)	6 : 3
Hughes	71	*Rickert Rice Mills v. Fontenot,* 297 U.S. 110 (1936)	9 : 0
Hughes	72	*Carter v. Carter Coal Co.,* 298 U.S. 238 (1936)	5 : 4
Hughes	73	*Ashton v. Cameron County Water Improvement District,* 298 U.S. 513 (1936)	5 : 4
Stone	74	*Tot v. United States,* 319 U.S. 463 (1943)	8 : 0
None[c]	75	*United States v. Lovett,* 328 U.S. 303 (1946)	8 : 0

[c] Mr. Chief Justice Stone had died before the case was heard and Mr. Chief Justice Vinson did not take his place on the bench until after it had been decided.

TABLE IX (*Continued*)

Under Chief Justice	Recorded Declaration Number	Citation of Case and Year Decided	Vote
Vinson	76	*United States v. Cardiff,* 344 U.S. 174 (1952)	8 : 1
Warren	77	*Bolling v. Sharpe,* 347 U.S. 497 (1954)	9 : 0
Warren	78	*United States ex rel Toth v. Quarles,* 350 U.S. 11 (1955)	6 : 3
Warren	79	*Reid v. Covert* and *Kinsella v. Krueger,*[d] 354 U.S. 1 (1957)	6 : 2
Warren	80	*Kinsella v. Singleton,*[d] 361 U.S. 234 (1960)	7 : 2
Warren	81	*Grisham v. Hagan,**** 361 U.S. 278 (1960) plus *McElroy v. United States,**** 361 U.S. 281 (1960)	6 : 2
Warren	82	*Trop v. Dulles,* 356 U.S. 86 (1958)	5 : 4
Warren	83	*Kennedy v. Mendoza-Martinez*[e]	
Warren	84	plus *Rusk v. Cort,*[e] 372 U.S. 144 (1963)	5 : 4
Warren	85	*Schneider v. Rusk,* 377 U.S. 163 (1964)	5 : 3
Warren	86	*Aptheker v. Secretary of State,* 378 U.S. 500 (1964)	6 : 3
Warren	87	*Lamont v. Postmaster-General* plus *Fixa v. Heilberg,* 381 U.S. 301 (1965)	8 : 0
Warren	88	*United States v. Brown,* 381 U.S. 437 (1965)	5 : 4
Warren	89	*United States v. Romano,* 382 U.S. 136 (1965)	9 : 0
Warren	90	*Afroyim v. Rusk,*[f] 387 U.S. 253 (1967)	5 : 4
Warren	91	*United States v. Robel,* 389 U.S. 258 (1967)	6 : 2

[d] See pp. 281–82, *supra,* for elaboration. Also see pp. 186–88, Ch. V, *supra.*
[e] The two cases were reported under the same citation, but there were two declarations of unconstitutionality involving segments of two separate statutes. (See p. 282, *supra.*)
[f] Although the holding refers specifically only to one aspect of the statute, its breadth may be interpreted as reaching several more.

TABLE IX *(Continued)*

Under Chief Justice	Recorded Declaration Number	Citation of Case and Year Decided	Vote
Warren	92	*Marchetti v. United States* and *Grosso v. United States,* 390 U.S. 39, 62 (1968)	7 : 1
Warren	93	*Haynes v. United States,* 390 U.S. 85 (1968)	7 : 1
Warren	94	*United States v. Jackson,* 390 U.S. 569 (1968)	6 : 2
Warren	95	*Washington v. Legrant,* 394 U.S. 618 (1969)	6 : 3
Warren	96/97[g]	*Leary v. United States,* 395 U.S. 6 (1969)	9 : 0
Burger	98	*Schacht v. United States,* 398 U.S. 58 (1970)	5 : 4
Burger	99	*Oregon v. Mitchell,* 400 U.S. 112 (1970)	5 : 4
Burger	100/101[h]	*Blount v. Rizzi* and *United States v. The Book Bin,* 400 U.S. 410 (1971)	9 : 0
Burger	102	*Tilton v. Richardson,* 403 U.S. 672 (1971)	9 : 0
Burger	103	*Chief of Capitol Police v. Jeannette Rankin Brigade,* 409 U.S. 972 (1972)	9 : 0
Burger	104	*Richardson v. Davis* and *Richardson v. Griffin,*[h] 409 U.S. 1069 (1972)	6 : 3
Burger	105	*United States Department of Agriculture v. Murry,* 413 U.S. 508 (1973)	5 : 4
Burger	106	*United States Department of Agriculture v. Moreno,* 413 U.S. 528 (1973)	7 : 2
Burger	107/108[g]	*Frontiero v. Richardson,* 411 U.S. 677 (1973)	8 : 1
Burger	109	*Jiminez v. Weinberger,* 418 U.S. 000 (1974)	8 : 1

[g] Same citation but involving two different statutes.
[h] Two separate cases but same statute.

JUDICIAL REVIEW ABROAD

As already indicated, the practice of judicial review is not likely to be found in nonfederal states. Hence the other two major subject-lands of this study either do not, as in the case of Britain, or did not, until the adoption of the Constitution of 1958, in the case of France, clothe their courts with the power of judicial review—and in the instance of the French Fifth Republic, it is judicial review only to a limited and tangential degree (if indeed it is classifiable as "judicial review" at all). But, as noted earlier, the Giscard d'Estaing government, which came into office in May 1974, pledged moves toward *bona fide* judicial review, and it did effect one that fall.

BRITAIN

In Britain, Parliament is supreme in the sense that *any* law that has been enacted by it and has received the routine approval of the Crown becomes the law of the land and is *ipso facto* beyond overturning by the British courts. By virtue of the ancient writ of *quo warranto*, the courts do, of course, possess the authority to *interpret* legislation, and particularly administrative action based upon it—for all government officials are potentially accountable to the courts for their actions—*but they may not strike down the law itself*. In the immortal words of Walter Bagehot, the famous British economist and journalist, "there is nothing the British Parliament cannot do except transform a man into a woman and a woman into a man." Although he expressed this fact of *governmental* life a century ago, it is still as true today as it was then. The more or less homogeneous people of Britain, deeply steeped in the common experience of centuries, tradition, custom, and a firm, if not uncritical, faith in Westminster and Whitehall, continue to be quite content to entrust their treasured freedoms to the good judgment of their representatives assembled in Parliament. These representatives are duly checked—"controlled" is a more appropriate term—by the powerful executive arm, the political parties, the continuing dedication to the "cricket" factor, and public opinion itself. The British courts are revered and esteemed as necessary concomitants of the democratic process, but *not* in the role of ultimate guardians of the Constitution.

FRANCE

The French, too, insisting that a law is the expression of the sovereign will, had not endowed their courts with authority to declare laws unconstitutional, even in a limited manner, until the proclamation of the Constitution of the Fifth Republic in 1958. However, prior to it they did devise a rather interesting safeguard in order to ascertain that suggested legislation of dubious constitutionality did not become law per se short of an amendment to the Constitution. That safeguard was established by the framers of the Constitution of the Fourth Republic in the form of a special thirteen-member committee known as the *Constitutional Committee (Comité Constitutionnel)*.

Chaired by the President of the Republic, the Constitutional Committee consisted, in addition to the President of the National Assembly and the President of the Council of the Republic, of three members selected by the latter and seven by the former branch of the legislature. In each instance these ten were chosen from personnel outside the membership of the respective chambers, usually professors of law in general concord with the several political parties represented in Parliament. Whenever it was requested to do so by the President of the Council of the Republic and an absolute majority of its members—and only then!—the committee was empowered to examine a law prior to its final promulgation to determine whether or not it was of such a nature as to require its recasting as a *constitutional amendment* rather than simply pass as a *law*. If the committee concurred that a law did in fact imply an amendment to the Constitution, it was referred back to the National Assembly for appropriate action. Not surprisingly, the Constitutional Committee was hardly a very busy institution; it was called upon in merely a few cases, and only one or two of these gave it an opportunity to perform a significant role. Whatever its performance, the institution was a far cry from bona fide judicial review.

The Constitutional Council. However, France moved a bit closer to bona fide judicial review—without actually attaining it—with the adoption of a provision in the de Gaulle Constitution of 1958 calling for a *Constitutional Council (Conseil Constitutionnel)*.[40] Not a court at all, it actually lies outside the judicial system of the government; neither individual citizens nor groups nor courts of law can appeal to it. The council is composed of all the ex-Presidents of France—regardless of which Republic they may have headed—plus nine other distinguished personages, of whom three each are selected by the President of the Republic, the President of the Senate, and the President of the National Assembly. M. *le président* of the council is chosen from among its membership by the incumbent President of the Republic. The members may hold no public office of any kind, other than al-

40 Title VII, Articles 56–63.

295

ready held civil service appointments, for it was the intention of the authors of the institution that its membership be wholly independent, exercising no outside remunerative public activity whatsoever.

The nine appointive members of the Constitutional Council—usually lawyers who have been active in politics (five of the original nine had been active Gaullists)—serve for one nonrenewable, staggered nine-year term of office, whereas all ex-Presidents of France serve for life. In theory, the latter may not resign, but one, the venerable Vincent Auriol, first President of the Fourth Republic, announced on July 2, 1960, that, in protest of three allegedly unconstitutional actions taken by President de Gaulle, he would no longer participate in the Council's work. The disputed actions were, first, a measure to increase vastly state aid to denominational schools; second, de Gaulle's refusal, in March 1960, to convene Parliament in special session despite a request by a majority of the deputies (who were duly backed by a constitutional provision); and third, the short-cut procedure employed to revise the Constitution on the structure of the French Community. The then seventy-five-year-old popular Socialist, who had done much to bring de Gaulle to power in the dark days of May 1958, concluded his letter of resignation to Council President Léon Noel as follows:

> This lack of deference for the national sovereignty and our fundamental charter orients the constitutional regime of 1958 toward a system of personal and arbitrary power in opposition to the essential rules and principles of democracy. . . . [T]hus, not wanting to remain powerless and mute before attacks on the national sovereignty, I regret to inform you that I will no longer sit with the Constitutional Council.[41]

The Council has the preventive power to declare unconstitutional all *organic laws* (e.g. appointment and removal of high officials; finance bills) and *standing orders* (rules of procedure) of the houses of Parliament; both these categories *must* be submitted to the council prior to their promulgation. It is also empowered to strike down those *ordinary laws, treaties*, and *protocols* which *may* be voluntarily referred to it by the President of the Republic, the Premier, or the Presidents of the two houses of Parliament. Thus, Senate President Alain Poher—who had unsuccessfully opposed President Georges Pompidou in the 1969 elections—referred an anti-freedom of association bill to it in 1971. It was a measure bitterly criticized by liberals and leftists, and had been passed over the Senate's objections. In a milestone decision, the Council declared it unconstitutional—marking the

[41] As reported by Robert C. Doty in *The New York Times* (International Edition), July 2, 1960.

first time that the body, dominated by the ruling Gaullist party, had effectively opposed the government on a fundamental point of law.[42]

Normally, the Council is expected to hand down a decision within one month, but if the government categorizes a referred measure as "urgent," it must rule on the matter within eight days. Among the other main functions of the Council are: supervision of the "regularity" of the elections of the President of the Republic, the members of Parliament—the Constitutional Council, not Parliament, establishes the credentials of the deputies[43] and senators—and of all popular referenda; it may decide disputes between the government (the Ministry) and Parliament regarding the "delimitation of executive and legislative competence";[44] and it *must* be consulted by the President of the Republic when he is contemplating the assumption of emergency powers under Article 16 of the Constitution—as de Gaulle did in April 1961—with regard to both the existence of the emergency and the measures he proposes to take under it.

The Council—which meets *in camera*—cannot itself initiate action in constitutional cases, but it is autonomous regarding the other delimited areas of its power just outlined. A quorum for a valid decision is seven members, yet an absolute majority is required to certify Presidential disability—another of its responsibilities. One opinion only is delivered in behalf of the entire body—there are no concurring or dissenting opinions—but all decisions of the Council must be written. Its decisions—which are based on written documents and briefs, there being no oral argument at all—are final and binding and are not appealable to "any jurisdiction whatsoever." Yet it has no power to enforce its decisions, other than the power to persuade.

Given this distinctly limited range of power and authority, it would be highly misleading to characterize the functions of the Constitutional Council as judicial review *per se*. There are three debilitating weaknesses: First, the inability of private individuals and groups to challenge the constitutionality of a law, since only the high public officers named above possess that right as an adjunct of their official station. Second, a challenge to the constitutionality of a law even by one of the latter is possible solely as to the substance of the law and not as to its procedural application (one of the

---

[42] Decision of July 16, 1971. (See the articles in the International Edition of the *Herald Tribune*, July 19, 1971 and *The New York Times*, July 18, 1971, p. 13.

[43] Thus, after the November 1962 elections to the National Assembly, the Council invalidated the results in four assembly districts.

[44] By the end of 1969, the Council had decided 66 such disputes. See Roy Pierce, *French Politics and Political Institutions*, 2d ed. (New York: Harper and Row, 1973), pp. 94–95. In only seven of the disputes did the Council side with Parliament.

most frequent causes of court review in the United States, for example). Third, the extremely short period of time permitted to the Council for its deliberation on a validly challenged measure makes all but a mockery of the concept of an appeal—especially since its power is exercisable only *prior* to promulgation. On the other hand, its record to date (Fall 1974) indicates a definite inclination to assert itself in the constitutional evaluation of the writing of parliamentary rules. It remains to be seen whether this inclination is a harbinger of more assertion in other areas of its presumed competence—but this is unlikely. In the opinion of one of the most astute commentators on the French scene, *le conseil constitutionnel* is best thought of as an adjunct to the President of the Republic in his endeavors to ensure respect for the 1958 Constitution.[45] This appraisal was assuredly vindicated when President de Gaulle in October 1962 called for a national referendum on direct election of the President—despite the Council's objections, and those by the *conseil d'état*—to such a referendum call on the obvious ground that the Constitution of 1958 did not provide for such direct action; and that, indeed, the President's call represented a patent violation of the letter and the spirit of the basic document. But when, predictably, de Gaulle refused to be stopped; held the referendum; won it (albeit by a narrow margin); and then saw his action and the attendant results challenged at the bar of the Council, the latter promptly declared itself "incompetent" to rule on the "subject matter approved" by and in the referendum. The French Constitutional Council is no Supreme Court of the United States—despite the Giscard d'Estaing reforms of 1974.

SOME OTHER SPECIAL CONSTITUTIONAL TRIBUNALS

Several countries—perhaps recognizing traditional distinctions between natural and positive law—have created judicial bodies that approach or even feature some of the manifestations of the power of judicial review, yet they are usually found *outside* or astride the ordinary court structure. Among the more visible of these bodies are the constitutional courts of West Germany, Italy, and Austria, all of which practice at least some measure of judicial review. There are others, but a brief treatment of these three will suffice to illustrate the point. The three states, each in a post–World War II development, empowered their special constitutional courts to guard against infringement of their constitutions by simple legislation and other governmental action—e.g. any action that would violate the constitutional guarantee,

---

[45] William Pickles, *The French Constitution, October 4, 1958* (London: Stevens & Co., Ltd., 1960), p. 33.

present in almost identical form in all three lands, that "all persons shall be equal before the law." There has been fairly general acceptance of their purpose and functions.[46]

By far the most active and most successful among the three is West Germany's *Federal Constitutional Court (Bundesverfassungsgericht)*, created in 1951 at United States insistence under the Basic Law of 1949, as amended in 1970, and seated in Karlsruhe. (The framers of the Weimar Republic had rejected judicial review because of what they regarded as the "stultifying actions" of the United States Supreme Court!) It consists of sixteen judges of at least forty years of age; all have considerable past judicial, legal, professional, or other high public experience and are eligible for judicial office as well as for election to the *Bundestag* (though they cannot be members of it). They are elected half by the lower house (*Bundestag*) by a special committee of twelve electors set up by it on the basis of proportional representation in the *Bundestag*—hence dominated by the major parties—with nine of the twelve votes necessary for selection, and half by the upper house (*Bundesrat*) of Parliament by a two-thirds majority. The *Bundesrat* is representative of the partisan and regional interests of the *Länder* (states). The selections by the two houses are made from a list provided by the Ministry of Justice. It comprises *all* federal judges eligible for elevation to the *Bundesverfassungsgericht* as well as any other legally trained candidates who are nominated by the federal government, by the *Länder* and by the political parties. Only six of those selected—three each from its two eight-member chambers—*must* come from the ranks of professionally trained, sitting federal judges; the others may, but need not, be drawn from such judgeships. As of 1970 all judges serve for non-renewable twelve-year terms of office; they must retire at age sixty-eight.

The Federal Constitutional Court possesses the extensive power to decide all disputes involving the meaning and effectiveness of the Basic Law (*Grundgesetz*); it decides the constitutional validity of any federal or state (*Land*) statute, whether or not a case involving it has already come before one of the regular courts; and it adjudicates disputes between organs of government at the national level. Out of these powers arise the Court's two most significant functions: jurisdiction over disputes between the Federal Republic and the *Länder* regarding the latter's administration of the for-

[46] See the informative article by Taylor Cole, "The Constitutional Courts: A Comparison," in 53 *American Political Science Review* 963–84 (December 1959). See also Mauro Cappelletti, *Judicial Review in the Contemporary World* (Indianapolis: The Bobbs-Merrill Co., Inc., 1971), Ch. III, "The Modern Systems of Judicial Review: The Organs of Control," pp. 45–68.

mer's statutes, and guardianship over the fundamental rights and privileges of citizens as determined by the Basic Law both on substantive and procedural grounds—like judicial review in the United States and unlike its restricted, if conceivably now widening, practice in France.

As indicated, the *Bundesverfassungsgericht*[47] is composed of two chambers or "senates" of eight judges each, one for all cases dealing with civil and constitutional rights, the other for the rest of the cases. The former senate's opinions are unsigned and no votes are recorded, but the latter now publishes the division in cases and has begun to identify dissenting judges. The *Bundesverfassungsgericht* has been a busy and assertive court, and to the surprise of many a skeptic it has acted with considerable courage and vigor. For example, it braved the wrath and power of Chancellor Konrad Adenauer when, in a momentous decision early in 1961, it declared unconstitutional, as a violation of principles of federalism guaranteed in Article 30 of the Basic Law, his executive action setting up a federally controlled, second television network that was to be financed largely through commercials[48]—a plan that had been expressly rejected by Parliament earlier! The decision was particularly remarkable since it resulted from a suit filed some months earlier by four *Länder* dominated by the Chancellor's opposition, the Social Democrats.

Two other significant decisions served to declare both the Communist party in 1956 and in 1952 the socialist *Reich* party—a neo-Nazi organization —unconstitutional as being detrimental to the constitutional and democratic order of the state.[49] And as another illustration of the Court's virility and assertiveness, it did not hesitate to strike down an executive decree based on what the Court viewed as unconstitutional delegation of legislative power by the *Bundestag* to the Executive.[50] The reasoning employed here was quite similar to that used by the United States Supreme Court in 1935, in the "Hot Oil" cases,[51] when it declared unconstitutional, as an illegal delegation of legislative power to the Chief Executive, an important section of the National Industrial Recovery Act which was soon to fall in its

---

[47] There are three modes of access to the *Bundesverfassungsgericht*: (1) *Richterklage*— request by an inferior court to have the BVG render a judgment on a constitutional question in a pending case. (2) *Parteienklage*—appeal by a constitutional organ (federal or state). (3) *Bürgerklage*—in cases concerning questions of violation of basic rights of individuals involving any statute, judicial decision, or administrative act, or, in the case of local governments, "the right of self-government."
[48] 12 BVerf GE 60 (1961).
[49] BVerf GE 85 (1956) and 2 BVerf GE 1 (1952).
[50] 1 BVerf GE 14 (1951).
[51] *Panama Refining Co. v. Ryan*, 293 U.S. 388 (1935).

entirety. And as a final example of the Court's versatile jurisdictional determination, in 1966 it declared unconstitutional the federal statutes under which the three major political parties had been subsidized from public funds to the tune of DMK 38,000,000 (about $14,500,000) annually. The Court held that such funds could be authorized only for legitimate election campaign expenses, not for general propaganda, and would have to be made available to splinter parties as well. "In a free society," said the tribunal, "the process of forming public opinion should be free of the state, and should move from the people themselves to the state institutions rather than from the state down to the people."[52] It is fair to say that the *Bundesverfassungsgericht* has assumed an importance hardly predictable, and that it has thus become a significant and prestigious element in the *modus operandi* of the new German federalism. In the judgment of one seasoned observer, "the Court clearly has become the most important source of judicial influence in German politics and the most active and powerful tribunal in Western Europe."[53]

Another modern special constitutional tribunal is Italy's *Constitutional Court* (*Corte Costituzionale*), established under the Italian Constitution of 1948—although it did not begin to function until January 1, 1956. This fifteen-member body is staffed with distinguished personages who have had at least twenty years of experience as practicing lawyers, or who are experienced judges or professors of law. (Once more we note the high esteem in which the professor is held in Europe.) The members of the Court are appointed for staggered twelve-year terms, five selected by the President of the Republic of Italy with the Premier's countersignature; five by a three-fifths vote of Parliament in joint session; and five by the "ordinary and administrative judiciary," i.e. three by the *Corte di Cassazione*, one by the *Consiglio di Stato*, and one by the *Corte dei Conti*. The Court is the final interpreter of the Constitution; it has the power to declare both national and regional laws unconstitutional—as it did in the case of a 1934 law that denied Sunday rest to shepherds[54]—and it serves as arbiter in disputes between organs of government at the national level. In that role it also serves as legitimator—e.g., it ruled in favor of Italy's controversial 1971 divorce law, holding that church weddings, like marriages, were liable to dissolution

[52] 20 BVerf GE 56–59, 119, 134 (1966).
[53] Lewis J. Edinger, *Politics in Germany: Attitudes and Processes* (Boston: Little, Brown and Co., 1968), p. 323.
[54] Decision of July 22, 1962. A few months earlier the *Corte Constituzionale* upheld the constitutionality of articles 559 and 560 of Italy's penal code which provides far sterner punishment for adulterous wives than for unfaithful husbands. (Decision of November 28, 1961.)

under that statute.[55] Access of individuals to it is considerably less readily available than in West Germany and that fact, plus a general tendency to tread much more gingerly, largely because of the open hostility to its ultimate power by Italy's Attorney General, at first rendered the *Corte Costituzionale* less of a peacemaker in matters of constitutional checks than its counterpart north of the Alps. The *Corte's* average annual caseload has been less than two hundred to date. Nevertheless, it has asserted itself, and particularly so when dealing with the now familiar illegal delegation of legislative power to the executive branch, prompting two knowledgeable commentators to conclude that the Court has not only "insisted upon its prerogatives and successfully defended its position," but that it has "become a bulwark for freedom in Italian society."[56] On the other hand, its decisions have at times been deliberately ignored by officials—one such instance in 1957 causing the resignation of Enrico De Nicola, the Court's first President, when a cabinet minister resolutely refused to adhere to decision of the Court.[57] Antagonism between the judicial and other branches of government have continued.

Austria, too, has its Constitutional Court, the *Verfassungsgericht*. This fourteen-member tribunal was re-instituted in 1945, based upon the Austrian Constitution of 1920, as amended in 1925 and 1929. Its members are appointed for life—unlike a majority of the German justices and all of the Italian justices—by the President of the Republic of Austria from nominees of the federal government, partly on the recommendations of the lower house (National Council) and the upper house (Federal Council) of Parliament. The tribunal has the power to review the constitutionality of legislation and to decide jurisdiction disputes between the courts and administrative authorities. Individuals have less ready access to the *Verfassungsgericht* than they do to its German counterpart yet somewhat more than to that of Italy. This center position of the Austrian tribunal applies also to its range of power and conception of functions. But it, too, has asserted itself and has not been loath to examine legislation, even legislation extending to the social realm; i.e. it held unconstitutional a section of the Income Tax Law of 1953 that differentiated between the sexes for tax purposes.[58]

Yet of all the issues that have confronted these three constitutional courts

[55] Decision of July 8, 1971. In 1974 it vetoed a government ban of foreign cable TV.

[56] Guglielmo Negri and Joseph La Palombara, "Principles of Italian Constitutional Law and the Structure of Central Government," in Negri, *Three Essays on Comparative Politics* (Milano: D. A. Ciuffre, 1964), pp. 33–7 and p. 8, respectively.

[57] See Norman Kogan, *The Government of Italy* (New York: Thomas Y. Crowell Co., 1965), p. 120.

[58] Decision of March 29, 1958.

of Europe, by far the greatest number has concerned the interpretation and application of respective constitutional provisions in the vexatious areas of delegation of legislative authority, federalism, and equality before the law. With varying emphasis, they are very much in the constitutional weather eye of the United States judiciary as well.

AN HISTORICAL NOTE

The notion that courts, or some other body, should exercise judicial review as the guardian of the theoretical primacy of a basic law or constitution[59] stems primarily from the early European rejection of the idea of the inviolability of an enacted law. One of the first statements clamoring for a type of judicial review in that connection was made in England—oddly enough in view of the subsequent rejection of the concept. It arose out of the famous *Dr. Bonham's Case* in 1610. The King, pursuant to an Act of Parliament, had granted to members of the London College of Physicians the exclusive right to issue licenses to practice medicine in that city. Dr. Bonham was charged with practicing medicine illegally, for he was not a member of that College—the latter having refused to license him. The College then fined him, confiscating half of the fine for itself! When the case came before Sir Edward Coke, the Lord Chief Justice, he declared the charter void as a violation of the common law. Holding the latter to be supreme, Sir Edward simply stated that the courts could declare acts of Parliament null and void; therefore, he held in the now so famous dictum: "When an act of Parliament is against common right and reason, or repugnant, or impossible to be performed, the common law will control it and adjudge such act to be void."[60] Parliament then simply re-enacted the statute! If Sir Edward's view of judicial review was ever seriously adopted at all anywhere in England, it was promptly superseded when the Glorious Revolution of 1688 clearly established the supremacy of Parliament. In fact, already in 1653 Lord Coke's peers had held in *Captain Streater's Case*[61] that ". . . we must submit to the legislative power else things would run around."[62]

---

[59] An intriguing development on that front, albeit a still somewhat unreliable one, in terms of its genuine role and meaning, is the establishment in 1964 of Yugoslavia's eleven-man Constitutional Court, elected by the Federal Assembly for a once renewable eight-year term of office. See Winston M. Fisk and Alvin Z. Rubinstein, "Yugoslavia's Constitutional Court," 15 *East Europe* 7 (July 1966).

[60] 8 Co. 188a.

[61] 5 How St. Trs. 365.

[62] However, there are those who argue—a bit tortuously—that, in effect, by their common law power of *interpreting* legislation, the courts of England *do* practice judicial review. See, for example, A. Wilson, in "The Doctrine and Practice of Judicial Review of Legislation," 4 *Me Judice* 20 (January 1962).

Nevertheless, the concept of judicial review—a product of our common western history and the "logical result of centuries of European thought and colonial experience"[63]—subsequently found its way across the Atlantic Ocean to the British Colonies, there to be nurtured by several colonial courts. In eight or nine separate early judgments these courts refused to enforce legislative enactments that they deemed to be against "the laws of nature" (shades of Locke and future events) or "the laws of natural equity" —in a sense against the latent, unwritten Constitution.

JUDICIAL REVIEW AT HOME

Yet if the principle of judicial review was imbedded in the minds of the American Founding Fathers, they assuredly failed to spell it out literally— although the records of the Constitutional Convention in Philadelphia in 1787 prove conclusively that the idea of judicial review was widely recognized and accepted; that the matter was very much on the minds of the delegates, who after all distrusted unrestrained popular government; and that it was widely debated. In any event, the massed evidence is quite persuasive that a vast majority of the delegates, anti-Federalists as well as Federalists, favored it—although for quite different reasons. Between 25 and 32 of the 40 delegates are generally considered to have called for it. Leading constitutional authorities such as Professors Beard, Corwin, and Mason are fully agreed on that interpretation of the wishes of the delegates[64] who, with less than a handful of dissenters, in effect concurred in the pronouncement by Gouverneur Morris of Pennsylvania that the courts should decline to give the weight of law to "a direct violation of the Constitution." Morris admitted that such control over the legislature might have "its inconveniences," but that it was nonetheless necessary because even the "most virtuous citizens will often as members of a legislative body concur in measures which afterwards in their private capacity they will be ashamed of."[65]

[63] Mauro Cappelletti, *Judicial Review in the Contemporary World, op. cit.* p. 25.
[64] See Charles Beard, "The Supreme Court—Usurper or Grantee?," 27 *Political Science Quarterly* 1 (1912); Max Farrand, *The Framing of the Constitution of the United States* (New Haven: Yale University Press, 1913); and John Schmidhauser, *The Supreme Court as Final Arbiter in Federal-State Relations, 1789–1957* (Chapel Hill: University of North Carolina Press, 1958), especially Chs. I and XI. See also Beard's classic, *The Supreme Court and the Constitution* rev. ed., with an introduction by Alan F. Westin (Englewood Cliffs, N.J.: Prentice-Hall, Inc., 1962).
[65] As quoted by Alpheus T. Mason and Richard H. Leach, *In Quest of Freedom* (Englewood Cliffs, N.J.: Prentice-Hall, Inc., 1959), p. 124.

So prominent a framer as Alexander Hamilton declared in his famous *Federalist Paper* #78 that judicial review was definitely meant to be incorporated into the prerogatives of the judiciary; that "the courts were designed to be an intermediate body between the people and the legislature, in order among other things, to keep the latter within the limits assigned to their authority. The interpretation of the laws is the proper and peculiar province of the courts." The "Father of the Constitution" himself, James Madison, wrote:

> Judiciary is truly the only defensive armor of the Federal Government, or rather for the Constitution and laws of the United States. Strip it of that armor and the door is wide open for nullification, anarchy and convulsion.[66]

And in his famed Philadelphia lectures of 1790–91, James Wilson, probably the most influential Founding Father after James Madison—and by then an Associate Justice of the United States Supreme Court—observed that the Constitution was supreme law; that it was for the judges to declare and apply it; that what was subordinate must give way; and that because one branch of the government infringed the Constitution was no reason why another should abet such infringement.[67] Despite this solid evidence it is still a matter of considerable academic dispute whether or not the framers intended the power of judicial review to be given to the courts. But there are sundry additional grounds for the conclusion that such doubts as still remain ought to be laid at rest—that the debate over the legitimacy of judicial review is settled by history.

FURTHER HISTORICAL ROOTS

The Constitution itself, while admittedly not providing for the power of judicial review in so many words, assuredly alludes to it by implication. The supremacy clause of Article VI, relating to the duty of state judges, may well be viewed as implying judicial review by federal tribunals over *state actions*. Moreover, that same provision of the Constitution requires acts of Congress to be made "in pursuance thereof," which would seem to call for someone to act as arbiter. It may be well to quote the entire supremacy clause:

[66] As quoted by Charles Warren in *The Supreme Court in United States History* (Boston: Little Brown, 1937), Vol. I, p. 740.
[67] *Ibid*. Vol. I, p. 460.

> This Constitution, and the laws of the United States which shall be made in pursuance thereof, and all treaties made or which shall be made under the authority of the United States, shall be the supreme law of the land; and the judges in every state shall be bound thereby, anything in the Constitution or laws of any state to the contrary notwithstanding.[68]

Another relevant provision of the basic document is to be found in Article III, which states:

> The judicial power shall extend to all cases, in law and equity, arising under this Constitution, the laws of the United States and treaties made or which shall be made, under the authority. . . .[69]

If nothing else, this section clearly indicated the authority of the judiciary over cases in a vast area of constitutional interpretation and thus implied its finite power as to the legality of those cases.

Moreover, as has already been briefly indicated, it is noteworthy that in the colonial period the British Privy Council had *established* judicial review over acts passed by the colonial legislatures. At least eight states' ratifying conventions expressly discussed and accepted the power to pronounce legislative acts null and void.[70] Furthermore, between 1789 and 1803 the courts in ten of the states had *exercised* that power by declaring state laws to be in conflict with state constitutions, and prior to 1789 eight instances[71] of state court judicial review deciding against their state legislature took place. And Section 25 of the Judiciary Act 1789, the law under which the First Congress created the national judiciary, *conferred* on the federal government specific authority to *reverse* provisions of state laws and state constitutions that conflicted with the "Constitution, treaty, statute, or commission of the United States."[72] Still, since neither the Constitution for any level of government, nor the Judiciary Act of 1789 for the national level, specifically provided for judicial review, it remained for the Supreme Court of the United States to do so. This it did in 1803, in *Marbury v. Madison*[73] —though, as Thomas Reed Powell noted in his *Vagaries and Varieties in Constitutional Interpretation*, no one "had any premonition that the point of judicial review would be relevant to the disposition of the controversy."[74]

[68] Constitution of the United States, Article VI, Sec. 2.
[69] Ibid. Article III, Sec. 2.
[70] Va., R.I., N.Y., Conn., Mass., N.J., N.C., S.C.
[71] E.g. *Holmes v. Walton* (New Jersey, 1780) and *Trevett v. Wheeden* (Rhode Island, 1786).
[72] Act of September 24, 1789, c.20, 25, 1 Statutes at Large 73, 87.
[73] 1 Cranch 137.
[74] (New York: Columbia University Press, 1956), p. 11.

With the possible exception of *McCulloch v. Maryland*[75]—of which James Bradley Thayer and Felix Frankfurter thought "that the conception of the nation which Marshall derived from the Constitution and set forth [in it] is his greatest single judicial performance"[76]—and, perhaps, *Gibbons v. Ogden*[77] (but for different reasons), no more important case at constitutional law exists than the hallowed and revered *Marbury v. Madison*—which has been called "the rib of the Constitution."[78] All three were written by that great national constitutionalist, Mr. Chief Justice John Marshall, who had himself been a delegate to the Ratifying Convention of Virginia and a one-term Congressman from that state. The background of the *Marbury* decision is so colorful, and the decision itself so important, that no treatment of the judicial process would be complete without at least a brief analysis of the case, which is one that is not only still frequently cited by courts in the United States, but also in other countries—for example, Italy and India!

Prompt enactment of the Judiciary Act of 1789 enabled the national judiciary to begin to function at once in the fledgling United States, but questions of the existence of the power of judicial review and any possible challenge of it did not arise immediately. However, the issue was simmering. For example, in *Hayburn's Case* two Supreme Court justices, riding circuit in Pennsylvania in 1792, had refused to carry out a congressional statute that they deemed contrary to the Constitution. Backed by the full Court, Associate Justices Blair and Wilson ruled that they could not perform certain duties imposed upon them by the law because they were not "judicial in nature."[79] Together with District Judge Peters they were to pass on disputed pension claims of invalid war veterans, with *their* determination subject to review by the Secretary of War and by Congress! If nothing else, this judicial refusal to carry out a legislative act called attention to the constitutional problem. Three years later, in *Van Horne's Lessee v. Dorrance*[80] Mr. Justice William Paterson—who had been a delegate from the Constitutional Convention in New Jersey—held for the Court: "Whatever may be the case in other countries, yet in this *there can be no doubt that every act*

---

[75] 4 Wheaton 316 (1819).
[76] "John Marshall and the Judicial Function," in *Government Under Law* (Cambridge: Harvard University Press, 1956), p. 8.
[77] 9 Wheaton 1 (1824).
[78] Glendon A. Schubert, *Constitutional Politics* (New York: Holt, Rinehart and Winston, 1960), p. 178.
[79] 2 Dallas 409 (1792).
[80] 2 Dallas 304 (1795).

of the Legislature repugnant to the Constitution, is absolutely void."[81] A similar judgment was expressed by Mr. Justice Samuel Chase on another occasion soon thereafter.[82]

Moreover, the Supreme Court had struck down at least two relatively minor *state* enactments[83]—although the second of these decisions was of considerable importance since it held state laws subject to treaties by ruling that the Anglo-American Peace Treaty overrode a Virginia law on the delicate and potentially explosive issue of debts owed to British subjects by Americans.[84] Furthermore, depending upon the historical source, the Supreme Court even held an insignificant *federal* pension claim law unconstitutional in the case of *U.S. v. Yale Todd*, which was decided in 1794 but not reported until it became a footnote almost sixty years later in *U.S. v. Ferreira*.[85] Nevertheless, this was evidently the first instance of the declaration of unconstitutionality of a federal statute. Finally, two years after *Yale Todd*, the Court—with three of its six justices not participating—expressly upheld a congressional statute imposing a duty on carriages as not being a "direct tax" and therefore not unconstitutional.[86] (Exactly ninety-nine years later the Supreme Court in effect overruled this decision in the *Second Income Tax Case*,[87] thus precipitating the Sixteenth Amendment.) Yet regardless of these aforegone instances of incipient concern with judicial review, it was not until 1803 and *Marbury v. Madison* that matters actually came to a climax.

The Factual Setting. The second President of the United States, John Adams, had been defeated in his bid for re-election in 1800 by his political arch-rival, Thomas Jefferson. Laboring desperately to salvage something for his prostrate Federalist party, Adams was determined to pack the federal judiciary with as many judgeships as humanly and statutorily possible. With the aid of a more than obliging lame-duck Federalist Congress, which passed both the Circuit Court Act[88] and the District of Columbia Organic

---

[81] Ibid. at 308. (Italics supplied.)
[82] *Cooper v. Telfair*, 2 Dallas 14 (1800), at 19.
[83] *Clerke v. Harwood*, 3 Dallas 342 (1797) and *Ware v. Hylton*, 3 Dallas 199 (1796).
[84] *Ware v. Hylton*, loc. cit.
[85] 13 Howard 40 (1851).
[86] *Hylton v. United States*, 3 Dallas 171 (1796).
[87] *Pollock v. Farmers Loan & Trust Co.*, 158 U.S. 601 (1895).
[88] The Act—which was repealed in March 1802 at Jefferson's insistence—also provided that the next vacancy on the Supreme Court should *not* be filled, thus reducing the Court's membership from six to five and thereby rendering impossible any automatic vacancy-filling appointment by the incoming Jefferson, a "Democratic-Republican" rather than a Federalist. Barely one year later the new President succeeded in having Congress re-establish the membership at six.

Law Act early in 1801, Adams, before leaving office on March 3, 1801, was able to nominate, have approved by the Senate, and commission the following into office: sixteen new circuit judges (under the Circuit Court Act); forty-two new justices of the peace (under the District of Columbia Act); and one Chief Justice of the United States Supreme Court—his own Secretary of State, the forty-five-year-old staunch Federalist John Marshall (who in 1798 had refused Washington's offer of an Associate Justiceship). These nominees have often been called "Adams' Midnight Judges" because the President devoted his waning hours in office to signing their commissions of appointment.

It fell to the outgoing premier of the cabinet—Marshall, whose appointment Adams came to regard as the single most important act of his Administration (just as Hoover would ultimately regard his own of Cardozo more than 125 years later)—to affix to them the Great Seal of the United States and then to deliver the new judgeship commissions to the various appointees. But Marshall, at once fatigued and exhilarated on Inauguration Eve, failed to deliver seventeen of the forty-two justices-of-the-peace commissions, although, aided by his brother James, he worked until late into the evening, and indeed had taken care of all the important new circuit judgeships plus most of the other appointments. However, he would begin his first full day as Chief Justice in the morning, a post to which he had been appointed almost two months earlier upon the resignation of the elderly and feeble Oliver Ellsworth in favor of a diplomatic position, and upon John Jay's summary refusal to accept Adam's proffered second appointment as Chief Justice because, as Jay felt, the Court lacked "energy, weight, and dignity." As head of the Court, Marshall would have the somewhat less than delightful duty of administering the oath of the Presidency to his avowed political enemy (and distant cousin) Thomas Jefferson—who would later frequently refer to Marshall as "that gloomy malignity." He left the undelivered commissions to the incoming Secretary of State, James Madison.[89] The stage was thus set for a towering battle of three veritable titans of the early days of Constitution and Nation.

Preliminaries. Angry because of the sustained packing of the judiciary with Federalist appointees, Jefferson upon taking office was delighted to

[89] For an unusually penetrating analysis of the more technical aspects of *Marbury v. Madison*, see Mr. Justice Harold H. Burton's article, "The Cornerstone of Constitutional Law: The Extraordinary Case of *Marbury v. Madison*," 36 *American Bar Association Journal* 805 (October 1950). See also the more historical piece by John A. Garraty, "The Case of the Missing Commissions," in his *Quarrels that Have Shaped the Constitution* (New York: Harper & Row, 1964).

find the seventeen undelivered justice-of-the-peace commissions on the desk of the Secretary of State—Madison arrived somewhat later. The new President, subsequently seconded enthusiastically by his new Secretary of State, determined not to deliver them, declaring that the ". . . nominations crowded in by Mr. Adams after he knew he was not appointing for himself I treat as mere nullities."[90] And, according to one account, the commissions at issue were "disposed of with the other waste paper and rubbish of the office."[91] Neither subsequent pleas nor threats by such disappointed office-seekers as William Marbury were to sway them. Marbury, a forty-one-year-old Washingtonian, and three other staunch Federalists—Denis Ramsay, William Harper, and Robert Townshend Hooe—subsequently sought aid of counsel and hired Charles Lee, Attorney General under George Washington and John Adams.

Lee turned to the law and to the courts. He found what he believed to be the law in a provision of the Judiciary Act of 1789: Section 13 of that important law extended to the Supreme Court of the United States the power to issue a *writ of mandamus—mandamus* being the Latin for "we command"—an old Anglo-Saxon writ used as early as the twelfth-century reign of Henry II, commanding a public official to perform his official, ministerial, nondiscretionary duty. Invoking that provision, Lee petitioned the Court for appropriate action—and, at the next term of the court in 1803, *Marbury v. Madison* reached the original docket of the highest court of the land. It could readily have dismissed the petition for want of jurisdiction under the 1789 statute in this type of case—but, as will become apparent, this would hardly have suited the purposes of the Chief Justice. For presiding over the Supreme Court now, of course, was Jefferson's mortal political enemy and Adam's loyal supporter, John Marshall, who had issued an order to Madison—who promptly ignored it—to show cause why the requested writ of mandamus should not be issued against him. Surely Marshall's decision would be in favor of Marbury, especially in view of the seemingly clear language of Section 13!

Marshall, C. J., for the Court. But both the Federalists and the Jeffersonian Republicans had underestimated the boldness and judiciousness, the craftsmanship and shrewd political acumen, the farsightedness and statesmanship, and, above all, the powerful dedication to the Constitution—*as he saw it and wanted to see it*—of the fourth Chief Justice of the United

90 Warren, op. cit. Vol. I, p. 201.
91 Charles S. Hyneman, *The Supreme Court on Trial* (New York: Atherton Press, 1963), p. 75.

States Supreme Court. And it was John Marshall who spoke for the unanimous Court in a twenty-seven-page opinion, despite the fact that he had a direct interest in the case at bar—which today would almost certainly result in self-disqualification from the case. Whatever one may think of his failure to abstain, it is not difficult to agree with Professor Corwin that "his compact presentation of the case marches to its conclusion with all the precision of a demonstration of Euclid."[92] The Chief Justice was confronted with a dilemma: If he were to grant the writ in the face of almost certain disobedience by Madison, the Court would be powerless, and if he were to refuse to grant it, Jefferson would triumph.

Marshall's heart, of course, was on the side of Marbury's cause—which happened to be that of his fellow Federalists—and he did not hesitate to chide Jefferson and Madison from the bench, to castigate them for their "rascality." Moreover, he distinctly concurred with the plaintiff's contention that (1) he had a legal right to the commission, and (2) the laws of the land afforded him a remedy. These 9000 words of *obiter dicta* consumed twenty of the twenty-seven pages! But as to the remedy, Marshall—an experienced political savant, here confronted with an utterly political situation—announced unmistakably that a writ of mandamus, issued by the Supreme Court under Section 13 of the Judiciary Act, was definitely *not* such a remedy, for it was *unconstitutional!*

It was unconstitutional, explained Marshall for himself and his unanimous Associated Justices, Paterson, Chase, Washington (Cushing and Moore not sitting), because *by incorporating it into the Judiciary Act of 1789 Congress had added to the original jurisdiction of the Supreme Court by law*—an action which Article III, the judicial article of the Constitution, does not sanction. And, continued Marshall in an unprecedented, pithy, 1500-word display of a combination of judicial self-abnegation and judicial assumption of power—for there is no doubt that judicial review, "the ultimate conservative response to the 'evils of democracy,'"[93] was a goal of the democracy-distrusting Federalists—in Section 13 Congress had given to the Court a power which it could not legally receive. (That section of the act had actually figured in earlier Supreme Court decisions, yet no one had chosen to raise the present constitutional issue.) *"An act repugnant to the Constitution is void,"* explained Marshall, thus echoing Hamilton's *Federalist* #78,

---

[92] A lecture at Princeton University, September 25, 1950.
[93] Wallace Mendelson, *Capitalism, Democracy, and the Supreme Court* (New York: Appleton-Century-Crofts, 1960), p. 20.

and, in so stating the matter, he enunciated clearly the doctrine of judicial review.[94] He elaborated:

> It is emphatically the province and duty of the judicial department to say what the law is. Those who apply the rule to particular cases, must of necessity expound and interpret that rule. . . . A law repugnant to the Constitution is void; . . . courts as well as other departments are bound by that instrument.[95]

Significance and Summary. In brief, John Marshall—thus ingeniously having managed to have his cake and eat it too, in what Senator Albert J. Beveridge of Indiana, his most famous biographer, perhaps somewhat extravagantly described as "a coup as bold in design and as daring as that by which the Constitution had been framed"[96]—clearly, cogently, and quite emphatically enunciated and interpreted three principles of the utmost significance to the young nation: (1) that the courts have the power of judicial review; (2) that the Constitution of the United States is the supreme law of the land; (3) that the *original* jurisdiction of the Supreme Court cannot be changed by simple law of Congress, since that particular jurisdiction is specifically limited by the language of the Constitution—although, plainly, the *appellate* jurisdiction can be changed by simple legislation because the letter of the Constitution so permits. (This, of course, has been done since, with the most pertinent illustration being the intriguing post-Civil War case of *ex parte McCardle*.[97] Here the Supreme Court had under consideration an appeal, already argued before it in an 1868 *habeas corpus* proceeding—having unanimously rejected the government's motion to dismiss it for want of jurisdiction—in which the constitutionality of one of the Reconstruction Acts was at issue. Fearful that the Court might declare the act at issue unconstitutional—and thus conceivably strike a mortal blow against the entire Reconstruction program—Congress, over President An-

---

[94] For a different view, though wholly "pro" judicial review, see Charles L. Black, Jr., *The People and the Court: Judicial Review in a Democracy* (New York: The Macmillan Co., 1960), pp. 25ff. Black contends that judicial review had already been firmly established by then, and he calls a "myth" the usual belief that it was Marshall who gave it authoritative expression.

[95] *Marbury v. Madison*, 1 Cranch 137 (1803).

[96] *The Life of John Marshall* (Boston: Houghton Mifflin Co., 1919), Vol. I, p. 223, and Vol. III, p. 142.

[97] 7 Wallace 506 (1869). Colonel William H. McCardle, editor of the *Vicksburg* [*Miss.*] *Times* in the Fourth Reconstruction District, whose paper had been vociferously critical of Reconstruction policies and forces under the command of General Edward O. C. Ord, had been charged with numerous offenses, court-martialed, and sentenced to be shot.

drew Johnson's courageous but fruitless veto that March quickly amended the statute defining the appellate jurisdiction of the Supreme Court in these cases. Congress did this—via a rider to a customs and revenue appeals bill— by withdrawing from that jurisdiction direct appeals to the Supreme Court from the circuit courts in certain classes of *habeas corpus* proceedings, including the present one.[98] Incidentally, the majority of the Court, which had simply postponed action pending the legislative and executive moves, was far from displeased about the congressional victory—although Associate Justices Field and Grier issued a bitter public dissent against what they viewed as an evasion of constitutional responsibility and deliberate procrastination. But the Court was unanimous in upholding the action of Congress—and the Reconstruction Acts were never tested by it.)

The importance of Marshall's decision in *Marbury v. Madison* to American constitutional development can hardly be overestimated.[99] There is no question that judicial review is crucial to the governmental process in the United States under its federal character and its separation of powers principle. Yet it cannot be gainsaid that Marshall strained the judicial process in making *Marbury v. Madison* his vehicle for the announcement of the doctrine of the judicial veto. We have already noted that he should probably have disqualified himself from sitting in the case because of his direct and personal involvement with both its fundamental issue and its personnel— after all, the case in effect arose out of his own negligence or apathy—and that, in any event, he did not really have to accept the case for review. He could readily have dismissed it for lack of original jurisdiction in this case. Moreover, based on available precedent, he could easily have interpreted Section 13 and its empowering provision—indeed, he probably should have —in such a manner as to raise no substantial questions regarding statutory additions to the Court's original jurisdiction. For a good case could be made for the contention, based on the intent of its framers in the First Congress (which included future Chief Justice Oliver Ellsworth), that Section 13 signified nothing more than that the Court had power to grant writs of mandamus in all instances when such a remedy would be appropriate in the disposition of cases duly and properly brought be-

---

[98] In a letter to his son, Battle, shortly before he died—he was never tried for his alleged crimes and lived to a ripe old age—McCardle wrote that the Supreme Court had actually agreed to decide the case in his favor before Congress acted, the vote being 6 : 3 to hold his arrest unconstitutional.

[99] Marbury and his fellow litigants disappeared into the obscurity whence they had come at the conclusion of the case. Marbury became president of a Georgetown bank in 1814 and died in 1835.

fore it, either on its original or its appellate docket. Specifically, the section stated that the Supreme Court could issue the writ to "persons holding office under the authority of the United States"—and the justices *had* issued that writ in earlier cases without questioning Section 13 for a moment. By no means was Section 13 thus necessarily intended to enlarge the original jurisdiction of the Court—but Marshall now claimed that the Court could not issue a writ of mandamus *except* in cases that came to it on appeal from a lower court.

Yet none of the above suggested alternate courses of action would have suited Marshall's purposes—one of which also was to avoid the potential embarrassment that would have resulted from the almost certain defiance by President Jefferson. Having said and recognized that, however, we should acknowledge the genius of that powerful figure in American history and of the great service he performed in expounding the doctrine of judicial review when he did. Far from being a usurpation, it has powerful claims to authenticity, based on more than a century of history, a strong line of precedents, and convincing contemporary literature. That debate on the justification and wisdom of the doctrine ensued almost at once, and that it has never really ceased, merely serves to add stature to its progenitor.

VIII
Judicial Review:
II   Controversy
and Limitations

JUDICIAL REVIEW IN A DEMOCRATIC STATE:
SAINT OR SINNER?

That no other federal law, or section thereof, was declared unconstitutional by the Supreme Court between *Marbury v. Madison*[1] in 1803 and the *Dred Scott case*,[2] a full fifty-four years later, did not lessen the debate on the doctrine of judicial review. That it has remained fresh, indeed, and has lost none of its controversial characteristics, is testified to vividly and contemporarily by the widespread public, often emotion-charged, debate surrounding the unanimous decision for the Court by Mr. Chief Justice Warren in the 1954 *Segregation Cases*[3]—in a sense the grandchildren of the Taney Court's decision in *Dred Scott*. The charge against the Warren Court: in holding compulsory segregation on account of race in the public schools to be a violation of the "equal protection of the laws" clause of the Fourteenth Amendment to the United States Constitution, the Court had not *judged*, not *interpreted*, not *reviewed*, but *legislated*. The indictment of judicial legislation is directly related, of course, to the power and doctrine of judicial review—once characterized as "the people's institutionalized means of self-control."[4]

[1] 1 Cranch 137.
[2] *Dred Scott v. Sandford*, 19 Howard 393 (1857).
[3] *Brown v. Board of Education*, 347 U.S. 483 (1954) and *Bolling v. Sharpe*, 347 U.S. 497 (1954).
[4] Charles L. Black, Jr., *The People and the Court: Judicial Review in a Democracy* (New York: The Macmillan Co., 1960), p. 20. For some other vital contemporary works on judicial review, with varying points of view, cf. Alexander M. Bickel, *The Least Dangerous Branch* (Indianapolis: The Bobbs-Merrill Co., Inc., 1962); Herbert Wechsler, *Principles, Politics and Fundamental Law* (Cambridge: Harvard University Press, 1961); Charles S. Hyneman, *The Supreme Court on Trial* (New York: Atherton Press, 1963); Howard E. Dean, *Judicial Review and Democracy* (New York: Random House, Inc., 1966); and Arthur A. North, S. J., *The Supreme Court: Judicial Process and Judicial Politics* (New York: Appleton-Century-Crofts, 1966).

INVOKING AUTHORITY

Unfortunately, all too few professional observers of the judicial process and quite naturally even fewer laymen, however informed they may be, are resolutely consistent in their attitude toward either judicial review or the institution that exercises the power. To abide by Paul A. Freund's exhortation that "criticism . . . be informed by perspective and informed by philosophy"[5] is difficult. More often than not "it all depends whose ox is being gored," to employ Al Smith's pungent phrase. Yet it is entirely feasible to determine both articulate and reasonable "con" and "pro" positions regarding the doctrine, without resorting to the more passionate partisans of the controversy. Although a great deal of literature on the subject is available, we may well permit two of America's most honored and most literate governmental personages to speak for the two sides. It is fair to say that, had they not lived and functioned considerably more than a century apart, they would have respected and admired one another and would have made a worthy set of opponents in any public debate on the issue—Thomas Jefferson against, and Benjamin Cardozo for! With due allowance for certain deviations, their points of view, even their verbiage, are today very much representative of the two divergent attitudes on the question.

Con: Although he was among the first to suggest judicial review as a means of harmonizing the federal system, and although evidence contained in at least two letters written from Paris to James Madison is persuasive that Thomas Jefferson had favored some type or degree of direct judicial control at the time of the framing of the Constitution in Philadelphia and even almost two years later,[6] the great Virginian certainly never accepted the notion of judicial review as it was subsequently expounded by his political opponent, John Marshall. Some observers[7] trace the genesis of his hostility to the enforcement of the hated Alien and Sedition Acts of 1798—prior thereto he was demonstrably not opposed to judicial review, at least in theory. In any event, Jefferson's opposition was based upon two major concepts: first, that the doctrine of judicial review—as applied by Marshall, for he saw no one else do it—violates that of the constitutionally mandated theory of the separation of powers; and second, that it represents a patent denial of the veritable popular will, the majority will, as expressed by the

[5] *The Supreme Court of the United States* (Cleveland and New York: The World Publishing Co., 1961), p. 77.
[6] Dec. 20, 1787, and March 15, 1789.
[7] E.g. Wallace Mendelson, "Jefferson on Judicial Review: Consistency through Change," 29 *University of Chicago Law Review* 327–37 (Winter 1962).

sovereign people through their duly elected representatives "in Congress assembled" (and in any other properly constituted legislative body). That the second assertion did not, however, blind him to the potential excesses of these representatives, is indicated clearly in one of his letters to Madison, to whom he voiced the fear that ". . . the tyranny of the legislatures is the most formidable dread at present and will be for many years."[8]

Nonetheless, Jefferson vehemently rejected the contention that the Founding Fathers had intended to give to one of the three branches the right to prescribe rules for the government of the others, "and to that one, too, which is unelected by and independent of the nation." He insisted that each of the three branches, being independent, "has an equal right to decide for itself the meaning of the Constitution in the cases submitted to its action; where it is to act ultimately without appeal."[9] To Jefferson, the doctrine of judicial review, with its inherent possibilities of leading to judicial *supremacy*, was both elitist and *anti*democratic—although, of course, on close examination one sees that *all* agencies of government have their "undemocratic" aspects.

This position has been echoed frequently since, but by none better than by a contemporary of Jefferson, Mr. Justice John B. Gibson of the Supreme Court of Pennsylvania—probably the most able adversary of judicial review in his day. From that bench in 1825, in his now famous dissenting opinion in *Eakin v. Raub*,[10] in which his colleagues upheld the power of Pennsylvania's state courts to declare state statutes unconstitutional, Gibson challenged the Marshallian argument in *Marbury v. Madison* lucidly and forcefully along the lines of the Jeffersonian response. One of his key points was the classic concept of popular democracy—that it is a "postulate in the theory of our government . . . that the people are wise, virtuous, and competent to manage their own affairs."[11] Yet Gibson had apparently modified his viewpoint twenty years later. When an attorney, pleading his case before the Pennsylvania Supreme Court, cited the Gibson dissent in *Eakin v. Raub*, that Justice replied from the bench that he had changed his opinion for two reasons: one, that the Pennsylvania Constitutional Convention of 1838, by remaining silent on judicial review, had "sanctioned the pretensions of the courts to deal freely with the acts of the legislature"; and two,

---

[8] Letter of March 15, 1789.
[9] From his letter to Judge Spencer Roane of the Virginia Supreme Court, September 6, 1819.
[10] 12 S. & R. (Pa. S. Ct.) 330.
[11] Ibid. at 355.

"from experience of the necessity of the case."[12] This does not necessarily connote a change of mind, but it assuredly does indicate at least that Mr. Justice Gibson, true to his philosophy of the representative legislative function, had accepted the latter's "surrender" to the doctrine.

Pro: Although he greatly admired Jefferson both as a man and as a political philosopher, Benjamin N. Cardozo, who served for many years on the New York State Court of Appeals as well as an Associate Justice of the United States Supreme Court for the regrettably brief period from 1932 to 1938, disagreed strongly with Jefferson's approach to, and rejection of, judicial review. Cardozo anchored his belief in that doctrine upon the firm conviction that while it must be employed cautiously and sparingly—as he himself did —it serves nonetheless as a necessary and proper check on possible excesses by both the federal and state legislatures. But it would be utterly wrong to label him a "judicial activist." More than a decade prior to his universally hailed appointment to the Supreme Court, where he mounted the seat vacated by Mr. Justice Oliver Wendell Holmes, Jr., Cardozo advanced his key contention that it is the *restraining influence of its presence* rather than the frequency of its application that renders judicial review so vital to the governmental process in the United States of America. His characteristically beautiful style and language must be quoted directly:

> By conscious or subconscious influence, the presence of this restraining power aloof in the background, but none the less always in reserve, *tends to stabilize and rationalize the legislative judgment,* to infuse it with the glow of principle, to hold the standard aloft and visible for those who must run the race and keep the faith. . . . The restraining power of the judiciary does not manifest its chief worth in the few cases in which the legislature has gone beyond the lines that mark the limits of discretion. Rather shall we find *its chief worth in making vocal and audible the ideals that might otherwise be silenced, in giving them continuity of life and expression, in guiding and directing choice within the limits where choice ranges.* This function should preserve to the courts the power that now belongs to them; if only the power is exercised with insight into social values, and with suppleness of adaption to changing social needs.[13]

The man whom Cardozo had succeeded was familiar with the above passage, fully concurred in its sentiment and credo, and had practiced it

---

12 See *Norris v. Clymer,* 2 Pa. St. 277 (1845), at 281, as reported by Robert E. Cushman and Robert F. Cushman, *Cases in Constitutional Law* (New York: Appleton-Century-Crofts, 1968), pp. 23–24.

13 *The Nature of the Judicial Process* (New Haven: Yale University Press, 1921), pp. 93–94. (Italics supplied.)

throughout his three decades on the highest bench of the land. However, although Holmes was willing to grant that the United States would not "come to an end if we lost our power to declare an Act of Congress void," he firmly insisted that ". . . the Union would be imperiled if we could not make that declaration as to the laws of the several states."[14] United States Circuit Court Judge Learned Hand, the great contemporary of Holmes and Cardozo, frequently echoed this Holmesian creed. But he went considerably further than Holmes when, writing several years after his retirement from the bench, he endeavored to devise a test which would provide another modification of the doctrine: While agreeing that the Supreme Court must have the power and authority to review *grants* of power to and by Congress, he believed that it should not possess these sanctions regarding "a review of how the power has been *exercised*."[15] It is difficult to see how such an amendment of the doctrine of judicial review would not wound it seriously, if not, in effect, fatally.

The Jefferson and Cardozo viewpoints—and their attempted modifications—have manifold ardent and articulate adherents.[16] Yet there is no longer any doubt that judicial review is a permanent fixture in the American structure and operation of government, notwithstanding the repeated frontal and guerilla attacks from both public and private sources.[17] It is, after all, an essential adjunct of democracy, a normal fact of American governmental life—ringingly reconfirmed in *United States v. Nixon* in 1974!

DRAWING THE LINE—OR ATTEMPTING TO DO SO

Directly and intimately related to the controversy over the doctrine of judicial review is the frequently voiced charge that the Supreme Court of the

[14] Oliver Wendell Holmes, Jr., "Law and the Court," in *Collected Legal Papers* (New York: Harcourt, Brace, 1920), p. 295.

[15] Learned Hand, *The Bill of Rights* (Cambridge: Harvard University Press, 1958), p. 66, pp. 93–94. (Italics supplied.)

[16] For a conveniently "tabularized" list of arguments in favor and against judicial review, see Alan F. Westin's "Introduction" to the paper edition of Charles A. Beard's classic, *The Supreme Court and the Constitution* (Englewood Cliffs, N.J.: Prentice-Hall, Inc., 1962), pp. 6–7.

[17] For summary analysis of attempted legislative checks on the power, see Sheldon D. Elliott, "Court-Curbing Proposals in Congress," 33 *Notre Dame Lawyer* 597–605 (August 1958). Four excellent books dealing with the problem are Walter F. Murphy, *Congress and the Court* (Chicago: University of Chicago Press, 1962); C. Herman Pritchett, *Congress versus the Supreme Court* (Minneapolis: University of Minnesota Press, 1961); Adam C. Breckenridge, *Congress Against the Court* (Lincoln: University of Nebraska Press, 1971); and John R. Schmidhauser and Larry L. Berg, *The Supreme Court and Congress: Conflict and Interaction, 1945–1968* (New York: The Free Press, 1972).

United States—and to a somewhat lesser degree the lower rungs of the judiciary—is guilty of *judicial legislating*; in other words, that many of its decisions are tantamount to legislating rather than judging. More often than not, this indictment of the judiciary admits, and indeed grants, that the Court must have the power to *interpret* legislation and, if "absolutely necessary," hold unconstitutional a law that is *clearly* contrary to the Constitution—although no yardstick is provided on the connotation of the modifier "clearly." But this school of thought insists that a line must be drawn between the exercise of judicial *judgment* and the imposition of judicial *will*. Judicial will is accordingly equated with legislating, presumably reserved to Congress and the legislatures of the fifty states. Like all fine lines, the one between "interpreting" or "judging" and "legislating" is highly tenuous. How is it to be drawn? By whom? Where? Under what circumstances? Clearly there is no simple or single response to these questions, so crucial to line-drawing in general, and the line at issue in particular.

JUDICIAL LEGISLATING

The polar extremes in the endless controversy over the absence or presence of the concept of judicial legislating become readily apparent by the following two quotes, taken from active and honorable participants on both sides of the aisle—institutionally as well as philosophically. Early in 1930, arising on the floor of the United States Senate, of which he was one of the finest and most purposeful members for many years, George W. Norris of Nebraska, the "gentle knight of progressive ideals," shouted:

> We have a legislative body, called the House of Representatives, of over 400 men. We have another legislative body, called the Senate, of less than 100 men. We have, in reality, another legislative body, called the Supreme Court, of nine men; and they are more powerful than all the others put together.[18]

The diametrically opposite point of view is represented in a passage from an address to the New York State Bar Association in 1893 by Mr. Justice David Brewer of the United States Supreme Court:

> They [courts and judges] make no law, they establish no policy, they never enter into the domain of popular action. They do not govern. Their functions in relation to the state are limited to seeing that popular action does not trespass upon right and justice as it exists in written constitutions and natural law.[19]

[18] *Congressional Record,* 71 Cong. 2d Sess., Vol. 72, Part 4, p. 3566 (February 13, 1930).

[19] Address to the New York State Bar Association, *Proceedings* (1893).

Both expressions are equally extreme in their thesis, of course; they represent gross oversimplifications, notwithstanding the sincerity and conviction of the two men involved. Indeed, most of the Justices of the highest tribunal do not claim to have a pat answer to the vexatious question presented by the controversy over *the line*. But they have often come to grips with the crux of the matter in recognizing the human element that is so inevitably involved in the judicial process. In the realistic words of Mr. Justice John H. Clarke:

> I have never known any judges, no difference how austere of manner, who discharged their judicial duties in an atmosphere of pure, unadulterated reason. Alas! we are all "the common growth of Mother Earth,"—even those of us who wear the long robe.[20]

The blunt-spoken Mr. Justice McReynolds insisted that a judge should not be "an amorphous dummy, unspotted by human emotions"—and he was more than a little spotted! "Judges are men, not disembodied spirits," once remarked Mr. Justice Frankfurter; ". . . as men they respond to human situations. They do not reside in a vacuum." "Our judges are not monks or scientists," wrote Mr. Chief Justice Warren, "but participants in the living stream of our national life, steering the law between the dangers of rigidity on the one hand and formlessness on the other."[21] He thus echoed the realistic appraisal made by Thomas Reed Powell four decades earlier. He had opined:

> Judges have preferences for social policies as you and I. They form their judgments after the varying fashions in which you and I form ours. They have hands, organs, dimensions, senses, affections, passions. They are warmed by the same winter and summer and by the same ideas as a layman is.[22]

In any event, the Justices are agreed that they judge the cases and controversies that reach the Court in accordance with the Constitution and the laws of the land. There is no doubt that the nine Justices—in fact the judges on all levels of the judicial process—necessarily "legislate" in interpreting constitutional phraseology. The question is how much and how far they are justified in such judicial legislating. The often quoted jurist, however apocryphal the story may be, who responded to the question of whether judges make law replied, "Of course we do; made some myself last Mon-

---

[20] Hoyt L. Warner, *The Life of Mr. Justice Clarke* (Cleveland: Western Reserve University Press, 1959), p. 69.
[21] "The Law and the Future," 52 *Fortune* 106 (November 1955).
[22] "The Logic and Rhetoric of Constitutional Law," 15 *Journal of Philosophy, Psychology, and Scientific Method* 656 (1918).

day," is undoubtedly close to the truth. One of the wisest among those who graced the bench of the Supreme Court, the revered Mr. Justice Holmes—who has been so well described as the official judicial philosopher for the modern age[23]—also recognized "without hesitation" that judges *do and must legislate*"; but he added that they ". . . can do so only interstitially; they are confined from molar to molecular motions."[24] In a valedictory interview, Mr. Chief Justice Warren readily acknowledged that the Court, in effect, does make law:

> It doesn't make it consciously, it doesn't do it by intending to usurp the role of Congress but because of the very nature of our job. When two litigants come into court, one says the act of Congress means this, the other says the act of Congress means the opposite of that, and we say the act of Congress means something—either one of the two or something in between. We are making law, aren't we?[25]

Mr. Chief Justice Marshall, however, who was fully aware of the problem at issue, nevertheless insisted on commenting in one case that "judicial power, as contradistinguished from the power of the law, has no existence. Courts are the mere instruments of the law, and can will nothing."[26] Yet this man, who is generally recognized as the most competent and successful of all the Chief Justices to date, and is ranked among the two or three most powerful and influential jurists ever to sit on the Supreme Court, was hardly one to be loath to interpret broadly the Constitution and legislation passed under its authority—and in accordance with what Mr. Justice Holmes later referred to as "the felt necessities of the time." After all, had not that same Marshall written, in the great *McCulloch v. Maryland* decision, that our laws were made under a Constitution that was "intended to endure for ages to come and, consequently, to be adapted to the various crises of human affairs"?[27] Probably not a single Justice did more of this "adapting," and more incisively, than did Mr. Chief Justice Marshall, who often reminded his countrymen that "we must never forget that it is a *Constitution* we are expounding!"[28] Did he *interpret* or did he *legislate?* Undoubtedly both.

[23] Fred V. Cahill, Jr., *Judicial Legislation* (New York: The Ronald Press, 1952), p. 32.
[24] *Southern Pacific Co. v. Jensen*, 244 U.S. 205 (1916), at 221. (Italics supplied.)
[25] Sacramento, Calif., June 26, 1969, as quoted in *The New York Times*, June 27, 1969, p. 17.
[26] *Osborn v. United States Bank*, 9 Wheaton 738 (1824).
[27] Wheaton 316 (1819).
[28] Mr. Justice Frankfurter considered this Marshall statement to be "the single most important utterance in the literature of constitutional law—most important because most comprehensive and comprehending." ("John Marshall and the Judicial Function," 69 *Harvard Law Review* 217, 1955, at 219.)

More on the Line and on the Goring of Oxen. Marshall's long-term successor, Mr. Chief Justice Roger B. Taney, stared into the heart of the problem when, in rendering the majority opinion in the *Dred Scott* case, he held:

> The Constitution speaks not only in the same words, but with the same meaning and intent with which it spoke when it came from the hands of its framers, and was voted on and adopted by the people of the United States. Any other rule of construction would abrogate the judicial character of this Court and make it the mere reflex of the popular opinion or passion of the day.[29]

But the *Dred Scott* decision has been denounced more often as sheer "legislation" than any other decision of the Court, with the possible exception of the 1954 *Segregation Cases*.[30] When he was informed of the decision in *Dred Scott*, Senator Hale of New Hampshire introduced a resolution to *abolish* the Supreme Court. Yet again depending upon the point of view, those people who hailed the *Dred Scott* judgment as "statesmanlike interpretation" would have violently denounced the *Segregation Cases* as "blatant legislation," whereas the champions of the latter decisions would have roundly denounced the former! Indeed, some of the torrent of abuse poured upon the Court by *Segregation Cases* critics is almost identical in verbiage to that employed by the enemies of their Southern ancestors, the Radical Republicans of the North, in attacking *Dred Scott!* Could it be that the popular judgment does, in fact, depend upon whose ox is being gored?

Mr. Justice Owen J. Roberts, always searching for, if not inevitably contributing to, a modicum of consistency on the bench, attempted to draw the line once and for all in 1936—"the slot machine theory," commented Roscoe Pound acidly—when he spoke for a majority of six in the significant case of *United States v. Butler*, in which the Court struck down the Agricultural Adjustment Act of 1933:

> When an act of Congress is appropriately challenged in the Courts as not conforming to the constitutional mandate the judicial branch of the Government has only one duty—*to lay the article of the Constitution which is invoked beside the statute which is challenged and to decide whether the latter squares with the former.*[31]

[29] *Dred Scott v. Sandford,* 19 Howard 393 (1857).
[30] *Brown v. Board of Education,* 347 U.S. 483 (1954) and *Bolling v. Sharpe,* 347 U.S. 497 (1954).
[31] 297 U.S. 1 (1936), at 62. (Italics supplied.)

323

"Bravo," applauded the *opponents* of the New Deal, "great judicial states-manship, proper and precise interpretation of the Constitution!" "An un-warranted, outrageous assumption of legislative authority," countered the *proponents* of the New Deal, "arrogant disregard of constitutional limita-tions of judicial power." And President Roosevelt, scarcely one year after *Butler*, moved—unsuccessfully—to pack the Court by statutory provision, setting off one of the most interesting, most heated, and most sustained controversies in the entire history of Court and Nation.[32]

It was in the *Butler* case that the issue was perhaps most nearly faced by Mr. Justice Harlan Fiske Stone, not too many years later to be the Chief Justice, when he dissented from the opinion of the majority and admon-ished the members on that side of the decision that

> . . . while unconstitutional exercise of power by the executive and legis-lative branches is subject to judicial restraint, *the only check on our own exercise of power is our own sense of self-restraint.* . . . Courts are not the only agency of government that must be assumed to have capacity to govern. . . . For the removal of unwise laws from the statute books ap-peal lies not to the courts but to the ballot and to the processes of demo-cratic government.[33]

This would seem to be as close to the facts of judicial life as is attainable. In a sense, and although he would very likely have disapproved of the com-parison, the Stone comment was almost an echo of a famous statement made twenty years earlier by Charles Evans Hughes while he was the Re-publican presidential nominee. He had just become an ex-Associate Justice of the United States Supreme Court; was an ex-Governor of New York; a future Secretary of State in the Administrations of Presidents Harding and Coolidge; and ultimately would ascend the Court for a second tenure, this time as Chief Justice. While stumping during the campaign, a campaign which almost won him the presidency, he publicly repeated a statement he had made some years earlier: "*We are under the Constitution, but the Con-stitution is what the judges say it is.*" That assertion represents both too drastic and too oversimplified an analysis of the complex position of the ju-diciary and the Court, and it is subject to considerable substantive modifi-cation. Surely, in the final analysis, the Constitution is or becomes what the people of the nation want it to be or to become—a fact of political life that is very much on the mind of judges—and it must be considered, as Holmes

[32] For an engagingly written account, see Joseph Alsop and Turner Catledge, *The 168 Days* (New York: Doubleday, Doran, 1938).

[33] *United States v. Butler*, 297 U.S. 1 (1936), at 78, 88. (Italics supplied.)

said, "in the light of our whole experience and not merely in that of what was said a hundred years ago." In the words of his long-time friend and colleague, Brandeis:

> Our Constitution is not a strait jacket. It is a living organism. As such it is capable of growth—of expansion and adaptation to new conditions. Growth implies changes, political, economic, and social. Growth which is significant manifests itself rather in intellectual and moral conceptions than in material things.[34]

Moreover, while the Constitution, for the sake of argument, may well be what the judges say it is, that does by no means ascertain appropriate compliance, as has been repeatedly demonstrated. With these essential qualifications in mind, however, the Hughes campaign statement, coupled with the Stone dissent in the *Butler* case, could serve by and large as the definitive view of the Court's attitude. It has frequently been echoed by other articulate members of the highest bench, such as that philosophical devotee of British legislative supremacy and majority rule, Mr. Justice Frankfurter, who, in dissenting in the controversial expatriation case of *Trop v. Dulles*, lectured that:

> All power is, in Madison's phrase, "of an encroaching nature." . . . Judicial power is not immune against this human weakness. It must also be on guard against encroaching beyond its proper bounds, and not the less so since *the only restraint upon it is self-restraint.* . . .[35]

Vast differences about this aspect of the vexatious line exist now and have always existed among the Justices themselves, but most, in fact probably all, would in candor subscribe to the essence of the suggested Stone-Hughes formula, however at variance their interpretation and application of it may be. One thing is clear above all: in the realistic words of Mr. Justice Cardozo—not only one of the most proficient and most beloved Justices ever to sit on the Supreme Court, but also one of its finest and most haunting stylists: *"The great tides and currents which engulf the rest of men, do not turn aside in their course, and pass the judges idly by."*[36]

Mr. Justice George Sutherland, one of the six-man majority in the *Butler* case, justified judicial activism—which he and his jurisprudential soulmates,

---

[34] An unpublished passage in *United States v. Moreland*, 258 U.S. 433 (1922), as quoted by Alexander Bickel in his *The Supreme Court and the Idea of Progress* (New York: Harper and Row, 1970), p. 20.

[35] 356 U.S. 86 (1958), at 113. (Italics supplied.)

[36] *The Nature of the Judicial Process*, op. cit. p. 168 (Italics supplied.)

Justices Van Devanter, McReynolds, and Butler applied chiefly in the economic *laisser faire* camp—as natural judicial involvement. As one student of Sutherland analyzed his posture, according to Sutherland the oath of office taken by each Justice required him to decide cases in terms of his own best judgment. "Self-restraint, therefore, had no place among judicial duties. To surrender one's deliberate judgment, indeed, except as it might be modified by the persuasion of those holding different views, would constitute a violation of his oath of office."[37] To quote Sutherland directly from his dissenting opinion in the 1937 "switch-in-time-that-saved-nine" *West Coast Hotel* case:

> Self-restraint belongs in the domain of will and not of judgment. The check upon the judge is that imposed of his oath of office, by the Constitution, and by his own conscience and informed convictions.[38]

It is delicious irony that his jurisprudential and philosophical opposite, Mr. Justice William O. Douglas, could just as easily have written these words—and applied them to his posture in the realm of civil rights and liberties! In any event, as Mr. Justice Frankfurter put the matter cogently, the Court cannot, in the long run, escape judging; it must adjudicate; it must decide. Not one to judge lightly or hastily—Professor Wallace Mendelson has aptly called him a "humilitarian" among jurists with respect to the legal process[39] —Frankfurter, while deeply dedicated to the concept of judicial self-restraint, nevertheless clearly met the problem in his concurring opinion in the well-known *Sweezy* case:

> To be sure, this [opinion] is a conclusion based on a judicial judgment in balancing two contending principles—the right of a citizen to political privacy, as protected by the Fourteenth Amendment, and the right of the State to self-protection. And striking the balance implies the exercise of judgment. This is the inescapable judicial task in giving substantive content, legally enforced, to the Due Process Clause, and it is a task ultimately committed to this Court. It must not be an exercise of whim or will. *It must be an overriding judgment founded on something much deeper and more justifiable than personal preference. As far as it lies within human limitations, it must be impersonal judgment. It must rest on fundamental presuppositions rooted in history to which widespread acceptance may*

[37] Carl Brent Swisher, *The Growth of Constitutional Power in the United States*, 2d ed. (Chicago: University of Chicago Press, 1963), p. 221.
[38] *West Coast Hotel Co. v. Parrish*, 300 U.S. 379, at 402.
[39] "Mr. Justice Frankfurter—Law and Choice," 10 *Vanderbilt Law Review* 333 (February 1957).

fairly be attributed. Such a judgment must be arrived at in a spirit of humility when it counters the judgment of the State's highest court. *But, in the end, judgment cannot be escaped—the judgment of this Court.*[40]

That this awesome and even agonizing duty of finding and drawing the line between judicial will and judicial judgment in rendering a necessary decision conscientiously is not confined to the highest level of the federal judiciary, may be illustrated by a decision of the Supreme Court of Michigan. In a consortium case replete with human factors, a closely divided (4 : 3) Court not only reversed a lower court decision but negated precedent of long standing. Speaking for the majority, Mr. Justice Talbot Smith recognized that the decision represented a drastic departure from the past and would surely be viewed as judicial legislating. Yet having braved the expected storm, he admitted that the decision to permit the wife of a man seriously injured in an automobile accident to sue for loss of consortium—i.e. marital comfort, affection, and companionship—marked a stride away from the "outworn legal views" derived from old English and Roman law that a wife is merely a "vassal, chattel, and household drudge." He concluded:

> Were we to rule upon precedent alone, we would have no trouble with this case. We would simply tell this woman to be gone, and take her shattered husband with her. . . . Legally today, the wife stands on a par with her husband. . . . *The obstacles to the wife's [court] action were judge-invented and they are herewith judge-destroyed.*[41]

The anticipated critical storm of charges of crass judicial legislating broke over the heads of author and Court at once. Yet, perhaps Mr. Justice Smith had simply been unusually frank in writing his opinion as he did—rather than disguising it in judicial semantics. Perhaps he had not been unaware of the famous statement of judicial philosophy expressed by Chancellor Kent of New York a century and a half earlier:

> I saw where justice lay, and the moral issue decided the court [Kent] half the time; and I then sat down to search the authorities. . . . I might once in a while be embarrassed by a technical rule, but I almost always found principles suited to my views of the case. . . .[42]

[40] *Sweezy v. New Hampshire, by Wyman, Attorney-General,* 354 U.S. 234 (1957). (Italics supplied.)

[41] *Montgomery v. Stephan,* 359 Mich. 33 (1960). Eight years later the New York Court of Appeals handed down an almost identical decision, and also by a 4 : 3 vote! (*Millington v. Southern Elevator Co.,* 293 N.Y.S. 2d 305.)

[42] William Kent (ed.), *The Memoirs and Letters of James Kent* (Boston: Little, Brown and Co., 1898), pp. 158–9.

327

In summary, depending, of course, upon the facts and posture of each individual case, both verbiage and line are very much matters of degree. But, as Mr. Justice Frankfurter took pains to admonish, to say that courts make law just as legislatures do is ". . . to deny essential features in the history of our democracy. It denies that legislation and adjudication have had different lines of growth, serve vitally different purposes, function under different conditions, and bear different responsibilities."[43]

JUDGES LIMITED: THE TAUGHT TRADITION OF THE LAW

Moreover, it must be clearly understood that judges are not free agents in rendering their decisions, regardless of the impression given by some. Again in Frankfurter's words: "We do not sit like kadi under a tree, dispensing justice according to considerations of individual expediency."[44] A deplorable tendency exists in the mind of the public to oversimplify the process of judicial decision-making, the area of government obviously least understood by the average citizen. Although it may perhaps overstate the case somewhat, there is much merit in the contention of the just-cited Mr. Justice Talbot Smith, that "we are rigidly bound within walls that are unseen" (by the layman).[45] These walls are built of the heritage of the law, the spirit of the Anglo-Saxon law, the impact of the cases as they come down through the years—in brief, *the taught tradition of the law*. No one expressed the heart of the matter better than Mr. Justice Cardozo:

> A jurist is not to innovate at pleasure. He is not a knight-errant, roaming at will in pursuit of his own ideal of beauty or of goodness. He is to draw his inspiration from consecrated principles. He is not to yield to spasmodic sentiment, to vague and unregulated benevolence. He is to exercise a discretion informed by tradition, methodized by analogy, disciplined by system, and subordinated to the primordial necessity of order in the social life.[46]

Among the vital aspects of this taught tradition are: an abiding sense of judicial integrity; a close and necessary regard for the rules of procedure; considerations of equal treatment before the law; the deference shown to legislative enactments; judicial recognition of the realities of the cultural,

[43] "Reflections on Reading Statutes," 2 *The Record* 213 (June 1947).
[44] *Terminiello v. Chicago*, 347 U.S. 1 (1949).
[45] Statement to author, August 15, 1958 (Madison, Wisconsin).
[46] *The Nature of the Judicial Process*, op. cit. p. 141.

ideological, and institutional setting which the judges share with their fellow citizens, not excluding the political realities; and *stare decisis*, the adherence to precedent.

STARE DECISIS

The desirability and, indeed, the need for certainty in planning our affairs, both in their internal (professional) and external aspects, render reliance on precedent an attractive and useful doctrine. "Imitation of the past," observed Mr. Justice Holmes, "until we have a clear reason for change, no more needs justification than appetite. It is a form of the inevitable to be accepted until we have a clear vision of what different things we want."[47] Yet, be it noted at once that *stare decisis* is a principle of policy and not a mechanical formula of adherence to the latest decision, "however recent and questionable, when such adherence involves collision with a prior doctrine more embracing in its scope, intrinsically sounder, and verified by experience."[48] "*Stare decisis*," in the words of Mr. Justice Brandeis,

> is usually the wise policy, because in most matters it is more important that the applicable rule of law be settled than that it be settled right. . . . This is commonly true even where the error is a matter of serious concern, provided correction can be had by legislation. But in cases involving the Federal Constitution, where correction through legislative action is practically impossible, this Court has often overruled its earlier decisions. The Court bows to the lessons of experience and the force of better reasoning, recognizes that the process of trial and error, so fruitful in the physical sciences, is appropriate also in the judicial function.[49]

The doctrine of *stare decisis* requires a careful weighing in each doubtful case "of the advantages of adherence to precedent and the necessity for judicially planned social and economic progress."[50] The law, as Dean Pound has stated, must be stable and yet it cannot stand still. Or, as Viscount Kilmuir, then the Lord High Chancellor of Britain, told a distinguished audience of legal scholars in 1960: "Critics are apt to allege that we treat exist-

[47] "Holdsworth's English Law," in *Collected Legal Papers* (Boston: A. Harcourt, 1920), p. 290.
[48] Mr. Justice Frankfurter, for the Court, in *Helvering v. Hallock*, 309 U.S. 106 (1940), at 110.
[49] *Burnet v. Coronado Oil & Gas Co.*, 285 U.S. 293 (1932), 406.
[50] Robert A. Sprecher, "The Development of the Doctrine of Stare Decisis and the Extent to Which It Should Be Applied," 31 *American Bar Association Journal* 501–9 (1945).

ing law with such reverence that every antique is replaced unaltered. I believe in an occasional spring cleaning."[51]

Reliance on precedent presents difficult problems to the judge, especially since the question to be resolved comes, normally speaking, to a *choice* of precedents. "Sometimes," commented Mr. Justice Jackson wistfully in his last book, "one is tempted to quote his former self, not only to pay his respects to the author, but to demonstrate the consistency of his views, if not their correctness."[52] Precedents abound and not all precedents are of equal rank; a good many judges generally seem to accord considerably more sanctity to very old and hallowed "precedents," such as most of Mr. Chief Justice John Marshall's decisions, than to those of relatively recent vintage. Progress, in any event, does not stand still, and a precedent may have to be overruled or reversed in time. "Our assurance that our children will live, as we have, under a constitutional democracy," commented the then U.S. Solicitor General Stanley F. Reed, "rests upon the power of the form of government to adjust itself. . . . The position of the Supreme Court on *stare decisis* makes that adjustment possible."[53] In at least 105 decisions made between 1810 and 1974, the Supreme Court of the United States *overruled* its own previous determinations.[54] Many additional cases are *distinguished* from precedent, which is somehow viewed as a less disrespectful device. "From age to age," commented Mr. Justice Douglas in an able treatment of the issue,

> the problem of constitutional adjudication is the same. It is to keep the power of government unrestrained by the social or economic theories that one set of judges may entertain. *It is to keep one age unfettered by the fears or limited vision of another.*[55]

Or, as Mr. Justice Potter Stewart admitted after eight years on the Court, in an important 1970 labor case, quoting Mr. Justice Frankfurter: "Wisdom too often never comes, and so one ought not to reject it merely because it comes late."[56] Precedents, as Mr. Justice Talbot Smith said, being "judge-

---

[51] Speech on the occasion of the dedication ceremony of the University of Chicago Law Center, April 30, 1960.

[52] Robert H. Jackson, *The Supreme Court in the American System of Government* (Cambridge: Harvard University Press, 1955), p. 11.

[53] "Stare Decisis," 35 *Pennsylvania Bar Association Journal Quarterly* 150 (1938).

[54] For a list of 90 of these instances and a discussion of the entire "overruling" problem, see A. P. Blaustein and A. H. Field, "Overruling Opinions in the Supreme Court," 57 *Michigan Law Review* 2 (1957).

[55] William O. Douglas, *Stare Decisis* (New York: The Association of the Bar of the City of New York, 1949), p. 31.

[56] *Boys Market v. Retail Clerks' Union*, 398 U.S. 235 (1970), at 255.

invented," may thus be "judge-destroyed." The judge must speak and through him society speaks. His function, as one leading student of constitutional law put it so lucidly, is "necessarily something more than to be a grammarian . . . [but] it is decidedly less than to be a zealot."[57] Lord Coke's practice to the contrary, few, if any, judges would today create a maxim out of whole cloth and then recite, "as the old maxim saith. . . ." (Yet it was the same Lord Coke who lauded *stare decisis* as "the known certaintie of the law which is the saftie of all."[58])

To sum up, the judge is assuredly not a free agent. Indeed, Mr. Justice John Marshall Harlan underscored that fact of judicial life poignantly, when he wrote a concurring memo in a coerced confession case:

> [D]espite my strong inclination to join in the dissent of my Brother White, I can find no acceptable avenue of escape from *Miranda v. Arizona*, 384 U.S. 436, 1966] in judging this case. . . . Therefore, and purely out of respect for *stare decisis*, I reluctantly feel compelled to acquiesce in today's decision of the Court, at the same time observing that the constitutional condemnation of this perfectly sensible, proper, and indeed commendable police work, highlights the unsoundness of *Miranda*.[59]

But Stewart joined White's dissent, responding to Harlan's action with the statement: "It seems to me that those who dissented [in *Miranda*] remain free not only to express our continuing disagreement with that decision, but also to oppose any broadening of its impact.[60]

No matter what it may be termed or how it may be styled, of necessity the judge "makes" the law—to some degree, at least. The delicate question will ever be how to aid its development without violating the confines of the constitutional structure. Let Mr. Justice Cardozo state the case:

> . . . [but] no doubt the limits for the judges are narrower. He legislates only between gaps. He fills the open spaces of the law. How far he may go without traveling beyond the walls of the interstices cannot be staked out for him upon a chart. He must learn it for himself as he gains the sense of fitness and proportion that comes with years of the practice of an art . . . None the less, within the confines of those open spaces and those of precedent and traditions, choice moves with a freedom which stamps its actions as creative. The law which is the resulting product is

[57] Paul A. Freund, *The Christian Science Monitor*, March 27, 1956, p. 16.
[58] Robert von Moschzisker, "Stare Decisis," 37 *Harvard Law Review* 409 (1924), at 429.
[59] *Orozco v. Texas*, 394 U.S. 324 (1969), at 327–8.
[60] *Ibid.* at 331.

not found, but made. The process, being legislative, demands the legislator's wisdom.[61]

Surely, to echo a comment once made by Max Lerner, ". . . judicial decisions are not babies brought by constitutional storks." They are the carefully considered, more or less practical, judgments by the human beings who, sensitive to their calling, wield judicial authority—as judges, not as legislators.

OTHER LIMITATIONS ON JUDICIAL POWER AND EFFECTIVENESS

Yet there remain several other qualifying considerations—checks may be a better term—upon judicial authority, even at the highest level of the federal courts. First, the Supreme Court's rulings may be effectively reversed by other participants in the process of government; second, they are almost inevitably responsive to over-all policy formulations, sooner or later; third, for enforcement they must look to the executive branch of the government; and fourth, as demonstrated in Chapter V, compliance with them is not necessarily automatic.

REVERSING THE COURT

In a variety of ways, although not without some toil and trouble, the Supreme Court of the United States may be reversed by direct or indirect action of other institutions in the political process. Although its decisions unquestionably constitute the supreme law of the land—as they must if government under law is to have any meaning in American society—and are thus final and binding, even that high body may have the last say "only for a time." This truth is readily documented by briefly examining the fate of the aforementioned 109 or 110 cases in which the Court, as of its 1974–75 term—and unanimously in almost one-third of these instances—had struck down as unconstitutional 115 provisions of federal laws.

No fewer than thirty-three times has Congress passed legislation that has had the effect of reversing the Court either totally or in substantial measure —as it did in passing the Federal Employers' Liability Act of April 22, 1908, designed to replace that of 1906 which the Court had declared unconstitutional 5 : 4 as an illegal invasion of intrastate commerce in the *First Employers' Liability Cases*[62] earlier in 1908. Since Congress seemed to have

[61] *The Nature of the Judicial Process*, op. cit. pp. 113–15.
[62] 207 U.S. 463.

corrected the alleged constitutional deficiency of the earlier statute, the Court found no difficulty in upholding it unanimously when the test came in the *Second Employers' Liability Cases*[63] in 1912.[64] In other instances the circumstances or situation of the controversy had either changed or become moot, thus rendering insignificant or totally unimportant the erstwhile decision handed down by the Court—as, for example, the withdrawal of improperly delegated legislative power by action of the legislature or the revocation or amendment of a challenged administrative or executive order, both actions coming prior to the full effect of the Court's decision.[65] In some instances it simply *distinguished* cases from often very similar earlier decisions—as it did when it upheld the second New Deal Agricultural Act of 1938 in *Mulford v. Smith*[66] in 1939 even though it struck down the first A.A.A. in *U.S. v. Butler*[67] three years earlier. True, the statutes were not exactly alike, and the personnel of the Court had changed, but the essential features, impact, and purpose of the statutes were unchanged. In other cases, the Court itself questioned, reversed, modified, or even negated its earlier judgments—by no means solely because of changes in its personnel— as it did so prominently in the four *Covert-Krueger Cases* between 1955 and 1960.[68] And in six to nine (depending upon one's point of view) instances— Amendments to the Constitution were passed in order to reverse the Court: the *Eleventh* (1798), reversing the 1793 decision in *Chisholm v. Georgia,*[69] by amending the original jurisdiction of the Supreme Court to hear certain suits against the several states; the *Thirteenth, Fourteenth,* and *Fifteenth* (the Civil War Amendments, adopted in 1865, 1868, and 1870, respectively), reversing various Supreme Court decisions—including the *Dred*

---

[63] 223 U.S. 1. A more recent example is the Court's declaration of unconstitutionality of a federal municipal bankruptcy act in 1936 (*Ashton v. Cameron County Water Improvement District,* 298 U.S. 513), which Congress "corrected" with the enactment of a slightly revised law that was upheld by the Court two years later (*United States v. Bekins,* 304 U.S. 27).

[64] For two tables concentrating on Congressional reversal action, see Robert A. Dahl's updated 1957 article (as explained in fn. 78, *infra*) & Thomas P. Jahnige and Sheldon Goldman (eds.), "The Supreme Court's Role in National Policy Making," in *The Federal Judicial System: Readings in Process and Behavior* (New York: Holt, Rinehart and Winston, Inc., 1968), pp. 358–63.

[65] E.g. *Lewis Publishing Co. v. Wyman,* 228 U.S. 610 (1913).

[66] 307 U.S. 38.

[67] 297 U.S. 1.

[68] *Kinsella v. Krueger,* 357 U.S. 470 and *Reid v. Covert,* 351 U.S. 487 (June 11, 1956); 352 U.S. 901 (November 5, 1956); 354 U.S. 1 (June 10, 1957); and *Kinsella v. Singleton* 361 U.S. 234 and *Grisham v. Hagan,* 361 U.S. 278 (January 18, 1960).

[69] 2 Dallas 419.

Scott Case[70]—dealing with suffrage, slavery, and civil rights; the *Sixteenth* (1913), the Income Tax Amendment, giving Congress power to tax incomes from whatever source derived, thereby effectively reversing the 1895 decisions in *Pollock v. Farmers' Loan and Trust Co.*[71] which had held various income tax *statutes*, designed to accomplish the same end, unconstitutional as a violation of Article 1, Section 9, Clause 4; and the *Twenty-Sixth*, overturning the Court's 1970 ruling in *Oregon v. Mitchell*[72] by granting the franchise to eighteen-year-olds in *state* elections (the Court having upheld the statute insofar as it dealt with *federal* elections). Some would include the *Seventeenth* (direct election of U.S. Senators); the *Nineteenth* (women suffrage, 1920); and the *Twenty-Fourth* (abolition of the poll tax in federal elections). The adoption of a constitutional amendment is the most authoritative and most certain method of reversing the Court, but it is also usually the most difficult politically to attain, and almost always the most time-consuming.

Going beyond the 115 provisions struck down by it, the Court *overruled* 87 of its decisions between 1937 and 1973, including the immediate post-"switch-in-time-that-saved-nine" era. Prior thereto, the Court had overruled itself at least forty-six times. (These two figures cover not only overrulings of provisions previously held unconstitutional, but also those made on other than constitutional grounds.)[73] Unless it seems to be absolutely necessary, however, the Court is disinclined to resort to the strong concept of *overruling*. Thus, in only ten instances among the aforementioned 115 did the Court in subsequent decisions *specifically and literally* acknowledge an overruling—as it did, for example, in upholding the entire federal Fair Labor Standards Act of 1938 in the case of *United States v. Darby*[74] in 1941. There, among others, addressing itself to the child labor provisions of that statute, it *specifically* overruled its 1918 decision in *Hammer v. Dagenhart*,[75] where it had declared the federal Keating-Owen Child Labor Law of 1916 unconstitutional. Overruling differs from reversing as a matter of definition: technically speaking, a case may be *reversed* only on rehearing; thus, the original decision and the reversing decision are applicable to the *identical case*. An example of that procedure is the Court's

---

[70] *Dred Scott v. Sandford*, 19 Howard 393 (1857).
[71] 158 U.S. 601 and 157 U.S. 429.
[72] 400 U.S. 112.
[73] For all overrulings between 1790 and 1972, see *The Constitution of the United States of America* (Washington, D.C.: U.S. Government Printing Office, 1973).
[74] 312 U.S. 100.
[75] 247 U.S. 251.

decision in *Jones v. Opelika*, 316 U.S. 584, on June 8, 1942, upholding 5 : 4 an Opelika, Alabama, statute which required payment of the usual license tax or fee even by those groups (here the Jehovah Witnesses) that claimed exemption on grounds of freedom of religion—a decision which the Court *vacated* 5 : 4 on rehearing less than eleven months later, in *Jones v. Opelika*, 319 U.S. 103, on May 3, 1943, and then *reversed* on the same day in *Murdock v. Pennsylvania*, 319 U.S. 105.

The various statistics just cited do not take into account the many instances in which the Court overrules precedents *sub silentio*—i.e. when it overrules an earlier decision without saying so, but where the effect is clearly the same as an expressed overruling—as it did on several occasions in the last quarter of the past century and the first quarter of this century in the realm of commerce and taxation. Nor do the above figures account for those instances in which Congress, disagreeing with the Supreme Court's reading of a statute, simply rewrites or repeals it. For example, between 1944 and 1974 alone, Congress took fifty-six actions in economic matters which collectively overturned eighty-three Supreme Court rulings.

Thus, although many of the Supreme Court's decisions on questions of constitutionality last, quite a few are ultimately modified or neutralized by the Court itself or by valid action of other branches of the government, led by Congress. America's system of judicial review, as Professor Freund has noted cogently, indeed produces frustrations, but it has a saving grace of resiliency.

POLICY FORMULATIONS AND CONSIDERATIONS

In any case, the policy views of the Court, the members of which, after all, are "children of their times,"[76] never remain for long out of line with the policy views of the lawmaking majority—with the probable, but not inevitable, exception of decisions involving the Bill of Rights, particularly those made between 1940–49 and 1954–57 when the Court on a good number of occasions stood as a veritable bastion against the popular majority viewpoint. On major public policy issues, both the Chief Executive and Congress may be expected to succeed—speaking generally and *in the long run*,[77] although in the short run they may well have to bow. If the Court is

---

[76] Robert G. McCloskey, *The American Supreme Court* (Chicago: University of Chicago Press, 1961), p. 182.

[77] ". . . and the run must not be too long either!," as Professor Edward S. Corwin once observed. (*Court Over Constitution*. Princeton: Princeton University Press, 1938, p. 127.)

to thrive, as Professor Wallace Mendelson has said so well, it "must respect the social forces that determine elections and other major political settlements. No court can long withstand the morals of its era."[78] It is the "child of its time." The Court, however, cannot be a mere register of public opinion; it must be the latter's sporadic molder and leader. Yet, in the final analysis, as Francis Biddle well said, its Justices "must not get away too far from life and should continually touch earth for renewed vitality."[79]

This judicial alignment with the other two major branches on overriding policy matters may not always follow axiomatically, but it comes very close to reality. Some observers of the scene have even contended that far from representing a dependable means of preventing "legislative tyranny," judicial review of national policy seems to have but marginal value.[80] Whatever the actual merits of this contentious judgment may be, the Court is well aware of the limitations upon its powers. Mr. Justice Frankfurter, the "conscience of the Court" during most of his lengthy tenure, thus addressed himself to the question of reversing the Supreme Court in his now well-known separate concurring opinion in the unanimously decided Little Rock School Case, *Cooper v. Aaron*,[81] in which he quoted at length from his concurring opinion in the *United Mine Workers Case* of 1947:

> Even this court has the last say only for a time. Being composed of fallible men, it may err. But revision of its errors must be by orderly process of law. The court may be asked to reconsider its decisions, and this has been done successfully again and again throughout our history. Or, what this court has deemed its duty to decide may be changed by legislation; as it often has been, and, on occasion, by constitutional amendment.[82]

He might have added that one of the major catalysts in revision and reconsideration is the inevitably changing personnel composition of the Court—yet any recognition of that crucial element in judicial decision-making must carefully guard against a pat and oversimplified catch-all analysis of its sig-

---

[78] *Justices Black and Frankfurter: Conflict in the Court*, 2d ed. (Chicago: University of Chicago Press, 1967), pp. 75–6. On this point see also the intriguing article by Robert A. Dahl, "Decision-Making in a Democracy: The Supreme Court as a National Policy-Maker," 6 *Journal of Public Law* 279 (1957), updated a decade later (see fn. 64, *supra*).

[79] *Justice Holmes, Natural Law, and the Supreme Court* (New York: The Macmillan Co., 1961), p. 73.

[80] E.g. S. Sidney Ulmer, "Judicial Review as Political Behavior: A Temporary Check on Congress," 4 *Administrative Science Quarterly* 426 (March 1960).

[81] 358 U.S. 1 (1958).

[82] *United States v. United Mine Workers*, 330 U.S. 258.

nificance. In any event, reversal of judicial action is possible, and it has frequently been effectuated. Decisions running counter to the broad concensus simply do not last *in the long run*. The toast offered in 1801 at a dinner honoring the Justices, "To the Judiciary of the United States—independent of party, independent of power, independent of popularity!,"[83] merits skeptical analysis. Still, time and again the Court has come through nobly when the constitutional chips have been down—as it did in July 1974, when it was confronted with the expansive claims of Executive privilege advanced by President Nixon during the "Watergate" controversy. Its unanimous 8 : 0 ruling against these claims constituted a—probably *the*—major catalyst in his subsequent resignation from office on August 9 of that fateful year.

COMPLIANCE AND ENFORCEMENT

But there is more to be said. Aspects of Chapter V demonstrated at some length that the judgments of the Supreme Court of the United States are not necessarily accepted as automatically binding by those who ought to be bound. A decision may be simply ignored, as was proved by, for example, the continuation of the practice of "released time"[84] in numerous public secondary schools in situations and settings identical to that struck down as an unconstitutional violation of the principle of separation of state and church in *McCollum v. Board of Education*.[85] In 1966, four years after the decisions in the *Prayer and Bible Reading Cases*,[86] some 60 per cent of the states reported continued violations of the Court's mandates.[87] Or a decision may be circumvented, and even opposed by force, to which the history of the 1954 and 1955 *Segregation Cases* and their progeny bear ample witness. And there is the already described host of calculated, interminable delays in compliance.[88]

Moreover, with the very few exceptions of its original jurisdiction docket

---

[83] As quoted in *Connecticut Courant*, February 9 and 16, 1801.

[84] For an explanation and an analysis of "released time" see my *Freedom and the Court: Civil Rights and Liberties in the United States* 2d ed. (New York: Oxford University Press, 1972), Ch. VI.

[85] 333 U.S. 203 (1948).

[86] *Engel v. Vitale*, 370 U.S. 421 (1962) and *Abington School District v. Schempp* and *Murray v. Curlett*, 374 U.S. 203 (1963).

[87] See Ellis Katz, "Patterns of Compliance with the *Schempp* Decision," 14 *Journal of Public Law* 2 (1966), and Henry J. Abraham and Robert R. Benedetti, "The State Attorney-General: A Friend of the Court?", 117 *University of Pennsylvania Law Review* 795 (April 1969).

[88] See Ch. V, pp. 223–30.

cases, the Court formulates *general* policy. It is the lower federal and state courts, as the case may be, that *apply* it, presumably "not inconsistent with this opinion," as the Supreme Court's mandate normally reads. In so applying the opinion, the lower courts may, and often do, materially modify the Supreme Court's determination. These modifications, moreover, are not at all astonishing in view of the not infrequent habit of Supreme Court Justices to mix dogma with dicta. On the other hand, some of the so-called "modifications" or "interpretations" clearly have been little short of outright defiance—especially by state courts.[89]

There is also the obvious fact that, lacking any source of physical power of its own, the Supreme Court depends on the political branches of the government for the enforcement of its mandates, in particular on the Chief Executive, who has the vital obligation to ascertain obedience to all court orders. If the Court fails to obtain that co-operation in those instances where it is vital for compliance, it necessarily stands helplessly on the sidelines. The most famous case in point is the comment, perhaps apocryphal, by President Andrew Jackson who, according to Mr. Chief Justice Marshall's biographer, exploded, "John Marshall has made his decision:—*now let him enforce it!*"[90] The outburst reputedly occurred as a result of Marshall's decision in *Worcester v. Georgia*,[91] in which his Court upheld the rights of the Cherokee Indians in a dispute with Georgia, and where he strongly implied in his opinion that it was the President's duty to honor and back the Cherokee Nation's rights under federal law. Apocryphal or not, the Jackson comment illustrates the Court's dependence and its quandary when the necessary executive support is not forthcoming. Its effectiveness in the absence of the executive sword is as limited as its operations in general would be without the necessary appropriations from the legislative purse, and the legislative assent to its jurisdictional and procedural needs. In essence, as Mr. Justice Jackson stated this fact of judicial life starkly, ". . . [the Court] can perform but one function—that of deciding litiga-

---

[89] On this general point see the informative article by Walter Murphy, "Lower Court in Supreme Court Power," 53 *American Political Science Review* 1017–31 (December 1959).

[90] Albert J. Beveridge, *The Life of John Marshall*, Vol. 4 (Boston: Houghton Mifflin Co., 1919), p. 551.

[91] 6 Peters 515 (1832). Worcester, a citizen of Vermont, was a missionary preaching the gospel, who had entered the territory of the Cherokee nation under President Jackson's authorization, but without the permission that the state of Georgia required by statute. The Court declared the statute unconstitutional; yet, ironically, Jackson now sided with Georgia! It may well be that he did so because he did not wish to drive Georgia into the South Carolina-led tariff nullification camp.

tions—and can proceed in no manner except by the judicial process."[92] Thus he echoed an oft-quoted remark by Mr. Justice Samuel Miller that "in the division of the powers of government between the three great departments, executive, legislative, and judicial, the judicial is the weakest for purposes of self-protection and for the enforcement of the power which it exercises."[93] But not only do we often expect too much from the Court, we let it—or wish it would—settle *policy* matters that ought to be settled by one of the other two branches, notably the legislative, but which for a variety of reasons, chiefly political, are not.[94] Glaring illustrations of such policy matters are reapportionment/redistricting; segregation/desegregation; and criminal justice. And there is a host of others where the proverbial buck has been passed eagerly to the judicial branch!

MACHTKAMPF: THE SUPREME COURT IN THE POLITICAL POWER STRUGGLE

Despite the implications of the preceding paragraphs, the Supreme Court has been a participant in what may be viewed as a continuous struggle by the three "separated branches" of the federal government to attain a position of dominance, if not ultimate control, in the American political system. Since it lacks the potent weapons of the other two branches, especially weapons that would aid its self-protection and its enforcement of the powers which it exercises, the Court has necessarily been less prominent in this *Machtkampf* (struggle for power); but its own important tool of judicial review has provided it with a genuine measure of authority. And, as just pointed out, it has often been propelled into action precisely because the other organs of government have failed to fulfill their own responsibilities.

Victory in the *Machtkampf* of the three branches has been in the form of supremacy which has alternated from branch to branch; although sometimes the struggle has been featured by a quasi-alliance of two branches against the third over a period of time. A pertinent example is the frustrated and frustrating protracted effort of the closely allied New Deal Legislature and New Deal Executive commencing in 1933, which, on many major is-

[92] *The Supreme Court in the American System of Government* (Cambridge: Harvard University Press, 1955), p. 12.
[93] *In re Neagle*, 135 U.S. 1 (1890), at 63.
[94] On that point see the address by Mr. Justice Harlan at dedication ceremonies of the American Bar Center at Chicago, Illinois, August 13, 1963.

sues, had to wait for victory over the Supreme Court until four years later, when the "switch-in-time-that-saved-nine" took place.

In general, however, the *tone* of dominance has been set by the person and personality of the elected Chief Executive, who, after all, is the sole individual in the American federal governmental process to have a nationwide constituency, and who, within limits, is in the position of interpreting his powers narrowly or broadly. In other words, whenever the President has been of the category commonly called "active" or "strong"—e.g. Washington, Jackson, Polk, Lincoln, Wilson, the two Roosevelts, and Lyndon Johnson—the Executive branch, *in the long run*, has been able to acquire supremacy. Where he has been "passive" or "weak"; perhaps did not manifest sufficient concern for, understanding of, or even interest in the political process; or simply lacked sufficient support in Congress or by the people—e.g. John Quincy Adams, Pierce, Buchanan, Andrew Johnson, Grant, McKinley, Harding, Coolidge, Hoover, and Eisenhower—supremacy was acquired by Congress or, on occasion, by the Supreme Court. In several instances no clear-cut supremacy can be pinpointed. This is true, for example, of the Presidencies of Madison and Monroe, Hayes, Cleveland, Taft, Truman, the end of Eisenhower's second term after the dismissal of Sherman Adams and the death of John Foster Dulles (there is no doubt about the presence of congressional supremacy during Eisenhower's first term in office), and Kennedy. It should also be noted that during some Presidencies, or at least parts thereof, the Executive has tended to dominate in foreign affairs and Congress in internal matters, e.g. Truman, Eisenhower, and Kennedy. The abortive Presidency of Richard M. Nixon falls into a special category: Expansive assertions and practices of Presidential power enabled him to engage in sundry policy innovations in foreign affairs at the expense of domestic tranquility and achievements. His perceptions of Executive power and privilege escalated until the "Watergate" syndrome engulfed him and his Administration, ultimately resulting in his resignation from office—he was the first President to do so in the history of the Republic. His precipitous "full, free, and absolute" pardon, granted but one month later by his self-selected successor, Gerald Ford, for all offenses "committed or that may have been committed" by Nixon in the course of his entire Presidency, exacerbated prevalent national frustrations and anger, and raised fundamental questions for the principle of "Equal Justice Under Law," as well as for the future of the separation of powers and checks and balances.

At the risk of some oversimplification and generalization—which inevitably attend categorization and classification—Table X is designed to indicate periods of American history in which existed fairly discernible tendencies toward supremacy by one branch or two allied branches against a third. Some periods are necessarily listed in more than one category: for example, the first four years of the New Deal era, when presidential supremacy was unquestioned—or, rather, when there was surrender by Congress to President Roosevelt, but during which time the Supreme Court proved to be a major roadblock to the New Deal program.

There is no doubt that the Supreme Court of the United States has sporadically *challenged* the authority of both President and Congress. But in spite of the four or five indicated periods of tendencies toward judicial supremacy, the Court has never really actively *bid* for the role of dominant governmental agency of the land—although a good case could be made for there having been such a bid during the era of Mr. Chief Justice Marshall. During that period, as well as during the heyday of the Hughes Anti-New Deal Court, we may speak of periodic "government by judiciary" or "judicial supremacy," yet even then there was never any genuine likelihood that the Court would *in the final analysis* effectively *dominate* the Executive and/or the Legislative branches. When all is said and done, the Supreme Court of the United States does not possess the political power, the arsenal of potent weapons of government, the tools of the publicity media, or the strategic position in the government or in the body politic generally enjoyed by the other two branches.

An Historical Note. If we take a closer look at the Supreme Court's role in the *Machtkampf* on the American political scene we see that the high tribunal began on a very inauspicious note. Its dozen or so pre-Marshall years, during which three Chief Justices came and went—the second of whom, John Rutledge, was not confirmed by the Senate—were characterized by a lack of popular esteem and understanding, little work, and dissatisfied personnel. The first Chief Justice, John Jay, so thoroughly disliked his job and so loathed circuit-riding that he not only spent one year during his tenure in England on a diplomatic mission, but twice ran for Governor of New York, succeeding on the second try, whereupon he happily resigned the Chief Justiceship! When President Adams offered to re-appoint him as Chief Justice in 1800, he refused categorically. And, as already pointed out, the third Chief Justice, Oliver Ellsworth, eagerly left his office for a diplomatic post in France, where he then resigned, allegedly because of ill health. The Court did, however, soon make clear that it intended to act as an arbiter in disputes between the states and the federal government; and it became quickly apparent that its judicial sympathies lay with the latter.

341

TABLE X
PERIODS OF DISCERNIBLE TENDENCIES TOWARD
SUPREMACY OF BRANCHES OF THE GOVERNMENT

Years	President(s)	Chief Justice(s)	Commentary
A. *Tendencies Toward Legislative Supremacy*			
1809–1829	Madison Monroe J. Q. Adams	Marshall	Supremacy facilitated and advanced by powerful Court.
1837–1845	Van Buren W. H. Harrison Tyler	Taney	Aided by strong Court and passive Presidents.
1849–1861	Taylor Fillmore Pierce Buchanan	Taney	Nadir of Presidency. *Dred Scott* case.
1865–1885	Johnson Grant Hayes Garfield Arthur	S. P. Chase Waite	Partially effective opposition by Johnson and Hayes.
1919–1921	Wilson	White	Defeat of League. President ill.
1921–1933	Harding Coolidge Hoover	Taft Hughes	Co-operative Court. Weak, passive Presidents.
1953–1959	Eisenhower	Warren	Strong Court. Passive President.
B. *Tendencies Toward Executive Supremacy*			
1789–1797	Washington	Jay Rutledge Ellsworth	Co-operative Congress. Weak, docile Court.
1801–1809	Jefferson	Marshall	Some doubt about Executive Supremacy, but generally present.
1829–1837	Jackson	Marshall Taney	President in high form. Last years of Marshall Court.
1845–1849	Polk	Taney	Underrated President.
1861–1865	Lincoln	Taney S. P. Chase	High-water mark of Presidency. Civil War.
1901–1908	T. Roosevelt	Fuller	Popular President. Assertive Court.

Years	President(s)	Chief Justice(s)	Commentary
1913–1919	Wilson	White	President lost control to Republican Congressional majority in 1919, however.
1933–1945	F. D. Roosevelt	Hughes	Revolution on Court, 1937. "Packing."
		Stone	Powerful President.
1945–1947	Truman	Vinson	Truman "Honeymoon."
1963–1968	L. B. Johnson	Warren	Powerful President.
1969–1974	Nixon	Burger	Vast claims to Presidential power—truncated by "Watergate."

C. *Tendencies Toward Judicial Supremacy*

Years	President(s)	Chief Justice(s)	Commentary
1801–1829	Jefferson Madison Monroe J. Q. Adams	Marshall	The greatest Chief Justice at power's peak.
1857	Pierce Buchanan	Taney	The *Dred Scott* fiasco.
1889–1910	B. Harrison Cleveland McKinley	Fuller	Some doubt re Cleveland term (his second).
1935–1936	F. D. Roosevelt	Hughes	13 New Deal Laws declared unconstitutional.
1954–1957	Eisenhower	Warren	Civil libertarian activism.

D. *Supremacy Tendencies Not Readily Discernible*

Years	President(s)	Chief Justice(s)	Commentary
1797–1801	John Adams	Ellsworth	President and Congress shared power.
1885–1889	Cleveland	Waite Fuller	Probably President, but . . .
1910–1913	Taft	White	Uncertainty.
1947–1953	Truman	Vinson	Divided foreign and domestic tendencies.
1959–1960	Eisenhower	Warren	Sudden assertion of power by President. Democratic Congressional majority.
1961–1963	Kennedy	Warren	Divided foreign and domestic tendencies. Strong Court.
1968–1969	Johnson	Warren	Vietnam war becomes Johnson's political Waterloo.
1974–	Ford	Burger	

The Marshall era, of course, brought about a drastic metamorphosis in the Court's stance. The Chief Justice completely dominated the Court[95]— with dissents confined almost solely to Mr. Justice William Johnson. It is quite clear that Marshall, more than any other man in the history of the judiciary, determined the character of America's federal constitutional system. From its lowly, if not discredited, level John Marshall raised the United States Supreme Court to a position of equality with the Executive and the Legislature—perhaps even one of dominance during the heyday of his Chief Justiceship. He called his constitutional interpretations as he saw them, always adhering to his previously discussed, oft-expressed doctrine that ". . . it is a *constitution* we are expounding . . . intended to endure for ages to come and, consequently, to be adapted to the various crises of human affairs."[96] Yet, as we know, he hastened to insist that "[j]udicial power, as contradistinguished from the power of law, has no existence. Courts are the mere instruments of the law, and can will nothing."[97] Thus, "willing nothing," Marshall handed down, among many others, four of the most momentous decisions in the history of, and the future for, Court, Constitution, and Country, without which it is at best doubtful that the nation would have grown and prospered as it has: (1) *Marbury v. Madison*[98] (judicial review, supremacy of the U.S. Constitution); (2) *McCulloch v. Maryland*[99] (implied powers of Congress, reaffirmation of the supremacy of the U.S. Constitution, federal immunity from involuntary state taxation, federal government held to have its powers directly from the people rather than from the states); (3) *Gibbons v. Ogden*[100] (plenary federal authority over interstate and foreign commerce); and (4) *Dartmouth College v. Woodward*[101] (inviolability of contracts). Truly, the Court led and, leading, gave the federal government the means to develop and work.

Whereas the Marshall Court had by its decisions placed the emphasis upon the national commercial-creditor-propertied classes, its successor, the also powerful Taney Court, pursued a different emphasis. The sanctity of

[95] Of a total of 1215 cases between 1801 and 1835 he delivered the opinion in 519, and of the 62 decisions involving constitutional questions he wrote 36. See Robert J. Heamer, *The Supreme Court in Crisis: A History of Conflict* (Amherst: The University of Massachusetts Press, 1971), p. 35.

[96] *Osborn v. United States Bank,* 9 Wheaton 738 (1824), at 866.

[97] *McCulloch v. Maryland,* 4 Wheaton 316 (1819).

[98] 1 Cranch 137 (1803).

[99] Loc. cit.

[100] 9 Wheaton 1 (1824).

[101] 4 Wheaton 518 (1819).

property remained a primary consideration of the tribunal, but it devolved upon a different segment of society and, incidentally, of the country. A Southerner from Maryland, the Jackson-appointed Roger B. Taney, a Democrat and a Catholic—the first of his religious persuasion to be on the bench —by his decisions favored "states' rights" and *agrarian* property, that is, land and slaves. From a totally different milieu than the great constitutional nationalist who preceded him, Taney, and with him a majority of his Court, demonstrated a faithful attachment to the economic interests of the South and the rapidly developing frontier of the West. But disaster loomed on the horizon: after pursuing the aforementioned policies determinedly, and with little, if any, interference from the other two branches for twenty years, Taney, then in his eightieth year, lonely and frustrated, met his and the Court's judicial Waterloo in 1857 with his opinion in *Dred Scott v. Sandford*[102]—the thrust of which was leaked in advance by Mr. Justice John Catron to President Buchanan,[103] the sole known such breach of secrecy on record.

This decision—"more than a crime . . . a blunder"[104]—by his Southern-dominated Court, with but two Justices dissenting, John McLean[105] and Benjamin Curtis (Curtis's opinion having been circulated in advance in the Northern press), featured nine separate opinions, including Taney's. It stipulated among other things: no Negro could be a citizen; that the Negro was "a person of an inferior order"; that he was a slave and thus his master's permanent property no matter whether the latter took him to slave or free parts of the country; that the Missouri Compromise was unconstitutional; and that no individual of African descent was "a portion of this American people." *Dred Scott* permanently beclouded Taney's reputation—notwithstanding his towering contributions to constitutional development—dragged the Supreme Court of the United States into its lowest depths, and has tened the dawn of the Civil War and with it the Emancipation Declaration and the Civil War Amendments (XIII, XIV, and XV). In the words of a Washington newspaperman, "If epithets and denunciations could sink a judicial body, the Supreme Court of the United States would never be heard of again."[106]

---

[102] 19 Howard 393.

[103] Mr. Justice Robert O. Grier was also *scienter* to the leak; indeed, it was he who encouraged Catron to spill the proverbial beans.

[104] Bickel, *The Least Dangerous Branch*, op. cit. p. 45.

[105] For a discussion of McLean's political motivations and aspirations see fn. 128, Ch. V, *supra*. See also Bickel's commentary in his *Politics and the Warren Court* (New York: Harper & Row, 1965), p. 135.

[106] As quoted by Hyneman, op. cit. p. 31.

With *Dred Scott*—which has been widely viewed as the most disastrous opinion ever issued by the high bench[107]—the Court invited a violent congressional reaction. While that took a while to take concrete form, the influence of the Court declined at once. The country as a whole was hardly willing to consider, let alone accept, Mr. Justice James M. Wayne's anxious explanation *cum* plea in his concurring opinion that

> . . . there had become such a difference of opinion that the peace and harmony of the country required the settlement of the slavery issues by judicial decision. . . . In our action we have only discharged our duty as a distinct and efficient department of the Government, as the framers of the Constitution meant the judiciary to be. . . .[108]

Far from alleviating the incipient sectional strife, the Court had promoted it. During and after the Civil War, with Taney's role reduced to one of bitterness and unhappiness, Congress demonstrated its utter contempt of the Supreme Court by *thrice* changing its size in six years; up from nine to ten in 1863; down from ten to seven in 1866; up again from seven to nine in 1869. Quite obviously, all this was done for policy purposes. And, as we have seen earlier in these pages, when in 1868–69 the post-Taney Court indicated a possible declaration of unconstitutionality of some of the military Reconstruction Acts, an angry Congress, acting under its powers derived from the Constitution to limit the Court's appellate jurisdiction, simply deprived it of the power to decide the case.[109] This was the beginning of the Chief Justiceship of the politically ambitious Salmon P. Chase (1864–74)[110] and of Morrison R. Waite (1874–88), both Northern Republicans, during whose tenure the Court, predictably, was chiefly concerned, in addition to safeguarding property, with maintaining the status quo: state authority over individuals and federal authority over interstate commerce—which represented the two great post-Civil War problems. The former included the Waite Court's nullification of the attempted use of the due process of law clause of the Fourteenth Amendment by the federal government as a national arm to protect civil rights in the states in the historic *Civil Rights Cases*[111]—something the Chase Court had already done in connection with

---

[107] E.g. McCloskey, op. cit. p. 94.

[108] *Dred Scott v. Sandford,* loc. cit. at 454–5.

[109] *Ex parte McCardle,* 7 Wallace 506 (1869).

[110] Prior to his assumption of the Chief Justiceship, Chase had been a candidate at the Republican presidential conventions of 1856 and 1860. In 1868, while on the highest bench, he unsuccessfully sought the presidential nomination on *both* tickets!

[111] 109 U.S. 3 (1883).

the Amendment's "privileges and immunities" clause when citizens of Louisiana attempted to invoke it.[112] Indeed, the Chase Court, in a burst of judicial activism, did declare nine acts of Congress unconstitutional; but, as explained above, in the final analysis it bowed before the power of the Radical Republicans in Congress, and it was effectively "packed" by President Grant in 1871, thus nullifying within fifteen months its briefly successful attempt to battle for what it had regarded as stable currency in the *Legal Tender Cases*.[113] One important contribution of the Waite Court to be noted, notwithstanding its generally proprietarian bent, was the highly significant development of the "affectation with the public interest" doctrine, announced by the Chief Justice himself in his opinion for a majority of seven in the leading *Granger* case of *Munn v. Illinois*.[114] There, while still clinging to the notion of due process laid down in *The Slaughterhouse Cases*,[115] Waite held that, under certain circumstances, the state police power could be employed to regulate private property in the public interest.

With the long Chief Justiceship of the Cleveland-appointed Melville W. Fuller of Illinois, however, the Court all but bid for policy leadership. It did this, above all, by striking out on a path designed to re-assure the sanctity of property, as the majority of the Court saw it. This majority was now composed of a group of highly conservative, property-conscious Justices, who, when given the opportunity, began to strike down as unconstitutional a fair number of federal and state laws in the economic and social sphere. *Laisser faire* seemed secure, indeed! Until roughly this time, state laws, for example, had been held unconstitutional largely because they were viewed as conflicting either with the interstate commerce or the obligation-of-contract clauses of the Constitution. Of 128 state laws invalidated by the federal courts *before* 1888, 50 involved the former clause, 50 the latter, and only one the taking of property "without due process of law." The Fuller Court, on the other hand, ultimately struck down a large number of state laws on that last ground, holding that the several legislative "experimentations" at issue deprived "persons" of liberty and property without *substantive* due process of law. Substantive due process had truly come of age! The Supreme Court had become the arbiter "between the voters on the one hand and the property owners on the other."[116] And the concept of "per-

---

[112] *The Slaughterhouse Cases,* 16 Wallace 36 (1873).
[113] 12 Wallace 457 (1871) and *Hepburn v. Griswold,* 8 Wallace 603 (1870).
[114] 94 U.S. 113 (1877).
[115] 16 Wallace 36 (1873).
[116] Arthur J. Hadley, "The Constitutional Position of Property in America," 64 *The Independent* 837 (1904).

sons" now also included *corporations*, thanks to a unanimous Court ruling in the *Santa Clara* case,[117] a decision invalidating assessments on portions of railroad property. It was featured by a casual *announcement* at the hearing stage by Mr. Chief Justice Waite, who did not even write the opinion: "The Court does not wish to hear argument on the question whether the provision in the Fourteenth Amendment to the Constitution, which forbids a State to deny to any person within its jurisdiction the equal protection of the laws, applies to these Corporations. We are all of the opinion that it does."[118] This was a rather cavalier manner of disposing of a highly significant constitutional issue—one that was neither before the Court nor had been argued in the case at bar!

The states, however, and—considerably later—the federal government insistently wished to pioneer in the realm of economic and social legislation, as they deemed that to be the desire of the majority of the voters. Yet in most areas—viz., maximum hours, minimum wages, working conditions, regulation of woman and child labor, compulsory arbitration, employer liability, and many others—the legislatures ran into the judicial vetoes not only of the Fuller Court, but also those of his successors, the White and Taft Courts and, until 1937, the Hughes Court—despite the established Waite "affectation with the public interest doctrine." Throughout this period the Supreme Court demonstrated again and again a remarkable regard for the protection of *property* under its interpretations of the "liberty and property" phases of the "due process of law" clauses of the Fifth and Fourteenth Amendments to the United States Constitution. But, oddly enough, the Court found these clauses no barrier against legislative invasions of the *cultural and political* realms, often referred to as "civil rights" or "civil liberties."

From the turn of the century on, when the great Mr. Justice Oliver Wendell Holmes, Jr., was appointed by President Theodore Roosevelt to what was to be his thirty-year tenure on the Court, dissenting voices to the majority's policies were increasingly heard. As of 1916 Holmes was joined in dissents, although frequently for different reasons, by his colleague Louis D. Brandeis; and with the advent of Justices Harlan F. Stone in 1925 and Benjamin N. Cardozo in 1932, the dissenting voices in this area had swelled to just one short of a majority. The previously described switch by Mr. Chief Justice Hughes, and, to a lesser extent, by Mr. Justice Owen D. Roberts, ultimately brought on what the eminent American constitutionalist Ed-

---

[117] *Santa Clara County v. Southern Pacific Railroad Co.*, 118 U.S. 394 (1886).
[118] *Ibid.* at 396.

ward S. Corwin aptly called "a Constitutional Revolution." Having lost the battle of packing the Court in February 1937, President F. D. Roosevelt won the war when fate, in the form of deaths and resignations, weeded out the remaining four ultra-conservative Justices on the bench between 1937 and 1941—Associate Justices Willis Van Devanter, George Sutherland, James C. McReynolds, and Pierce Butler—ultimately allowing him to fill nine vacancies on the Court.[119]

By no means all of these Roosevelt appointees saw the law as he had hoped they would; but certainly the New Deal now had clear sailing, and there was no doubt that the new Justices rejected outright the "thou-shalt-not-pass" doctrines of their predecessors relative to legislative experimentation in the economic-proprietarian sphere. As Mr. Justice Black was to comment later: "Whether the legislature takes for its textbook Adam Smith, Herbert Spencer, Lord Keynes, or some other is no concern of ours."[120] Judicial self-restraint on legislative policy-making in these areas of public life became the avowed policy of the Court—just as the "Old Court" had practiced a similar restraint on legislative policies in the cultural and political realms (e.g. the "separate but equal" concept and abridgement on speech, press, and assembly). Yet, interestingly enough, the "New Court" immediately commenced to complete the cycle of policy reversal by throwing up judicial vetoes in the face of a good many legislative encroachments —as the Court saw these—on civil rights and liberties. Thus the nature and character of the Court's labors began to change dramatically. Of the 160 decisions in which it had written opinions in the 1935–36 term, a *mere two* had dealt with civil rights and liberties. That ratio began to climb steadily so that a decade later 20 times as many opinions fell into that category, and 15 years later fully 54 cases dealt with that vital area of public life—a fact of judicial life that has not only continued to the present, but has accelerated, with more than half (85 of 156 in 1972–73) of the Court's written opinions now concerning the libertarian sector.

When Justices Murphy and Wiley Rutledge joined Mr. Chief Justice Stone and Justices Black and Douglas in the early 1940's, these "libertarian activists" were generally in firm control—certainly until the death of the Chief Justice in April 1946. They briefly relinquished that control during the last four years of the Vinson Court upon the death of Justices Murphy and Rutledge in 1949 and their replacement by Justices Clark and Minton,

[119] Black, Reed, Frankfurter, Douglas, Murphy, Stone (promotion to Chief Justice), Byrnes, Jackson, and Rutledge.
[120] *Ferguson v. Skrupa*, 372 U.S. 726 (1963), at 732.

when the Court tended—broadly speaking—to side with government rather than the individual in the general field of national security, that so difficult and emotion-charged "Cold War" problem. But they more or less regained it during the first four years of the Warren Court, from 1953 to 1957, Mr. Chief Justice Warren having replaced Mr. Chief Justice Vinson on Vinson's death. However, with the Court led by the consistently "nonactivist" Mr. Justice Frankfurter, the 1957–58 term saw a return to readily discernible judicial self-restraint even in *that* area of public and constitutional policy—some would contend largely as a result of the veritable barrage of congressional and public criticism against the Court following its spate of "pro-civil liberty" decisions in 1956–57. Yet with the retirement of Justices Whittaker and Frankfurter in 1962, and their replacement by Justices Byron White and Arthur Goldberg, the latter in turn yielding to Abe Fortas in 1965, plus the Thurgood Marshall replacement of Mr. Justice Clark, the libertarian image of the Warren Court was restored. It continued and indeed mounted until the Chief Justice's resignation in 1969. His replacement by Warren Earl Burger has been characterized by a somewhat moderating tenor and by some retrenchment in the criminal justice sector, but there are no indications of a general return to pre-Warren Court doctrine. The overriding concern for civil rights and liberties will almost surely continue to characterize a majority of cases reaching the highest tribunal for adjudication.

Finally, when the great issues of Executive power that had arisen in the "Watergate" affair reached the Burger Court in July 1974, it took on President Nixon, in *United States, Petitioner, v. Richard M. Nixon, President of the United States*.[121] In an 8 : 0 decision, the unanimous Court, including three of the Nixon appointees (the fourth, Mr. Justice Rehnquist, having disqualified himself), ruled, in effect, that no man was above the law, that the President was duty-bound to comply with a valid judicial order to turn over evidence desired in a criminal trial, and that there was no "absolute, unqualified presidential privilege of immunity from judicial process under all circumstances." Here, fifteen days prior to Nixon's resignation, Mr. Chief Justice Burger, resorting to John Marshall's immortal words, told the President, the nation, and the world: "We therefore reaffirm that it is 'emphatically the province and the duty' of this Court 'to say what the law is.' "

If we reflect on these several considerations in this analysis of the *Machtkampf*, the work of the Supreme Court and the force and implications of its decisions come into closer focus. At times the Court has clearly led the

[121] 417 U.S. 683.

country (e.g. the Marshall era); at other times it has more or less held the line (e.g. the Chase-Waite era—with important qualifications); at times it has deliberately stimulated social and economic progress (e.g. the post-1937 Court); at others it has deliberately delayed it (e.g. the Fuller Court). At times it has looked to a majority sentiment, as it were, by following the election returns (e.g. the *Insular* decisions at the turn of the last century);[122] at others it has defied majority sentiment (e.g. some of the 1956–57 term "civil liberties" decisions).[123] At times its decisions have been seemingly motivated by "sectional" or "class" considerations (e.g. *Dred Scott*,[124] proclaiming corporations as "persons,"[125] and the 1954 *Segregation Cases*);[126] at others they have been truly "national" in spirit and effect (e.g. the first two major Marshall decisions, cited earlier). In a very real sense, the Court through the years has thus been the conscience of the country. In a measure, it has represented the *volonté générale* of the land, in a qualitative rather than a quantitative sense. It has done this through its decisions, speaking through its Justices, who—almost always of a rather high caliber—have interpreted the Constitution as they saw it, in line with the taught tradition of the law.

Of course, the Supreme Court of the United States is engaged in the political process—but, in Mr. Justice Frankfurter's admonitory prose, it is "the Nation's ultimate judicial tribunal, not a super-legal aid bureau."[127] His jurisprudential heir, Mr. Justice John Marshall Harlan, seconded and extended this salient point by observing that the "Constitution is not a panacea for every blot upon the public welfare, nor should this Court, ordained as a judicial body, be thought of as a general haven for reform movements."[128] Of course, the Justices who, in the words of E. V. Rostow, are "inevitably teachers in a vital national seminar"[129]—consult their own policy preferences. But they do so in an institutional setting that forces responsibility upon them. They must meet and maintain high standards of integrity, intelligence, logic, reflectiveness, and consistency. They must ever

[122] *Downes v. Bidwell,* 182 U.S. 244 (1901) and *De Lima v. Bidwell,* 182 U.S. 1 (1901).

[123] E.g. *Watkins v. United States,* 354 U.S. 178; *Jencks v. United States,* 353 U.S. 657; *Yates v. United States,* 354 U.S. 298.

[124] *Dred Scott v. Sandford,* loc. cit.

[125] *Santa Clara County v. Southern Pacific Railroad Co.,* loc. cit.

[126] *Brown v. Board of Education,* 347 U.S. 483 and *Bolling v. Sharpe,* 347 U.S. 497.

[127] *Uveges v. Pennsylvania,* 335 U.S. 437, (1948) at 450.

[128] *Reynolds v. Sims,* 377 U.S. 533 (1964), dissenting opinion, at 624.

[129] "The Democratic Character of Judicial Review," 66 *Harvard Law Review* 195 (1952).

demonstrate a sense of history complete with the realities and vagaries of public affairs, a task that Judge C. Hutcheson, Jr., of Texas once called "the hunch of intuition about the inner life of American democracy."[130] They have the exciting, yet delicate task of heeding the "felt necessities of the time"—to employ once again Mr. Justice Holmes's inspired phrase— while holding aloft the banner of constitutional fundamentals. It was Daniel Webster, not a present-day observer or participant of the governmental process, who put his finger on what should be obvious: Speaking in the House of Representatives in support of a judiciary bill, he intoned that "the maintenance of the judicial power is essential and indispensable to the very being of this government. The Constitution without it would be no constitution; the government no government."[131]

[130] As quoted by Rostow in his *The Sovereign Prerogative: The Supreme Court and the Quest for Law* (New Haven: Yale University Press, 1962), p. 110.
[131] As quoted by Mr. Chief Justice Earl Warren, "Webster and the Court," *Dartmouth College Alumni Magazine*, May 19, 1969, p. 34.

IX
Coda:
A Realistic Bulwark

If the foregoing analysis of the role of the Supreme Court of the United States in the political process has proved anything at all, it ought to be that there is a recognition of the overriding need for judicial self-restraint. Its acceptance plays an omnipresent and omnipotent part in the attitude of the nine members of the highest court in the United States. No matter how the judicial record of these nine individuals may appear on a chart or graph; no matter how predictable or unpredictable their position on certain issues may be—a factor that on balance is probably far more of a blessing than a curse—they are fully aware of their role in, and responsibility to, the democratic body politic which they serve with such dedication. They serve as a collective institution of government; but it is an institution that is characterized by individual absorption in the tasks at hand, an absorption that calls for direct personal evaluation and decision-making. As has been demonstrated throughout these pages, *each member of the Supreme Court* normally participates in every stage of the consideration of a case—from the review stage through the evaluation of briefs, through oral argument, through discussion and vote in Conference, to the writing of or participation in the ultimate opinion of the Court. At every stage of the life of a case the Justices are fully aware of their responsibilities as members of the governmental process, and thus practice much procedural as well as substantive judicial self-restraint—both in the type of cases they will hear and in the kind of decisions they will render. This emphasis on what Alexander Bickel wisely termed "passive virtues"[1] is a simple, and yet immensely complicated,

---

[1] *The Least Dangerous Branch: The Supreme Court at the Bar of Politics* (Indianapolis: The Bobbs-Merrill Co., 1962), title of Ch. IV.

fact of judicial life—whatever the opinion of expert as well as laymen outsiders on judicial legislating may be. But there is little doubt that the Justices believe with Johann Wolfgang von Goethe that "self-limitation is the first mark of the master."[2]

Throughout the almost two centuries of its existence, the Court has developed a host of unwritten laws, practices, precedents, and attitudes which we may well view as a code of behavior for the highest judicial body in the United States—a series of significant *maxims of judicial self-restraint*. In analyzing the most commonly accepted of these, the reader should be aware that any such enumeration will necessarily involve some generalization— and that maxims, like rules, are sometimes broken quite deliberately.

THE SIXTEEN GREAT MAXIMS OF JUDICIAL SELF-RESTRAINT

There is nothing holy about either the number of these maxims or the order in which they will appear below. They are presented roughly in the order in which they would normally confront the Justices as an issue reaches the Supreme Court in the form of a case of controversy—presumably when it has become "ripe" for adjudication.

ONE: *Before the Court will even glance at a particular issue or dispute officially, a definite "case" or "controversy" at law or in equity between bona fide adversaries under the Constitution must exist, involving the protection or enforcement of valuable legal rights, or the punishment, prevention, or redress of wrongs directly concerning the party or parties bringing the justiciable suit.* Mr. Justice Jackson viewed this maxim as "perhaps the most significant and least comprehended limitation upon the judicial power."[3] The judicial system of the United States is constructed upon specific cases with specific facts. Thus, when a group of federal employees endeavored to join one George P. Poole in a suit testing the validity of that portion of the Hatch Act of 1939 which forbids members of the executive civil service to take an active part in "political management or in political campaigns," the Supreme Court disqualified them as appellants since they, unlike Poole, had not violated the provision in question.[4] Refusing to take jurisdiction, the Court thereby reiterated its oft-expressed stand against "every form of

---

[2] From the sonnet "Was Wir Bringen," 1802. ("In der Beschränkung zeigt sich erst der Meister.")

[3] Robert H. Jackson, *The Supreme Court in the American System of Government* (Cambridge: Harvard University Press, 1955), p. 11.

[4] *United Public Workers of America v. Mitchell,* 330 U.S. 75 (1947).

pronouncement on abstract, contingent, or hypothetical issues."[5] Except for Poole's claims, no case or controversy directly involving the interest of the appellants was involved here in the face of the Supreme Court's first maxim—regardless of what lower tribunals might have held. Probably the most famous illustration of the "case or controversy" problems is the Court's 1911 decision in *Muskrat v. United States*.[6] At issue was an act of Congress that had authorized Muskrat and others to bring suit in the U.S. Court of Claims, with an appeal to the Supreme Court *to determine the validity of certain acts of Congress* which altered the terms of some prior allotments of Cherokee Indian lands. Speaking for a unanimous Court, Mr. Justice Day rejected the appeal as not meeting the "case or controversy" requirement. "If such actions as are here attempted, to determine the validity of legislation are sustained," lectured Day, "the result will be that this court, instead of keeping within the limits of judicial power and deciding cases or controversies arising between opposing parties, as the Constitution intended it should, will be required to give opinions in the nature of advice concerning legislative action, *a function never conferred upon it by the Constitution. . . .*[7]

TWO: Closely related to the need for the presence of a case or controversy is the logical demand that *the party or parties bringing suit must have* "*standing.*" The gist of the question of standing, as the Court elucidated it in *Baker v. Carr*, "is whether the party seeking relief has alleged such a personal stake in the outcome of the controversy as to assure that concrete adverseness which sharpens the presentation of issues upon which the court so largely depends for illumination of difficult constitutional questions."[8] There are two major aspects to the difficult and intricate concept[9] of standing. The *first*, to raise a constitutional issue with proper standing, is that it must be shown that the one who seeks to challenge the statute or action is

---

[5] Jackson, loc. cit. p. 12.

[6] 219 U.S. 346.

[7] Ibid. at 362. (Italics supplied.) President Nixon's counsel unsuccessfully argued the absence of a "case" or "controversy" in *United States v. Nixon*, 417 U.S. 683 (1974).

[8] 369 U.S. 186 (1962), at 204.

[9] The doctrine of "standing" was dramatically invoked, in an entirely different context, by the International Court of Justice at The Hague in 1966 when it narrowly ruled (8 : 7) that it could not accept a case concerning South Africa's racial practices brought by Ethiopia and Libya because these two complainants lacked sufficient *legal* (as distinguished from emotional) interests in the subject of their complaint. (The decisive eighth vote was cast by Court President Sir Percy Spender, who under the tribunal's rules, was empowered to cast a second vote to break the 7 : 7 tie—which, ironically, had been created by Sir Percy's initial vote *against* assuming jurisdiction!)

personally and substantially injured by it, or is in substantial danger of such injury. A relaxation of that rule, at least in the so sensitive free speech area, was introduced with the Court's landmark 1965 ruling in *Dombrowski v. Pfister*, where it held 5 : 2 that federal district judges should have the power to enjoin the enforcement of unconstitutional laws—i.e. laws presumed unconstitutional "on their face"—if these laws, as per Justice Brennan's majority opinion, pose a "chilling effect" upon freedom of expression by the mere "fact of prosecution, unaffected by the prospects of its success or failure. . . . [Thus, courts may] avoid making vindication of freedom of expression await the outcome of protracted litigation."[10] But the relaxation was short-lived. District judges, prodded by aggressive attorneys for litigants, followed the Supreme Court's *Dombrowski* ruling with such gusto that state laws on obscenity, abortion, subversion, homosexuality, vagrancy, etc., began to fall like tenpins—and in 1971 the Burger Court called a halt, in a significant decision which instructed the lower federal courts to halt state prosecutions *only* when state officials were "cynically harassing" defendants, causing "irreparable injury."[11] In other words, six years after *Dombrowski* the Court substituted a test of "irreparable injury" for "chilling effect."

The *second* aspect of standing is that a petitioner must not only have a personal and substantial interest infringed by the statute or action, but that he must also "bring himself, by proper averment and showing, within the class as to whom the act thus attacked is unconstitutional."[12] Thus the Su-

---

[10] 380 U.S. 479, at 487.

[11] *Younger v. Harris*, 401 U.S. 37 (1971). The Court applied its *Younger* ruling to six cases before it on the same day as the parent case (February 23, 1971). The opinions in *Younger* and the six were written by Mr. Justice Black, with but Mr. Douglas in dissent.

[12] *Southern Railroad Co. v. King*, 217 U.S. 524 (1910) at 534. The reference to "class" in the quotation points to the vexatious legal phenomenon called a "class action"—that is, a suit filed by the person allegedly wronged on behalf of himself and perhaps hundreds or thousands of unnamed others who can be classified with him as *similarly* wronged. Thus, class actions, when successful, provide a way for the claims of many individuals to be settled at one time, eliminating repetitious litigation and establishing an economical route to obtaining redress, since the legal fees can be taken from the total damages awarded. Celebrated illustrations of successful class action suits are the school desegregation cases of 1954 and the one-man, one-vote cases of 1964. In the decade that followed more and more class action suits were brought, and finally the Burger Court began to draw a line. The first such decision was rendered late in 1973, in a 6 : 3 vote against the plaintiff in a pollution case. Certain kinds of class actions, such as those involving antitrust and civil rights suits, will not be affected by the Court's limitation since they have no $10,000 minimum requirement. But henceforth, when parties from *different* states are involved (i.e. in "diversity of citizenship" cases, which do call for a $10,000 minimum—see Ch. IV, *supra*), *every* plaintiff must meet the $10,000 damage allegation requirement *sepa-*

preme Court ruled 6 : 3 in late 1970 that the Commonwealth of Massachusetts lacked *standing* to litigate the question of the constitutionality of the Vietnam war by attempting to challenge it in behalf of its individual citizens.[13] A lower appellate court did accept the war-legality question as a justiciable controversy a year later, and then upheld its legality, but the Supreme Court, predictably, denied *certiorari*.[14]

One of the most famous illustrations of a *lack of standing* on record is the case of Dr. Wilder Tileston, a Connecticut physician who wanted to challenge the constitutionality of that state's statutory prohibition[15]—enforced but three times between the time of its birth in 1879 and its death at the bar of the United States Supreme Court in 1965[16]—of the "use of drugs or instruments to prevent conception, and the giving of assistance or counsel in their use." Having lost his appeal in the Connecticut Supreme Court of Errors below, he endeavored to get federal Supreme Court review. Because of their importance to the concept of standing, the pertinent sections of that court's *per curiam* decision should be quoted:

> Appellant [Dr. Tileston] alleged that the statute, if applicable to him, would prevent his giving professional advice concerning the use of contraceptives to three patients whose condition of health was such that their lives would be endangered by child-bearing, and that appellees [Abraham S. Ullman and other law enforcement officers of the state], intend to prosecute any offense against the statute and "claim or may claim" that the proposed professional advice would constitute such an offense. The complaint set out in detail the danger to the lives of appellant's patients in the event that they should bear children, but *contained no allegation asserting any claim under the Fourteenth Amendment of infringement of appellant's liberty or his property rights*. The relief prayed was a declaratory judgment [to be explained in the next maxim] as to whether the statutes are applicable to appellant and if so whether they constitute a valid exercise of constitutional power "within the meaning and intent of Amend-

---

rately. No longer will a "collective" total of $10,000 bring proper class action standing. (*Zahn v. International Paper Co.*, 414 U.S. 291.) A further narrowing of class action availability came with a unanimous ruling, handed down in May 1974, that henceforth a person bringing such a suit must notify all members of the class potentially benefited, *and* bear the cost of such notice, even if it is prohibitively high. (*Eisen v. Carlisle & Jacqueline*, 416 U.S. 979).

13 *Massachusetts v. Laird*, 400 U.S. 886, Justices Douglas, Harlan, and Stewart dissenting.
14 *Orlando v. Laird*, 404 U.S. 869 (1971), Justices Douglas and Brennan dissenting. (The Circuit Court's citation was 443 F. 2d 1039.)
15 *Tileston v. Ullman*, 318 U.S. 44 (1943).
16 *Griswold v. Connecticut*, 381 U.S. 479.

ment XIV of the Constitution of the United States prohibiting a state from depriving any person *of life* without due process of law." . . .

We are of the opinion that the proceedings in the state courts *present no constitutional question which appellant has standing to assert. The sole constitutional attack upon the statutes under the Fourteenth Amendment is confined to their deprivation of life—obviously not appellant's but his patients'.* There is no allegation or proof that appellant's life is in danger. *His patients are not parties to this proceeding* and there is no basis on which we can say that he has standing to secure an adjudication of his patient's constitutional right to life, *which they do not assert in their own behalf.* . . . *No question is raised in the record with respect to the deprivation of appellant's liberty or property in contravention of the Fourteenth Amendment.* . . . Since the *appeal must be dismissed on the grounds that appellant has no standing to litigate the constitutional question which the record presents,* it is unnecessary to consider whether the record shows the existence of a genuine case or controversy essential to the exercise of jurisdiction of this Court. . . . Dismissed.[17]

In short, Dr. Tileston had no standing to sue: his patients might well have had such, but *they* did not bring suit; *he* might have had such, but he brought suit on nonjusticiable grounds. Of course, the Court was not about to get into the delicate matter of birth control if it could avoid doing so, and it had every judicial right to do just that—at least at this stage of the process.

Not to be outdone, opponents of the Connecticut statute tried again in 1961, and this time with patients *and* a physician as plaintiffs. The Supreme Court was hard pressed to reject the appeal for adjudication of the issue and thus to continue to refuse to get involved in the sticky problem. But it managed: Led, not surprisingly, by Mr. Justice Frankfurter, and narrowly dividing 5 : 4, the majority held the controversy *not* to be "fit for adjudication"; that no one had in fact been injured, such as being jailed or fined; and that consequently, ". . . this Court cannot be umpire to debates concerning harmless, empty shadows."[18] Frankfurter pointed out that the law in question had rarely been the subject of a prosecution, that perhaps it had died of disuse and would therefore not ever be enforced. Yet the statute's opponents were not mollified: more determined than ever to test its constitutionality, they continued to try to obtain standing to challenge it. They opened a birth-control clinic in New Haven, frankly advertising its existence —and, to their utter delight, the state decided to prosecute them! Best of

17 *Tileston v. Ullman,* loc cit. at 46. (Italics supplied.)
18 *Poe v. Ullman and Buxton v. Ullman,* 367 U.S. 497 (1961).

all, Mrs. Estelle T. Griswold, the Executive Director of the Planned Parenthood League of Connecticut, and Dr. C. Lee Buxton, a licensed physician, who served as medical director for the league's New Haven Center, found themselves convicted and fined $100 each. Now they had standing at last! Losing in the courts below, they appealed to the Supreme Court on the ground that the Connecticut statute, as applied to them, violated the Fourteenth Amendment. In 1965 the Court granted their appeal, pointing out that persons prosecuted under a relevant statute must surely have standing to challenge it. And by a vote of 7 : 2 in an opinion by Mr. Justice Douglas, plus three concurring and two dissenting opinions, it declared the law to be an unconstitutional infringement not only of Amendment XIV, but also of Amendment I, III, IV, V, and IX.[19] Whatever the merits of the Connecticut case may be, standing is assuredly essential to an orderly and efficacious judicial process.[20]

[19] *Griswold v. Connecticut*, 381 U.S. 479 (1965).
[20] Another fascinating and contentious aspect of this problem is the precedent established by the Supreme Court ruling in *Frothingham v. Mellon*, 262 U.S. 447 (1923), which determined that an "ordinary tax payer" is generally precluded from contesting the constitutionality of *federal* expenditures—such as expenditures to sectarian schools and other institutions—on the ground that he does not possess "sufficient interest" to bring suit. In *Frothingham* (often identified as *Massachusetts v. Mellon*, for the two were argued, considered, and disposed of together), Mr. Justice Sutherland held for the unanimous Court that a taxpayer's interest in the moneys of the Treasury (here regarding the Federal Maternity Act) "is shared with millions of others; is comparatively minute and indeterminable; the effect upon future taxation . . . is so remote . . . that no basis is afforded for an appeal to the preventive power of the Court." As a consequence, a *federal* taxpayer (but not necessarily a *state* taxpayer in his capacity as a state citizen, for many states do allow such "taxpayer suits"), whose rights guaranteed by, for example, the First Amendment, are actually deemed violated, may be without a judicial remedy. This dilemma became particularly acute with the passage of the Federal Elementary and Secondary Aid to Education Act of 1965, with its attendant overtones of the Separation of Church and State controversy. Consequently, legislation to provide for judicial review of the constitutionality of grants and loans under seven specific federal statutes—including the aid-to-education measure just mentioned, plus any other statute administered by the Department of Health, Education, and Welfare—was introduced in and passed by the Senate on four occasions, only to die in the House in each instance. But in a dramatic development the Court in October 1967 agreed to hear arguments of seven taxpayers (*Flast v. Gardner*, 389 U.S. 895) who contended that they had a right as federal citizens to challenge the constitutionality of federal aid to parochial schools, notwithstanding the *Frothingham* precedent. In June 1968 the Court agreed, 8 : 1 (*Flast v. Cohen*, 392 U.S. 83); *provided* that the taxpayer can establish a two-part "nexus": (1) That he establish a "logical link between that [taxpayer] status and the type of legislative enactment attacked; and (2) that he can show that the challenged enactment exceeds specific constitutional limitations imposed upon the exercise of the congressional taxing and spending power. . . ." (at 102–3.) Abuse of legislative power *must* be demonstrated.

*THREE: The Court does not render advisory opinions, i.e. judicial rulings
upon the constitutionality of governmental action in the absence of a case
or controversy requiring such a ruling for its disposition*—nor do the lower
federal constitutional courts. In effect, this was settled as early as 1793,
when President Washington addressed the members of the Supreme Court,
asking them to define for him the authority given him by the Constitution
to decide certain questions involved in the United States policy of neutral-
ity with respect to a war such as the one then in progress in Europe. Mr.
Chief Justice Jay responded for the Court that it would not and could not
tender legal advice—that its role was confined to the decision of cases that
arose in the course of bona fide litigation. *Legislative* courts, however, give
advisory opinions, and so do many of the courts of the fifty states—such as
Colorado, Massachusetts, and South Dakota.

All courts, on the other hand, are empowered to render *declaratory judgments*—a device that enables courts generally to enter a final judgment between litigants *in an actual controversy*, defining their respective rights
under a statute, contract, will, or other document, *without* attaching to the
otherwise binding judgment any consequential or coercive relief. The crucial distinction between a declaratory judgment and an advisory opinion is
the presence of an actual controversy in the case of a declaratory judgment,
whereas an advisory opinion would deal with an abstract, hypothetical question insofar as the judicial process is concerned. Today, three-quarters of the
states and the federal government under the Federal Declaratory Judgment
Act of 1934, permit declaratory judgments. In the words of the federal
statute, such a judgment—which is reviewable above—answers the following
question in an actual controversy: ". . . whether or not further relief is or
could be prayed." It was for just such a declaratory judgment that Dr.
Tileston had pleaded initially, and unsuccessfully, because he then lacked
standing.

The Supreme Court itself has admitted the obvious: that the line between advisory opinions and declaratory judgments is a thin one, and that
"it would be difficult, if it would be possible, to fashion a precise test for
determining in every case whether there is such a controversy [as is demanded by a declaratory judgment]."[21] But it insisted in the *Ashwander*
case[22] that the Federal Declaratory Judgment Act "does not attempt to
change the essential requisites for the exercise of judicial power"; and, on

---

[21] *Maryland Casualty Co. v. Pacific Coal & Oil Co.*, 312 U.S. 270 (1941), at 273.
[22] *Ashwander v. Tennessee Valley Authority*, 297 U.S. 288 (1936), at 325.

another occasion, it stated that it cannot be invoked to "obtain" an advisory decree upon a hypothetical state of facts."[23]

FOUR: *Not only must the complainant in federal court expressly declare that he is invoking the Constitution of the United States—"the ultimate* touchstone of constitutionality," in Mr. Justice Frankfurter's phrase—*but a specific live rather than dead constitutional issue citing the particular provision on which he relies in that document must be raised by him; the Court will not entertain generalities.* Indeed, it has held specifically that an attack upon a statute as "violative of the Constitution of the United States" is insufficient on its face.[24] Nor will a simple contention that a statute is "in violation of the Fifth or Seventh Amendments to the Constitution" do.[25] Specific, careful, closely reasoned documentation is essential. Moreover, the issue must be raised *seasonably;* that is, *timely* assertion of the constitutional issue must be made before a tribunal having proper jurisdiction, and it must be reasserted at every opportunity in the course of the litigation. The Court is not concerned with dead or moot and thus inappropriate problems—as, for example, one caused by the death of an essential party, here the defendant, in an appeal in a criminal action.[26]

FIVE: The Court looks askance upon any attempt to have the judicial decision-cake and eat it too. Thus, *it will not pass upon the constitutionality of a statute or of an official action at the instance of one who has availed himself of its benefits, but then decides to challenge its legality anyway.* An illustration is the case of a St. Louis, Missouri, casting company, in the role of owner of property within a special sewer district who connected his premises with a freshly constructed sewer and availed himself of its benefits. But then he challenged the validity of the statute that permitted a tax levy against him as a recipient of the services, as being an unconstitutional infringement of his property rights under the Fourteenth Amendment.[27] The Supreme Court held unanimously that by accepting and availing himself of the benefits of the construction and zoning involved, the owner was "estopped from maintaining a suit" on the grounds and under the circumstances here involved.

SIX: *All remedies in the pertinent lower federal and/or state courts must have been exhausted, and prescribed lower court procedure duly followed,*

---

[23] *Electric Bond & Share Co. v. Securities & Exchange Commission,* 303 U.S. 419 (1938), at 443.
[24] *Herndon v. Georgia,* 295 U.S. 441 (1935).
[25] *Chapin v. Frye,* 179 U.S. 127 (1900).
[26] *List v. Pennsylvania,* 131 U.S. 396 (1888).
[27] *St. Louis v. Prendergast Co.,* 260 U.S. 459 (1923).

before making application to the United States Supreme Court for review.
As Judge Augustus N. Hand of the Second Circuit Court of the United
States once observed, "the rule of exhaustion is the only rule which is consistent with orderly government." Thus, the highest court of the land will
not review a judgment of a state court unless on the face of the record it
affirmatively appears that a *federal question constituting an appropriate
ground* for such review was presented in, and expressly or necessarily decided by, such a state court. For example, in 1963 the Court ruled 6 : 3 that
a New York state judgment had not been taken to the highest New York
court empowered to consider it, as statutorily required for Supreme Court
review. Hence it dismissed a writ it had granted earlier to hear the case as
having been "improvidentially granted."[28] A decade later, the Court sternly
and unanimously rejected a challenge by a group of legal rights organizations to a new system of New York State court registration and supervision
being applied to charitable corporations practicing law in that state by the
Appellate Division of the New York State Supreme Court. The U.S. Supreme Court held that the groups had to apply to the Appellate Division
for an exception to the registration requirements and be refused *before* they
could bring a constitutional challenge to the supervision system.[29] No
matter how vital, inviting, timely, or attractive the issue involved may be,
the Supreme Court will not accept a case unless the remedies below have
been exhausted; nor does it matter that a lower tribunal might not be
"friendly" to the substance of a suit—as has occurred frequently in connection with state court adjudication of such contentious problems as desegregation, criminal justice, and Bible-reading in the public schools.[30] Orderly
procedure is of the very essence of the judicial process; judicial and administrative chaos is the alternative.

SEVEN: Assuming it has been properly raised, *the federal question at issue
must be substantial rather than trivial; it must be the pivotal point of the
case; and it must be part of the plaintiff's case rather than a part of his adversary's defense.* Whatever the subjective overtones of the term "substantial" may be, it is normally not an overwhelming job to distinguish between
a "substantial" and a "trivial" federal question. For example, the controversies surrounding the extent of the federal government's authority in connection with the Tennessee Valley Authority projects, raised in sundry respects in the famous case of *Ashwander v. T.V.A.*,[31] the attempt by the

---

[28] *Gotthilf v. Sills,* 375 U.S. 79. See also *United States v. Raines,* 362 U.S. 17 (1960),
at 21.

[29] *Young Lords Party v. Supreme Court of New York,* 414 U.S. 1088 (1973).

[30] E.g. *Michel v. Louisiana,* 350 U.S. 91 (1955), and *Say v. Noia,* 372 U.S. 319 (1963)

State of California to close its borders to a destitute non-citizen traveling in interstate commerce, and that by Connecticut and others to deny welfare benefits to persons recently migrated from other states,[32] are pertinent instances of substantial federal questions. On the other hand, the endeavors of some Greek-letter fraternities on various campuses in New York and Colorado to have the Supreme Court review requirements by the Trustees of the State University of New York and those of the University of Colorado, setting deadlines on removing restrictive racial and/or religious clauses from fraternity "constitutions" on pain of revocation of campus privileges, were summarily—and quite predictably—turned aside as not involving a substantial question.[33]

EIGHT: Although it would be an oversimplification, if not entirely incorrect, to state that the Supreme Court reviews only questions of law, it is nonetheless generally true that *questions of fact—as distinct from questions of law—are not normally accepted as proper bases for review.* This is especially true of the area of judicial review of administrative construction of statutes, where a *purely* factual question has no chance of a hearing, for Congress has statutorily provided for the finality of administrative finding of fact.

However, it is axiomatic that the problem of which questions are of "law," which of "fact," and which "mixtures" is a difficult one. Any attempt to draw a rigid line poses a genuine problem because of the very nature of the two concepts—as was demonstrated again in a station house "show-up" identification case in late 1972, where the Court, dividing 5 : 3, held that the dispute between the litigants was not so much over "the elemental facts" as over the "constitutional significance to be attached to them."[34] In the words of one seasoned student of the subject, ". . . matters of law grow downward into roots of fact, and matters of fact reach upward, without a break, into matters of law."[35] In any event, the Court will not permit administrative procedures—which most frequently are at issue in this particular dichotomy—to fall below what it is prone to regard as a "constitutional

---

[32] *Edwards v. California*, 314 U.S. 160 (1941) and *Shapiro v. Thompson*, 349 U.S. 618 (1969), respectively.

[33] *Webb v. State University of New York*, 348 U.S. 867 (1954), and *The New York Times*, September 21, 1966.

[34] *Neil v. Biggers*, 409 U.S. 188. The majority comprised the Chief Justice and Associate Justices Powell (the author of the opinion), White, Blackmun, and Rehnquist; in dissent were Douglas, Brennan, and Stewart. (Marshall did not participate.)

[35] John Dickinson, *Administrative Justice and the Supremacy of Law* (Cambridge: Harvard University Press, 1927), p. 55.

minimum," a concept that is clearly a matter of law subject to judicial review.

NINE: While Britain's highest tribunal, the House of Lords, considered itself *bound* by its own prior decisions until it publicly and expressly modified that doctrine in 1966,[36] *the Supreme Court of the United States has never held itself absolutely bound by its precedents.* It has often adhered to many of these, of course, and will presumably continue to do so, but it has not permitted itself to become enslaved by past decisions. Nor could it do so— the law does not stand still; Mr. Justice Holmes's "felt necessities of the times" are ever compelling facts of governmental life. We must not expect from the Court, in Mr. Chief Justice Hughes's trenchant warning, "the icy stratosphere of certainty." But a decision of the Supreme Court is utterly binding *in federal matters* on all courts below, state as well as federal—regardless of sporadic foot-dragging and aberrations.[37]

TEN: The Court has been inclined to defer to certain legislative or executive actions by classifying an issue otherwise quite properly before it as a political question—hence refusing to come to grips with it. Depending upon one's point of view—after all, is not every constitutional question or decision "political" to some extent?—this intriguing practice or formula is either a mere *device* for transferring the responsibility for a question or decision to another branch of the government, or it is in fact *required* by the constitutionally explicit or implicit realities and necessities of the presence of the separation of powers principle. What really *is* a "political question"? Giving short shrift to this inquiry, Mr. Justice Holmes, coming to the core of an issue briskly and pithily as always, once characterized it as ". . . little more than a play on words."[38] He would have no part of the concept as a judicial mechanism—while nevertheless fully recognizing, of course, the realities of the political facts of life. Jefferson—*au contraire*—regarded all questions involving the constitutionality of acts of Congress which might come before the Court as "political questions."

Professor Edward S. Corwin essayed the following, perhaps not entirely helpful, definition of the vexatious verbiage in his last monumental annotation of the Constitution:

---

36 See the Lord Chancellor's (Lord Gardiner's) announcement, in *House of Lords Official Reports,* Vol. 276, No. 43, col. 677, July 26, 1966. *Parliamentary Debate (Hansard Weekly)* and 1 W.L.R. 1234 (1966). For an interesting, pertinent, recent House of Lords decision, see *Broome v. Cassell & Co.* [1972] 2 W.L.R. 645, in particular Lord Diplock, at 721.
37 See pp. 223–30 and 337–39, *supra.*
38 *Nixon v. Herndon,* 273 U.S. 536 (1927), at 540.

. . . a political question relates to the possession of political power, of sovereignty, of government, the determination of which is vested in Congress and the President, and whose decision are binding on the courts.[39]

In a different vein, Professor J. W. Peltason, one of the students of the revered Princeton scholar, preferred to view political questions as "those which judges choose not to decide, and a question becomes political by the judges' refusal to decide it."[40] And Judge Learned Hand labeled it—insofar as its scope is undefined—as a "stench in the nostrils of strict constructionists,"[41] a description eminently applicable to the stance taken by his ardent admirer Frankfurter! A good many of the Supreme Court's decisions, while not necessarily invalidating Corwin's analysis, would seem to support Peltason's more realistic evaluation. However, judges can, and do, change their minds, depending upon the posture and setting of an issue; what may be rejected or avoided as a political question today may quite conceivably be accepted for review on its merit at a later date—of which the legislative reapportionment-redistricting decisions are pertinent illustrations, indeed.

For years—to be precise, until its precedent-shattering decision in what must be regarded as one of the two or at most three most significant Supreme Court decisions of the twentieth century, namely *Baker v. Carr* in 1962[42]—the Court simply would not get involved in the question of the constitutionality or even the justiciability of the way in which legislatures and constitutions either did or did not apportion or district state and/or congressional districts—no matter how obvious, how outrageous, and yes, even how illegal the apportionment or districting or lack of it might have been! The Court, in the words of the main advocate of this Bastille-like stand, Mr. Justice Frankfurter—to whom Fred Rodell liked to refer as "the Court's Emily Post"—was not going to get itself involved in such a "patently political question," in such a "political thicket," which in his view was, after all, an area of the "exclusive authority" of legislatures.[43]

Thus, the constitutionality of the well-known county unit system of

---

[39] Edward S. Corwin, *The Constitution of the United States*, revised and annotated (Washington, D.C.: United States Government Printing Office, 1953), p. 547.

[40] Jack W. Peltason, *Federal Courts in the Political Process* (Garden City, N.Y.: Doubleday, 1955), p. 10.

[41] *The Bill of Rights* (Cambridge: Harvard University Press, 1958), p. 15, n. 3.

[42] 369 U.S. 186. An earlier case was *Gomillion v. Lightfoot*, 364 U.S. 339 (1960). The latter was argued on October 9, 1961, and was decided in favor of plaintiff, 6 : 2, on March 26, 1962, as 369 U.S. 186 (1962).

[43] See his opinion for the Court in *Colegrove v. Green*, 328 U.S. 549 (1946), discussed below.

Georgia—a prime example of anti-urban, pro-rural legislative gerrymander-ing—had been before the Court on several occasions. Under that system, each of the various counties received a minimum of two and a maximum of six electoral votes for the eight most populous counties, including Fulton County (Atlanta), with each county's electoral vote going to the candidate receiving the highest popular vote therein. The net effect had been that the one million inhabitants of Fulton County—a considerable proportion of whom were registered Negroes—received but one-third more votes than the handful of residents in numerous small rural counties. In other words a vote in the small counties of Georgia had from 11 to 120 times as much weight as one in Fulton! Yet attempts to have the Supreme Court come to grips with the matter had come to naught as recently as 1950, 1951, 1958, and 1959. The Court stood by its pronouncement in the first of these cases, *South v. Peters*,[44] that "a state's geographical distribution of electoral strength among its political subdivision" is a political question. Thereby the Court continued to cling to the general philosophy and tactics it had enun-ciated in *Colegrove v. Green* in 1946,[45] a case concerning congressional dis-tricts in Illinois. Here appellants had contended that the Illinois law appor-tioning congressional districts was unconstitutional because the various districts were characterized by rank inequalities. For example, a Chicago congressional district had 914,053 inhabitants, whereas one in southern Illi-nois comprised a mere 112,116. But in its decision the Supreme Court, with only seven Justices participating, and these split three ways, nevertheless held—through Mr. Justice Frankfurter and Associate Justices Reed and Burton—that it could not intervene in such a political question, one that it regarded as being up to the legislature to determine and alleviate. If the Court did intervene, wrote Frankfurter, it would be entering into a "politi-cal thicket," and that, anyway, it is "hostile to a democratic system to in-volve the judiciary in the politics of the people."[46] Mr. Justice Black, speak-ing also for Justices Douglas and Murphy, dissented vigorously, contending that the State of Illinois's failure to redistrict was tantamount to "willful legislative discrimination" and constituted a denial of the equal protection

[44] 339 U.S. 276 (1950).
[45] 328 U.S. 549.
[46] Ibid. at 554. The decisive fourth vote in the case was provided by Mr. Justice Rut-ledge who, in effect, agreed with the three dissenters that the issue per se was justici-able, but nonetheless chose to concur in the Frankfurter opinion for the Court in view of "the shortness of time remaining" before the next election and the difficulties of an election at large in a state with so many Congressional districts. Mr. Justice Jackson did not sit; he was at the Nuremberg war crimes trials. Mr. Chief Justice Stone had just died, and his successor, Fred M. Vinson, had not yet been sworn in.

of the laws presumably guaranteed by the Fourteenth Amendment to the Constitution of the United States.

But the days of the "political question" doctrine in *this* sector of public law were clearly numbered when the Court, after twice having noted probable jurisdiction in its 1960–61 term, agreed to hear argument in 1961 in a Tennessee case involving that state's outright refusal to reapportion the General Assembly among its ninety-five counties, seats that had been arbitrarily and capriciously apportioned by a 1901 statute—and never touched since, despite an almost fivefold growth of eligible voters and major shifts of population from rural to urban areas generally. The case was *Baker v. Carr.* Knowing its significance, the Supreme Court ordered three and a half hours of oral argument,[47] with United States Solicitor General Archibald Cox arguing as *amicus curiae* on the side of the plaintiff on behalf of the United States Government. The mere willingness to accept *Baker v. Carr* for review served notice of the possibility, if not the probability, of a dramatic "political question" shift. And it was dramatic indeed! There were six opinions, covering a total of 165 pages, with Mr. Justice Frankfurter's agitated and angry dissenting opinion for Mr. Justice Harlan and himself consuming 65 pages alone! Still, what Mr. Justice Brennan actually decided in his opinion for the Court can be described quickly: (1) that the federal courts *do* have jurisdiction in apportionment-districting cases; (2) that the Baker complaint did present a *justiciable controversy;* and (3) that Baker and his co-appellants had *standing* to bring the suit. Notwithstanding Frankfurter's deeply felt warnings—in what was to prove his last opinion prior to his retirement for reasons of health later that year (1962)—that the judiciary was damaging itself by getting into such "political matters," that it was immersing itself dangerously and wrongly in a "mathematical quagmire," the Court majority of six (Mr. Justice Whittaker had not participated in the case), without addressing itself to the specific merits of Baker's contentions, (a) regarded them as eminently justiciable in the courts, i.e. capable of adjudication, and (b) remanded the case to the lower federal court whence it came for purposes of such adjudication. (Ultimately, Tennessee was ordered to redistrict. It complied, albeit haltingly.) In short, rejecting the Frankfurter admonition that ". . . in a democratic society like ours, relief [for political mischief] must come through an aroused popular conscience that sears the conscience of the people's representatives,"[48] the highest court in the land in effect reformulated the "political question"

[47] *Baker v. Carr,* 368 U.S. 804 (1961).
[48] Ibid. 369 U.S. 186 (1962), at 270.

concept and doctrine. No longer would it apply to the matter at issue. In Brennan's words, the political question doctrine relates properly to "the relationship between the judiciary and the coordinate branches of the Federal Government, and not the federal judiciary's relationship to the states. . . ."[49] Over Frankfurter's specific disagreement on the point, Brennan thus confined "political questions," by way of the *Baker v. Carr* decision, to "a function of the separation of powers."[50]

As a logical result of the decision, the Supreme Court subsequently struck down as unconstitutional the infamous, although by then somewhat revised, Georgia County Unit System for state legislative apportionment in *Gray v. Sanders* in 1963,[51] plus state legislative malapportionment of congressional districts in 1964 in *Wesberry v. Sanders*.[52] Later in 1964, in the most far-reaching and most contentious of all of the myriad of post-*Baker v. Carr* decisions, the Court required that *both* houses of state legislatures be apportioned on the basis of *population*—a decision handed down in a six-case "package" known by its lead-case, *Reynolds v. Sims*.[53] In 1968 the principle was extended to local government,[54] and in 1969 the Court made clear, 6 : 3, that states would have to justify *any* numerical deviation between districts on pain of findings of unconstitutionality.[55] Decisions in 1970 held the one-man one-vote rule to apply to all *elective* bodies exercising "general governmental authority"[56]—even school boards—but *not* to those that, like the New York City Board of Estimate, do not possess that kind of power,[57] nor, accordingly, to elected *judges*.[58] Ultimately, deviations were sanctioned for certain political boundaries at the state level[59]—but not even so much as 4 per cent for congressional districts.[60]

It should be clear, however, that the important contraction brought about by *Baker v. Carr* has by no means removed the concept of "political question" doctrine as such. A case like the well-known 1849 *Luther v. Borden*[61]

[49] Ibid. at 210.
[50] Ibid. at 217.
[51] 372 U.S. 368.
[52] 376 U.S. 1.
[53] 377 U.S. 533.
[54] *Avery v. Midland County*, 390 U.S. 474.
[55] *Wells v. Rockefeller*, 394 U.S. 542.
[56] E.g. *Hadley v. Junior College District of Metropolitan Kansas City*, 397 U.S. 50.
[57] *Bergerman v. Lindsay*, 398 U.S. 955.
[58] *Wells v. Edwards*, 409 U.S. 1095 (1973).
[59] *City of Virginia Beach v. Howell*, 410 U.S. 315 (1973), *Gaffney v. Cummings*, 412 U.S. 735 (1973), and *White v. Regester*, 412 U.S. 755 (1973).
[60] *White v. Regester*, 412 U.S. 755 (1973).
[61] 7 Howard 1.

would today assuredly continue to be treated—in line with the new Brennan formula announced in *Baker v. Carr*—as a political question. *Luther v. Borden* arose out of the Rhode Island Dorr Rebellion, early in America's history. Very briefly, the facts of the case were such that the Supreme Court found itself confronted with the crucial decision as to *which one* of two governments battling for legal supremacy in Rhode Island in 1842 was *the* legal one. The Court concluded that this was clearly a "political question" since the President of the United States, in exercising the power conferred upon him by Congress to send federal troops to aid states in suppressing insurrection, had indicated that he regarded the original—the "charter"—government as the lawful one of the two, and that this judgment was binding upon the judiciary.

If one accepts the concept of the political question at all, the *Luther* example is obviously a much more clear-cut one than those involving legislative apportionment. Yet what a political question *is* remains difficult to determine. Generalization of the doctrine is still virtually impossible. Moreover, as Mr. Justice Brennan pointed out in *Baker v. Carr*, ". . . the mere fact that [a] suit seeks protection of a political right does not mean it presents a political question. Such an objection is little more than a play upon words."[62] And as his colleague Clark put the matter in his concurring opinion, ". . . national respect for the courts is more enhanced through the forthright enforcement of [basic national rights such as fair legislative apportionment] than by rendering them nugatory through the interposition of subterfuges."[63] However attractive in theory, the "political question" maxim is a treadmill; perhaps to a fatal degree its supporting logic is circular.

ELEVEN: *In the event of a validly challenged statute, the presumption of its constitutionality is always in its favor.* As early as 1827, Mr. Justice Bushrod Washington wrote:

> It is but a decent respect to the wisdom, integrity, and patriotism of the legislative body, by which any law is passed, to presume in favor of its validity, until its violation of the Constitution is proved beyond a reasonable doubt.[64]

Hence, as the history of the Court shows, if a legislative enactment can be construed to be in reasonable harmony with the Constitution, a majority of the Court will almost always do so. Obviously, the views of the Justices

[62] Opinion for the Court, 369 U.S. 186, at 209.
[63] Ibid. at 261–62.
[64] *Ogden v. Saunders*, 12 Wheaton 213 (1827).

have differed somewhat, often drastically, on the meaning of the word "reasonable." Thus, while there is today practically no judicial interference with legislation dealing with economic and social matters, the Court remains seriously divided on what constitutes "reasonable" legislative restrictions in certain areas of civil rights and liberties, such as the national security sector in the face of the specific guarantees under the First Amendment. For example, generally speaking, a hard core of five members of the 1966–67 Warren bench—the Chief Justice himself and Justices Black, Douglas, Brennan, and Fortas—would brook little, if any, legislative encroachments in this sector, whereas a hard core of three—Justices Clark, Harlan, and White—would exercise more or less judicial self-restraint, with Mr. Justice Stewart more unpredictable here, given his pronounced concern for freedom of expression.

In any event, the Court will not normally formulate a rule of constitutional law broader than is required by the precise facts to which it is to be applied. "The cardinal principle of statutory construction," wrote Mr. Chief Justice Hughes in a famous case,

> is to save and not to destroy. We have repeatedly held that as between two possible interpretations of a statute, by one of which it would be unconstitutional and the other valid, our plain duty is to adopt that which will save the act. Even to avoid a serious doubt the rule is the same.[65]

On the other hand, Mr. Justice Stone—normally a firm adherent to the philosophy of presumption of constitutionality—implied an important exception to the general rule in his footnote in the otherwise rather unimportant *Carolene Products* case[66]—which footnote became one of the most famous of all time! It was there that he stated that perhaps there might be occasion for departing from the normal presumption of constitutionality for legislation in cases *where the legislative action in question involved a restriction or curtailment of the ordinary political processes which could generally be expected to be employed to bring about the negation of undesirable legislation,* or *where it appeared to be within* "*a specific prohibition of the Constitution, such as those of the first ten amendments,* which are deemed equally specific when held to be embraced within the Fourteenth."[67] And as of the late 1960s, the Burger Court adopted a posture of

---

[65] *N.L.R.B. v. Jones & Laughlin Steel Corporation,* 301 U.S. 1 (1937).

[66] *United States v. Carolene Products Co.,* 304 U.S. 144 (1938), at 152–53, fn. 4.

[67] Ibid. (Italics supplied.) On the issue of what has been regarded as a judicial "double standard," see my *Freedom and the Court: Civil Rights and Liberties in the United States,* op. cit. Ch. II.

judicial "suspicion" under which it began to regard legislative activity in certain categories as "suspect," notably in those of race, national origin, and sex. In those areas, legislatures (and executives) would henceforth have to prove the existence of a *"compelling* state interest" rather than, as heretofore, a mere "rational relationship" in order to see their actions survive judicial scrutiny.

TWELVE: In the exercise of what some commentators have been fond of styling "judicial parsimony," *if a case or controversy can be decided upon any other than constitutional grounds—such as by statutory construction, which constitutes the greatest single area of the Court's work, or if it can rest on an independent state ground—the Court will be eager to do so.* For it will not decide questions of a constitutional nature unless absolutely necessary to the decision of the case, and even then it will draw such a decision as narrowly as possible, being ever loath to formulate a rule of constitutional law broader than is clearly required by the precise facts to which it is to be applied. Nor will it anticipate a question of constitutional law in advance of the necessity of deciding it. As Mr. Justice White put it in an "obscenity" case, the proper approach is "not to invalidate . . . but to construe . . . narrowly."[68] Mr. Justice Frankfurter succinctly underscored the point of anticipation in an edifying exchange with Thurman Arnold, who was acting as counsel for Dr. J. P. Peters, petitioner in the loyalty-security case of *Peters v. Hobby.*[69] Mr. Arnold pleaded with the Court that he would not like to win the case on the narrow procedural, statutory ground to which a majority of the members of the bench was evidently inclining. Responded Mr. Justice Frankfurter: "The question is not whether you want to win the case on that ground or not. This Court reaches constitutional issues last, not first."[70] He might well have quoted Mr. Justice Brandeis's famous assertion that the ". . . most important thing we do is not doing."

The loyalty-security field affords a host of pertinent illustrations of the Court's preference for a resort to its potent weapon of statutory construction rather than to constitutional grounds. This delicate and emotion-laden area of public policy is tailor-made for such an approach, which preserves the statute while sometimes smoothing certain ragged edges. Thus the Court effects a gain, however moderate it may be, for individual civil rights,

---

[68] *United States v. Thirty-Seven (37) Photographs,* 402 U.S. 363 (1971), at 375, plurality opinion.
[69] 349 U.S. 311 (1955).
[70] As reported in 23 *U.S. Law Week* 265–66 (1955).

while retaining the generally popular and politically desirable law. To cite some instances: it is precisely what the Court did in narrowing executive authority to dismiss government employees under the Summary Suspension Act of 1950 by holding that the act did not authorize dismissal of employees holding "non-sensitive" positions;[71] in limiting the power of the Secretary of State to withhold a passport from a citizen "for any substantive reason he may choose," holding that the Immigration and Nationality Act of 1952 did not authorize such sweeping discretionary powers;[72] and in holding that, while the Magnuson Seaman's Act of 1950 had given the executive branch the authority to act to prevent sabotage, it had emphatically not provided it with the authority to inquire into seamen's beliefs and associations before granting them seamen's licenses.[73] In each of these instances, congressional reaction was to the effect that "we did *so* intend to authorize what you say we did not," but in the absence of the passage of any clarifying or amplifying amendments the two statutes stood as judicially construed. After all, statutory construction is an act of judgment and, as Mr. Justice Holmes once observed succinctly, applies to cases "in which there is a fair contest between two readings."

THIRTEEN: The Court will not ordinarily impute illegal motives to the lawmakers. "So long as Congress acts in pursuance of its constitutional power," explained Mr. Justice Harlan in a much-debated decision upholding certain aspects of the investigative authority of the House Committee on Un-American Activities,[74] "the judiciary lacks authority to intervene *on the basis of the motives* which spurred the exercise of that power." This sentiment was echoed by Mr. Justice Black in one of his last opinions, in which he wrote that no precedent existed for holding a law violative of "equal protection solely because of the motivations of the men who voted for it."[75] And as early as 1810 Mr. Chief Justice Marshall had written that it "may well be doubted how far the validity of a law depends upon the motives of its framers."[76] Indeed, the Court is not supposed to consider *motives* at all; but, as Max Radin once wrote, that concept is indeed a "transparent and absurd fiction"[77]—to which the decision in the *Child Labor Tax Case*[78] of 1922, for example, bears eloquent witness.

[71] *Cole v. Young,* 351 U.S. 536 (1956).
[72] *Kent and Briehl v. Dulles,* 357 U.S. 116 (1958).
[73] *Schneider v. Smith,* 390 U.S. 17 (1968).
[74] *Barenblatt v. United States,* 360 U.S. 109 (1959). (Italics supplied.)
[75] *Palmer v. Thompson,* 403 U.S. 217 (1971), majority opinion at 224.
[76] *Fletcher v. Peck,* 6 Cranch 87, at 130.
[77] "Statutory Interpretation," 43 *Harvard Law Review* 863 (April 1930).
[78] *Bailey v. Drexel Furniture Co.,* 259 U.S. 20.

However, to compound the problem, the Supreme Court is expected to, and very frequently does, take legislative *intent* or *purpose* into account—yet, it is no easy task to separate motives and intent, and Mr. Justice Frankfurter, for one, consistently refused to do so. Mr. Justice Holmes wrote, "I only want to know what the words mean." Still, ". . . words are not crystals," and he found *policy* in words.[79] Or, as Mr. Justice Cardozo wrote so appropriately, "a great principle of constitutional law is not susceptible of comprehensive statement in an adjective."[80] The *Steel Seizure Case*[81] of 1952, in which seven separate opinions were written, provided a basis for an opinion for the Court only because a sufficient number of Justices was able to agree on the single point that Congress, in enacting the Taft-Hartley Act, had deliberately *intended* not to provide for presidential authority to seize struck plants. Here the intent of Congress proved to be the basis for the Court's judgment that the Chief Executive had usurped legislative power, with the Justices—as is their custom—equating intent with legislative history.

This approach is sometimes styled "psychoanalyzing Congress" by some of the less reverent observers of the governmental scene, who have considerable—and perhaps well-grounded—doubt of the infallibility of the contention, frequently quoted by Mr. Justice Frankfurter, that ". . . a page of history is worth a volume of logic." Yet whatever their merits otherwise, for this purpose at least the *Congressional Record* and the reports of the various committees of Congress are a constant and evidently fertile source of reference for the members of the Supreme Court. Thus, in unanimously upholding the Voting Rights Act of 1965, the Court repeatedly referred to congressional intent to eradicate the "substantial voting discrimination" in *specific* sections of the country because it "knew" about these and wanted to remove them. Again and again Mr. Chief Justice Warren used the term "Congress knew," thus underscoring its intent or purpose.[82]

FOURTEEN: *If the Court does find that it must hold a law unconstitutional, it will usually try hard to confine the holding to that particular section of the statute which was successfully challenged on constitutional grounds*—provided such a course of action is at all feasible. It would not be feasible, of course, if the section at issue constituted the veritable heart of the legislation, in which case the Court would follow a well-established rule of statutory construction: if the various parts of a statute are inextricably

---

[79] See Felix Frankfurter, "Some Reflections on the Readings of Statutes," Sixth Annual Benjamin N. Cardozo Lecture before the Association of the Bar of the City of New York, March 8, 1947. (Reprinted in 47 *Columbia Law Review* 527–46.)
[80] *Carter v. Carter Coal Co.*, 298 U.S. 238 (1936), at 327.
[81] *Youngstown Sheet and Tube Co. v. Sawyer*, 343 U.S. 579.
[82] *South Carolina v. Katzenbach*, 383 U.S. 301 (1966), opinion for the Court, *passim.*

connected to such degrees as to warrant the assumption that the legislature intended the law to function as a whole, then if some portions of the statute are unconstitutional the law must be treated as unconstitutional in its entirety.[83] "Sectionalized" unconstitutionality is known as *separability*, for which Congress now customarily, and quite specifically, provides in its statutes—although it neither always does so, nor is it required by the courts to do so.[84] A typical separability clause—taken from the War Powers Resolution of 1973—reads:

> If any provision of this joint resolution or the application thereof to any person or circumstance is held invalid, the remainder of the joint resolution and the application of such provision to any other person or circumstance shall not be affected thereby.

This not only serves to save those sections not affected by the Court's particular decision, but it may also act to preserve the law's entire structure for a test involving different litigants.

The series of decisions declaring portions of the Uniform Code of Military Justice Act of 1950 unconstitutional[85] are cases in point; certain powers delegated to the armed services under it are no longer valid, but the balance of the act stands and is enforced. On the other hand, although initially it was merely the "hot oil" provisions of the National Industrial Recovery Act of 1933—standing apart from those provisions of the act dealing with codes of fair competition—that fell as an unconstitutional delegation of legislative power in January 1935,[86] four months later the codes, too, and with them the entire structure of the act, fell on similar grounds.[87]

FIFTEEN: A *legislative enactment—or an executive action—may be unwise, unjust, unfair, undemocratic, injudicious, ". . . if you like . . . even tyrannical,"*[88] *or simply stupid, but still be constitutional in the eyes of the Court.* Much deference is thus paid to the legislature, and justly so under the American system of separation of powers and division of powers. In the clipped language of a Holmes opinion: "We fully understand . . . the very

---

[83] For example, see *Pollock v. Farmers' Loan and Trust Co.*, 158 U.S. 601 (1895).

[84] See Mr. Chief Justice Burger's opinion in *Tilton v. Richardson*, 403 U.S. 672 (1971), in which a portion of a federal statute was declared unconstitutional despite the acknowledged "absence of an express separability provision."

[85] *United States ex rel Toth v. Quarles*, 350 U.S. 11 (1955) *Reid v. Covert* 354 U.S. 1 (1957), *Kinsella v. Singleton*, 361 U.S. 234 (1960), among others.

[86] *Panama Refining Co. v. Ryan*, 293 U.S. 388.

[87] *Schechter v. United States*, 295 U.S. 495.

[88] Mr. Justice Holmes, dissenting in *Lochner v. United States*, 198 U.S. 45 (1905).

powerful argument that can be made against the wisdom of this legislation, but on that point we have no concern."[89] Mr. Justice Holmes once stated this constitutional and judicial philosophy in typically colorful fashion to the then sixty-one-year-old Mr. Justice Stone:

> Young man, about 75 years ago I learned that I was not God. And so, when the people . . . want to do something I can't find anything in the Constitution expressly forbidding them to do, I say, whether I like it or not, "Goddamit, let 'em do it."[90]

Or, as he said to John W. Davis on another occasion: "Of course I know, and every other sensible man knows, that the Sherman law [the Sherman Anti-Trust Act of 1890] is damned nonsense, but if my country wants to go to hell, I am here to help it."[91] The man who was appointed to the Holmes seat on the Court after Mr. Justice Cardozo's death in 1938, Mr. Justice Frankfurter, continued to champion that philosophy of judicial self-restraint eloquently, repeatedly, and consistently. Thus, he dissented vigorously from the majority's declaration of unconstitutionality of a section of the Immigration and Nationality Act of 1940 in *Trop v. Dulles:*

> It is not easy to stand aloof and allow want of wisdom to prevail, to disregard one's own strongly held view of what is wise in the conduct of affairs. But it is not the business of this Court to pronounce policy. It must observe a fastidious regard for limitations on its own power, and this precludes the Court's giving effect to its own notions of what is wise or politic. That self-restraint is of the essence in the observance of the judicial oath, for the Constitution has not authorized the judges to sit in judgment on the wisdom of what Congress and the Executive Branch do.[92]

But once again much, if not all, depends upon how the Justices see the line between self-restraint, which they indubitably all recognize as an essential element in the judicial process, and *ultra vires* legislative and executive actions. If, in drawing this line, some Justices, on some issues, are prone to address themselves more to the judicial heart than the judicial mind, who is to say where and how the Founding Fathers of the Constitution of the

---

[89] *Noble State Bank v. Haskell*, 219 U.S. 575 (1910), opinion for the Court, at 580.
[90] As quoted by Charles P. Curtis in his *Lions Under the Throne* (Boston: Houghton Mifflin Co., 1947), p. 281.
[91] As told by Francis Biddle, *Justice Holmes, Natural Law and the Supreme Court* (New York: The Macmillan Co., 1961), p. 9.
[92] 356 U.S. 86 (1958), at 120.

United States would today distinguish between that document's heart and mind? They too were men, just as judges are men, "not disembodied spirits," in Mr. Justice Frankfurter's words; they are men who "respond to human situations . . . [who] do not reside in a vacuum." And his mentor, Holmes, believed that judges "should not be too rigidly bound to the tenets of judicial self-restraint in cases involving civil liberties."[93] Of course, even pedigreed champions of the latter may well disagree on the point in certain specific cases—as is intriguingly demonstrated by Justices Black and Douglas in the *Connecticut Birth Control Case* of 1965.[94] There, speaking for the seven-man majority that held the state's anti-birth-control law unconstitutional on a host of grounds, Douglas insisted that ". . . we do not sit [in rendering this decision] as a super-legislature to determine the wisdom, need, and propriety of laws that touch economic problems, business affairs, or social conditions. This law, however, operates directly on an intimate relation of husband and wife, and their physician's role in one aspect of that relation."[95] Black, however, dissenting together with his colleague Stewart, regarded the Court's action as one "based on subjective considerations of 'natural justice' [a formula that] is no less dangerous when used to enforce this Court's views about personal rights than those about economic rights."[96] Judges are men. . . .

SIXTEEN: *The Supreme Court* has reiterated time and again that it *is not designed to serve as a check against inept, unwise, emotional, unrepresentative legislators.* Mr. Chief Justice Waite put it well when he wrote in 1876 that for *"protection against abuses by legislatures the people must resort to the polls, not the courts."*[97] Some eighty years later, Mr. Justice Douglas reiterated this point of view forcefully: "Congress acting within its constitutional powers, has the final say on policy issues. If it acts unwisely the electorate can make a change."[98] This fundamental truth lies at the very core of the democratic process—a process which enables the people and their representatives at once to rise to soaring heights of wisdom and magnanimity and to descend to the depths of folly and pettiness. Yet that process, under law, proscribes *unconstitutional* action.

93 As quoted by Mr. Chief Justice Stone to Professor Clinton Rossiter, April 12, 1941, related by Alpheus T. Mason in *Harlan Fiske Stone: Pillar of the Law* (New York: The Viking Press, 1956), p. 516.
94 *Griswold v. Connecticut*, 381 U.S. 479.
95 Ibid. at 482.
96 Ibid. at 522.
97 *Munn v. Illinois*, 94 U.S. 113, at 134. (Italics supplied.)
98 *Railway Employees' Department v. Hansen*, 351 U.S. 225 (1956).

THE BULWARK

The Supreme Court of the United States of America—which Woodrow Wilson reviewed as "the balance wheel of our whole constitutional system . . . a vehicle of the Nation's life . . ."[99]—may be perpetually steeped in controversy; it may not always have exercised all of its power, or exercised it wisely when it did; it may on occasion have gone well beyond its presumed functions; it may have deliberately avoided issues that might have proved to be potentially troublesome; it may not always have been able to make its decisions "stick"; and there may well be considerable room for improvement. No institution of government can be devised by human beings that will be satisfactory to all people at all times. The Court is much better at saying what the government may *not* do than in prescribing what the government must do and how it must go about doing it. Indeed, the Court should resolutely shun prescriptive policy-making.[100] It has quite enough to do in statutory and constitutional application and interpretation. To reiterate the second Mr. Justice Harlan's often-quoted admonition: "The Constitution is not a panacea for every blot upon the public welfare; nor should this Court, ordained as a judicial body, be thought of as a general haven for reform movements."[101] Paraphrasing Professor Freund, the question is not whether the Court can do everything, but whether it can do something. Of course, it can escape neither controversy nor criticism—nor should it. In Mr. Justice Holmes's oft-quoted words: "We are very quiet there, but it is the quiet of a storm center, as we all know." As an institution at once legal, political, governmental, and human, the Court possesses both the assets and the liabilities that attend these descriptive characteristics.

Yet, when all is said and done, the Court, at the head of the United States judiciary, is not only the most fascinating, the most influential, and the most powerful judicial body in the world, it is also the "living voice of [the] Constitution," as Lord Bryce, who knew America well indeed, once phrased it. As such it is both arbiter and educator and, in essence, represents the sole solution short of anarchy under the American system of government as we know it. It acts, in the words of one commentator, "as the instrument of national moral values that have not been able to find other

---

[99] *Constitutional Government in the United States* (New York: Columbia University Press, 1907), p. 142.
[100] On this point see Alexander M. Bickel's *The Supreme Court and the Idea of Progress* (New York: Harper & Row, 1970), *passim.*
[101] *Reynolds v. Sims,* 377 U.S. 533 (1964), dissenting opinion, at 624.

377

governmental expression"[102]—assuming, of course, that it functions within its authorized sphere of constitutional adjudication. In that role it operates "as the collective conscience of a sovereign people."[103] And, as Alexander Meiklejohn once observed, no other institution "is more deeply decisive in its effect upon our understanding of ourselves and our government."[104] It defines values and proclaims principles. It is a corrective force in our life.

Beyond that, moreover, the Supreme Court of the United States is the chief protector of the Constitution, of its great system of balances—as *United States v. Nixon* proved again in 1974—and of the peoples' liberties. It is the greatest institutional safeguard we possess. It may have retreated, even yielded to pressures now and then, but without its vigilance our liberties would scarcely have survived. Few have sounded this call more eloquently than did Mr. Justice Black in his memorable opinion for the Court in *Chambers v. Florida:*

> Under our constitutional system, courts stand against any winds that blow as havens of refuge for those who might otherwise suffer because they are helpless, weak, outnumbered, or because they are non-conforming victims of prejudice and public excitement. No higher duty, no more solemn responsibility, rests upon this Court, than that of translating into living law and maintaining this constitutional shield deliberately planned and inscribed for the benefit of every human being subject to our Constitution—of whatever race, creed, or persuasion.[105]

Within the limits of procedure and deference to the presumption of constitutionality of legislation, the Court—our "sober second thought," as Professor Charles Black calls it[106]—is the natural forum in our society for the individual and for the small group. The Court's essential function, as Mr. Chief Justice Warren told the Centennial Convocation of the New York School of Law, "is to act as the final arbiter of minority rights."[107] It thereby serves as a primary rather than an auxiliary check. In Mr. Justice Douglas's words: "The people should know that when filibusters occupy the forums,

[102] Anthony Lewis, *The New York Times Magazine*, June 17, 1962, p. 28.
[103] Judge J. Shelby Wright, "The Role of the Courts: Conscience of a Sovereign People," 29 *The Reporter* 5 (September 29, 1963).
[104] *Free Speech and Its Relation to Self-Government* (New York: Harper & Brothers, 1948), p. 32.
[105] 309 U.S. 227 (1940), at 241.
[106] Charles L. Black, Jr., *The People and the Court: Judicial Review in a Democracy* (New York: The Macmillan Co., 1960), p. 12.
[107] New York City, October 3, 1968.

when oppressions are great, when the clash of authority between the individual and the State is severe, they can still get justice in the courts."[108] It represents a power that so astute an observer of the American scene as Alexis de Toqueville viewed as "one of the most powerful barriers that have ever been devised against tyranny of political assemblies."[109]

Thus the Court must be prepared to say "no" to the government—which Madison, the father of the Bill of Rights, hoped fervently it would always do. There are many citizens—indeed, most citizens, once they have given the problem the careful thought it merits—who will feel far more secure in the knowledge of *that* guardianship, one generally characterized by common sense, than if it were primarily exercised by the far more easily pressured, more impulsive, and more emotion-charged legislative or executive branches. Far too easily do these two yield to the politically expedient and the popular—for they are close, indeed, to what Judge Learned Hand called "the pressure of public hysteria, public panic, and public greed." Hence—and again in Earl Warren's words—the Court must always stand ready to advance the rights of . . . minority interests if the executive and the legislative branches falter."[110] His Court did just that, moving dramatically from deference to the prerogatives of the other two branches and of the states to aggressive protection of the constitutional rights of the individual —as the Court perceived these.

The Court, which often has had to act as a "moral goad" to public panic and public greed, is neither engaged nor interested in a popularity contest— its function is *not* one of counting constituents. Should the time ever arrive when that is the Court's function, the supreme judicial tribunal will have lost its meaning. "[W]e have no constituency," mused Warren on the last day of his sixteen-year tenure as Chief Justice of the United States, just prior to swearing in his successor, Warren Earl Burger. "We serve no minority. We serve only the public interest as we see it, guided only by the Constitution and our own conscience."[111]

Even if a transfer of that guardianship to other institutions of government were theoretically desirable, which few thoughtful citizens believe, it would be politically impossible. "Do we desire constitutional questions," asked Charles Evans Hughes when off the bench, in his fine book on the Court, ". . . to be determined by political assemblies and partisan divi-

---

[108] *Bell v. Maryland*, 378 U.S. 226 (1964), concurring opinion, at 242–43.
[109] *Democracy in America* (New York: Alfred A. Knopf, 1948), Vol. I, p. 103.
[110] As quoted in *The Philadelphia Inquirer*, October 4, 1968, p. 2.
[111] As quoted in *The New York Times*, June 24, 1969, p. 24.

sion?"[112] The response must be a ringing "no!" In the 1955 Godkins Lectures, which he was preparing to deliver at Harvard University when death intervened, Mr. Justice Jackson expressed this conviction eloquently and ably:

> The people have seemed to feel that the Supreme Court, whatever its defects, is still the most detached, dispassionate, and trustworthy custodian that our system affords for the translation of abstract into concrete constitutional commands.[113]

And we may well agree with Thomas Reed Powell that the logic of American constitutional law is the common sense of the Supreme Court.

As a commentary on the point, that distinguished observer of Court and Constitution reported an incident that took place after the turn of the century in a debate on the floor of the United States Senate between Senators John C. Spooner of Wisconsin and "Pitchfork Ben" Tillman of South Carolina. At one juncture of the proceedings, Tillman exclaimed: "I am tired of hearing what the Supreme Court says. What I want to get at is the common sense of the matter." Rejoined Spooner: "I too am seeking the common sense of the matter. But, as for me, I prefer the common sense of the Supreme Court of the United States to that of the Senator from South Carolina."[114]

In the long run common sense has always served the Supreme Court of the United States well in its ceaseless striving, as a voice of reason, to maintain the blend of change and continuity which is the *sine qua non* for desirable stability in the governmental process of a democracy. In that role it will live in history.

[112] *The Supreme Court of the United States* (New York: Columbia University Press, 1928), p. 236.
[113] Jackson, op. cit. p. 23.
[114] "The Logic and Rhetoric of Constitutional Law," 15 *Journal of Philosophy, Psychology, and Scientific Method* 656 (1918).

Appendices

Appendix A

MEMBERS OF THE SUPREME COURT OF THE UNITED STATES†

Name	Place of Birth	Year of Birth	State App't From	Appointed by President	(A) Judicial Oath Taken	Date Service Terminated	(B) Service Terminated By:	(C) Years of Service	Year of Death
Chief Justices:									
Jay, John	N.Y.	1745	N.Y.	Washington	(a) Oct. 19, 1789	June 29, 1795	resigned	5	1829
Rutledge, John	So. Car.	1739	So. Car.	Washington	Aug. 12, 1795	Dec. 15, 1795	rejected	(D) 0	1800
Ellsworth, Oliver	Conn.	1745	Conn.	Washington	Mar. 8, 1796	Dec. 15, 1800	resigned	4	1807
Marshall, John	Va.	1755	Va.	Adams, J.	Feb. 4, 1801	July 6, 1835	Death	34	1835
Taney, Roger Brooke	Md.	1777	Md.	Jackson	Mar. 28, 1836	Oct. 12, 1864	Death	28	1864
Chase, Salmon Portland	N.H.	1808	Ohio	Lincoln	Dec. 15, 1864	May 7, 1873	Death	8	1873
Waite, Morrison Remick	Conn.	1816	Ohio	Grant	Mar. 4, 1874	Mar. 23, 1888	Death	14	1888
Fuller, Melville Weston	Maine	1833	Illinois	Cleveland	Oct. 8, 1888	July 4, 1910	Death	21	1910
White, Edward Douglass	La.	1845	La.	Taft	Dec. 19, 1910	May 19, 1921	Death	(D)10	1921
Taft, William Howard	Ohio	1857	Conn.	Harding	July 11, 1921	Feb. 3, 1930	retired	8	1930
Hughes, Charles Evans	N.Y.	1862	N.Y.	Hoover	Feb. 24, 1930	June 30, 1941	RETIRED	(D)11	1948
Stone, Harlan Fiske	N.H.	1872	N.Y.	Roosevelt, F.	July 3, 1941	Apr. 22, 1946	Death	4	1946
Vinson, Frederick Moore	Ky.	1890	Ky.	Truman	June 24, 1946	Sept. 8, 1953	Death	7	1953
Warren, Earl	Calif.	1891	Calif.	Eisenhower	Oct. 5, 1953	June 23, 1969	RETIRED	15	1974
Burger, Warren Earl	Minn.	1907	Va.	Nixon	June 23, 1969				
Associate Justices:									
Rutledge, John	So. Car.	1739	So. Car.	Washington	(c) Feb. 15, 1790	Mar. 5, 1791	resigned	1	1800
Cushing, William	Mass.	1732	Mass.	Washington	(b) Feb. 2, 1790	Sept. 13, 1810	Death	20	1810
Wilson, James	Scotland	1742	Penn.	Washington	(b) Oct. 5, 1789	Aug. 21, 1798	Death	8	1798
Blair, John	Va.	1732	Va.	Washington	(c) Feb. 2, 1790	Jan. 27, 1796	resigned	5	1800
Iredell, James	England	1751	No. Car.	Washington	(b) May 13, 1790	Oct. 20, 1799	Death	9	1799
Johnson, Thomas	Md.	1732	Md.	Washington	(c) Aug. 6, 1792	Feb. 1, 1793	resigned	0	1819
Paterson, William	Ireland	1745	N.J.	Washington	(a) Mar. 11, 1793	Sept. 9, 1806	Death	13	1806
Chase, Samuel	Md.	1741	Md.	Washington	Feb. 4, 1796	June 19, 1811	Death	15	1811
Washington, Bushrod	Va.	1762	Va.	Adams, J.	(c) Feb. 4, 1799	Nov. 26, 1829	Death	30	1829
Moore, Alfred	No. Car.	1755	No. Car.	Adams, J.	(c) Aug. 9, 1800	Jan. 26, 1804	resigned	3	1810
Johnson, William	So. Car.	1771	So. Car.	Jefferson	May 7, 1804	Aug. 4, 1834	Death	30	1834
Livingston, Henry Brockholst	N.Y.	1757	N.Y.	Jefferson	Jan. 20, 1807	Mar. 18, 1823	Death	16	1823
Todd, Thomas	Va.	1765	Ky.	Jefferson	(a) May 4, 1807	Feb. 7, 1826	Death	18	1826
Duvall, Gabriel	Md.	1752	Md.	Madison	(a) Nov 23, 1811	Jan. 14, 1835	resigned	23	1844

Name	Birthplace	Born	President	Term began	Term ended	Reason		
Story, Joseph	Mass.	1779	Madison	(c)Feb. 3, 1812	Sept. 10, 1845	Death	33	1845
Thompson, Smith	N.Y.	1768	Monroe	(b)Sept. 1, 1823	Dec. 18, 1843	Death	20	1843
Trimble, Robert	Va.	1777	Adams, J. Q.	(a)June 16, 1826	Aug. 25, 1828	Death	2	1828
McLean, John	N.J.	1785	Jackson	Jan. 11, 1830	Apr. 4, 1861	Death	31	1861
Baldwin, Henry	Penn.	1780	Jackson	Jan. 18, 1830	Apr. 21, 1844	Death	14	1844
Wayne, James Moore	Georgia	1790	Jackson	Jan. 14, 1835	July 5, 1867	Death	32	1867
Barbour, Philip Pendleton	Va.	1783	Jackson	May 12, 1836	Feb. 25, 1841	Death	4	1841
Catron, John	Penn.	1786	Van Buren	May 1, 1837	May 30, 1865	Death	28	1865
McKinley, John	Va.	1790	Van Buren	(c)Jan. 9, 1838	July 19, 1852	Death	14	1852
Daniel, Peter Vivian	Va.	1784	Van Buren	(c)Jan. 10, 1842	May 31, 1860	Death	18	1860
Nelson, Samuel	N.Y.	1792	Tyler	Feb. 27, 1845	Nov. 28, 1872	retired	27	1873
Woodbury, Levi	N.H.	1789	Polk	(b)Sept. 23, 1845	Sept. 4, 1851	Death	5	1851
Grier, Robert Cooper	Penn.	1794	Polk	Aug. 10, 1846	Jan. 31, 1870	retired	23	1870
Curtis, Benjamin Robbins	Mass.	1809	Fillmore	(b)Oct. 10, 1851	Sept. 30, 1857	resigned	5	1874
Campbell, John Archibald	Georgia	1811	Pierce	(c)Apr. 11, 1853	Apr. 30, 1861	resigned	8	1889
Clifford, Nathan	N.H.	1803	Buchanan	Jan. 21, 1858	July 25, 1881	Death	23	1881
Swayne, Noah Haynes	Va.	1804	Lincoln	Jan. 27, 1862	Jan. 24, 1881	retired	18	1884
Miller, Samuel Freeman	Ky.	1816	Lincoln	July 21, 1862	Oct. 13, 1890	Death	28	1890
Davis, David	Md.	1815	Lincoln	Dec. 10, 1862	Mar. 4, 1877	resigned	14	1886
Field, Stephen Johnson	Conn.	1816	Lincoln	May 20, 1863	Dec. 1, 1897	retired	34	1899
Strong, William	Conn.	1808	Grant	Mar. 14, 1870	Dec. 14, 1880	retired	10	1895
Bradley, Joseph P.	N.J.	1813	Grant	Mar. 23, 1870	Jan. 22, 1892	Death	21	1892
Hunt, Ward	N.Y.	1810	Grant	Jan. 9, 1873	Jan. 27, 1882	disabled	9	1886
Harlan, John Marshall	Ky.	1833	Hayes	Dec. 10, 1877	Oct. 14, 1911	Death	33	1911
Woods, William Burnham	Ohio	1824	Hayes	Jan. 5, 1881	May 14, 1887	Death	6	1887
Matthews, Stanley	Ohio	1824	Garfield	May 17, 1881	Mar. 22, 1889	Death	7	1889
Gray, Horace	Mass.	1828	Arthur	Jan. 9, 1882	Sept. 15, 1902	Death	20	1902
Blatchford, Samuel	N.Y.	1820	Arthur	Apr. 3, 1882	July 7, 1893	Death	11	1893
Lamar, Lucius Quintus C.	Georgia	1825	Cleveland	Jan. 18, 1888	Jan. 23, 1893	Death	5	1893
Brewer, David Josiah	Asia Minor	1837	Harrison	Jan. 6, 1890	Mar. 28, 1910	Death	20	1910
Brown, Henry Billings	Mass.	1836	Harrison	Jan. 5, 1891	May 28, 1906	retired	15	1913
Shiras, George, Jr.	Penn.	1832	Harrison	Oct. 10, 1892	Feb. 23, 1903	retired	10	1924
Jackson, Howell Edmunds	Tenn.	1832	Cleveland	Mar. 4, 1893	Aug. 8, 1895	Death	2	1895
White, Edward Douglass	La.	1845	Cleveland	Mar. 12, 1894	Dec. 18, 1910	promoted	16	1921
Peckham, Rufus Wheeler	N.Y.	1838	McKinley	Jan. 6, 1896	Oct. 24, 1909	Death	13	1909
McKenna, Joseph	Penn.	1843	Roosevelt, T.	Jan. 26, 1898	Jan. 5, 1925	retired	26	1926
Holmes, Oliver Wendell	Mass.	1841	Roosevelt, T.	Dec. 8, 1902	Jan. 12, 1932	retired	29	1935
Day, William Rufus	Ohio	1849	Roosevelt, T.	Mar. 2, 1903	Nov. 13, 1922	retired	19	1923

MEMBERS OF THE SUPREME COURT OF THE UNITED STATES (Continued)

Name	Place of Birth	Year of Birth	State App't From	Appointed by President	(A) Judicial Oath Taken	Date Service Terminated	(B) Service Terminated By:	(C) Years of Service	Year of Death
Moody, William Henry	Mass.	1853	Mass.	Roosevelt, T.	Dec. 17, 1906	Nov. 20, 1910	disabled	3	1917
Lurton, Horace Harmon	Ky.	1844	Tenn.	Taft	Jan. 3, 1910	July 12, 1914	Death	4	1914
Hughes, Charles Evans	N.Y.	1862	N.Y.	Taft	Oct. 10, 1910	June 10, 1916	resigned	5	1948
Van Devanter, Willis	Indiana	1859	Wyo.	Taft	Jan. 3, 1911	June 2, 1937	RETIRED	26	1941
Lamar, Joseph Rucker	Georgia	1857	Georgia	Taft	Jan. 3, 1911	Jan. 2, 1916	Death	4	1916
Pitney, Mahlon	N.J.	1858	N.J.	Taft	Mar. 18, 1912	Dec. 31, 1922	disabled	10	1924
McReynolds, James Clark	Ky.	1862	Tenn.	Wilson	Oct. 12, 1914	Jan. 31, 1941	RETIRED	26	1946
Brandeis, Louis Dembitz	Ky.	1856	Mass.	Wilson	June 5, 1916	Feb. 13, 1939	RETIRED	22	1941
Clarke, John Hessin	Ohio	1857	Ohio	Wilson	Oct. 9, 1916	Sept. 18, 1922	resigned	5	1945
Sutherland, George	England	1862	Utah	Harding	Oct. 2, 1922	Jan. 17, 1938	RETIRED	15	1942
Butler, Pierce	Minn.	1866	Minn.	Harding	Jan. 2, 1923	Nov. 16, 1939	Death	16	1939
Sanford, Edward Terry	Tenn.	1865	Tenn.	Harding	Feb. 19, 1923	Mar. 8, 1930	Death	7	1930
Stone, Harlan Fiske	N.H.	1872	N.Y.	Coolidge	Mar. 2, 1925	July 2, 1941	promoted	16	1946
Roberts, Owen Josephus	Penn.	1875	Penn.	Hoover	June 2, 1930	July 31, 1945	RESIGNED	15	1955
Cardozo, Benjamin Nathan	N.Y.	1870	N.Y.	Hoover	Mar. 14, 1932	July 9, 1938	Death	6	1938
Black, Hugo Lafayette	Ala.	1886	Ala.	Roosevelt, F.	Aug. 19, 1937	Sept. 17, 1971	RETIRED	34	1971
Reed, Stanley Forman	Ky.	1884	Ky.	Roosevelt, F.	Jan. 31, 1938	Feb. 25, 1957	RETIRED	19	
Frankfurter, Felix	Austria	1882	Mass.	Roosevelt, F.	Jan. 30, 1939	Aug. 28, 1962	RETIRED	23	1965
Douglas, William Orville	Minn.	1898	Conn.	Roosevelt, F.	Apr. 17, 1939				
Murphy, Frank	Mich.	1890	Mich.	Roosevelt, F.	Feb. 5, 1940	July 19, 1949	Death	9	1949
Byrnes, James Francis	So. Car.	1879	So. Car.	Roosevelt, F.	July 8, 1941	Oct. 3, 1942	resigned	1	1972
Jackson, Robert Houghwout	Penn.	1892	N.Y.	Roosevelt, F.	July 11, 1941	Oct. 9, 1954	Death	13	1954
Rutledge, Wiley Blount	Ky.	1894	Iowa	Roosevelt, F.	Feb. 15, 1943	Sept. 10, 1949	Death	6	1949
Burton, Harold Hitz	Mass.	1888	Ohio	Truman	Oct. 1, 1945	Oct. 13, 1958	RETIRED	13	1964
Clark, Thomas Campbell	Texas	1899	Texas	Truman	Aug. 24, 1949	June 12, 1967	RETIRED	17	
Minton, Sherman	Indiana	1890	Indiana	Truman	Oct. 12, 1949	Oct. 15, 1956	RETIRED	7	1965
Harlan, John Marshall	Illinois	1899	N.Y.	Eisenhower	Mar. 28, 1955	Sept. 23, 1971	RETIRED	16	1971
Brennan, William Joseph, Jr.	N.J.	1906	N.J.	Eisenhower	Oct. 16, 1956				
Whittaker, Charles Evans	Kansas	1901	Mo.	Eisenhower	Mar. 25, 1957	Mar. 31, 1962	DISABLED*	5	1973
Stewart, Potter	Mich.	1915	Ohio	Eisenhower	Oct. 14, 1958				
White, Byron Raymond	Colo.	1917	Colo.	Kennedy	Apr. 16, 1962				
Goldberg, Arthur Joseph	Illinois	1908	Illinois	Kennedy	Oct. 1, 1962	July 25, 1965	resigned	2	
Fortas, Abe	Tenn.	1910	Tenn.	Johnson, L.	Oct. 4, 1965	May 14, 1969	resigned	3	

Marshall, Thurgood	Md.	1908	N.Y.	Johnson, L.	Nixon	Oct. 2, 1967
Blackmun, Harry A.	Illinois	1908	Minn.	Nixon		June 9, 1970
Powell, Lewis Franklin, Jr.	Va.	1907	Va.	Nixon		Jan. 7, 1972
Rehnquist, William Hubbs	Wisc.	1924	Ariz.	Nixon		Jan. 7, 1972

NOTES: The acceptance of the appointment and commission by the appointee, as evidenced by the taking of the prescribed oaths, is here implied; otherwise the individual is not carried on this list of the Members of the Court. Examples: Robert Hanson Harrison is not carried, as a letter from President Washington of February 9, 1790, states Harrison declined to serve. Neither is Edwin M. Stanton, who died before he could take the necessary steps toward becoming a Member of the Court. Chief Justice Rutledge is included because he took his oaths, presided over the August Term of 1795, and his name appears on two opinions of the Court for that term.

(A) The date a Member of the Court took his judicial oath (the Judiciary Act provided "That the Justice of the Supreme Court, and the district judges, before they proceed to execute the duties of their respective offices, shall take the following oath . . .") is here used as the date of the beginning of his service, for until that oath is taken he is not vested with the prerogatives of his office. Dates without small-letter references are taken from the Minutes of the Court or from the original oath which is in the Clerk's file. The small letter (a) denotes the date is from the Minutes of some other court: (b) from some other unquestionable authority; (c) from authority that is questionable, and better authority would be appreciated.

(B) Explanation of terms used in identifying nature of termination of services:

1. A Member of the Court of 70 or more years of age and of 10 or more years of service who, pursuant to the Act of April 10, 1869, on or subsequent acts, retired or resigned and continued to receive the salary which he was receiving when he retired or resigned, is here carried as "retired."

2. A Member retiring since the Act of March 1, 1937 (50 Stat. 24) is granted the same privileges with regard to retiring, instead of resigning, that are granted to judges other than Justices of the Supreme Court. He may be assigned to perform such judicial duties as he is willing to undertake, and during the remainder of his lifetime continues to receive the salary of the office. Such Member is here carried as "RETIRED."

3. A Member of less than 70 years of age or having less than 10 years of service, who resigned and who thereafter did not continue to draw pay based on his age or service, or who resigned before the Act of April 10, 1869, became effective, as Justice Duvall did, is here carried as "resigned."

4. A Member of 70 or more years of age and 10 or more years of service, resigning since the Act of March 1, 1937, who continues to receive the salary he was receiving when he resigned is here carried as "RESIGNED."

5. Justices Hunt, Moody, and Pitney, who retired under Special Acts, are here carried as "disabled."

6. A Member retiring for disability under the general provisions of 28 U.S. Code 372 is here carried as "DISABLED."

(C) All calculations regarding ages or years of service are based on the age or service of the individual on his latest anniversary. Example: Chief Justice Rutledge actually served from August 12, 1795, to December 15, 1795, and is here carried as "0" years of service; and Mr. Justice Blair served from February 2, 1790 to his resignation on January 27, 1796—5 years, 11 months, and 25 days—but is here carried as 5 years.

(D) For service as Associate Justice, see below.

* Resigned September 30, 1965.

† ADAPTED FROM A TABLE REVISED BY FRANK M. HEPLER, MARSHAL OF THE SUPREME COURT OF THE UNITED STATES, 1972.

Appendix B

TABLE OF SUCCESSION OF THE JUSTICES OF THE SUPREME COURT OF THE UNITED STATES †
Showing Years of Active Service on the Court

Judiciary Act of 1789 provided for a Chief Justice and 5 Associate Justices

Year	(Chief Justice)			(Associate Justices)		
1789 1790	John Jay 1789-1795	John Rutledge 1789-1791	William Cushing 1789-1810	James Iredell 1790-1799	James Wilson 1789-1798	John Blair 1789-1796
1800	John Rutledge 1795 / Oliver Ellsworth 1796-1799 / John Marshall 1801-1835	Thomas Johnson 1791-1793 / William Paterson 1793-1806		Alfred Moore 1799-1804 / William Johnson 1804-1834	Bushrod Washington 1798-1829	Samuel Chase 1796-1811
1810		Henry B. Livingston 1806-1823	Joseph Story 1811-1845			Gabriel Duval 1811-1836
1820		Smith Thompson 1823-1843				
1830					Henry Baldwin 1830-1844	
	Roger B. Taney 1836-1864			James M. Wayne 1835-1867		Philip P. Barbour 1836-1841
1840		Samuel Nelson 1845-1872	Levi Woodbury 1846-1851		Robert C. Grier 1846-1870	Peter V. Daniel 1841-1860
1850			Benjamin R. Curtis 1851-1857 / Nathan Clifford 1858-1881			
1860	Salmon P. Chase 1864-1873					Samuel F. Miller 1862-1890
1870	Morrison R. Waite 1874-1888	Ward Hunt 1872-1882			William Strong 1870-1880	
1880	Melville W. Fuller 1888-1910	Samuel Blatchford 1882-1893	Horace Gray 1881-1902		William B. Woods 1880-1887 / Lucius Q. C. Lamar 1888-1893	Henry B. Brown 1890-1906
1890		Edward D. White J 1894 CJ 1910-1921			Howell E. Jackson 1893-1895 / Rufus W. Peckham 1895-1909	
1900			Oliver Wendell Holmes 1902-1932			William H. Moody 1906-1910
1910	Edward D. White J 1894 CJ 1910-1921	Willis Van Devanter 1910-1937			Horace H. Lurton 1909-1914 / James C. McReynolds 1914-1941	Joseph R. Lamar 1910-1916 / Louis D. Brandeis 1916-1939
1920	William H. Taft 1921-1930		Benjamin N. Cardozo 1932-1938 / Felix Frankfurter 1939-1962			
1930	Charles E. Hughes 1930-1941					
1940	Harlan F. Stone J 1925 CJ 1941-1946	Hugo L. Black 1937-1971			James F. Byrnes 1941-1942 / Wiley Rutledge 1943-1949 / Sherman Minton 1949-1956	William O. Douglas 1939
1950	Fred M. Vinson 1946-1953					
	Earl Warren 1953-1969				William J. Brennan 1956	
1960			Arthur J. Goldberg 1962-1965 / Abe Fortas 1965-1969			
1970	Warren E. Burger 1969	Lewis F. Powell, Jr. 1972	Harry A. Blackmun 1970			
1980						

Act of July 23, 1866, provided for reduction of the Court to 7 members as vacancies should occur.

† ADAPTED FROM A TABLE REVISED BY FRANK M. HEPLER, MARSHAL OF THE SUPREME COURT OF

TABLE OF SUCCESSION OF THE JUSTICES OF THE SUPREME COURT OF THE UNITED STATES

Column 1	Column 2	Column 3	Column 4	Column 5	Column 6	Year
						1789
						1790
Act of February 24, 1807, provided for increase of the Court to 7 members.						
						1800
Thomas Todd 1807-1826		Act of March 3, 1837, provided for increase of the Court to 9 members.	Act of March 3, 1863, provided for increase of the Court to 10 members.	Act of April 10, 1869, provided for increase of the Court to 9 members.		1810
Robert Trimble 1826-1828						1820
John McLean 1829-1861						1830
	John Catron 1837-1865	John McKinley 1837-1852	Act of March 3, 1866, provided for reduction of the Court to 7 members as vacancies should occur. (Actually the Court fell to 8.)			
						1840
						1850
		John A. Campbell 1853-1861				
						1860
Noah H. Swayne 1862-1881	Act of July 23, 1866, provided for reduction of the Court to 7 members as vacancies should occur.	David Davis 1862-1877	Stephen J. Field 1863-1897	Act of July 23, 1866, provided for reduction of the Court to 7 members as vacancies should occur.	Joseph P. Bradley 1870-1892	1870
		John M. Harlan 1877-1911				1880
Stanley Matthews 1881-1889						
David J. Brewer 1889-1910						1890
					George Shiras, Jr. 1892-1903	
			Joseph McKenna 1898-1925			1900
					William R. Day 1903-1922	
Charles E. Hughes 1910-1916						1910
		Mahlon Pitney 1912-1922				
John H. Clarke 1916-1922						1920
George Sutherland 1922-1938		Edward T. Sanford 1923-1930	Harlan F. Stone J 1925 CJ 1941-1946	Pierce Butler 1922-1939		
		Owen J. Roberts 1930-1945				1930
Stanley F. Reed 1938-1957				Frank Murphy 1940-1949		1940
			Robert H. Jackson 1941-1954			
		Harold H. Burton 1945-1958		Tom C. Clark 1949-1967		1950
Charles E. Whittaker 1957-1962		Potter Stewart 1959	John M. Harlan 1955-1971			
Byron R. White 1962						1960
				Thurgood Marshall 1967		
						1970
			Wm. H. Rehnquist 1972			
						1980

THE UNITED STATES, 1972.

Four
Selected
Bibliographies

ADMINISTRATIVE JUSTICE

(*Administrative law and agencies in the United States;*
independent regulatory commissions.)

Association of American Law Schools, *Selected Essays on Constitutional Law* (Foundation Press, 1938).

Cushman, R. E., *The Independent Regulatory Commissions* (Oxford, 1941).

Davis, K. C., *Administrative Law and Government* (West, 1960).

———, *Discretionary Justice: A Preliminary Inquiry* (Louisiana State U., 1969).

Dickinson, J., *Administrative Justice and the Supremacy of Law* (Russell, 1959).

Fesler, J. W., *Area and Administration* (U. of Alabama, 1949).

Frank, J. F., *If Men Were Angels* (Harper, 1942).

Friendly, H. J., *The Federal Administration Agencies: The Need for Definition of Standards* (Harvard, 1962).

Gellhorn, E., *Administrative Law and Process in a Nutshell* (West, 1960).

Gellhorn, W., *Federal Administrative Proceedings* (Johns Hopkins, 1941).

Jaffe, L., and N. Nathanson, *Administrative Law: Cases and Materials* (Little, Brown, 1961).

Landis, J. M., *The Administrative Process* (Yale, 1938).

Langallatag, A., *The Department of Justice of the United States* (Johns Hopkins, 1927).

Lorch, R. S., *Democratic Justice and Administrative Law* (Wayne State U., 1969).

McFarland, C., *Judicial Control of the F.T.C. and the I.C.C.* (Harvard, 1933).

Mayers, L., *The American Legal System*, rev. ed. (Harper, 1964).

Nichols, P., *Power of Eminent Domain* (Boston Book Co., 1909).

Nonet, P., *Administrative Justice: Advocacy and Change in Government Agencies* (Sage, 1969).

Paulson, M. C. (ed.), *Legal Institutions Today and Tomorrow* (Columbia, 1959).

Pennock, J. R., *Administration and the Rule of Law* (Rinehart, 1941).

Pound, R., *Administrative Law: Its Growth, Procedure, Significance* (U. of Pittsburgh, 1942).

Schwartz, B., *An Introduction to American Administrative Law*, 2nd ed. (Oceana, 1962).

———, and H. W. R. Wade, *Legal Control of Government: Administrative Law in Britain and the United States* (Oxford, 1972).

———, *The Professor and the Commissions* (Knopf, 1959).

Shapiro, M., *The Supreme Court and Administrative Agencies* (Free Press, 1968).

APPORTIONMENT, GERRYMANDERING, AND REDISTRICTING

Bain, C. W., *Annexation in Virginia: The Use of the Judicial Process for Readjusting City-County Boundaries* (U. of Virginia, 1966).

Baker, G. E., *The Reapportionment Revolution: Representation, Political Power, and the Supreme Court* (Random House, 1966).

———, *Rural Versus Urban Political Power* (Random House, 1955).

———, *State Constitutions: Reapportionment*, rev. ed. (National Municipal League, 1962).

Boyd, W. J. D., *Changing Patterns of Apportionment* (National Municipal Review, 1965).

Bushnell, E. B. (ed.), *Impact of Reapportionment on the Thirteen Western States* (U. of Utah, 1970).

Claude, R., *The Supreme Court and the Electoral Process* (Johns Hopkins, 1970).

Commission on Intergovernmental Relations, *Apportionment of State Legislatures* (U.S. G.P.O., 1962).

Congressional Quarterly, *Representation and Apportionment* (C.Q., 1966).

Cortner, R. C., *The Apportionment Cases* (U. of Tennessee, 1970).

de Grazia, A., *Apportionment and Representative Government* (Praeger, 1963).

Dixon, R. G., Jr., *Democratic Representation* (Oxford, 1968).

Goldwin, R. A. (ed.), *Representation and Misrepresentation* (Rand McNally, 1968).

Graham, G. S., *One Man, One Vote: Baker v. Carr and the American Levelers* (Little, Brown, 1972).

Hacker, A., *Congressional Districting: The Issue of Equal Representation*, rev. ed., (Brookings, 1964).

Hamilton, H. (ed.), *Legislative Apportionment: Key to Power* (Harper & Row, 1964).

Hanson, R., *The Political Thicket: Reapportionment and Constitutional Democracy* (Prentice-Hall, 1963).

Havard, W. C., and L. C. Beth, *The Politics of Mis-Representation* (Atherton, 1962).

Jewell, M. E. (ed.), *The Politics of Reapportionment* (Atherton, 1962).

Larson, J. E., *Reapportionment and the Court* (U. of Alabama, 1962).

Lee, C. B. T., *One Man, One Vote: WMCA and the Struggle for Equal Representation* (Scribner's, 1967).

McKay, R. B., *Reapportionment: The Law and Politics of Equal Representation* (20th Century Fund, 1965).

———, *Reapportionment and the Federal Analogy* (National Municipal Review, 1962).

National Municipal Review, *Court Decisions on Legislative Reapportionment* (National Municipal Review, 1962).

O'Rourke, T. B., *Reapportionment* (A.E.I., 1972).

Polsby, N. W. (ed.), *Reapportionment in the 1970s* (U. of California, 1971).

Schubert, G. A. (ed.), *Reapportionment* (Scribner's, 1965).

Taper, B., *Gomillion v. Lightfoot: Apartheid in Alabama* (McGraw-Hill, 1962).

———, *Gomillion v. Lightfoot: The Tuskegee Gerrymander Case* (McGraw-Hill, 1962).

Wieck, W. M., *The Guarantee Clause of the United States Constitution* (Cornell, 1972).

CASEBOOKS–AMERICAN CONSTITUTIONAL LAW AND CONSTITUTIONAL HISTORY

Aqueduct Books (eds.), *Decisions of the United States Supreme Court, 1963–1964 Term ff* (Aqueduct, 1965 ff).

Barrett, E. L., and P. W. Bruton, *Constitutional Law: Cases and Materials*, 4th ed. (Foundation Press, 1973).

Bartholomew, P. C., *Ruling American Constitutional Law* (Littlefield, Adams, 1970).

Berman, H. J., and W. R. Greiner, *The Nature and Functions of Law*, 3rd ed. (Foundation Press, 1972).

Berns, W. F., *Constitutional Cases in American Government* (Cornell, 1963).

Cahil, P. V., and R. J. Steamer, *The Constitution: Cases and Comments* (Ronald, 1959).

Chase, H. W., and C. R. Ducat, *Constitutional Interpretation* (West, 1974).

Conant, M., *The Constitution and Capitalism* (West, 1974).

Dodd, W. F., *Cases and Materials on Constitutional Law* (West, 1954).

Dowling, N. T., *Cases on Constitutional Law*, 6th ed. (Foundation Press, 1959).

———, and R. A. Edwards, *American Constitutional Law* (Foundation Press, 1954).

———, and G. Gunther, *Constitutional Law*, 7th ed. (Foundation Press, 1968).

Evans, L. B., *Cases on American Constitutional Law*, 6th ed. (Callaghan, 1952).

Fairman, C., *American Constitutional Decisions* (Holt, 1950).

Fenwick, C. G., *Evans Cases on Constitutional Law*, 7th ed. (Callaghan, 1957).

Forkosch, M. D., *Constitutional Law*, 2nd ed. (Foundation Press, 1969).

Frank, J. P., *Cases and Materials on Constitutional Law*, rev. ed. (McGraw-Hill, 1952).

Freund, P. A., *et al.*, *Constitutional Law* (Little, Brown, 1961).

Friedelbaum, S. H., *Contemporary Constitutional Law* (Houghton Mifflin, 1972).

Garrity, J. A. (ed.), *Quarrels that Have Shaped the Constitution* (Harper & Row, 1964).

Grad, F. P., *Environmental Law: Sources and Problems* (Bender, 1972).

Grossman, J. B., and R. S. Wells (eds.), *Constitutional Law and Judicial Policy Making* (Wiley, 1972).

Gunther, G., and N. T. Dowling, *Constitutional Law: Cases and Materials*, 8th ed. (Foundation Press, 1970).

Hall, J. P., *Cases on Constitutional Law* (West, 1913).

Hare, J. I. C., *American Constitutional Law* (Brown, 1889).

Heller, F. H., *Introduction to American Constitutional Law* (Harper, 1952).

Jackson, P. E., *Dissent in the Supreme Court: A Chronology* (U. of Oklahoma, 1969).

Jones, R. W., *The Law of Journalism* (Washington Law Book Co., 1940).

Kauper, P. G., *Constitutional Law–Cases and Materials* (Little, Brown, 1961).

Ketcham, O. W., and M. G. Paulsen, *Cases and Materials Relating to Juvenile Courts* (Foundation Press, 1967).

Kutler, S. I., *The Supreme Court and the Constitution: Readings in American Constitutional History* (Houghton Mifflin, 1969).

Lockhart, W. B., Y. Kamisar, and J. H. Choper, (eds.), *American Constitutional Law*, 4th ed. (West, 1975).

———, *Cases and Materials on the American Constitution*, 4th ed. (West, 1975).

———, *Dodd's Cases on Constitutional Law* (West, 1962).

387

Mason, A. T., and W. B. Beaney, *American Constitutional Law: Introductory Essays and Selected Cases*, 5th ed. (Prentice-Hall, 1972).

McKay, R. B. (ed.), *The American Constitutional Law Reader* (Oceana, 1958).

Mendelson, W., *The Constitution and the Supreme Court*, 2nd ed. (Dodd, Mead, 1965).

Mishkin, P. J., and C. Morris, *On Laws and Courts: An Introduction to Judicial Development of Case and Statute Study* (Foundation Press, 1965).

Pollak, L. H. (ed.), *The Constitution and the Supreme Court* (Meridian, 1965).

Polsky, S. (ed.), *Medico-Legal Reader* (Oceana, 1956).

Pritchett, C. H., *American Constitutional Issues* (McGraw-Hill, 1962).

————, and A. F. Westin (eds.), *The Third Branch of Government* (Harcourt, Brace & World, 1963).

Rosenblum, V. G., and A. D. Castberg, *Cases on Constitutional Law: Political Roles of the Supreme Court* (Dorsey, 1973).

Saye, A. B., *Cases and Materials on Constitutional Law*, 2nd ed. (Callaghan, 1974).

Schechter, A. H., *Contemporary Constitutional Issues* (McGraw-Hill, 1972).

Schmidhauser, J. R., *Constitutional Law in the Political Process* (Rand-McNally, 1963).

Schwartz, B., *American Constitutional Law* (Cambridge, 1955).

Scott, J. B., *Judicial Settlement of Controversies Between States of the American Union* (Clarendon, 1918).

Shapiro, M., and D. S. Hobbs, *The Politics of Constitutional Law* (Winthrop, 1974).

Shuman, S. I., and N. D. West, *American Law: An Introductory Survey of Some Principles, Cases, and Text* (Wayne State U., 1971).

Sigler, J. A., *Courts and Public Policy: Cases and Essays* (Dorsey, 1969).

Spaeth, H. J., *The Warren Court: Cases and Commentary* (Chandler, 1966).

Swisher, C. B., *Historic Decisions of the Supreme Court* (Toronto, 1958).

Thayer, J. B., *Cases on Constitutional Law* (Macmillan, 1959).

Tresolini, R. J., *Justice and the Supreme Court* (Lippincott, 1963).

————, *American Constitutional Law*, 3rd ed. (Macmillan, 1970).

————, *Constitutional Decisions in American Government* (Lippincott, 1965).

Tucker, E. W., *Text, Cases and Problems on Legal Regulation of the Environment* (West, 1972).

————, *Text, Cases and Problems on the Adjudication of Social Issues* (West, 1971).

Ziegler, B. M., *The Supreme Court and American Economic Life* (Row, Peterson, 1962).

COMPARATIVE ASPECTS

(*Chiefly* domestic *aspects; for comparative aspects overseas, see Bibliography III.*)

Abraham, H. J., *Courts and Judges: An Introduction to the Judicial Process* (Oxford, 1959).

————, *The Judicial Process: An Introductory Analysis of the Courts of the United States, England, and France*, 3rd ed. (Oxford, 1975).

Andrews, W. G. (ed.), *Constitutions and Constitutionalism*, 2nd ed. (Van Nostrand, 1963).

Becker, T. L., *Comparative Judicial Politics* (Rand McNally, 1970).

Black, C. L., Jr., *Impeachment: A Handbook* (Yale, 1974).
Borchard, E. M., *Declaratory Judgments*, 2nd ed. (Bands-Baldwin, 1941).
Bowie, R. R. and C. J. Friedrich (eds.), *Studies in Federalism* (Little, Brown, 1954).
Burgess, J. W., *Political Science and Comparative Constitutional Law* (Ginn, 1890).
Dawson, J. P., *A History of Lay Judges* (Doubleday, 1956).
Douglas, W. O., *We the Judges* (Doubleday, 1956).
Friedrich, C. J., *Constitutional Government and Democracy*, 5th ed. (Blaisdell, 1968).
Glick, H. R., *Supreme Courts in State Politics* (Basic Books, 1971).
Gray, C. M., *Copyhold, Equity, and the Common Law* (Harvard, 1963).
Harding, A. L. (ed.), *The Administration of Justice in Retrospect* (S.M.U., 1957).
Haynes, E., *The Selection and Tenure of Judges* (National Press Conf. of Judicial Councils, 1944).
Karlen, D., *Appellate Courts in the United States and England* (N.Y.U., 1956).
Kempin, F. G., Jr., *Legal History: Law and Social Changes* (Prentice-Hall, 1963).
Macmahon, A. W., *Federalism Mature and Emergent* (Doubleday, 1953).
McWhinney, E., *Judicial Review in the English-Speaking World*, 4th ed. (U. of Toronto, 1969).
Murphy, W. F., and J. Tanenhaus, *The Study of Public Law* (Random House, 1971).
Newan, R. A., *Equity and Law: A Comparative Study* (Oceana, 1961).
Pollock, Sir F., *Essays in the Law* (Macmillan, 1922).
Read, C. (ed.), *The Constitution Reconsidered* (Columbia, 1938).
Robson, W. A., *Justice and Administrative Law: A Study of the British Constitution* (Stevens, 1951).
Schubert, G., and D. J. Danelski, *Comparative Judicial Behavior* (Oxford, 1969).
Schwartz, B., *The Code Napoleon and the Common Law World* (N.Y.U., 1956).
Spiro, H., *Government By Constitution* (Random House, 1959).
Stannard, H., *The Two Constitutions: A Comparative Study of British and American Constitutional Systems* (Van Nostrand, 1959).
Sutherland, A. E. (ed.), *Government Under Law* (Harvard, 1956).
Wagner, W. J., *Federal States and their Judiciary: Comparative Study in Constitutional Law and Organization of Courts in Federal States* (Mouton, 1959).
Wheare, K. C., *Federal Government*, 4th ed. (Oxford, 1964).
——, *Modern Constitutions* (Oxford, 1951).

THE CONGRESS

(*The legislative branch of our national government.*)

A.F.L.-C.I.O., *Why Richard M. Nixon Must Be Impeached—Now* (A.F.L.-C.I.O., 1974).
American Civil Liberties Union, *Why President Richard Nixon Should Be Impeached* (A.C.L.U., 1974).
Americans for Democratic Action, *The Case for Impeachment* (A.D.A., 1974).
Benedict, M. L., *The Impeachment and Trial of Andrew Johnson* (Norton, 1973).
Berger, R., *Congress versus the Supreme Court* (Harvard, 1969).
——, *Impeachment: The Constitutional Problem* (Harvard, 1973).
Brant, I., *Impeachment: Trials and Errors* (Knopf, 1972).
Breckenridge, A. C., *Congress Against the Court* (U. of Nebraska, 1971).

Committee on the Judiciary, U.S. House of Representatives, *Impeachment: Selected Materials* (Superintendent of Documents, 1974).

Congressional Quarterly Guide to American Government, *Impeachment* (C.Q., 1974).

Deantonio, E., and D. Talbot, *Point of Order! A Documentary of the Army-McCarthy Hearings* (Norton, 1964).

Dionisopousos, P. A., *Rebellion, Racism, and Representation: The Adam Clayton Powell Case and Its Antecedents* (Northern Illinois U., 1970).

Dobrovir, W. A., *The Offenses of Richard M. Nixon: A Lawyer's Guide for the People of the United States of America* (A. B. Zill, 1974).

Ehrlich, W., *Presidential Impeachment: An American Dilemma* (Forum Series, 1974).

Ettrude, D. J. (ed.), *The Power of Congress To Nullify Supreme Court Decisions* (H. W. Wilson, 1924).

Fisher, L., *The President and Congress: Power and Policy* (Free Press, 1972).

Goldfarb, R. L., *The Contempt Power* (Columbia, 1963).

Harris, J. P., *The Advice and Consent of the Senate: A Study of the Confirmation of Appointments by the United States Senate* (Berkeley, 1953).

Hurst, J. W., *The Growth of American Law: The Lawmakers* (Little, Brown, 1950).

Lawson, J. F., *The General Welfare Clause* (J. F. Lawson, 1934).

Lowi, T. J. (ed.), *Legislative Politics USA*, 2nd ed. (Little, Brown, 1965).

Lurie, L., *The Impeachment of Richard Nixon* (Berkeley Publ. Co., 1973).

Mason, A. T., and W. B. Beaney, *The Supreme Court in a Free Society* (Prentice-Hall, 1959).

Morgan, D. L., *Congress and the Constitution: A Study of Responsibility* (Harvard, 1967).

Murphy, W. F., *Congress and the Court* (U. of Chicago, 1962).

New Priorities, *The Constitutional Crisis: Congress vs. the Executive* (Gordon & Breach, 1974).

Nichols, E. R., *Congress or the Supreme Court: Which Shall Rule America?* (Noble, 1935).

Paulson, M. C. (ed.), *Legal Institutions Today and Tomorrow* (Columbia, 1959).

Polsby, N. W., *Congress and the Presidency* (Prentice-Hall, 1963).

Pritchett, C. H., *Congress versus the Supreme Court* (U. of Minnesota, 1961).

Schmidhauser, J. R., and L. L. Berg, *The Supreme Court and Congress: Conflict and Interaction, 1945–1968* (Free Press, 1972).

Vinyard, D., *Congress* (Scribner's, 1969).

Weeks, K. M., *Adam Clayton Powell and the Supreme Court* (Dunellen, 1971).

Wilson, W., *Congressional Government* (Houghton, Mifflin, 1885).

FEDERALISM

GENERAL WORKS

Allen, R. S., *Our Sovereign States* (Vanguard, 1949).

Ames, H. V. (ed.), *State Documents on Federal Relations, 1789–1861* (U. of Pennsylvania, 1900).

Anderson, W., *The Nation and the States: Rivals or Partners?* (U. of Minnesota, 1955).

Association of American Law Schools, *Selected Essays on Constitutional Law* (Foundation Press, 1938).

Benson, G. C. S., *The New Centralization* (Rinehart, 1941).

Bloch, C., *States Rights: The Law of the Land* (Harrison, 1958).

Bordon, M. (ed.), *The Anti-Federalist Papers* (Michigan State U., 1965).

Bowie, R. R., and D. J. Friedrich (eds.), *Studies in Federalism* (Little, Brown, 1954).

Brannon, H., *A Treatise on the Rights and Privileges Guaranteed by the Fourteenth Amendment to the Constitution of the United States* (Anderson, 1901).

Clark, J. P., *The Rise of a New Federalism* (Columbia, 1938).

Cooley, R. M., *Constitutional Limitations*, 17th ed. (Little, Brown, 1954).

Corwin, E. S., *The Doctrine of Judicial Review* (Princeton, 1914).

————, *National Supremacy: Treaty Power versus State Power* (H. Holt & Co., 1913).

Dietze, G., *The Federalist: A Classic on Federalism and Free Government* (Johns Hopkins, 1960).

Douglas, W. O., *We the Judges* (Doubleday, 1956).

Engdahl, D. E., *Constitutional Power: Federal and State* (West, 1974).

Guthrie, W. D., *Lectures on the 14th Article of Amendment to the Constitution of the United States* (Little, Brown, 1898).

Hamilton, A., Jay, J., and Madison, J., *The Federalist Papers* (McLcan, 1788).

Harris, R. J., *The Judicial Power of the United States* (Kennikat, 1940).

Hart, H. M., Jr., and H. Wechsler, *The Federal Court and the Federal System* (Foundation Press, 1953).

Heins, A. J., *Constitutional Restrictions Against State Debt* (U. of Wisconsin, 1963).

Hopkins, V. C., *Dred Scott's Cases* (Fordham, 1951).

Hutchins, R. M., *Two Faces of Federalism* (Center for the Study of Democratic Institutions, 1962).

Kilpatrick, J. J., *The Sovereign States* (Regnery, 1957).

Lien, A. J., *Concurring Opinion* (Washington U., St. Louis, 1957).

Livingston, W. S., *Federalism and Constitutional Change* (Oxford, 1956).

Macmahon, A. W. (ed.), *Federalism Mature and Emergent* (Doubleday, 1955).

Main, J. T., *The Antifederalist Critics of the Constitution, 1781–1788* (Quadrangle, 1964).

Mason, A. T., *Free Government in the Making*, 3rd ed. (Oxford, 1965).

————, *The States Rights Debate: Antifederalism and the Constitution*, 2nd ed. (Oxford, 1972).

Merriam, C. E., *The Written Constitution and the Unwritten Attitude* (R. R. Smith, 1931).

Miller, A. S., *The Supreme Court and American Capitalism* (Free Press, 1968).

Morley, F., *Freedom and Federalism* (Regnery, 1959).

Orfield, L. B., *The Amending of the Federal Constitution* (Calahan, 1942).

Peltason, J. W., *Fifty-Eight Lonely Men: Southern Federal Judges and School Desegregation* (Harcourt, Brace & World, 1961).

Pound, R., C. H. McIlwain, and R. F. Nichols, *Federalism as a Democratic Process* (Rutgers, 1942).

Powell, T. R., *Vagaries and Varieties in Constitutional Interpretations* (Columbia, 1956).

Ramaswamy, M., *The Creative Role of the Supreme Court of the United States* (Stanford, 1956).

Roberts, O. J., *The Court and the Constitution* (Harvard, 1951).

Rockefeller, N. A., *The Future of Federalism* (Harvard, 1962; Atheneum, 1963).

Schmidhauser, J. R., *The Supreme Court as Final Arbiter of Federal-State Relations* (U. of North Carolina, 1958).

Sprague, J. D., *Voting Patterns of the United States Supreme Court: Cases in Federalism, 1889–1959* (Bobbs-Merrill, 1968).

Ten-Broek, J., *Anti-Slavery Origins of the Fourteenth Amendment* (Berkeley, 1951).

Warren, C., *The Supreme Court and Sovereign States* (Princeton, 1924).

Wheare, K., *Federal Government*, 4th ed. (Oxford, 1964).

White, L. D., *The States and the Nation* (Louisiana State U., 1956).

Wiecek, W. M., *The Guarantee Clause of the United States Constitution* (Cornell, 1972).

Wilcox, T., *States Rights v. The Supreme Court* (Little, Brown, 1960).

THE COMMERCE CLAUSE

Baxter, M. G., *Daniel Webster and the Supreme Court* (U. of Mass., 1967).

Benson, P. R., Jr., *The Supreme Court and the Commerce Clause, 1937–1970* (Dunellen, 1971).

Cooke, F. H., *The Commerce Clause of the Federal Constitution* (Baker, Voolins, 1908).

Corwin, E. S., *The Commerce Power versus States' Rights* (Princeton, 1936).

Frankfurter, F., *The Commerce Clause Under Marshall, Taney and Waite* (U. of North Carolina, 1937).

Gavit, B. C., *The Commerce Clause of the United States Constitution* (Principia, 1956).

Hartman, J. P., *State Taxation of Interstate Commerce* (Dennis, 1953).

Kallenbach, J. E., *Federal Cooperation with the States under the Commerce Clause* (U. of Michigan, 1942).

Lerner, M., *The Supreme Court and American Capitalism* (Yale Law Journal, 1933).

Mahany, M. M., *Commerce Clause Tax Problems* (Wilkinson, 1940).

Melder, F. E., *State and Local Barriers to Interstate Commerce in the United States* (U. of Maine, 1937).

Ramaswamy, M., *The Commerce Clause in the Constitution of the United States* (Longmans, Green, 1948).

Ribble, F. D. G., *State and National Power Over Commerce* (Columbia, 1937).

Rottschaefer, H., *The Constitution and Socio-Economic Change* (U. of Michigan, 1948).

Rutledge, W. B., *A Declaration of Legal Faith* (U. of Kansas, 1947).

Wood, S. B., *Constitutional Politics in the Progressive Era* (U. of Chicago, 1967).

THE CONTRACT CLAUSE

Magrath, P. B., *Yazoo: Law and Politics in the New Republic, the Case of Fletcher v. Peck* (Brown U., 1967).

Wright, B. F., *The Contract Clause of the Constitution* (Harvard, 1938).

FULL FAITH AND CREDIT

Jackson, R. H., *Full Faith and Credit: The Lawyer's Clause in the Constitution* (Columbia, 1945).

THE GUARANTEE CLAUSE

Wiecek, W. M., *The Guarantee Clause of the United States Constitution* (Cornell, 1972).

POLICE POWER

Roettinger, R., *The Supreme Court and the State Police Power: A Study in Federalism* (Public Affairs Press, 1957).

RELATIONSHIPS AMONG THE STATES

Leach, R. H., and R. S. Sugg, Jr., *The Administration of Interstate Compacts* (Louisiana State U., 1959).

Ridgeway, M. E., *Interstate Compacts: A Question of Federalism* (Southern Illinois U., 1971).

Scott, J. B., *Judicial Settlement of Controversies between States of the American Union* (Clarendon, 1918).

Thursby, V. B., *Interstate Cooperation: A Study of the Interstate Compact* (Public Affairs Press, 1953).

Warren, C., *The Supreme Court and Disputes Between States* (William and Mary, in *Bulletin of the College of Virginia*, vol. 34, no. 5, June, 1940).

Zimmerman, F. L., and M. Wendell, *The Interstate Compact Since 1925* (Council of State Governments, 1951).

STATE COURTS AND FEDERAL RELATIONSHIPS

Council of State Governments, *Courts of Last Resort of the States* (Council of State Governments, 1955).

Elliott, S. D., *Improving Our Courts* (Oceana, 1959).

Glick, H. R., *Supreme Courts in State Politics* (Basic, 1970).

Jacobs, C. E., *The Eleventh Amendment and Sovereign Immunity* (Greenwood, 1972).

Mitchel, W., *Relations between Federal and State Courts* (Columbia, 1950).

Vanderbilt, A. T., *Minimum Standards of Judicial Administration* (N.Y.U., 1949).

Wendell, M., *Relations Between the Federal and State Courts*, rev. ed. (Columbia, 1953).

THE TAXING POWER AND OTHER MONETARY PROBLEMS

Dunne, G. T., *Monetary Decisions of the Supreme Court* (Rutgers, 1960).

Hansen, A., and H. Perloff, *State and Local Finance in the National Economy* (Norton, 1944).

Heins, A. J., *Constitutional Restrictions Against State Debt* (U. of Wisconsin, 1963).

Maxwell, J. A., *Fiscal Impact of Federalism in the United States* (Harvard, 1946).

ASPECTS OF AMERICAN CONSTITUTIONAL DEMOCRACY:

General Works

(*Works dealing with many areas of our system, but not specifically with any one feature —many are cross-referenced in other categories.*)

Association of American Law Schools, *Selected Essays on Constitutional Law* (Foundation Press, 1938).

Aumann, F. A., *The Instrumentalities of Justice: Their Forms, Functions, and Limitations* (Ohio State U., 1956).

Beard, C. A., *The Republic* (Viking, 1943).

Berman, H. J., *Talks on American Law* (Random House, 1961).

Black, C. L., Jr., *Perspectives in Constitutional Law* (Prentice-Hall, 1963).

Burdick, C. K., *The Law of the American Constitution: Its Origins and Development* (Putnam, 1922).

Burlingame, R., *The American Conscience* (Knopf, 1957).

Cardozo, B. N., *Law and Literature and Other Essays* (Harcourt, Brace, 1931).

Cohen, L. K. (ed.), *The Legal Conscience: Selected Papers of Felix S. Cohen* (Yale, 1960).

Collyer, R. (comp.), *In Defense of the Constitution: Excerpts from Addresses and Opinions of Chief Justices of the U.S.* (Yale, 1960).

Commager, H. S., *The American Mind* (Yale, 1950).

Corwin, E. S., *A Constitution of Powers in a Secular State* (U. of Virginia, 1951).

———, *Our Expendable Constitution* (U. of Illinois, 1955).

Curtis, C. P., *It's Your Law* (Harvard, 1954).

Dahl, R. A., *A Preface to Democratic Theory* (U. of Chicago, 1956).

Daniels, J., *Frontier on the Potomac* (Macmillan, 1946).

Denning, A., *The Road to Justice* (Stevens, 1955).

Dewey, D. O., *Union and Liberty: A Documentary History of American Constitutionalism* (McGraw-Hill, 1969).

Dietze, G. (ed.), *Essays on the American Constitution* (Prentice-Hall, 1964).

Dilliard, I. (ed.), *The Spirit of Liberty: Papers and Addresses of Learned Hand* (Knopf, 1959).

Douglas, W. O., *Being an American* (Day, 1948).

———, *We the Judges* (Doubleday, 1956).

Edwards, N., *The Courts and the Public Schools* (U. of Chicago, 1962).

Fainsod, M., and L. Gordon, *Government and the American Economy* (Norton, 1948).

Fesler, J. W., *Area and Administration* (U. of Alabama, 1949).

Frankfurter, F., *Law and Politics* (Harcourt, Brace, 1939).

———, *Of Law and Men: Papers and Addresses*, ed. by Phillip Elman (Harcourt, Brace, 1956).

———, *The Public and Its Government* (Oxford, 1930).

Freedman, V., *Society on Trial: Current Court Decision and Social Change* (Thomas, 1965).

Garrison, L. K., *et al.*, *The Legal Process*, rev. ed. (Chandler, 1961).

Garvey, G., *Constitutional Bricolage* (Princeton, 1971).

The Gaspar Bacon Lectures on the Constitution of the United States, 1940–1950 (Boston U., 1953).

Gordon, R. M., *Nine Men Against America* (Devin-Adair, 1958).

Hagrath, E. P. (ed.), *The Constitutional System* (Scott, Foresman, 1966).

Hare, J. I. C., *American Constitutional Law* (Brown, 1889).

Holcombe, A. N., *The Constitutional System*, rev. ed. (Scott-Foresman, 1968).

Kaplan, B., and L. Hall (eds.), *Judicial Administration and the Common Man* (Lippincott, 1953).

Kauper, P. G., *Frontiers of Constitutional Liberty* (U. of Michigan, 1956).

Laski, H. J., *The American Democracy* (Viking, 1948).

Lasswell, H. D., *Power and Personality* (Norton, 1948).

McCloskey, R. G., *Essays in Constitutional Law* (Knopf, 1957).

McKay, R. B. (ed.), *The American Constitutional Law Reader* (Oceana, 1958).

McLaughlin, A. S., *The Courts, the Constitution, and Parties* (U. of Chicago, 1912).

Marshall, G., *Constitutional Theory* (Oxford, 1971).

Mason, A. T., and W. M. Beaney, *The Supreme Court in a Free Society*, rev. ed. (Prentice-Hall, 1968).

Matthews, J. M., *The American Constitutional System* (McGraw-Hill, 1940).

Mayers, L., *The American Legal System*, rev. ed. (Harper & Row, 1964).

Morlan, R. L., *Capitol, Courthouse and City Hall*, 3rd ed. (Houghton, Mifflin, 1966).

Paulson, M. C. (ed.), *Legal Institutions Today and Tomorrow* (Columbia, 1959).

Pekelis, A. H., *Law and Social Action* (Cornell, 1950).

Pomeroy, J. N., *An Introduction to the Constitutional Law of the United States* (Hurd and Houghton, 1886).

Pritchett, C. H., *The American Constitutional System*, 3rd ed. (McGraw-Hill, 1971).

Read, C. (ed.), *The Constitution Reconsidered*, rev. ed., preface by R. B. Morris (Columbia, 1968).

Rickard, J. A., and J. H. McCrocklin, *Our National Constitution* (Stackpole, 1956).

Rottschaefer, H., *The Constitution and Socio-Economic Change* (U. of Michigan Law School, 1949).

Schechter, A. H., *Contemporary Constitutional Issues* (McGraw-Hill, 1972).

Schoulder, J., *Constitutional Studies* (Dodd, Mead, 1897).

Schwartz, B., *American Constitutional Law* (Harvard, 1955).

———, *A Commentary on the Constitution of the U.S.* Part I: *The Powers of Government* (Macmillan, 1963).

———, *The Powers of Government* (Macmillan, 1965).

Shapiro, M. M. (ed.), *The Supreme Court* (Scott, Foresman, 1967).

———, *The Supreme Court and Constitutional Law* (Scott, Foresman, 1965).

Smith, H. R., *Democracy and the Public Interest* (U. of Georgia, 1960).

Sutherland, A. E. (ed.), *Constitutionalism in America* (Blaisdells, 1964).

———, *Government Under Law* (Harvard, 1956).

———, *The Law and One Man Among Many* (U. of Wisconsin, 1956).

Taft, W. H., *Popular Government* (Yale, 1913).

Tiffany, J., *A Treatise on Government and Constitutional Law* (W. C. Little, 1867).

Truman, D. B., *The Governmental Process* (Knopf, 1951).

Vanderbilt, A. T., *The Doctrine of Separation of Powers and Its Present Day Significance* (U. of Nebraska, 1963).

Warren, E., *The Law in the Future* (Fortune Magazine, 1955).

Watson, D. K., *The Constitution of the United States: Its History, Application, and Construction* (Callaghan, 1910).

Weaver, S. P., *Constitutional Law and Its Administration* (Callaghan, 1946).

Wechsler, H., *Principles, Politics, and Fundamental Law: Selected Essays* (Harvard, 1961).

Welch, J., *The Constitution* (Houghton, Mifflin, 1956).

Westin, A. F., *The Uses of Power: 7 Cases in American Politics* (Harcourt, Brace & World, 1962).

Wilson, W., *Constitutional Government in the United States* (Columbia, 1908).
Wright, B. F., *Growth of American Constitutional Law* (Reynal and Hitchcock, 1942; Phoenix, 1967).

THE JUDICIAL PROCESS: General Works

(The federal judicial process and court system; especially the Supreme Court and its jurisprudence.)

Abraham, H. J., *Courts and Judges: An Introduction to the Judicial Process* (Oxford, 1959).
———, *The Judicial Process: An Introductory Analysis of the Courts of the United States, England, and France*, 3rd ed. (Oxford, 1975).
———, *The Judiciary: The Supreme Court in the Governmental Process*, 3rd ed. (Allyn & Bacon, 1973).
Acheson, P. C., *The Supreme Court: America's Judicial Heritage* (Dodd, Mead, 1961).
Alfange, D., *The Supreme Court and the National Will* (Kennikat, 1937).
Arneson, B. A., *Elements of Constitutional Law* (Harper, 1928).
Auerbach, C. A., L. D. Garrison, W. Hurst, and S. Mermin, *The Legal Process*, rev. ed. (Chandler, 1961).
Aumann, F. R., *The Changing American Legal System* (DaCapo, 1969).
Baade, H. W. (ed.), *Jurimetrics* (Duke, 1963).
Baldwin, S. E., *The American Judiciary* (Morgantown, 1925).
Beck, C. (ed.), *Law and Justice: Essays in Honor of Robert T. Rankin* (Duke, 1969).
Becker, T. L., and M. M. Feeley, *The Impact of Supreme Court Decisions*, 2nd ed. (Oxford, 1973).
———, and V. Murray, *Government Lawlessness in America* (Oxford, 1971).
Bent, J. A., *The Independent Judiciary* (Morgantown, 1925).
Bickel, A. M., *The Least Dangerous Branch: The Supreme Court at the Bar of Politics* (Bobbs-Merrill, 1963).
———, *The Supreme Court and the Idea of Progress* (Harper & Row, 1970).
Black, C. L., *Structure and Relationship in Constitutional Law* (Louisiana State U., 1969).
Callison, I. P., *Courts of Injustice* (Twayne, 1956).
Clayton, J. E., *The Making of Justice: The Supreme Court in Action* (Dutton, 1964).
Cook, B. B., *The Judicial Process in California* (Dickinson, 1961).
Cook, W. W. (ed.), *Fundamental Legal Concepts as Applied in Judicial Reasoning* (Yale, 1964).
Cooley, R. M., *Constitutional Limitations* (Putnam's, 1868).
Cooley, T. M., *Principles of Constitutional Law*, 2nd ed. (Little, Brown, 1891).
Cox, A., *The Warren Court: Constitutional Decision as an Instrument of Reform* (Harvard, 1968).
Coy, H., *The First Book of the Supreme Court* (Watts, 1958).
Curtis, C. P., *Lions Under the Throne* (Houghton, Mifflin, 1947).
Dolbeare, K. M., *Trial Courts in Urban Politics* (Wiley, 1967).
———, and P. E. Hammond, *The School Prayer Decisions: From Court Policy to Local Practice* (U. of Chicago, 1971).

Douglas, W. O., *We, The Judges* (Doubleday, 1956).

Eisenstein, J., *Politics and the Legal Process* (Harper & Row, 1973).

Ernst, M. L., *The Great Reversals: Tales of the Supreme Court* (Weybright and Talley, 1973).

Ervin, S. J., Jr., and R. Clark, *Role of the Supreme Court: Policy-Maker or Adjudicator* (Amer. Ent. Inst., 1972).

Farnsworth, E. A., *An Introduction to the Legal System of the United States* (Oceana, 1963).

Felscher, H., and M. Rosen, *The Press in the Jury Box* (Macmillan, 1966).

Fish, P. G., *The Politics of Federal Judicial Administration* (Princeton, 1973).

Fleming, M., *The Price of Perfect Justice* (Basic Books, 1974).

Forte, D. F., *The Supreme Court in American Politics: Judicial Activism v. Judicial Restraint* (Heath, 1972).

Frank, J. F., *Courts on Trial: Myth and Reality in American Justice* (Princeton, 1959).

———, *If Men Were Angels* (Harvard, 1942).

Frank, J. P., *Marble Palace: The Supreme Court in American Life* (Knopf, 1958).

Frankfurter, F., and J. W. Landis, *The Business of the Supreme Court: A Study of the Federal Judicial System* (Macmillan, 1928).

Freund, P. A., *On Understanding the Supreme Court* (Little, Brown, 1949).

———, *The Supreme Court of the United States: Its Business, Purposes, and Performance* (Meridian, 1961).

Garvey, G., *Constitutional Bricolage* (Princeton, 1971).

Glick, H. R., *Supreme Courts in State Politics* (Basic Books, 1971).

Goldberg, A. J., *Equal Justice: The Warren Era of the Supreme Court* (Northwestern, 1971).

Goldman, S., and T. P. Jahnige, *The Federal Courts as a Political System* (Harper & Row, 1971).

Gray, D. L., *The Supreme Court and the News Media* (Northwestern, 1968).

Grossman, J. B., and J. Tanenhaus (eds.), *Frontiers of Judicial Research* (Wiley, 1969).

———, and R. S. Wells (eds.), *Constitutional Law and Judicial Policy-Making* (Wiley, 1972).

Harvard Law Review, *Social Science Approaches to the Judicial Process* (Da Capo, 1971).

Hirschfield, R., *The Constitution and the Court* (Random House, 1960).

Horn, R. A., *Groups and the Constitution* (Stanford, 1956).

Hughes, C. E., *The Supreme Court of the United States* (Columbia, 1928).

Hyneman, C. S., *The Supreme Court on Trial* (Atherton, 1963).

Jackson, P. E. (ed.), *The Wisdom of the Supreme Court* (U. of Oklahoma, 1962).

Jackson, R. H., *The Supreme Court in the American System of Government* (Harvard, 1955).

Jacob, H., *Debtors in Court: The Consumption of Governmental Services* (Rand McNally, 1969).

———, *Justice in America: Courts, Lawyers, and the Judicial Process*, 2nd ed. (Little, Brown, 1972).

——— (ed.), *Law, Politics and the Federal Courts* (Little, Brown, 1968).

Jahnige, T. P., and S. Goldman (eds.), *The Federal Judicial System: Readings in Process and Behavior* (Holt, Rinehart & Winston, 1968).

397

Johnson, G. W., *The Supreme Court* (Morrow, 1962).

Johnson, R. M., *The Dynamics of Compliance: Supreme Court Decision-Making from a New Perspective* (Northwestern, 1968).

Journal of Public Law (Symposium), "Policy-Making in a Democracy: The Role of the United States Supreme Court" (1957).

Judson, R. N., *The Judiciary and the People* (Yale, 1913).

Karlen, D., *Appellate Courts in the United States and England* (N.Y.U., 1963).

Kirschheimer, O., *Political Justice: The Use of Legal Procedure for Political Ends* (Princeton, 1961).

Klonoski, J. R., and R. I. Mendelsohn, *The Politics of Local Justice* (Little, Brown, 1970).

Kohlmeier, L. M., Jr., *"God Save this Honorable Court!"* (Scribner's, 1973).

Krislov, S., *The Supreme Court in the Political Process* (Macmillan, 1965).

———, et al., *Compliance and the Law: A Multidisciplinary Approach* (Sage, 1971).

Kurland, P. (ed.), *The Supreme Court Review* (U. of Chicago, 1960 ff).

Kurland, P. B., *Politics, the Constitution, and the Warren Court* (U. of Chicago, 1973).

Kutler, S. I. (ed.), *The Dred Scott Decision: Law or Politics* (Houghton, Mifflin, 1967).

Llwellyn, K. N., *The Bramble Bush* (Oceana, 1960).

Lyttle, C. M., *The Warren Court and Its Critics* (U. of Arizona, 1968).

McCloskey, R. G., *The Modern Supreme Court*, ed. by Martin Shapiro (Harvard, 1972).

MacKenzie, J. P., *The Appearance of Justice* (Scribner's, 1974).

McRuer, J. C., *The Evolution of the Judicial Process* (Clark, Irvin, 1959).

Magrath, C. P. (ed.), *Constitutionalism and Politics: Conflict and Concerns* (Scott, Foresman, 1968).

Manwaring, D. R., D. R. Reich, and S. L. Wasby, *The Supreme Court as Policy Maker: Three Studies on the Impact of Judicial Decisions* (Public Affairs Research Bureau, 1968).

Mason, A. T., *The Supreme Court: Instrument of Power or of Revealed Truth?* (Boston U., 1953).

———, *The Supreme Court: Palladium of Freedom* (U. of Michigan, 1962).

Mayers, L., *The Machinery of Justice: An Introduction to Legal Structure and Process* (Prentice-Hall, 1963).

Mendelson, W., *The Supreme Court: Law versus Discretion* (Bobbs-Merrill, 1967).

Milner, N. A., *The Court and Local Law Enforcement: The Political Impact of Miranda* (Sage, 1970).

Moreland, C. C., *Equal Justice Under the Law* (Oceana, 1957).

Murphy, W. F., *Elements of Judicial Strategy* (U. of Chicago, 1973).

———, and J. Tanenhaus, *The Study of Public Law* (Random House, 1971).

———, J. Tanenhaus, and D. Kastner, *Public Evaluation of Constitutional Courts* (Sage, 1974).

———, and C. H. Pritchett (eds.), *Courts, Judges, and Politics*, 2nd ed. (Random House, 1974).

Nagel, S. S., *The Legal Process from a Behavioral Perspective* (Dorsey, 1969).

Newman, R. P., and D. R. Newman, *Evidence* (Houghton, Mifflin, 1971).

North, A. A., *The Supreme Court: Judicial Process and Judicial Politics* (Appleton-Century-Crofts, 1966).

Norton, T. J., *Losing Liberty Judicially* (Macmillan, 1928).

———, *Undermining the Constitution* (Devin Adair, 1950).

Peltason, J. W., *Federal Courts in the Political Process* (Doubleday, 1955).

Post, C. G., Jr., *The Supreme Court and Political Questions* (Da Capo, 1969).

Ramaswamy, M., *The Creative Role of the Supreme Court of the United States* (Stanford, 1956).

Roche, J. P., and L. W. Levy (eds.), *The Judiciary: Documents in American Government* (Harcourt, Brace & World, 1964).

Rosen, P. L., *The Supreme Court and Social Science* (U. of Illinois, 1972).

Salomon, L. I. (ed.), *The Supreme Court* (H. W. Wilson, 1961).

Sayer, R. H., B. B. Boyer, and R. E. Gooding, Jr., *The Warren Court: A Critical Analysis* (Chelsea House, 1968).

Schmidhauser, J. R., *The Supreme Court: Its Politics, Personalities, and Procedures* (Holt, 1960).

Schubert, G. A., *Constitutional Politics* (Holt, Rinehart & Winston, 1960).

———, *The Constitutional Polity* (Boston U., 1970).

———, *Judicial Policy Making*, 2nd ed. (Scott, Foresman, 1974).

———, and D. J. Danelski, *Comparative Judicial Behavior* (Oxford, 1969).

———, "Judicial Process and Behavior, 1963–1971" in J. A. Robinson (ed.), *Political Science Annual*, III (Bobbs-Merrill, 1972).

Schwartz, B., *A Commentary on the Constitution of the United States: Part I, The Powers of Government* (Macmillan, 1963).

———, *The Supreme Court: Constitutional Revolution in Retrospect* (Ronald, 1954).

Scigliano, R. G., *The Courts: A Reader in the Judicial Process* (Little, Brown, 1962).

Shapiro, M. M., *Law and Politics in the Supreme Court: New Approaches to Political Jurisprudence* (Stanford, 1964).

——— (ed.), *The Supreme Court and Public Policy* (Scott, Foresman, 1969).

———, and D. Hobbs, *The Politics of Constitutional Law* (Winthrop, 1972).

Sheldon, C. H., *The Judicial Process: Models and Approaches* (Dodd, Mead, 1974).

Sigler, J. A., *An Introduction to the Legal System* (Dorsey, 1968).

Spaeth, H. J., *An Introduction to Supreme Court Decision Making* (Chandler, 1965).

Starr, I., *The Federal Judiciary* (Oxford Social Studies, 1957).

Steamer, R. J., *The Supreme Court: Constitutional Revision and the New "Strict Constructionism"* (Burgess, 1973).

Swisher, C. B., *The Growth of Constitutional Power in the United States*, 2nd ed. (U. of Chicago, 1963).

———, *The Supreme Court in Modern Role* (N.Y.U., 1958).

Tully, A., *Supreme Court* (Simon & Schuster, 1963).

Ulmer, S. S., *Courts as Small and Not So Small Groups* (General Learning Press, 1971).

——— (ed.), *Political Decision Making* (Van Nostrand, 1971).

Vanderzell, J. H. (ed.), *The Supreme Court and American Government* (Crowell, 1968).

Vines, K. N., and H. Jacob, *Studies in Judicial Politics* (Tulane, 1962).

Warren, E., *A Republic . . . If You Can Keep It* (Quadrangle, 1972).

Wasby, S. L., *The Impact of the United States Supreme Court* (Dorsey, 1970).

Wasserstrom, R. A., *The Judicial Decision: Toward a Theory of Legal Justification* (Stanford, 1969).

Westin, A. F., *The Supreme Court: Views from Inside* (Norton, 1961).

Willoughby, W. F., *Principles of Judicial Administration* (Brookings, 1929).

HISTORY

GENERAL WORKS

(*Sweeping surveys as well as specific eras and institutions.*)

Alfange, D., *The Supreme Court and the National Will* (Doubleday, 1937).

Alloway, C. C., *United States Constitutional Law, 1850–1875* (Oceana, 1958).

Angell, E., *Supreme Court Primer* (Reynal and Hitchcock, 1937).

Bates, E. S., *The Story of the Supreme Court* (Bobbs-Merrill, 1936; Cornerstone, 1963).

Bauer, E. K., *Commentaries on the Constitution, 1790–1860* (Columbia, 1952).

Beck, J. M., *The Constitution of the United States* (Doran, 1922).

Beth, L. P., *The Development of the American Constitution, 1877–1917* (Harper & Row, 1971).

Beitzinger, A. J., *A History of American Political Thought* (Dodd, Mead, 1972).

Boudin, L. B., *Government by Judiciary* (Godwin, 1932).

Brown, E. S., *Ratification of the 21st Amendment to the Constitution of the U.S.* (Da Capo, 1970).

Burdick, C. K., *The Law of the American Constitution: Its Origins and Development* (Putnam, 1922).

Carson, H. L., *The History of the Supreme Court of the United States* (Keller, 1891).

Commager, H. S. (ed.), *Documents of American History*, 6th ed. (Appleton-Century-Crofts, 1948).

Cooley, T. M., *Constitutional History of the United States* (Putnam's, 1889).

Crosskey, W. W., *Politics and the Constitution in the History of the United States* (U. of Chicago, 1953).

Cummings, H. S., and C. McGarland, *Federal Justice* (Macmillan, 1937).

Donald, P., *The Politics of Reconstruction* (Louisiana State U., 1966).

Edmunds, P. D., *Law and Civilization* (Public Affairs Press, 1959).

Ernst, M. L., *The Ultimate Power* (Doubleday, 1937).

Fairman, C., *The Bacon Lectures on the Constitution of the United States, 1940–1950* (Boston U., 1953).

——, *Reconstruction and Reunion, 1864–1888*, Part One (Vol. VI of the *Oliver Wendell Holmes Devise History of the Supreme Court of the United States*) (Macmillan, 1973).

Fenn, P. T., *The Development of the Constitution* (Appleton-Century-Crofts, 1948).

Flack, H. B., *The Adoption of the Fourteenth Amendment* (Johns Hopkins, 1908).

Fox, J. C., *The History of Contempt of Court* (Oxford, 1927).

Frankfurter, F., *The Commerce Clause Under Marshall, Taney, and Waite* (U. of North Carolina, 1937).

Freund, P. A. (gen. ed.), *The Oliver Wendell Holmes Devise History of the Supreme Court of the United States*, 11 vols. (Macmillan, 1973 ff).

Fribourg, M. G., *The Supreme Court in American History* (Macrae Smith, 1965).

Friedman, L. M., *A History of American Law* (Simon & Schuster, 1973).

Friedrich, C. J., and R. G. McCloskey, *From the Declaration of Independence to the Constitution* (Bobbs-Merrill, 1964).

Fuess, C. M., *Daniel Webster* (Little, Brown, 1930).

Haines, C. G., *The Role of the Supreme Court in American Government and Politics, 1789–1835* (U.C.L.A., 1944).

――――, and F. H. Sherwood, *The Role of the Supreme Court in American Government and Politics, 1835–1864* (Berkeley, 1957).

Hamilton, W. H., and D. Adair, *The Power to Govern: The Constitution Then and Now* (Norton, 1937).

Hartz, L., *Economic Policy and Democratic Thought* (Harvard, 1948).

Hendrick, B. J., *Bulwark of the Republic* (Little, Brown, 1939).

Hockett, C. H., *The Constitutional History of the United States, 1826–1876* (Macmillan, 1939).

Jackson, R. H., *The Struggle for Judicial Supremacy* (Knopf, 1941).

Jacobs, C. E., *Law Writers and the Courts* (Berkeley, 1954).

James, J. B., *The Framing of the Fourteenth Amendment* (U. of Illinois, 1956 and 1965).

Jensen, M. D., *The Articles of Confederation* (U. of Wisconsin, 1940).

Kelly, A. H., and W. Harbison, *The American Constitution—Its Origin and Development*, 4th ed. (Norton, 1970).

Kempin, F. G., Jr., *Historical Introduction to Anglo-American Law in a Nutshell*, 2nd ed. (West, 1973).

――――, *Legal History: Law and Social Change* (Prentice-Hall, 1963).

Kendrick, B. J., *Journal of the Joint Committee of Fifteen on Reconstruction* (Scribner's, 1914).

Kutler, S. I., *Judicial Power and Reconstruction Politics* (U. of Chicago, 1968).

Lacy, C., *The Meaning of the American Revolution* (New American Library, 1960).

Lasson, N. B., *The History of the Development of the Fourteenth Amendment* (Johns Hopkins, 1937).

Leedham, C., *Our Changing Constitution* (Dodd, Mead, 1964).

McCloskey, R. G., *The American Supreme Court* (U. of Chicago, 1960).

McCune, W., *The Nine Young Men* (Harper & Bros., 1947).

McIlwain, C. H., *Constitutionalism, Ancient and Modern*, rev. ed. (Cornell, 1947).

McLaughlin, A. C., *The Constitutional History of the United States* (Appleton-Century, 1935).

Mason, A. T., *The Supreme Court from Taft to Warren*, rev. & enl. (Louisiana State U., 1968).

Maverick, M., *In Blood and Ink* (Modern Age, 1939).

Mendelson, W., *Capitalism, Democracy, and the Supreme Court* (Appleton-Century-Crofts, 1960).

Miller, P. (ed.), *The Legal Mind in America: From Independence to the Civil War* (Doubleday, 1962).

Morgan, E. S., *The Birth of the Republic* (U. of Chicago, 1956).

Munro, W. B., *The Makers of the Unwritten Constitution* (Macmillan, 1930).

Murray, W. H., *The Supreme Court, The President, and Seven Senators* (Meador, 1959).

Myers, G., *History of the Supreme Court of the United States* (Kerr, 1912).

Padover, S. K., *The Living United States Constitution* (New American Library, 1953).

Paul, A. M., *Conservative Crisis and the Rule of Law: Attitudes of Bar and Bench, 1887–1895* (Cornell, 1960).

Pollak, L. H. (ed.), *The Constitution and the Supreme Court: A Documentary History* (World, 1966).

Pomeroy, J. N., *An Introduction to the Constitutional Law of the United States* (Houghton, Mifflin, 1886).

Pritchett, C. H., *The American Constitution* (McGraw-Hill, 1959).

Rachlis, F., *They Came to Kill* (Random House, 1961).

Randall, J. G., *The Civil War and Reconstruction* (Heath, 1937).

———, *Constitutional Problems Under Lincoln*, rev. ed. (Peter Smith, 1963).

Read, C. (ed.), *The Constitution Reconsidered* (Columbia, 1938).

Ribble, F. D. G., *State and National Power Over Commerce* (Columbia, 1937).

Rodell, F., *Nine Men: A Political History of the Supreme Court from 1790 to 1955* (Random House, 1955).

Rodick, B. C., *American Constitutional Custom: A Forgotten Factor In the Founding* (Philosophical Library, 1953).

Rogers, H. S. (ed.), *Constitutional History of the United States as Seen in the Development of American Law* (Bender, 1890).

Rosen, P. L., *The Supreme Court and Social Science* (U. of Illinois, 1972).

Schovler, J., *Constitutional Studies* (Dodd, Mead, 1897).

Schubert, G., *The Constitutional Polity* (Boston U., 1970).

Schwartz, B., *The Reins of Power: A Constitutional History of the United States* (Hill & Wang, 1963).

Silver, D. M., *Lincoln's Supreme Court* (U. of Illinois, 1956).

Smith, J. M., and P. L. Murphy, *Liberty and Justice* (Knopf, 1958).

Steamer, R. J., *The Supreme Court in Crisis: A History of Conflict* (U. of Massachusetts, 1971).

Story, J., *A Familiar Exposition on the Constitution of the United States: Containing a Brief Commentary* (Petersburgh, 1840).

Swindler, W. F., *Court and Constitution in the Twentieth Century: The Old Legality, 1889–1932* (Bobbs-Merrill, 1969).

———, *Court and Constitution in the Twentieth Century: The New Legality, 1932–1968* (Bobbs-Merrill, 1970).

Swisher, C. B., *American Constitutional Development*, 2nd ed. (Houghton, Mifflin, 1954).

Tocqueville, A. de, *Democracy in America* (H. G. Langley, 1841).

Towle, N., *A History and Analysis of the Constitution of the United States* (Little, Brown, 1860).

Twiss, B. R., *Lawyers and the Constitution: How Laissez Faire Came to the Supreme Court* (Princeton, 1942).

Wallace, H. A., *Whose Constitution?* (Reynal and Hitchcock, 1936).

Warren, C., *The Supreme Court in United States History*, rev. ed. (Little, Brown, 1926).

Wright, B. F., *The Contract Clause of the Constitution* (Harvard, 1938).

SPECIFIC WORKS—TWO AREAS OF MAJOR HISTORICAL INTEREST

1. The Franklin D. Roosevelt Era

Alsop, J., and T. Catledge, *The 168 Days* (Doubleday, 1938).

Baker, L., *Back to Back: The Duel Between FDR and the Supreme Court* (Macmillan, 1967).

Barnes, W. R., and A. W. Littlefield, *The Supreme Court Issue and the Constitution* (Barnes & Noble, 1937).

Brant, I., *Storm Over the Constitution* (Bobbs-Merrill, 1936).

Burns, J. M., *The Lion and the Fox* (Harcourt, Brace, 1956).

Committee on the Judiciary, U.S. Senate, 75th Cong., 1st sess., *Reorganization of the Federal Judiciary* (1937).

Cope, A. H., and F. Krinsky, *Franklin D. Roosevelt and the Supreme Court* (Heath, 1952).

Cortner, R., *The Wagner Act Cases* (U. of Tennessee, 1964).

Corwin, E. S., *Constitutional Revolution, Ltd.* (Clarmont, 1941).

Ericksson, E. M., *The Supreme Court and the New Deal* (U.C.L.A., 1940).

Goldberg, L., and E. Levenson, *Lawless Judges* (Rand School Press, 1935).

Jackson, R. H., *The Struggle for Judicial Supremacy* (Knopf, 1941).

Johnson, J. E., *Reorganization of the Supreme Court* (H. W. Wilson, 1937).

Lippmann, W., *The Supreme Court: Independent or Controlled?* (Harper, 1937).

Mason, A. T., *The Supreme Court: Vehicle of Revealed Truth or Power Group, 1930–1937* (Boston U., 1953).

Pearson, D., and R. S. Allen, *The Nine Old Men* (Doubleday, 1936).

Pritchett, C. H., *The Roosevelt Court: A Study in Judicial Politics and Values, 1937–1947* (Macmillan, 1947).

Pusey, T. R., *The Supreme Court Crisis* (Macmillan, 1937).

Sommer, F. H., *Reforming the Supreme Court* (N.Y.U., 1951).

2. Origin, Formation, and Ratification of the Constitution

Baldwin, H., *A General View of the Origin and Nature of the Constitution and Government of the United States* (Clark, 1837).

Bancroft, G., *History of the Formation of the Constitution of the United States of America* (Appleton, 1882).

Beard, C. A., *An Economic Interpretation of the Constitution of the United States* (Macmillan, 1913).

Becker, C. L., *The Declaration of Independence: A Study in the History of Political Ideas* (Knopf, 1942).

Bowen, C. D., *Miracle at Philadelphia: The Story of the Constitutional Convention, May to September 1787* (Little, Brown, 1966).

Brant, I., *The Bill of Rights* (Bobbs-Merrill, 1965).

——, *James Madison: Father of the Constitution, 1787–1800* (Bobbs-Merrill, 1950).

Brown, R. E., *Charles Beard and the Constitution: A Critical Analysis of an Economic Interpretation of the Constitution* (Princeton, 1956).

Buchanan, J. M., and G. Tullock, *The Calculus of Consent: Logical Foundations of Constitutional Democracy* (U. of Michigan, 1966).

Butzner, J., *Constitutional Chaff: Suggestions of the Constitutional Convention of 1787* (Columbia, 1941).

Corwin, E. S., *American Constitutional History*, essays ed. by A. T. Mason and G. Harvey (Harper & Row, 1963).

Dietze, G., *The Federalist: A Classic on Federalism and Free Government* (Johns Hopkins, 1960).

Elliot, J. (ed.), *The Debates in the Several State Conventions on the Adoption of the Federal Constitution*, 2nd ed. (Lippincott, 1854).

Farrand, M., *The Framing of the Constitution of the United States* (Yale, 1926).

————, *The Records of the Federal Convention of 1787* (Yale, 1911).

Fiske, J., *The Critical Period of American History, 1783–1789* (Houghton, Mifflin, 1888).

Goebel, J., Jr., *Antecedents and Beginnings to 1801* (Vol. I of the *Oliver Wendell Holmes Devise History of the Supreme Court of the United States*) (Macmillan, 1973).

Hamilton, A., Jay, J., and Madison, J., *The Federalist Papers* (McLean, 1788; Random House, 1972).

Hunt, C., and J. B. Scott (eds.), *The Debates in the Federal Convention of 1787* (Oxford, 1920).

Hyneman, C. S., and G. W. Davy, *A Second Federalist, Congress Creates a Government* (Appleton-Century-Crofts, 1966).

Jaffa, H. V., *Equality and Liberty: Theory and Practice in American Society* (Oxford, 1965).

Jameson, J. F., *Essays in the Constitutional History of the United States in the Formative Period, 1775–1789* (Houghton, Mifflin, 1889).

Jensen, M. O., *The Making of the American Constitution* (Anvil, 1964).

Konefsky, S. S., *John Marshall and Alexander Hamilton: Architects of the American Constitution* (Macmillan, 1965).

Kruschke, E. R., *An Introduction to the Constitution of the United States* (American Book Co., 1968).

Latham, E. (ed.), *The Declaration of Independence and the Constitution* (Heath, 1956).

Levy, L. W. (ed.), *Essays on the Making of the Constitution* (Oxford, 1972).

Long, B., *Genesis of the Constitution of the United States of America* (Macmillan, 1926).

Lyon, W., *The Constitution and the Men Who Made It* (Houghton, Mifflin, 1936).

McCloskey, P. N., Jr., *The United States Constitution* (Addison Wesley, 1964).

McDonald, F., *We the People: The Economic Origins of the Constitution* (U. of Chicago, 1958).

McLaughlin, A. C., *The Confederation and the Constitution, 1783–1789* (Harper, 1905).

Madison, J., *Journal of the Federal Convention* (Laugtree and O'Sullivan, 1840).

Mason, A. T., *The States Rights Debate: Antifederalism and the Constitution*, 2nd ed. (Prentice-Hall, 1972).

Miller, J. C., *Origins of the American Revolution* (Little, Brown, 1943).

Montross, L., *Reluctant Rebels: The Story of the Continental Congress* (Harper Bros., 1950).

Morrison, S. F., *Sources and Documents Illustrating the American Revolution, 1764–1788, and the Formation of the Federal Constitution*, 2nd ed. (Oxford, 1929).

Prescott, A. T. (comp.), *Drafting the Federal Constitution* (Louisiana State U., 1941).

Rossiter, C., *Seedtime of the Republic* (Harcourt, Brace, 1953).

————, *1787: The Grand Convention* (Macmillan, 1966).

Schachner, N., *The Founding Fathers* (Putnam's, 1954).

Schuyler, R. N., *The Constitution of the United States: An Historical Survey of its Formation* (Macmillan, 1923).

Scott, J. B., *The Declaration of Independence, The Articles of Confederation, the Constitution of the United States* (Oxford, 1917).

Shapiro, M. (ed.), *The Constitution of the United States and Related Documents* (Appleton-Century-Crofts, 1966).

Solberg, W. N., *The Federal Convention and the Formation of the Union of American States* (Liberal Arts, 1958).

Stevens, C. E., *Sources of the Constitution of the United States* (Macmillan, 1894).

Story, J., *Commentaries on the Constitution of the United States* (Little, 1833).

Van Doren, C. C., *The Great Rehearsal: The Story of the Making and Ratifying of the Constitution of the United States* (Viking, 1948).

Warren, C., *The Making of the Constitution* (Little, Brown, 1937).

Wright, B. F., *Consensus and Continuity, 1776–1787* (Boston U., 1958).

INTERPRETATIONS OF THE CONSTITUTION

(Analysis and interpretations of the written Constitution, clause by clause. Also, aspects of the "unwritten" Constitution: practices which modify the written document.)

Antieua, C. J., *Commentaries on the Constitution of the United States* (U. of Buffalo, 1960).

Baldwin, L. D., *Reframing the Constitution: An Imperative for Modern America* (American Bibliographical Center, 1972).

Brannon, H., *A Treatise on the Rights and Privileges Guaranteed by the Fourteenth Amendment to the Constitution of the United States* (Anderson, 1961).

Burgess, J. W., *Reconstruction and the Constitution* (Scribner's, 1905).

Cooke, E. F., *Detailed Analysis of the Constitution* (Littlefield, Adams, 1965).

Corwin, E. S., *The Constitution and What It Means Today*, 13th ed., ed. by H. W. Chase and C. R. Ducat (Princeton, 1973).

———, *Constitution of the United States: Analysis and Interpretation*, ed. by L. S. Jayson (U.S. G.P.O., 1973).

Dumbauld, E., *The Constitution of the United States* (U. of Oklahoma, 1964).

Eidelberg, P., *The Philosophy of the American Constitution: A Re-Interpretation of the Intentions of the Founding Fathers* (Free Press, 1968).

Gunther, G. (ed.), *John Marshall's Defense of McCulloch v. Maryland* (Stanford, 1969).

Guthrie, W. D., *Lectures on the 14th Amendment to the Constitution of the United States* (Little, Brown, 1898).

Hamilton, A., Jay, J., and Madison, J., *The Federalist Papers* (McLean, 1788; Random House, 1972).

Heathcock, C. L., *The United States Constitution in Perspective* (Allyn & Bacon, 1963).

Henkin, L., *Foreign Affairs and the Constitution* (Foundation Press, 1972).

Horwill, H. W., *The Usages of the American Constitution* (Oxford, 1925).

Jacobs, C. E., *The Eleventh Amendment and Sovereign Immunity* (Greenwood, 1972).

Jones, P. F. (ed.), *The Constitution of the United States, 1787–1962* (U. of Pittsburgh, 1963).

Kruschke, E. R., *An Introduction to the Constitution of the United States* (American Book Co., 1968).

Leedham, C., *Our Changing Constitution* (Dodd, Mead, 1964).

Levy, L. W., *Judgments: Essays on American Constitutional History* (Quadrangle, 1972).

Lieberman, J. K., *Understanding the Constitution* (Walker, 1967).

Liston, R. A., *The Tides of Justice—The Supreme Court and the Constitution in Our Time* (Delacorte, 1966).

McBain, H. L., *The Living Constitution* (Macmillan, 1927).

Merrian, C. C., *The Written Constitution and the Unwritten Attitude* (R. R. Smith, 1931).

Michigan Law Review, "The Article V Convention Process: A Symposium" (Da Capo, 1970).

Mitchell, B., and L. P. Mitchell, *A Biography of the Constitution of the United States* (Oxford, 1964).

Murphy, P. L., *The Constitution in Crisis Times* (Harper & Row, 1972).

Orfield, L. B., *The Amending of the Federal Constitution* (Callaghan, 1942).

Peltason, J. W., *Corwin and Peltason's Understanding the Constitution*, 6th ed. (Dryden, 1973).

Pritchett, C. H., *The American Constitution* (McGraw-Hill, 1968).

Schouler, J., *Constitutional Studies* (Dodd, Mead, 1897).

Schwartz, B., *A Commentary on the Constitution of the United States*, Part I, The Powers of Government (Macmillan, 1963).

Shogan, R., *A Question of Judgment: The Fortas Case and the Struggle for the Supreme Court* (Bobbs-Merrill, 1972).

Small, N. J. (ed.), *Constitution of the United States of America*, rev. & ann. (U.S. G.P.O., 1964).

Smith, O. G., *The Convention and the Constitution: The Political Ideas of the Founding Fathers* (St. Martin's, 1964).

Story, J., *Commentaries on the Constitution of the United States* (Little, Brown, 1833).

———, *A Familiar Exposition on the Constitution of the U.S.: Containing a Brief Commentary* (Marsh, Capen, Lyon, and Webb, 1840).

Ten-Broek, J., *Anti-Slavery Origins of the Fourteenth Amendment* (Berkeley, 1951).

Tiffany, J., *A Treatise on Government and Constitutional Law* (W. C. Little, 1867).

Towel, N., *A History and Analysis of the Constitution of the United States* (Little, Brown, 1860).

Tugwell, R. G., *The Emerging Constitution* (Harper & Row, 1974).

———, *Model for a New Constitution* (Freel, 1970).

Vose, C., *Constitutional Change* (Heath, 1972).

Willoughby, W. W., *The Constitutional Law of the United States* (Baker, 1929).

JUDGES AND JUSTICES

(The men and their behavior in their decision-making function; see also Bibliography II.)

Abraham, H. J., *Justices and Presidents: A Political History of Appointments to the Supreme Court* (Oxford, 1974).

Asch, S. H., *The Supreme Court and Its Great Justices* (Arco, 1971).

Ashman, C., *The Finest Judges Money Can Buy* (Nash, 1973).

Baxter, M. G., *Daniel Webster and the Supreme Court* (U. of Massachusetts, 1967).

Becker, T., *Political Behavioralism and Modern Jurisprudence* (Rand McNally, 1965).

Bickel, A. M., *Politics and the Warren Court* (Harper & Row, 1966).

Borkin, J., *The Corrupt Judge* (Potter, 1962).

Botein, B., *Trial Judge* (Simon & Schuster, 1952; Cornerstone, 1963).

Bruce, A. A., *The American Judge* (Macmillan, 1924).

Cardozo, B. N., *The Nature of the Judicial Process* (Yale, 1921).

Chase, H. W., *Federal Judges: The Appointing Process* (U. of Minnesota, 1973).

Danelski, D. J., "The Chief Justices of the Supreme Court" (Unpublished Ph.D. Dissertation, U. of Illinois, 1961).

Davenport, W. H. (ed.), *Voices in Court* (Macmillan, 1958).

Douglas, W. O., *We, The Judges* (Doubleday, 1956).

Ewing, C. A. M., *The Judges of the Supreme Court, 1789–1937* (U. of Minnesota, 1938).

Frankfurter, F., *Of Law and Men: Papers and Addresses of Felix Frankfurter*, ed. by Philip Elman (Harcourt, Brace, 1956).

Freund, P. A., *On Law and Justice* (Harvard, 1968).

Friedman, L., and F. L. Israel (eds.), *The Justices of the United States Supreme Court, 1789–1969: Their Lives and Major Opinions* (Chelsea & Bowker, 1969).

Friendly, H. J., *Benchmarks* (U. of Chicago, 1967).

Goldberg, L., and L. Levenson, *Lawless Judges* (Rand School Press, 1935).

Harris, R., *Decision* (Dutton, 1971).

Hurst, J. S., *The Growth of American Law: The Lawmakers* (Little, Brown, 1950).

Jaffee, L. L., *British and American Judges as Lawmakers* (Oxford, 1970).

Kirchheimer, O., *Political Justice: The Use of Legal Procedure for Political Ends* (Princeton, 1961).

Klein, F. W., and J. S. Lee (eds.), *Selected Writings of Arthur T. Vanderbilt* (Oceana, 1966).

Knox, K. C., *A Judge Comes of Age* (Scribner's, 1940).

Kristein, B. F. (ed.), *A Man's Reach: The Philosophy of Judge Jerome Frank* (Macmillan, 1965).

Levy, L. W., *The Law of the Commonwealth and Chief Justice Shaw* (Harvard, 1957).

Lide, L. D., *The Trial Judge in South Carolina* (U. of South Carolina, 1953).

Lummus, H. T. *The Trial Judge* (Foundation Press, 1937).

Nagel, S., "Judicial Characteristics and Judicial Decision-making" (Unpublished Ph.D. Dissertation, Northwestern, 1961).

Peltason, J. W., *Fifty-eight Lonely Men: Southern Federal Judges and School Desegregation*, rev. ed. (Harcourt, Brace & World, 1971).

Porter, E. S., *Conscience of the Court* (Prentice-Hall, 1962).

Pritchett, C. H., *The Roosevelt Court: A Study in Judicial Politics and Values, 1937–1947* (Macmillan, 1947).

Roe, C. E., *Our Judicial Oligarchy* (Huebsch, 1912).

Rosenblum, V. G., *Law as a Political Instrument* (Doubleday, 1955).

Schick, M., *Learned Hand's Court* (Johns Hopkins, 1970).

Schubert, G. A., *Constitutional Politics* (Holt, Rinehart & Winston, 1960).

———, *Judicial Behavior: A Reader in Theory and Research* (Rand McNally, 1964).

————, *The Judicial Mind: The Attitudes and Ideologies of the Supreme Court, 1943–1963* (Northwestern, 1965).

————, *The Judicial Mind Revisited: Psychometric Analysis of Supreme Court Ideology* (Oxford, 1974).

————, *Quantitative Analysis of Judicial Behavior* (Free Press, 1959).

———— (ed.), *Judicial Decision-making* (Free Press, 1959).

Shanks, H., *The Art and Craft of Judging* (Macmillan, 1968).

Shientag, B. L., *Moulders of Legal Thought* (Viking, 1943).

Shogan, R., *A Question of Judgment: The Fortas Case and the Struggle for the Supreme Court* (Bobbs-Merrill, 1972).

Simon, J. F., *In His Own Image: The Supreme Court in Richard Nixon's America* (McKay, 1973).

Stansbury, A. J., *Report of the Trial of James H. Peck* (Hilliard, Gray, 1833).

Steamer, R. J., *The Supreme Court: Constitutional Revision and the New "Strict Constructionism"* (Burgess, 1973).

Todd, A. L., *Justice on Trial: The Case of Louis D. Brandeis* (McGraw-Hill, 1964).

Tomkins, D. C., *The Supreme Court of the United States: A Bibliography* (Berkeley, 1959).

Tresolini, R. J., *Justice and the Supreme Court* (Lippincott, 1963).

Ulc, O., *The Judge in a Communist State* (Ohio State U., 1972).

Ulman, J. N., *A Judge Takes the Stand* (Knopf, 1933).

Vanderbilt, A. T., *Judges and Jurors: Their Functions, Qualifications, and Selection* (Boston U., 1956).

Westin, A. F., *The Supreme Court: Views from Inside* (Norton, 1961).

Wyzanski, C. E., Jr., *Whereas—A Judge's Premise: Essays in Judgment, Ethics, and the Law* (Atlantic, Little, Brown, 1965).

JUDICIAL REVIEW

Abraham, H. J., *The Judicial Process: An Introductory Analysis of the Courts of the United States, England, and France*, 3rd ed. (Oxford, 1975).

Association of American Law Schools, *Selected Essays on Constitutional Law* (Foundation Press, 1938).

Beard, C. A., *The Supreme Court and the Constitution*, rev. ed., with a new introduction by Alan F. Westin (Prentice-Hall, 1962).

Beck, J. M., *The Changed Conception of the Constitution* (U. of Rochester, 1925).

Becker, T. L., *The Supreme Court Decisions: Readings on Causes and Effects* (Oxford, 1969).

Black, C. L., Jr., *The People and the Court: Judicial Review in a Democracy* (Macmillan, 1960).

————, *Old and New Ways in Judicial Review* (Bowdoin, 1957).

Boudin, L. B., *Government by Judiciary* (Godwin, 1932).

Cahn, E., *Supreme Court and Supreme Law* (Indiana U., 1954).

Carr, R. K., *The Supreme Court and Judicial Review* (Farrar and Rinehart, 1942).

————, *Democracy and the Supreme Court* (U. of Oklahoma, 1936).

Cooley, T. M., *Constitutional Limitations* (Putnam's, 1868).

Corwin, E. S., *Court Over Constitution: A Study of Judicial Review as an Instrument of Popular Government* (Princeton, 1938).

————, *The Doctrine of Judicial Review* (Princeton, 1914).

————, *The Establishment of Judicial Review* (Princeton, 1930).

————, *Our Constitutional Revolution and How To Round It Out* (Philadelphia Brandeis Lawyer Society, 1951).

Coxe, B., *Judicial Power and Unconstitutional Legislation* (Kay, 1893; Da Capo, 1970).

Crosskey, W. W., *Politics and the Constitution in the History of the United States* (U. of Chicago, 1953).

Cushman, R. E., *The Role of the Supreme Court in a Democratic Nation* (Public Affairs Comm., 1938).

————, *The Supreme Court and the Constitution* (Public Affairs Comm., 1940).

————, *What's Happening to Our Constitution* (Public Affairs Comm., 1940).

Davis, H. A., *The Judicial Veto* (Houghton, Mifflin, 1914).

Dean, H., *Judicial Review and Democracy* (Random House, 1966).

Dougherty, J. H., *The Power of the Federal Judiciary over Legislation* (Putnam's, 1912).

Fennell, W. G., *The "Reconstructed Court"* (N.Y.U., 1942).

Forte, D. F. (ed.), *The Supreme Court in American Politics: Judicial Activism v. Judicial Restraint* (Heath, 1972).

Freedman, M., W. H. Beaney, and E. V. Rostow, *Perspectives on the Court* (Northwestern, 1967).

Garvey, G. *Constitutional Bricolage* (Princeton, 1971).

Gilbert, W. C. (comp.), *Provisions of Federal Law Held Unconstitutional by the Supreme Court of the United States* (U.S. G.P.O., 1936).

Haines, C. G., *The American Doctrine of Judicial Supremacy*, 2nd ed., rev. and enl. (Berkeley, 1959).

————, *A Government of Laws or a Government of Men* (U.C.L.A., 1929).

Hand, L., *The Bill of Rights* (Harvard, 1958; Atheneum, 1964).

Henry, J. M., *Nine Above the Law: Our Supreme Court* (Lewis, 1936).

Hyneman, C. S., *The Supreme Court on Trial* (Atherton, 1963).

Johnson, J. E. (ed.), *Limitation of the Power of the Supreme Court To Declare Acts of Congress Unconstitutional* (H. W. Wilson, 1935).

Johnston, R. E., *The Effect of Judicial Review in Federal-State Relations in Australia, Canada, and the United States* (Cambridge, 1970).

Levy, B. H., *Our Constitution: Toll or Testament* (Knopf, 1941).

Lewinson, J. L., *Limiting Judicial Review* (Parker, Stane and Braid, 1937).

Loewenstein, K., *Political Power and the Government Process*, Ch. VIII (U. of Chicago, 1956).

Long, H. A., *Usurpers, Foes of Free Men* (Post, 1957).

McCloskey, R. G., *American Conservatism in the Age of Enterprise* (Harvard, 1957).

————, *The American Supreme Court* (U. of Chicago, 1960).

McKay, R. B. (ed.), *The American Constitutional Law Reader* (Oceana, 1958).

McLaughlin, A. C., *The Courts, Constitution and Parties* (U. of Chicago, 1912).

McWhinney, E., *Judicial Review in the English-Speaking World*, 4th ed. (U. of Toronto, 1969).

Mason, A. T., *The Supreme Court: Palladium of Freedom* (U. of Michigan, 1962).

Meigs, W. M., *The Relation of the Judiciary to the Constitution* (Neale, 1919).

Moore, B. F., *The Supreme Court and Unconstitutional Legislation* (Columbia, 1913).

Nichols, E. R., *Congress or the Supreme Court: Which Shall Rule America* (Noble, 1935).

Notre Dame Lawyer, Symposium, "The Role of the Supreme Court in the American Constitutional System" (Notre Dame Law School, 1959).

Powell, T. R., *Vagaries and Varieties in Constitutional Interpretations* (Columbia, 1956).

Roe, G. E., *Our Judicial Oligarchy* (Huebsch, 1912).

Rostow, E. V., *The Sovereign Prerogative: The Supreme Court and the Quest for Law* (Yale, 1962).

Senior, M. R., *The Supreme Court: Its Power of Judicial Review with Respect to Congressional Legislation* (George Washington U., 1937).

Smith, F. A., *Judicial Review of Legislation in New York, 1906–1938* (Columbia, 1952).

Syracuse Law Review, "Controversy Over the Supreme Court" (A Symposium) (Spring, 1959).

Tompkins, D. C., *The Supreme Court of the United States: A Bibliography* (Berkeley, 1959).

Von Moschzisker, R., *Judicial Review of Legislation* (National Assoc. for Constitutional Government, 1923).

Warren, C., *Congress, the Constitution, and the Supreme Court* (Little, Brown, 1935).

Wechsler, H., *Principles, Politics and Fundamental Law* (Harvard, 1961).

Wright, B. F., *The Growth of American Constitutional Law* (Reynal and Hitchcock, 1942).

JURIES

Abraham, H. J., *The Judicial Process: An Introductory Analysis of the Courts of the United States, England, and France*, 3rd ed. (Oxford, 1975).

Bentham, J., *The Elements of the Art of Packing as Applied to Special Juries* (Effingham-Wilson, 1821).

Bloomstein, M. J., *Verdict: The Jury System* (Dodd, Mead, 1968).

Busch, F. X., *Law and Tactics in Jury Trials* (Bobbs-Merrill, 1963).

Chester, G., *The Ninth Juror* (Random House, 1971).

Clementson, G. B., *Special Verdicts and Special Findings by Juries* (West, 1905).

Crook, J., *Law and Life of Rome* (Cornell, 1967).

Dawson, J. P., *A History of Lay Judges* (Harvard, 1960).

Devlin, Sir P., *Trial by Jury* (Methuen, 1966).

Forsyth, W., *History of Trial by Jury*, new ed. (Cockcroft, 1875).

Francis, P., *How To Serve on a Jury* (Oceana, 1953).

Frank, J., *Courts on Trial: Myth and Reality in American Justice* (Princeton, 1949).

Gleisser, M., *Juries and Justice* (A. S. Barnes, 1968).

Green, L., *Judge and Jury* (Vernon, 1930).

Joiner, C. W., *Civil Justice and the Jury* (Prentice-Hall, 1962).

Kalven, H., Jr., and H. Zeisel, *The American Jury* (U. of Chicago, 1966).

Keeney, B. C., *Judgment by Peers* (Harvard, 1949).

McCart, S., *Trial by Jury: A Complete Guide to the Jury System* (Chilton, 1965).

Mathes, W. C., and E. J. Devitt, *Federal Jury Practice and Instructions, Civil and Criminal* (West, 1965).

Osborn, A. S., *The Mind of the Juror* (Boyd, 1937).

Polier, J. W., A View from the Bench (National Council on Crime and Delinquency, 1964).

Scigliano, R. G., The Michigan One-Man Grand Jury (Michigan State U., 1957).

Shields, D. C., and J. F. Cragan, Justice and the Jury (Campus, 1971).

Simon, R. J., The Jury and the Plea of Insanity (Little, Brown, 1966).

Vanderbilt, A. T., Judges and Jurors: Their Functions, Qualifications, and Selection (Boston U., 1956).

Wellman, F. L., Gentlemen of the Jury (Macmillan, 1936).

Winters, G. R., The Jury: Selected Readings (American Judic. Soc., 1971).

Younger, R. D., The People's Panel: The Grand Jury in the United States, 1634–1941 (Brown U., 1963).

JURISDICTION AND ORGANIZATION OF COURTS

Abraham, H. J., The Judicial Process: An Introductory Analysis of the Courts of the United States, England, and France, 3rd ed. (Oxford, 1975).

Annual Reports of the Director of the Administrative Office of the United States Courts.

Brennan, W. J., Modernizing the Courts (Inst. of Jud. Ad., 1957).

Bunn, C. W., A Brief Survey of the Jurisdiction and Practice of the Courts of the United States, 5th ed. (West, 1949).

Bureau of Municipal Research, The Magistrate Courts of Philadelphia, rev. ed. (Pennsylvania Economy League, 1958).

Callender, C. M., American Courts: Their Organization and Procedure (McGraw-Hill, 1927).

Comer, J. P., The Forging of the Federal Indigent Code (Principia, 1966).

Countryman, E., The Supreme Court of the United States (Bender, 1913).

Dobie, A. N., Handbook of Federal Jurisdiction and Procedure (West, 1928).

Ferguson, J. H., and D. L. Cowells, Minor Courts in Pennsylvania: A Study of the Justices of the Peace and Aldermen (Pennsylvania State U., 1962).

Fins, H. G., Federal Jurisdiction and Procedure (Bobbs-Merrill, 1960).

Frank, J. F., Courts on Trial (Princeton, 1959).

Glick, H., Supreme Courts in State Politics: An Investigation of the Judicial Role (Basic Books, 1971).

———, and K. N. Vines, State Court Systems (Prentice-Hall, 1973).

Goldman, S., and T. Jahnige, The Federal Courts as a Political System (Harper & Row, 1971).

Gressman, E., and R. L. Stern, Supreme Court Practice, 4th ed. (Bureau of National Affairs, 1969).

Harding, A. L., (ed.), The Administration of Justice in Retrospect (S.M.U., 1957).

Harris, R. J., The Judicial Power of the United States (Louisiana State U., 1940).

Hart, H. M., Jr., and H. Wechsler, The Judicial Code and Rules of Procedure in the Federal Courts (Foundation Press, 1954).

Institute of Public Administration, The Minor Courts in Pennsylvania (Pennsylvania State U., 1962).

Kalven, D., Appellate Courts in the United States and England (N.Y.U., 1956).

Lepawsky, A., The Judicial System of Metropolitan Chicago (U. of Chicago, 1932).

McGowan, C., The Organization of Judicial Power in the United States (Northwestern, 1969).

411

Moley, R., *Our Criminal Courts* (Minton, Balch, 1930).

Post, C. G., Jr., *The Supreme Court and Political Questions* (Johns Hopkins, 1936).

Pound, R., *Organization of Courts* (Little, Brown, 1940).

Richardson, R. W., and K. N. Vines, *Politics of the Federal Courts* (Little, Brown, 1970).

Robertson, R., *Jurisdiction of the Supreme Court of the United States* (Bender, 1951).

Rose, J. C., *Jurisdiction and Procedure of Federal Courts* (Bender, 1938).

Rosenheim, M. K., *Justice for the Child: The Juvenile Court in Transition* (Macmillan, 1962).

Sayre, W. S. (ed.), *State Court Systems* (Prentice-Hall, 1973).

Schick, M., *Learned Hand's Court* (Johns Hopkins, 1970).

Sunderland, E. R., *Judicial Administration* (Callaghan, 1939).

United States Senate, Committee on the Judiciary, *Composition and Jurisdiction of the United States Supreme Court* (Superintendent of Documents, 1954).

————, *Reorganization of the Federal Judiciary* (Superintendent of Documents, 1937).

Warren, G., *Traffic Courts* (Little, Brown, 1942).

Wolfson, R. F., and P. Kurland, *Jurisdiction of the Supreme Court of the United States*, rev. ed. (Bender, 1951).

Wright, B. F., *Federal Courts* (West, 1963).

LABOR LAW AND LEGISLATION

Fleming, R. W., *The Labor Arbitration Powers* (U. of Illinois, 1967).

Frankfurter, F., with Nathan Greene, *The Labor Injunction* (Macmillan, 1930).

Groat, G. C., *Attitude of American Courts in Labor Cases* (Longmans, Green & Co., 1911).

Mueller, S. J., and A. H. Myers, *Labor Law and Legislation*, 3rd ed. (Southwestern, Publishing Co., 1962).

Myers, A. H., *Labor Law and Legislation*, 4th ed. (Southwestern, Publishing Co., 1968).

Oberer, W. E., and K. L. Hanslowe, *Collective Bargaining and the Law—An Overview* (West, 1972).

Parker, R. A., *A Guide to Labor Law* (Praeger, 1961).

Raushenbush, C., and E. Stein, *Labor Cases and Materials* (Crofts, 1941).

Taylor, A. G., *Labor and the Supreme Court*, 2nd ed. (U. of Michigan, 1960).

Wellington, H. H., *Labor and the Legal Process* (Yale, 1969).

THE LAW

(Principles of law. What the law is. Development of the law.)

Allen, C. K., *Law in the Making*, 7th ed. (Oxford, 1964).

Arens, R., and H. D. Lasswell, *In Defense of Public Order: The Emerging Field of Sanction Law* (Columbia, 1961).

Arneson, B. A., *Elements of Constitutional Law* (Harper Bros., 1928).

Aumann, F. R., *The Changing American Legal System* (Ohio State U., 1940).

Barkun, M., *Law Without Sanctions: Order in Primitive Societies and the World Community* (Yale, 1968).

Belli, M. M., *Ready for the Plaintiff* (Holt, 1956).

Berman, H. J. (ed.), *Talk on America's Law* (Random House, 1961).

————, and W. R. Greiners, *The Nature and Function of Law* (Foundation Press, 1966).

Black, C. L., Jr., *The Occasions of Justice: Essays Mostly in Law* (Macmillan, 1964).

Bloustein, E. J. (ed.), *Nuclear Energy, Public Policy and the Law* (Oceana, 1964).

Blumberg, A. S. (ed.), *Law and Order* (Aldine, 1970).

Bodenheimer, E., *Jurisprudence* (McGraw-Hill, 1947).

Borchard, E. M., *Declaratory Judgments*, 2nd ed. (Banks-Baldwin, 1941).

Brownell, E. A., *Legal Aid in the United States* (with Supplement) (Lawyers' Coop. Publ. Co., 1961).

Buckland, W. W., and A. D. McNair, *Roman Law and the Common Law*, rev. ed. (Cambridge, 1952).

Carpenter, W. S., *Foundations of Modern Jurisprudence* (Appleton-Century-Crofts, 1958).

Cataldo, B. F., *et al.*, *Introduction to Law and the Legal Process* (Wiley, 1965).

Cooley, T. M., *Constitutional Limitations* (Putnam's, 1868).

Cooper, F. E., *Living the Law* (Bobbs-Merrill, 1958).

Corry, J. A., *The Power of the Law* (CBS Learning Systems, 1971).

Daube, D., *Roman Law: Linguistic, Social, and Philosophical Aspects* (Aldine, 1969).

Davenport, W. H. (ed.), *Voices in Court* (Macmillan, 1958).

Davis, F. J., *et al.*, *Society and the Law: New Meaning for an Old Profession* (Free Press, 1962).

Desmond, C. S., *Through the Courtroom Window* (West, 1959).

Donnelly, R. C., J. Goldstein, and R. D. Schwartz, *Criminal Law* (Free Press, 1962).

Edmunds, P. D., *Law and Civilization* (Public Affairs Press, 1959).

Edwards, N., *The Courts and the Public Schools* (U. of Chicago, 1962).

Ehrlich, J. W. (ed.), *Blackstone* (Capricorn, 1959).

Eisenstein, J., *Politics and the Legal Process* (Harper & Row, 1973).

Evan, W. M. (ed.), *Law and Sociology* (Free Press, 1962).

Field, O. P., *The Effect of an Unconstitutional Statute* (U. of Minnesota, 1935).

Ford, S., *The American Legal System—Its Dynamics and Limits* (West, 1970).

Fordham, J. B., *Local Government Law* (Foundation Press, 1949).

Freund, E., *The Police Power, Public Policy, and Constitutional Rights* (Callaghan, 1904).

Friedman, L., and S. Macauley, *Law and the Behavioral Sciences* (Stanford, 1970).

Fuller, L. L., *The Anatomy of Law* (Modern Library, 1969).

————, *Legal Fictions* (Stanford, 1967).

————, *The Morality of Law* (Yale, 1964).

Gavong, C. K., and R. W. Pearce, *Law and Society* (Irwin, 1965).

Grad, F. P., A. L. Goldberg, and B. A. Shapiro, *Alcoholism and the Law* (Oceana, 1971).

Gray, C. M., *Copyhold, Equity, and the Common Law* (Harvard, 1963).

Gray, J. C., *The Nature and Sources of the Law*, 2nd ed. (Macmillan, 1948; Beacon, 1963).

Green, L., *Judge and Jury* (Vernon Law Book Co., 1930).

Griswold, E. N., *Law and Lawyers in the United States: The Common Law under Stress* (Harvard, 1964).

Hare, J. I. C., *American Constitutional Law* (Brown, 1889).

Hartland, E. S., *Primitive Law* (Kennikat, 1924).

Havighurst, C. C. (ed.), *Air Pollution Control* (Oceana, 1969).

———, *Medical Progress and the Law* (Oceana, 1969).

Hazard, G. C., Jr., *Law in a Changing Society* (Prentice-Hall, 1968).

Henderson, G. C., *The Position of Foreign Corporations in American Constitutional Law* (Harvard, 1960).

Henson, R. D. (ed.), *Landmarks of Law: Highlights of Legal Opinion from 1890 to the Present* (Harper & Bros., 1960; Beacon, 1963).

Hoebel, E. A., *The Law of Primitive Man* (Harvard, 1964).

Hogue, A. R., *Origins of the Common Law* (U. of Indiana, 1966).

Hohfeld, W. N., *Fundamental Legal Conceptions* (Yale, 1964).

Holdsworth, Sir W., *A History of English Law* (Goodhart and Hanbury, 1956).

Holmes, O. W., Jr., *The Common Law* (Little, Brown, 1881; new ed., Harvard, 1963, ed. by Mark De Wolfe Howe).

Honnold, J., *The Life of the Law: Readings on the Growth of Legal Institutions* (Free Press, 1964).

Hurst, J. W., *The Law of Treason in the United States: Collected Essays* (Greenwood, 1971).

Jackson, P. E., *Justice and the Law* (Michie, 1964).

Jahr, A. D., *The Law of Eminent Domain—Valuation and Procedure* (C. Boardman, 1953).

Jones, H. W., *The Efficacy of Law* (Northwestern, 1969).

Keeton, R. E., *Legal Cause in the Law of Torts* (Ohio State U., 1963).

Kent, J., *Commentaries on American Law*, 5th ed. (Little, Brown, 1830).

Kirchheimer, O., *Political Justice: The Use of Legal Procedure for Political Ends* (Princeton, 1961).

Lee, L. T., *Consular Law and Practice* (Praeger, 1961).

Lefcourt, R. (ed.), *Law Against the People: Essays to Demystify Law, Order, and the Courts* (Knopf, 1971).

Lobenthal, J., *Power and Put-On: The Law in America* (Outerbridge & Dienstfrey, 1970).

London, E., *The World of Law* (Simon & Schuster, 1960).

Lunt, D. C., *The Road to Law* (Norton, 1962).

McCormick, C. T., *Handbook of the Law of Evidence* (West, 1954).

McKean, D., *The Integrated Bar* (Houghton, Mifflin, 1963).

Macmillan, H. P., *Law and Other Things* (Cambridge, 1937).

Maine, Sir H., *Ancient Law* (Murray, 1917).

Manning, B., *Federal Conflict of Interest Law* (Harvard, 1964).

Marshall, J., *Law and Psychology in Conflict* (Bobbs-Merrill, 1966 and Anchor, 1969).

Mellinkoff, D., *The Language of the Law* (Little, Brown, 1963).

Morris, C., *The Justification of the Law* (U. of Pennsylvania, 1971).

Morris, R. B., *Studies in the History of American Law* (Lippincott, 1959).

Muir, W. K., Jr., *Law and Attitude Change* (U. of Chicago, 1973).

New York Times (eds.), *American Law: The Formative Years* (Arno, 1971).

Newan, R. A., *Equity and Law: A Comparative Study* (Oceana, 1961).

Nice, R. W. (ed.), *Treasury of Law* (Philosophical Library, 1964).

Oceana Publications, Inc. (eds.), *Annual Survey of American Law* (1960 ff).

————, *The Legal Almanac Series* (1955ff).

Palmer, E. E. (ed.), *Current Law and Social Problems* (U. of Toronto, 1963).

Paton, G. W., *A Textbook of Jurisprudence* (Claredon, 1951).

Perkins, R. M., *Cases on Criminal Law and Procedures* (Foundation Press, 1959).

Phelps, C. E., *Elements of Judicial Equity* (King, 1890).

Plucknett, F. T. A., *A Concise History of the Common Law*, 3rd ed. (Butterworth, 1940).

Pollock, Sir F., *Essays in the Law* (Macmillan, 1922).

————, *The Expansion of the Common Law* (Macmillan, 1904).

————, *A First Book in Jurisprudence*, 4th ed. (Macmillan, 1918).

————, *Jurisprudence and Legal Essays* ed. by A. L. Goodhart (St. Martin's, 1962).

Post, C. G., *An Introduction to the Law* (Prentice-Hall, 1963).

Pound, R., *The Formative Era of American Law* (Little, Brown, 1938).

Radin, M., *The Law and Mr. Smith* (Bobbs-Merrill, 1938).

————, *The Law and You* (Mentor, 1948).

Rawls, J., *A Theory of Justice* (Harvard, 1971).

Raz, J., *The Concepts of a Legal System* (Oxford, 1970).

Rodell, F., *Woe Unto You Lawyers*, rev. ed. (Pageant, 1956).

Rogers, H. S., *Constitutional History of the United States as Seen in the Development of American Law* (Bender, 1890).

Ross, M. J., *Handbook of Everyday Law*, rev. and enl. (Harper & Row, 1967).

Rostow, E. V., (ed.), *Is Law Dead?* (Simon & Schuster, 1972).

Rottschaefer, H., *Handbook of American Constitutional Law* (West, 1939).

Schnapper, M. B., *Constraint by Copyright* (Public Affairs Press, 1962).

Schur, E. M., *Law and Society: A Sociological View* (Random House, 1969).

Schwartz, B., *The Law in America* (American Heritage, 1974).

Seagle, W., *Law, the Science of Inefficiency* (Macmillan, 1952).

————, *The Quest for Law* (Knopf, 1941).

Shartel, B., *Our Legal System and How It Operates* (U. of Michigan Law School, 1950).

Simon, T. R., *The Tradition of Natural Law* (Fordham, 1965).

Simpson, S. P., and J. Stone, *Law and Society* (West, 1948–49).

Sloan, I. J., *Environment and the Law* (Oceana, 1971).

————, *Youth and the Law* (Oceana, 1970).

Steigleman, W. A., *The Newspaperman and the Law* (W. C. Brown, 1950).

Surrency, E., B. Field, and J. Crea, *A Practical Guide to Legal Research*, 2nd ed. (Oceana, 1959).

Sutherland, A. E., *An Introduction to Law* (Harvard, 1957).

————, *Statutes and Statutory Construction*, 3rd ed. (Horack, 1943).

Thayer, J. B., *Legal Essays* (Boston Book Co., 1908).

United States Code, Title 28 (comprising the *Federal Judicial Code*), (U.S. G.P.O.).

University of Michigan Law School 1955 Conference, *Aims and Methods of Legal Research* (U. of Michigan, 1958).

Vanderbilt, A. T., *Studying Law*, 2nd ed. (N.Y.U., 1955).

Vinogradoff, P., *Common Sense in Law*, 3rd ed., rev. by H. G. Hanbury (Oxford, 1949).

————, *Outlines of Historical Jurisprudence* (Oxford, 1920).

Wasserstein, B., and M. J. Green, *With Justice for Some* (Beacon, 1970).

Weaver, S. P., *Constitutional Law and Its Administration* (Callaghan, 1946).

415

Weissman, J., *Law in a Business Society* (Prentice-Hall, 1963).
Wigmore, J. H., *Wigmore on Evidence*, 3rd ed. (Little, Brown, 1940).
Willoughby, W. W., *The Constitutional Law of the United States* (Baker, 1929).
Wolff, H., *Roman Law: A Historical Introduction* (U. of Oklahoma, 1951).
Wormser, R. A., *The Story of Law* (Simon & Schuster, 1962).
Wortley, B. A., *Jurisprudence* (Oceana, 1966).
Wright, C. A., *Handbook of the Law of Federal Courts* (West, 1970).

THE LEGAL PROFESSION

(Attorneys, court officers: the men, their work, their education.)

Arnold, T., *Fair Fights and Foul: A Dissenting Lawyer's Life* (Harcourt, Brace & World, 1965).
Bishop, J. W., Jr., *Obiter Dicta: Opinions, Judicial and Otherwise, on Lawyers and the Law* (Atheneum, 1971).
Black, J. (ed.), *Radical Lawyers: Their Role in the Movement and in the Courts* (Avon, 1971).
Blaustein, A. D., and C. O. Porter, *The American Lawyer* (Chicago, 1954).
Bloom, M. T., *The Trouble with Lawyers* (Simon & Schuster, 1969).
Botein, B., *The Prosecutor* (Simon & Schuster, 1956).
Bowen, C. D., *The Lion and the Throne: The Life and Times of Sir Edward Coke, 1552–1634* (Little, Brown, 1957).
Brown, C. G., *You May Take the Witness* (U. of Texas, 1955).
Brown, E. L., *Lawyers, Law Schools and the Public Service* (Russell Sage Foundation, 1948).
Butler, C. H., *A Century at the Bar of the Supreme Court* (Putnam's, 1942).
Carlin, J. E., *Lawyer's Ethics: A Survey of the New York City Bar* (Russell Sage Foundation, 1966).
———, *Lawyers on Their Own: A Study of Individual Practitioners in Chicago* (Rutgers, 1964).
Casper, J. D., *Lawyers Before the Warren Court: Civil Liberties and Civil Rights, 1957–1966* (U. of Illinois, 1972).
Chambers, M. M., *Colleges and the Courts* (Columbia, 1952).
Choust, A. H., *The Rise of the Legal Profession in America* (U. of Oklahoma, 1965).
Curtis, C. P., *It's Your Law* (Harvard, 1954).
Davenport, W. H. (ed.), *Voices in Court* (Macmillan, 1958).
Donovan, J. W., *Modern Jury Trials* (Jennings, 1929).
Drinker, H. S., *Legal Ethics* (Columbia, 1953).
Elliff, J. T., *Crime, Dissent and the Attorney General: The Justice Department in the 1960's* (Sage, 1971).
Eulau, A., and J. D. Sprague, *Lawyers in Politics: A Study in Professional Convergence* (Bobbs-Merrill, 1964).
Fordham, E. W., *Notable Cross-Examinations* (Macmillan, 1957).
Frank, J. P., *Lincoln as a Lawyer* (U. of Illinois, 1961).
Frank, M. M., *The Diary of a D. A.* (Holt, Rinehart & Winston, 1960).
Garland, A. H., *Experience in the United States Supreme Court* (J. Byrne & Co., 1898).
Goodhart, A. L., *Five Jewish Lawyers of the Common Law* (Oxford, 1959).

Goulden, J. C., *The Superlawyers: The Small and Powerful World of the Great Washington Law Firms* (Weybright & Tally, 1972).

Greenbaum, E. S., *A Lawyer's Job: In Court—in the Army—in the Office* (Harcourt, Brace & World, 1968).

Grossman, J., *Lawyers and Judges* (Wiley, 1965).

Handler, J. F., *The Lawyer and His Community: The Practicing Bar in a Middle-Sized City* (U. of Wisconsin, 1968).

Harbaugh, W. H., *Lawyer's Lawyer: The Life of John W. Davis* (Oxford, 1973).

Harris, R., *Justice: The Crisis of Law, Order, and Freedom in America* (Dutton, 1970).

Hine, R. L., *Confessions of an Un-Common Attorney* (Macmillan, 1945).

Horton, J. T., *James Kent: A Study in Conservatism* (Appleton-Century, 1939).

Hurst, J. W., *The Growth of American Law: The Lawmakers* (Little, Brown, 1950).

Huston, L. A., *et al.*, *Roles of the Attorney General of the United States* (L.R.S., 1968).

Karlen, D., *The Citizen in Court: Litigant, Witness, Juror, Judge* (Holt, Rinehart, & Winston, 1964).

Knox, J. C., *A Judge Comes of Age* (Scribner's, 1940).

Kutner, L., *The Lawyer* (Dodd, Mead, 1966).

Lewis, W. D. (ed.), *Great American Lawyers* (Winston, 1907).

Llewellyn, K. N., *The Bramble Bush: On Our Law and Its Study* (Oceana, 1957).

McKean, C., *The Integrated Bar* (Houghton, Mifflin, 1963).

Marks, F. R., *The Lawyer, the Public, and Professional Responsibility* (American Bar Fund, 1972).

Mayer, M., *The Lawyer* (Harper & Row, 1966).

Morris, C., *How Lawyers Think* (Swallow, 1962).

Musmanno, M. M., *Verdict* (Doubleday, 1958).

Navasky, V. S., *Kennedy Justice* (Atheneum, 1971).

Nizer, L., *My Life in Court* (Doubleday, 1961).

Paulson, M. C. (ed.), *Legal Institutions Today and Tomorrow* (Columbia, 1959).

Pike, J. A., *Beyond the Law: The Religious and Ethical Meaning of the Lawyer's Vocation* (Doubleday, 1963).

Pound, R., *The Lawyer from Antiquity to Modern Times* (West, 1953).

Rossman, G., *Advocacy and the King's English* (Bobbs-Merrill, 1960).

Rutherford, M. L. S., "The Influence of the American Bar Association on Public Opinion and Legislation" (Unpublished Ph.D. Dissertation, U. of Pennsylvania, 1937).

St. John, A. R., *Final Verdict* (Doubleday, 1962).

Schientag, B. L., *Moulders of Legal Thought* (Viking, 1943).

Schmidhauser, J. R., *The Supreme Court: Its Politics, Personalities and Procedures* (Holt, Rinehart and Winston, 1960).

Smigel, E. O., *The Wall Street Lawyer* (Free Press, 1964).

Smith, T., *Lawyer: Opportunities for Careers in the Legal Profession* (Macmillan, 1961).

Stryker, L. P., *The Art of Advocacy* (Simon & Schuster, 1954; Cornerstone, 1963).

Sunderland, E. R., *Judicial Administration* (Callaghan, 1939).

Taylor, G. C., *Fifty Years in the Law* (Philosophical Library, 1963).

Vanderbilt, A. T., *Men and Measures in the Law* (Knopf, 1949).

——, *Studying Law*, 2nd ed. (N.Y. U., 1955).

Warkov, S., *Lawyers in the Making* (Aldine, 1966).

Warren, C., *A History of the American Bar* (Little, Brown, 1911).

Wellman, F. L., *The Art of Cross-Examination*, 4th ed. (Macmillan, 1936).
———, *Day in Court* (Macmillan, 1910).
Weinberg, A., and I. Weinberg (eds.), *Clarence Darrow's Verdicts Out of Court* (Quadrangle, 1963).
Weyrauch, W. O., *The Personality of Lawyers* (Yale, 1964).
Whitney, H. C., *Life on the Circuit with Lincoln* (Estes-Lauriat, 1892).
Williston, S., *Life and Law* (Little, Brown, 1940).
Winters, G. R., *Bar Association Organization and Other Activities* (Amer. Judic. Soc., 1954).
Wood, A. L., *Criminal Lawyer* (Yale, 1967).

THE MILITARY

(*Law, courts, control.*)

Ambrose, S. E., and J. A. Barber, Jr. (eds.), *The Military and American Society* (Free Press, 1972).
Aycock, W. B., and B. W. Wurfel, *Military Law Under the Uniform Code of Military Justice* (U. of North Carolina, 1955).
Bishop, J. W., Jr., *Justice Under Fire: A Study of Military Law* (Charterhouse, 1974).
Corwin, E. S., *Total War and the Constitution* (Knopf, 1947).
Davis, J. W., Jr., and K. M. Dolbeare, *Little Groups of Neighbors: the Selective Service System* (Markham, 1968).
Edwards, M. O., and C. L. Decker, *The Serviceman and the Law* (Stackpole, 1951).
Everett, R. O., *Military Justice in the Armed Forces of the United States* (Military Service Publication Co., 1956).
Feld, B. A., *A Manual of Courts-Martial Practice and Appeal* (Oceana, 1957).
Generous, W. T., Jr., *Swords and Scales: The Development of the Uniform Code of Military Justice* (Kennikat, 1973).
Huntington, S. P., *The Soldier and the State* (Vintage, 1963).
Levantrossier, W. F., *Congress and the Citizen-soldier: Legislative Policy Making for the Federal Armed Forces Reserve* (Ohio State U., 1968).
McNair, L., and A. D. Watts, *The Legal Effects of War*, 4th ed. (Cambridge, 1966).
Mayers, J. C., III (ed.), *Why the Draft? The Case for a Volunteer Army* (Penguin, 1968).
Millis, W., *The Constitution and the Common Defense* (Fund for the Republic, 1959)
Pusey, M. J., *The Way We Go To War* (Houghton, Mifflin, 1969).
Smith, L., *American Democracy and Military Power: A Study of Civil Control of the Military Power in the United States* (U. of Chicago, 1951).
Spanier, J. W., *The Truman-MacArthur Controversy and the Korean War* (Harvard, 1959).
Wiener, F. B., *The Uniform Code of Military Justice* (Combat Forces Press, 1950).

PHILOSOPHICAL AND THEORETICAL ASPECTS OF LAW (JURISPRUDENCE)

Anderson, W. R. (ed.), *Studies in Legal Philosophy* (Vanderbilt Law School, 1961).
Arnold, T. W., *The Symbols of Government* (Yale, 1935).

Association of the Bar of the City of New York, *Conflict of Interest and Federal Service* (Harvard, 1960).

Berman, H. J., *Talks on American Law* (Random House, 1961).

Blackstone, W., *Commentaries* (Beacon, 1962).

———, *Of Public Wrongs* (Beacon, 1963).

Bodenheimer, E., *Jurisprudence* (McGraw-Hill, 1947).

———, *Jurisprudence: The Philosophy and Method of the Law* (Harvard, 1962).

Boorstin, D. J., *The Mysterious Science of the Law* (Beacon, 1963).

Brandt, R. B. (ed.), *The Concept of Social Justice* (Prentice-Hall, 1962).

Brown, B. F. (ed.), *The Natural Law Reader* (Oceana, 1960).

Burgess, J. W., *Political Science and Comparative Constitutional Law* (Ginn, 1890).

———, *Recent Changes in American Constitutional Theory* (Columbia, 1923).

Burin, F. S., and K. L. Shell (eds.), *Politics, Law and Social Change: Selected Essays of Otto Kirchheimer* (Columbia, 1969).

Cahill, F. V., *Judicial Legislation: A Study in American Legal Theory* (Ronald, 1952).

Cahn, E., *The Moral Decision: Right and Wrong in the Light of American Law*, 2nd ed. (Indiana U., 1959).

———, *The Sense of Injustice* (N.Y.U., 1951).

——— (ed.), *The Predicament of Democratic Man* (Macmillan, 1961).

Cahn, L. (ed.), *Confronting Justice: The Edward Cahn Reader* (Little, Brown, 1966).

Calhoun, J. C., *A Disquisition on Government* (Appleton, 1854; Political Science Classics, 1947).

Cardozo, B. N., *The Growth of the Law* (Yale, 1924).

———, *Law and Literature and Other Essays* (Harcourt, Brace, 1931).

———, *The Nature of the Judicial Process* (Yale, 1921).

———, *The Paradoxes of Legal Science* (Columbia, 1928).

Carlin, J. E., J. Howard, and S. Messenger, *Civil Justice and the Poor* (Sage, 1968).

Carpenter, W. S., *Foundations of Modern Jurisprudence* (Appleton-Century-Crofts, 1958).

Chambliss, W. J., and R. B. Seidman, *Law, Order and Power* (Addison-Wesley, 1971).

———, *Sociology of the Law: A Research Bibliography* (Glendessary Press, 1970).

Cohen, L. K., (ed.), *The Legal Conscience: Selected Papers of Felix S. Cohen* (Yale, 1960).

Cohen, M. R., *Law and Social Order* (Harcourt, Brace, 1933)

———, *My Philosophy of Law* (West, 1941).

———, *Reason and Law* (Collier, 1961).

———, *Reason and Nature* (Harcourt, Brace, 1931).

Corwin, E. S., *Constitutional Revolution, Ltd.* (Claremont, 1941).

———, *The Higher Law Background of American Constitutional Law* (Cornell, 1929).

———, *The Twilight of the Supreme Court: A History of Our Constitutional Theory* (Yale, 1934).

Cowan, T., (ed.), *The American Jurisprudence Reader* (Oceana, 1955).

Currie, B., *Selected Essays on the Conflict of Laws* (Drake U., 1963).

Curtis, C. P., *Law as Large as Life* (Simon & Schuster, 1959).

Dalzell, G. W., *Benefit of Clergy in America and Related Matters* (Blair, 1955).

Davis, K. C., *Discretionary Justice: A Preliminary Inquiry* (U. of Illinois, 1972).

Davitt, T. E., *The Basic Values in Law* (Amer. Phil. Soc., 1968).

Dias, R. M. W., and G. B. J. Hughes, *Jurisprudence* (Butterworth, 1957).

Dilliard, I. (ed.), *The Spirit of Liberty: Papers and Addresses of Learned Hand* (Knopf, 1959).

Duster, T., *The Legislation of Morality* (Free Press, 1970).

Ehrenzweig, A. A., *Psychoanalytic Jurisprudence* (Oceana, 1971).

Ehrlich, E., *Fundamental Principles of the Sociology of Law* (Harvard, 1936).

Einaudi, M., *The Physiocratic Doctrine of Judicial Control* (Harvard, 1938).

Evan, W. M. (ed.), *Law and Sociology* (Free Press, 1962).

Frank, J. F., *Law and the Modern Mind*, 2nd ed. (Brentano's, 1949; Anchor, 1963).

Friedman, L., and B. Neuborne, *Unquestioning Obedience to the President* (Norton, 1972).

Friedmann, W., *Law in a Changing Society* (Berkeley, 1959).

———, *Legal Theory*, 5th ed. (Columbia, 1967).

Friedrich, C. J., and J. W. Chapman (eds.), *Justice* (Atherton, 1963).

———, *The Philosophy of Law in Historical Perspective*, 2nd ed. (U. of Chicago, 1962).

———, *Transcendent Justice: The Religious Dimensions of Constitutionalism* (Duke, 1963).

Gerhart, E. C., *American Liberty and National Law* (Beacon, 1953).

Gierke, O. von, *Natural Law and the Theory of Society*, trans. by E. Barker (Cambridge, 1934; Beacon, 1963).

Ginsberg, M., *On Justice in Society* (Penguin, 1965).

Golding, M. P. (ed.), *The Nature of Law: Readings in Legal Philosophy* (Random House, 1966).

Haines, C. G., *The Revival of Natural Law Concepts* (Harvard, 1930).

Hall, J., *Readings in Jurisprudence* (Bobbs-Merrill, 1938).

Harding, A. L. (ed.), *The Administration of Justice in Retrospect* (S.M.U., 1957).

Hare, J. I. C., *American Constitutional Law* (Brown, 1889).

Harris, R. W., *Justice: The Crisis of Law, Order, and Freedom in America* (Dutton, 1970).

Hart, H. L. A., *The Concept of Law* (Oxford, 1961).

Hayek, F. A., *Law, Legislation, and Liberty* (U. of Chicago, 1973).

Henson, R. D. (ed.), *Landmarks of Law: Highlights of Legal Opinion from 1890 to the Present* (Harper, 1960).

Holcombe, A. N., *Our More Perfect Union: From Eighteenth-Century Principles to Twentieth-Century Practice* (Harvard, 1950).

Holmes, O. W., Jr., *The Common Law* (Little, Brown, 1881; new ed., Harvard, 1963, ed. by Mark DeWolfe Howe).

Hook, S. (ed.), *Law and Philosophy: A Symposium* (N.Y.U., 1964).

Jackson, P. E. (comp.), *Justice and the Law* (Michie, 1964).

Kelsen, H., *General Theory of Law and State* (Harvard, 1945).

———, *What Justice?* (Berkeley, 1957).

Lefcourt, R. (ed.), *Law Against the People: Essays to Demystify Law, Order and the Courts* (Random House, 1971).

Levi, E. H., *An Introduction to Legal Reasoning* (U. of Chicago, 1949).

Levitt, M., and B. Rubenstein, *Orthopsychiatry and the Law* (Wayne State U., 1971).

Llewellyn, K. N., *Jurisprudence: Realism in Theory and Practice* (U. of Chicago, 1962).

Lloyd, D. (ed.), *Introduction to Jurisprudence* (Praeger, 1960).

McCloskey, R. G., *American Conservatism in the Age of Enterprise* (Harvard, 1957).

McIlwain, C. H., *The American Revolution: A Constitutional Interpretation* (Macmillan, 1928).

———, *Constitutionalism, Ancient and Modern*, rev. ed. (Cornell, 1947).

———, *Constitutionalism and the Changing World* (Macmillan, 1939).

Maine, Sir H., *Ancient Law* (J. Murray, 1930; Beacon, 1963).

Marshall, J., *Intention in Law and Society* (Funk & Wagnalls, 1968).

Mason, A. T., and R. H. Leach, *In Quest of Freedom: American Political Thought and Practice* (Prentice-Hall, 1959).

Moore, R. G., *Stare Decisis* (Simmons-Broadman, 1958).

Morris, C. (ed.), *The Great Legal Philosophers: Selected Readings in Jurisprudence*, rev. ed. (U. of Pennsylvania, 1971).

———, *The Justification of the Law* (U. of Pennsylvania, 1972).

Nader, L. (ed.), *Law in Culture and Society* (U. of California, 1971).

Nagel, S. S., *Law and Social Change* (Sage, 1970).

Nice, R. W. (ed.), *Treasury of Law* (Philosophical Library, 1965).

Northrup, F. C. S., *The Complexity of Legal and Ethical Experience* (Little, Brown, 1959).

Olafson, F. A., *Society, Law, and Morality* (Prentice-Hall, 1961).

——— (ed.), *Justice and Social Policy* (Prentice-Hall, 1965).

Paton, G. W., and D. P. Durham (eds.), *A Textbook of Jurisprudence*, 4th ed. (Oxford, 1972).

Patterson, C. P., *Constitutional Principles of Thomas Jefferson* (U. of Texas, 1953).

Paul, A. M., *The Conservative Crisis and the Rule of Law*, 2nd ed. (Harper, 1969).

Petrazycke, L. J., *Law and Morality* (Harvard, 1955).

Pollock, Sir F., *Essays in the Law* (Macmillan, 1922).

———, *Jurisprudence and Legal Essays*, ed. by A. L. Goodhart (St. Martin's, 1961).

Pound, R., *Contemporary Juristic Theory* (Claremont, 1940).

———, *The Future of the Common Law* (Harvard, 1937).

———, *Interpretations of Legal History* (Harvard, 1946).

———, *An Introduction to the Philosophy of Law*, rev. ed. (Yale, 1959).

———, *Justice According to Law* (Yale, 1951).

———, *Law and Morals* (U. of North Carolina, 1924).

———, *Law-Finding Through Experience and Reason* (U. of Georgia, 1960).

———, *New Paths of the Law* (U. of Nebraska, 1950).

———, *Social Control Through Law* (Yale, 1942).

———, *The Spirit of the Common Law* (Marshall, Jones, 1931; Beacon, 1963).

———, *The Task of Law* (Franklin and Marshall, 1944).

Radin, M., *The Law as Logic and Experience* (Yale, 1940).

Reagan, R., *Private Conscience and Public Law: The American Experience* (Fordham, 1972).

Reuschlein, H. G., *Jurisprudence—Its American Prophets: A Survey of Taught Jurisprudence* (Greenwood, 1951).

Robson, W. S., *Civilization and the Growth of Law* (Macmillan, 1935).

Ross, A., *On Law and Justice* (Stevens, 1959).

———, *Towards a Realistic Jurisprudence* (Munksgaard, 1946).

Rossiter, C. A., *Seedtime of the Republic* (Harcourt, Brace, 1953).

Rostow, E. V., *The Sovereign Prerogative: The Supreme Court and the Quest for Law* (Yale, 1962).

Rumble, W. E., Jr., *American Legal Realism: Skepticism, Reform, and the Judicial Process* (Cornell, 1968).

Sawer, G., *Law in Society* (Oxford, 1965).

Selznick, R., *Law, Society, and Industrial Justice* (Sage, 1969).

Shklar, J. N., *Legalism* (Harvard, 1964).

Shuman, S. I., *Legal Positivism: Its Scope and Limitations* (Wayne State U., 1963).

Simpson, S. P., and J. Stone, *Law and Society* (West, 1948–49).

Smith, J. A., *The Spirit of American Government* (Macmillan, 1907).

Stone, J., *Human Law and Human Justice* (Stanford, 1965).

———, *Law and the Social Sciences in the Second Half Century* (U. of Minnesota, 1966).

———, *Legal Systems and Lawyers' Reasonings* (Stanford, 1964).

———, *The Province and Function of Law* (Harvard, 1950).

Sutherland, A. B. (ed.), *Government Under Law* (Harvard, 1956).

———, *The Law and One Man Among Many* (U. of Wisconsin, 1956).

Tiedman, C. G., *The Unwritten Constitution of the United States* (Putnam's, 1890).

Timasheff, N. S., *An Introduction to the Sociology of Law* (Harvard, 1938).

Toqueville, A. de, *Democracy in America* (H. G. Langley, 1841).

Tuolmin, S., *The Place of Reason in Ethics* (Cambridge, 1953).

Vinogradoff, P., *Common Sense in Law*, 3rd ed., rev. by H. G. Hanbury (Oxford, 1949).

———, *Outlines of Historical Jurisprudence* (Oxford, 1920).

Von Moschzisker, R., *Stare Decisis, Res Judicata, and Other Essays* (Cyrus Dixon, 1929).

Wasserstrom, R. A., *The Judicial Decision: Toward a Theory of Legal Justification* (Stanford, 1961).

Whitehead, A. N., *Symbolism* (Macmillan, 1927).

Wormuth, F. D., *The Origins of Modern Constitutionalism* (Harper, 1949).

Wright, B. F., *American Interpretations of Natural Law* (Harvard, 1931).

Wu, J. C. H., *Foundation of Justice* (Sheed & Ward, 1959).

Zelermyer, W., *The Process of Legal Reasoning* (Prentice-Hall, 1963).

THE PRESIDENCY

(The executive branch of our national government.)

Abraham, H. J., *Justices and Presidents: A Political History of Appointments to the Supreme Court* (Oxford, 1974).

A.F.L.-C.I.O., *Why Richard M. Nixon Must Be Impeached—Now* (A.F.L.-C.I.O., 1974).

Alley, R. S., *So Help Me God: Religion and the Presidency* (John Knox Press, 1972).

American Civil Liberties Union, *Why President Richard Nixon Should Be Impeached* (A.C.L.U., 1974).

Americans for Democratic Action, *The Case for Impeachment* (A.D.A., 1974).

Barber, J. D., *The Presidential Character* (Prentice-Hall, 1973).

Black, C. L., Jr., *Impeachment: A Handbook* (Yale, 1974).

Benedict, M. L., *The Impeachment and Trial of Andrew Johnson* (Norton, 1973).

Berger, R., *Executive Privilege: A Constitutional Myth* (Harvard, 1974).

———, *Impeachment: The Constitutional Problem* (Harvard, 1973).

Binkley, W. E., *President and Congress*, 3rd rev. ed. (Knopf, 1962).

Blackman, J. L., Jr., *Presidential Seizure in Labor Disputes* (Harvard, 1967).

Brant, I., *Impeachment: Trials and Errors* (Knopf, 1972).

Breckenridge, Adam Carlyle, *The Executive Privilege: Presidential Control over Information* (U. of Nebraska, 1974).

Burns, J. M., *Presidential Government: The Crucible of Leadership* (Houghton, Mifflin, 1973).

Committee on the Judiciary, U.S. House of Representatives, *Impeachment: Selected Materials* (Superintendent of Documents, 1974).

Congressional Quarterly Guide to American Government, *Impeachment* (C.Q., 1974).

Corwin, E. S., *The President: Office and Powers*, 4th ed. (N.Y.U., 1957).

———, *Total War and the Constitution* (Knopf, 1947).

Cotter, C. P., and J. M. Smith, *Powers of the President During National Crisis* (Public Affairs Press, 1959).

Cronin, T. E. (ed.), *The Presidential Advisory System* (Harper & Row, 1969).

D'Amato, A. A., and R. M. O'Neil, *The Judiciary and Vietnam* (St. Martin's, 1972).

Dobrovir, W. A., *The Offenses of Richard M. Nixon: A Lawyer's Guide for the People of the U.S.A.* (A. B. Zill, 1974).

Egger, R., *The President of the United States*, 2nd ed. (McGraw-Hill, 1972).

———, and J. P. Harris, *The President and Congress* (McGraw-Hill, 1963).

Ehrlich, W., *Presidential Impeachment: An American Dilemma* (Forum Series, 1974).

Feerick, J. D., *From Failing Hands: The Story of Presidential Succession* (Fordham, 1965).

Finer, H., *The Presidency: Crisis and Regeneration* (U. of Chicago, 1973).

Fisher, L., *President and Congress: Power and Policy* (Free Press, 1972).

Gilbert, A. M., *Executive Agreements and Treaties, 1946–1973* (Thomas-Newell, 1973).

Glaser, W. A., *Pretrial Discovery and the Adversary System* (Sage, 1969).

Grundstein, N. D., *Presidential Delegation of Authority in Wartime* (U. of Pittsburgh, 1961).

Hardin, C. M., *Presidential Power and Accountability* (U. of Chicago, 1974).

Haight, D., and L. Johnston (eds.), *The Presidency* (St. Martin's, 1967).

———, *The Presidency: Roles and Powers* (Rand McNally, 1965).

Henkin, L., *Foreign Affairs and the Constitution* (Foundation Press, 1973).

Hirschfield, R. S., *The Power of the Presidency*, 2nd ed. (Aldine, 1973).

Hughes, E. J., *The Living Presidency* (Coward, McCann & Geoghegan, 1973).

Hurst, J. W., *The Growth of American Law: The Lawmakers* (Little, Brown, 1950).

James, D. B., *The Contemporary Presidency*, 2nd ed. (Bobbs-Merrill, 1974).

Kallenbach, J. E., *The American Chief Executive* (Harper & Row, 1966).

Koenig, L. W., *The Chief Executive*, rev. ed. (Harcourt, Brace & World, 1968).

———, *The President and the Crisis: Powers of the Office from the Invasion of Poland to Pearl Harbor* (King Crown, 1944).

Latham, E., *Kennedy and Presidential Power* (Heath, 1972).

Learned, H. B., *The President's Cabinet* (Yale, 1912).

Lurie, L., *The Impeachment of Richard Nixon* (Berkeley Publishing Co., 1973).

McConnell, G., *The President Seizes the Steel Mills* (U. of Alabama, 1960).
————, *Steel and the Presidency, 1962* (Norton, 1963).
McKay, R. B. (ed.), *The American Constitutional Law Reader* (Oceana, 1958).
Mason, A. T., and W. B. Beaney, *The Supreme Court in a Free Society* (Prentice-Hall, 1959).
May, E. R., *The Ultimate Decision: The President as Commander in Chief* (Braziller, 1960).
Morgan, R. P., *The President and Civil Rights* (St. Martin's, 1970).
Mosler, P. (ed.), *Judicial Protection Against the Executive* (Heymanns/Oceana, 1972).
New Priorities, *The Constitutional Crisis: Congress vs. the Executive* (Gordon & Breach, 1974).
New York Times, *The Assassination of a President* (Viking, 1964).
Polsby, N. W., *Congress and the Presidency* (Prentice-Hall, 1963).
Randall, J. G., *Constitutional Problems Under Lincoln*, rev. ed. (U. of Delaware, 1956; U. of Illinois, 1964).
Rankin, R. S., and W. R. Dallmayr, *Freedom and Emergency Powers in the Cold War* (Appleton-Century-Crofts, 1964).
Reedy, G., *The Presidency in Flux* (Columbia, 1972).
Rich, B. N., *The President and Civil Disorder* (Brookings, 1941).
Rossiter, C. L., *Constitutional Dictatorship: Crisis Government in the Modern Democracies* (Princeton, 1948).
————, *The Supreme Court and the Commander-in-Chief* (Cornell, 1951).
Schlesinger, A. M., Jr., *The Imperial Presidency* (Houghton Mifflin, 1973).
Schubert, G. A., *The Presidency in the Courts* (U. of Minnesota, 1957).
Scigliano, R., *The Supreme Court and the Presidency* (Free Press, 1970).
Small, N. J., *Some Presidential Interpretations of the Presidency* (Da Capo, 1970).
Smith, M. J., and C. P. Cotter, *Powers of the President During Crisis* (Public Affairs Press, 1960).
Taft, W. H., *Our Chief Magistrate and His Powers* (Columbia, 1916).
Thomas, N., and H. W. Baade, *The Institutionalized Presidency* (Oceana, 1972).
Tugwell, R. G., and T. E. Cronin, *The Presidency Reappraised* (Praeger, 1974).
Vinyard, D., *The Presidency* (Scribner's, 1971).
Westin, A. F., *Anatomy of a Constitutional Law Case* (Macmillan, 1958).
Winter, R. K., Jr., *Watergate and the Law: Political Campaigns and Presidential Power* (Amer. Ent. Inst., 1974).
Wolk, A., *The Presidency and Black Civil Rights: Eisenhower to Nixon* (Fairleigh Dickinson, 1971).

PROCEDURE IN THE COURTS

Alfini, J. J., and G. R. Winters (comps and eds.), *Selected Readings on Courtroom Design* (Amer. Judic. Soc., 1973).
American Bar Association, *The Improvement of the Administration of Justice: A Handbook*, 4th ed. (A.B.A., 1961).
Annual Reports of the Director of the Administrative Office of the United States Courts (U.S. G.P.O.).
Balbus, I. D., *The Dialectics of Legal Repression: Black Rebels Before the American Criminal Courts* (Russell-Sage, 1973).

424

Barron, W. W., and A. Holtzoff, *Federal Practice and Procedure* (Thompson, 1950–58).

Blumberg, A. S., *Criminal Justice* (Quadrangle, 1968).

Borchard, E. M., *Convicting the Innocent* (Yale, 1932).

Bureau of Municipal Research, *The Magistrate Courts of Philadelphia*, rev. ed. (Pennsylvania Economy League, 1958).

Bush, F. X., *Law and Tactics in Jury Trials* (Bobbs-Merrill, 1963).

Callendar, C. N., *American Courts: Their Organization and Procedure* (McGraw-Hill, 1927).

Clark, R., *Contempt* (Swallow, 1970).

Dangel, E. M., *Contempt* (National Lawyers Manual Co., 1939).

Davenport, W. H. (ed.), *Voices in Court* (Macmillan, 1958).

Doble, A. M., *Handbook of Federal Jurisdiction and Procedure* (West, 1928).

Dolbeare, K. M., *Trial Courts in Urban Politics: State Court Policy Impact and Functions in a Local Political System* (Wiley, 1967).

Douglas, W. O., *Stare Decisis* (Assoc. of Bar of City of N.Y., 1949).

Finns, H. G., *Federal Jurisdiction and Procedure* (Bobbs-Merrill, 1960).

Fleming, M., *The Price of Perfect Justice* (Basic Books, 1974).

Fox, J. C., *The History of Contempt of Court* (Oxford, 1927).

Fox, S. J., *Juvenile Courts in a Nutshell* (West, 1971).

Frank, J. F., *Courts on Trial* (Princeton, 1959).

———, and B. Frank, *Not Guilty* (Doubleday, 1957).

Gavit, B. C., *Procedure in State Courts* (Practicing Law Institute, 1946).

Goldfarb, R. L., *The Contempt Power*, rev. ed. (Doubleday, 1971).

Gressman, E., and R. L. Stern, *Supreme Court Practice*, 4th ed. (Washington Bureau of National Affairs, 1969).

Grey, D. L., *The Supreme Court and the News Media* (Northwestern, 1968).

Hall, L., and Y. Kamisar, *Modern Criminal Procedure* (West, 1965).

Harding, A. L. (ed.), *The Administration of Justice in Retrospect* (S.M.U., 1957).

Hart, H. M., Jr., and H. Wechsler, *The Judicial Code and Rules of Procedure in the Federal Courts* (Foundation Press, 1954).

James, F., *Criminal Procedure* (Little, Brown, 1965).

Karlen, D., *The Citizen in Court: Litigant, Witness, Juror, Judge* (Holt, Rinehart & Winston, 1964).

———, *Judicial Administration: The American Experience* (Oceana, 1970).

———, *Primer of Procedure* (Campus Publ. Co., 1950).

Kunstler, W. M., *First Degree* (Oceana, 1970).

Laurent, F. W., *The Business of a Trial Court* (U. of Wisconsin, 1959).

Llewellyn, K. N., *The Common Law Tradition: Deciding Appeals* (Little, Brown, 1960).

McCarty, D. G., *Psychology for the Lawyer* (Prentice-Hall, 1929).

MacDougal, C. D., *Covering the Courts* (Prentice-Hall, 1946).

Matthews, P., *How To Try a Criminal Case* (Dennis, 1960).

Meador, D. J., *English Practices and American Reforms* (U. of Virginia, 1973).

Moore, R. F., *Stare Decisis* (Simmons Boardman, 1958).

Munsterberg, H., *On the Witness Stand* (Simmons Boardman, 1925).

Newman, R. P., and D. R. Newman, *Evidence* (Houghton, Mifflin, 1970).

Oswald, J. F., *Contempt of Court* (Butterworth, 1911).

425

Peck, D. A., *Decision at Law* (Dodd, Mead, 1961; Cornerstone, 1963).

Perkins, R. M., *Cases on Criminal Law and Procedure* (Foundation Press, 1959).

Porter, E. S., *Conscience of the Court* (Prentice-Hall, 1962).

Pound, R., *Appellate Procedure in Civil Cases* (Little, Brown, 1941).

Rose, J. C., *Jurisdiction and Procedure of Federal Courts* (Bender, 1938).

Rosenberg, M., *The Pretrial Conference and Effective Justice* (Columbia, 1965).

Saari, D. J., *Modern Court Management: Trends in the Role of the Court Executive* (U.S. G.P.O., 1970).

St. John, A. R., *Final Verdict* (Doubleday, 1962).

Stryker, L. P., *Courts and Doctors* (Macmillan, 1932).

Taylor, G. C., *Fifty Years in the Law* (Philosophical Library, 1963).

Thomas, C. H., *Problems of Contempt of Court* (Horn-Shafer, 1943).

Tierney, K., *How to be a Witness* (Oceana, 1971).

Vanderbilt, A. T., *Cases and Other Materials on Modern Procedure and Judicial Administration* (Wash. Sq., 1952).

———, *Men and Measures in the Law* (Knopf, 1949).

Von Moschzisker, R., *Stare Decisis, Res Judicata, and Other Essays* (Cyrus Dixon, 1929).

Wright, B. F., *Federal Courts* (West, 1963).

Zeisel, H., H. Kalven, Jr., and B. Buchholz, *Delay in the Court* (Little, Brown, 1959).

REFORMS

(Discussions of change in the Constitution and the courts.)

American Bar Association, *The Improvement of the Administration of Justice* (A.B.A., 1971).

———, *Ten Cures for Court Congestion* (A.B.A., 1959).

Association of the Bar of the City of New York, *Conflict of Interest and Federal Service* (Harvard, 1960).

Bureau of Municipal Research, *The Magistrate Courts of Philadelphia*, rev. ed. (Pennsylvania Economy League, 1958).

Cohn, R. G., *To Judge with Justice: The History and Politics of Illinois Judicial Reform* (U. of Illinois, 1973).

Downie, L., Jr., *Justice Denied: The Case for Reform of the Courts* (Praeger, 1971).

Elliot, W. Y., *The Need for Constitutional Reform* (Whittlesey House, 1935).

Federal Judicial Center, *Report of the Study Group on the Caseload of the Supreme Court* (Adm Off. of the U.S. Courts, 1972).

Fleming, M., *The Price of Perfect Justice* (Basic Books, 1973).

Friendly, H. J., *Federal Jurisdiction: A General View* (Columbia, 1973).

Friesen, E. C., Jr., E. C. Gallas, and N. M. Gallas, *Managing the Courts* (Bobbs-Merrill, 1971).

Goodnow, F. J., *Social Reform and the Constitution* (Macmillan, 1911).

Hazlitt, H., *A New Constitution Now* (McGraw-Hill, 1942).

Hehmeyer, A., *Time for a Change: A Proposal for a Second Constitutional Convention* (Rinehart, 1943).

James, H., *Crisis in the Courts*, 2nd ed. (McKay, 1971).

Seymour, W. N., *Why Justice Fails* (Morrow, 1973).

Vanderbilt, A. T., *The Challenge of Law Reform* (Princeton, 1955).
Wheeler, J. P. (ed.), *Salient Issues of Constitutional Revision* (National Municipal League, 1960).

STAFFING THE COURTS

(Selection and tenure.)

Abraham, H. J., *The Judicial Process: An Introductory Analysis of the Courts of the United States, England, and France*, 3rd ed. (Oxford, 1975).
————, *Justices and Presidents: A Political History of Appointments to the Supreme Court* (Oxford, 1974).
Bashful, E., *The Florida Supreme Court: A Study in Judicial Selection* (Florida State U., 1958).
Carpenter, W. S., *Judicial Tenure in the United States* (Yale, 1918).
Chase, H. W., *Federal Judges: The Appointing Process* (U. of Minnesota, 1972).
Danelski, D. J., *A Supreme Court Justice is Appointed* (Random House, 1964).
Davis, J. W., *Selecting Judges* (Andrews, 1933).
Harris, J. P., *The Advice and Consent of the Senate: A Study of the Confirmation of Appointments by the United States Senate* (Berkeley, 1953).
Harris, R., *Decision* (Dutton, 1971).
Haynes, E., *The Selection and Tenure of Judges* (National Conference of Judicial Councils, 1944).
McHargue, D. J., *Factors Influencing the Selection and Appointment of Members of the United States Supreme Court, 1784–1932* (Unpublished Ph.D. Dissertation, U.C.L.A., 1949).
Nagel, S. S., *Comparing Elected and Appointed Judicial Systems* (Sage, 1973).
Rae, D., *The Political Consequences of Electoral Laws* (Yale, 1967).
Schlesinger, J., *Ambition and Politics: Political Careers in the United States* (Rand McNally, 1966).
Schmidhauser, J. R., *The Supreme Court: Its Politics, Personalities and Procedures* (Holt, 1960).
Scigliano, R. G., *The Courts: A Reader in the Judicial Process* (Little, Brown, 1962).
Shogan, R., *A Question of Judgment: The Fortas Case and the Struggle for the Supreme Court* (Bobbs-Merrill, 1972).
Simon, J. F., *In His Own Image: The Supreme Court in Richard Nixon's America* (McKay, 1973).
Todd, A. L., *Justice on Trial: The Case of Louis D. Brandeis* (McGraw-Hill, 1964).
Vanderbilt, A. T., *Judges and Jurors: Their Functions, Qualifications, and Selection* (Boston U., 1956).
Watson, R. A., and R. G. Downing, *The Politics of Bench and Bar: Judicial Selection Under the Missouri Non-Partisan Court Plan* (Wiley, 1969).
Wilkinson, J. H., III, *Serving Justice* (Charterhouse, 1974).

II AMERICAN CONSTITUTIONAL LAW: BIOGRAPHIES, AUTOBIOGRAPHIES, AND RELATED WORKS OF AND BY JUSTICES OF THE SUPREME COURT OF THE UNITED STATES

GENERAL

Abraham, H. J., *Justices and Presidents: A Political History of Appointments to the Supreme Court* (Oxford, 1974).

Asch, S. H., *The Supreme Court and Its Great Justices* (Arco, 1971).

Barbar, J., *The Honorable Eighty-Eight* (Vanguard, 1957).

Bates, E. S., *The Story of the Supreme Court* (Bobbs-Merrill, 1936).

Brown, J. M., *Through These Men* (Harper, 1956).

Cahn, E. (ed.), *The Great Rights* (Macmillan, 1963).

Campbell, T. W., *Four-Score Forgotten Men* (Pioneer, 1950).

Danelski, D. J., *A Supreme Court Justice is Appointed* (Random House, 1964).

Dunham, A., and P. B. Kurland (eds.), *Mr. Justice*, rev. and enl. (Phoenix, 1964).

Ewing, C. A. M., *Judges of the Supreme Court, 1789–1938* (U. of Minnesota, 1938).

Flanders, H., *The Lives and Times of the Chief Justices of the Supreme Court of the United States* (Lippincott, 1858).

Frank, J. P., "The Appointment of Supreme Court Justices: Prestige Principles and Politics," *Wisconsin Law Review*, March, 172, May, 343, July, 461 (1941).

Freund, P. A., *On Law and Justice* (Harvard, 1968).

Friedman, L., and F. L. Israel (eds.), *The Justices of the United States Supreme Court, 1789–1969*, 4 vols. (Chelsea, 1970).

Harris, R., *Decision* (Dutton, 1971).

Lewis, W. D., *Great American Lawyers* (Winston, 1908).

McCune, W., *The Nine Young Men* (Harper, 1947).

Merryman, J. H., *The Civil Law Tradition* (Stanford, 1970).

Seagle, W., *Men of Law: From Hammurabi to Holmes* (Macmillan, 1947).

Tresolini, R. J., *Justice and the Supreme Court* (Lippincott, 1962).

Umbreit, K. B., *Our Eleven Chief Justices: A History of the Supreme Court in Terms of Their Personalities* (Harper, 1938).

Vanderbilt Law Review, Symposium, "Studies in Judicial Biography" (Vol. X, No. 2, 1957).

Van Santvoord, G., *Sketches of the Lives and Judicial Services of the Chief Justices of the Supreme Court of the United States* (Scribner's, 1854).

Westin, A. F. (ed.), *An Autobiography of the Supreme Court* (Macmillan, 1963).

PHILIP P. BARBOUR (1783–1841)

Scott, W. W., *History of Orange County* (Waddey, 1907).

HUGO LAFAYETTE BLACK (1886–1971)

Black, H. L., *A Constitutional Faith* (Knopf, 1969).

Dilliard, I., *One Man's Freedom: Mr. Justice Black and the Bill of Rights* (Knopf, 1963).

Frank, J. P., *Mr. Justice Black: The Man and His Opinions* (Knopf, 1949).
Hamilton, V. V. de V., *Hugo Black: The Alabama Years* (L.S.U., 1972).
Mason, G. L., *Hugo Black and the United States Senate* (U. of Kansas, 1964).
Meador, D. J., *Mr. Justice Black and His Books* (U. of Virginia, 1974).
Mendelson, W. (ed.), *Justices Black and Frankfurter*, 2nd ed. (U. of Chicago, 1966).
Strickland, S. P. (ed.), *Hugo Black and the Supreme Court* (Bobbs-Merrill, 1967).
United States Congress, Joint Committee on Printing, *Hugo Lafayette Black, 1886–1971: Memorial Addresses and Tributes* (U.S. G.P.O., 1972).
Williams, C., *Hugo L. Black: A Study in the Judicial Process* (Johns Hopkins, 1950).
Yale Law Journal, Symposium, "Mr. Justice Black" (February 1956).

JOSEPH P. BRADLEY (1813–1892)
Bradley, C. (ed.), *Miscellaneous Writings of Joseph P. Bradley* (Harham, 1901).

LOUIS DEMBITZ BRANDEIS (1856–1941)
Bickel, A. M., *The Unpublished Opinions of Mr. Justice Brandeis: The Supreme Court at Work* (Harvard, 1957; Phoenix, 1967).
DeHaas, J., *Louis D. Brandeis* (Block, 1929).
Dilliard, I. (ed.), *Mr. Justice Brandeis: Great American* (Modern View Press, 1941).
Fraenkel, O. K. (ed.), *The Curse of Bigness: Miscellaneous Papers of Louis D. Brandeis* (Viking, 1934).
Frankfurter, F., *Mr. Justice Brandeis* (Yale, 1932).
Freund, P. A., *The Writings of Louis D. Brandeis* (Bobbs-Merrill, 1966).
Goldman, S. (ed.), *The Words of Mr. Justice Brandeis* (Schuman, 1953).
Konefsky, S. J., *The Legacy of Holmes and Brandeis: A Study in the Influence of Ideas* (Macmillan, 1956).
Lief, A. (ed.), *Brandeis: The Personal History of an American Ideal* (Stackpole, 1936).
Mason, A. T., *Brandeis—A Free Man's Life* (Viking, 1946).
———, *Brandeis and the Modern State* (National Home Library, 1936).
———, *Brandeis: Lawyer and Judge in the Modern State* (Princeton, 1933).
———, *The Brandeis Way* (Princeton, 1938).
Noble, I., *Firebrand for Justice: A Biography of Louis Dembitz Brandeis* (Westminister, 1969).
Peare, C. O., *The Louis D. Brandeis Story* (Crowell, 1970).
Pollack, E. H. (ed.), *The Brandeis Reader* (Oceana, 1956).
Todd, A. L., *Justice on Trial: The Case of Louis D. Brandeis* (McGraw-Hill, 1964).
Urofsky, M. I., *A Mind of One Piece: Brandeis and American Reform* (Scribner's 1971).
———, and D. W. Levy (eds.), *Letters of Louis D. Brandeis*, Vol. I (1870–1897): *Urban Reformer;* Vol. II (1907–1912): *People's Attorney* (State University of New York Press, 1972).
Yale Law Library, *Louis Dembitz Brandeis, 1856–1941: A Bibliography* (New Haven, 1958).

HENRY BILLINGS BROWN (1836–1913)
Kent, C. A., *Memoir of Henry Billings Brown* (Dunfield, 1915).

HAROLD H. BURTON (1888–1964)
Hudon, E. G. (ed.), *The Occasional Papers of Mr. Justice Burton* (Bowdoin, 1969).

Marquardt, R. G., "The Judicial Justice: Mr. Justice Burton and the Supreme Court" (Unpublished Ph.D. Dissertation, U. of Wisconsin, 1973).

PIERCE BUTLER (1866–1939)
Brown, F. J., *The Social and Economic Philosophy of Pierce Butler* (Catholic U., 1945).

JAMES F. BYRNES (1879–1972)
Byrnes, J. F., *All in One Lifetime* (Harper, 1958).

JOHN A. CAMPBELL (1811–1889)
Conner, H. G., *John A. Campbell, Associate Justice of the United States Supreme Court, 1853–1861* (Houghton Mifflin, 1920).

BENJAMIN N. CARDOZO (1870–1938)
Bender, N. (ed.), *The Benjamin N. Cardozo Memorial Lectures* (Bender, 1971).
Hall, M. E. (ed.), *Selected Writings of B. N. Cardozo* (Fallon, 1947).
Hellman, G. S., *Benjamin N. Cardozo—American Judge* (Whittlesey, 1940).
Levy, B. H., *Cardozo and Legal Thinking* (Oxford, 1938).
————, *Cardozo and the Frontiers of Legal Thinking: With Selected Opinions*, 2nd ed. (Case Western Reserve, 1970).
Pollard, J. P., *Mr. Justice Cardozo: A Liberal Mind in Action* (Yorktown Press, 1935).

SALMON PORTLAND CHASE (1808–1873)
Chase, S. P., *Diaries and Correspondence* (Da Capo, 1971).
Hart, A. B., *Salmon Portland Chase* (Houghton Mifflin, 1899).
Schuckers, J. W., *The Life and Public Services of Salmon Portland Chase* (Appleton, 1874).

SAMUEL CHASE (1741–1811)
United States Senate, *Trial of Samuel Chase, An Associate Justice of the Supreme Court Impeached by the House of Representatives for High Crimes and Misdemeanors Before the Senate of the United States* (1805), 8th Cong., 2nd sess.

TOM C. CLARK (1899–   )
Dorin, D. D., "Justice Tom Clark and the Right of Defendants in State Courts" (Unpublished Ph.D. Dissertation, U. of Virginia, 1974).

JOHN H. CLARKE (1857–1945)
Warner, H. L., *The Life of Mr. Justice Clarke: A Testimony to the Power of Liberal Dissent in America* (Western Reserve U., 1959).

NATHAN CLIFFORD (1803–1881)
Clifford, P. G., *Nathan Clifford, Democrat* (Putnam's, 1922).

BENJAMIN ROBBINS CURTIS (1809–1874)
Curtis, B. R., Jr., *A Memoir of Benjamin Robbins Curtis, L.L.D.* (Little, Brown, 1879).

PETER V. DANIEL (1784–1860)
Frank, J. P., *Justice Daniel Dissenting: A Biography of Peter V. Daniel, 1784–1860* (Harvard, 1964).
Hendricks, B. M., *Bulwark of the Republic: A Biography of the Constitution* (Little, Brown, 1957).

DAVID DAVIS (1815–1886)
King, W. L., *Lincoln's Manager: David Davis* (Harvard, 1960).

WILLIAM RUFUS DAY (1849–1923)
McLean, F. J., *William Rufus Day, Supreme Court Justice from Ohio* (Johns Hopkins, 1947).

WILLIAM O. DOUGLAS (1898–   )
Countryman, V. (ed.), *Douglas of the Supreme Court: A Selection of His Opinions* (Doubleday, 1959).
Douglas, W. O., *Go East, Young Man* (Random House, 1974).
———, *We the Judges* (Doubleday, 1956).
University of Chicago Law Review, "Justices Frankfurter and Douglas" (Autumn 1958).

OLIVER ELLSWORTH (1745–1807)
Brown, W. G., *The Life of Oliver Ellsworth* (Macmillan, 1905; Da Capo, 1970).

STEPHEN J. FIELD (1816–1899)
Swisher, C. B., *Stephen J. Field: Craftsman of the Law* (Brookings, 1930; Phoenix, 1969).

ABE FORTAS (1910–   )
Heckart, R. J., "Justice Fortas and the First Amendment" (Unpublished Ph.D. Dissertation, S.U.N.Y., Albany, 1973).
Shogan, R., *A Question of Judgment: The Fortas Case and the Struggle for the Supreme Court* (Bobbs-Merrill, 1972).

FELIX FRANKFURTER (1882–1965)
Baker, L., *Felix Frankfurter* (Coward-McCann, 1969).
Frankfurter, F., *Extrajudicial Essays on the Court and Constitution*, ed. by P. B. Kurland (Harvard, 1970).
———, *Mr. Justice Brandeis* (Yale, 1932).
———, *Mr. Justice Holmes and the Constitution* (Harvard, 1938).
———, *Mr. Justice Holmes and the Supreme Court*, 2nd ed. (Atheneum, 1965).
———, *Of Law and Men* (Harcourt, Brace, 1956).
———, *The Public and Its Government* (Beacon, 1964).
——— (ed.), *Mr. Justice Holmes* (Coward-McCann, 1931).
Freedman, M., *Roosevelt and Frankfurter: Their Correspondence, 1928–1945* (Little, Brown, 1968).
Jacobs, C. E., *Justice Frankfurter and Civil Liberties* (Berkeley, 1961).
Konefsky, S. J. (ed.), *The Constitutional World of Mr. Justice Frankfurter* (Macmillan, 1949).

431

Kurland, P. B., *Mr. Justice Frankfurter and the Constitution* (U. of Chicago, 1971).

——— (ed.), *Mr. Justice Frankfurter on the Supreme Court* (Harvard, 1970).

———, *Of Law and Life and Other Things that Matter: Papers and Addresses of Felix Frankfurter, 1956–1963* (Harvard, 1965).

MacLeish, A., and E. F. Richard (eds.), *Law and Politics: Occasional Papers of Mr. Justice Frankfurter* (Harcourt, Brace, 1939).

Mendelson, W. (ed.), *Felix Frankfurter: A Tribute* (Reynal, 1964).

———, *Felix Frankfurter: The Judge* (Reynal, 1964).

———, *Justice Black and Frankfurter*, 2nd ed. (U. of Chicago, 1966).

Phillips, H. B. (ed.), *Felix Frankfurter Reminisces* (Reynal, 1960).

Thomas, H. S., *Felix Frankfurter: Scholar on the Bench* (Johns Hopkins, 1960).

University of Chicago Law Review, "Justices Frankfurter and Douglas" (Autumn 1958).

Yale Law Journal, Symposium, "Mr. Justice Felix Frankfurter" (December 1957).

MELVILLE WESTON FULLER (1833–1910)

King, W. L., *Melville Weston Fuller: Chief Justice of the United States, 1888–1910* (Macmillan, 1950 and Phoenix, 1967).

ARTHUR J. GOLDBERG (1908–   )

Goldberg, A. J., *Equal Justice: The Supreme Court in the Warren Era* (Northwestern, 1971).

Moynihan, D. P. (ed.), *The Defense of Freedom: The Public Papers of Arthur J. Goldberg* (Harper & Row, 1966).

HORACE GRAY (1828–1902)

Mitchell, S. R., "Mr. Justice Horace Gray" (Unpublished Ph.D. Dissertation, U. of Wisconsin, 1961).

JOHN MARSHALL HARLAN (1833–1911)

Clark, F. B., *The Constitutional Doctrines of Justice Harlan* (Johns Hopkins, 1915).

Kentucky Law Journal, Symposium, "John Marshall Harlan, 1833–1911" (Spring 1958).

Porter, M. C. A., "John Marshall Harlan and the Laissez-Faire Court" (Unpublished Ph.D. Dissertation, U. of Chicago, 1970).

OLIVER WENDELL HOLMES, JR. (1841–1935)

Bander, E. J. (comp.), *Justice Holmes ex Cathedra* (Michie, 1966).

Bent, S., *Justice Oliver Wendell Holmes* (Vanguard, 1932).

Biddle, F., *Justice Holmes, Natural Law, and the Supreme Court* (Macmillan, 1961).

———, *Mr. Justice Holmes* (Scribner's, 1942).

Bowen, C. D., *A Yankee from Olympus: Justice Holmes and His Family* (Little, Brown, 1944).

Frankfurter, F., *Mr. Justice Holmes and the Supreme Court*, 2nd ed. (Atheneum, 1965).

———, *et al.*, *Mr. Justice Holmes* (Coward, McCann, 1931).

Holmes, O. W., Jr., *Collected Legal Papers* (Harcourt, 1920).

———, *The Common Law* (Little, Brown, 1881; new ed. Harvard, 1962, ed. by Mark de Wolfe Howe).

————, *Speeches* (Little, Brown, 1913).

Howe, M. de W., *Justice Holmes to Dr. Wu: An Intimate Correspondence, 1921–1932* (Central Bk., 1935).

————, *Justice Oliver Wendell Holmes: The Proving Years, 1870–1882* (Harvard, 1963).

————, *Justice Oliver Wendell Holmes: The Shaping Years, 1841–1870* (Harvard, 1957).

————, *Touched with Fire: Civil War Letters and Diary of Oliver Wendell Holmes, Jr., 1861–1864* (Da Capo, 1969).

————, *The Holmes-Laski Letters, 1916–1935* (Harvard, 1953; Atheneum, 1963).

————, *The Holmes-Pollock Letters, 1874–1932*, rev. ed. (Harvard, 1941; Atheneum, 1963).

———— (ed.), *The Occasional Speeches of Justice Oliver Wendell Holmes* (Harvard, 1963).

Hurst, W. J., *Justice Holmes on Legal History* (Macmillan, 1964).

Konefsky, S. J., *The Legacy of Holmes and Brandeis: A Study in the Influence of Ideas* (Macmillan, 1956).

Lerner, M. (ed.), *The Mind and Faith of Justice Holmes* (Little, Brown, 1943).

Lief, A. (ed.), *The Dissenting Opinions of Mr. Justice Holmes* (Vanguard, 1943).

Marke, J. (ed.), *The Holmes Reader*, 2nd ed. (Oceana, 1964).

Morse, J. T., Jr. (ed.), *Life and Letters of Oliver Wendell Holmes* (Houghton, Mifflin, 1896).

CHARLES EVANS HUGHES (1862–1948)

Danelski, D. J., and J. S. Tulchin (eds.), *The Autobiographical Notes of Charles Evans Hughes* (Harvard, 1973).

Hendel, S., *Charles Evans Hughes and the Supreme Court* (Columbia, 1951).

Hughes, C. E., *Addresses*, 2nd ed. (Harper & Bros., 1916).

Kornberg, H. R., "Charles Evans Hughes in the Supreme Court: A Study in Judicial Philosophy and Voting Behavior" (Unpublished Ph.D. Dissertation, Brown U., 1972).

Perkins, D., *Charles Evans Hughes and American Democratic Statesmanship* (Little, Brown, 1956).

Pusey, M. J., *Charles Evans Hughes* (Macmillan, 1951).

Ransom, W. L., *Charles Evans Hughes: The Statesman as Shown in the Opinions of the Jurist* (Dutton, 1916).

Warren, E., *Hughes and the Court* (Colgate, 1962).

Wesser, R. F., *Charles Evans Hughes: Politics and Reform in New York, 1905–1910* (Cornell, 1967).

WARD HUNT (1810–1886)

Wyman, T. B., *Geneology of the Name and Family of Hunt* (Wilson, 1862).

JAMES IREDELL (1751–1799)

McRee, G. F. (ed.), *The Life and Correspondence of James Iredell* (Peter Smith, 1949).

ROBERT H. JACKSON (1892–1954)

Gerhart, E. C., *Robert H. Jackson: Lawyer's Judge* ("Q" Corp., 1961).

————, *America's Advocate: Robert H. Jackson* (Bobbs-Merrill, 1958).

Schubert, G. (ed.), *Dispassionate Justice: A Synthesis of the Judicial Opinions of Robert H. Jackson* (Bobbs-Merrill, 1969).

Stanford Law Review, Symposium, "Mr. Justice Jackson" (December 1955).

Steamer, R. J., "The Constitutional Doctrine of Mr. Justice Robert H. Jackson" (Unpublished Ph.D. Dissertation, Cornell, 1954).

JOHN JAY (1745–1829)

Jay, W., *The Life of John Jay* (Harper & Bros., 1833).

Johnston, H. P. (ed.), *The Correspondence and Public Papers of John Jay, 1763–1826* (Putnam's, 1890).

Monaghan, F., *John Jay: Defender of Liberty* (Bobbs-Merrill, 1935).

Morris, R. B., *John Jay, the Nation and the Court* (Boston U., 1967).

THOMAS JOHNSON (1732–1819)

Delaplaine, E. S., *The Life of Thomas Johnson* (Hitchcock, 1927).

WILLIAM JOHNSON (1771–1834)

Morgan, D. G., *Justice William Johnson: The First Dissenter* (U. of South Carolina, 1954).

JOSEPH RUCKER LAMAR (1857–1916)

Lamar, C. P., *The Life of Joseph Rucker Lamar, 1857–1916* (Putnam's, 1926).

LUCIUS Q. C. LAMAR (1825–1893)

Cate, W. A., *Lucius Q. C. Lamar* (U. of North Carolina, 1935).

Mayes, E., *Lucius Q. C. Lamar* (Barbee, 1895).

Merrill, H. S., *Bourbon Leader* (Little, Brown, 1957).

HENRY BROCKHOLST LIVINGSTON (1757–1823)

Livingston, E. B., *The Livingstons of Livingston Manor* (Knickerbocker, 1910).

JOSEPH McKENNA (1843–1926)

McDevitt, M., *Joseph McKenna* (Catholic U., 1946).

JOHN McLEAN (1785–1861)

Weisenburger, F. P., *The Life of John McLean: A Politician on the United States Supreme Court* (Ohio State U., 1937).

JAMES CLARK McREYNOLDS (1862–1946)

Blaisdell, Donald P., "Mr. Justice James Clark McReynolds" (Unpublished Ph.D. Dissertation, U. of Wisconsin, 1948).

Early, S. T., Jr., "James Clark McReynolds and the Judicial Process" (Unpublished Ph.D. Dissertation, U. of Virginia, 1954).

JOHN MARSHALL (1755–1835)

Adams, J. S. (ed.), *An Autobiographical Sketch by John Marshall* (U. of Michigan, 1937).

Baker, L., *John Marshall: A Life in Law* (Macmillan, 1974).

Beveridge, A. J., *The Life of John Marshall* (Houghton Mifflin, 1916).

Corwin, E. S., *John Marshall and the Constitution: A Chronicle of the Supreme Court* (Yale, 1921).

Cotton, J. P., Jr. (ed.), *The Constitutional Decisions of John Marshall* (Putnam's 1905; Da Capo, 1969).

Dillon, J. M. (ed.), *John Marshall: Complete Constitutional Decisions* (Callaghan, 1903).

Faulkner, R. K., *The Jurisprudence of John Marshall* (Princeton, 1968).

Jones, W. N. (ed.), *Chief Justice John Marshall: A Reappraisal* (Cornell, 1956).

Konefsky, S. J., *John Marshall and Alexander Hamilton: Architects of the American Constitution* (Macmillan, 1965).

Loth, D. G., *Chief Justice: John Marshall and the Growth of the Republic* (Norton, 1949).

Mason, F. N., *My Dearest Polly: Letters of Chief Justice Marshall to His Wife, 1779–1831* (Garrett & Massie, 1961).

Palmer, B. W., *Marshall and Taney: Statesmen of the Law* (U. of Minnesota, 1939).

Rhodes, I. S., *The Papers of John Marshall: A Descriptive Calendar* (U. of Oklahoma, 1970).

Roche, J. P. (ed.), *John Marshall: Major Opinions and Other Writings* (Bobbs-Merrill, 1966).

Services, J. A., *A Bibliography of John Marshall* (U.S. Commission for Celebration of 200th Anniv. of Birth of John Marshall, 1956).

Severn, B., *John Marshall: The Man Who Made the Court Supreme* (McKay, 1969).

Surrency, E. (ed.), *The Marshall Reader* (Oceana, 1955).

Sutherland, A. E., *Government Under Law* (Harvard, 1956).

Thayer, J. B., *John Marshall* (Houghton Mifflin, 1901; Phoenix, 1967).

THURGOOD MARSHALL (1908–   )

Bland, R. W., *Private Pressure on Public Law: The Legal Career of Justice Thurgood Marshall* (Kennikat, 1973).

Fenderson, L. H., *Thurgood Marshall* (McGraw-Hill, 1969).

SAMUEL FREEMAN MILLER (1816–1890)

Fairman, C., *Mr. Justice Miller and the Supreme Court, 1862–1890* (Harvard, 1939).

Gregory, C. N., *Samuel Freeman Miller* (State Hist. Soc. Iowa, 1907).

WILLIAM HENRY MOODY (1853–1917)

Weiner, F. B., *The Life and Judicial Career of William Henry Moody* (Harvard, 1937).

FRANK MURPHY (1890–1949)

Howard, J. W., Jr., "Frank Murphy: A Liberal's Creed" (Unpublished Ph.D. Dissertation, Princeton, 1959).

————, *Mr. Justice Murphy: A Political Biography* (Princeton, 1968).

Lunt, R. D., *The High Ministry of Government: The Political Career of Frank Murphy* (Wayne State U., 1965).

Michigan Law Review, Symposium, "Mr. Justice Frank Murphy" (April 1950).
Norris, H., *Mr. Justice Murphy and the Bill of Rights* (Oceana, 1965).

WILLIAM PATERSON (1745–1806)
Wood, G. S., *William Paterson of New Jersey, 1745–1806* (Fair Lawn Press, 1933).

STANLEY F. REED (1884–   )
Fitzgerald, M. J., "Justice Reed: A Study of a Center Judge" (Unpublished Ph.D. Dissertation, U. of Chicago, 1950).
O'Brien, F. W., *Justice Reed and the First Amendment: The Religion Clauses* (Georgetown U., 1958).

OWEN J. ROBERTS (1875–1955)
Leonard, C. A., *A Search for a Judicial Philosophy: Mr. Justice Roberts and the Constitutional Revolution of 1937* (Kennikat, 1971).

JOHN RUTLEDGE (1739–1800)
Barry, R., *Mr. Rutledge of South Carolina* (Duell, Sloan & Pierce, 1942).

WILEY B. RUTLEDGE (1894–1949)
Harper, F. W., *Justice Rutledge and the Bright Constellation* (Bobbs-Merrill, 1965).
Iowa Law Review, Symposium, "Wiley B. Rutledge" (Summer 1950).
Rutledge, W. B., *A Declaration of Legal Faith* (U. of Kansas, 1947).

GEORGE SHIRAS, JR. (1832–1924)
Shiras, G., III (ed.), *Justice George Shiras, Jr., of Pittsburgh* (U. of Pittsburgh, 1953).

HARLAN FISKE STONE (1872–1946)
Konefsky, S. J., *Chief Justice Stone and the Supreme Court* (Macmillan, 1946).
Mason, A. T., *Harlan Fiske Stone: Pillar of the Law* (Viking, 1956).

JOSEPH STORY (1779–1845)
Commager, H. S., *The Writings of Justice Joseph Story* (Bobbs-Merrill, 1966).
Dunne, G. F., *Justice Joseph Story and the Rise of the Supreme Court* (Simon & Schuster, 1971).
McClellan, J., *Joseph Story and the American Constitution* (U. of Oklahoma, 1971).
Schwartz, M. D., and J. C. Hogan, *Joseph Story: A Collection of Writings by an Eminent American Jurist* (Oceana, 1959).
Story, W. W. (ed.), *Life and Letters of Joseph Story* (Little, 1851).
———, *The Miscellaneous Writings of Joseph Story* (Little, 1852).

GEORGE SUTHERLAND (1862–1942)
Paschal, J. F., *Mr. Justice Sutherland: A Man Against the State* (Princeton, 1951).

NOAH H. SWAYNE (1804–1884)
Swayne, N. W. (comp.), *The Descendants of Francis Swayne and Others* (Lippincott, 1921).

WILLIAM HOWARD TAFT (1857–1930)
McHale, F., *President and Chief Justice: The Life and Public Services of William Howard Taft* (Dorrance, 1931).
Mason, A. T., *William Howard Taft: Chief Justice* (Simon & Schuster, 1965).
Pringle, H., *The Life and Times of William Howard Taft* (Farrow & Rinehart, 1939).

ROGER BROOKE TANEY (1777–1864)
Lewis, W., *Without Fear or Favor: A Biography of Chief Justice Roger Brooke Taney* (Houghton Mifflin, 1965).
Palmer, B. W., *Marshall and Taney: Statesmen of the Law* (U. of Minnesota, 1939).
Smith, C. W., *Roger B. Taney: Jacksonian Jurist* (U. of North Carolina, 1936).
Steiner, B. C., *Life of Roger Brooke Taney, Chief Justice of the United States Supreme Court* (Williams & Wilkin, 1922).
Swisher, C. B., *Roger B. Taney* (Macmillan, 1935).
Tyler, S., *Memoir of Roger Brooke Taney: Chief Justice of the Supreme Court of the United States* (J. Murphy, 1872).

FRED M. VINSON (1890–1953)
Bolner, J., "Chief Justice Vinson: A Study of His Politics and His Constitutional Law" (Unpublished Ph.D. Dissertation, U. of Virginia, 1962).

MORRISON R. WAITE (1816–1888)
Magrath, C. P., *Morrison R. Waite: The Triumph of Character* (Macmillan, 1963).
Trimble, B. R., *Chief Justice Waite: Defender of the Public Interest* (Princeton, 1938).

EARL WARREN (1891–1974)
Bozell, L. B., *The Warren Revolution* (Arlington House, 1966).
Christman, H. M. (ed.), *The Public Papers of Chief Justice Earl Warren* (Simon & Schuster, 1959).
Frank, J. P., with Y. Karsh, *The Warren Court* (Macmillan, 1964).
Katcher, L., *Earl Warren: A Political Biography* (McGraw-Hill, 1967).
Stone, I., *Earl Warren* (Prentice-Hall, 1948).
Warren, E., *A Republic . . . If You Can Keep It* (Quadrangle, 1972).
Weaver, J. D., *Warren: The Man, The Court, The Era* (Little, Brown, 1967).

BUSHROD WASHINGTON (1762–1829)
Binney, H., *Bushrod Washington* (Sherman, 1858).

JAMES MOORE WAYNE (1790–1867)
Lawrence, A. A., *James Moore Wayne: Southern Unionist* (U. of North Carolina, 1943).

EDWARD DOUGLAS WHITE (1845–1921)
Hill, A. B., "The Constitutional Doctrine of Chief Justice White" (Unpublished Ph.D. Dissertation, U. of California, 1922).
Klinkhamer, Sister M. C., "Edward Douglas White, Chief Justice of the United States" (Unpublished Ph.D. Dissertation, Catholic U., 1948).

JAMES WILSON (1742–1798)
Smith, C. H., *James Wilson, Founding Father* (U. of North Carolina, 1956).
Wilson, J., *The Works of the Hon. James Wilson* (Bronson & Chaunch, 1804).

LEVI WOODBURY (1789–1851)
Woodbury, C. L. (ed.), *Writings of Levi Woodbury* (Little, Brown, 1852).

III COMPARATIVE CONSTITUTIONAL AND ADMINISTRATIVE LAW

Abel-Smith, E., and R. Stevens, *Lawyers and the Courts: A Sociological Study of the English Legal System, 1750–1965* (Heinemann, 1966; Harvard, 1967).
Abrahams, G., *Police Questioning and the Judges' Rules* (Oyez, 1964).
Adams, M., *Censorship: The Irish Experience* (U. of Alabama, 1968).
Alderfer, H. F., *Public Administration in New Nations* (Praeger, 1968).
Alexander, L. N., *The Law of the Sea* (U. of Rhode Island, 1970).
Alexandrowicz, C. H., *Constitutional Developments in India* (Oxford, 1957).
Allen, Sir C. K., *Administrative Jurisdiction* (Stevens, 1956).
———, *Law and Orders: An Inquiry into the Nature and Scope of Delegated Legislative and Executive Powers in England*, 3rd ed. (Stevens, 1953).
———, *Law in the Making*, 7th ed. (Oxford, 1964, 1967).
———, *The Queen's Peace* (Stevens, 1956).
Allott, A. N. (ed.), *Judicial and Legal Systems in Africa* (Butterworth, 1962).
Almond, G., and J. L. Coleman (eds.), *The Politics of the Developing Areas* (Princeton, 1960).
———, and S. Verba, *The Civic Culture* (Little, Brown, 1963, 1965).
Amery, L. S., *Thoughts on the Constitution*, 2nd ed. (Oxford, 1953).
Amos, Sir M., *British Criminal Justice*, rev. ed. (Longmans, Green, 1957).
Amos, Sir M. S., and Walton, *Introduction to French Law* (Oxford, 1935).
Anderson, J. N. D. (ed.), *Changing Law in Developing Countries* (Praeger, 1963).
———, *Islamic Law in the Modern World* (N.Y.U., 1959).
Andrews, J. A., *Criminal Justice* (U. of Wales, 1968).
Anson, Sir W. R., *Law and Custom of the Constitution* (Oxford, 1922–35).
Appleman, J. A., *Military Tribunals and International Crimes* (Bobbs-Merrill, 1954).
Archer, P., *The Queen's Courts*, 2nd ed. (Pelican, 1963).
Arendt, H., *Eichmann in Jerusalem* (Viking, 1963, 1966).

Bagehot, W., *The English Constitution*, 2nd ed. (World's Classics, 1928).
Bain, K. B., *Banned!* (MacGibbon & Kee, 1967).
Baker, H. C., *Legal Systems of Israel* (Israel University Press, 1968).
Baker, R. D., *Judicial Review in Mexico: A Study of the Camparo Suit* (U. of Texas, 1971).
Banerjee, D. N., *Our Fundamental Rights: Their Nature and Extent (As Judicially Determined)* (World Press, 1960).
Banton, M., *The Policeman in the Community* (Basic, 1964).

Barker, Sir E., *Church, State, and Education* (U. of Michigan, 1957).

Barkun, M., *Law Without Sanctions: Order in Primitive Societies, and The World Community* (Yale, 1968).

Barlow, R. B., *Citizenship and Conscience: A Study in the Theory and Practice of Religious Toleration in England During the Eighteenth Century* (U. of Pennsylvania, 1963).

Bartholomew, P. C., *The Irish Judiciary* (U. of Notre Dame, 1972).

Bar-Yaacov, N., *Dual Nationality* (Praeger, 1961).

Bataille, A., *Inside the French Courts* (Hutchinson, 1941).

Bathurst, M. E., *et al.*, *Legal Problems of an Enlarged European Community* (Stevens, 1972).

Bayley, D. H., *The Police and Political Development in India* (Princeton, 1969).

———, *Public Liberties in the New States* (Rand McNally, 1964).

———, and H. Mendelsohn, *Minorities and the Police* (Free Press, 1969).

Bebr, G., *Judicial Control of the European Communities* (Praeger, 1962).

Becker, T. L., *Comparative Judicial Politics: The Political Functionings of Courts* (Rand McNally, 1964).

——— (ed.), *Political Trials* (Bobbs-Merrill, 1970).

Bedford, S., *The Faces of Justice: A Traveller's Report* (Simon & Schuster, 1961).

Bedi, A. S., *Freedom of Expression and Security: A Comparative Study of the Function of the Supreme Courts of the United States of America and India* (Asia Publ. House, 1966).

Benewick, R., *Political Violence and Public Order* (Allen Lane, 1969).

Bentham, J., *Rationale of Judicial Evidence* (Hunt and Clarke, 1827).

Benton, W. E., and G. Grimm (eds.), *Nuremberg: German Views of the War Trials* (S.M.U., 1955).

Berkley, G. E., *The Democratic Policeman* (Beacon, 1969).

Berman, H. J., *Justice in Russia: An Interpretation of Soviet Law*, rev. ed., enl. (Vintage, 1963).

———, and J. W. Spindler, *Soviet Criminal Law and Procedure: The RSFSR Codes* (Harvard, 1966).

———, and J. B. Quigley, Jr., *Basic Laws on the Structure of the Soviet State* (Harvard, 1968).

Berry, B., *Race and Ethnic Relations*, 3rd ed. (Houghton Mifflin, 1965).

Birch, A. H., *Federalism, Finance and Social Legislation in Canada, Australia, and the United States* (Oxford, 1955).

Bishop, W., *International Law: Cases & Materials*, 2nd ed. (Dennis, 1962).

Blackstone, Sir W., *Commentaries on the Laws of England* (Harper, 1854; Beacon, 1962).

Blanshard, P., *Freedom and Catholic Power in Spain and Portugal* (Beacon, 1962).

Blaustein, A. P., and G. H. Flanz, *Constitutions of the Countries of the World* (Oceana, 1971).

Bloomfield, L. P., *International Military Forces* (Little, Brown, 1964).

Bodde, E., and C. Morris, *Law in Imperial China Exemplified by 190 Ch'ing Dynasty Cases* (Harvard, 1968).

Bonner, R. J., *Lawyers and Litigants in Ancient Athens* (Barnes & Noble, 1969).

Bosch, W. J., *Judgment on Nuremberg* (U. of North Carolina, 1970).

439

Boutmy, E. G., *Studies in Constitutional Law: France, England, United States*, 2nd ed. (Macmillan, 1891).

Bowett, D. W., *The Law of International Institutions* (Praeger, 1963).

Bozeman, A. B., *The Future of Law in a Multicultural World* (Princeton, 1971).

Brierly, J. L., *The Law of Nations*, 6th ed. (Oxford, 1963).

Brohi, A. K., *Fundamental Law of Pakistan* (Din Muhammadi Press, 1958).

Brookes, E. H., and J. B. Macaulay, *Civil Liberty in South Africa* (Oxford, 1958).

Brown, E. G., *British Statutes in American Law, 1776–1836* (U. of Michigan, 1965).

Brownlie, I., *Principles of Public International Law* (Oxford, 1968).

Bunn, R., and W. G. Andrews (eds.), *Basic Documents in Human Rights* (Oxford, 1971).

———, *Civil Liberties in Europe* (Van Nostrand, 1967).

Cam, H. M., *Law-Finders & Law-Makers in Medieval England* (Barnes & Noble, 1963).

Cameron, J. R., *Frederick William Maitland and the History of English Law* (U. of Oklahoma, 1961).

Campbell, C. M., and R. Wilson, *Lawyers and their Public* (Martin Robertson, 1974).

Cantor, N. F., *William Stubbs on the English Constitution* (Cromwell, 1967).

Cappelletti, M., *Judicial Review in the Contemporary World* (Bobbs-Merrill, 1971).

———, J. H. Merryman, and J. M. Perillo, *The Italian Legal System* (Stanford, 1967).

Carey, J. (ed.), *Race, Peace, Law and Southern Africa* (Oceana, 1967).

——— (ed.), *UN Protection of Civil and Political Rights* (Syracuse U., 1969).

Carlston, K. S., *Law and Organization in World Society* (U. of Illinois, 1962).

Carr, Sir T., *Concerning English Administrative Law* (Columbia, 1941).

Castaneda, J., *Legal Effects of United Nations Resolutions* (Columbia, 1941).

Casteberg, F., *Freedom of Speech in the West* (Oceana, 1960).

———, *Problems of Legal Philosophy* (Allen & Unwin, 1958).

Cavenaugh, W. E., *Juvenile Courts, The Child and the Law* (Penguin, 1967).

Central Office of Information, *The English Legal System* (H.M.S.O., 1964).

Chanders, J., *To Deprave and Corrupt* (Souvenir, 1962).

Chapman, B., *The Profession of Government* (Allen & Unwin, 1959).

Charles, R., *La Justice en France* (Presses Universitaires, 1958).

Chloros, A. G., *Yugoslav Civil Law: History, Family, Property* (Oxford, 1970).

Christoph, J. B., *Capital Punishment and British Politics* (U. of Chicago, 1962).

Claglett, H., *Administration of Justice in Latin America* (Oceana, 1952).

Clyde, W. M., *The Struggle of the Freedom of the Press from Caxton to Cromwell* (Oxford, 1964).

Cohen, M. (ed.), *Law and Politics in Space* (McGill, 1964).

Conrad, J. P., *Crime and Its Correction: An International Survey of Attitudes and Practices* (Berkeley, 1965).

Conquest, R. (ed.), *Justice and the Legal System in the U.S.S.R.* (Praeger, 1968).

———, *The Soviet Police System* (Praeger, 1968).

Corbett, P. E., *The Growth of World Law* (Princeton, 1971).

Cowen, Z., *Federal Jurisdiction in Australia* (Oxford, 1959).

Cracknell, D. G., *Constitutional Law and the English Legal System* (Butterworth, 1968).

Craig, A., *The Banned Books of England and Other Countries* (Allen & Unwin, 1967).

————, *Suppressed Books* (World, 1963).

Cramer, J., *The World Police* (Cassell & Co., 1964).

Crick, B., and W. A. Robson (eds.), *Protest and Discontent* (Penguin, 1970).

Critchley, T. A., *The Conquest of Violence: Order and Liberty in Britain* (Schocken, 1970).

————, *A History of Police in England and Wales* (Constable, 1967).

Cropper, I., *Criminal Evidence* (Butterworth, 1965).

Cross, R., *An Introduction to Criminal Law*, 5th ed. (Butterworth, 1964).

————, *Precedent in English Law*, 2nd ed. (Oxford, 1968).

D'Amato, A. A., *The Concept of Custom in International Law* (Cornell, 1971).

Daniel, W. W., *Racial Discrimination in England* (Penguin, 1968).

Daube, D., *Roman Law: Linguistic, Social, and Philosophical Aspects* (Aldine, 1969).

David, R., and H. P. de Vries, *The French Legal System: An Introduction to Civil Law Systems* (Oceana, 1958).

————, and J. E. C. Brierly, *Major Legal Systems in the World Today* (Free Press, 1969).

Davidson, E., *The Trial of the Germans: Nuremberg 1945–1946* (Macmillan, 1967).

Davis, H. E., *Government and Politics in Latin America* (Ronald, 1958).

Dawson, F. P., *A History of Lay Judges* (Harvard, 1960).

de Lolme, J. L., *The Constitution of England* (Kearsly, 1775).

Denning, Sir A., *The Changing Law* (Stevens, 1953).

Devlin, Sir P., *The Criminal Prosecution in England* (Yale, 1958).

————, *The Enforcement of Morals* (Oxford, 1965).

————, *Trial by Jury* (Stevens, 1956).

Diamond, A. S., *The Evolution of Law and Order* (Watts, 1951).

Dicey, A. V., *Introduction to the Study of the Law on the Constitution*, 10th ed. (Macmillan, 1959).

————, *Law and Public Opinion in England During the Nineteenth Century* (Torch, 1958).

Donner, A., *The Role of the Lawyer in the European Community* (Northwestern, 1968).

Dowrick, F. E., *Justice According to the English Common Lawyers* (Butterworth, 1961).

Driver, G. R., and J. C. Miles, *The Babylonian Laws* (Clarendon, 1952).

Du Cann, R., *The Art of the Advocate* (Penguin, 1964).

Duchacek, I., *Rights and Liberties in the World Today: Constitutional Promise and Reality* (Amer. Bibliogr. Ctr., 1973).

Duffet, J. (ed.), *Against the Crime of Silence: Proceedings of the International War Crimes Tribunal* (Bertrand Russell Peace Foundation, 1968).

Duguit, L., *Law in the Modern State* (Huebsch, 1919).

Dumbauld, E., *The Life and Legal Writings of Ango Grotius* (U. of Oklahoma, 1970).

Eaves, J., Jr., *Emergency Powers and the Parliamentary Watchdog* (Hansard Soc., 1957).

Eder, P. J., *A Comparative Survey of Anglo-American and Latin-American Law* (N.Y.U., 1950).

441

Eldersveld, S. J., V. Jagannadham, and A. P. Barnabas, *The Citizen and the Administrator in a Developing Democracy* (Scott, Foresman, 1968).

Emden, C. S., *The People and the Constitution*, 2nd ed. (Oxford, 1956).

Engel, S., with R. A. Metall (eds.), *Law, State, and International Legal Order: Essays in Honor of Hans Kelsen* (U. of Tennessee, 1964).

Ensor, R. C. K., *Courts and Judges in France, Germany, and England* (Oxford, 1933).

Erades, L., and W. L. Gould, *The Relations between International Law and Municipal Law in the Netherlands and in the United States* (Oceana, 1960).

Esmein, A., *A History of Continental Criminal Procedure* (Parkhill, 1914).

Evan, W. M. (ed.), *Law and Sociology: Exploratory Essays* (Free Press, 1962).

Falk, R. A., *The Role of Domestic Courts in the International Legal Order* (Syracuse U., 1964).

———, and C. E. Black (eds.), *The Future of the International Legal Order* (Princeton, 1970).

———, *The Status of Law in International Society* (Princeton, 1970).

———, and S. H. Mendlovitz (eds.), *The Strategy of World Order* (World Law Fund, 1966).

———, G. Kolko, and R. J. Lifton (eds.), *Crimes of War* (Viking, 1971).

———, *Legal Order in a Violent World* (Princeton, 1968).

———, *et al.*, *Essays on International Jurisdiction* (Ohio State U., 1961).

Fazal, M. A., *Judicial Control of Administrative Action in India and Pakistan* (Oxford, 1969).

Fellman, D., *The Defendant's Rights Under English Law* (U. of Wisconsin, 1966).

Fitzgibbon, R. H. (ed.), *The Constitution of the Americas* (U. of Chicago, 1951).

Flecher, J. K., *The British Courts: Traditions and Ceremonial* (Cassell, 1953).

Flender, H., *Rescue in Denmark* (Macfadden-Bartell, 1964).

Fliess, P. J., *Freedom of the Press in the German Republic, 1918–1933* (Louisiana State U., 1955).

Foot, P., *Immigration and Race in British Politics* (Penguin, 1967).

———, *The Rise of Enoch Powell* (Penguin, 1970).

Foreign Languages Publishing House, *Fundamentals of Soviet Criminal Legislation, The Judicial System, and Criminal Court Procedure* (For. Lang. Publ. House, 1960).

Fosdick, R. B., *European Police Systems* (The Century Co., 1915).

Fouilee, A., *et al.*, *Modern French Legal Philosophy* (Macmillan, 1921).

Franck, T. M., *Comparative Constitutional Processes: Cases and Materials* (Praeger, 1968).

———, and E. Weisband, *Word Politics and Verbal Strategy Among the Super Powers* (Oxford, 1971).

Freedeman, C. E., *The Conseil d'État in Modern France* (Columbia, 1961).

Friedland, M. L., *Double Jeopardy* (Oxford, 1969).

Friedmann, W., *The Changing Structure of International Law* (Columbia, 1964).

———, *Law and Social Change in Contemporary Britain* (Stevens, 1951).

———, *Law in a Changing Society*, 2nd ed. (Penguin, 1965).

Friedrich, C., *The Impact of American Constitutionalism Abroad* (Boston U., 1967).

Galeotti, S., *The Judicial Control of Public Authorities in England and in Italy* (Stevens, 1954).

Garsia, M., *Criminal Law and Procedure in a Nutshell* (Sweet & Maxwell, 1964).

Geldart, W. M., *Elements of English Law,* 7th ed. (Oxford, 1966).

Gide, A., *Recollections of the Assize Court* (Hutchinson, 1941).

Gilbert, G. M., *Nuremberg Diary* (New American Library, 1960).

Giles, F. T., *The Criminal Law,* 3rd ed. (Penguin, 1963).

———, *The Juvenile Courts: Their Work and Problems* (Allen & Unwin, 1946).

———, *The Magistrates' Courts,* rev. ed. (Stevens, 1964).

Ginsberg, M. (ed.), *Law and Opinion in England in the Twentieth Century* (Berkeley, 1959).

Giuttari, T. R., *The American Law of Sovereign Immunity: An Analysis of Legal Interpretation* (Praeger, 1970).

Gledhill, A., *The Republic of India: The Development of Its Laws and Constitution,* 2nd ed. (Stevens, 1964).

Gluckman, M., *The Judicial Process Among the Barotse of Northern Rhodesia* (U. of Manchester, 1955).

———, *Politics, Law and Ritual in Tribal Society* (Aldine, 1964).

Golay, O. F., *The Founding of the Federal Republic of Germany* (U. of Chicago, 1958).

Golyakov, I. T., *The Role of the Soviet Court* (Public Affairs Press, 1948).

Goodhart, A. H., *English Law and the Moral Law* (Stevens, 1953).

———, *Precedent in English and Continental Law* (Stevens, 1934).

Gough, J. W., *Fundamental Law in English Constitutional History* (Oxford, 1955).

Graveson, R. H., *The Conflict of Laws* (Sweet & Maxwell, 1965).

Green, A. W., *Political Integration by Jurisprudence* (Sijthoff, 1969).

Green, E., *Judicial Attitudes Toward Sentencing* (Macmillan, 1961).

Griffith, J. H. G., and J. Street, *Principles of Administrative Law,* 2nd ed. (Pitman, 1958).

Groves, H. E., *Comparative Constitutional Law* (Oceana, 1963).

Grzybowski, K., *The Socialist Commonwealth of Nations, Organizations and Institutions* (Yale, 1964).

———, *Soviet Legal Institutions* (U. of Michigan, 1962).

Gsovsky, V., and K. Grzybowski (eds.), *Government, Law, and the Courts in the Soviet Union and Eastern Europe* (Praeger, 1960).

Guins, G. C., *Soviet Law and Soviet Society* (Nijhoff, 1954).

Haas, E. B., *Human Rights and International Action* (Stanford, 1970).

Hale, Sir M. (ed.), *The History of the Common Law of England* (U. of Chicago, 1971).

Haley, A. G., *Space Law and Government* (Appleton-Century-Crofts, 1963).

Hall, J., *Comparative Law and Social Theory* (Louisiana State U., 1963).

Hamson, C. J., *Executive Discretion and Judicial Control: An Aspect of the French Conseil d'État* (Stevens, 1954).

———, and T. F. T. Plucknett, *The English Trial and Comparative Law* (Heffner, 1952).

Hanbury, H. G., *English Courts of Law,* 4th ed. (Oxford, 1967).

Harding, A., *A Social History of English Law* (Penguin, 1966).

Hargrove, J. L. (ed.), *Law, Institutions and the Global Environment* (Oceana, 1972).

Harris, W. R., *Tyranny on Trial: The Evidence at Nuremberg* (S.M.U., 1954).

Harrison, B. F., *The Work of a Magistrate* (Shaw & Sons, 1964).

Harrison, W., *The Government of Britain*, 6th ed. (Hutchinson, 1960).

Hart, H. L. A., *Punishment and Responsibility: Essays in the Philosophy of Law* (Oxford, 1968).

Hart, J. M., *The British Police* (Allen & Unwin, 1951).

Hauriou, M., *Droit Constitutionnel et Institutions Politiques* (Monchrestien, 1966).

Hausner, G., *Justice in Jerusalem* (Harper & Row, 1966).

Havighurst, C. C. (ed.), *International Control of Propaganda* (Oceana, 1967).

Hawgood, J. A., *Modern Constitutions Since 1787* (Macmillan, 1939).

Hay, P., *Federalism and Supranational Organizations: Patterns for New Legal Structures* (U. of Illinois, 1966).

Hazard, J. N., *Communists and Their Law* (U. of Chicago, 1969).

———, *Law and Social Change in Soviet Society* (U. of Toronto, 1953).

———, *Settling Disputes in Soviet Society: The Formative Years in Legal Institutions*, rev. ed. (Columbia, 1960).

———, I. Shapiro, and P. B. Waggs, *The Soviet Legal System: Post-Stalin Documentation and Historical Commentary*, 2nd ed. (Oceana, 1969).

Henderson, E. G., *Foundations of English Administrative Law: Certiorari and Mandamus in the Seventeenth Century* (Harvard, 1963).

Heuss, Th., *Verfassungsrecht und Verfassungspolitik* (Scherpe-Verlag, 1950).

Heuston, R. F. V., *Essays in Constitutional Law* (Stevens, 1961).

Hiro, D., *Black British, White British* (Rampart, 1974).

Hoffmann, S., *et al.*, *In Search of France* (Harvard, 1960).

Holdsworth, Sir W., *A History of English Law*, 7th ed. (Goodhart & Hanbury, 1956).

———, *Some Makers of English Law* (Cambridge, 1966).

Holloway, K., *Modern Trends in Treaty Law: Constitutional Law, Reservations and the Three Modes of Legislation* (Oceana, 1967).

Hutchison, T. W. (ed.), *Africa and Law: Developing Legal Systems in African Commonwealth Nations* (U. of Wisconsin, 1968).

Hyde, H. Montgomery, Lord Justice, *The Life and Time of Lord Birkett of Ulverston* (Random House, 1965).

Inns of Court, The, *Rule of Law: A Study by the Inns of Court* (Conservative Pol. C., 1956).

Ioffe, O. S., *Soviet Civil Law* (International Arts and Sciences Press, 1961).

———, and M. D. Shargorodskii, *Problems of Legal Theory* (International Arts and Sciences Press, 1961).

Jackson, R. H., *The Nuremberg Case* (Knopf, 1947).

Jackson, R. M., *Enforcing the Law* (Pelican, 1972).

———, *The Machinery of Justice in England*, 6th ed. (Cambridge, 1972).

Jacobini, H. B., *International Law: A Text*, rev. ed. (Dorsey, 1968).

Jaffe, L. L., *English and American Judges as Lawmakers* (Oxford, 1970).

James, P. S., *Introduction to English Law*, 4th ed. (Butterworth, 1959).

Jenks, C. W., *The Common Law of Mankind* (Praeger, 1959).

———, *Law in the World Community* (McKay, 1967).

———, *The Proper Law of International Organization* (Oceana, 1962).

444

————, *Space Law* (Praeger, 1965).

Jenks, E., *The Book of English Law*, 6th ed. (Ohio State U., 1967).

Jennings, Sir W. I., *The British Constitution*, 3rd ed. (Cambridge, 1950).

————, *Constitutional Law and the Commonwealth*, 3rd ed. (Oxford, 1957).

————, *The Law and the Constitution*, 4th ed. (U. of London, 1958).

Jessup, P. C., *The Price of International Justice* (Columbia, 1971).

Johnston, R. E., *The Effect of Judicial Review on Federal-State Relations in Australia, Canada, and the United States* (Louisiana State U., 1970).

Johnstone, Q., and D. Hopson, Jr., *Lawyers and Their Work* (Bobbs-Merrill, 1967).

Jones, A. H. M., *Studies in Roman Government and Law* (Praeger, 1960).

Kahin, G. McT., *Major Governments of Asia* (Cornell, 1958).

Karlen, D., *Appellate Courts in the United States and England* (N.Y.U., 1963).

————, in collaboration with G. Sawyer and E. M. Wise, *Anglo-American Criminal Justice* (Oxford, 1967).

Katz, M., *The Relevance of International Adjudication* (Harvard, 1968).

Katznelson, I., *Black Men, White Cities* (Oxford, 1974).

Keeton, G. W., *The Norman Conquest and the Common Law* (Barnes & Noble, 1966).

————, *The Passing of Parliament*, 2nd ed. (Benn, 1954).

————, et al., *The United Kingdom, The Development of Its Laws and Constitution: England, Wales, Northern Ireland, The Isle of Man; Scotland; the Channel Islands* (Stevens, 1955).

Keir, Sir D. L., *The Constitutional History of Modern Britain Since 1485*, 6th ed. (Black, 1960).

Keir, Sir D. L., and F. H. Lawson (eds.), *Cases in Constitutional Law*, 5th ed. (Oxford, 1967).

Kelsen, H., *The Communist Theory of Law* (Praeger, 1960).

————, *Principles of International Law*, 2nd ed. (Holt, Rinehart & Winston, 1966).

Kempin, F. G., Jr., *Legal History: Law and Social Change* (Prentice-Hall, 1963).

Kidd, R., *British Liberty in Danger* (Lawrence & Wishart, 1942).

Kili, S., *Turkish Constitutional Developments and Assembly Debates on the Constitutions of 1924 and 1961* (Robert College Press, Univ. Center, 1972).

Kinnane, C. H., *Anglo-American Law*, 2nd ed. (Bobbs-Merrill, 1952).

Kiralfy, A. K., *The English Legal System*, 3rd ed. (Sweet & Maxwell, 1960).

Kirschheimer, O., *Political Justice* (Princeton, 1961).

Konstantinovsky, B. A., *Soviet Law in Action: The Recollected Cases of a Soviet Lawyer* (Harvard, 1953).

Kucherov, S., *Courts, Lawyers, and Trials Under the Last Three Tsars* (Praeger, 1953).

Kunkel, W., *An Introduction to Roman Legal and Constitutional History* (Oxford, 1966).

Kutner, L., *The Human Right to Individual Freedom: A Symposium on World Habeas Corpus* (U. of Miami, 1970).

————, *World Habeas Corpus* (Oceana, 1962).

La Fave, W. R., *Law in the Soviet Society* (U. of Illinois, 1966).

La Forest, G. V., *Extradition to and from Canada* (Hauser, 1962).

Lambert, J., *Crime, Police and Race Relations* (Oxford, 1970).

La Nauze, J. A., *The Making of the Australian Constitution* (U. of Melbourne, 1972).

Lapenna, I., *State and Law: Soviet and Yugoslav Theory* (Yale, 1964).

Lasky, H. J., *Studies in Law and Politics* (Allen & Unwin, 1932).

Laufer, H., *Verfassungsgerichtsbarkeit und Politischer Prozess* (J. C. B. Mohr, 1968).

Lauterpacht, Sir H., *The Development of International Law in the International Court* (Praeger, 1958).

———, *The Function of Law in the International Community* (Oxford, 1933).

Lawson, F. H., *A Common Lawyer Looks at the Civil Law* (Oxford, 1955).

Lawson, F. H. (ed.), *The Rational Strength of English Law* (Stevens, 1951).

———, *The Roman Law Reader* (Oceana, 1969).

———, *et al.*, *Amos and Walton's Introduction to French Law*, 2nd ed. (Oxford, 1963).

Leech, N. E., C. T. Oliver, and J. M. Sweeney, *The International Legal System: Cases and Materials* (Foundation Press, 1973).

Letourneur, M., J. Bauchet, and J. Meric, *Le Conseil d'État et les Tribunaux Administratifs* (Armand Colin, 1970).

Levy, H. P., *The Press Council: History, Procedure, and Cases* (St. Martin's, 1968).

Lewin, J., *Studies in African Law* (U. of Pennsylvania, 1971).

Lewis, J. R., *Law in Action* (Allman, 1965).

Lewy, C., *et al.*, *Essays on French Law* (Washington Law Soc., 1958).

Liang, H. H., *The Berlin Police Force in the Weimar Republic* (U. of California, 1970).

Lloyd, D. (ed.), *Introduction to Jurisprudence*, rev. ed. (Praeger, 1966).

Luard, E., *Conflict and Peace in the Modern International System* (Little, Brown, 1968).

——— (ed.), *The International Protection of Human Rights* (Praeger, 1967).

MacDonald, R. St. J. (ed.), *Changing Legal Objectives* (U. of Toronto, 1963).

MacGuigan, M. R., *Jurisprudence: Readings and Cases*, 2nd ed. (U. of Toronto, 1966).

MacMillan, W. M., *The Road to Self-Rule: A Study in Colonial Evolution* (Taber, 1969).

Maggs, P. B., *The Soviet Legal System* (Oceana, 1966).

Maitland, F. W., *The Constitutional History of England* (Cambridge, 1961).

———, *Selected Historical Essays* (Beacon, 1963).

Maki, J. M., *Court and Constitution in Japan: Selected Supreme Court Decisions, 1948–60* (U. of Washington, 1964).

Mallory, J. R., *The Structure of Canadian Government* (St. Martin's, 1971).

Mann, A., *Judgment at Nuremberg* (New American Library, 1960).

Marsh, S. B., *Outlines of English Law* (Sweet & Maxwell, 1967).

Marshall, G., and G. C. Moodle, *Some Problems of the Constitution* (Hutchinson, 1959).

Marshall, G., *Constitutional Theory* (Oxford, 1971).

———, *Police and Government: The Status and Accountability of the British Constable* (Methuen, 1965, 1967).

Mason, P., *Race Relations* (Oxford, 1970).

Mathews, A. S., *Law, Order and Liberty in South Africa* (Berkeley, 1974).

McDougal, M. S., and F. Feliciano, *Law and Minimum World Public Order* (Yale, 1962).

McIlwain, C. H. *The High Court of Parliament* (Yale, 1910).
McLennan, B. (ed.), *Political Opposition and Dissent* (Dunellen, 1973).
McRuer, J. C., *The Evolution of the Judicial Process* (Clarke, Irwin, 1957).
McWhinney, E., *Comparative Federalism: States' Rights and National Power* (U. of Toronto, 1963).
———, *Constitutionalism in Germany and the Federal Constitutional Court* (Sythoff, 1962).
——— (ed.), *Canadian Jurisprudence: The Civil Law and the Common Law in Canada* (Toronto, 1958).
———, *Judicial Review in the English-Speaking World*, 4th ed. (U. of Toronto, 1969).
———, and M. A. Bradley, *New Frontiers in Space Law* (Oceana, 1969).
Meador, D. J., *Criminal Appeals: English Practices and American Reforms* (U. of Virginia, 1972).
Mecham, J. L., *Church and State in Latin America; A History of Politico-Ecclesiastical Relations*, rev. ed. (U. of North Carolina, 1966).
Megarry, Q. C., *Lawyer and Litigant in England* (Stevens, 1962).
Merrilat, H. C. L., *Land and Constitution in India* (Columbia, 1970).
Merryman, J. H., *The Civil Law Tradition* (Stanford, 1969).
Millard, E. L., *Freedom in a Federal World*, 9th ed. (Oceana, 1966).
Milner, A., *African Legal Systems* (Praeger, 1968).
Milner, J. B. (ed.), *Community Planning: A Casebook on Law and Administration* (U. of Toronto, 1963).
Milton, F., *The English Magistracy* (Oxford, 1967).
Minear, R. H., *Victors' Justice: The Tokyo War Crimes Trial* (Princeton, 1971).
Morgan, G. G., *Soviet Administrative Legality: The Role of the Attorney General's Office* (Stanford, 1962).
Morris, N., and C. Howard, *Studies in Criminal Law* (Oxford, 1964).
Morrison, F. L., *Courts and the Political Process in England* (Sage, 1974).
Moskowitz, M., *Human Rights and World Order* (Oceana, 1958).
———, *The Politics and Dynamics of Human Rights* (Oceana, 1968).
Mosler, P. (ed.), *Judicial Prosecution Against the Executive* (Heymanns/Oceana, 1972).
Mueller, C. O. W. (ed.), *The French Criminal Procedure Code* (Rothman, 1964).
———, *The German Criminal Procedure Code* (Rothman, 1965).
Muhammad, V. A. S., *The Legal Framework of World Trade* (Praeger, 1958).

Napley, D., *Crime and Criminal Procedure* (Oyer, 1963).
———, *A Guide to Law and Practice Under the Criminal Justice Act of 1967* (Sweet & Maxwell, 1967).
Newman, K. J., *Essays on the Constitution of Pakistan* (Dacca, 1956).
Newman, R. A., *Equity and Law: A Comparative Study* (Oceana, 1960).
Nicholas, B., *An Introduction to Roman Law* (Oxford, 1962).

Ogilvie, Sir C., *The King's Government and the Common Law, 1471–1641* (Oxford, 1958).
Ostrower, A., *Language Law and Diplomacy* (U. of Pennsylvania, 1965).
O'Sullivan, R., *The Inheritance of the Common Law* (Stevens, 1950).

447

Page, L., *Justice of the Peace* (Faber & Faber, 1967).

Papadatos, P., *The Eichmann Trial* (Praeger, 1965).

Parker, J., *Some Aspects of French Law* (Scribner's, 1929).

Parry, C., *Nationality and Citizenship Laws of the Commonwealth* (Stevens, 1960).

Paton, G. W., and D. P. Derham (eds.), *A Textbook of Jurisprudence* (Oxford, 1972).

Patterson, S., *Immigration and Race Relations in Britain, 1960–1967* (Oxford, 1969).

Peaslee, A. J., *Constitutions of Nations*, 2nd ed. (Nijhoff, 1956).

Phillips, O. H., *The Constitutional Law of Great Britain and the Commonwealth*, 2nd ed. (Sweet & Maxwell, 1957).

Plischke, E., *Contemporary Government of Germany* (Houghton Mifflin, 1961).

Plucknett, T. F. T., *A Concise History of the Common Law*, 4th ed. (Butterworth, 1948).

———, *Early English Legal Literature* (Cambridge, 1958).

Podgorecki, A., *et al.*, *Knowledge and Opinion About Law* (Martin Robertson, 1974).

Pollard, R. S. W. (ed.), *Administrative Tribunals at Work: A Symposium* (Stevens, 1950).

Pollock, Sir F., and F. W. Maitland, *History of English Law* (Cambridge, 1898).

Pompe, C. A., *Aggressive War: An International Crime* (Nijhoff, 1953).

Popisil, L., *Anthropology of Law: A Comparative Theory* (Harper & Row, 1971).

Potter, H., *An Historical Introduction to English Law and Its Institutions*, 3rd ed. (Sweet & Maxwell, 1948).

Pound, R., *The Lawyer from Antiquity to Modern Times* (International Publ. Co., 1953).

Pratt, O. C., *Tort Liability of the State* (U. of Illinois, 1947).

Pritchard, J. L., *A History of Capital Punishment* (Kennikat, 1932).

Proehl, P. O. (ed.), *Legal Problems of International Trade* (U. of Illinois, 1959).

Pylee, M. V., *Constitutional Government in India*, 2nd ed. (Asia Publ. House, 1965).

Rackman, E., *Israel's Emerging Constitution, 1948–1951* (Columbia, 1951).

Radcliffe, G. R. Y., and G. Cross, *The English Legal System*, 3rd ed. (Butterworth, 1954).

Radzinowicz, Sir L., and M. E. Wolfgang, *Crime and Justice* (Basic Books, 1971).

Reith, C., *A Short History of the British Police* (Oxford, 1948).

Rendel, M., *The Administrative Functions of the French Conseil d'État* (Weiderfeld & Nicolson, 1970).

Report of the (Franks) Committee on Administrative Tribunals and Enquiries (H.M.S.O., Cmd. 218 of 1957).

Reuschemeyer, D., *Lawyers and Their Society: A Comparative Study* (Harvard, 1974).

Rice, W. G., *Law Among States in Federacy: A Survey of Decisions of the Swiss Federal Tribunal in Intercantonal Controversies* (Nelson, 1959).

———, *A Tale of Two Courts: Judicial Settlement of Controversies Between the State of the Swiss and American Federation* (U. of Wisconsin, 1967).

Richardson, H. G., and G. O. Sayles, *Law and Legislation from Aethelbert to Magna Carta* (U. of Edinburgh, 1966).

Roberts, G. D., *Law and Life* (W. H. Allen, 1964).

Robertson, A. H., *European Institutions* (Praeger, 1959).

———, *Human Rights in Europe* (Manchester U., 1963).

————— (ed.), *Human Rights in National and International Law* (Oceana, 1968).

Robinson, J., *And the Crooked Shall Be Made Straight: The Eichmann Trial, the Jewish Catastrophe, and Hannah Arendt's Narrative* (Macmillan, 1965).

Robson, W. A., *Justice and Administrative Law: A Study of the English Constitution* 3rd ed. (Stevens, 1951).

Rogger, H., and E. Weber, *The European Right: A Historical Profile* (U. of California, 1966).

Romashkin, P. S. (ed.), *Fundamentals of Soviet Law* (For. Lang. Publ. House, 1961).

Ronning, C. N., *Law and Politics in Inter-American Diplomacy* (Wiley, 1963).

Rose, E. J. B., *Colour and Citizenship: A Report on British Race Relations* (Oxford, 1969).

Rosenne, S., *The Law and Practice of the International Court* (Sijthoff, 1965).

—————, *The World Court: What It Is and How It Works* (Oceana, 1962).

Rothchild, D., *Racial Bargaining in Independent Kenya: A Study of Minorities and Decolonization* (Oxford, 1973).

Royal Comm. on the Police, *Final Report* (H.M.S.O., 1962).

Rudd, G. R., *The English Legal System* (Butterworth, 1962).

Runes, D. D., *The Disinherited and the Law* (Philosophical Library, 1964).

Runes, D. D., *The World Court* (Oceana, 1962).

Sachs, A., *Justice in South Africa* (U. of California, 1973).

Sandifer, D. V., and L. R. Scheman, *The Foundations of Freedom* (Praeger, 1966).

Sawer, G., *Australian Federalism in the Courts* (Cambridge, 1969).

—————, and E. M. Wise, *Anglo-American Criminal Justice* (Oxford, 1967).

Schact, J., *An Introduction to Islamic Law* (Oxford, 1964).

Schlesinger, R. B., *Comparative Law*, 2nd ed. (Foundation Press, 1960).

—————, *Formation of Contracts: A Study of the Common Core of Legal Systems* (Oceana, 1968).

—————, *Soviet Legal Theory* (Kegan Paul, 1964).

—————, *Soviet Legal Theory: Its Social Background and Development* (Humanities, 1951).

Schmeiser, D. A., *Civil Liberties in Canada* (Oxford, 1964).

Schubert, C., and D. J. Danelski, *Comparative Judicial Behavior: Cross Cultural Studies in Political Decision-Making in the East and West* (Oxford, 1969).

Schur, E. M., *Narcotics Addiction in Britain and America* (U. of Indiana, 1962).

Schuyler, R. L., *British Constitutional History Since 1832* (Van Nostrand, 1962).

Schwartz, B. (ed.), *The Code Napoleon and the Common-Law World* (N.Y.U., 1956).

—————, *French Administrative Law and the Common-Law World* (N.Y.U., 1954).

—————, *Law and the Executive in Britain* (N.Y.U., 1949).

—————, *The Root of Freedom: A Constitutional History of England* (Hill & Wang, 1967).

Schwartz, B., and H. W. R. Wade, *Legal Control of Government: Administrative Control in Great Britain and the United States* (Oxford, 1972).

Schwarzenberger, G., and C. Holland (eds.), *Law, Justice and Equity: Essays in Tribute to G. W. Keefon* (Oceana, 1967).

Schwelb, E., *Human Rights and International Community* (Quadrangle, 1964).

Scofield, C. L., *A Study of the Court of Star Chamber* (U. of Chicago, 1960).

Scott, F. R., *Civil Liberties and Canadian Federalism* (U. of Toronto, 1959).

Segal, R., *The Race War: The World-Wide Clash of White and Non-White* (Viking, 1967).

Sharma, J. D., *Modern Constitutions at Work* (Asia Publ. House, 1962).

Sharswood, G., *Blackstone's Commentaries on the Laws of England* (Lippincott, 1891).

Shawcross, Sir H. W., *The Functions and Responsibilities of an Advocate* (Assn. of Bar of City of N.Y., 1958).

Shientag, B. L. *Moulder of Legal Thought* (Kennikat, 1943).

Shoolbred, C. F., *The Administration of Criminal Justice in England and Wales* (Pergamon, 1966).

Siebert, F. S., *Freedom of the Press in England: 1476–1776* (U. of Illinois, 1952, 1965).

Sieghart, M. A., *Government by Decree* (Stevens, 1950).

Silvert, K. H. (ed.), *Churches and States: The Religious Institution and Modernization* (Amer. Univ. Field Staff, 1967).

Simpson, J. L., and H. Fox, *International Arbitration: Law and Practice* (Praeger, 1959).

Singer, P., *Democracy and Disobedience* (Oxford, 1974).

Siyar, S., *The Islamic Law of Nations* (Johns Hopkins, 1966).

Smith, D. E. (ed.), *South Asian Politics and Religion* (Princeton, 1966).

Smith, G., *A Constitutional and Legal History of England* (Scribner's, 1955).

Smith, M., *The Developments of European Law* (Columbia, 1928).

de Smith, S. A., *Judicial Review of Administrative Action* (Stevens, 1960).

Sommerich, O. C., and B. Busch, *Foreign Law—A Guide to Its Pleading and Proof* (Oceana, 1959).

Sorenson, M. (ed.), *Manual of Public International Law* (St. Martin's, 1968).

Sowle, C. R. (ed.), *Police Power and Individual Freedom* (Aldine, 1965).

St. John-Stevas, N., *Life, Death, and the Law: Law and Christian Morals in England and the United States* (Indiana U., 1961).

Stanger, R. J. (ed.), *Essays on Espionage and International Law* (Ohio State U., 1962).

Stannard, H., *The Two Constitutions: A Comparative Study of British and American Constitutional Systems* (Van Nostrand, 1949).

Starke, J. G., *Introduction to International Law*, 5th ed. (Butterworth, 1963).

Stead, P. J., *The Police of Paris* (Staples, 1957).

Stein, P., *Regulae Juris: From Juristic Rules to Legal Maxims* (U. of Edinburgh, 1966).

Stephen, J. F., *A History of the Criminal Law of England* (Macmillan, 1883).

Stephenson, C., and F. G. Marcham (eds.), *Sources of English Constitutional History* (Harper, 1937).

Stevens, R. B., *Questions and Answers on Constitutional Law and Legal History*, 7th ed. (Sweet & Maxwell, 1959).

Stewart, Z. (ed.), *The Ancient World: Justice, Heroism and Responsibility* (Prentice-Hall, 1966).

Stone, J., *Human Law and Human Justice* (Stevens, 1965).

———, *The International Court and World Crisis* (Carnegie Endowment, 1962).

———, *Legal System and Lawyers' Reasoning* (Stevens, 1964).

———, *Social Dimensions of Law and Justice* (Stanford U., 1966).

Strayer, B. L., *Judicial Review of Legislation in Canada* (U. of Toronto, 1968).

Street, H., *Freedom, The Individual and the Law*, 3rd ed. (Penguin, 1972).

———, *Governmental Liability: A Comparative Study* (Cambridge, 1953).

Strong, C. F., *A History of Modern Political Constitutions: An Introduction to the Comparative Study of the History and Existing Form* (Capricorn, 1964).

Stumpf, S. E., *Morality and the Law* (Vanderbilt U., 1966).

Syatauw, J. J. G., *Decisions of the International Court of Justice* (Oceana, 1963).

Szirmai, A. (ed.), *Law in Eastern Europe* (Hillary, 1959).

Szladits, C., *Bibliography of Foreign and Comparative Law Books and Articles in English* (Oceana, 1955, 1961, 1969).

————, *A Guide to Foreign Legal Materials—French, German, Swiss* (Oceana, 1959).

Taswell-Langmead, T. P., *English Constitutional History*, 11th ed., rev. by T. F. T. Pluckett (Houghton Mifflin, 1961).

Taylor, T., *Nuremberg and Vietnam: An American Tragedy* (Quadrangle, 1970).

Triska, J. F., and R. M. Susser, *The Theory, Law, and Policy of Soviet Treaties* (Stanford, 1962).

Turner, R. V., *The King and His Courts* (Cornell, 1968).

Tuttle, E. O., *The Struggle Against Capital Punishment in Great Britain* (Stevens, 1961).

Ulc, O., *The Judge in a Communist State* (Ohio State U., 1972).

United Nations, *International Court of Justice* (U.N. Publications, 1971).

Vallat, Sir F. (ed.), *An Introduction to the Study of Human Rights* (Europa, 1972).

Van Dyke, V., *Human Rights, the United States, and World Community* (Oxford, 1970).

Vedel, G., *Droit Administratif* (Presses Université de France, 1968).

Verba, S., *Law and the Indo-China War* (Princeton, 1972).

Vile, M. J. C., *Constitutionalism and the Separation of Powers* (Oxford, 1967).

Vinogradoff, Sir P., *Common Sense in Law*, 3rd ed. (Oxford, 1959).

Von der Mehden, F. R., *Comparative Political Violence* (Prentice-Hall, 1973).

Von Glahn, G., *Law Among Nations*, 2nd ed. (Macmillan, 1970).

Von Knieriem, A., *The Nuremberg Trials* (Regnery, 1959).

Von Mehren, A. T., *The Civil Law Systems: Cases and Materials for the Comparative Study of Law* (Little, Brown, 1957).

———— (ed.), *Law in Japan: The Legal Order in a Changing Society* (Harvard, 1963).

Vyshinsky, A. Y., *Law of the Soviet State* (Macmillan, 1948).

Wade, E. C. S., *Administrative Law* (Oxford, 1961).

————, *Dicey's Introduction to the Study of the Law of the Constitution*, 10th ed. (Macmillan, 1959).

————, and G. C. Phillips (eds.), *Constitutional Law*, 7th ed. (Longmans, Green, 1965).

Wade, H. W. R., *Towards Administrative Justice* (U. of Michigan, 1963).

Wagner, W. J., *Federal States and Their Judiciary: Comparative Study* (Mouton, 1959).

Walker, D. M., *The Scottish Legal System* (W. Green, 1959).

Walker, M. G., *Criminal Law* (Sweet & Maxwell, 1964).

Walker, N., *Crimes, Courts, and Figures: An Introduction to Criminal Statistics* (Penguin, 1971).

451

————, *Crime and Insanity in England: The Historical Perspective* (U. of Edinburgh, 1968).

————, *Crime and Punishment in Britain* (U. of Edinburgh, 1965).

Walvin, J., *The Black Presence: A Documentary History of the Negro in England* (Schocken, 1972).

Watkins, R. D., *The State as a Party Litigant* (Johns Hopkins, 1927).

Watson, J. Steven, and W. C. Costin, *The Law and Working of the Constitution: Documents, 1660–1914* (Adam and Charles Black, 1952).

Weil, G., *The European Convention on Human Rights* (Sythoff, 1963).

Welch, C. E., Jr. (ed.), *Soldier and State in Africa: A Comparative Analysis of Military Intervention and Political Change* (Northwestern, 1970).

Weyrauch, W. O., *The Personality of Lawyers* (Yale, 1964).

Wheare, K. G., *The Constitutional Structure of the Commonwealth* (Oxford, 1961).

————, *Modern Constitutions*, 2nd ed. (Oxford, 1966).

Whitaker, B., *The Police* (Eyre & Spottiswoode, 1964).

Whitaker, H. G., *Politics and Power: A Text in International Law* (Harper & Row, 1964).

White, G. M., *The Use of Experts by International Tribunals* (Syracuse U., 1965).

White, I. L., *et al.*, *Law and Politics in Outer Space: A Bibliography* (U. of Arizona, 1971).

Whittemore, E. P., *The Press in Japan Today: A Case Study* (U. of South Carolina, 1968).

Wiener, F. B., *Civilians Under Military Justice: The British Practice Since 1689, Especially in North America* (U. of Chicago, 1967).

Wigmore, J. H., *A Panorama of the World's Legal Systems* (West, 1928).

Williams, G. L., *The Proof of Guilt*, 3rd ed. (Stevens, 1963).

————, *A Treatise on the Anglo-American System of Evidence* (Little, Brown, 1961).

Williams, W. J., *Moriarty's Police Law*, 18th ed. (Butterworth, 1965).

Williams, W. L., *Intergovernmental Military Forces and World Public Order* (Oceana, 1971).

Wilson, H. H., and H. Glickmann, *The Problem of Internal Security in Great Britain, 1948–1953* (Random House, 1954).

Wilson, R. R. (ed.), *International and Comparative Law of the Commonwealth* (Duke, 1969).

Wiseman, H. V., *The Cabinet in the Commonwealth* (Stevens, 1958).

Woetzel, R., *The Nuremberg Trials in International Law*, rev. ed. (Praeger, 1962).

Wolf-Phillips, L., *Constitutions and Modern States: Selected Texts and Commentary* (Praeger, 1968).

Wolfenden, Sir John, *et al.*, *The Wolfenden Report* (Stein & Day, 1963).

Woodhouse, A. S. P., *Puritanism and Liberty*, 2nd ed. (U. of Chicago, 1951).

Wortley, B. A., *Jurisprudence* (Oceana, 1967).

Wright, G., and A. Mejia, Jr., *An Age of Controversy* (Dodd, Mead, 1963).

Zaitsev, Y., and O. Poltorak, *The Soviet Bar* (For. Lang. Publ. House, 1959).

Zile, Z. R., R. Sharlet, and J. C. Love, *The Soviet Legal System and Arms Inspection* (Praeger, 1972).

Zurcher, A. J., *Constitutions and Constitutional Trends Since World War II*, 2nd ed. (N.Y.U., 1955).

IV AMERICAN CONSTITUTIONAL LAW: CLASSIFIED WORKS ON CIVIL RIGHTS AND LIBERTIES

I. GENERAL BACKGROUND

A. HISTORY.

Avins, A. (ed.), *The Reconstruction Amendment Debates: The Legislative History and Contemporary Debates in Congress on the Thirteenth, Fourteenth, and Fifteenth Amendments* (Va. Comm. on Const'l. Gov't., 1967).

Barrington, B. C., *Magna Charta*, 2nd ed. (Campbell, 1900).

Becker, C. L., *The Declaration of Independence* (Harcourt, Brace, 1922).

Berman, W. C., *The Politics of Civil Rights in the Truman Administration* (Ohio State U., 1970).

Brant, I., *The Bill of Rights: Its Origin and Meaning* (Bobbs-Merrill, 1965).

Brown, S. G., *The First Republicans: Political Philosophy and Public Policy in the Party of Jefferson and Madison* (Syracuse U., 1954).

Carter, H., *The Angry Scar: The Story of Reconstruction* (Doubleday, 1959).

Casper, J. D., *Lawyers Before the Warren Court: Civil Liberties and Civil Rights, 1957–66* (U. of Illinois, 1972).

Castberg, F., *Freedom of Speech in the West* (Oceana, 1960).

Chafee, Z., *How Human Rights Got into the Constitution* (Boston U., 1952).

Chicago, University of, *The People Shall Judge*, 2 vols. (U. of Chicago, 1949).

Commager, H. S., and L. W. Levy, *The Bill of Rights* (Bobbs-Merrill, 1966).

Cranston, M., *Freedom: A New Analysis* (Longmans, Green, 1953).

Daube, D., *Civil Disobedience in Antiquity* (Aldine, 1973).

Dietze, G., *Magna Carta and Property* (U. of Virginia, 1965).

Dollard, J., *Mr. Lincoln and the Negroes: The Long Road to Equality* (Atheneum, 1963).

Duchacek, I. D., *Rights and Liberties in the World Today: Constitutional Promise and Reality* (Clio, 1973).

Dumbauld, E., *The Bill of Rights and What It Means Today* (U. of Oklahoma, 1957).

———, *The Declaration of Independence and What It Means Today* (U. of Oklahoma, 1965).

Eaton, C., *Freedom of Thought in the Old South* (Duke U., 1940).

Ekirch, A. A., *The Decline of American Liberalism* (Longmans, Green, 1955).

Flack, H. B., *The Adoption of the Fourteenth Amendment* (Johns Hopkins, 1908).

Grant, J. (ed.), *Black Protest: History, Documents and Analysis, 1619 to the Present* (Fawcett, 1968).

Harlan, L. B., *Separate and Unequal* (U. of North Carolina, 1958).

Harris, R. J., *The Quest for Equality: The Constitution, Congress, and the Supreme Court* (L.S.U., 1960).

Harvey, J. C., *Civil Rights During the Kennedy Administration* (U. of Mississippi, 1971).

Holt, J. C., *Magna Carta* (Columbia, 1966).

————, *The Making of Magna Carta* (U. of Virginia, 1965).

Howard, A. E. D., *The Road from Runnymede: Magna Carta and Constitutionalism in America* (U. of Virginia, 1968).

Hurst, J. W., *Law and the Conditions of Freedom in the Nineteenth-Century United States* (U. of Wisconsin, 1956).

Hyman, H. M., *To Try Men's Souls: Loyalty Tests in American History* (U. of California, 1959).

————, *Era of the Oath: Northern Loyalty Tests During the Civil War and Reconstruction* (U. of Pennsylvania, 1954).

James, J. B., *The Framing of the Fourteenth Amendment* (U. of Illinois, 1956).

Jensen, M., *The Articles of Confederation* (U. of Wisconsin, 1960).

Johnson, D., *The Challenge to American Freedoms* (U. of Kentucky, 1963).

Kelley, A. H., *Where Constitutional Liberty Came From* (Catt Mem. Fund, 1954).

Kemper, D. J., *Decade of Fear: Senator Hennings and Civil Liberties* (U. of Missouri, 1965).

Knight, H., *With Liberty and Justice for All: The Meaning of the Bill of Rights Today* (Oceana, 1967).

Konvitz, M. R., *A Century of Civil Rights* (Columbia, 1961).

Lasson, N. B., *The History of the Development of the Fourteenth Amendment* (Johns Hopkins, 1937).

Levy, L. W., *Legacy of Suppression: Freedom of Speech and Press in Early American History* (Harvard, 1960).

Lewis, A., and The New York Times, *Portrait of a Decade* (Random House, 1965).

MacIver, R. M. (ed.), *Great Expressions of Human Rights* (Harper & Bros., 1950).

McPherson, J. M., *The Struggle for Equality: Abolitionists and the Negro in the Civil War and Reconstruction* (Princeton, 1965).

Markmann, C. L., *The Noblest Cry: A History of the American Civil Liberties Union* (St. Martin's, 1965).

Meador, D. J., *Habeas Corpus and Magna Carta: Dualism of Power and Liberty* (U. of Virginia, 1966).

Mennix, D. P., and M. Cowley, *Black Cargoes: A History of the Atlantic Slave Trade, 1581–1865* (Viking, 1962).

Metz, H. W., and C. A. H. Thomson, *Authoritarianism and the Individual* (Brookings, 1950).

Meyer, H. N., *The Amendment that Refused To Die* (Chilton, 1973).

Muller, H. J., *Freedom in the Ancient World* (Harper, 1961).

————, *Freedom in the Western World* (Harper, 1964).

Myers, H. A., *Are Men Equal?* (Cornell, 1955).

Nye, R. B., *Fettered Freedom: Civil Liberties and the Slavery Controversy, 1830–1860* (Michigan State College, 1949).

Pallister, A., *Magna Carta: The Heritage of the Law* (Oxford, 1971).

Pound, R., *The Development of Constitutional Guarantees of Liberty* (Yale, 1957).

Preston, W., Jr., *Aliens and Dissensus: Federal Suppression of Radicals, 1903–1933* (Harvard, 1963).

Quarles, B., *Lincoln and the Negro* (Oxford, 1961).

Randall, J. G., *The Civil War and Reconstruction* (D. C. Heath, 1937).

————, *Constitutional Problems under Lincoln* (U. of Illinois, 1951).

Raphael, D. D. (ed.), *Political Theory and the Rights of Man* (Indiana U., 1967).

Roche, J. P., *The Quest for the Dream: The Development of Civil Rights and Human Relations in Modern America* (Macmillan, 1963).

Rossiter, C., *Seedtime of the Republic: The Origin of the American Tradition of Political Liberty* (Harcourt, Brace, 1953).

Rutland, R. A., *The Birth of the Bill of Rights, 1776–1791* (Collier, 1962).

Scheiber, H. N., *The Wilson Administration and Civil Liberties* (Cornell, 1960).

Schwartz, B., *The Fourteenth Amendment: A Century in American Law and Life* (N.Y.U., 1970).

Schwartz, B., *The Roots of Freedom* (Hill & Wang, 1967).

Shotwell, J. T., *The Long Way to Freedom* (Bobbs-Merrill, 1960).

Silver, D. M., *Lincoln's Supreme Court* (U. of Illinois, 1956).

Smith, J. M., *Freedom's Fetters: The Alien and Sedition Laws and American Civil Liberties* (Cornell, 1956).

Stenton, D. M., *After Runnymede: Magna Carta in the Middle Ages* (U. of Virginia, 1965).

Stevens, W. O., *Footsteps to Freedom* (Dodd, Mead, 1954).

Swindler, W. F., *Magna Carta: Legend and Legacy* (Bobbs-Merrill, 1965).

Tenbroek, J., E. N. Barnhart, and F. W. Matson, *The Anti-Slavery Origins of the Fourteenth Amendment* (Berkeley, 1951).

———, *Equal under Law* (Collier, 1965).

Thorne, S. E., *et al.*, *The Great Charter* (Mentor, 1969).

Weyl, N., *Treason: The Story of Disloyalty and Betrayal in American History* (Public Affairs Press, 1950).

Whipple, L., *The Story of Civil Liberty in the United States* (Vanguard, 1927).

White, W., *How Far the Promised Land?* (Viking, 1955).

Woodward, C. V., *The Strange Career of Jim Crow*, rev. ed. (Oxford, 1957).

Wright, E., *Fabric of Freedom, 1763–1800* (Hill & Wang, 1961).

Wynes, C. E., *Race Relations in Virginia, 1870–1902* (U. of Virginia, 1961).

Zabel, O. H., *God and Caesar in Nebraska: A Study of the Legal Relationship of Church and State, 1854–1954* (U. of Nebraska, 1955).

B. DOCUMENTS AND REPORTS.

American Civil Liberties Union, *Annual Report(s)* (A.C.L.U.).

Angle, P., *By These Words* (Rand McNally, 1954).

Bardolph, R., *The Civil Rights Record: Black Americans and the Law, 1849–1970* (Crowell, 1971).

Becker, C. L., *The Declaration of Independence* (Harcourt, Brace, 1922).

Berman, D. M., *A Bill Becomes a Law: The Civil Rights Act of 1960* (Macmillan, 1962).

Boyd, J. P., *The Declaration of Independence* (Princeton, 1945).

Brookes, A. D. (ed.), *Civil Rights and Liberties in the United States* (Civil Libs. Educ. Foundation, 1962).

Brown, S. G. (ed.), *We Hold These Truths* (Harper & Bros., 1948).

Chafee, Z., *Documents on Fundamental Human Rights: The Anglo-American Tradition* (Harvard, 1952; Atheneum, 1963).

———, *Three Human Rights in the Constitution of 1787* (U. of Kansas, 1956, 1968).

Cohen, W., M. Schwartz, and D. Sobul, *The Bill of Rights: A Sourcebook* (Benziger, 1968).

Commager, H. S. (ed.), *Documents of American History*, 4th ed. (Appleton-Century-Crofts, 1949).

————, *Living Ideas in America* (Harper & Bros., 1951).

Davis, J. P. (ed.), *The American Negro Reference Book* (Prentice-Hall, 1966).

Dixon, R. G., and E. Plischke (eds.), *American Government: Basic Documents and Materials* (Van Nostrand, 1950).

Dorsen, N., *Frontiers of Civil Liberties* (Pantheon, 1968).

Grant, J. (ed.), *Black Protest: History, Documents and Analysis, 1619 to the Present* (Fawcett, 1968).

Hamilton, A., J. Madison, and J. Jay, *The Federalist*, ed. by B. F. Wright (Harvard, 1961).

Hanson, H. A., *et al.*, *Fighting for Freedom* (Winston, 1947).

Hurst, J. W., *The Law of Treason in the United States: Collected Essays* (Greenwood, 1971).

King, D. B., and C. W. Quick (eds.), *Legal Aspects of the Civil Rights Movement* (Wayne State, 1965).

Monaghan, F., *Heritage of Freedom* (Princeton, 1947).

Murray, P., *Human Rights U.S.A., 1948–1966* (Board of Missions, The Methodist Church, 1967).

————, *State Laws on Race and Color* (Christian Service, 1950).

Perry, R. L., *Sources of Our Liberties: Documentary Origins of Individual Liberties in the United States Constitution and the Bill of Rights* (American Bar F., 1959).

———— (ed.), *Sources of Our Liberties: English and American Documents from Magna Charta to the Bill of Rights* (McGraw-Hill, 1964).

Pious, R. M. (ed.), *Identity and Authority: Civil Rights and Liberties in the 1970s* (Random House, 1973).

President's National Advisory Commission on Civil Disorders, Report (Bantam, 1968).

Rankin, R. S., *State Constitutions: The Bill of Rights* (Nat'l. Mem. Lea., 1960).

Reitman, A. (ed.), *The Price of Liberty* (Norton, 1968).

Rodgers, H. R., Jr., and C. S. Bullock III, *Law and Social Change: Civil Rights, Laws and Their Consequences* (McGraw-Hill, 1972).

Schwartz, B. (ed.), *The Fourteenth Amendment: A Century in American Law and Life* (N.Y.U., 1969).

Skolnick, J. H. (ed.), *The Politics of Protest: A Task Force Submitted to the NCCPV* (Simon & Schuster, 1969).

Smith, J. M., and P. L. Murphy, *Liberty and Justice—An Historical Record of American Constitutional Development* (Knopf, 1958).

Sobul, D., *The Bill of Rights, A Handbook* (Benziger, 1968).

Witherspoon, J. P., *Administrative Implementation of Civil Rights* (U. of Texas, 1968).

Zarr, M., *The Bill of Rights and the Police* (Oceana, 1970).

c. CASEBOOKS. (General and specific.)

Abernathy, G. M., *Civil Liberties Under the Constitution*, 2nd ed. (Dodd, Mead, 1972).

Amaker, N. C., *Civil Liberty and Civil Rights*, 4th ed. (Oceana, 1966).

Barker, L. J., and T. W. Barker, *Civil Liberties and the Constitution: Cases and Commentary* (Prentice-Hall, 1970).

———, *Freedoms, Courts, Politics: Studies in Civil Liberties* (Prentice-Hall, 1972).

Catterell, H. H. (ed.), *Judicial Cases Concerning American Slavery and the Negro* (Carnegie Inst., 1926–37).

Cortner, R. S., and C. M. Lytle, Jr., *Modern Constitutional Law: Commentary and Case Studies* (Free Press, 1971).

Cushman, R. F., *Cases in Civil Liberties* (Appleton-Century-Crofts, 1968).

Dorsen, N. (ed.), *Discrimination and Civil Rights: Cases, Texts and Materials* (Little, Brown, 1969).

Emerson, T. I., and D. Haber, *Political and Civil Rights in the United States*, 3rd ed. (Little, Brown, 1967).

Fairman, C., *American Constutitional Decisions* (Holt, 1950).

Freedman, W., *Society on Trial: Current Constitutional Decisions and Social Change* (Thomas, 1965).

Gordon, W. I., *Nine Men Plus: Supreme Court Opinions on Free Speech and Free Press* (W. C. Brown, 1971).

Gunther, G., and N. T. Dowling, *Cases and Materials on Individual Rights in Constitutional Law* (Foundation Press, 1970).

Gweck, S., *Cases on Criminal Law and Its Enforcement* (West, 1951).

Haiman, F. S., *Freedom of Speech: Issues and Cases* (Random House, 1965).

Hays, A. C., *Let Freedom Ring* (Boni & Liverright, 1937).

Inbau, F. E., and C. Sowle, *Cases and Comments on Criminal Justice* (Foundation Press, 1960).

Israel, J. H., and W. R. LaFave, *Criminal Procedure in a Nutshell: Constitutional Limitations* (West, 1971).

Kaplan, J., *Criminal Justice: Introductory Cases and Materials* (Foundation Press, 1973).

Kerper, H. B., *Introduction to the Criminal Justice System* (West, 1972).

Konvitz, M. R., *Bill of Rights Reader: Leading Constitutional Cases*, 4th ed. (Cornell, 1968).

———, *Expanding Liberties: The Emergence of New Civil Liberties and Civil Rights in Postwar America* (Viking, 1967).

Lockhart, W. B., Y. Kamisar, and J. H. Choper, *Cases and Materials on Constitutional Rights and Liberties*, 3rd ed. (West, 1970).

Mason, A. T., and W. M. Beaney, *American Constitutional Law: Introductory Essays and Selected Cases*, 3rd ed. (Prentice-Hall, 1964).

Micheall, J., and H. Wechsler (eds.), *Criminal Law and Its Administration: Cases, Statutes, and Commentaries* (Foundation Press, 1940).

Newman, E. S., *Civil Liberty and Civil Rights*, 5th ed. (Oceana, 1970).

Parker, K., R. M. O'Neil, and N. Econopouly, *Civil Liberties: Case Studies and the Law* (Houghton Mifflin, 1965).

Paulsen, M. G., and S. H. Kadish, *Criminal Law and Its Processes* (Little, Brown, 1962).

Pritchett, C. H., *American Constitutional Issues* (McGraw-Hill, 1962).

Reimel, T., *Handbook on Criminal Law in Pennsylvania* (Bisel, 1958).

Sheldon, C., *The Supreme Court: Politicians in Robes* (Free Press, 1970).

Sovern, M. I., *Cases and Materials on Racial Discrimination in Employment* (West, 1969).

Spinard, W., *Civil Liberties* (Quadrangle, 1970).

Sweet, E. C., *Civil Liberties in America: A Casebook* (Van Nostrand, 1966).

Tresolini, R. J., *These Liberties: Case Studies in Civil Rights* (Lippincott, 1968).

Weinberger, A. D., *Freedom and Protection: The Bill of Rights* (Chandler, 1962).

Weinreb, L. L., *Leading Constitutional Cases on Criminal Justice* (Foundation Press, 1973).

D. GENERAL OUTLINES. (See also: III. B. Theories and Aspects of Freedom, Rights, and Liberties; also see under specific rights.)

Asch, S., *Civil Rights and Responsibilities Under the Constitution* (Arco, 1968).

Antieau, C. J., *Rights of Our Fathers* (Coiner, 1968).

Association of the Bar of the City of New York, *Freedom to Travel: Report of the Special Committee to Study Passport Procedures* (Dodd, Mead, 1958).

Barker, L. H., and T. W. Barker, Jr., *Freedoms, Courts, Politics: Studies in Civil Liberties* (Prentice-Hall, 1965).

Bishop, H. M., and S. Handel, *Basic Issues of American Democracy* (Appleton-Century-Crofts, 1961).

Bontecou, E. (ed.), *Freedom in the Balance: Opinions of Judge Henry W. Edgeton Relating to Civil Liberties* (Cornell, 1953).

Brannon, H. A., *Treaties on the Rights and Privileges Guaranteed by the Fourteenth Amendment to the Constitution of the United States* (Anderson, 1901).

Brennan, W. J., Jr., *The Bill of Rights and the States* (Center for the Study of Dem. Insts., 1961).

Brooks, A. D., *Civil Rights and Liberties in the United States: An Annotated Bibliography* (Civil Liberties Educational Foundation, 1962).

Brookes, E. H., and J. B. Maculay, *Civil Liberty in South Africa* (Oxford, 1959).

Cahn, E., *Can the Supreme Court Defend Civil Liberties?* (Sidney Hillman Foundation, 1956).

———— (comp.), *Confronting Injustice: The Edmond Cahn Reader* (Little, Brown, 1966).

————, *The Great Rights* (Macmillan, 1963).

Columbia University Teachers College, Citizenship Education Project, *When Men Are Free: Premises of American Liberty* (Houghton, Mifflin, 1955).

Commager, H. S., et al., *Civil Liberties Under Attack* (U. of Virginia, 1943).

Congressional Quarterly, *Revolution in Civil Rights*, 3rd ed. (C.Q. Service, 1968).

Creamer, J. S., *A Citizen's Guide to Legal Rights* (Holt, Rinehart, Winston, 1971).

Cushman, R. E., *Civil Liberties in the United States: A Guide to Current Problems and Experience* (Cornell, 1956).

Davis, E., *But We Were Born Free* (Bobbs-Merrill, 1954).

Donovan, J. C., *The Politics of Poverty* (Pegasus, 1967).

Dorsen, N., *Frontiers of Civil Liberties* (Pantheon, 1968).

Douglas, W. O., *The Anatomy of Liberty* (Trident, 1963).

————, *A Living Bill of Rights* (Doubleday, 1961).

————, *The Rights of the People* (Doubleday, 1958).

Edman, I., *Fountainhead of Freedom* (Reynal & Hitchcock, 1941).

Edwards, R. A., *The Fourteenth Amendment and Civil Liberty* (Catt Mem. Fund, 1955).

Fairman, C., and S. Morrison, *The Fourteenth Amendment and the Bill of Rights: The Incorporation Theory* (Da Capo, 1970).

Fernando, E. M., *The Bill of Rights* (Oceana, 1971).

Fleishman, H., *Let's Be Human* (Oceana, 1960).

Frankel, O. K., *Our Civil Liberties* (Viking, 1964).

————, *The Rights We Have: A Handbook of Civil Liberties* (Cornell, 1971).

Friedman, L., *The Civil Rights Reader: Basic Documents of the Civil Rights Movement* (Walker, 1967).

Gellhorn, W., *American Rights: The Constitution in Action* (Macmillan, 1960).

Hanely, T. O. B., *Their Rights and Liberties* (Newman Press, 1959).

Humphrey, H. H., *Beyond Civil Rights: A New Day for Equality* (Random House, 1968).

Hutchins, R. M., *Freedom, Education and the Fund: Essays and Addresses, 1946–1956* (Meridian Books, 1956).

Jacobs, C. E., *Justice Frankfurter and Civil Liberties* (Berkeley, 1961).

Kauper, P. G., *Civil Liberties and the Constitution* (U. of Michigan, 1962).

————, *Frontiers of Constitutional Liberty* (U. of Michigan, 1956).

Kemper, D. J., *Decade of Fear: Senator Hennings and Civil Liberties* (U. of Missouri, 1956).

Konvitz, M. R., *First Amendment Freedom: Selected Cases on Freedom of Religion, Speech, Press, Assembly* (Cornell, 1963).

————, and C. Rossiter (eds.), *Aspects of Liberty: Essays Presented to Robert E. Cushman* (Cornell, 1958).

Kunstler, W. M., *. . . and Justice for All* (Oceana, 1962).

Lamont, C., *The Right To Travel* (Basic Pamphlet, 1957).

Lewis, A., *Portrait of a Decade* (Random House, 1964).

MacLeish, A., *A Continuing Journey* (Houghton, Mifflin, 1967).

Newman, E. S. (ed.), *Civil Liberty and Civil Rights*, 5th ed. (Oceana, 1970).

————, *The Freedom Reader*, 2nd ed. (Oceana, 1963).

————, *The Hate Reader* (Oceana, 1964).

————, *The Law of Civil Rights and Civil Liberties* (Oceana, 1958).

Penrose, W. O., *Freedom Is Ourselves* (U. of Delaware, 1952).

Pious, R. M. (ed.), *Civil Rights and Liberties in the 1970s* (Random House, 1973).

Reppy, A., *Civil Rights in the United States* (Central Books, 1951).

Roche, J. P., *Courts and Rights: The American Judiciary in Action*, 2nd ed. (Random House, 1966).

Rodgers, H. R., Jr., and C. S. Billock, *Law and Social Change: Civil Rights, Law and Their Consequences* (McGraw-Hill, 1972).

Schechter, A. H., *Contemporary Constitutional Issues* (McGraw-Hill, 1972).

Schwartzman, R., and J. Stein, *Law of Personal Liberties* (Oceana, 1955).

Senser, R., *Primer on Interracial Justice* (Hellicon, 1962).

Shapiro, M., *The Court and Civil Rights* (Scott, Foresman, 1966).

Smith, T. V., *The Bill of Rights and Our Individual Liberties* (Catt Mem. Fund, 1954).

Starr, I., *Human Rights in the United States*, rev. ed. (Oxford, 1964).

Starzinger, V., *Civil Rights* (St. Martin's, 1965).

Superintendent of Documents, *The Report of the United States Commission on Civil Rights* (1959, ff.).

Thomas, N. C., *Politics, Administration and Civil Rights* (Random House, 1966).

Wattenberg, W. W. (ed.), *All Men Are Created Equal* (Wayne, 1966).

Way, H. F., *Liberty in the Balance: Current Issues in Civil Liberties*, 3rd ed. (McGraw-Hill, 1971).

Wilcox, C. (ed.), *Civil Liberties Under Attack* (U. of Pennsylvania, 1952).

Wirt, F. M., and W. D. Hawley, *New Dimensions of Freedom in America* (Chandler, 1969).

Yeager, F. B., and J. R. Stark, *Your Inalienable Rights* (Public Affairs Press, 1960).

II. PHILOSOPHY OF CIVIL RIGHTS AND LIBERTIES

A. GENERAL.

1. Due Process. (See also: IV. A. Procedural Due Process Generally.)

Collins, F. L., *The F.B.I. in Peace and War*, rev. & enl. by L. Dember (Ace, 1962).

Cunningham, M., et al., *Free Man versus his Government* (S.M.U., 1958).

Francis, P., *Protection Through the Law* (Oceana, 1965).

Graham, F. P., *The Due Process Revolution* (Hayden, 1970).

Nagel, S. S. (ed.), *The Rights of the Accused: In Law and Action* (Sage, 1972).

Newman, E. S., *Police, the Law and Personal Freedom* (Oceana, 1965).

Williams, E. B., *One Man's Freedom* (Atheneum, 1962).

Wood, V., *Due Process of Law, 1932–1949* (Louisiana State U., 1951).

2. Equal Protection. (See also: IV. Criminal Law and Procedure.)

Association of the Bar of the City of New York, *Equal Justice for the Accused* (Dodd, Mead, 1959).

Berger, M., *Equality by Statute: The Revolution in Civil Rights*, rev. ed. (Doubleday, 1967).

Dye, T. R., *The Politics of Equality* (Bobbs-Merrill, 1971).

Foundation of Federal Bar Association, *Equal Justice Under the Law* (Grosset, 1965).

Harris, R. J., *The Quest for Equality: The Constitution, Congress, and the Supreme Court* (Louisiana State U., 1960).

North Carolina Law Review, *Civil Rights and the South* (Da Capo, 1971).

Rainwater, L. (ed.), *Inequality and Justice* (Aldine, 1974).

Warsoff, L. A., *Equality and the Law* (Greenwood, 1938).

B. THEORIES AND ASPECTS OF FREEDOM. RIGHTS AND LIBERTIES.

Abraham, H. J., *Freedom and the Court: Civil Rights and Liberties in the United States*, 2nd ed. (Oxford, 1972).

Adler, M., *The Idea of Freedom*, Vols. I and II (Doubleday, 1958, 1961).

American Civil Liberties Union, *Freedom Through Dissent* (Oceana, 1963).

Angle, P. M. (ed.), *Created Equal—The Complete Lincoln-Douglas Debates of 1858* (U. of Chicago, 1958).

Anshen, R. N., *Freedom: Its Meaning* (Harcourt, Brace, 1940).

Bachrach, P., *Problems in Freedom* (Stackpole, 1953).

Barth, A., *Law Enforcement Versus the Law* (Collier, 1963).

Bay, C., *The Structure of Freedom* (Stanford, 1958).

Bayley, D. H., *Public Liberties in the New States* (Rand McNally, 1964).

Berdau, H. A. (ed.), *Civil Disobedience: Theory and Practice* (Pegasus, 1969).

Berlin, I., *Four Essays on Liberty* (Oxford, 1969).

Chafee, Z., *The Blessings of Liberty* (Lippincott, 1956).

Chagla, M. C., *The Individual and the State* (Asia Publication House, 1961).

Coffin, W. S., Jr., and C. E. Whitaker, *Law, Order, and Civil Disobedience* (Amer. Enterpr. Inst., 1967).

Cohen, M. P., *The Faith of A Liberal* (Holt, 1946).

Collins, C. W., *The Fourteenth Amendment and the States* (Little, Brown, 1912).

Commager, H. S., *Freedom and Order: A Commentary on the American Political Science* (Braziller, 1966).

Corwin, E. S., *Liberty Against Government: The Rise, Flowering and Decline of a Famous Juridical Concept* (Louisiana State U., 1948).

Cowling, M., *Mill and Liberalism* (Cambridge, 1963).

Cranston, M., *Freedom: A New Analysis* (Longman, Green, 1953).

Dahl, N. (ed.), *The Rights of Americans: What They Are—What They Should Be* (Vintage, 1971).

Douglas, W. O., *An Almanac of Liberty* (Doubleday, 1954).

——, *The Anatomy of Liberty* (Trident, 1963).

Dowden, W. S., and T. N. March (eds.), *The Heritage of Freedom: Essays on the Rights of Free Men* (Harper & Row, 1962).

Ekirch, A. A., Jr., *The Decline of American Liberalism* (Longman, Green, 1955; Atherton, 1966).

—— (ed.), *Voices in Dissent: An Anthology of Individualist Thought in the United States* (Citadel, 1961).

English, R. (ed.), *The Essentials of Freedom* (Kenyon, 1960).

Filler, L. (ed.), *Wendell Phillips on Civil Rights and Freedom* (Hill & Wang, 1965).

Fortas, A., *Concerning Dissent and Civil Disobedience* (New American Library, 1968).

Fosdick, D., *What Is Liberty?* (Harper, 1939).

Foster, A., *A Measure of Freedom* (Doubleday, 1950).

Friedman, D., *The Machinery of Freedom* (Harper & Row, 1973).

Friedrich, C. J., *Authority* (Harvard, 1958).

Gerhart, E. C., *American Liberty and Natural Law* (Beacon, 1953).

Graham, H. J., *Everyman's Constitution: Historical Essays on the Fourteenth Amendment, the "Conspiracy Theory" and American Constitutionalism*

Green, J. F., *The United Nations and Human Rights* (Brookings, 1956).

Hand, L., *The Spirit of Liberty: Papers and Addresses of Learned Hand*, 3rd ed. (Knopf, 1960).

Handlin, O., and M. Handlin, *The Dimensions of Liberties* (Harvard, 1961).

Harris, R., Justice, *The Crisis of Law, Order and Freedom in America* (Dutton, 1970).

Hartz, L., *The Liberal Tradition in America* (Harcourt, Brace, 1955).

Horn, R. A., *Groups and the Constitution* (Stanford, 1956).

Johnson, G. W., *This American People* (Harper & Bros., 1951).

Kallen, H. M., *A Study of Liberty* (Antioch, 1959).

Kennedy, R. E., *The Pursuit of Justice* (Harper & Row, 1965).

Laski, R., *Liberty in the Modern State* (Viking, 1930).

Levy, L. W., *Jefferson and Civil Liberties: The Darker Side* (Harvard, 1963).

Lieber, F., *Civil Liberty and Self-Government*, 3rd ed. (Lippincott, 1875).

MacIver, R. M., *Conflict of Loyalties* (Harper, 1952).

MacLeish, A., *Freedom in the Right To Choose* (Beacon, 1951).

Madden, E., *Civil Disobedience and Moral Law* (U. of Washington, 1968).

Maritain, J., *Man and the State* (U. of Chicago, 1951).

Markman, C. L., *The Noblest Cry* (St. Martin's, 1965).

Mayer, M. (ed.), *The Tradition of Freedom* (Oceana, 1960).

Medina, H. R., *The Anatomy of Freedom* (Holt, 1959).

Meiklejohn, A., *Political Freedom: The Constitutional Powers of the People* (Oxford, 1965).

Meiklejohn, D., *Freedom and the Public: Public and Private Morality in America* (Syracuse U., 1965).

Mill, J. S., *On Liberty* (Appleton-Century-Crofts, 1851).

——, *Prefaces to Liberty: Selected Writings of John Stuart Mill*, ed. by B. Wishy (Beacon, 1959).

Miller, H. H., *The Case for Liberty* (U. of North Carolina, 1965).

Milton, J., *Areopagitica*, 1644 ed. (Saifer, 1972).

Mims, E., Jr., *The Majority of the People* (Modern Age Books, 1941).

Morgan, C., *A Time to Speak* (Harper & Row, 1964).

——, *Liberties of the Mind* (Macmillan, 1952).

Muller, H. J., *The Individual in a Revolutionary World* (Ryerson, 1964).

——, *Issues of Freedom: Paradoxes and Promises* (Harper & Bros., 1960).

Newman, E. S., *Civil Liberty and Civil Rights*, 5th ed. (Oceana, 1970).

Nock, A. J., *Our Enemy the State* (Capton, 1946).

O'Neil, R. M., *The Price of Dependency: Civil Liberties in the Welfare State* (Dalton, 1970).

Oppenheim, F. E., *Dimensions of Freedom* (St. Martin's, 1961).

Orton, W. A., *The Liberal Tradition: Social and Spiritual Conditions of Freedom* (Oxford, 1945).

Patterson, B. B., *The Forgotten Ninth Amendment* (Bobbs-Merrill, 1955).

Pennock, J. R., *Liberal Democracy* (Rinehart, 1950).

——, and J. W. Chapman, *Political and Legal Obligations*, Nomos XII (Atherton, 1970).

Pfeffer, L., *The Liberties of an American: The Supreme Court Speaks* (Beacon, 1956, 1963).

Rogge, O. J., *The First and the Fifth* (Nelson, 1959).

Russell, B., *Authority and the Individual* (Simon & Schuster, 1949).

Smith, B., *The Democratic Spirit* (Knopf, 1941).

Spenser, H., *Man Versus the State* (Appleton, 1884).

Spinrad, W., *Civil Liberties* (Quadrangle, 1970).

Spitz, D., *Essays on the Liberal Idea of Freedom* (U. of Arizona, 1964).

Stouffer, S. A., *Communism, Conformity and Civil Liberties: A Cross-Section of the Nation Speaks Its Mind* (Doubleday, 1955).

Tawney, R. H., *Equality* (Barnes and Noble, 1965).

Thomas, N., *Great Dissenters* (Norton, 1954).

Thoreau, H. D., *On the Duty of Civil Disobedience* (Yale, 1849).

Trueblood, D. E., *Declaration of Freedom* (Harper & Bros., 1955).

Truman, H. S., *Freedom and Equality* (U. of Missouri, 1960).

Tussman, J., *Obligation and the Body Politic* (Oxford, 1960).
United Nations, *Yearbook on Human Rights* (annual).
Walker, P. G., *Restatement of Liberty* (Hutchinson, 1951).
Whipple, L., *Our Ancient Liberties* (H. W. Wilson, 1927).
Wild, J., *Human Freedom and Social Order* (Duke, 1961).
Woetzel, R. K., *The Philosophy of Freedom* (Oceana, 1966).
Woodhouse, A. S. P., *Puritanism and Liberty*, 2nd ed. (U. of Chicago, 1951).

C. THE ROLE OF THE SUPREME COURT. (SEE ALSO: II. D., "LINE DRAWING.")

Abraham, H. J., *Freedom and the Court: Civil Rights and Liberties in the United States*, 2nd ed. (Oxford, 1972).
———, *The Judiciary: The Supreme Court in the Governmental Process*, 3rd ed. (Allyn & Bacon, 1973).
Acheson, P. C., *The Supreme Court: America's Judicial Heritage* (Dodd, Mead, 1961).
Asch, S. H., *Civil Rights and Responsibilities Under the Constitution* (Arco, 1969).
Becker, C. L., *et al.*, *Safeguarding Civil Liberty Today* (Cornell, 1945).
Bickel, A. M., *Politics and the Warren Court* (Harper & Row, 1965).
Cahn, E., *Can the Supreme Court Defend Civil Liberties?* (Sidney Hillman Found., 1956).
Carr, R. K., *Federal Protection of Civil Rights: Quest for a Sword* (Cornell, 1945).
Casper, J. D., *Lawyers Before the Warren Court: Civil Liberties and Civil Rights* (U. of Illinois, 1956).
Cox, A. M., D. Howe, and J. R. Wiggins, *Civil Rights, the Constitution, and the Courts* (Harvard, 1967).
Cushman, R. E. (ed.), *Safeguarding Civil Liberty Today* (Cornell, 1945).
Fraenkel, O. K., *The Supreme Court and Civil Liberties*, 2nd ed. (Oceana, 1962) (Suppl. 1966).
Freedmen, M., W. M. Beaney, and E. V. Rostow, *Perspectives on the Court* (Northwestern, 1967).
Goldberg, A. J., *The Warren Era of the Supreme Court* (Northwestern, 1971).
Gordon, R., *Nine Men Against America: The Supreme Court and Its Attack on American Liberties* (Devin-Adair, 1958).
Johnson, D., *The Challenge to American Freedom* (U. of Kentucky, 1963).
Konvitz, M. R., *Expanding Liberties: The Emergence of New Civil Liberties and Rights in Postwar America* (Viking, 1967).
Laponce, J. A., *The Protection of Minorities* (U.C.L.A., 1960).
Lee, F. F., *Negro and White in Connecticut Town* (Bookman, 1961).
McCloskey, R. G. (ed.), *The American Supreme Court* (U. of Chicago, 1960).
Mason, A. T., and W. M. Beaney, *The Supreme Court in Free Society* (Prentice-Hall, 1959).
Mitau, G. T., *Decade of Decicions, 1954–1964* (Scribner's, 1968).
Pritchett, C. H., *Congress Versus the Supreme Court, 1957–1960* (U. of Minnesota, 1961).
———, *The Political Offender and the Warren Court* (Boston U., 1958).
Roche, J. P., *Courts and Rights* (Random House, 1961).
Shapiro, H. H., *Federal Enforcement of the Criminal Civil Rights Statutes* (Rutgers, 1960).

Spicer, G. W., *The Supreme Court and Fundamental Freedom*, 2nd ed. (Appleton, Century, 1967).
Tussman, J., *The Supreme Court on Racial Discrimination* (Oxford, 1963).
Ziegler, B. M., *Desegregation and the Supreme Court* (Heath, 1958).

D. "LINE DRAWING." (SEE ALSO: ii. C., THE ROLE OF THE SUPREME COURT.)

Abraham, H. J., *Freedom and the Court: Civil Rights and Liberties in the United States*, 2nd ed. (Oxford, 1972).
Buckley, W. F., Jr., *God and Man at Yale* (Regnery, 1951).
Commager, H. S., *Majority Rule and Minority Rights* (U. of Virginia, 1943).
————— (ed.), *Freedom and Order: A Commentary on the American Political Scene* (Braziller, 1966).
Cook, T. I., *Democratic Rights Versus Communist Activity* (Doubleday, 1954).
Dorsen, N. (ed.), *The Rights of Americans* (Pantheon, 1970).
Hand, L., *The Bill of Rights* (Harvard, 1958).
Hofstadter, R., and M. Wallace, *American Violence: A Documentary History* (Knopf, 1970).
Hook, S., *Heresy, Yes—Conspiracy, No!* (Day, 1953).
—————, *The Paradoxes of Freedom* (Berkeley, 1962).
Kariel, H., *The Decline of American Pluralism* (Stanford, 1961).
Kerner Commission, *Report of the National Advisory Commission on Civil Disorder* (Bantam, 1968).
King, D. B., and C. W. Quick (eds.), *Legal Aspects of the Civil Rights Movement* (Wayne State, 1964).
Masotti, L. H., and D. R. Bowen, *Riots and Rebellion* (Sage, 1968).
Mendelson, W., *Justices Black and Frankfurter: Conflict in the Court*, 2nd ed. (U. of Chicago, 1967).
Murphy, P. L., *The Constitution in Crisis Times, 1918–1969* (Harper & Row, 1972).
Robb, H. E., and R. Sobel, *From Left to Right: Readings on the Sociopolitical Spectrum* (Benziger, 1968).
Sheldon, C. H., *The Supreme Court: Politicians in Robes* (Glencoe Press, 1970).
Skolnick, J. H. (ed.), *The Politics of Protest* (Simon & Schuster, 1969).
Sloan, I. H., *Youth and the Law: Rights, Privileges and Obligations* (Oceana, 1970).
Sowle, C. R. (ed.), *Police, Power and Individual Freedom: The Quest for Balance* (Aldine, 1962).
Street, H., *Freedom, the Individual and the Law* (Penguin, 1964).
Sutherland, J. N., and M. G. Werthiman, *Comparative Concepts in Law and Order* (Scott, Foresman, 1971).
Veysey, L. (ed.), *Law and Resistance: American Attitudes Toward Authority* (Harper Torchbooks, 1970).
Walker Commission, *Rights in Conflict: The Walker Report on Violence in Chicago* (Bantam, 1969).
Witherspoon, J. P., *Administrative Implementation of Civil Rights* (U. of Texas, 1969).

E. STATES' RIGHTS. (SEE ALSO: III. D., THE SOUTH AND ITS VIEWPOINT.)

Bloch, C. J., *States' Rights: The Law of the Land* (Harrison, 1958).
Brady, T. P., *Black Monday* (Miss. Assoc. of Citizens Councils, 1955).

Eastland, J. C., *The Supreme Court's Modern Scientific Authorities in the Segregation Cases* (1957).

Kilpatrick, J. J., *The Sovereign States: Notes of a Citizen of Virginia* (Regnery, 1957).

Marshall, B., *Federalism and Civil Rights* (Columbia, 1964).

Pittman, R. C., *The Supreme Court, the Broken Constitution, and the Shattered Bill of Rights* (Dalton, Ga., 1956).

Putnam, C., *Race and Reason* (Public Affairs Press, 1961).

Virginia State Committee for Courts of Justice, *The Doctrine of Interposition: Its History and Application* (1957).

Williams, J. B., *Interposition: The Barrier Against Tyranny* (1956).

F. THE ECONOMIC SPHERE.

Baldwin, R. N., *Civil Liberties and Industrial Conflict* (Harvard, 1938).

Becker, C. L., *Freedom and Responsibility in the American Way of Life* (Knopf, 1945).

Berle, A. A., Jr., *Economic Power and the Free Society* (Fund for the Republic, 1957).

Cousins, F. R., *Public Civil Rights Agencies and Fair Employment* (Praeger, 1969).

Gellhorn, W., *Individual Freedom and Governmental Restraints* (Louisiana State U., 1956).

Gregory, C. O., *Labor and Law* (Norton, 1958).

Hale, R. L., *Freedom Through Law* (Columbia, 1952).

Hayek, F. V., *The Constitution of Liberty* (U. of Chicago, 1960).

Lieberman, E., *Unions Before the Bar* (Harper & Bros., 1950).

Lien, A. J., *Concurring Opinion: The Privileges or Immunities Clause of the Fourteenth Amendment* (Washington U., 1957).

Lockard, D., *Toward Equal Opportunity: A Study of State and Local Anti-Discrimination Laws* (Macmillan, 1960).

Mason, A. T., *Security Through Freedom: American Political Thought and Practice* (Cornell, 1955).

Mason, L., *The Language of Dissent* (World, 1959).

Millis, H. A., and E. C. Brown, *From the Wagner Act to Taft-Hartley* (U. of Chicago, 1950).

Morison, S. E., *Freedom in Contemporary Society* (Little, Brown, 1956).

Parker, R., *A Guide to Labor Law* (Praeger, 1961).

Polsky, S. (ed.), *The Medico-Legal Reader* (Oceana, 1956).

Rostow, E. V., *Planning for Freedom* (Yale, 1963).

Rottschaefer, H., *The Supreme Court and Socio-Economic Change* (U. of Michigan, 1948).

Schnapper, M. B., *Constraint by Copyright* (Public Affairs Press, 1962).

Tawney, R. H., *Equality*, 5th ed. (Putnam's, 1961).

Thomas, N. C., *Politics, Administration and Civil Rights* (U. of Michigan, 1966).

III. PHILOSOPHIES OF PREJUDICE: MINORITY GROUPS
AND RACE RELATIONS
(SEE ALSO: VI. SEGREGATION/DESEGREGATION)

A. GENERAL.

Allport, G. W., *The Nature of Prejudice* (Doubleday, 1960).

———, *Personality and Social Encounter: Selected Essays* (Beacon Press, 1960).

Barron, M. L., (ed.), *Minorities in a Changing World* (Knopf, 1967).

Baruch, D. W., *Glass House of Prejudice* (William Morrow, 1946).

Barzun, J., *Race: A Study in Modern Superstition* (Harcourt, Brace, 1937).

Bellush, J., and S. David, *Race and Politics in New York City: Six Studies in Policy-Making* (Praeger, 1971).

Benedict, R., *Race: Science & Politics* (Viking, 1947).

Berger, M., *Equality by Statute: Legal Controls Over Group Discrimination* (Columbia, 1954).

Berson, L. E., *The Negro and the Jews* (Random House, 1971).

Bibby, C., *Race, Prejudice and Education* (Praeger, 1961).

Brink, W., and L. Harris, *Black and White: A Study of United States Racial Attitudes Today* (Simon & Schuster, 1967).

Burlingame, R., *The Sixth Column* (Lippincott, 1962).

Clark, K. B., *Prejudice and Your Child* (Beacon Press, 1955).

Cox, O. C., *Caste, Class and Race: A Study in Social Dynamics* (Doubleday, 1948).

Davis, A., B. B. Gardner, and M. R. Gardner, *Deep South: A Social Anthropological Study of Caste and Class* (U. of Chicago, 1954).

Dexter, H. H., *What's Right With Race Relations* (Harper & Bros., 1959).

Dollard, J., *Caste and Class in a Southern Town*, 3rd ed. (Doubleday, 1957).

Dykeman, W., and J. Stokely, *Neither Black nor White* (Rinehart, 1957).

——, *Seeds of Southern Change: The Life of Will Alexander* (U. of Chicago, 1962).

Fineberg, S. A., *Punishment Without Crime: What You Can Do About Prejudice* (Doubleday, 1949).

Gittler, J. P., *Understanding Minority Groups* (Wiley, 1956).

Glazer, N., and D. P. Monihan, *Beyond the Melting Pot* (M.I.T., 1965).

Glock, C. Y., and E. Siegelman (eds.), *Prejudice U.S.A.* (Praeger, 1969).

Goodman, M. E., *Race Awareness in Young Children* (Addison-Wesley, 1952).

Gordon, M. M., *Assimilation in American Life: The Role of Race, Religion, and National Origins* (Oxford, 1964).

Greenberg, J., *Race Relations and American Law* (Columbia, 1959).

Grimes, A. P., *Equality in America: Religion, Race and the Urban Majority* (Oxford, 1964).

Handlin, O., *Race and Nationality in American Life* (Little, Brown, 1957).

——, *The Uprooted* (Little, Brown, 1951).

Hansen, M. L., *The Immigrant in American History* (Harvard, 1940).

Herzog, S. J. (ed.), *Minority Group Politics: A Reader* (Holt, Rinehart & Winston, 1971.).

Hirsh, S. G., *The Fears Men Live By* (Harper & Bros., 1955).

Jahoda, M., *Race Relations and Mental Health* (Columbia, 1960).

Katz, S. (ed.), *Negro and Jew: An Encounter in America* (Macmillan, 1967).

Laponee, J. A., *The Protection of Minorities* (U.C.L.A., 1960).

Lee, F. F., *Negro and White in Connecticut Town* (Bookman, 1961).

Lubell, S., *White and Black: Test of a Nation* (Harper & Row, 1964).

Marcus, L., *The Treatment of Minorities in Secondary School Textbooks* (Anti-Defamation League, 1961).

Mason, P., *Common Sense About Race* (Macmillan, 1961).

Masuoka, J., and P. Valien, *Race Relations: Problem and Theory* (U. of North Carolina, 1961).

Myers, G. A., *History of Bigotry in the United States* (Random House, 1943).
Newman, E. S. (ed.), *The Hate Reader* (Oceana, 1964).
Raab, E., *American Race Relations Today* (Anchor, 1962).
———, and S. Lipset, *Prejudice and Society* (A.D.L., 1967).
Rose, A. M., *Race Prejudice & Discrimination: Readings in Inter-Group Relations in the United States* (Knopf, 1951).
Rose, P. I., *They and We: Racial and Ethnic Relations in the U.S.* (Random House, 1964).
Roy, R. L., *Apostles of Discord* (Beacon, 1953).
Saenger, G., *The Social Psychology of Prejudice* (Harper, 1953).
Simpson, G. E., and J. M. Yinger, *Racial and Cultural Minorities* (Harper & Bros., 1958).
Snyder, L. L., *The Idea of Racialism: Its Meaning and History* (Van Nostrand, 1962).
Steinfield, M., *Cracks in the Melting Pot: Readings in Racism and Discrimination in American History* (Glencoe, 1970).
Thompson, E. T., and E. C. Hughes, *Race: Individual and Collective Behavior* (Free Press, 1958).
———, *Race Relations and the Race Problem* (Duke, 1939).
Trager, H. G., and M. R. Yarrow, *They Learn What They Live: Prejudice in Young Children* (Harper & Bros., 1952).
Tumin, M. M. (ed.), *Race and Intelligence* (A.D.L., 1963).
UNESCO, *Race and Science: The Race Question in Modern Science* (Columbia, 1961).
———, *The Race Question in Modern Science* (Morrow, 1956).
U.S. Commission on Civil Rights, *Justice* (U.S. G.P.O., 1961).
Vanderbilt University School of Law, *The Race Relations Law Reporter* (1956 ff.).
Vander Zanden, J. W., *American Minority Relations: The Sociology of Peace and Ethnic Groups*, 2nd ed. (Ronald, 1966).
Westin, A. F. (ed.), *Freedom Now: The Civil Rights Struggle in America* (Basic Books, 1964).
Wood, F. G., *Black Scare: The Racist Response to Emancipation and Reconstruction* (Berkeley, 1970).
Young, W. M., Jr., *To Be Equal* (McGraw-Hill, 1964).
Zubaida, S. (ed.), *Race and Racialism* (Barnes & Noble, 1970).

B. THE BLACKS. (SEE ALSO: VI. SEGREGATION/DESEGREGATION.)

Aptheker, H., *Soul of the Republic: The Negro Today* (Marzani & Munsell, 1964).
Barbour, F. B. (ed.), *The Black Power Revolt* (Porter, Sargent, 1968).
——— (ed.), *The Black Seventies* (Horizon, 1971).
Bardolph, R. (ed.), *The Civil Rights Record: Black Americans and the Law, 1849–1970* (Cornell, 1970).
———, *The Negro Vanguard* (Rinehart & Co., 1961).
Barker, L. B., *The Black in the American Political System* (Winthrop, 1974).
Bittker, B. I., *The Case for Black Freedom* (Random House, 1972).
Bontemps, A., *100 Years of Negro Freedom* (Dodd, Mead, 1961).
Booker, S., *Black Man's America* (Prentice-Hall, 1964).
Brink, W., and L. Harris, *The Negro Revolution in America* (Simon & Schuster, 1964).
Brown, I. C., *The Story of the American Negro* (Friendship Press, 1957).

467

Burkey, R. M., *Racial Discrimination and Public Policy in the United States* (Heath, 1971).

Burns, W. H., *The Voices of Negro Protest in America* (Oxford, 1963).

Conrad, E., *Jim Crow America* (Duell, Sloan and Pearce, 1947).

Davie, M. R., *Negroes in American History* (McGraw-Hill, 1949).

Davis, J., *Character Assassination* (Philosophical Library, 1951).

Draper, R., *The Rediscovery of Black Nationalism* (Viking, 1970).

Du Bois, W. E. B., *The Philadelphia Negro* (Blom, 1967).

Essien-Udom, E. U., *Black Nationalism: A Search for Identity in America* (U. of Chicago, 1962).

Farmer, J., *Freedom—When?* (Random House, 1966).

Fischel, L. H., Jr., and B. Quarles, *The Negro American: A Documentary History* (Morrow, 1968).

Franklin, J. H., *From Slavery to Freedom: A History of American Negroes* (Knopf, 1967).

———, and I. Harr (eds.), *The Negro in the Twentieth Century: A Reader* (Vintage, 1967).

Frazier, E. F., *Black Bourgeoisie* (Free Press, 1957).

Ginzberg, E., and A. S. Eichner, *The Troublesome Presence: American Democracy and the Negro* (Free Press, 1964).

Glenn, N. D., and C. M. Bonjean (eds.), *Blacks in the United States: An Anthology* (Chandler, 1969).

Goldwin, R. A., *100 Years of Emancipation* (Rand McNally, 1964).

Graham, H. D., *Violence: The Crisis of American Confidence* (Johns Hopkins, 1971).

Greenberg, E. S., N. Milner, and D. M. Olson, *Black Politics: The Inevitability of Conflict* (Holt, Rinehart & Winston, 1970).

Greger, R., and E. McDonald, *A Look Down the Lonesome Road* (Doubleday, 1964).

Grier, W. H., and T. M. Cobbs, *Black Rage* (Basic Books, 1968).

Griffin, J. H., *Black Like Me* (Houghton Mifflin, 1960).

Hamilton, C. V., *The Politics of Civil Rights* (Random House, 1968).

Handlin, O., *The Dimensions of Liberties* (Harvard, 1958).

Hansberry, L., *The Movement: Documentary of a Struggle for Equality* (Simon & Schuster, 1965).

Harvey, J. C., *Black Civil Rights During the Johnson Administration* (Jackson State U., 1973).

———, *Civil Rights During the Kennedy Administration* (Jackson State U., 1971).

Hentoff, N., *The New Equality* (Viking, 1964).

Herskovits, M. J., *The American Negro* (Indiana U., 1968).

Isaacs, H. R., *The New World of Negro Americans* (Day, 1963).

Jacob, P., *Prelude to Riot: A View of Urban America from the Bottom* (Random House, 1968).

Javits, J. K., *Discrimination—U.S.A.* (Harcourt, Brace, 1960).

Kalven, H., Jr., *The Negro and the First Amendment* (Ohio State U., 1965).

Kardiner, A., and L. Ovesey, *The Mark of Oppression* (Meridian, 1962).

Katz, W. L. (ed.), *Eyewitness: The Negro in American History* (Pitman, 1968).

Kephart, W. M., *Racial Factors and Urban Law Enforcement* (U. of Pennsylvania, 1958).

Killian, L., and C. Grigg, *Racial Crisis in America: Leadership in Conflict* (Prentice-Hall, 1964).

King, L. L., *Confessions of a White Racist* (Viking, 1971).

Ladd, E., *Negro Political Leadership in the South* (Cornell, 1966).

Lane, A. J., *The Brownsville Affair: National Crisis and Black Reaction* (Kennikat, 1972).

Lincoln, E. R., *The Black Muslims in America* (Beacon, 1961).

Litwack, L. F., *North of Slavery: The Negro in the Free States, 1790–1860* (U. of Chicago, 1961).

Logan, R. W., *The Negro in the United States* (Van Nostrand, 1957).

Lomax, L. E., *The Negro Revolt* (Harper & Row, 1962).

McKissick, F., *Three Fifths of a Man* (Macmillan, 1969).

Mangum, C. S., *The Legal Status of the Negro* (U. of North Carolina, 1940).

Mannix, D. P., and M. Cowley, *Black Cargoes: A History of the Atlantic Slave Trade, 1581–1865* (Viking, 1962).

Marx, G. T., *Protest and Prejudice: A Study of Belief in the Black Community*, rev. ed. (Harper & Row, 1970).

Matthews, D. R., and J. W. Prothro, *Negroes and the New Southern Politics* (Harcourt, Brace & World, 1966).

Mitchell, G. E., and W. H. Peace III, *The Angry Black South: Southern Negroes Tell Their Own Story* (Citadel, 1962).

Morcland, L. B., *White Racism and the Law* (Merrill, 1970).

Morris, M. D., *The Politics of Black America: An Annotated Bibliography* (Public Affairs Press, 1971).

Myrdahl, G., *An American Dilemma: The Negro Problem and Modern Democracy* (Harper & Bros., 1962).

Newby, I. A., *Challenge to the Court* (Louisiana State U., 1967).

Nolan, V. A., *Communism Versus the Negro* (Regnery, 1951).

Nordhalt, J. W., *The People that Walk in Darkness: A History of the Negro People in America* (Ballantine, 1960).

Panetta, L. E., and P. Gall, *Bring Us Together: The Nixon Team and the Civil Rights Retreat* (Lippincott, 1971).

Parsons, T., and K. B. Clark (eds.), *The Negro American* (Beacon, 1967).

President's National Advisory Commission on Civil Disorders, *Report* (Bantam, 1968).

Putnam, C., *Race and Reality* (Public Affairs Press, 1961).

Redding, J. S., *On Being Negro in America* (Bobbs-Merrill, 1951).

Rose, A., *The Negro in America* (Beacon, 1956).

Rowan, C., *Go South to Sorrow* (Random House, 1957).

————, *South of Freedom* (Knopf, 1952).

Shade, W. G., and R. C. Herrenkohl, *Seven on Black: Reflections on the Negro Experience in America* (Lippincott, 1969).

Sickels, R. J., *Race, Marriage and the Law* (U. of New Mexico, 1972).

Silberman, C. E., *Crisis in Black and White* (Random House, 1965).

Sloan, I. J., *The American Negro: A Chronology and Fact Book* (Oceana, 1965).

Storing, H. J. (ed.), *What Country Have I? Political Writings by Black Americans* (St. Martin's, 1970).

Warren, R. P., *Who Speaks for the Negro?* (Random House, 1965).

Welsch, E. K., *The Negro in the United States: A Research Guide* (Indiana U., 1965).
Weyl, N., *The Negro in American Civilization* (Public Affairs Press, 1960).
Yinger, J. M., *A Minority Group in American Society* (McGraw-Hill, 1965).

C. OTHER MINORITY GROUPS: JAPANESE, AMERICAN INDIANS, JEWS.

Belth, N. C. (ed.), *Barriers: Patterns of Discrimination Against Jews* (Friendly House, 1958).
Bloom, L., and R. Riemer, *Removal and Return* (U. of California, 1949).
Bosworth, A. R., *America's Concentration Camps* (Norton, 1967).
Burnette, R., *The Tortured American* (Prentice-Hall, 1971).
Daniels, R., *Concentration Camps, USA: Japanese Americans and World War II* (Holt, Rinehart & Winston, 1971).
———, *The Politics of Prejudice: The Anti-Japanese Movement in California and the Struggle for Exclusion* (Berkeley, 1962).
Davis, E., *But We Were Born Free* (Bobbs-Merrill, 1954).
Deloria, V., Jr., *Custer Died for Your Sins: An Indian Manifesto* (Macmillan, 1969).
Epstein, B. R., and A. Forster, *"Some of My Best Friends . . ."* (Farrar, Strauss, 1962).
Forster, A., and B. R. Epstein, *Cross-Currents* (Doubleday, 1957).
———, *The New Anti-Semitism* (McGraw Hill, 1974).
———, *The Trouble-Makers* (Doubleday, 1952).
Girdner, A., and A. Loftis, *The Great Betrayal* (Macmillan, 1969).
Glock, C. Y., G. J. Selznick, and J. L. Spaeth, *The Apathetic Majority: A Study Based on Public Responses to the Eichmann Trial* (A.D.L., 1968).
———, and R. Stark, *Christian Beliefs and Anti-Semitism* (A.D.L., 1966).
Grodzins, M., *Americans Betrayed: Politics and the Japanese Evacuations* (U. of Chicago, 1949).
Handlin, O., *The Dimensions of Liberties* (Harvard, 1961).
Herzog, S. J. (ed.), *Minority Group Politics* (Holt, Rinehart & Winston, 1971).
Higham, J., *Strangers in the Land: Patterns of American Nativism, 1869–1929* (Rutgers, 1955).
Howard, J. R. (ed.), *The Awakening Minorities: American Indians, Mexican-Americans and Puerto Ricans* (Aldine, 1970).
Javits, J. K., *Discrimination—U.S.A.* (Harcourt, Brace, 1960).
Josephy, A. M., *Red Power: The American Indians' Fight for Freedom* (McGraw-Hill, 1971).
Kanowitz, L., *Women and the Law* (U. of New Mexico, 1969).
Konvitz, M. R., *The Aliens and Asiatics in American Law* (Cornell, 1946).
Kramer, J. R., and S. Leventman, *Children of the Gilded Ghetto* (Yale, 1961).
Leathers, N. L., *The Japanese in America* (Lerner, 1967).
Leighton, A. H., *The Governing Men* (Princeton, 1945, 1964).
McWilliams, C., *A Mask for Privilege* (Little, Brown, 1948).
———, *North from Mexico* (Lippincott, 1949).
———, *Prejudice—Japanese-American—Symbols of Racial Intolerance* (Little, Brown, 1944).
Mack, R. W., and T. S. Duster, *Patterns of Minority Relations* (A.D.L., 1965).
Mears, E. G., *Resident Orientals of the American Pacific Coast* (U. of Chicago, 1928).

Parkes, J., *Anti-Semitism* (Quadrangle, 1969).

Reel, A. F., *The Case of General Yamashita* (U. of Chicago, 1949).

Rosenstock, M., *Louis Marshall: Defender of Jewish Rights* (Wayne State, 1966).

Samora, J. (ed.), *La Raza: Forgotten Americans* (Notre Dame, 1966).

Seldes, G., "*We Hold These Truths . . .*" (League of Amer. Writers, 1939).

Selznick, G. J., and S. Steinberg, *The Tenacity of Prejudice: Anti-Semitism in Contemporary America* (A.D.L., 1969).

Sindler, A. P., *Change in the Contemporary South* (Duke, 1964).

Smith, B., *Americans from Japan* (Lippincott, 1948).

Ten Broek, J., E. N. Barnhart, and F. W. Matson, *Prejudice, War and the Constitution: Causes and Consequences of the Japanese-Americans in World War II*, rev. ed. (Berkeley, 1968).

Thomas, D. S., *The Salvage* (U. of California, 1952).

———, and R. S. Nishimito, *The Spoilage* (Berkeley, 1946).

Tumin, M. M., *An Inventory and Appraisal of Research on American Anti-Semitism* (A.D.L., 1961).

Van Every, D., *Disinherited: The Lost Birthright of the American Indian* (Morrow, 1966).

Weintraub, R. G., *How Secure These Rights?* (Doubleday, 1949).

Yinger, J. M., *Anti-Semitism: A Case Study in Prejudice and Discrimination* (A.D.L., 1964).

D. THE SOUTH AND ITS VIEWPOINT. (See also: II. E., States' Rights.)

Bartley, N., *The Rise of Massive Resistance* (Louisiana State U., 1969).

Carter, H., *The South Strikes Back* (Doubleday, 1959).

———, *Southern Legacy* (Louisiana State U., 1950).

Cash, W. J., *The Mind of the South* (Knopf, 1956).

Chaze, E., *Tiger in the Honeysuckle* (Scribner's, 1965).

Clark, T. D., *The Emerging South* (Oxford, 1961).

Cousins, R. E., et al., *South Carolinians Speak: A Moderate Approach to Race Relations* (U. of North Carolina, 1957).

Dabbs, J. H., *The Southern Heritage* (Knopf, 1958).

Eaton, C., *The Mind of the Old South* (Louisiana State U., 1964).

Gates, R. L., *The Making of Massive Resistance* (U. of North Carolina, 1965).

Graham, H. D., *Crisis in Print: Desegregation and the Press in Tennessee* (Vanderbilt U., 1967).

Grantham, D. W., Jr., *Hoke Smith and the Politics of the New South* (Louisiana State U., 1967).

Hays, B. A., *A Southern Moderate Speaks* (U. of North Carolina, 1959).

Highsaw, R. B. (ed.), *The Deep South in Transformation* (U. of Alabama, 1964).

Leiserson, A. (ed.), *The American South in the 1960's* (Praeger, 1965).

McGill, R., *The South and the Southerner* (Little, Brown, 1963).

McKean, K. F., *Cross Currents in the South* (Swallow, 1963).

Morris, W., *The South Today: 100 Years After Appomattox* (Harper, 1965).

Newby, I. A., *Challenge to the Court: Social Scientists and the Defense of Segregation, 1954–1966* (Louisiana State U., 1969).

———, *Jim Crow's Defenses! Anti-Negro Thought in America, 1900–1930* (Louisiana State U., 1965).

Nicholls, W. A., *Southern Tradition and Regional Progress* (U. of North Carolina, 1960).

Norris, H. (ed.), *We Dissent* (St. Martin's, 1962).

Rubin, L. D., and J. J. Kilpatrick, *The Lasting South* (Regnery, 1957).

Savage, H., Jr., *The Seeds of Time: The Background of Southern Thinking* (Holt, 1959).

Silver, J. W., *Mississippi: The Closed Society*, enl. ed. (Harcourt, Brace & World, 1966).

Simkins, F. R., *Pitchfork Ben Tillman* (Louisiana State U., 1967).

Sindler, A. P. (ed.), *Change in the Contemporary South* (Duke, 1964).

Thorp, W., *A Southern Reader* (Knopf, 1955).

Tisdale, J. W., *A Southerner's Reflection about the 1954 Supreme Court Decision Concerning Racial Segregation in the Public Schools* (Jarrett's Press, 1956).

Warren, R. P., *Who Speaks for the Negro?* (Random House, 1965).

Watters, P., *The South and the Nation* (Pantheon, 1970).

Wirt, F. M., *Politics of Southern Equality: Law and Social Change in a Mississippi County* (Aldine, 1970).

Wood, F. G., *Black Scare: The Racist Response to Emancipation and Reconstruction* (U. of California, 1968).

Workman, W. D., Jr., *The Case for the South* (Devin-Adair, 1960).

Zinn, H., *The Southern Mystique*, 2nd ed. (Simon & Schuster, 1972).

IV. CRIMINAL LAW AND PROCEDURE

A. DUE PROCESS AND CRIMINAL JUSTICE GENERALLY. (See also: Specific aspects below.)

Alexander, F., *The Criminal, the Judge, and the Public* (Free Press, 1961).

Barth, A., *The Price of Liberty* (Viking, 1962).

Beck, C., *Law and Justice: Essays in Honor of Robert S. Rankin* (Duke, 1970).

Belli, M., *The Law Revolution* (Sherbourne, 1969).

Bent, A. E., *The Politics of Law Enforcement* (Lexington, 1974).

Blumberg, A. S. (ed.), *The Scales of Justice*, 2nd ed. (Dutton, 1974).

Casper, J. D., *American Criminal Justice* (Prentice-Hall, 1972).

Chambliss, W. J., *Crime and the Legal Process* (McGraw-Hill, 1969).

Chute, C. L., and M. Bell, *Crime, Courts and Probation* (Macmillan, 1956).

Cole, G. (ed.), *Criminal Justice: Law and Politics* (Duxbury, 1972).

Columbia Law Review, *Criminal Law and Its Administration* (Da Capo, 1971).

Cray, E., *The Big Blue Line* (Coward-McCann, 1967).

Dienstein, W., *Are You Guilty?* (Thomas, 1954).

Donigan, R. L., *Chemical Tests and the Law* (Traffic Institute, 1966).

Downie, L., Jr., *Justice Denied* (Penguin, 1972).

Eldridge, W. B., *Narcotics and the Law* (N.Y.U., 1962).

Fellman, D., *The Defendant's Right* (Rinehart, 1958).

Felsher, H., and M. Rosen, *The Press in the Jury Box* (Macmillan, 1966).

Francis, P., *Protection Through the Law* (Oceana, 1965).

Frankel, S., *Beyond a Reasonable Doubt* (Stein & Day, 1971).

George, B. J., Jr., *Constitutional Limitations on Evidence in Criminal Cases* (U. of Michigan, 1966).

Gillers, S., *Getting Justice: The Rights of the People* (Basic Books, 1971).

Goldfarb, R. L., *The Contempt Power* (Columbia, 1963).

Grant, J. A., *Our Common Law Constitution* (Boston U., 1960).

Griswold, E. N., *The Fifth Amendment Today* (Harvard, 1955).

Harding, A. L. (ed.), *Fundamental Law in Criminal Prosecutions* (S.M.U., 1959).

Harris, W. R., *Tyranny on Trial: The Evidence at Nuremberg* (S.M.U., 1954).

Jacob, H. (ed.), *The Potential for Reform of Criminal Justice* (Sage, 1974).

———, *Urban Justice: Law and Order in American Cities* (Prentice-Hall, 1973).

Kamisar, Y., F. E. Inbau, and T. Arnold, *Criminal Justice in Our Time* (U. of Virginia, 1965).

Kaplan, J., *Criminal Justice: Introductory Cases and Materials* (Foundation Press, 1973).

Karlen, D., *Anglo-American Criminal Justice* (Oxford, 1968).

Kirchheimer, O., *Political Justice: The Use of Legal Procedure for Political Ends* (Princeton, 1961).

Levin, A. L., *Evidence and the Behavioral Sciences* (U. of Pennsylvania, Institute of Legal Research, 1966).

Lieberman, J. K., *How the Government Breaks the Law* (Penguin, 1973).

Moreland, C. C., *Equal Justice Under Law* (Oceana, 1965).

Mott, R. L., *Due Process of Law* (Bobbs, 1926).

Nagel, S. S., *Rights of the Accused* (Sage, 1972).

Navasky, J. S., *Kennedy Justice* (Atheneum, 1971).

Neubauer, D. W., *Criminal Justice in Middle America* (General Learning Press, 1974).

Newman, D. J., *Conviction: The Determination of Guilt or Innocence Without Trial* (Little, Brown, 1967).

Newman, E. S., *Police, the Law and Personal Freedom* (Oceana, 1964).

Oaks, D. H., and W. Lehman, *Criminal Justice System and the Indigent* (U. of Chicago, 1953).

Orton, W. A., *The Liberal Tradition: Social and Spiritual Conditions of Freedom* (Oxford, 1945).

Paulsen, M. G., *Equal Justice for the Poor Man* (Public Affairs Pamphlets, 1965).

Peterson, V. W., *Barbarians in Our Midst* (Little, Brown, 1952).

Ploscowe, M., *The Truth About Divorce* (Hawthorne, 1955).

Pound, R., *Criminal Justice in America* (Holt, 1945).

Putkammer, E. W., *Administration of Criminal Law* (U. of Chicago, 1953).

Richette, L. A., *The Throwaway Children* (Lippincott, 1969).

Schaefer, W. V., *The Suspect and Society: Criminal Procedure and Converging Constitutional Doctrines* (Northwestern, 1967).

Seagle, W., *Acquitted of Murder* (Regnery, 1958).

Silverstein, L., *Defense of the Poor* (A.B.A., 1965).

Taylor, T., *Two Studies in Constitutional Interpretation* (Ohio State U., 1968).

Trebach, A. S., *The Rationing of Justice: Constitutional Rights and the Criminal Process* (Rutgers, 1964).

Young, R. B., *Criminal Law* (McGraw-Hill, 1972).

Zinn, H., *The Responsibilities of Civil Disobedience: Nine Fallacies on Law and Order* (Random House, 1968).

B. FAIR TRIAL.

Blackburn, S. (ed.), *White Justice: Black Experience Today in America's Courtrooms* (Harper & Row, 1971).

Busch, F. X., *Law and Tactics in Jury Trial* (Bobbs-Merrill, 1961).

Carter, D. T., *Scottsboro: A Tragedy of the American South* (Louisiana State U., 1969).

Forer, L. G., *"No One Will Lissen": How Our Legal System Brutalizes the Youthful Poor* (John Day, 1970).

Friendly, A., and R. L. Goldfarb, *Crime and Publicity: The Impact of News on the Administration of Justice* (20th Century Fund, 1967).

Heller, F. H., *The Sixth Amendment to the Constitution of the United States: A Study in Constitutional Development* (U. of Kansas, 1951).

Lassers, W. J., *Scapegoat Justice: Lloyd Miller and the Failure of the American Legal System* (Indiana U., 1974).

Morris, R. B., *Fair Trial: Fourteen Who Stood Accused, from Anne Hutchinson to Alger Hiss* (Knopf, 1952).

Newman, D. J., *Conviction: The Determination of Guilt or Innocence Without Trial* (Little, Brown, 1966).

Orfield, L. B., *Criminal Procedure from Arrest to Appeal* (N.Y.U., 1947).

Strouse, V., *Up Against the Law: The Legal Right of People Under Twenty-One* (Signet, 1970).

Sullivan, H. W., *Trial by Newspaper* (Patriot Press, 1961).

Wigmore, J. H., *A Treatise on the Anglo-American System of Evidence in Trials at Common Law*, 3rd ed. (Little, Brown, 1940).

Williams, E. B., *One Man's Freedom* (Atheneum, 1962).

C. SELF-INCRIMINATION.

Griswold, E. N., *The Fifth Amendment Today* (Harvard, 1955).

Hook, S., *Common Sense and the Fifth Amendment* (Criterion, 1959).

Inbau, F. E., *Self-Incrimination* (Thomas, 1950).

Levy, L. W., *Origins of the Fifth Amendment* (Oxford, 1968).

Maguire, J. N., *Evidence of Guilt: Restrictions upon Its Discovery or Compulsory Disclosure* (Little, Brown, 1959).

Mayers, L., *Shall We Amend the Fifth Amendment?* (Harper, 1959).

Rogge, O. J., *When Men Confess* (Nelson, 1959).

Schwartzman, R., and J. Stein, *The Law of Personal Liberties* (Oceana, 1955).

D. CONFESSIONS.

Beisel, A. R., *Control Over Illegal Enforcement of the Criminal Law: Role of the Supreme Court* (Boston U., 1955).

George, J. B. (ed.), *A New Look at Confessions: Escobedo—The Second Round* (U. of Michigan, 1966).

Graham, F. P., *The Self-Inflicted Wound* (Macmillan, 1970).

Inbau, F. E., and J. E. Inbau, *Criminal Interrogation and Confessions* (Williams & Wilkins, 1962).

———, *Lie Detection and Criminal Interrogation* (Williams & Wilkins, 1953).

Milner, N. A., *The Court and Local Law Enforcement: The Political Impact of Miranda* (Sage, 1971).

Reid, J. E., and F. E. Inbau, *Truth and Deception: The Polygraph ("Lie Detector") Technique* (Williams & Wilkins, 1966).

Reik, T., *The Compulsion to Confess* (Farrar, Straus & Cudahy, 1959).

Rogge, O. J., *Why Men Confess* (Nelson, 1959).

Sobel, N. R., *The New Confession Standards: "Miranda v. Arizona"* (Gould, 1966).
Stephens, O. H., Jr., *The Supreme Court and Confessions of Guilt* (U. of Tennessee, 1973).
Tompkins, D. C. (comp.), *The Confession Issue: From Nabb to Miranda: A Bibliography* (Berkeley, 1968).
United States Commission on Civil Rights, *Justice* (U.S. G.P.O., 1961).

E. SEARCHES AND SEIZURES.

Ashley, P. P., *Say It Safely* (U. of Washington, 1956).
Beisel, A. R., *Control Over Illegal Enforcement of the Criminal Law: Role of the Supreme Court* (Boston U., 1955).
Breckenridge, A. C., *The Rights to Privacy* (U. of Nebraska, 1971).
Cantey, R. C., *The Law of Search and Seizure* (U. of Georgia, 1957).
Cogan, J. J., *Law of Search and Seizure* (Oceana, 1950).
Donovan, J. B., *Strangers on a Bridge: The Case of Colonel Abel* (Atheneum, 1964).
Garrison, O. V., *Spy Government* (Lyle Stuart, 1967).
Landynski, J. W., *Search and Seizure and the Supreme Court* (Johns Hopkins, 1966).
Lasson, N. A., *The History and Development of the Fourth Amendment to the United States Constitution* (Da Capo, 1970).
Maguire, J. M., *Evidence of Guilt: Restrictions upon Its Discovery or Compulsory Disclosure* (Little, Brown, 1959).
Packard, V., *The Naked Society* (McKay, 1964).
Ringel, W. E., *Arrests, Searches, Confessions* (Gould, 1966).
———, *Lawyers Guide to Legal and Illegal Searches* (Gould, 1965).
Taylor, T., *Two Studies in Constitutional Interpretation: Search, Seizure, and Surveillance . . .* (Ohio State U., 1969).
Tiffany, L. P., D. M. McIntyre, Jr., and D. L. Rotenberg, *Detection of Crime: Stopping and Questioning, Search and Seizure, Encouragement and Entrapment* (Little, Brown, 1967).
Varon, J. A., *Searches, Seizures and Immunities* (Bobbs-Merrill, 1961).

F. WIRETAPPING, EAVESDROPPING AND PRIVACY.

Barth, A., *The Price of Liberty* (Viking, 1961).
Beisel, A. R., *Control Over Illegal Enforcement of the Criminal Law: Role of the Supreme Court* (Boston U., 1955).
Breckenridge, A. C., *The Right to Privacy* (U. of Nebraska, 1970).
Brenton, M., *The Privacy Invaders* (Coward-McCann, 1964).
Cowan, P., et al. (eds.), *State Secrets: Police Surveillance in America* (Viking, 1974).
Dash, S., R. Schwartz, and R. E. Knowlton, *The Eavesdroppers* (Rutgers, 1959).
Dienes, C. T., *Law, Politics, and Birth Control* (U. of Illinois, 1972).
Dorsen, N., and S. Gillers (eds.), *None of Your Business: Government Secrecy in America* (Viking, 1974).
Engberg, E., *The Spy in the Corporate Structure and the Right to Privacy* (World, 1967).
Ernst, M. L., and A. U. Schwartz, *Privacy: The Right To Be Let Alone* (Macmillan, 1962).

Fogarty, M. S., *Issues of Privacy and Security in the Urban Informational System* (Northwest Regional Educational Laboratory, 1969).

Goldberg, E. M., *Privacy Problems in Municipal Informational Systems* (Claremont, 1972).

Gross, H., *Privacy—Its Legal Protection* (Oceana, 1965).

Hofstadter, S. H., and G. Horowitz, *The Right to Privacy* (Central Books, 1964).

Long, E. V., *The Intruders: The Invasion of Privacy by Government and Industry* (Praeger, 1967).

Michigan Law Review, *The Right of Privacy* (Da Capo, 1971).

Miller, A. R., *The Assault on Privacy: Computers, Data Banks, and Dossiers* (U. of Michigan, 1971).

Murphy, W. F., *Wiretapping on Trial* (Random House, 1965).

Pennock, J. R., and J. W. Chapman (eds.), *Privacy* (Atherton, 1971).

Rosenberg, J. M., *The Death of Privacy* (Random House, 1969).

Rule, J. B., *Private Lives and Public Surveillance: Social Control in the Computer Age* (Schocken, 1974).

Westin, A. F. (ed.), *Information Technology in a Democracy* (Harvard, 1971).

———, *Privacy and Freedom* (Atheneum, 1967).

———, and M. A. Bakers, *Databanks in a Free Society* (Quadrangle, 1973).

Zelermeyer, W., *Invasion of Privacy* (Syracuse U., 1959).

G. COUNSEL.

Beaney, W. M., *The Right to Counsel in American Courts* (U. of Michigan, 1955).

Carter, D. T., *Scottsboro: A Tragedy of the American South* (Louisiana State U., 1969).

Graham, F. P., *The Self-Inflicted Wound* (Macmillan, 1970).

Heller, F. H., *The Sixth Amendment to the Constitution of the United States: A Study in Constitutional Development* (U. of Kansas, 1951).

Lewis, A., *Gideon's Trumpet* (Random House, 1964).

Medalie, R. J., *From Escobedo to Miranda: The Anatomy of a Supreme Court Decision* (Leore Law Book, Inc., 1966).

Milner, N. A., *The Court and Local Law Enforcement: The Political Impact of Miranda* (Sage, 1971).

Ulmer, S. S., *Military Justice and the Right to Counsel* (U. of Kentucky, 1970).

H. DOUBLE JEOPARDY.

Friedland, M. L., *Double Jeopardy* (Oxford, 1969).

Miller, L. G., *Double Jeopardy and the Federal System* (U. of Chicago, 1968).

Sigler, J. A., *Double Jeopardy: The Development of a Legal and Social Policy* (Cornell, 1969).

I. JURIES. (SEE ALSO: BIBLIOGRAPHY I, JURIES.)

Busch, F. X., *Law and Tactics in Jury Trials* (Bobbs-Merrill, 1961).

Heller, F. H., *The Sixth Amendment to the Constitution of the United States: A Study in Constitutional Development* (U. of Kansas, 1951).

Kalven, H., Jr., and H. Zeisel, *The American Jury* (Little, Brown, 1966; Phoenix Books, 1971).

Orfield, L. B., *Criminal Procedure from Arrest to Appeal* (N.Y.U., 1947).
Simon, R. J., *The Jury and the Defense of Insanity* (Little, Brown, 1968).
Zeisel, H., H. Kalven, Jr., and B. Buchholz, *Delay in the Courts* (Little, Brown, 1959).

J. BAIL.

Beeley, A. L., *The Bail System in Chicago* (U. of Chicago, 1927, 1966).
De Hass, E., *Antiquities of Bail: Origin and Historical Development in Criminal Cases to the Year 1275* (Columbia, 1940).
Foote, C., *Studies in Bail* (International Press, 1967).
Freed, D. J., and P. M. Wald, *Bail in the United States* (Dept. of Justice and Vera Foundation, 1964).
Goldfarb, R., *Ransom: A Critique of the American Bail System* (Harper & Row, 1965).
Thompkins, D. C. (ed.), *Bail in the United States: A Bibliography* (Berkeley, 1964).

K. CRUEL AND UNUSUAL PUNISHMENT.

Anslinger, H. J., and W. Oursler, *The Murderers* (Cudahy, 1961).
Barnes, H. E., *The Story of Punishment* (Stratford, 1930).
Beccaria, C., *On Crime and Punishment* (Indianapolis, 1963).
Chambliss, W. J., *The Deterrent Influence of Punishment* (Indiana U., 1972).
Eldridge, W. B., *Narcotics and the Law* (N.Y.U., 1962).
Hawkins, G., *Punishment and Deterrence* (Indiana U., 1972).
Honderich, T., *Punishment: The Supposed Justifications* (Pelican, 1972).
Meltsner, M., *Cruel and Unusual* (Random House, 1973).
Newfield, J., *Cruel and Unusual Justice* (Holt, Rinehart & Winston, 1974).
Prettyman, B. E., Jr., *Death and the Supreme Court* (Harcourt, Brace, 1961).

L. POLICE AGENCIES AND ENFORCEMENT.

Ahern, J. F., *Police in Trouble* (Hawthorne, 1972).
Asch, S. H., *Police Authority and the Rights of the Individual* (Arco, 1967).
Banton, M., *The Policeman in the Community* (Basic Books, 1965).
Bayley, D. H., and H. Mendelsohn, *Minorities and the Police: Confrontation in America* (Free Press, 1969).
Becker, T. L. (ed.), *Government Lawlessness in America* (Oxford, 1971).
Berkeley, G. E., *The Democratic Policeman* (Beacon, 1969).
Black, A., *The People and the Police* (McGraw-Hill, 1968).
Blumberg, A. S. (ed.), *The Scales of Justice*, 2nd ed. (Dutton, 1974).
Bordua, D. J., *The Police* (Wiley, 1967).
Chevigny, P., *Police Power: Police Abuses in New York City* (Pantheon, 1969).
Chicota, R. A., and M. C. Moran (eds.), *Riot in the Cities: An Analytical Symposium on the Causes and Effects* (Fairleigh, 1970).
Cole, G. F., *Politics and the Administration of Justice* (Sage, 1973).
Collins, F. L., *The F.B.I. in Peace and War*, rev. and enl. by L. Demles (Ace Books, 1962).
Cray, E., *The Big Blue Line: Police Power v. Human Rights* (Coward-McCann, 1967).
Deutsch, A., *The Trouble With Cops* (Crown, 1955).
Edwards, G., *The Police on the Urban Frontier* (Inst. of Human Rels. Press, 1968).

Eldiff, T. J. (ed.), *Crime, Dissent, and the Attorney General: The Justice Department in the 1960s* (Sage, 1971).

Gardiner, J. A., *Traffic and the Police: Variations in Law Enforcement Policy* (Harvard, 1969).

Hahn, H. (ed.), *Police in Urban Society* (Sage, 1971).

Harris, R., *Justice: The Crisis of Law, Order and Freedom in America* (Dutton, 1970).

Hopkins, E., *Our Lawless Police* (Viking, 1931).

Inbau, F. E., and J. R. Thompson (eds.), *The Supreme Court and the Police* (Sept. and Dec. issues of *The Journal of Criminal Law, Criminology and Social Sciences,* 1966).

Leonard, V. A. (ed.), *Academy Lectures on Lie Detection* (Thomas, 1950).

Lipsky, M. (ed.), *Law and Order: Police Encounters,* 2nd ed. (Dutton, 1974).

Lowenthal, M., *The Federal Bureau of Investigation* (Sloane, 1950).

Miller, F. W., *et al., The Police Function* (Foundation Press, 1971).

Millspaugh, A. C., *Crime Control by the National Government* (Brookings, 1937).

Navasky, V. S., *Kennedy Justice* (Atheneum, 1971).

Niederhoffer, A., *Behind the Shield: The Police in Urban Society* (Doubleday, 1967).

Radano, G., *Walking the Beat: A New York Policeman Tells What It's Like on His Side of the Law* (World, 1968).

Reiss, A. J., Jr., *The Police and the Public* (Yale, 1971).

Rolph, C. H. (ed.), *The Police and the Public* (Heinemann, 1962).

Ruchelman, L. (ed.), *Who Rules the Police?* (N.Y.U., 1972).

Saunders, C. B., Jr., *Upgrading the American Police* (Brookings, 1970).

Smith, B., *Police Systems in the United States,* rev. ed. (Harper, 1945).

Solmes, A., *The English Policeman, 1871–1935* (Allen & Unwin, 1935).

Sowle, C. R. (ed.), *Police Power and Individual Freedom: The Quest for Balance* (Aldine, 1972).

Steadman, R. F. (ed.), *The Police and the Community* (Johns Hopkins, 1972).

Steer, D., *Police Caution: A Study in the Exercise of Police Discretion* (Blackwells, 1971).

Summers, M. R. (ed.), *Law and Order in a Democratic Society* (Merrill, 1970).

Turner, W. W., *Invisible Witness: The Use and Abuse of the New Technology of Crime Investigation* (Bobbs-Merrill, 1968).

———, *The Police Establishment* (Putnam, 1968).

United States Commission on Civil Rights, *Justice* (U.S. G.P.O., 1961).

Whitehead, D., *The F.B.I. Story: A Report to the People* (Random House, 1956).

Whittemore, L. H., *Cop! A Closeup of Violence and Tragedy* (Holt, Rinehart & Winston, 1969).

Wilson, J. Q., *Varieties of Police Behavior: The Management of Law and Order in Eight Communities* (Harvard, 1968).

Wilson, O. W., *Police Administration,* 2nd ed. (McGraw-Hill, 1963).

Zarr, M., *The Bill of Rights and the Police* (Oceana, 1970).

M. ARRESTS AND PRELIMINARIES.

Boudin, K., B. Glick, E. Raskin, and G. Reichbach, *The Dust Book: What To Do till the Lawyer Comes* (Grove, 1970).

Dalbey, D., *Police Interrogation and the Miranda Rule* (F.B.I. National Academy, 1967).

Lafave, W. R., *Arrest: The Decision To Take a Suspect Into Custody* (Little, Brown, 1965).

Machen, E. W., Jr., *The Law of Arrest* (U. of North Carolina, 1950).

Miller, F. W., *Prosecution: The Decision To Charge a Suspect with a Crime* (Little, Brown, 1969).

Moenssens, A., *Fingerprints and the Law* (Chilton, 1969).

Newman, D., *Conviction: The Determination of Guilt or Innocence Without a Trial* (Little, Brown, 1966).

Orfield, L. B., *Criminal Procedure from Arrest to Appeal* (N.Y.U., 1947).

Schwartzmen, R. and J. Stein, *The Law of Personal Liberties* (Oceana, 1955).

Smith, H. M., *Arrest, Search and Seizure* (Thomas, 1959).

N. CAPITAL PUNISHMENT.

Beccaria, C., *On Crime and Punishment* (Indianapolis, 1963).

Bedau, H. A. (ed.), *The Death Penalty in America*, 2nd ed. (Aldine, 1968).

Bok, C., *Star Wormwood* (Knopf, 1959).

Bresler, F., *Reprieve: A Study of a System* (G. G. Harrap, 1965).

Brown, W., *Women Who Died in the Chair* (Collier, 1963).

Calvert, E. R., *Capital Punishment in the Twentieth Century* (Kennikat, 1927).

Chessman, C., *Cell 2455 Death Row* (Prentice-Hall, 1954).

Chevigny, P. G., *Police Power: Police Abuses in New York City* (Pantheon, 1968).

Christoph, J. B., *Capital Punishment and British Politics* (U. of Chicago, 1962).

DiSalle, M. V., *The Power of Life or Death* (Random House, 1965).

Duffy, H. S., with A. Hirshberg, *88 Men and 2 Women* (Doubleday, 1962).

Gower, W. E., *A Life for a Life* (Chatto & Windus, 1956).

Joyce, J. A., *Capital Punishment* (Nelson, 1961).

Karpman, B., *The Sexual Offender and His Offenses: Etiology, Pathology, Psychodynamics and Treatment* (Julian, 1954).

Koestler, A., *Reflections on Hanging* (Macmillan, 1957).

Laurence, J., *A History of Capital Punishment* (Citadel, 1960).

Lawes, L. E., *Man's Judgment of Death* (Putnam, 1924).

McCafferty, J. A., (ed.), *Capital Punishment* (Aldine-Atherton, 1972).

McClellan, S. G., *Capital Punishment* (Wilson, 1961).

Prettyman, E. B., Jr., *Death and the Supreme Court* (Harcourt, Brace & World, 1961).

Pritchard, J. L., *A History of Capital Punishment* (Kennikat, 1932).

St. John-Stevas, N., *Life, Death, and the Law* (Secker & Warburg, 1956).

Schuessler, K. F., *The Deterrent Influence of the Death Penalty* (Indiana U., 1972).

Sellin, T., *Capital Punishment* (Harper & Row, 1967).

Williams, B., *Due Process* (Morrow, 1960).

O. SENTENCING.

Dawson, R. O., *Sentencing* (Little, Brown, 1969).

Frankel, M., *Criminal Sentences/Law Without Order* (Hill & Wang, 1973).

Green, E., *Judicial Attitudes Toward Sentencing* (Macmillan, 1961).

Hogarth, J., *Sentencing as a Human Process* (U. of Toronto, 1971).

Sharples, K. S., *The Legal Framework of Judicial Sentencing Policy* (U. of Amsterdam, 1972).

P. PRINCIPLES OF CRIME AND CRIMINOLOGY.

Alexander, F., and H. Staub, *The Criminal, the Judge and the Public: A Psychological Analysis* (Macmillan, 1963).

Allen, F. A., *The Borderland of Criminal Justice* (U. of Chicago, 1964).

Allen, R. C. (ed.), *Readings in Law and Psychiatry* (Johns Hopkins, 1968).

Bakal, C., *The Right To Bear Arms* (McGraw-Hill, 1966).

Barnes, H. E., and N. K. Teeters, *New Horizons in Criminology* (Prentice-Hall, 1944).

Blumberg, A. S., *Criminal Justice* (Quadrangle, 1967).

Caughey, J. W., *Their Majesties the Mob* (U. of Chicago, 1960).

Clark, R., *Crime in America: Observations on its Nature, Causes, Prevention and Control* (Simon & Schuster, 1970).

Committee for Economic Development, *Reducing Crime and Assuring Justice* (C.E.D., 1972).

Cook, F. J., *The F.B.I. Nobody Knows* (Macmillan, 1964).

Cressy, D. R. (ed.), *Crime and Criminal Justice* (Quadrangle, 1971).

Douglas, J. D., *Crime and Justice in American Society* (Bobbs-Merrill, 1971).

Edelhertz, H., and G. Geis, *Public Compensation to Victims of Crime* (Praeger, 1974).

Eldridge, W. B., *Narcotics and the Law*, rev. ed. (Aldine, 1967).

Elliff, J. T., *Crime, Dissent, and the Attorney General* (Sage, 1971).

Evans, M. S., and M. Morre, *The Law Breakers: America's Number One Domestic Problem* (Arlington House, 1968).

Glaser, D., *The Effectiveness of a Prison and Parole System* (Bobbs-Merrill, 1964).

Glueck, S. (ed.), *Law and Psychiatry: Cold War or Entente* (Johns Hopkins, 1962).

Goldstein, A. S., *The Insanity Defense* (Viking, 1967).

Grad, F. P., *Alcoholism and the Law* (Oceana, 1971).

Hart, H. L. A., *Punishment and Responsibility* (Oxford, 1968).

Hartung, F. E., *Crime, Law and Society* (Wayne State U., 1971).

Jeffery, C. R., *Crime Prevention through Environmental Design* (Sage, 1971).

Kefauver, E., *Crime in America* (Doubleday, 1951).

Law Forum, New York Law School, *Symposium: Violence and the Law* (Vol. XIV, 1969).

McLennan, B. N. (ed.), *Crime in Urban Society* (Dunellen, 1970).

Mannheim, H., *Criminal Justice and Social Reconstruction* (Paul, French, Teubner, 1946).

Menninger, K., *The Crime of Punishment* (Viking, 1968).

Mitchell, R. S., *The Homosexual and the Law* (Arco, 1969).

Mueller, G. O. W., *Crime, Law and the Scholars* (U. of Washington, 1968).

Overstreet, H., and B. Overstreet, *The F.B.I. in Our Open Society* (Norton, 1969).

Packer, H. L., *The Limits of the Criminal Sanction* (Stanford, 1968).

Pincoffs, E., *The Rationale of Legal Punishment* (Humanities Press, 1966).

Polier, J. W., *The Rule of Law and the Role of Psychiatry* (Johns Hopkins, 1968).

President's Commission on Law Enforcement and Administration of Justice, *The Challenge of Crime in a Free Society* (Superintendent of Documents, 1967).

Quinney, R. (ed.), *Crime and Justice in Society* (Little, Brown, 1969).

Radzinowicz, Sir L. (ed.), *Crime and Justice*, 3 vols. (Basic, 1971).
Robitscher, J. B., *Pursuit of Agreement: Psychiatry and the Law* (Lippincott, 1966).
Rubin, S., *Crime and Juvenile Delinquency*, 3rd ed. (Oceana, 1970).
————, *Illusion, Fiction and Myths* (Oceana, 1965).
————, *Psychiatry and Criminal Law* (Oceana, 1965).
Schever, J. H., *To Walk the Streets Safely* (Doubleday, 1969).
Schur, E. M., *Crimes Without Victims* (Prentice-Hall, 1965).
Skolnick, J. H., *The Politics of Protest* (Simon & Schuster, 1969).
————, *Justice Without Trial: Law Enforcement in Democratic Society* (Wiley, 1966).
Sutherland, E. M., and D. R. Cressey, *Principles of Criminology* (Lippincott, 1960).
Szasz, T. S., *Law, Liberty and Psychiatry* (Macmillan, 1964).
————, *Psychiatric Justice* (Macmillan, 1965).
Tappan, R. W., *Crime, Justice and Correction* (McGraw-Hill, 1960).
University of Chicago Law Review Staff, *Criminal Justice in Extremis: Administration of Justice During the April 1968 Chicago Disorders* (American Bar Found., 1970).
Whitlock, F. A., *Criminal Responsibility and Mental Illness* (Buttersworth, 1963).

V. MILITARY JUSTICE AND SELECTIVE SERVICE IN PEACE AND WAR (See also: X., Religion.)

A. GENERAL.

American Friends' Service Committee, *The Draft?* (Hill & Wang, 1968).
Anthony, J. G., *Hawaii Under Army Rule* (Stanford, 1955).
Coffin, T., *The Passion of the Hawks* (Macmillan, 1964).
Corwin, E. S., *Total War and the Constitution* (Knopf, 1947).
Ellsberg, D., *Papers on the War* (Simon & Schuster, 1972).
Fairman, C., *The Law of Martial Rule* (Callaghan, 1943).
Finn, J. (ed.), *A Conflict of Loyalties: The Case for Selective Conscientious Objection* (Pegasus, 1968).
Herring, P., *The Impact of War* (Farrar & Rinehart, 1941).
Huntington, S. P., *The Soldier and the State: The Theory and Politics of Civil-Military Relations* (Belknap of Harvard, 1957).
Jacobs, C. E., and J. F. Gallagher, *The Selective Service Act* (Dodd, Mead, 1967).
Lovell, J. P., and P. S. Kronenberg, *New Civil-Military Relations* (Dutton, 1974).
Lynn, C. J., *How To Stay Out of the Army: A Guide to Your Rights Under the Draft Laws* (Grove, 1968).
McNair, L., and A. D. Watts, *The Legal Effects of War* (Cambridge U., 1966).
Marmion, H. A., *Selective Service: Conflict and Compromise* (Wiley, 1968).
Miller, J. C., III, *et al.* (eds.), *Why the Draft? The Case for a Volunteer Army* (Penguin, 1968).
Millis, W., *et al.*, *Arms and the State: Civil-Military Elements in National Policy* (20th Century Fund, 1958).
————, *Individual Freedom and the Common Defense* (Fund for the Republic, 1957).
Mincar, R. H., *Victors' Justice: The Tokyo War Crimes Trial* (Princeton, 1971).
Oppenheimer, Martin (ed.), *The American Military*, 2nd ed. (Dutton, 1974).
Paxon, F. C., *America at War, 1917–1918* (Houghton Mifflin, 1939).

481

Peterson, H. C., and G. C. Fita, *Opponents of War, 1917–1918* (U. of Wisconsin, 1957).

Rankin, R. S., *When Civil Law Fails: Martial Law and its Legal Basis in the U.S.* (Duke, 1939).

Reel, A. F., *The Case of General Yamashita* (U. of Chicago, 1949).

Rossiter, C., *The Supreme Court and the Commander-in-Chief* (Cornell, 1951).

Scheiber, H. N., *The Wilson Administration & Civil Liberties* (Cornell, 1960).

Sherrill, K. S., *Military Justice Is to Justice as Military Music Is to Music* (Harper, 1970).

Smith, L., *American Democracy and Military Power* (U. of Chicago, 1951).

Stein, H. (ed.), *American Civil-Military Establishment* (U. of Alabama, 1963).

Summers, R. E., *Wartime Censorship of Press and Radio* (Wilson, 1942).

Swomley, J. M., Jr., *The Military Establishment* (Beacon, 1964).

Tatum, A., and J. S. Tuchinsky, *Guide to the Draft* (Beacon, 1969).

Tax, S. (ed.), *The Draft: A Handbook of Facts and Alternatives* (U. of Chicago, 1968).

Taylor, T., *Nuremberg and Vietnam: An American Tragedy* (Quadrangle, 1970).

Velvel, L. R., *Undeclared War and Civil Disobedience* (Dunellen, 1970).

Walzer, M., *Obligations: Essays on Disobedience, War and Citizenship*

Zahn, G. C., *War, Conscience and Dissent* (Hawthorne, 1967).

B. CIVILIANS.

Barnes, P., *Pawns: The Plight of the Citizen Soldier* (Knopf, 1972).

Bloom, L., and R. Riemer, *Removal and Return* (U. of California, 1949).

Cable, J. L., *Loss of Citizenship: Denaturalization—the Alien in Wartime* (National Law Book Co., 1943).

Davis, J. W., Jr., and K. M. Dolbeare, *Little Groups of Neighbors: The Selective Service System* (Markham, 1968).

Gaylin, W., *In the Service of Their Country: War Resisters in Prison* (Viking, 1970).

Gerhardt, J. M., *The Draft and Public Policy: Issues in Military Manpower Procurement* (Ohio State U., 1971).

Girdner, A., and A. Loftis, *The Great Betrayal: The Evacuation of the Japanese-Americans During World War II* (Macmillan, 1969).

Grodzins, M., *The Loyal and the Disloyal: Social Boundaries of Patriotism and Treason* (U. of Chicago, 1956).

McWilliams, C., *Prejudice—Japanese-American—Symbols of Racial Intolerance* (Little, Brown, 1944).

Marmion, H. A., *Selective Service: Conflict and Compromise* (Wiley, 1970).

Sibley, M. Q., and P. E. Jacob, *Conscription of Conscience: The American State and the Conscientious Objector* (Cornell, 1952).

Tenbroek, J., et al., *Japanese-American Evacuation and Resettlement* (Berkeley, 1944).

——, *Prejudice, War and the Constitution* (Berkeley, 1954).

Thomas, D. S., *The Salvage* (U. of California, 1952).

——, and R. S. Nishimito, *The Spoilage* (Berkeley, 1946).

Wamsley, G. L., *Selective Service and a Changing America* (Merrill, 1969).

Wiener, F. B., *Civilians Under Military Justice: The British Practice Since 1689, Especially in North America* (U. of Chicago, 1967).

Willoughby, G., *Handbook for Conscientious Objectors* (Larchwood, 1964).

C. MILITARY PERSONNEL.

Avins, A., *The Law of AWOL* (Oceana, 1957).

Aycock, W. B., and S. W. Wurfel, *Military Law Under the Uniform Code of Military Justice* (U. of North Carolina, 1962).

DiMona, J., *Great Court-Martial Cases* (Grosset & Dunlap, 1972).

Edwards, M. O., and C. L. Decker, *The Serviceman and the Law* (Stockpole, 1951).

Everett, R. O., *Military Justice in the Armed Forces of the U.S.* (Mil. Sv. Pub. Co., 1956).

Finn, J. (ed.), *Conscience and Command: Justice and Discipline in the Military* (Viking, 1971).

Thieml, P. M., *The Legal Status of Participants in Unconventional Warfare* (Special Operations Research Office, 1961).

Ulmer, S. S., *Military Justice and the Right to Counsel* (U. of Kentucky, 1970).

Walker, D. (ed.), *Military Law* (Prentice-Hall, 1954).

VI. SEGREGATION/DESEGREGATION (See also: III., Philosophies of Prejudice.)

A. GENERAL.

Ashmore, H. S., *Epitaph for Dixie* (Norton, 1957).

———, *The Other Side of Jordan: Negroes Outside the South* (Norton, 1960).

Balbus, I. D., *The Dialectics of Legal Repression: Black Rebels Before the American Criminal Courts* (Russell Sage, 1973).

Blaustein, A. P., and R. S. Zangrando, *Civil Rights and the American Negro: A Documentary History* (Trident, 1968).

Brink, W., and L. Harris, *Black and White: A Study of Racial Attitudes Today* (Simon & Schuster, 1967).

Brown, H. R., *Die, Nigger, Die!* (Dial Press, 1969).

Cable, G. W., *The Negro Question: A Selection of Writings on Civil Rights in the South* (Doubleday, 1890).

Carmichael, P. A., *The South and Segregation* (Public Affairs Press, 1965).

Clark, K. B., *Dark Ghetto: Dilemmas of Social Power* (Harper & Row, 1965).

Coles, R., *The Desegregation of Southern Schools: A Psychiatric Study* (S.R.C. and A.D.L., 1963).

Commager, H. S. (ed.), *The Struggle for Racial Equality* (Harper, 1967).

Countryman, J. (ed.), *Discrimination and the Law* (U. of Chicago, 1965).

Crain, R., and D. Kirby, *Political Strategies in Northern Desegregation* (Lexington, 1973).

Dabbs, J. M., *Who Speaks for the South?* (Funk & Wagnalls, 1965).

Dalfiume, R. M., *Desegregation of the U.S. Armed Forces: Fighting on Two Fronts, 1939–1953* (U. of Missouri, 1969).

Fortune Magazine, *The Negro and the City* (A.D.L., 1968).

Freedman, L. (ed.), *Southern Justice* (Pantheon, 1965).

Graham, H. D., *Crisis in Print: Desegregation and the Press in Tennessee* (Vanderbilt, 1967).

Greenberg, J. A. (ed.), "Blacks and the Law," Special vol. of *The Annals* Vol. 407, May 1973.

Handlin, O., *Fire-Bell in the Night: The Crisis in Civil Rights* (Little, Brown, 1964).

Hill, H., and J. Greenberg, *Citizen's Guide to De-Segregation* (Beacon, 1955).

Hoffman, N. J., *Mississippi Notebook* (White, 1965).

Hopkins, V. C., *Dred Scott Case* (Atheneum, 1967).

Huie, W. B., *Three Lives for Mississippi* (W.C.C., 1965).

Jacobs, P., *Prelude to Riot* (Random House, 1967).

Johnson, C. S., *Patterns of Negro Segregation* (Harper, 1943).

Kutler, S. I., *Judicial Power and Reconstruction Politics* (U. of Chicago, 1968).

——— (ed.), *The Dred Scott Decision: Law or Politics* (Houghton Mifflin, 1967).

Latham, F. B., *The Dred Scott Decision, March 6, 1857* (Watts, 1857).

Leiserson, A. (ed.), *The American South in the 1960's* (Praeger, 1964).

Lockard, D., *Toward Equal Opportunity: A Study of State and Local Anti-Discrimination Laws* (Macmillan, 1968).

Loth, D., and H. Flemming, *Integration North and South* (Fund for the Republic, 1956).

Lubell, S., *White and Black: Test of a Nation* (Harper & Row, 1964).

MacIver, R. M. (ed.), *Discrimination and National Welfare* (Harper & Bros., 1949).

Mendelson, W., *Discrimination* (Prentice-Hall, 1963).

Michael, W. E., *The Age of Error* (Vantage, 1957).

Mitchell, G. E., and W. H. Peace III, *The Angry Black South: Southern Negroes Tell Their Own Story* (Citadel, 1962).

Molotch, H. L., *Managed Integration: Dilemmas of Doing Good in the City* (U. of California, 1973).

Morgan, C., Jr., *A Time to Speak* (Harper & Row, 1964).

Morris, W., *Yazoo: Integration in a Deep Southern Town* (Harper's Magazine Press, 1971).

Muse, B., *Ten Years of Prelude* (Viking, 1964).

Nichols, L., *Breakthrough on the Color Front* (Random House, 1954).

Olsen, O. H. (ed.), *The Thin Disguise: Plessy v. Ferguson, A Documentary Presentation, 1864–1896* (Humanities Press, 1968).

O'Neill, J. E. (ed.), *The Breaking of the Wall: Aspects of Segregation* (Macmillan, 1961).

———, *A Catholic Case Against Segregation* (Macmillan, 1961).

Osofsky, G., *The Burden of Race: A Documentary History of Negro-White Relations in America* (Harper & Row, 1968).

Peters, W., *The Southern Temper* (Doubleday, 1959).

Pettigrew, T. F., *Epitaph for Jim Crow* (A.D.L., 1964).

———, *Racially Separate or Together* (A.D.L., 1969).

Reid, I. (ed.), *Racial Desegregation and Integration* (Amer. Acad., 1956).

Romero, P. (ed.), *In Black America* (United Publ. Co., 1969).

Silberman, C. E., *Crisis in Black and White* (Random House, 1964).

Silver, J. W., *Mississippi: The Closed Society* (Harcourt, Brace & World, 1966).

Simkins, F. B., *The Everlasting South* (Louisiana State U., 1963).

Sindler, A. P. (ed.), *Change in the Contemporary South* (Duke, 1964).

Southern Regional Council, *Intimidation, Reprisal and Violence in the South's Racial Crisis* (S.R.C., 1959).

Stahl, D., F. B. Sussman, and N. J. Bloomfield, *The Community and Racial Crisis* (Practicing Law Institute, 1966).

Stampp, K., *The Peculiar Institution* (Knopf, 1963).

Stoff, S., *The Two-Way Street: Guideposts to Peaceful School Desegregation* (David-Hewart, 1967).

Suchman, E. A., J. P. Dean, and R. M. Williams, Jr., *Desegregation* (A.D.L., 1963).

Talmadge, H. E., *You and Segregation* (Vulcan, 1955).

Townsend, C., *Old Age: The Last Segregation* (Grossman, 1970).

Tucker, S., *Mississippi From Within* (Arco, 1965).

Tumin, N. M., *Desegregation: Readiness and Resistance* (Princeton, 1958).

Tussman, J., *The Supreme Court on Racial Discrimination* (Oxford, 1963).

U.S. Commission on Civil Rights, *Enforcement: A Report on Equal Protection in the South* (U.S. G.P.O., 1965).

——, *With Liberty and Justice for All* (U.S. G.P.O., 1959).

Urban America Inc. and The Urban Coalition, *One Year Later* (Praeger, 1969).

Vander Zander, J. W., *Race Relations in Transition: The Segregation Crisis in the South* (Random House, 1965).

Warren, R. P., *Segregation: The Inner Conflict in the South* (Random House, 1956).

Williamson, J. (comp.), *The Origins of Segregation* (Heath, 1968).

Wirt, F. M., *Politics of Southern Equality: Law and Social Change in a Mississippi County* (Aldine-Atherton, 1972).

Wolk, A., *The Presidency and Black Civil Rights: Eisenhower to Nixon* (Fairleigh Dickinson, 1971).

Woodward, C. V., *The Strange Career of Jim Crow*, 3rd rev. ed. (Oxford, 1974).

Woofter, T. J., *Southern Race Progress: The Wavering Color Line* (Public Affairs Press, 1957).

Young, W. M., *Beyond Racism: Building an Open Society* (McGraw-Hill, 1969).

——, *To Be Equal* (McGraw-Hill, 1964).

Ziegler, B. M., *Desegregation and the Supreme Court* (Heath, 1953).

Zinn, H., *The Southern Mystique* (Knopf, 1965).

B. EDUCATION.

Alexander, K., and K. F. Jordan, *Constitutional Reform of School Finance* (Lexington, 1973).

Anderson, M., *The Children of the South* (Farrar, Straus & Giroux, 1966).

Ashmore, H. S., *The Negro and the Schools*, rev. ed. (U. of North Carolina, 1954).

Barrett, R. H., *Integration at Ole Miss* (Quadrangle, 1965).

Bates, D., *The Long Shadow of Little Rock: A Memoir* (McKay, 1963).

Berman, D. M., *It Is So Ordered* (Norton, 1966).

Blaustein, A. P., and C. C. Ferguson, Jr., *Desegregation and the Law* (Vintage, 1962).

Blossom, V., *It Has Happened Here* (Harper, 1959).

Bork, R. H., *Constitutionality of the President's Busing Proposals* (Amer. Enterpr. Inst., 1972).

Boyle, S. P., *The Desegregated Heart* (Morrow, 1962).

Brady, T. P., *Black Monday* (Miss. Assoc. of Citizens Councils, 1955).

Brickman, W. W., and S. Lehrer, *The Countdown on Segregated Education* (Society for the Advancement of Ed., 1960).

Brown, R. R., *Bigger than Little Rock* (Seabury, 1958).

Buchheimer, N., and A. Buchheimer, *Equality through Integration* (A.D.L., 1969).

Campbell, E. A., *When a City Closes Its Schools* (U. of North Carolina, 1960).

485

————, and T. F. Pettigrew, *Christians in Racial Crisis: A Study of Little Rock's Ministry* (Public Affairs Press, 1959).

Carmichael, O., and W. James, *The Louisville Story* (Simon & Schuster, 1957).

Caughey, J., and L. Caughey, *School Segregation on Our Doorstep: The Los Angeles Story* (Quail, 1966).

Coles, R., *The Desegregation of Southern Schools: A Psychiatric Study* (A.D.L., 1963).

Coons, J. E., S. Sugarman, and W. Clune, *Private Wealth and Public Education* (Harvard, 1971).

Cox, E. S., *The School Situation at Clinton* (1957).

Crain, R. L., *The Politics of School Desegregation* (Aldine, 1968).

Daly, C. V. (ed.), *The Quality of Inequality: Urban and Suburban Public Schools* (U. of Chicago, 1969).

Damerell, R. G., *Triumph in a White Suburb: The Dramatic Story of Teaneck, N.J.* (Morrow, 1968).

Dean, J. P., and A. Rosen, *A Manual of Intergroup Relations* (U. of Chicago, 1955).

Dentler, R. A., B. Mackler, and M. A. Warshauer (eds.), *The Urban R's: Race Relations as the Problem in Urban Education* (Praeger, 1967).

Dobbs, F. M., *The Southern Heritage* (Knopf, 1958).

Edwards, N., *The Courts and the Public Schools: The Legal Basis of School Organization and Administration* (U. of Chicago, 1971).

Edwards, T. B., and F. M. Wirt (eds.), *School Desegregation in the North: The Challenge and the Experience* (Chandler, 1968).

Faulkner, W., B. Mays, and C. Sims, *The Segregation Decisions: Three Views* (S.R.C., 1956).

Fellman, D. (ed.), *The Supreme Court and Education*, rev. ed. (Columbia, 1969).

Fleming, H. C., and J. Constable, *What's Happening in School Integration* (Public Affairs Comm., 1956).

Fletcher, J. L., Jr., *The Segregation Case and the Supreme Court* (Boston U., 1958).

Friedman, L. (ed.), *Argument: The Oral Argument Before the Supreme Court in Brown v. Board of Education of Topeka, 1952–1955* (Chelsea, 1970).

Fuchs, E., *Pickets at the Gates: The Challenge of Civil Rights in Urban Schools* (Free Press, 1966). NYC problems.

Gates, R. L., *The Making of Massive Resistance: Virginia; Politics of Public School Desegregation, 1954–1956* (U. of North Carolina, 1964).

Giles, H. H., *The Integrated Classroom* (Basic Books, 1959).

Ginzberg, E., *The Negro Potential* (Columbia, 1956).

Green, D. R., and W. E. Guaerke, *If the Schools Are Closed* (S.R.C., 1959).

Gwaltney, F. I., *The Numbers of Our Days* (Random House, 1959).

Harlan, L. R., *Separate and Unequal* (U. of N. Carolina, 1958).

Hill, R., and M. Feeley, *Affirmative School Integration: Efforts to Overcome De Facto Segregation in Urban Schools* (Sage, 1969).

Hogan, J. C., *The Schools, the Courts, and the Public Interest* (Lexington, 1973).

Holley, J. W., *Education and the Segregation Issue* (W. Frederick, 1955).

Humphrey, H. H. (ed.), *School Desegregation: Documents and Commentaries* (Crowell, 1964).

Ivey, H., and J. Corey, *Action Patterns in School Desegregation: A Guidebook* (Phi Delta Kappa, Inc., 1959).

Jones, L. G. E., *Negro Schools in the Southern States* (Oxford, 1928).

Kilpatrick, J. J., *The Southern Case for School Segregation* (Crowell, Collier, 1962).

Lanoue, G. R., and B. L. R. Smith, *The Politics of School Decentralization* (Heath, 1972).

Levy, F., *Northern Schools and Civil Rights: The Racial Imbalance Act of Massachusetts* (Markham, 1971).

Lord, W., *The Past That Would Not Die* (Harper & Row, 1965).

McCauley, P., and E. D. Bell (eds.), *Southern Schools: Progress and Problems* (Southern Educational Reporting Service, 1959).

McCord, J. H. (ed.), *With All Deliberate Speed* (U. of Illinois, 1969).

Mack, R. W. (ed.), *Our Children's Burden: Studies of Desegregation in Nine American Communities* (Random House, 1968).

Martin, J. B., *The Deep South Says Never* (Ballantine, 1957).

Maston, T. B., *Segregation and Desegregation: A Christian Approach* (Macmillan, 1959).

Miller, A. S., *Racial Discrimination and Private Education* (U. of North Carolina, 1957).

Miller, L., *The Petitioners: The Story of the Supreme Court of the United States and the Negro* (Pantheon, 1966).

Mills, N. (ed.), *The Great School Bus Controversy* (Teachers College Press, 1974).

Muse, B., *Virginia's Massive Resistance* (Indiana U., 1961).

Orfield, G., *The Reconstruction of Southern Education: The Schools and the 1964 Civil Rights Act* (Wiley, 1964).

Peltason, J. W., *Fifty-Eight Lonely Men*, rev. ed. (U. of Illinois, 1971).

Pierce, T. M., *et al.*, *White and Negro Schools in the South* (Prentice-Hall, 1955).

Pincus, J. (ed.), *School Finance in Transition: The Courts and Educational Reform* (Ballinger, 1974).

President's Commission for the Observance of Human Rights Year, *Racism and American Education* (Harper & Row, 1970).

Quint, H. H., *Profile of Black and White: A Frank Portrait of South Carolina* (Public Affairs Press, 1958).

Record, W., *Little Rock, U.S.A.* (Chandler, 1960).

Reutter, E. E., *Schools and the Law* (Oceana, 1965).

Rubin, L., *Busing and Backlash: White Against White in an Urban School District* (U. of California, 1972).

Scott, J. I. E., *Negro Students and Their Colleges* (Meador, 1949).

Shannon, K. M., *Integration Decision Unconstitutional* (Little Rock Arkansas Demo., 1956).

Shoemaker, D. (ed.), *With All Deliberate Speed* (Harper & Bros., 1957).

Silverman, C., *The Little Rock Story* (U. of Alabama, 1959).

Smith, L., *Now Is the Time* (Viking, 1955).

Southern Educational Reporting Service, *Southern Schools: Progress and Problems* (Nashville, 1959).

Spurlock, C., *Education and the Supreme Court* (U. of Illinois, 1955).

Sterling, D., and D. Gross, *Tender Warriors* (Hill & Wang, 1958).

Stoff, S., *The Two-Way Street: Guideposts to Peaceful School Desegregation* (David-Stewart, 1967).

Sullivan, N. V., *et al.*, *Bound for Freedom: An Educator; Adventures in Prince Edward County* (Little, Brown, 1965).

Swanson, B. E., *The Struggle for Equality* (Hobbs, Dorwin, 1966).

Swanson, E. W., and J. A. Griffin, *Public Education in the South Today and Tomorrow* (U. of North Carolina, 1955).

Tipton, J. H., *Community in Crisis: The Elimination of Segregation from a Public School System* (Columbia, 1953).

Trillin, C., *An Education in Georgia* (Viking, 1964).

U.S. Commission on Civil Rights, *Education: Book 2 of 1961 Report* (U.S. G.P.O., 1961).

————, *Equal Protection of the Laws in Public Higher Education* (U.S. G.P.O., 1960).

University of North Carolina Press, *When a City Closes Its Schools* (U. of North Carolina, 1960).

Weinberg, M. (ed.), *Integrated Education* (Glencoe, 1968).

Williams, R. J., and M. W. Ryan (eds.), *Schools in Transition: Community Experience in Desegregation* (U. of North Carolina, 1954).

C. EMPLOYMENT.

Becker, G. S., *The Economics of Discrimination* (U. of Chicago, 1957).

Buffalo Law Review, *Toward Equal Opportunity in Employment: The Role of the State and Local Government* (Da Capo, 1971).

Bullock, R., *Merit Employment: Non-Discrimination in Industry* (Inst. of Ind. Relations, U.C.L.A., 1960).

Edwards, G. F., *The Negro Professional Class* (Free Press, 1959).

Ferman, L. A., J. L. Kornbluth, and J. A. Miller, *Negroes and Jobs: A Book of Readings* (U. of Michigan, 1968).

Fisher, P. L., and R. L. Loewenstein, *Race and the News Media* (Praeger, 1967).

Ginzberg, E., *The Negro Potential* (Columbia, 1956).

Graves, W. B., *Fair Employment Practice Legislation in the U.S.: Federal-State-Municipal* (Library of Congress, 1951).

Greer, S., *Last Man In: Racial Access to Union Power* (Free Press, 1959).

Hope, J., II., *Equality of Opportunity: A Union Approach to Fair Employment* (Public Affairs, 1956).

Jacobson, J. (ed.), *The Negro and the American Labor Movement* (Doubleday, 1968).

Kesselman, L. C., *The Social Politics of the FEPC: A Study in Reform Pressure Movement* (U. of North Carolina, 1948).

Krislov, S., *The Negro in Federal Employment: The Quest for Equal Opportunity* (U. of Minnesota, 1957).

Mandelbaum, D. G., *Soldier Groups and Negro Soldiers* (U. of California, 1952).

Moon, B., *The High Cost of Prejudice* (Messner, 1947).

Nelson, D. D., *The Integration of the Negro into the United States Navy* (Farrar, Straus, 1951).

Norgren, P. H., *Employing the Negro in American Industry: A Study of Management Practices* (Ind. Rel. Counselors, 1959).

Reitzes, D. C., *Negroes and Medicine* (Harvard, 1958).

Ross, M., *All Manner of Men* (Reynal and Hitchcock, 1948).

Ruchames, L., *Race, Jobs and Politics: The Story of F.E.P.C.* (Columbia, 1953).

Smith, H. S., *Freedom to Work* (Vantage, 1955).

Southall, S. E., *Industry's Unfinished Business: Achieving Sound Industrial Relations and Fair Employment* (20th Century Fund, 1966).

Sovern, M. I., *Legal Restraints on Racial Discrimination in Employment* (20th Century Fund, 1966).

D. HOUSING.

Abrams, C., *Forbidden Neighbors: A Study of Prejudice in Housing* (Harper, 1955).

Black, A., *Who's My Neighbor* (Public Affairs Comm., 1956).

Bradburn, N. M., S. Sudman, and G. L. Gockel, *Side by Side: Integrated Neighborhoods in America* (Quardrangle, 1971).

Braden, A., *The Wall Between* (Monthly Review Press, 1958).

Casstevens, T. W., *Politics, Housing and Race Relations: California's Rumford Act and Proposition 14* (Berkeley, 1965).

Clark, K. B., *Dark Ghetto* (Harper & Row, 1965).

————, *Prejudice and Your Child* (Beacon, 1955).

Commission on Race and Housing, *Where Shall We Live? Report of the Commission on Race and Housing* (U. of California, 1958).

Deutsch, M., *Interracial Housing* (U. of Minnesota, 1951).

Eley, L. W., and T. W. Casstevens, *The Politics of Fair Housing Legislation: State and Local Case Studies* (Chandler, 1968).

Foley, E. P., *The Achieving Ghetto* (National Press, 1967).

Glazer, N., and D. McEntire (eds.), *Studies in Housing and Minority Groups* (U. of California, 1961).

Grier, E., and G. Grier, *Equality and Beyond: Housing Segregation and the Goals of the Great Society* (Quadrangle, 1968).

————, *Privately Developed Interracial Housing: An Analysis of Experience* (U. of California, 1961).

Hesslink, G. K., *Black Neighbors: Negroes in a Northern Rural Community* (Bobbs-Merrill, 1968).

Laurenti, L., *Property Value and Race: Studies in Seven Cities* (Berkeley, 1960).

Long, H. H., and C. S. Johnson, *People v. Property: Race Restrictive Covenants in Housing* (Fisk U., 1947).

McEntire, D., *Residence and Race: Final and Comprehensive Report to the Commission on Race and Housing* (U. of California, 1961).

Messner, S. D. (ed.), *Minority Groups and Housing: A Selected Bibliography, 1950–1967* (U. of Connecticut, 1967).

Northwood, L. K., and E. A. E. Barth, *Urban Desegregation: Negro Pioneers and Their White Neighbors* (U. of Washington, 1965).

Rabkin, C., and W. G. Grigsby, *The Demand for Housing in Racially Mixed Areas: A Study of Neighborhood Change* (U. of California, 1961).

Rabkin, S., *A Landmark Decision of Segregation in Housing: Jones v. Mayer* (A.D.L., 1969).

Rainwater, L., *Behind Ghetto Walls: Black Family Life in a Federal Slum* (Aldine, 1970).

Rosen, H., and C. Rosen, *But Not Next Door* (Obolensky, 1962).

Schroeder, O., Jr., and D. T. Smith (eds.), *De Facto Segregation and Civil Rights* (Hein, 1963).

Thomas, N. C., *Rule 9: Politics, Administration, and Civil Rights* (Random House, 1966).

Vose, C. E., *Caucasians Only: The Supreme Court, The NAACP and the Restrictive Covenant Cases* (Berkeley, 1959).

Warren, R. L. (ed.), *Politics and the Ghetto* (Aldine-Atherton, 1970).

Weaver, R. C., *The Negro Ghetto* (Harcourt, Brace, 1948).

Wheeler, K., *Peaceable Lane* (Simon & Schuster, 1960).

E. TECHNIQUES OF THE NEGRO CIVIL RIGHTS MOVEMENT. (The NAACP, sit-ins, and other "ins": The leaders of the general "civil rights" activities; violent responses.)

Altshuler, A., *Community Control: The Black Demand for Participation in Large American Cities* (Pegasus, 1970).

Bailey, H. A., Jr. (ed.), *Negro Politics in America* (Merrill, 1967).

Barbour, F. B., (ed.), *The Black Power Revolt* (Sargent, 1968).

Belfrage, S., *Freedom Summer* (Viking, 1965).

Boskin, J., *Urban Racial Violence in the Twentieth Century* (Glencoe Press, 1969).

Burns, W. H., *The Voices of Negro Protest in America* (Oxford, 1963).

Carmichael, S., and C. Hamilton, *Black Power: The Politics of Liberation in America* (Random House, 1967).

Clark, K. B. (ed.), *The Negro Protest* (Beacon, 1963).

Clarke, C. J., *These Rights They Seek* (Public Affairs, 1962).

Coffin, W. S., and E. E. Whitaker, *Law, Order and Civil Disobedience* (Amer. Ent. Inst., 1967).

Cohen, J., and W. S. Murphy, *Burn Baby Burn: The Los Angeles Race Riot, August, 1965* (Dutton, 1966).

Cone, J. H., *Black Theology and Black Power* (Seabury, 1969).

Daly, C. U., *Urban Violence* (U. of Chicago, 1969).

Ehle, N., *The Free Men* (Harper & Row, 1965).

Ellis, W. W., *White Ethics and Black Power* (Aldine, 1969).

Fisher, P. L., and R. L. Loewenstein, *Race and the News Media* (A.D.L., 1967).

Foner, P. S., *The Black Panthers Speak* (Lippincott, 1970).

Garfinkel, H., *When Negroes March* (Free Press, 1959).

Gilbert, B. W., *Ten Blocks from the White House: Anatomy of the Washington Riots of 1968* (Praeger, 1968).

Greer, E. (ed.), *Black Liberation Politics: A Reader* (Allyn & Bacon, 1971).

Grimshaw, A. D., *Racial Violence in the United States* (Aldine, 1969).

Guerin, D., *Negroes on the March* (Weissman, 1956).

Hamilton, C. V., *The Politics of Civil Rights* (Random House, 1967).

Hayden, T., *Rebellion in Newark: Official Violence and Ghetto Response* (Random House, 1967).

Hughes, L., *Fight for Freedom: The Story of the NAACP* (Norton, 1963).

Jacobs, P., *Prelude to Riot: A View of Urban America from the Bottom* (Vintage, 1969).

Killian, L. M., *The Impossible Revolution: Black Power and the American Dream* (Random House, 1968).

King, M. L., *Stride Toward Freedom: The Montgomery Story* (Harper, 1958).

————, *Where Do We Go From Here? Chaos or Community?* (Harper & Row, 1967).

Ladd, E. C., Jr., *Negro Political Leadership in the South* (Cornell, 1961).

Lincoln, E. R., *The Black Muslims in America* (Beacon, 1961).

Locke, H. G., *The Detroit Riots of 1967* (Wayne State U., 1971).

Lomax, L. E., *The Negro Revolt* (Harper & Row, 1962).

McWorther, G. (ed.), *The Political Sociology of the Negro: A Selective Review of the Literature* (A.D.L., 1968).

Marx, G., *Protest and Prejudice* (Harper & Row, 1969).

Masotti, L. H., and D. R. Bowen (eds.), *Riots and Rebellion* (Sage, 1969).

Matthews, D. R., and J. W. Prothro, *Negroes and the New Southern Politics* (Harcourt, Brace & World, 1966).

Meier, A. (ed.), *Black Experience II: The Transformation of Activism* (Aldine, 1969).

————, and E. Rudwick, *CORE: A Study in the Civil Rights Movement, 1942–1968* (Oxford, 1973).

————, and F. L. Broderick, *Negro Protest Thought in the Twentieth Century* (Bobbs-Merrill, 1966).

Muse, B., *The American Negro Revolutionary from Nonviolence to Black Power, 1963–1967* (Indiana U., 1968).

Oppenheimer, M., *The Urban Guerilla* (Quadrangle, 1969).

Patterson, E., *Black City Politics* (Dodd, Mead, 1974).

Peck, J., *Freedom Ride* (Simon & Schuster, 1962).

Peeks, E., *The Long Struggle for Black Power* (Scribner's, 1971).

Powledge, F., *Black Power—White Resistance: Notes on the New Civil War* (World, 1967).

Proudfoot, M., *Diary of a Sit-In* (U. of North Carolina, 1962).

Record, W., *The NAACP and the Communist Party in Conflict* (Cornell, 1964).

Reddick, L. D., *Crusader Without Violence* (Harper, 1959).

Rossi, P. H. (ed.), *Ghetto Revolts* (Aldine, 1970).

Shepherd, G. W., Jr. (ed.), *Racial Influences on American Foreign Policy* (Basic Books, 1970).

Sutherland, F. (ed.), *Letters from Mississippi* (McGraw-Hill, 1965).

Tucker, S., *For Blacks Only: Black Strategies for Change in America* (Eerdmans, 1971).

Von Hoffman, N., *Mississippi Notebook* (David White, 1965).

Wagstaff, T., *Black Power: The Radical Response to White America* (Glencoe Press, 1968).

Wakefield, D., *Revolt in the South* (Grove, 1960).

Waskow, I., *From Race-Riot to Sit-Ins: 1919 and the 1960's* (Doubleday, 1966).

Wilkinson, D. Y. (ed.), *Black Revolt: Strategies of Protest* (McCutchan, 1969).

Wright, N., Jr., *Black Power and Urban Unrest* (Hawthorn, 1967).

Zinn, H., *Disobedience and Democracy: Nine Fallacies on Law and Order* (Random House, 1968).

————, *SNCC: The New Abolitionists* (Beacon, 1964).

VII. VOTING AND SUFFRAGE

Aikin, C., *The Negro Votes* (Chandler, 1962).

Catt, C. C., and N. R. Shuler, *Women Suffrage and Politics: The Inner Story of the Suffrage Movement* (U. of Washington, 1923).

Claude, R., *The Supreme Court and the Electoral Process* (Johns Hopkins, 1970).

Elliott, W. E. Y., *The Rise of Guardian Democracy: The Supreme Court's Role in Voting Rights Disputes, 1845–1969* (Harvard, 1974).

Gillette, W. M., *The Right to Vote: Politics and the Passage of the Fifteenth Amendment* (Johns Hopkins, 1965).

Grimes, A. P., *The Puritan Ethic And Woman Suffrage* (Oxford, 1967).

Hamilton, C. V., *The Bench and the Ballot: Southern Federal Judges and Black Voters* (Oxford, 1973).

Keech, W. R., *The Impact of Negro Voting: The Role of the Vote in the Quest for Equality* (Rand-McNally, 1968).

Key, V. O., Jr., *Southern Politics in State and Nation* (Knopf, 1949).

Lewinson, P., *Race, Class and Party: A History of Negro Suffrage and White Politics in the South* (Grosset & Dunlap, 1964).

Mitchell, W. C., *Why Vote?* (Markham, 1971).

Ogden, A. R., *The Poll Tax in the South* (Catholic U., 1958).

Pomper, G. M., *Elections in America: Control and Influence in American Politics* (Dodd, Mead, 1968).

President's Committee on Civil Rights, *To Secure These Rights* (U.S. G.P.O., 1947).

Price, H. D., *The Negro in Southern Politics* (N.Y.U., 1957).

Reitman, A., and R. B. Davidson, *The Election Process—Voting Laws and Procedures* (Oceana, 1972).

Smith, C. E., *Voting and Election Laws* (Oceana, 1960).

Strong, S. D., *Negroes, Ballots, and Judges* (U. of Alabama, 1968).

Taper, B., *Gomillion Versus Lightfoot: The Tuskegee Gerrymander Case* (McGraw-Hill, 1962).

Williamson, C., *American Suffrage from Property to Democracy. 1760–1860* (Princeton, 1968).

VIII. EXPRESSION: SPEECH, PRESS, AND PETITION: speech, subversion, conspiracy, civil disobedience, the press, radio, television, motion pictures, books, libel, petition. (See also: IV., Criminal Law and Procedure; IX., Assembly and Association; XI., Academic Freedom; XII., Morals and Censorship.)

Alexander, J., *A Brief Narrative of the Case and Trial of John Peter Zenger*, ed. by S. N. Katz (Belknap, 1963).

American Newspaper Publishers Association, *Fair Trial and Free Press* (A.B.A., 1966).

Anastaplo, G., *The Constitutionalist: Notes on the First Amendment* (S.M.U., 1971).

Angoff, C., *The Book of Libel*, 2nd ed. (Barnes & Noble, 1966).

Arendt, H., *On Violence* (Harcourt, Brace & World, 1969).

Arthur, W. A., and R. L. Crossman. *The Law of Newspapers* (McGraw-Hill, 1940).

Barron, J. A., *Freedom of the Press For Whom: The Right of Access to Mass Media* (Indiana U., 1973).

Becker, C. L., *Freedom and Responsibility in the American Way of Life* (Knopf, 1945).

Berns, W., *Freedom, Virtue, and the First Amendment* (L.S.U., 1957).

Blumer, H., and P. Houser, *Movies, Delinquency and Crime* (Macmillan, 1933).

Bollan, W., *The Freedom of Speech and Writing Upon Public Affairs Considered* (Da Capo, 1970).

Bosmajian, H. (ed.), *The Principles and Practice of Freedom of Speech* (Houghton Mifflin, 1971).

Brucker, H., *Freedom of Information* (Macmillan, 1949).

Buranelli, V. (ed.), *The Trial of Peter Zenger* (N.Y.U., 1957).

Bush, C. R. (ed.), *Free Press and Fair Trial* (U. of Georgia, 1970).

Capaldi, N. (ed.), *Clear and Present Danger: The Free Speech Controversy* (Pegasus, 1969).

Casey, R. D. (ed.), *The Press in Perspective* (Louisiana State U., 1963).

Castberg, F., *Freedom of Speech in the West* (Oceana, 1960).

Caughey, J. W., *In Clear and Present Danger: The Critical State of Our Freedoms* (U. of Chicago, 1958).

Chafee, Z., *Free Speech in the United States* (Harvard, 1941).

———, *Freedom of Speech* (Harcourt, 1920).

———, *Freedom of Speech and Press* (Harvard, 1955).

———, *Government and Mass Communication: A Report from the Commission on Freedom of the Press*, rev. ed. (Anchor, 1965).

———, *Thirty-five Years with Freedom of Speech* (Harvard, 1952).

Chener, W. L., *Freedom of the Press* (Harcourt, Brace, 1955).

Childress, J. F., *Civil Disobedience and Political Obligation* (Yale, 1971).

Clark, D. G., and E. R. Hutchinson, *Mass Media and the Law: Freedom and Restraint* (Wiley, 1970).

Clor, H. M. (ed.), *Civil Disorder and Violence: Essays on Causes and Cures* (Rand-McNally, 1972).

Clyde, W., *The Struggle for Freedom of the Press from Caxton to Cromwell* (Oxford, 1934).

Cogley, J., *Report on Blacklisting*, Vol. I.: *Movies*; Vol. II.: *Radio-TV* (Fund for the Republic, 1956).

Cohen, C., *Civil Disobedience: Conscience, Tactics and the Law* (U. of California, 1971).

Commager, H. S., *Freedom, Loyalty, Dissent* (Oxford, 1954).

Commission on Freedom of the Press, *American Radio: A Report on Broadcasting in the United States* (U. of Chicago, 1947).

———, *A Free and Responsible Press: A General Report on Mass Communication* (U. of Chicago, 1947).

———, *Freedom of the Movies: A Report on Self-Regulation from the Commission on Freedom of the Press*, ed. by Ruth A. Inglias (U. of Chicago, 1947).

———, *Freedom of the Press: A Framework of Principle* (U. of Chicago, 1947).

———, *People Speaking to People: A Report on International Mass Communication* (U. of Chicago, 1948).

Cooper, K., *The Right to Know: An Exposition of the Evils of News Suppression and Propaganda* (Farrar, Straus & Cudahy, 1956).

Cord, R. L., *Protest, Dissent and the Supreme Court* (Winthrop, 1971).

Cowen, Z., *Fair Trial v. a Free Press* (Center for the Study of Democratic Institutions, 1965).

Craig, A., *The Banned Books of England and Other Countries* (Allen and Unwin, 1962).

Cross, H. L., *The People's Right to Know* (Columbia, 1953).

Daniels, W. M. (ed.), *The Censorship of Books* (Wilson, 1954).

Davis, D. B. (ed.), *The Fear of Conspiracy: Images of Un-American Subversion from the Revolution to the Present* (Cornell, 1971).

Davis, J. C. (ed.), *When Men Revolt—and Why* (Free Press, 1970).

Dawson, S. A., *Freedom of the Press* (Columbia, 1924).

Dean, J., *Hatred, Ridicule, or Contempt: A Book of Libel Cases* (Constable, 1953).

DeGrazia, E., *Censorship Landmarks* (Bowker, 1970).

Douglas, W. O., *Points of Rebellion* (Random House, 1970).

Downs, R. B. (ed.), *The First Freedom, Liberty, and Justice in the World of Books and Readings* (A.D.A., 1960).

Drinker, H. S., *Some Observations of the Freedoms of the First Amendment* (Boston U., 1957).

Eidenberg, E., and R. D. Morey, *An Act of Congress: The Legislative Process and the Making of Education Policy* (Norton, 1969).

Emerson, T. I., *The System of Freedom of Expression* (Random House, 1972).

———, *Toward a General Theory of the First Amendment* (Random House, 1967).

Ernst, M. L., *The First Freedom* (Macmillan, 1946).

Faulk, J. H., *Fear on Trial* (Simon & Schuster, 1964).

Fellman, D., *The Limits of Freedom* (Rutgers, 1959).

Felsher, H., and M. Rosen, *The Press in the Jury Box* (Macmillan, 1966).

Fisher, P., and R. Lowenstein (eds.), *Race and the News Media* (A.D.L., 1967).

Fliess, P. J., *Freedom of the Press in the German Republic, 1918–1933* (L.S.U., 1955).

Fortas, A., *Concerning Dissent and Civil Disobedience* (New American Library, 1968).

Freeman, H. A., *et al.*, *Civil Disobedience* (Center for the Study of Democratic Institutions, 1966).

Friedman, L., *The Wise Minority: An Argument for Draft Resistance and Civil Disobedience* (Dial, 1971).

Friendly, A., and R. L. Goldfarb, *Crime and Publicity: The Impact of News on the Administration of Justice* (20th Century Fund, 1967).

Georgetown Law Journal, *Media and the First Amendment in a Free Society* (U. of Massachusetts, 1974).

Gerald, J. E., *The Press and the Constitution, 1931–1947* (U. of Minnesota, 1948).

Gill, J., *Tide Without Turning: Elijah P. Lovejoy and Freedom of the Press* (Starr King, 1958).

Gillett, C. R., *Banned Books*, Vols. 1 and 2 (Columbia, 1932).

Gillmor, D. M., *Free Press and Fair Trial* (Public Affairs Press, 1966).

Glessing, R. J., *The Underground Press in America* (Indiana U., 1971).

Goldfarb, R. L., *The Contempt Power* (Columbia, 1963).

Goldstein, M. J., *et al.*, *Pornography and Sexual Deviance* (U. of California, 1970).

Goldwin, R. A. (ed.), *Civil Disobedience: Essays Old and New* (Rand McNally, 1969).

Goodman, W., *The Committee: The Extraordinary Career of the House Committee on Un-American Activities* (Farrar, Straus, 1968).

Grey, D. L., *The Supreme Court and the News Media* (Northwestern, 1968).

Gurr, T. R., *Why Men Rebel* (Princeton, 1970).

Hachten, W. A., *The Supreme Court and the Press* (Public Affairs Press, 1965).

———, *The Supreme Court on Freedom of the Press: Decisions and Dissents* (Iowa State U., 1968).

Haight, A. L., *Banned Books* (Bowker, 1956).

Haiman, F. S., *Freedom of Speech: Issues and Cases* (Random House, 1965).

Haney, R. W., *Comstockery in America* (Houghton-Mifflin, 1956).

Hay, G., *Two Essays on the Liberty of the Press* (Da Capo, 1970).

Hocking, W. E., *Freedom of the Press: A Framework of Principle* (U. of Chicago, 1945).

Hohenberg, J., *Free Press: Free People: The Best Cause* (Columbia, 1971).

Hudon, E. G., *Freedom of Speech and Press in America* (Public Affairs Press, 1963).

Hughes, F., *Prejudice and the Press* (Devin-Adair, 1950).

Hyde, H. M., *Privacy and the Press* (Butterworth, 1947).

Ickes, H. L., *Freedom of the Press Today* (Vanguard, 1941).

Inglis, R. A., *Freedom of the Movies* (U. of Chicago, 1947).

Jackson, H., *The Fear of Books* (London, 1932).

Jennison, P., *Freedom To Read* (Public Affairs Pamphlets, 1965).

Johnson, G. W., *Peril and Promise: An Inquiry into Freedom of the Press* (Harper, 1958).

Kadish, M. R., and S. H. Kadish, *Discretion To Disobey* (Stanford, 1973).

Kahn, G., *Hollywood on Trial* (Boni and Gear, 1948).

Kalven, H., Jr., *The Negro and the First Amendment* (U. of Chicago, 1965).

Kaplan, M. A., *Dissent and the State in Peace and War* (Dunellen, 1970).

Konvitz, M. R., *First Amendment Freedoms: Selected Cases on Freedom of Religion, Speech, Press, Assembly* (Cornell, 1963).

——, *Fundamental Liberties of a Free People: Religion, Speech, Press, Assembly* (Cornell, 1957).

Krislov, S., *The Supreme Court and Political Freedom* (Free Press, 1968).

Lacy, D., *Freedom and Communication* (Illinois U., 1961).

Levy, L. W., *Freedom of the Press from Zenger to Jefferson* (Bobbs-Merrill, 1967).

——, *Legacy of Suppression: Freedom of Speech and Press in Early American History* (Harvard, 1960).

Lofton, J., *Justice and the Press* (Beacon, 1967).

Luskin, J., *Lippmann, Liberty and the Press* (U. of Alabama, 1972).

McClennan, G. S., *Censorship in the United States* (Wilson, 1967).

McCoy, R. E., *Freedom of the Press: An Annotated Bibliography* (Southern Illinois U., 1968).

Medina, H. R., *Freedom of the Press and Fair Trial: Final Report with Recommendations*, Columbia, 1967).

Meiklejohn, A., *Free Speech and Its Relation to Self-Government* (Harper, 1948).

——, *Political Freedom: The Constitutional Powers of the People* (Oxford, 1960, 1965).

Miller, J. O., *Crisis in Freedom: The Alien and Sedition Acts* (Little, Brown, 1951).

Miller, M., *The Judges and the Judged* (Doubleday, 1952).

Morloon, S. E., F. Merck, and F. Freidel, *Dissent in Three American Wars* (Harvard, 1971).

Murphy, P. L., *The Meaning of Freedom of Speech: First Amendment Freedom from Wilson to FDR* (Greenwood, 1973).

Nelson, H. L. (ed.), *Freedom of the Press from Hamilton to the Warren Court* (Bobbs-Merrill, 1967).

————, *Libel in News of Congressional Investigating Committees* (U. of Minnesota, 1961).

Nizer, L., *The Jury Returns* (Doubleday, 1966).

O'Neil, R. M., *Free Speech* (Bobbs-Merrill, 1972).

Patterson, G., *Free Speech and a Free Press* (Little, Brown, 1939).

Pember, D. R., *Privacy and the Press: The Law, the Mass Media and the First Amendment* (U. of Washington, 1972).

Phelps, R. E., and E. D. Hamilton, *Libel* (Macmillan, 1967).

Randall, R. S., *Censorship of the Movies: The Social and Political Control of a Mass Medium* (U. of Wisconsin, 1968).

Raymond, A., *The People's Right to Know: A Report on Government News Suppression* (A.C.L.U., 1955).

Rose, A. M., *Libel and Academic Freedom: A Lawsuit Against Political Extremists* (U. of Minnesota, 1968).

Royal Commission on the Press, *Report of the Royal Commission on the Press, 1947–1949* (H.M.G.P.O., 1949).

Rucker, B. W., *The First Freedom* (Southern Illinois U., 1968).

Schroeder, T., *Constitutional Free Speech: Defined and Defended* (Da Capo, 1970).

Seldes, G., *Freedom of the Press* (Bobbs-Merrill, 1935).

————, *The People Don't Know* (Gaer Association, 1949).

Shapiro, M., *Freedom of Speech: The Supreme Court and Judicial Review* (Prentice-Hall, 1966).

————, *The Pentagon Papers and the Courts* (Chandler, 1972).

Short, J. F. (ed.), *Collective Violence* (Aldine-Atherton, 1972).

Shuman, S. I. (comp.), *Law and Disorder: The Legitimacy of Direct Action as an Instrument of Social Policy* (Wayne State U,. 1971).

Siebert, F. S., *Freedom of the Press in England, 1476–1776* (U. of Illinois, 1952).

————, *The Rights and Privileges of the Press* (Appleton-Century, 1934).

Smead, E. E., *Freedom of Speech by Radio and Television* (Public Affairs Press, 1958).

Smith, H. L., *Behind the Press in South Africa* (Stewart, 1947).

Smith, J. M., *Freedom of Speech by Radio and Television* (Public Affairs Press, 1958).

Sorel, G., *Reflections on Violence* (Collier, 1961).

Special Committee on Radio and Television of the Association of the Bar of the City of New York, *Radio, Television, and the Administration of Justice* (Columbia, 1967).

Spicer, G. W., *The Supreme Court and Fundamental Freedom* (Appleton-Century, 1959).

Spring, S., *Risks and Rights in Publishing, Television, Radio, Motion Pictures, Advertising, and the Theatre* (Allen & Unwin, 1952).

Sullivan, H., *Trial by Newspaper* (Patriot, 1961).

Swayze, H., *Political Control of Literature in the U.S.S.R.: 1946–1959* (Howard, 1962).

Taylor, T., *Two Studies in Constitutional Interpretation . . . and Fair Trial and Free Press* (Ohio State U., 1969).

Thayer, F., *Legal Control of the Press* (Foundation Press, 1944).

Thomas, E. C., *Law of Libel and Slander*, 3rd ed. (Oceana, 1973).

Thoreau, H. D., *The Variorum Civil Disobedience*, ed. by W. Harding (Twayne, 1967).

Van Den Haag, E., *Political Violence and Civil Disobedience* (Harper, 1972).

Von Der Mehden, F. R., *Comparative Political Violence* (Prentice- Hall, 1973).

Walzer, M., *Obligations: Essays on Disobedience, War and Citizenship* (Harvard, 1970).

Wasserstrom, W., *Civil Liberties and the Arts* (Syracuse U., 1964).

White, L., *The American Radio* (U. of Chicago, 1947).

Wiggins, J. R., *Freedom or Secrecy* (Oxford, 1956).

Williams, F., *Press, Parliament and People* (Heinemann, 1946).

Wittenberg, P. (ed.), *Dangerous Words: A Guide to the Law of Libel* (Columbia, 1960).

Wolff, R. P., *In Defense of Anarchism* (Harper & Row, 1970).

Yankewich, L. R., *It's Libel or Contempt If You Print It* (Parker, 1950).

Young, A. F. (ed.), *Dissent: Explorations in the History of American Radicalism* (Northern Illinois U., 1968).

Zashin, E. M., *Civil Disobedience and Democracy* (Free Press, 1971).

Zinn, H., *Disobedience and Democracy* (Random House, 1968).

IX. ASSEMBLY AND ASSOCIATION (See also: VIII., Expression: Speech, Press, and Petition.)

Abernathy, G., *The Right of Assembly and Association* (Amer. Jewish Comm., 1957).

American Jewish Committee, *Assault Upon Freedom of Association* (Amer. Jewish Comm., 1957).

Fellman, D., *The Constitutional Right of Association* (U. of Chicago, 1963).

Mintz, B., with R. Spenser and J. R. Robinson, *Assault Upon Freedom of Association* (Amer. Jewish Comm., 1959).

Rice, C. E., *Freedom of Association* (N.Y.U., 1962).

Robertson, D. B. (ed.), *Voluntary Associations: A Study of Groups in Free Societies* Knox, 1966).

Smith, B., *A Dangerous Freedom* (Lippincott, 1954).

X. RELIGION (See also: V., Military Justice in Peace and War; VIII., Expression: Speech, Press, and Petition; XII., Morals and Censorship.)

A. FREE EXERCISE.

Allport, G. W., *The Individual and His Religion* (Macmillan, 1954).

Bates, M. S., *Religious Liberty: An Inquiry* (Harper, 1954).

Blackham, H. J., *Religion in a Modern Society* (Ungar, 1966).

Blakely, W. A., *American State Papers and Related Documents on Freedom in Religion* (Religious Liberty Assoc., 1949).

Blau, J. L. (ed.), *Cornerstones of Religious Freedom in America* (Beacon, 1949).

Brady, J. H., *Confusion Twice Confounded: The First Amendment and the Supreme Court* (Seton Hall U., 1954).

Burstein, A., *Law Concerning Religion in the United States* (Oceana, 1950).

Cogley, J. (ed.), *Religion in America* (Meridian, 1958).

Cohen, R., *Sunday in the Sixties* (Public Affairs Pamphlet, 1965).

Davis, J. W., Jr., and K. M. Dolbeare, *Little Groups of Neighbors: The Selective Service System* (Markham, 1968).

Drinker, H. S., *Some Observations on the Freedoms of the First Amendment* (Boston U., 1957).

Dunn, W. K., *What Happened to Religious Education: The Decline of Religious Teaching in the Public Elementary School, 1776–1861* (Johns Hopkins, 1958).

Educational Policies Commission, *Moral and Spiritual Values in the Public Schools* (N.E.A., 1951).

Fellman, D., *The Limits of Freedom* (Rugters, 1959).

Fenton, J. H., *The Catholic Vote* (Hauser, 1960).

Finn, J. (ed.), *A Conflict of Loyalties: The Case for Selective Conscientious Objection* (Pegasus, 1968).

Hartford, E. F., *Moral Values in Public Education: Lessons from the Kentucky Experience* (Harper, 1958).

Henry, V., *The Place of Religion in Public Schools: A Handbook To Guide Communities* (Harper, 1950).

Herberg, W., *Protestant-Catholic-Jew*, rev. ed. (Doubleday, 1960).

Hudson, W. S., *Religion in America* (Scribner's, 1968).

Johns, W. L., *Dateline Sunday, U.S.A.* (Pacific Press Publ. Assn., 1967).

Konvitz, M. R., *Religious Liberty and Conscience: A Constitutional Inquiry* (Viking, 1969).

Lincoln, C. E., *The Black Muslims in America* (Beacon, 1961).

McCollum, V., *One Woman's Fight*, rev. ed. (Beacon, 1961).

McGrath, J. J. (ed.), *Church and State in American Law* (Bruce, 1962).

Manwaring, D. R., *Render Unto Caesar: The Flag Salute Controversy* (U. of Chicago, 1962).

Marnell, W. H., *The First Amendment: The History of Religious Freedom in America* (Doubleday, 1966).

———, *The First Amendment: Religious Freedom in America from Colonial Days to the School Prayer Controversy* (Anchor, 1966).

Miller, P., *Roger Williams* (Bobbs-Merrill, 1953).

Miller, W. L., *Religion and the Free Society* (Fund for the Republic, 1958).

O'Brien, F. W., *Justice Reed and the First Amendment: The Religion Clauses* (Georgetown U., 1958).

Pike, E. R., *Jehovah's Witnesses* (Philosophical Library, 1954).

Porter, E. S., *Conscience and the Court* (Prentice-Hall, 1962).

Raab, E. (ed.), *Religious Conflict in America: Studies of the Problem Beyond Bigotry* (Doubleday, 1964).

Rodgers, H. R., Jr., *Community Conflict, Public Opinion and the Law: The Amish Dispute in Iowa* (Merrill, 1969).

Rutherford, J. F., *Enemies* (Watchtower Society, 1937).

Simon, G., *Church, State and Opposition in the U.S.S.R.* (U. of California, 1973).

Stevick, D. B., *Civil Disobedience and the Christian* (Seabury, 1969).

Stroup, H., *The Jehovah's Witnesses* (Columbia, 1945).

Torpey, W. G., *Judicial Doctrines of Religious Rights in America* (U. of North Carolina, 1948).

B. SEPARATION OF CHURCH AND STATE.

Acton, J. E. E. Dalberg-Acton, 1st Baron, *Esays on Church and State* (Viking, 1953).

Adams, J. L., *The Growing Church Lobby in Washington* (Eerdmans, 1970).

Alley, R. S., *So Help Me God: Religion and the Presidency* (John Knox Press, 1972).
American Association of School Administrators, *Religion in the Public Schools* (A.A.S.A., 1964).
Antieau, D. J., *Freedom From Federal Establishment* (Bruce, 1964).
Bailey, S. K., and E. K. Mosher, *ESEA: The Office of Education Administers a Law* (Syracuse U., 1968).
Balk, A., *The Religion Business* (John Knox Press, 1969).
Barker, Sir E., *Church, State, and Education* (U. of Michigan, 1957).
Barnes, R. P., *Under Orders: The Churches and Public Affairs* (Doubleday, 1961).
Beth, L. P., *The American Theory of Church and State* (U. of Florida, 1958).
Blanshard, P., *American Freedom and Catholic Power* (Beacon, 1958).
———, *Communism, Democracy and Catholic Power* (Beacon, 1951).
———, *God and Man in Washington* (Beacon, 1960).
———, *Religion and the Schools: The Great Controversy* (Beacon, 1963).
Blum, V. C., *Freedom in Education: Federal Aid for All Children* (Doubleday, 1965).
Boles, D. E., *The Two Swords: Commentaries and Cases on Religion and Education* (Iowa State U., 1967).
———, *The Bible, Religion and the Public Schools*, 3rd ed. (Iowa State U,. 1965).
Brady, J. H., *Confusion Twice Confounded: The First Amendment and the Supreme Court* (Seton Hall U., 1954).
Brickman, W. W., and S. Lehrer, *Religion, Government and Education* (Soc. for Adv. of Education, 1961).
Brown, N. C. (ed.), *The Study of Religion in the Public Schools: An Appraisal* (Amer. Council on Education, 1958).
Butts, R. F., *The American Tradition in Religion and Education* (Beacon, 1950).
Callahan, D. J. (ed.), *Federal Aid and Catholic Schools* (Helicon, 1964).
Cogdell, G. D., *What Price Parochaid?* (Amer. United for Sep. of Church and State, 1970).
Cogley, J. (ed.), *Religion in America* (Meridian, 1958).
Corwin, E. S., *A Constitution of Power in a Secular State* (Michie, 1951).
Costanzo, J., S.J., *This Nation Under God: Church, State and Schools in America* (Herder and Herder, 1964).
Dawson, J. M., *America's Way in Church, State and Society* (Macmillan, 1953).
———, *Separate Church and State Now* (R. R. Smith, 1948).
Dierenfield, R., *Religion in American Public Schools* (Public Affairs Press, 1962).
Doerr, E., *The Conspiracy That Failed* (Amer. United for Sep. of Church and State, 1968).
Dolbeare, K. M., and P. E. Hammond, *The School Prayer Decisions: From Court Policy to Local Practice* (U. of Chicago, 1971).
Douglas, W. O., *The Bible and the Schools* (Little, Brown, 1966).
Drinan, R. F., *Religion, the Courts and Public Policy* (McGraw-Hill, 1963).
Drinker, H. S., *Some Observations on the Freedoms of the First Amendment* (Boston U., 1957).
Drovin, E. G., *The School Question: A Bibliography and Church-State Relationship in American Education, 1940–1960* (Catholic U., 1963).
Dulce, B., and E. J. Richter, *Religion and the Presidency* (Macmillan, 1962).
Dunn, W. K., *What Happened to Religious Education?* (Johns Hopkins, 1965).

Ebersole, L., *Church Lobbying in the Nation's Capitol* (Macmillan, 1951).

Edwards, N., *The Courts and the Public Schools* (U. of Chicago, 1971).

Ehler, S. E., and J. B. Morrall, *Church and State Through the Centuries* (Newman, 1954).

Eidenberg, E., and R. D. Morey, *An Act of Congress* (Norton, 1969).

Erickson, D. A. (ed.), *Public Controls for Nonpublic Schools* (U. of Chicago, 1969).

Fellman, D., *Religion in American Public Law* (Boston U., 1965).

—— (ed.), *The Supreme Court and Education* (Columbia, 1960).

Frazier, E. F., *The Negro Church in America* (Schocken, 1969).

Freund, P. A., and R. Ulich, *Religion and the Public Schools* (Harvard, 1965).

Frommer, A. (ed.), *The Bible and the Public Schools* (Liberal Press, 1963).

Fuchs, L. H., *John F. Kennedy and American Catholicism* (Meredith, 1967).

Gabel, R. J., *Public Funds for Church and Private Schools* (Catholic U., 1937).

Gellhorn, W., and R. K. Greenawalt, *The Sectarian College and the Public Purse: Fordham—A Case Study* (Oceana, 1970).

Georgetown University Institute for Church-State Law, *Freedom from Federal Establishment* (Bruce, 1964).

Gianella, D. A. (ed.), *Religion and the Public Order* (U. of Chicago, 1964 ff).

Gordis, R., *Religion and the Schools* (Fund for the Republic, 1959).

Greene, E. B., *Religion and the State: The Making and Testing of an American Tradition* (Cornell, 1959).

Griffiths, W. E., *Religion, the Courts, and the Public Schools* (Anderson, 1966).

Healey, R. M., *Jefferson on Religion in Public Education* (Yale, 1964).

Heeley, A. V., *Why the Private School?* (Harper, 1951).

Herzog, A., *The Church Trap* (Macmillan, 1969).

Hook, S., *Religion in a Free Society* (U. of Nebraska, 1967).

Howe, M. de W., *Cases on Church and State in the United States* (Harvard, 1952).

——, *The Garden and the Wilderness: Religion and Government in American Constitutional History* (U. of Chicago, 1965).

Johnson, A. W. and F. Yost, *Separation of Church and State in the United States* (U. of Minnesota, 1948).

Johnson, F. E. (ed.), *American Education and Religion: The Problem of Religion in the Schools* (Harper, 1952).

Kallen, J. M., *Secularism Is the Will of God: An Essay in the Social Philosophy of Democracy and Religion* (Twayne, 1954).

Katz, W. G., *Religion and American Constitutions* (Northwestern, 1964).

Kauper, P. G., *Civil Liberties and the Constitution* (U. of Michigan, 1962).

——, *Religion and the Constitution* (L.S.U., 1964).

Kerwin, J. G., *Catholic Viewpoint on Church and State* (Hanover House, 1960).

Kik, J. M., *The Supreme Court and Prayer in the Public Schools* (Presbyterian, 1963).

Kilpatrick, J. J., *The Southern Case for School Segregation* (Crowell, Collier, 1962).

Krinsky, F., *The Politics of Religion in America* (Glencoe,, 1968).

Kurland, P. B., *Religion and the Law: Of Church and State and the Supreme Court* (Aldine, 1962).

Lanove, G., *Public Funds for Parochial Schools?* (N.C.C.C., U.S.A., 1963).

Laubach, J. H., *School Prayers: Congress, the Courts and the Public* (Public Affairs Press, 1969).

Lekachman, R., *et al.*, *The Churches and the Public* (Center for the Study of Democratic Institutions, 1960).

Lenski, G., *The Religion Factor* (Doubleday, 1961).

Lo Bello, N., *The Vatican Empire* (Trident, 1969).

Lowell, C. S., *The Embattled Wall* (Americans United, 1966).

——, *The Great Church-State Fraud* (Luce, 1973).

McCluskey, N. G., *Catholic Viewpoint on Education* (Hanover House, 1959).

McGill, R., *A Church, A School* (Abingdon, 1959).

Madden, W., *Religious Values and Secular Education* (Columbia, 1950).

Manwaring, D., *Religion, Liberty and the State* (Bobbs-Merrill, 1971).

Mason, R. E., *Moral Values and Secular Education* (Columbia, 1950).

Masters, N. A., R. H. Salisbury, and T. H. Eliot, *State Politics and the Public Schools* (Knopf, 1964).

Meranto, P., *The Politics of Federal Aid to Education in 1965: A Study in Political Innovation* (Syracuse U., 1967).

Michaelson, R., *Piety in the Public School* (Macmillan, 1970).

Moehlman, C., *Wall of Separation Between Church and State* (Beacon, 1951).

Morgan, R. E., *The Politics of Religious Conflict: Church and State in America* (Pegasus, 1968).

——, *The Supreme Court and Religion* (Free Press, 1972).

Muir, W. K., *Prayer in the Public Schools: Law and Attitude Change* (U. of Chicago, 1967).

Nichols, R. F., *Religion and American Democracy* (L.S.U., 1959).

Northwestern University Law Review, *Contemporary Problems in Church-State Relations* (Da Capo, 1971).

Oaks, D. H. (ed.), *The Wall Between Church and State* (U. of Chicago, 1963).

Odegard, P. H., *Religion and Politics* (Oceana, 1960).

O'Neill, J. M., *Catholicism and American Freedom* (Harper, 1952).

——, *Religion and Education Under the Constitution* (Harper, 1949).

Parsons, W. P., S.J., *The First Freedom: Considerations on Church and State in the United States* (McMullen, 1948).

Pfeffer, L., *Church, State and Freedom*, rev. enl. ed. (Beacon, 1967).

——, *Creeds in Competition* (Harper, 1959).

Pike, J. A., *A Roman Catholic in the White House* (Doubleday, 1960).

Powell, T., *The School Bus Law: A Case Study in Education, Religion, and Politics* (Wesleyan, 1960).

Pratt, J. W., *Religion, Politics, and Diversity: The Church-State Theme in New York History* (Cornell, 1967).

Raab, E. (ed.), *Religious Conflict in America* (Anchor, 1964).

Reutter, E. E., Jr., *Schools and the Law* (Oceana, 1965).

Rice, C. E., *The Supreme Court and Public Prayers: The Need for Restraint* (Fordham, 1964).

Robertson, D. B., *Should Churches Be Saved?* (Westminster, 1969).

Robison, J. B., *The Case Against Parochaid* (A.C.L.U., 1972).

Rock, J., *The Time Has Come* (Knopf, 1963).

St. John-Stevas, N., *Birth Control and Public Policy* (Center for the Study of Democratic Institutions, 1960).

Schultz, H. E., *Religious Education and the Public Schools* (Berkeley, 1955).

Shaver, E. L., *The Weekday Church School* (Pilgrim, 1956).

Shields, C., *Democracy and Catholicism in America* (McGraw-Hill, 1958).

Silvert, K. H., *Churches and States: The Religious Institution and Modernization* (Amer. U. Field Staff, 1967).

Smith, E. A., *Religious Liberty in the United States: The Development of Church-State Thought Since the Revolutionary Era* (Fortress Press, 1972).

Stallo, J. B., *The Bible in the Public Schools* (R. Clarke, 1870).

Stedman, M. S., Jr., *Religion and Politics in America* (Harcourt, Brave & World, 1964).

Stokes, A. P., and L. Pfeffer, *Church and State in the United States*, rev. ed. (Harper & Row, 1964).

———, *Church and State in the United States*, 3 vols. (Harper, 1950).

Swomley, J. M., Jr., *Religion, the State and the Schools* (Pegasus, 1969).

Thayer, V. T., *The Attack upon the American Secular School* (Beacon, 1951).

———, *The Role of the School in American Society* (Dodd, Mead, 1966).

Tussman, J., *The Supreme Court on Church and State* (Oxford, 1962).

Umbret, L., *Render Unto the People* (Abingdon, 1946).

Walter, E. A. (ed.), *Religion and the State University* (U. of Michigan, 1958).

Ward, H. H., *Space-Age Sunday* (Macmillan, 1960).

Ward, L. R., *Federal Aid to Private Schools* (Newman, 1964).

———, *Religion in All the Schools* (Fides, 1960).

Wilson, J. F. (ed.), *Church and State in American History* (Heath, 1965).

Wolf, D. J., S.J., *Toward Consensus: Catholic-Protestant Interpretations of Church and State* (Doubleday, 1968).

Zabel, O. H., *God and Caesar in Nebraska: A Study of the Legal Relationship of Church and State, 1854–1954* (U. of Nebraska, 1955).

XI. ACADEMIC FREEDOM (See also: VIII., Speech, Press and Petition; XII., Morals and Censorship.)

Baade, H. W., and R. O. Everett (eds.), *Academic Freedom: The Scholar's Place in Modern Society* (Oceana, 1964).

Barth, A., *The Loyalty of Free Men*, new ed. (Anchor, 1965).

Beale, H. K., *Are American Teachers Free?* (Scribner's, 1936).

Byse, C., and L. Joughin, *Tenure in American Higher Education* (Cornell, 1959).

Caughey, J. W., *In Clear and Present Danger: The Critical State of Our Freedoms* (U. of Chicago, 1960).

Chambers, M. M., *The Colleges and the Courts, 1946–1950: Judicial Decisions Regarding Higher Education in the United States* (Columbia, 1952).

Countryman, V., *Un-American Activities in the State of Washington* (Cornell, 1951).

Douglas, W. O., *Freedom of the Mind* (Doubleday, 1964).

Earle, J., et al., *On Academic Freedom* (L.R.S., 1971).

Ehlers, H., and C. L. Gordon (eds.), *Crucial Issues in Education* (Holt, 1959).

Fellman, D. (ed.), *The Supreme Court and Education* (Columbia, 1960).

Gardner, D. P., *The California Oath Controversy* (U. of California, 1967).

Hofstadter, R., and W. P. Metzger, *The Development of Academic Freedom in the United States* (Columbia, 1955).

Hook, S., *Academic Freedom and Academic Tenure* (Cowles, 1969).
———, *Heresy, Yes—Conspiracy, No!* (Day, 1953).
Hurburd, D., *This Happened in Pasadena* (Macmillan, 1951).
Iversen, R. W., *The Communists and the Schools* (Harcourt, Brace, 1959).
Jones, H. M. (ed.), *Primer of Intellectual Freedom* (Harvard, 1959).
Joughin, L. (ed.), *Academic Freedom and Tenure: A Handbook for the AAUP* (U. of Wisconsin, 1969).
Kahn, J., *The Threat to Academic Freedom* (Horizon, 1956).
Kirk, R., *Academic Freedom: An Essay in Definition* (Regnery, 1955).
Kruytbosch, C. E., and S. L. Messinger, *The State of the University: Authority and Change* (Sage, 1970).
Lamont, C., *Freedom Is as Freedom Does: Civil Liberties Today* (Horizon, 1956).
Lipset, S. M. (ed.), *Student Politics* (Basic Books, 1967).
MacIver, R. M., *Academic Freedom in Our Time* (Columbia, 1955).
Melby, E. O., and M. Puner, *Freedom and Public Education* (Praeger, 1953).
Metzger, W. P., and R. Hofstadter, *Academic Freedom in the United States* (Columbia, 1955).
Metzger, W. P., et al., *Dimensions of Academic Freedom* (U. of Illinois, 1968).
Moos, M., and F. Rourke, *The Campus and the State* (Johns Hopkins, 1959).
Morison, S. E., *Freedom in Contemporary Society* (Little, Brown, 1956).
National Council of Teachers of English, *The Student's Right to Read* (N.C.T.E., 1963).
Nelson, J., and G. Roberts, Jr., *The Censor and the Schools* (Little, Brown, 1963).
Reutter, E. E., Jr., *The School Administrator and Subversive Activities* (Columbia, 1951).
Rose, A. M., *Libel and Academic Freedom* (U. of Minnesota, 1968).
Stewart, G. R., *The Year of the Oath: The Fight for Academic Freedom at the University of California* (Doubleday, 1950).
Summers, R. E. (ed.), *Freedom and Loyalty in Our Colleges* (Wilson, 1954).
Taylor, H., *On Education and Freedom* (Abelard-Schuman, 1954).
Van Doren, M., *Man's Rights to Knowledge, and the Free Use Thereof* (Columbia, 1954).
Walter, E. A. (ed.), *Religion and the State University* (U. of Michigan, 1958).
Williamson, E. G., and J. L. Cowan, *The American Student's Freedom of Expression: A Research Appraisal* (U. of Minnesota, 1966).

XII. MORALS, OBSCENITY AND CENSORSHIP (See also: VIII., Speech, Press and Petition; X., Freedom of Religion; XI., Academic Freedom.)

Beman, L., *Selected Articles on Censorship of the Theatre and Moving Pictures* (Wilson, 1961).
Blanshard, P., *The Right to Read: The Battle Against Censorship* (Beacon, 1955).
Boyer, P. S., *Purity in Print: The Nice Society's Movement and Book Censorship in America* (Scribner's, 1968).
Broun, H., and M. Leech, *Anthony Comstock: Roundsman of the Lord* (Boni, 1927).
Brucker, H., *Freedom of Information* (Macmillan, 1945).
Carmen, I. H., *Movies, Censorship and the Law* (U. of Michigan, 1966).

Chafee, Z., *Government and Mass Communication* (U. of Chicago, 1947).

Chandos, J. (ed.), *To Deprave and Corrupt* (Associated Press, 1963).

Clor, H. M., *Obscenity and Public Morality: Censorship in a Liberal Society* (U. of Chicago, 1969).

———— (ed.), *Censorship and Freedom of Expression: Essays on Obscenity and Law* (Rand McNally, 1971).

Cogley, J., *Report on Blacklisting*, Vol. I: *Movies*; Vol. II: *Radio-TV* (Fund for the Republic, 1956).

Commission on Freedom of the Press, *People Speaking to People: A Report on International Mass Communication* (U. of Chicago, 1948).

————, *Mass Communication: A Report from the Commission on Freedom of the Press* (U. of Chicago, 1947).

Craig, A., *The Banned Books of England and Other Countries* (Allen and Unwin, 1962).

————, *Suppressed Books: A History of the Conception of Literary Obscenity* (World, 1963).

Crowther, B., *Movies and Censorship* (Public Affairs Pamphlets, 1965).

Daniels, W. M., (ed.), *The Censorship of Books* (Wilson, 1954).

Dennett, M. W., *Birth Control Laws: Shall We Keep Them, Change Them or Abolish Them?* (Hitchcock, 1926).

Devlin, Sir P., *The Enforcement of Morals* (Oxford, 1968).

Ernst, M. L., and A. Lindley, *The Censor Marches On* (Doubleday, Doran, 1940).

————, and U. Schwartz, *Censorship: The Search for the Obscene* (Macmillan, 1964).

————, and W. Seagle, *To the Pure: A Study of Obscenity and the Censor* (Viking, 1928).

Fellman, D., *The Censorship of Books* (Hauser, 1957).

Fiske, M., *Book Selection and Censorship* (Berkeley, 1959).

Ford, J., *Criminal Obscenity: A Plea for Its Suppression* (Revell, 1926).

Gardiner, R. C., *Catholic Viewpoints on Censorship* (Hanover House, 1957).

Gerber, A. B., *Sex, Pornography and Justice* (Lyle Stewart, 1965).

Haight, A. L., *Banned Books* (Bowker, 1956).

Haney, R. W., *Comstockery in America* (Beacon, 1960).

Hart, H. L. A., *Law, Liberty and Morality* (Stanford, 1963).

Hyde, H. M., *A History of Pornography* (Farrar, Straus & Giroux, 1965).

Inglis, R. A., *Freedom of the Movies* (U. of Chicago, 1947).

Kauper, P. G., *Civil Liberties and the Constitution* (U. of Michigan, 1962).

Kerr, W., *Criticism and Censorship* (Bruce, 1954).

Kilpatrick, J. J., *The Smut Peddlers* (Doubleday, 1960).

Kronhausen, E., and P. Kronhausen, *Pornography and the Law*, rev. ed. (Ballantine, 1965).

Kuh, R. H., *Foolish Figleaves? Pornography in—and out of—Court* (Macmillan, 1967).

Kyle-Keith, R., *The High Price of Pornography* (Public Affairs Press, 1961).

Lindesmith, A. R., *The Addict and the Law* (Indiana U., 1965).

McCormick, J., and M. MacInnes (eds.), *Versions of Censorship* (Doubleday, 1962).

McKeown, R., R. D. Merton, and W. Gellhorn, *The Freedom to Read: Perspective and Program* (Bowker, 1957).

Marcuse, L., *Obscene* (MacGibbon & Key, 1965).

504

Meiklejohn, D., *Freedom and the Public: Public and Private Morality in America* (Syracuse U., 1965).

Mueller, G., *Legal Regulation of Sexual Conduct* (Oceana, 1960).

Mumford, H. (ed.), *Primer of Intellectual Freedom* (Harvard, 1949).

Murphy, The Rev. T. J., *Censorship: Government and Obscenity* (Helicon, 1963).

Nelson, J., and G. Roberts, Jr., *The Censor and the Schools* (Little, Brown, 1963).

Okudaira, Yasuhiro, *Political Censorship in Japan, 1931–1945* (Inst. of Legal Research, U. of Pennsylvania, 1962).

Paul, J. C. N., and M. L. Schwartz, *Federal Censorship: Obscenity in the Mail* (Free Press, 1961).

Putnam, G. H., *The Censorship of the Church of Rome* (Putnam's, 1906).

Randall, R. S., *Censorship of the Movies: The Social and Political Control of a Mass Medium* (U. of Wisconsin, 1968).

Rembar, C., *The End of Obscenity: The Trials of "Lady Chatterley," "Tropic of Cancer," and "Fanny Hill"* (Random House, 1968).

St. John-Stevas, N., *Obscenity and the Law* (Secker & Warburg, 1956).

Sanger, M., *An Autobiography* (Norton, 1938).

Schumach, M., *The Face on the Cutting Room Floor: The Story of Movie and Television Censorship* (Morrow, 1964).

Smead, E. E., *Freedom of Speech by Radio and Television* (Public Affairs Press, 1958).

Spring, S., *Risks and Rights in Publishing, Television, Radio, Motion Pictures, Advertising and the Theatre* (Allen & Unwin, 1952).

Stumpf, S. E., *Morality and the Law* (Vanderbilt, 1966).

Summers, R. E., *Wartime Censorship of Press and Radio* (Wilson, 1942).

Thomas, J. L., *Lotteries, Frauds and Obscenity in the Mails* (E. W. Stephens, 1900).

Vidal, G., *The City and the Pillar*, rev. ed. (Dutton, 1965).

Wertham, R., *Seduction of the Innocent* (Rinehart, 1954).

XIII. IMMIGRATION, CITIZENSHIP AND ALIENAGE

Alexander, N., *The Rights of Aliens Under the Federal Constitution* (Capitol, 1931).

The Annals (E. B. Hutchinson, spec. ed.), "The New Immigration," (AAPS, Sept., 1966).

Averbach, F. L., *The Immigration and Nationality Act* (Common Council for Amer. Unity, 1952).

———, *Immigration Laws of the United States* (Bobbs-Merrill, 1961).

Bennett, M. T., *American Immigration Policies* (Public Affairs Press, 1964).

Bernard, W. S. (ed.), *American Immigration Policies* (Public Affairs Press, 1969).

Bouscaren, A. T., *The Security Aspects of Immigration Work* (Marquette U., 1959).

Bruce, J. C., *The Irony of Our Immigration Policy* (Random House, 1954).

Cable, J. L., *Loss of Citizenship: Denaturalization—the Alien in Wartime* (National Law Book Co., 1943).

Clark, J. P., *The Deportation of Aliens from the United States to Europe* (Columbia, 1931).

Divine, R. A., *American Immigration Policy, 1924–25* (Yale, 1957).

Gettys, C. L., *The Law of Citizenship in the United States* (U. of Chicago, 1934).

Gordon, C., and H. Rosenfield, *Immigration Law and Procedure* (Banks & Co., 1959).

Gordon, M. M., *Assimilation in American Life: The Role of Race, Religion and National Origins* (Oxford, 1964).

Handlin, O., *Immigration as a Factor in American History* (Prentice-Hall, 1959).

———, *The Uprooted* (Little, Brown, 1951).

Hansen, M. L., *The Immigrant in American History* (Harvard, 1940).

Hicks, J. D., *The American Nation* (Houghton, Mifflin, 1959).

Higham, J., *Strangers in the Land: Patterns of American Nativism, 1860–1929* (Rutgers, 1955).

Hutchinson, E. P., *Immigrants and Their Children, 1850–1950* (Wiley, 1956).

Jones, M. A., *American Immigration* (U. of Chicago, 1960).

Kansas, S., *U.S. Immigration; Exclusion, Deportation, and Citizenship of the United States of America*, 2nd ed. (Bender, 1940).

Kent, D. P., *The Refugee Intellectual: The Americanization of the Immigrants of 1933–1941* (Columbia, 1953).

Knauff, E. R., *The Ellen Knauff Story* (Norton, 1952).

Konvitz, M. R., *The Alien and Asiatic in American Law* (Cornell, 1946).

———, *Civil Rights in Immigration* (Cornell, 1953).

Kraus, M., *Immigration, the American Maxims from Pilgrims to Modern Refugees* (Van Nostrand, 1966).

Lowenstein, E. (ed.), *The Alien and the Immigration Law* (Oceana, 1958).

Post, L. F., *The Deportation Delirium of Nineteen-Twenty* (Kerr, 1923).

President's Commission on Immigration and Naturalization, *Whom We Shall Welcome* (U.S. G.P.O., 1953).

Schrieke, B., *Alien Americans* (Viking, 1936).

Schwartz, A. P., *The Open Society* (Clarion, 1969).

Sellen, H. (ed.), *Practice and Procedure Under the Immigration and Nationality Act* (New York, 1954).

Silving, H., *Immigration Laws of the United States* (Oceana, 1949).

Solomon, B. M., *Ancestors and Immigrants: A Changing New England Tradition* (Harvard, 1956).

Taiang, I. M., *The Question of Expatriation in America Prior to 1907* (Johns Hopkins, 1942).

Tyler, P., *Immigration and the United States* (Wilson, 1956).

Van Vleck, W. C., *The Administrative Control of Aliens: A Study in Administrative Law and Procedure* (Commonwealth Fund, 1932).

Ziegler, B. M. (ed.), *Immigration: An American Dilemma* (Heath, 1953).

XIV. INTERNAL SECURITY: LOYALTY, SECURITY, THOUGHT CONTROL, CLASSIFIED DATA

A. GENERAL.

Association of the Bar of the City of New York, *Equal Justice for the Accused* (Dodd, Mead, 1959).

Biddle, F., *The Fear of Freedom* (Doubleday, 1951).

Bontecou, E. (ed.), *The Federal Loyalty-Security Program* (Cornell, 1953).

Brookings Institution, *Suggested Standards for Determining Un-American Activities* (1945).

Chafee, Z., *Watchman, What of the Night?* (University, 1942).

Chapin, B., *The American Law of Treason: Revolutionary and Early National Origin* (U. of Washington, 1964).

Chase, H. W., *Security and Liberty: The Problem of Native Communists, 1947–1955* (Doubleday, 1955).

Collins, F. L., *The F.B.I. in Peace and War*, rev. and enl. by L. Demles (Ace Books, 1962).

Commager, H. S., *Freedom, Loyalty, Dissent* (Oxford, 1954).

Cook, T. I., *Democratic Rights Versus Communist Activity* (Doubleday, 1943).

Curtil, M., *The Roots of American Loyalty* (Columbia, 1946).

Davis, D. B., *The Fear of Conspiracy* (Cornell, 1972).

Davis, J., *Character Assassination* (Philosophical Library, 1951).

Dowell, S. F., *A History of Criminal Syndicalism Legislation in the United States* (Johns Hopkins, 1939).

Gellhorn, W., *Security, Loyalty and Science* (Cornell, 1950).

Ginzberg, B., *Rededication to Freedom* (Simon & Schuster, 1959).

Goldbloom, M., *American Security and Freedom* (American Jewish Committee, 1955).

Grodzins, M., *The Loyal and the Disloyal: Social Boundaries of Patriotism and Treason* (U. of Chicago, 1956).

Guttman, A., and B. M. Ziegler, *Communism, the Courts and the Constitution* (Heath, 1964).

Harper, A. D., *The Politics of Loyalty: The White House and the Communist Issue 1946–1952* (Greenwood, 1970).

Laswell, H. D., *National Security and Individual Freedom* (McGraw-Hill, 1950).

Miller, J. C., *Crisis in Freedom* (Little, Brown, 1951).

Mitchell, D., *1919: Red Mirage* (Macmillan, 1970).

Murphy, The Rev. T. J., *Censorship: Government and Obscenity* (Helicon, 1963).

Murray, R. K., *Scare: A Study in National Hysteria 1919–1920* (U. of Minnesota, 1955).

Peltason, J., *Constitutional Liberty and Seditious Activity* (Catt Memorial Fund, 1954).

Peters, C., and T. Branch (eds.), *Blowing the Whistle* (Praeger, 1973).

Rankin, R. S., and W. R. Dallmayr, *Freedom and Emerging Powers in the Cold War* (Appleton-Century-Crofts, 1963).

Rourke, R. E., *Secrecy and Publicity: Dilemmas of Democracy* (Johns Hopkins, 1961).

Schaar, J. H., *Loyalty to America: The Background and Consequences* (U.C.L.A., 1957).

Schwartz, A. P., *The Open Society* (Simon & Schuster, 1968).

Seidman, J., *Communism in the United States: A Bibliography* (Cornell, 1967).

Shapiro, M., *The Pentagon Papers and the Courts* (Chandler, 1973).

Shils, E. A., *The Torment of Secrecy: American Security Policies* (Free Press, 1956).

Summers, R. E., *Federal Information Controls in Peacetime* (Wilson, 1949).

Thayer, G., *The Farther Shores of Politics* (Simon & Schuster, 1968).

Wahlke, J. C., *Loyalty in a Democratic State* (Heath, 1952).

Weyl, N., *The Battle Against Disloyalty* (Crowell, 1951).

———, *Treason: The Story of Disloyalty and Betrayal in American History* (Public Affairs Press, 1950).

Wilson, H. H., and H. Glickman, *The Problem of Internal Security in Great Britain, 1948–1953* (Doubleday, 1954).

B. FEDERAL AND STATE STATUTES.

Gellhorn, W. (ed.), *The States and Subversion* (Cornell, 1952).

Preston, W., Jr., *Aliens and Dissenters: Federal Suppression of Radicals, 1903–1933* (Harvard, 1963).

Weinstein, S., and H. S. Brown, Jr., *Personnel Security Programs of the Federal Government* (Fund for the Republic, 1954).

C. GOVERNMENT EMPLOYMENT.

Andrews, B., and P. Andrews, *A Tragedy of History: A Journalist's Confidential Role in the Hiss-Chambers Case* (McKay, 1963).

Brown, R. S., Jr., *Loyalty and Security: Employment Tests in the United States* (Yale, 1958).

Chambers, W., *Witness* (Random House, 1956).

Hiss, A., *In the Court of Public Opinion* (Knopf, 1957).

Hook, S., *The Paradoxes of Freedom* (Berkeley, 1962).

Lamont, C., *Freedom Is as Freedom Does: Civil Liberties Today* (Horizon, 1956).

Westin, A., *The Constitution and Loyalty Program* (Catt Memorial Fund, 1954).

Yarmolinsky, A., *Case Studies in Personnel Security* (Bureau of National Affairs, 1955).

D. LEGISLATIVE INVESTIGATION. (McCarthyism, HUAC, Alger Hiss.)

Alsop, J. W., Jr., and S., *We Accuse: The Story of American Justice in the Case of Robert Oppenheimer* (Simon & Schuster, 1954).

Anderson, J., and R. W. May, *McCarthy: The Man, the Senator, the "Ism"* (Beacon, 1952).

Andrews, B., and P. Andrews, *A Tragedy of History: A Journalist's Confidential Role in the Hiss-Chamber Case* (McKay, 1962).

———, *Washington Witch Hunt* (Random House, 1948).

Barrett, E. L., Jr., *The Tenney Committee: Legislative Investigation of Subversive Activities in California* (Cornell, 1951).

Barth, A., *Government by Investigation* (Viking, 1955).

———, *The Loyalty of Free Men*, rev. ed. (Archon, 1965).

———, *When Congress Investigates Loyalty and Security in a Democracy* (Public Affairs Comm., 1956).

Beck, C., *Contempt of Congress* (Hauser, 1959).

Belfrage, C., *The American Inquisition, 1945–1960* (Bobbs, Merrill, 1973).

Bessie, A., *Inquisition in Eden* (Macmillan, 1965).

Buckley, W. F., Jr., and the Editors of the National Review, *The Committee and Its Critics* (Putnam, 1962).

———, and L. B. Bozell, *McCarthy and His Enemies* (Regnery, 1953).

Carr, R. K., *The Constitution and Congressional Investigation Committees* (Cornell, 1954).

———, *The House Committee on Un-American Activities, 1945–50* (Cornell, 1952).

Chamberlain, L. H., *Loyalty and Legislative Action: A Survey of Activity by the New York State Legislature, 1919–1949* (Cornell, 1952).

Chambers, W., *Witness* (Random House, 1956).

Cohn, R., *McCarthy* (New American Library, 1968).

Cook, F. J., *The Nightmare Decade: The Life and Times of Senator Joe McCarthy* (Random House, 1971).
———, *The Unfinished Story of Alger Hiss* (Morrow, 1958).
Cooke, A., *A Generation on Trial: U.S.A. v. Alger Hiss* (Knopf, 1950).
Cornell University Study, *The Tenney Committee: Study of Legislative Investigations of Subversive Activities in California* (1962).
DeAntonio, E., and D. Talbot, *Point of Order! Documentary of the Army-McCarthy Hearings* (Norton, 1964).
Dimock, M. E., *Congressional Investigating Committees* (Johns Hopkins, 1929).
Donner, F. J., *The Un-Americans* (Ballantine, 1961).
Eberling, E. J., *Congressional Investigations* (Columbia, 1928).
Freeland, R. M., *The Truman Doctrine and the Origin of McCarthyism* (Knopf, 1971).
Gellerman, W., *Martin Dies* (John Day, 1944).
Gillmor, D., *Fear the Accuser* (Abelard-Schuman, 1954).
Goldfarb, R. L., *The Contempt Power* (Columbia, 1963).
Goodman, W., *The Committee: The Extraordinary Career of the House Committee on Un-American Activities* (Farrar, Straus, 1968).
Gore, L., *Joe Must Go* (Messner, 1954).
Griffith, R., *The Politics of Fear: Joseph McCarthy and the Senate* (U. of Kentucky, 1971).
Hiss, A., *In the Court of Public Opinion* (Knopf, 1957).
Hook, S., *Political Power and Personal Freedom: Critical Studies in Democracy, Communism, and Civil Rights* (Criterion, 1959).
Jaffe, J. F., *Crusade Against Radicalism: New York During the Red Scare, 1914–1924* (Kennikat, 1972).
Johnson, J. E., *Investigation Powers of Congress* (Wilson, 1951).
Jowitt, W. A. Jowitt, 1st Earl, *The Strange Case of Alger Hiss* (Doubleday, 1953).
Kallen, H. M., *The Lamont Case: History of a Congressional Investigation* (Horizon, 1957).
Kemper, D. J., *Decade of Fear* (U. of Missouri, 1965).
Lamb, E., *Trial by Battle* (Center for the Study of Democratic Institutions, 1964).
Lamont, C., *Freedom Is as Freedom Does: Civil Liberties Today* (Horizon, 1956).
Lattimore, O., *Ordeal by Slander* (Little, Brown, 1950).
McGeary, M. N., *The Development of Congressional Investigative Power* (Columbia, 1940).
McWilliams, C., *Witch Hunt: The Revival of Heresy* (Little, Brown, 1950).
Matusow, H., *False Witness* (Cameron & Kahn, 1955).
Merson, M., *The Private Diary of a Public Servant* (Macmillan, 1955).
Nelson, H. L., *Libel in News of Congressional Investigating Committees* (U. of Minnesota, 1961).
Ogden, A. R., *The Dies Committee*, 2nd ed. (Catholic U., 1946).
Oxnam, G. B., *I Protest: My Experience with the House Committee on Un-American Activities* (Harper, 1954).
Packer, H. L., *Ex-Communist Witnesses: Four Studies in Fact-Finding* (Stanford, 1962).
Potter, C. E., *Days of Shame* (Coward-McCann, 1965).
Rogin, M. P., *The Intellectuals and McCarthy: The Radical Specter* (M.I.T., 1969).
Rorty, J., and M. Decter, *McCarthy and the Communists* (Beacon, 1954).

509

Rovere, R., *Senator Joe McCarthy* (Harcourt, Brace, 1959).

Seldes, G., *Witch Hunt* (Modern Age Books, 1940).

Sommerville, J., *The Communist Trials and the American Tradition: Expert Testimony on Force and Violence* (Cameron, 1956).

Straight, M., *Trial by Television: The Army-McCarthy Hearings* (Beacon, 1954).

Taylor, T., *Grand Inquest: The Story of Congressional Investigations* (Simon & Schuster, 1955).

Thomas, L., *When Even Angels Wept: The Senator Joseph McCarthy Affair—A Story Without a Hero* (Morrow, 1973).

Thomas, N., *The Test of Freedom* (Norton, 1954).

Uphaus, W., *Commitment* (McGraw-Hill, 1964).

Warren, F. A., *Liberals and Communism: The "Red Decade" Revisited* (Indiana U., 1966).

Watkins, A. V., *Enough Rope* (U. of Utah, 1970).

Wittenberg, P., *The Lamont Case: History of a Congressional Investigation* (Horizon, 1957).

E. THE COMMUNISTS.

Almond, G. A., *The Appeals of Communism* (Princeton, 1954).

Blanshard, P., *Communism, Democracy and Catholic Power* (Beacon, 1951).

Bochenski, J. M., and G. Niemeyer, *Handbook on Communism* (Praeger, 1963).

Decter, M. (ed.), *The Profile of Communism: A Fact-by-Fact Primer* (Collier, 1962).

Dennis, E., *Ideas They Cannot Jail* (International, 1950).

Draper, T., *The Roots of American Communism* (Viking, 1957).

Eberling, E. J., *Congressional Investigations* (Columbia, 1928).

Ernst, M. L., and D. Loth, *Report on the American Communist* (Holt, 1952).

Fund for the Republic, *Bibliography on the Communist Problem in the United States* (Fund for the Republic, 1955).

Gates, J., *The Story of an American Communist* (Nelson, 1958).

Hoover, J. E., *Masters of Deceit* (Holt, 1958).

———, *A Study of Communism* (Holt, Rinehart & Winston, 1962).

Howe, I., and L. Coser, *The American Communist Party: A Critical History, 1919–1960*, rev. ed. (Praeger, 1962).

Hunt, R. N. G. (ed.), *Books on Communism* (Amperstand Ltd., 1959).

Iversen, R. W., *The Communists and the Schools* (Harcourt, Brace, 1959).

Johnsen, J. E., *Should the Communist Party Be Outlawed?* (Wilson, 1949).

Latham, E., *The Communist Controversy in Washington: From the New Deal to McCarthy* (Harvard, 1966).

Miller, W. J., H. L. Roberts, and M. D. Shulman, *The Meaning of Communism* (Simon & Schuster, 1963).

Monnerot, J., *Sociology and Psychology of Communism* (Beacon, 1953).

Murray, R. K., *Red Scare* (McGraw-Hill, 1955).

Overstreet, H., and B. Overstreet, *What We Must Know About Communism* (Norton, 1958).

Palmer, E. E. (ed.), *The Communist Problems in America* (Crowell, 1951).

Record, W., *Race and Radicalism: The NAACP and the Commuist Party in Conflict* (Cornell, 1964).

Roy, R. L., *Communism and the Churches* (Harcourt, Brace, 1960).

Shannon, D. A., *The Decline of American Communism: A History of the Communist Party of the United States Since 1945* (Harcourt, Brace, 1959).

Sutherland, A. E., *Two Reference Volumes on Communism in the United States* (Harvard, 1956).

Wechsler, J. A., *The Age of Suspicion* (Random House, 1953).

F. THE RIGHT WING.

Alexander, C. C., *The Ku Klux Klan in the Southwest* (U. of Kentucky, 1965).

Bell, D. (ed.), *The Radical Right* (Doubleday, 1963).

Broyles, J. A., *The John Birch Society: Anatomy of a Protest* (Beacon, 1966).

Cain, E., *They'd Rather Be Right* (Macmillan, 1963).

Chalmer, D. M., *Hooded Americanism: The First Century of the Ku Klux Klan* (Doubleday, 1965).

Ellsworth, R. E., and S. M. Harris, *American Right Wing* (U. of Illinois, 1960).

Epstein, B. R., and A. Forster, *The Radical Right: Report on the John Birch Society and Its Allies* (Random House, 1967).

Forster, A., and B. R. Epstein, *Danger on the Right* (Random House, 1964).

Hapgood, N. (ed.), *Professional Patriots* (Boni, 1927).

Hofstadter, R., *The Paranoid Style: American Politics and Other Essays* (Knopf, 1965).

Jackson, K. T., *The Ku Klux Klan in the City* (Oxford, 1967).

Janson, D., and B. Eisman, *The Far Right* (McGraw-Hill, 1963).

Lindbergh, C. A., *The Wartime Journals of Charles A. Lindberg* (Harcourt, Brace, Jovanovich, 1970).

Lipset, S. M., and E. Raab, *The Politics of Unreason: Right-Wing Extremism in America, 1790–1970* (Harper & Row, 1970).

Lowe, D., *KKK: The Invisible Empire* (Norton, 1967).

McEvoy, J., III, *Radicals or Conservatives: The Contemporary American Right* (Rand McNally, 1971).

New York Times (eds.), *The Right-Wing Individualist Tradition in America* (Arno, 1971).

Overstreet, H., and B. Overstreet, *The Strange Tactics of Extremism* (Norton, 1964).

Randel, W. P., *The Ku Klux Klan: A Century of Infamy* (Chilton, 1965).

Redekopf, H., *The American Far Right: A Case Study of Billy James Hargis and Christian Crusade* (Eerdmans, 1968).

Rice, A. S., *The KKK in American Politics* (Public Affairs Press, 1962).

Rogger, H., and E. Weber, *The European Right: A Historical Profile* (U. of California, 1966).

Rosenstone, R. A. (ed.), *Protest from the Right* (Glencoe Press, 1968).

Roy, R. L., *Apostles of Discord* (Beacon, 1953).

Schoenberger, R. A. (ed.), *The American Right Wing: Readings in Political Behavior* (Holt, Rinehart, Winston, 1969).

Sheinberg, M., and A. Kraditor, *Peddlers of Fear* (Public Affairs, 1966).

Sherwin, M., *The Extremists* (St. Martin's, 1953).

Steiner, G., *The Roots of the Right* (Harper & Row, 1971).

Thayer, G., *The Farther Shores of Politics* (Simon & Schuster, 1968).

Turner, W. W., *Power on the Right* (Ramparts Press, 1971).

Walker, B. R., *The Christian Fright Peddlers* (Doubleday, 1964).
Welch, R., *Blue Book of the John Birch Society* (The John Birch Society, 1958).

XV. FAMOUS CASES INVOLVING CIVIL RIGHTS AND LIBERTIES.

A. SACCO-VANZETTI.

Apple, P. P., *The Sacco-Vanzetti Case: A Transcript*, 6 vols., w/bibl. (Holt, 1928–29).
Burlingham, C. C., and B. Flexner (eds.), *The Sacco-Vanzetti Case: Transcript of the Trial of Nicola Sacco and Bartolomeo Vanzetti in the Courts of Massachusetts and Subsequent Proceedings, 1920–1927* (Holt, 1928).
Bush, M., *Ben Shalin: The Passion of Sacco and Vanzetti* (Syracuse U., 1969).
Ehrmann, H. B., *The Case That Will Not Die* (Little, Brown, 1969).
——, *The Untried Case: The Sacco-Vanzetti Case and the Morelli Gang*, 2nd ed. (Vanguard, 1960).
Feliciani, A., and G. Jackson, *The Sacco-Vanzetti Case: Twenty Years Later* (Privately published, 1947).
Felix, D., *Protest: Sacco-Vanzetti and the Intellectuals* (Indiana U., 1965).
Frankel, O. K., *The Sacco-Vanzetti Case* (Knopf, 1931).
Frankfurter, F., *The Case of Sacco and Vanzetti: A Critical Analysis for Lawyers and Laymen* (Little, Brown, 1927, 1961, 1962).
Joughin, L., and E. M. Morgan, *The Legacy of Sacco and Vanzetti* (Quadrangle, 1964).
Lyons, E., *The Life and Death of Sacco and Vanzetti* (Never, 1927; Da Capo, 1970).
Montgomery, R. H., *Sacco-Vanzetti: The Murder and the Myth* (Devin-Adair, 1960).
Musmanno, M. S., *After Twelve Years: The Sacco-Vanzetti Case* (Knopf, 1939).
Russell, F., *Tragedy in Dedham—The Story of the Sacco-Vanzetti Case* (McGraw-Hill, 1962).
Stark, L., *We Saw It Happen* (Simon & Schuster, 1939).
Valenti, M., *Question of Guilt* (Paperback Library, 1966).

B. LOEB-LEOPOLD.

Darrow, C. S., *The Story of My Life* (Scribner's, 1958).
Leopold, N. F., *Life Plus 99 Years* (Doubleday, 1958).
McKernan, M., *The Amazing Crime and Trial of Leopold and Loeb* (New American Library, 1958).
Weinberg, A., *Attorney for the Damned* (Simon & Schuster, 1957).

C. JOHN PETER ZENGER.

Alexander, J., *A Brief Narrative of the Case and Trial of John Peter Zenger*, ed. by S. N. Katz (Belknap, 1963).
Buranelli, V. (ed.), *The Trial of Peter Zenger* (N.Y.U., 1957).
Galt, T., *Peter Zenger, Fighter for Freedom* (Crowell, 1951).
James, A., *A Brief Narrative of the Case and Trial of Peter Zenger, Printer of the New York Weekly Journal*, rev. ed. (Harvard, 1963).
Levy, L. W. (ed.), *Freedom of the Press from Zenger to Jefferson* (Bobbs-Merrill, 1967).
Rutherford, L., *John Peter Zenger* (Peter Smith, 1904).

D. JOHN SCOPES—"THE MONKEY TRIAL."

Darrow, C. S., *The Story of My Life* (Scribner, 1958).
De Camp, L. S., *The Great Monkey Trial* (Doubleday, 1968).
Ginger, R., *Six Days or Forever: Tennessee v. John Thomas Scopes* (Signet, 1960).
Grebstein, S. H. (ed.), *Monkey Trial: The State of Tennessee v. John Thomas Scopes* (Houghton, Mifflin, 1960).
Scopes, J. T., and J. Presley, *Center of the Storm: Memoirs of John T. Scopes* (Holt, Rinehart & Winston, 1967).
Tompkins, J. R. (ed.), *John Scopes and Others: D-Days at Dayton—Reflections on the Scopes Trial* (L.S.U., 1965).
Weinberg, A., *Attorney for the Damned* (Simon & Schuster, 1957).

E. LEE HARVEY OSWALD, JACK RUBY, AND THE WARREN COMMISSION.

Belli, M. M., *Dallas Justice: The Real Story of Jack Ruby and His Trial* (McKay, 1964).
Epstein, E. J., *Inquest: The Warren Commission and the Establishment of Truth* (Viking, 1967).
Kaplan, J., and J. R. Walz, *The Trial of Jack Ruby* (Macmillan, 1965).
Lane, M., *A Citizen's Dissent: Mark Lane Replies* (Holt, Rinehart & Winston, 1968).
———, *Rush to Judgment: A Critique of the Warren Commission Inquiry* (Holt, Rinehart & Winston, 1966).
Meagher, S., *Accessories After the Fact: The Warren Commission, the Authorities and the Report* (Bobbs-Merrill, 1968).
Newman, A. H., *The Assassination of John F. Kennedy: The Reason Why* (Potter, 1970).
Sauvage, L., *The Oswald Affair: An Examination of the Contradictions and Omissions of the Warren Report* (World, 1966).
Thompson, J., *Six Seconds in Dallas: A Micro Study of the Kennedy Assassination* (Random House, 1968).
Warren Commission, *Official Warren Commission Report on the Assassination of President John F. Kennedy* (Doubleday, 1964).
Wills, G., and O. Demaris, *Jack Ruby* (New American Library, 1968).

F. JAMES EARL RAY.

Blair, C., Jr., *The Strange Case of James Earl Ray: The Man Who Murdered Martin Luther King, Jr.* (Bantam, 1969).
Frank, G., *An American Death: The True Story of the Assassination of Dr. Martin Luther King, Jr., and the Greatest Manhunt of Our Time* (Doubleday, 1972).

G. "CHICAGO SEVEN."

Epstein, J., *The Great Conspiracy Trial* (Random House, 1970).
Lukas, J. A., *The Barnyard Epithet and Other Obscenities: Notes on the Chicago Conspiracy Trial* (Perennial, 1970).
Schultz, J., *Motion Denied: A New Report on the Chicago Conspiracy Trial* (Morrow, 1973).

H. OTHERS.

Bailey, F. L., and H. Aronson, *The Defense Never Rests* (Stein & Day, 1971).

Bannan, J. F., and R. S. Bannan, *Law, Morality and Vietnam: The Peace Militants and the Courts* (Indiana U., 1974).

Becker, T. L., *Political Trials* (Bobbs-Merrill, 1971).

Boskin, J., and F. Krinsky, *The Oppenheimer Affair: A Political Play in Three Acts* (Glencoe, 1968).

Chalmers, A. K., *They Shall Be Free* (Doubleday, 1961).

Chessman, C., *Cell 2455 Death Row* (Prentice-Hall, 1954).

Cooke, A., *A Generation on Trial: U.S.A. v. Alger Hiss* (Penguin, 1968).

Cornell, J., *The Trial of Ezra Pound* (Day, 1966).

Davidson, I. D., and R. Gehman, *The Jury Is Still Out* (Harper, 1959).

Dickler, G., *Man on Trial* (Delta, 1964).

Dinnerstein, L., *The Leo Frank Case* (Columbia, 1968).

Donovan, J. B., *Strangers on a Bridge: The Case of Colonel Abel* (Atheneum, 1964).

Fineberg, S. A., *The Rosenberg Case: Fact and Fiction* (Oceana, 1953).

Flynn, E. G., *The Alderson Story: My Life as a Political Prisoner* (Intern, 1963).

Foner, P. S., *The Case of Joe Hill* (International Publishers, 1965).

Franklin, C., *World Family Trials* (Tapliner, 1966).

Frost, R. H., *The Monkey Case* (Stanford, 1969).

Furneaux, R., *Courtroom USA: 1* (Penguin, 1964).

———, *Courtroom USA: 2* (Penguin, 1964).

Garrison, J., *A Heritage of Stone* (Putnam, 1970).

Gentry, K., *Frame-Up* (Norton, 1967).

Golden, H., *A Little Girl is Dead* (World, 1965).

Grover, D. H., *Debaters and Dynamiters: The Story of the Haywood Trial* (Oregon State U., 1964).

Hersey, J., *The Algiers Motel Incident* (Knopf, 1968).

Hopkins, V. C., *Dred Scott's Case* (Fordham, 1951).

Huie, W. B., *Three Lives for Mississippi* (W. C. C. Books, 1965).

Hunt, H. P., *The Case of Thomas J. Mooney and Warren K. Billings* (Da Capo, 1971).

Kirkwood, J., *American Grotesque: The Account of the Clay Shaw—Jim Garrison Affair* (Simon & Schuster, 1970).

Kunstler, W. M., *The Minister and the Choir Singer: The Hall-Mills Murder Case* (Morrow, 1964).

———, *The Case for Courage* (Morrow, 1962).

Lustgarten, E., *The Murder and the Trial* (Scribner, 1958).

Marke, J. J., *Vignettes of Legal History* (Rothman, 1965).

Nizer, L., *The Implosion Conspiracy* (Doubleday, 1973).

———, *The Jury Returns* (Doubleday, 1966).

———, *My Life in Court* (Doubleday, 1961).

O'Brien, F. W., *Was Justice Done? Historic Trials on Review* (Rockford College, 1971).

Patterson, H., and E. Conrad, *Scottsboro Boy* (Doubleday, 1950).

Prettyman, E. B., Jr., *Death and the Supreme Court* (Avon, 1964).

Raines, J. C. (ed.), *Conspiracy: The Implications of the Harrisburg Trial for the Democratic Tradition* (Harper & Row, 1974).

Reynolds, Q., *Courtroom* (Farrar, Straus, 1950).

Rosenberg, C. E., *The Trial of the Assassin Guiteau: Psychiatry and Law in the Gilded Age* (U. of Chicago, 1968).

Rubin, W. A., *The Mark Fein Case* (Dial, 1966).

Schneir, W., and M., *Invitation to an Inquest: Reopening the Rosenberg Atom Spy Case* (Penguin, 1973).

Schrag, P., *Test of Loyalty: Daniel Ellsberg and the Rituals of Secret Government* (Simon & Schuster, 1974).

Schultz, J., *Motion Will Be Denied: A New Report on the Chicago Conspiracy Trial* (Morrow, 1973).

Sharp, M. P., *Was Justice Done? The Rosenberg-Sobell Case* (Monthly Review Press, 1956).

Stern, P. M., *The Oppenheiner Case: Security on Trial* (Harper & Row, 1969).

Witmer, L., *The Nearing Case* (Da Capo Reprint of 1915 ed., 1970).

I
General
Subject
Index

II
Name
Index

527

III
Court
Case
Index